FACE *To* FACE

As part of Houghton Mifflin's ongoing commitment to the environment, this text has been printed on recycled paper.

FACE *To* FACE

Readings on Confrontation and Accommodation in America

JOSEPH ZAITCHIK
University of Massachusetts, Lowell

WILLIAM ROBERTS
University of Massachusetts, Lowell

HOLLY ZAITCHIK
Boston University

HOUGHTON MIFFLIN COMPANY BOSTON TORONTO
Geneva, Illinois *Palo Alto* *Princeton, New Jersey*

To our forebears and families—Algonquin, Cambodian, Canadian, English, French, German, Irish, Jewish, Russian, Vietnamese, Welsh—who, from 1635 to 1991, came from many nations to this nation of nations:

Moses Cleveland (arrived 1635)
William Frederick Roberts and
Etta May Low Roberts
Maria Spellman
Max Hagedorn
Johanna Rymarzick
Mary McNeil
Napoleon Richard
Augustyn Mroz
Christina Hemke
Alfred Howell and
Harriet Roberts Howell
Irene Howell
Maier Zaitchik and
Malka Lifschitz Zaitchik
Viet Pham
Hon Horn
Yakov Zaitchik (arrived 1991)

Sponsoring Editor: Kristin Watts Peri
Special Projects Editor: Lynn Walterick
Associate Project Editor: Danielle Carbonneau
Electronic Publishing Supervisor: Victoria Levin
Production/Design Coordinator: Jill Haber
Senior Manufacturing Coordinator: Priscilla Bailey
Marketing Manager: George Kane

Interior Design: Sandra Rigney
Cover Design: Judy Arisman
Cover Image: *The Witnesses*, 1969, Romare Bearden. Collage 16″ × 21″. Collection of the Ciba-Geigy Corporation.

ACKNOWLEDGMENTS

Carlos Bulosan "Filipino Fruit Pickers," from *America Is in the Heart, A Personal History* by Carlos Bulosan, reprinted by permission of Harcourt Brace & Company.

Samuel Sewall From the *Diary of Samuel Sewall*, Volumes I & II edited by M. Halsey Thomas. Copyright © 1973 by Farrar, Straus & Giroux, Inc. Reprinted by permission of Farrar, Straus & Giroux, Inc.

Luther Standing Bear "What the Indian Means to America." Reprinted from *Land of the Spotted Eagle*, by Luther Standing Bear, by permission of the University of Nebraska Press. Copyright © 1933, by Luther Standing Bear. Renewal copyright, 1960, by May Jones.

Acknowledgments are continued on pages 559–562, which constitute a continuation of the copyright page.

Printed in the U.S.A.

Library of Congress Catalog Card Number: 93-78662

ISBN: 0-395-63686-8

123456789-AM-98 97 96 95 94

Contents

Rhetorical Table of Contents

Description

Narration

Illustration and Example

Definition

Classification and Division

Comparison and Contrast

Cause and Effect

Argument and Persuasion

Process Analysis

Analysis

Journals, Letters, Speeches, Dialogue, and Interview

Preface for Instructors

Face to Face: Readings on Confrontation and Accommodation in America examines the way ethnic and cultural groups have confronted and accommodated each other and how their interactions have shaped America and brought about its current problems, controversies, and opportunities. The readings, which represent a broad spectrum of opinion, were carefully chosen to help students avoid simplistic slogans, instant certainties, sentimental evasions, counterproductive stereotypes, and doctrinaire ideologies and to face current multicultural issues in an informed way. The book presents a range of perspectives—from the militant separatism of the early Malcolm X to the individualistic accommodation of Shelby Steele, from the English Only advocacy of Ronald Saunders to the multi-lingual inclusiveness of Harvey A. Daniels. Students are thus encouraged to reexamine their preconceptions and consider new ideas and options and then formulate their own responses to important issues.

Organization

Part 1, **National Identity and Cultural Pluralism,** explores the relationship between cultural pluralism and national identity and the possible consequences of our increasing multicultural awareness. Many other books ignore this issue, perhaps on the assumption—not necessarily shared by many students—that increasing ethnic consciousness is "good for the country."

Part 2, **Ethnic Journeys,** gives the background of ethnic groups who emigrated to America from all over the world, tracing their history and special problems and concerns from the earliest arrivals from Europe to the most recent from Asia.

Part 3, **Living in Multicultural America,** is arranged thematically in five chapters: Neighborhoods, Family, Language, Education, and Confrontations. This unit provides a wealth of social and cultural background and brings students into current debates on such issues as bilingualism, racial tension on college campuses, and ethnic responses to the first Rodney King verdict and its aftermath. Students can thereby evaluate the effects of such issues and events on their own lives.

Part 4, **Controversy: A Casebook on Multicultural Education,** discusses the current debate on multicultural education at the primary, secondary, and college levels. It provides students with an opportunity to enter into the conversation on an important issue in contemporary American society.

Features

- Substantial **introductions** to each chapter provide historical and cultural contexts for the readings that follow.

- **Freewriting assignments** precede and suggestions for discussion and writing follow each selection.

- **End-of-unit questions** encourage critical thinking, class discussion, and informed writing, as students are asked to integrate the ideas and approaches of the readings.

- **Ongoing journal projects** ask students to make connections between the readings and current events and issues.

- A **Rhetorical Table of Contents** provides convenient reference for instructors who wish to emphasize a rhetorical approach to the teaching of writing.

- The **Casebook** on the debate on multicultural education, with the accompanying apparatus on the mechanics of bibliography and in-text citations, provides the basis for a controlled research project. Since the materials the students will be using are included in the text itself, the instructor can do the close monitoring that is virtually impossible in open-ended research projects.

- The text includes **many genres**—essays, research studies, personal narratives, fiction, speeches, arguments—and suggestions for a variety of approaches to the material through discussion and writing. The readings and writing assignments are representative of the kinds of academic reading and writing that students will be doing in many other college courses.

Overview of Apparatus

To promote critical reading and creative thinking, we have designed **discussion questions** and **writing activities** that should inspire students to engage with and respond to the texts. We usually suggest a focused freewriting activity that is relevant to the readings. In the suggested assignments that follow the selections, we emphasize the writing process. For example, we ask students to write essays that incorporate their preliminary thoughts from their freewriting with their thoughts after they have read the selections. In this way, they can establish their own authority by connecting personal experience with academic discourse.

Some assignments encourage collaborative small-group responses, and others ask the student to explore the communities outside the classroom—campus, family, neighborhood—for discoveries that can be useful in discussion and writing.

We encourage students to keep a **Reaction Journal,** in which they have an opportunity to bring their own experiences and insights into their responses. The journal assignments that follow each selection vary in context and audience, but they almost always emphasize personal response and direct dialogue with the text. We sometimes ask students to write a letter to the author or to assume the role of a member of another group. For the more formal writing assignments, students may draw from these Reaction Journals by using them as part of the prewriting process.

While many of the assignments encourage reader response and personal dialogue with the text, we have not lost sight of the importance of formal exposition. The **end-of-section assignments** often call for the analysis and synthesis of readings through more formal discussion questions and writing assignments that utilize traditional modes of discourse. Here we emphasize expository and persuasive writing as well as such skills as summary and the use of secondary sources.

In brief, there is a wealth of material in the readings that can be mined in a number of ways. We hope your students will learn to read intelligently, summarize coherently the ideas to which they are exposed, and articulate their own values and developing perspectives. What matters most is that they write about things that matter.

Acknowledgments

We are deeply appreciative of the encouragement, advice, and assistance of many people:

Professors Cliff Lewis, George Luter, Hai B. Pho (University of Massachusetts, Lowell), Mark Zaitchik (Salem State College), and Patsy Roberts (Rivier College) for helpful suggestions in choosing readings and organizing the text.

Professor F. William Forbes (University of New Hampshire) for review and glossing of Spanish language material.

Carolyn Wolf and Ann Tevnan for their patience, kind words, and hard work with manuscript preparation.

The editorial staff at Houghton Mifflin, especially Carolyn Potts, Lynn Walterick, Danielle Carbonneau, and Kristin Watts Peri for their guidance, helpful suggestions, and, when appropriate, gentle prodding.

The academic reviewers—Katya Amato, Portland State University; Jeanne Anderson, University of Louisville; Valerie Babb, Georgetown University; Sylvia Charshoodian, Boston University; David Cope, Grand Rapids Community College; Cynthia Cox, Belmont University; Juan Delgado, California State University, San Bernadino; Mary Helen Dunlop, Iowa State University; Rhonda Levine, University of California, Santa Barbara; Clifford Marks, University of Wyoming; Margaret Marron, University of Wyoming; Judy Merrell, Community College of Allegheny County, Boyce Campus; Ann A. Merrill, Emory University; Shirley Moore, College of Charleston; Sarah-Hope Parmeter, University of California, Santa Cruz; Madeleine Picciotto, Spelman College; Theresa Redd, Howard University; Julie Tilton, San Bernardino Valley College; Linda Woodson, University of Texas at San Antonio; and Frances Zorn, University of Michigan, Ann Arbor—for perceptive evaluations of our proposal and good advice at several stages of the project.

Finally, our students in our composition, ESL, and cross-cultural courses at the University of Massachusetts, Lowell, and Boston University for their help in teaching us how to teach in a multicultural classroom.

Preface for Students

Writing instructors will use the material in this book in a variety of ways, with different emphases, applications, and assignments. As editors, we see ourselves as partners in a teacher-student-textbook collaborative. The teachers teach; the textbook is a teacher's aide.

When we decided to put together a multicultural reader, we found that while we did not always agree on particulars, we did share some important basic assumptions:

Student Audience

One way or another, for better and for worse, we are members of groups. We are born into a family, and are immediately identified by gender, race, nationality, residence, and religion. As we grow older we take on other group identities, becoming teenagers, college students, psychology majors, music lovers, baseball fans—the list is endless. We seldom go through a day without several group references to our age, education, profession, annual income, sexuality, special interests, enthusiasms, or relationships. What makes us different from each other is not only that we are members of *different* groups but that we do not necessarily feel the same way about our memberships *within* the groups. What is important is our *degree* of group commitment, the *level* of group consciousness, the *intensity* of group identity. But we also believe that all students—whether with strong or moderate or weak group identities—should be aware of at least some of the significant events in the cultural-political-economic history and life of individuals who identify or are identified with particular groups.

Selections

We have collected readings that reflect both intergroup and intragroup diversity in our pluralistic society and have tried to provide a spectrum of perspectives on some of the important events in this nation's multiethnic development and the problems we face today. Objectivity, of course, does not mean indifference. Our view is that it is possible for textbook editors to be fair and open-minded, that is, to recognize that reasonable, decent people can often disagree. We cannot claim to have achieved perfect balance, pro and con, on all issues. We have tried not to slant this book to the left or to the right, and we do not believe that such objectivity results in an ineffective, noncommitted middle.

We have tried to be as inclusive as possible within our space limitations. In six hundred pages we could not find room for even a third of the 106 ethnic groups described in the *Harvard Encyclopedia of American Ethnic Groups.* Our limitation in including readings about particular groups does not imply that they are not significant, and we encourage you to supplement this text with other easily available material and make use of your own experiences as they relate to issues raised here.

Focus

Our pluralistic society has been described in a number of ways—as a melting pot, a salad bowl, a patchwork quilt, a mosaic, a kaleidoscope. In this book we see the evolution of American society not as pieces or layers that are added with the arrival of new groups but as a dialectic of confrontation and accommodation as groups come into contact with each other. From the arrival of the first immigrants to the present day, ethnicity has played an important role in the shaping of America. Instances of confrontation can be seen from the time of the Puritan Nathaniel Ward, who declared, "My heart has naturally detested . . . foreigners dwelling in my country" to the exclusionary laws and nativist agitation of the nineteenth century to the variety of contemporary forms of confrontation—segregation, discrimination, chauvinism, separatism, hostility, and violence. The equally significant thread of accommodation is traceable from Roger Williams's affirmation of the "liberty of conscience" of all human beings and his respect for the traditions of Native Americans to the civil rights legislation of the 1960s to a variety of contemporary forms of accommodation—toleration, inclusion, compromise, acculturation, commonality, unity. This dialectic—between groups, within groups (intergenerationally and socioeconomically), and within individuals—is evident throughout the book from the first unit, "National Identity and Cultural Pluralism," to the last unit on the current controversy over multicultural education.

We believe that reading about where we come from (culturally as well as geographically), how we've interacted in confrontation and accommodation, and how this interaction has brought us to current problems, controversies and opportunities will contribute to a society in which, in the words of Martin Luther King, "all of God's children will be able to join hands." Although it is impossible to be definitive in a single text, we have tried to bring together materials that will meet the needs of an informed citizenry still looking for answers.

You will discover, if you have not already, that some multicultural issues elicit strong responses. Several readings in this book address questions now being debated on many college campuses. It is best that such debate be based on knowledge and analysis rather than on easy slogans, quick certainties, and sentimental evasions. A recent survey of over 200,000 first-year college students reported that 42 percent agreed that "helping to promote racial harmony" is an essential or very important goal. It is the hope of the editors that this book will help make it possible for you to move all of us closer to that goal.

PART

I

NATIONAL IDENTITY AND CULTURAL PLURALISM

He *is an American, who, leaving behind him all his ancient prejudices and manners, receives new ones from the new mode of life he has embraced, the new government he obeys, and the new rank he holds. He becomes an American by being received in the broad lap of our great* Alma Mater.

Here individuals of all nations are melted into a new race of men, whose labours and posterity will one day cause great change in the world. Americans are the western pilgrims, who are carrying along with them that great mass of arts, sciences, vigour, and industry, which began long since in the east; they will finish the great circle. The Americans were once scattered all over Europe; here they are incorporated into one of the finest systems of population which has ever appeared, and which will hereafter become distinct by the power of the different climates they inhabit. The American ought, therefore, to love this country much better than that wherein either he or his forefathers were born. . . .

—"WHAT IS AN AMERICAN?" *Michel Guillaume St. Jean de Crèvecoeur*

National Identity and Cultural Pluralism

"WHAT THEN IS THE American, this new man?" Crèvecoeur asked at the end of the eighteenth century. In speaking of "this new man"—today, more inclusively, this new human being—Crèvecoeur had no doubt that Americans were, in fact, different from their ancestors and their contemporaries in the Old World, their character molded by replacing "old prejudices and manners" with new ideals born of freedom and equality. Crèvecoeur envisioned "all individuals of all nations . . . melted into a new race of men." Such a creation of a "new race" implies the giving up of former identifications and allegiances. It implies as well a universal process in which all are changed and all willingly take on a shared identity with others who might seem to be very different from themselves. Crèvecoeur's vision found popular expression in Israel Zangwill's play *The Melting Pot*, which had a successful run in New York in 1908. But a glance at American society today may yield an impression of diversity rather than unity—one finds a climate in which the notion of "melting," with its associations of becoming indistinguishable, is to many people unacceptable. Indeed, as Andrew T. Kopan points out in "Melting Pot: Myth or Reality?" the notion of a melting pot in which diversity would be erased was never a popular concept among ethnic groups in the United States. Nor has it proven to be an accurate social vision. In "A Rap on Race," Margaret Mead and James Baldwin agree that the melting pot has "a very unfortunate image," representing a concept that people naturally resist. In "How American Are You?" Michael Novak speaks strongly against the kind of "psychic repression" that such a concept of a "homogenized America" imposes on the individual.

The face of America continues to change and with it the expectations of how much ethnicity should remain visible in the behavior and allegiance of new Americans. As the ideal has shifted from assimilation to cultural pluralism, the metaphors used to describe our cultural mix have changed to mirror an increasing emphasis on and acceptance of diversity. As Richard Rodriguez has observed, "The melting pot has been retired, clanking, into the museum of quaint disgrace." In its place have appeared successively the metaphors of "stew" (one unified flavor, with recognizable contributing entities, each altered by the cooking process) and then "salad bowl" (distinctly separate entities, contributing to a colorful and varied whole and perhaps bathed in a dressing of general culture, yet undergoing none of the internal changes that cooking would bring about). If one were to continue the evolution of the culinary metaphor, one might observe that at its most radical, the call for cultural pluralism rearranges the salad bowl into a kind of vegetable platter, with ethnic groups asserting their rights to retain their own flavors and textures discrete from the others grouped around a central bowl of "general culture" dip. Each variety remains distinct, yet all have in common proximity to something which, as we share in it, unites us all.

In many obvious ways the United States is a pluralistic society and must therefore continually answer the question of whether such pluralism is antithetical to the existence of a unified national identity. What is it that defines the United States, in Walt Whitman's words, as a "nation of nations" rather than a gathering of separate groups sharing little more than geography? In this nation, where the people do not share a common ethnic, linguistic, religious, or political ancestry, and where there is more ethnic diversity than in any other country, nationhood is defined primarily in terms of ideological commitment. In *Democracy in America* (1835–1840), Alexis de Tocqueville identified what has continued to be the glue that holds together and defines the diverse American population when he observed that being participants in their own governing can arouse in people an interest in and commitment to national welfare. Patriotism, he noted, "grows by the exercise of civil rights." The principles of freedom and democracy upon which the nation was founded require that people work together, making compromises and forming coalitions beyond their small circles of kin and neighbors. The political freedom to effect changes grants individuals the possibility of improving their lot, and thus the pursuit of personal and group interest and loyalty to national community become one.

As Louis H. Lapham observes in "Who and What Is American?", "We protect the other person's liberty in the interest of protecting our own." The exercise of civic responsibility fosters recognition of common interests. Thus, the national consciousness of the United States derives from its political process. We are, as Lapham points out, voluntarily bound together by the freedoms we enjoy. Political scientists Gabriel Almond and Sidney Verba gave the name "civic culture" to this sort of politically based culture, which is marked by (1) a people's agreement on the legitimacy of their political institutions and the course of public policy, (2) tolerance for and belief in the reconcilability of religious and cultural differences, and (3) trust in the ability of citizens to make competent political decisions. The ideological core of the civic culture is buttressed by participation in national rituals (observation of such holidays as the Fourth of July, singing of a national anthem, reciting of a pledge of allegiance), by consensus on national heroes, and by belief in national myths (in this case the concept of the United States as an asylum offering freedom and opportunities for achievement).

Because the opportunities and freedoms promised in this underlying creed applied initially to whites only, the national myth of the United States failed from the beginning to include Native and African-Americans, a situation that both Tocqueville and John Stuart Mill recognized as jeopardizing the entire enterprise. Tocqueville saw the exclusion of blacks from the exercise of civil rights as a dangerous threat to the survival of the nation. Mill, while not referring specifically to black slavery in the United States observed that denial of participation to any persons within an otherwise free society is a contradiction that results in the creation of a group of the permanently disaffected. Indeed, the source of many of the black/white and black/ethnic tensions existing today is the history of enslavement and disenfranchisement that excluded blacks from participation in the civic culture, from the process of self-definition in a national context.

The ideological nature of American nationality is particularly significant to a nation whose growth has depended on immigration. Gaining a legal American identity does not require any particular ethnic, linguistic, or religious credentials. One has simply to renounce hereditary titles and political allegiance to any other state, fulfill a residency requirement, and declare support for the ideals of liberty, equality, and representative government as expressed in the Constitution. Legal identification, however, does not always guarantee emotional attachment, especially for individuals from groups that have experienced exclusion and denigration and for whom, as Andrew Kopan remarks, "the price of success was often the severing of group ties." Being and becoming American is therefore at once a simple procedure and a profoundly complex experience, as individuals protected by the unifying civic culture seek their own ways of expressing their ethnic sensibilities.

Today one finds ethnic diversity celebrated even by Americans several generations from the immigrant experience. Surely one of the most obvious surface features of the American population is the existence of many distinct ethnic and racial groups. Clustered within and on the periphery of our cities are vibrant communities of Vietnamese, Haitians, Cubans, Russians, Thais, Koreans, Cambodians, Puerto Ricans, Colombians, Chinese, Latinos, and immigrants from many other nations, each contributing to the general culture its own foods, styles, vocabulary, music. In response to new waves of immigration in the past twenty years and also to renewed interest in ethnicity among second- and third-generation Americans, our supermarkets are now filled with a dazzling array of ethnic specialties previously found only within ethnic enclaves. Television advertising and programming feature representatives of minority cultures. Bumper stickers announcing pride in national origin are a common sight. Some second- and third- generation Americans are seeking out and readopting family names once discarded by forefathers at ports of entry as part of the process of moving from "ethnic" to "American." Now, it seems, the message is that one can be both.

Still, the nature of the coexistence of ethnic consciousness with national unity raises important questions. Does the insistence on maintaining ethnicity as the central fact of one's identity threaten the unity forged by an ideologically defined national character? Does not pluralism easily devolve into factionalism and worse? The past two decades have provided frightening examples of ethnic conflict. Beirut, which once seemed a model of multicultural harmony, became in the 1980s synonymous with ethnic warfare, and the "ethnic cleansing" of Moslems by Bosnian Serbs after the political dissolution of Yugoslavia is a grim reminder of ethnic consciousness run amok. The 1992 riots in Los Angeles following the Rodney King verdict bring the specter closer to home (see McPherson, Hu, Kim, and Terkel in "*Confrontations,*" pp. 461).

Early in the twentieth century, Theodore Roosevelt warned about threats to U.S. national unity posed by "hyphenated Americans" vacillating between dual allegiances. Similarly, Louis Lapham regrets the current fashion of qualifying our American-ness by announcing our identity as white Americans, female Americans, and the like. "The subordination of the noun to the adjectives," according to Lapham, "makes a mockery of both the American premise and the democratic spirit." Dividing ourselves up according to race, ethnicity, gender, age, and similar interest-group units highlights our differences, thereby muting our common interests and lessening what Lawrence H. Fuchs calls our sense of "we-ness." Defining our common ground becomes more difficult and, ironically, in debates over such issues as culturally inclusive curricula, more divisive (see "A Casebook on Multicultural Education," pp. 507).

"What then is the American, this new man?" The answer perhaps must be twofold. On one hand the national character is defined by allegiance to ideals. And therein lies our unity. But these very ideals allow for a cultural diversity that makes American society appear to be in a continual process of redefinition —accommodation—and, unfortunately, confrontation.

FROM A RAP ON RACE

MARGARET MEAD AND JAMES BALDWIN

Margaret Mead (1901–1978) is widely known for her work in social anthropology. She was curator of ethnology at the Museum of Natural History in New York City, taught at Columbia and Fordham, and served on various government commissions. Mead, who was particularly interested in patterns of child rearing, adolescence, and sexual behavior, conducted research in New Guinea, Samoa, and Bali. She also studied American character and culture and analyzed problems in contemporary American society. Among her writings are Coming of Age in Samoa *(1928),* Growing Up in New Guinea *(1930),* Culture and Commitment: A Study of the Generation Gap *(1970).*

James Baldwin (1924–1987) emerged as a leading black commentator on the condition of blacks in the United States with the publication of his first novel, Go Tell It on the Mountain, *in 1953. His novels* Tell Me How Long the Train's Been Gone *(1968) and* Just Above My Head *(1979) are concerned with black identity. Baldwin's nonfiction works include* Notes of a Native Son *(1955),* Nobody Knows My Name *(1961), and* The Fire Next Time *(1963).*

Mead and Baldwin first met on the evening of August 25, 1970. The following evening they began a seven-and-one-half-hour discussion on race and society, which they continued on the following day and night. The entire conversation was recorded and published as A Rap on Race. *In the following excerpt from that conversation, Mead and Baldwin touch on the mixed ancestry of so many Americans, the ability to in a sense choose our ancestors—our "mythical ancestors"—from among all people who came to this country and the natural resistance of people to the melting pot image.*

◆ FREEWRITING

In the epigraph at the opening of this section, Crèvecoeur says that the new American is, indeed, a new person, that ancient prejudices and manners of distant ancestors are far less important than those one acquires from being an American. Before reading "A Rap on Race" freewrite for ten or fifteen minutes about your ancestry and how it has or has not shaped your notion of who you are as an American.

Mead: Years ago, if we had a group of Italians in a city, we'd try to put Italian in as a course at the university but they wouldn't take Italian. Their parents spoke a dialect and were nonliterate, and taking Italian made them feel inferior whereas taking French made them feel superior. So you can break the connection of a people at any point by picking them up bodily and taking them somewhere else and separating them all from their former relatives and countrymen.

Now, I want to tell you about the other funny people in my class. I get a student who says, "Well, I don't know very much about my ancestors. I think they were sort of English, or Scotch or Welsh, or maybe some Dutch. I don't really know much about them." They are almost always Junior League–D.A.R. people. They actually know in every case. They probably can trace eight lines of ancestry, and they have been taught to be ashamed of it. So, they muddle around and look down.

"We're sort of monglers," I was taught to say as a child. Monglers is a Pennsylvania dialect word for a dog of mixed background. My mother would say that we were members of the intellectual proletariat. In the next breath she would say what she thought of the people in Pennsylvania that hadn't come over here until sixteen eighty!

There was one girl in one of my classes who had the most extraordinary mixed ancestry: she was partly Cuban, partly Mexican, but she had one West Virginia old American ancestor. And she had an absolute tone of voice that she had gotten from this grandmother. So, she said she really didn't know where she came from exactly. She knew perfectly well about these other ancestors but they didn't come in. She had the tone of voice of people who play down their ancestors that they are too proud of.

You see, I think we have to get rid of people being proud of their ancestors, because after all they didn't do a thing about it. What right have I to be proud of my grandfather? I can be proud of my child if I didn't ruin her, but nobody has any right to be proud of his ancestors.

Baldwin: Yes. I was just wondering about my own, in fact. I don't know anything about my black ancestors, obviously, and nothing at all about the white ancestors.

Mead: You don't know who they were at all?

Baldwin: No, I just know I have an English name, and God knows how I got that! But I think you are right. That is a very, very tricky thing, though, isn't it? Let us say I can claim Frederick Douglass as one of my ancestors. I am very proud of him because I think he was a great man and in some way handed something down: his indignation was handed down; his clarity was handed down.

Mead: Well, the fact that you claim him is important. The fact that you were brought up with the general idea that he was an ancestor can be important, because that gave you a style of thinking and pride.

Baldwin: That is what I mean when I say it is very tricky. I can see what you mean perfectly well: no one has a right to be proud because you have nothing to do with it and yet—

Mead: And you don't even know whether you have any particular genes or not.

Baldwin: No, you don't even know that. You have no idea what is handed down or how. It does not make a difference now, anyway. And yet one's ancestors have given one something, just the same. It is something difficult to get at.

You know it when you are in trouble, in real trouble. It's true for me and I am sure it must be true for everybody else, one way or another. It is not exactly that you hear a voice. It's just that you pull yourself together to confront whatever it is according to some principle which does not exactly exist in your memory but which has been given to you.

Mead: In the name of your ancestors.

Baldwin: In the name of your ancestors; let us put it that way. I have heard myself walking around the house singing a song I had forgotten, or didn't even know I knew, because I had to get through something and I had to find the only weapons I had. You reach out behind you and pick up whatever there is to confront this moment and to get past it. There is something very mysterious about it. Mystery is the only way I can define it. It is not mystical, but it seems to me that your ancestors give you, if you trust them, something to get through the world.

Mead: Which means in effect that your parents gave you trustworthy ancestors to be proud of. Suppose you had been adopted as a child and never heard about them? Then you'd have no access to them, though they could be just as real biologically.

Baldwin: Yes, but that kind of adoption would mean the breaking of the connection, wouldn't it? What about someone who's a bastard?

Mead: Bastards specialize in knowing who their fathers are. In many parts of the world they know better than their legitimate cousins. They pay more attention to it.

Baldwin: Because it is much more important.

Mead: Yes, well, this is the father that hasn't owned you. So this can become a terribly important thing. But I think that one of the things we have got to sort out in America is the recognition of whatever we know about our ancestors. That is the reason I was talking about the woman legislator, Mrs. Hamilton, recognizing her grandfather. This is important, and people should recognize their mixed ancestry if they have mixed ancestry. How much access they have through a kind of physical identification is different. But they also have to realize that all people who came to this country can be treated as our ancestors.

Baldwin: In fact, have to be.

Mead: We can take Thomas Jefferson and we can take Crispus Attucks and we can take—

Baldwin: The American Indian.

Mead: And the American Indian. The one thing you really ought to be allowed to do is to choose your ancestors.

Baldwin: Because finally, in a sense you do, don't you?

Mead: Sure. You pick the people that you care about. How they wrote, in your case. American scientists usually put up in their offices their genealogy, their scientific genealogy. And orthodox American psychoanalysts always have a picture of Freud. There are virtually as many views of Freud as there are of Christ, and which one they pick is very interesting—the young Freud, the old Freud and so forth—whichever, he's there. He's their ancestor. Now, we have a term for this in anthropology: mythical ancestors. And scientists—say you're a chemist; you line up the whole line that you go back to: your teacher and his teacher and his teacher. They are spiritual and mental ancestors, they're not biological ancestors, but they are terribly important.

Baldwin: We are talking about the models that the human race chooses to work from in effect. It is difficult to imagine anyone choosing Hitler as an ancestor, for example.

Mead: There are people who would.

Baldwin: Who do, yes.

Mead: Quite a few of them.

Baldwin: It gets to be rather frightening when you think about it, because it runs very close to the terms in which one elects to live and the reasons for that election. It reveals that depth of whatever dreams you have, and everyone lives by his dreams, really.

Mead: You know, de Gaulle created a great deal of confusion by remarking to some unimaginative American in the beginning of the Free French Movement: "I'm not Joan of Arc." The American couldn't understand why he said it. What was he talking about? he wondered. And, of course, in a sense he was Joan of Arc.

Baldwin: Of course he was!

Mead: He was just trying to separate himself a little from Joan of Arc.

Baldwin: Churchill said, "I know he thinks he is Joan of Arc, but you won't let me burn him."

Mead: So that one of the problems in this country is knowing who you are biologically. Some people have this biological access to Indians and Africans and Europeans, so they have access to three traditions. Some have only two and some have only one. There are very, very few black people, of course, who don't have some white ancestors. There are a few.

Baldwin: There are a few but very few.

Mead: They are very isolated, usually. A few have moved around. There are a few people in upper New York State, for example, who dropped off from the underground railroad, enough of them to marry each other and form a little community. But it is very rare. A lot of studies have been made, and we know it is exceedingly rare.

Baldwin: I suppose it is like that in Puerto Rico, too. That is a curious situation, the whole Puerto Rican thing. I do not know what they are going to do with it. When the boy you mentioned said, "I'm from Puerto Rico," I know what he meant. When they got here they looked like me and they had come off an island where everybody looks more or less like me and where everybody speaks Spanish. Then suddenly they find themselves in America next to the American Negro, whose existence they had never really heard of. And he didn't speak Spanish—that's one shock. On the other hand, the American Negro next to the Puerto Rican thought the Puerto Rican was speaking Spanish in order not to be identified with him. And when the boy said, "I'm from Puerto Rico," the American Negro thought, He means he is better than I am. Now, the boy didn't mean that, at least not in the beginning.

Mead: He did later.

Baldwin: He did later, yes. But in the beginning he only meant that he was from Puerto Rico and, I suppose, he had to hold on to that because that was the only thing he had. And, suddenly, here is this incredible melting pot, or whatever it is—

Mead: Well, it isn't a melting pot, is it?

Baldwin: No, it isn't. Nobody ever got melted. People aren't meant to be melted.

Mead: That old image from World War I is a bad image: to melt everyone down.

Baldwin: Because people don't want to be melted down. They resist it with all their strength.

Mead: Of course! Who wants to be melted down?

Baldwin: Melted down into what? It's a very unfortunate image.

Mead: Sometimes there are images. . . . They made a cover for a magazine once in Hawaii, where you have people from everywhere in the world. Around the edges they put faces that were unmistakably Asian, African, Polynesian, Caucasian. Then as you moved toward the center the faces became less and less definite, until you reached the center, where you had a face that you couldn't place. It was beautiful. And of course you see this all the time in Hawaii.

Baldwin: That's very beautiful.

Mead: But you couldn't have that face in the center representing the human race if you did not have all the extremes which contributed to it.

QUESTIONS FOR DISCUSSION

1. Margaret Mead suggests that ancestral pride is a right we don't have because we "didn't do a thing about it" (5). James Baldwin agrees to a point. But he promotes the notion that "one's ancestors have given one something, just the same . . . something to get through the world" (11, 14). Respond to these positions, and discuss whether or not they are mutually exclusive.

2. Mead suggests that it is important to realize that "all people who came to this country can be treated as our ancestors" (19). Baldwin adds that we select our ancestors as "models that the human race chooses to work from" (26). Discuss these ideas about ancestry, and try to think of your own ancestry in this context.

3. Both Mead and Baldwin reject the popular image of America as a melting pot. Discuss what that image suggests, and describe why Mead and Baldwin object to it. What sort of image would they prefer to use to represent our national character?

WRITING ASSIGNMENTS

1. Reaction Journal: The purpose of the reaction journal is to provide you with an opportunity to react privately to the content and/or style of a selection. For the above selection, write a personal response to what Mead and Baldwin imply about the role of ancestors in shaping individual character.

2. Baldwin and Mead agree that we, as human beings and as Americans, have every right to define ourselves by the ancestry we choose. Mead asserts, "The one thing you really ought to be allowed to do is to choose your ancestors" (23). Write an essay in which you define Mead's and Baldwin's notions of ancestors; then proceed to discuss the "ancestors" you have chosen to define you. Defend your choices, and demonstrate how they characterize your sense of being American.

3. "Rap" with one or two of your classmates about relationships between national character and ancestors. Feel free to draw from your readings and from your experience and observation.

MELTING POT: MYTH OR REALITY?

ANDREW T. KOPAN

Andrew T. Kopan (b. 1924) is a professor of Education at De Paul University. In the following essay, he describes the "two-way process" of immigration in which immigrants both change and are changed by America. In the not always welcoming response to new waves of immigrants Kopan notes "an ambivalence in the American character," for the ideal of equality frequently exists alongside the practice of discrimination. "Melting Pot: Myth or Reality" originally appeared in Cultural Pluralism *(1974), edited by Edgar G. Epps. Kopan was coeditor of* Rethinking Educational Equality *(1974).*

◆ FREEWRITING

Andrew Kopan employs two images to describe America's national identity: the melting pot and the mosaic. Before reading Kopan's essay, freewrite for ten or fifteen minutes. Describe what each image suggests to you, and discuss why each one does or does not define our national character.

Every nation has had its immigration and emigration problems. But the mass immigration that took place to the United States is unmatched elsewhere. In the more than 350 years since the English established their first permanent settlement at Jamestown, some 45 million people have migrated to these shores. This figure is many times greater than the American population in 1776. It is several times the number of people now living in the eight Rocky Mountain states. The peopling of America adds up to the greatest migration of all time, dwarfing all other population movements before or since.

Just a little more than a century ago Walt Whitman, the poet of democracy, hailed the United States as a "nation of nations." No phrase better sums up this country's cosmopolitan history. America was discovered by Scandinavians, named by a German mapmaker in honor of a Florentine explorer, and opened for colonization by a Genoese sea captain in the Spanish service. Captain Columbus' crew was a preview of things to come. It included an Englishman, a Negro, an Irishman, a Jew, and probably several Greeks.[1]

Non-Europeans got here long before Columbus. Will Rogers, the Oklahoma humorist who was part Cherokee, liked to say that his ancestors met the Mayflower when it was docked. Yet, like the Pilgrims, the first Indians were immigrants. In the distant past, according to anthropologists, the Indians migrated from Siberia across the Bering Strait and displaced the aboriginal American population. Where the earlier population originated has not been determined.

But the question of who came first is irrelevant. What is important is that, whether one traces his family back to Ellis Island, Plymouth Rock, the Bering Strait, or Africa, every American realizes that his ancestors came here from somewhere else. That is what President Franklin D. Roosevelt, who was of Dutch ancestry, meant when he reminded the Daughters of the American Revolution: "Remember, remember always, that all of us . . . are descended from immigrants. . . ."

But Americans have not just come from somewhere; they have come from 5
almost everywhere. Immigration explains why the people of this nation are unique in the diversity of their ancestry. They spring from a multitude of stocks that have made their way to this land from Europe, Asia, Africa, the Middle East, and Latin America.

This diversity has affected almost every aspect of United States history. Like the westward movement, to which is was related, immigration was a creative force in the shaping of American society. American culture emerged from the interplay between immigrant heritages and the New World environment.

Our language; our government, politics, and economy; our religions, music, arts, literature, and sciences; our educational systems; our sports, entertainment, even much of the food we eat—all testify, in one way or another, to immigrant cultural backgrounds.

But immigration was, and remains, a two-way process. To know that immigrants altered America is not enough. We also have to see how America altered the immigrants. Otherwise, we fail to understand the meaning of the journey for the immigrant and for his children as well. The wilderness and the frontier changed the institutions the immigrants brought with them,[2] as did the melting pot theory and the concept of cultural pluralism.

Long before the American colonies were settled, Spanish and French explorers left their mark on the vast American wilderness. The Spanish influence is found in a wide arc across the southern part of the country, from Florida through Texas and New Mexico to California. The French influence is apparent up and down the Mississippi and Ohio River valleys.

The first wave of settlement came with the colonists at Jamestown in 1607 and at Plymouth in 1620. It was predominantly English in origin. The urge for greater economic opportunity together with the desire for religious freedom led these people to leave their homes. Of all the groups that have come to America, they had the most difficult physical environment to master, but the easiest social adjustment to make. They fought a rugged land, which was hard, but they built a society in their own image, never knowing the hostility of the old toward the new that would face succeeding groups. Although the original states were former English colonies, the inhabitants were by no means wholly English in origin, customs, or religion. The southern back country was settled by Germans, Scotch, Scotch-Irish, and Welsh. Along the southern seaboard, however, the English predominated. Similar backgrounds characterized the people of Pennsylvania. French Huguenots were conspicuous in Charleston, South Carolina; Swedish Lutherans in Delaware; Dutch Calvinists in New Amsterdam and Albany, New York; Roman Catholics in Maryland; and Greek Orthodox in Florida. By 1750 New York City was already on its way to becoming the most cosmopolitan city in the world. Forty years later, when the first U.S. census was taken, a little more than half the people in this country were of African, Scottish, Scotch-Irish, Welsh, German, Dutch, Swedish, Spanish, French, and other non-English stock, and they were divided into more than a hundred religious denominations.

Shortly after 1820, the first year in which the Census Bureau records foreign immigration, there was a considerable Irish influx. This movement reached its height in the late 1840's and the 1850's, owing chiefly to the severe potato famine and other causes of internal discontent and unrest in Ireland. About the same time the first considerable migration of Germans to this country began—a migration that was to continue in increasingly large numbers down to the early 1880's. The crushing of the liberals in Germany in 1848 (when Carl Schurz came to America and Karl Marx went to England), together with the economic difficulties at about the same time, were the motivating factors in this move- 10 ment. During the same period, or a little later, many Swedes, Norwegians, and Danes also came to the United States, settling mostly in the upper Midwest.

Until 1885, by far the major number of foreign immigrants to the United States came from the countries of northwestern Europe. With few exceptions these settlers were of Teutonic and Celtic origin, possessing ideals, customs, standards of living, modes of thought, and religious beliefs similar to those of the earlier settlers: illiteracy was uncommon; education was highly esteemed; for the most part, homes were established in farming communities; and, except for the Germans, and, to some extent, the Irish, there was little tendency among the newcomers to settle in ethnic groups. Before 1880 immigration presented few obstacles to successful Americanization.

A major group that did meet obstacles, even though they were of Celtic origin, were the Irish Catholics. The advent of large numbers of these people in the eastern cities, and the establishment of their church schools, was looked upon by many Americans (themselves descended from earlier immigrant groups) as a menace to national security, and it resulted in a strong nativist movement. Protestant America's fear of Irish Catholics and of popery led to the burning of schools and convents and to riots in cities such as Boston, Philadelphia, and New York. In New York City an extended controversy over the use of public school funds by Irish Catholics resulted in the establishment of the first real public schools there in 1852. A political party, the Know-Nothing party, was even organized in 1853 to oppose Catholics and immigrants, especially Irish and Germans who urged that the United States intervene politically in their homelands. The party urged restriction of immigration, but the outbreak of the Civil War diverted the attention of the country.[3]

About 1885 America's immigration patterns changed. No longer did the majority of immigrants come from northwestern Europe; instead, larger and larger waves came from southern and eastern Europe. Where before 1885 nine-tenths of the immigrants had come from northwestern Europe, by 1905 three-fourths of them came from countries in southern and eastern Europe. Their religion was predominantly Roman Catholic, Greek Orthodox, or Jewish; customs, habits, and, to some extent, ideals formed striking contrasts to those of northern and western Europe. Illiteracy ranged from 13.7 percent to 78.9 percent in Serbia. Moreover, the various Slavic groups such as the Ruthenians, the Czechs, Croatians, Ukrainians, and Poles were a "subject people" unfamiliar with the democratic processes of western Europe and the United States. Furthermore, this "new" immigration, including Italians, Greeks, and the Jews, tended to settle in ethnic colonies in large cities, thus isolating themselves from the mainstream of American life. Most serious, perhaps, was the fact that, unlike earlier immigrants, many of the latecomers did not intend to make America a permanent home, and they had no desire to become Americans. . . .

All of these migrations were regarded as unwelcome and socially destructive by groups already settled and partially acculturated. Those of English or Anglo-Saxon origins looked down upon the Irish, the Germans, and the Scandinavians, who, in turn, looked down upon the Italians, the Slavs, the Greeks, and the Jews.

Today, their descendants look down upon the Puerto Ricans, the Mexican-Americans, and the Negroes, who, as the most recent immigrants or migrants are often considered inferior and a threat to what is "American," whatever that means. Thus, a recurring nativism continues to afflict our nation, creating numerous social, political, and educational problems. And yet, all the migrations had one purpose—the uprooting of peoples in order that they and their children might have a better chance, truly a part of the American dream!

The idea of the melting pot is as old as the Republic. "I could point out to 15
you a family," wrote the naturalized New Yorker, Jean de Crèvecoeur, in 1782, "whose grandfather was an Englishman, whose wife was Dutch, whose son married a Frenchwoman, and whose present four sons have now four wives of different nations. *He* is an American, who leaving behind him all his ancient prejudices and manners, receives new ones from the new mode of life he has embraced. . . . Here individuals of all nations are melted into a new race of men. . . ." It was an idea close to the heart of the American self-image. But as a century passed, and the number of individuals and nations involved grew, the confidence that they could be fused together waned, as did the conviction that it would be a good thing if they were to be. In 1882 the Chinese were excluded, and the first general immigration law was enacted, to be followed by a steady succession of new and more selective barriers. Then, in the National Origins Act of 1924, the nation formally adopted the policy of using immigration to reinforce, rather than further dilute, the racial stock of early America. . . .

It was once believed that the system of public education with its almost universal use of English would produce a nation unilingual and unicultural at base. The successful operation of this principle was taken for granted, for the public schools did help to acculturate and Americanize untold thousands of immigrants. Revisionist writers now question such statements,[4] but it was World War I that clearly established that the nation was not of one culture and one language and that neither Jacksonian democracy, with its assertion of the similarity and equality of all, nor the later theory of the melting pot had worked effectively. While the public schools were teaching in English, private schools, particularly certain parochial groups, Protestant, Roman Catholic, and some Greek Orthodox, were carrying out instruction in various foreign tongues. Both industrial centers and rural regions contained communities culturally distinct from their American surroundings and conscious of their separate identity.

These communities, especially those of the so-called "new" immigration, added constantly to their ranks from streams of newly arrived immigrants and from the American people's failure to practice their national theory of equality. These immigrants congregated for mutual protection in ethnic colonies, especially in the large cities, because they were denied entry (like the blacks later) into the broader community. The ethnic colonies served as decompression chambers or mutual protective groups, where "wops," "hunkies," or "kikes" (as they were often branded), forced by social pressure back into their ghettos, could seek their place among their own kind. Of low economic status and without an intelligentsia (except in the case of the Jews), leaderless and with a tendency to lose successful members since the price of success was often the severing of group ties, these immigrant communities hung on in most American cities, ignored by many and condemned by others as un-American.

Thus there is ambivalence in the American character: the proclamation of the equality of all people as exemplified in the Declaration of Independence and the Federal Constitution, on the one hand; and the practice of discrimination and the denial of equality, on the other hand. It is this ambivalence that contributed in part to the development of ethnic communities. Rebuffed socially and often economically, the immigrant groups developed certain characteristics. Mutual benefit societies have been formed to assist members at times of sickness or death and, incidentally, to serve as social gathering places. Food stores and restaurants purveying familiar food have served as gossip centers where news is shared and stereotypes of thought and action are reinforced and preserved. In most communities a church follows the first signs of prosperity, as soon as the group is able to support a minister or priest. To many an immigrant his religion is the only experience that he can carry unchanged from his old home to his new. Whether or not a school follows the establishment of the church depends largely upon the leadership, for the demand for education is far from universal among immigrants, who are often illiterate. The development of schools is most apt to be stimulated by religious authorities seeking either to preserve the religious affiliation of a group exposed to alien ways or to enable a particular church to survive. Such schools, whether supplementary or full-time, have been organized by evangelical Scandinavians, Polish Catholics, German Lutherans, Greek Orthodox, and Orthodox Jews, to name some. In these schools, the ethnic language, history, and traditions are taught to second and third generations of immigrants, sometimes alongside English studies. When not supported by religious leaders, such schools are usually the work of organization officials who see in the younger generation the only way to maintain organizations that originally grew up to protect newcomers.

When a community is sufficiently large and literate, there are publications in the native tongue to spread news of the old country and of the community itself and to interpret the affairs of the nation at large. Professional men within the group perform necessary services. Traditional forms of entertainment develop. The community in many instances becomes so complete that its members practically never leave it (except to move from one such community to another). They do not think in other terms, hardly read American news, rarely meet other people or make contact with the outer community. Such isolation as this exists most conspicuously in more or less separate industrial communities, but it is almost as characteristic of blocks in the ghettos of large cities (for example, Jewtown, Little Italy, Greektown, Little Lithuania, Little Warsaw, and Chinatown, among others, in Chicago). Although it can hardly remain so complete for more than one generation in a city, a new generation does not see the end of the old isolation.

These separate communities consist of a solid, group-conscious nucleus sur- 20
rounded by a fringe that is gradually being worn away by intermarriage, educa-

tion, participation in activities such as sports, and economic change. They are torn by internal conflicts between the generations, for the first generation of native-born children, subjected to external influences, differs sharply in ways and attitudes from the parents. The internal factors holding the communities together are weakened whenever immigration is reduced, and the attitude of the broader community gains strength and becomes the perpetuating force.

Of course, the force of economic pressure is constantly at work, breaking down isolation, producing physical mobility, encouraging contacts among members of different groups, and rewarding those who achieve financial success with scant regard for the group from which they come. Sociologists tell us that, from among the people of the "new" immigration, the Jews, Greeks, Syrians, and Armenians were the first to reach middle-class status, and this was due chiefly to their mercantile background.[5] Yet even as these groups climbed the socioeconomic ladder and moved out of the ethnic community, they retained much of their ancestral ethnicity down to the third and fourth generation.

We may argue whether it is "nature" that returns to frustrate continually the imminent creation of a single American nationality. The fact is that, in every generation throughout the history of the American republic, the merging of the varying streams of population, differentiated from one another by origin, religion, and outlook, has seemed to lie just ahead—a generation yet to come, perhaps. This continual deferral of the final melting of the different ingredients (or at least of the different white ingredients) into a seamless national web such as is found in the major national states of Europe suggests that we must search for some systematic and general causes for this American pattern of subnationalities and subcultures. It is not the temporary upsetting inflow of new and unassimilated immigrants that creates a pattern of ethnic groups within the nation; rather it is some central tendency in the national ethos that structures people, whether those coming in afresh or the descendants of those who have been here for generations, into groups of different status and character.

Fifty years after mass immigration from Europe ended, the ethnic pattern is still strong in the United States. Four major factors appear to have contributed to the survival of ethnicity:

1. After every wave of immigration strong sentiments of "nativism" resulted in prejudice against immigrants, forcing them to close ranks for protection and to isolate themselves into ethnic colonies.

2. Cultural conservatives in the ethnic communities exhorted their compatriots to remain loyal to their religion, language, customs, and traditions. These flames were generally fanned by the immigrant press, whose editors were usually culturally conservative, as well as by the organized church.

3. Politicians exploited immigrants for their vote, and ethnic political organizations were courted by both political parties.

4. Third and fourth generation descendants of immigrants desired to seek out their ancestral roots and to perpetuate ethnic traditions—foods, songs, dances—which gave them identity. This is not unlike the current movement among Negroes in their search for identity and an acceptable self-concept.

The mosaic of subcultures that thus characterizes the United States has given rise to the concept of "cultural pluralism." . . .

Cultural pluralism has given America its strength. Immigration has made the United States a world power of over 200 million people. The immigrants that came to America, both white and black, tilled the fields, manned the industries, built the railroads, and did many other things that made the country the industrial giant that it is. As its motto—*E pluribus unum*—proclaims, the United States remains truly one nation out of many people.

Notes

1. Arthur Mann, *Immigrants in American Life* (Boston: Houghton Mifflin Co., 1968), 2; Seraphim G. Canoutas, *Hellenism in America* (New York: Cosmos Publishing Co., 1918), 20–21. I am indebted to Professor Mann for this section of the paper.

2. For a general account of the difficulties experienced by immigrants and the impact of the American social order upon them see Oscar Handlin, *The Uprooted* (New York: Grosset and Dunlap, 1951); Michael Kraus, *Immigration: The American Mosaic* (Princeton, New Jersey: D. Van Nostrand Co., 1966).

3. A standard work on this topic is Ray A. Billington, *The Protestant Crusade, 1800–1860: A Study of the Origins of American Nativism* (New York: Macmillan Co., 1918).

4. Colin Greer, "Public Schools: The Myth of the Melting Pot," *Saturday Review* 52 (November 15, 1969), 84–85; see also Colin Greer, *Cobweb Attitudes: Essays on Educational and Cultural Mythology* (New York: Teachers College Press, Columbia University, 1970), ch. 1; Charles E. Silberman, *Crisis in the Classroom* (New York: Vantage Books, 1970), 53–61.

5. Bernard C. Rosen, "Race, Ethnicity, and the Achievement Syndrome," *American Sociological Review* 24 (February 1959), 47-60.

QUESTIONS FOR DISCUSSION

1. In paragraph 7 Kopan states his thesis and reinforces his title. Discuss how effectively he prepares his readers for his thesis. Discuss the rhetorical strategies in the preceding six paragraphs.

2. Kopan points out that America's immigration patterns changed about 1885. Explain why. Discuss why the image of America as melting pot was no longer appropriate after this shift in patterns.

3. Discuss the significance of each of the following:
   a. "But immigration was, and remains, a two-way process" (7).
   b. "Before 1880 immigration presented few obstacles to successful Americanization" (11).
   c. "Thus there is ambivalence in the American character" (18).

d. "Rather it is some central tendency in the national ethos that structures people" (22).

4. In paragraph 14 Kopan describes the "recurring nativism" that continues to afflict our nation. Explain what he means. Point to examples of such nativism in your region.

WRITING ASSIGNMENTS

1. Reaction Journal: Write a personal response to Kopan's essay. Try to focus on how Kopan's thoughts are or are not consistent with your private thoughts on whether you live in a nation or a group of subnations.

2. Write an essay in which you describe the cultural and ethnic backgrounds of your ancestors. You may have to interview elder family members as you gather your information. Organize your essay chronologically. Use the organization of paragraphs 8–13 of Kopan's essay as a model.

3. Certainly a key point in Kopan's essay is the "recurring nativism" that he mentions in paragraph 14. Indeed, such nativist sentiment still afflicts our nation as we move closer to the twenty-first century. Write an essay in which you give current examples of such nativism. You may wish to include a section on how the popular media exploit or condemn this attitude in cinema and television.

HOW AMERICAN ARE YOU?

MICHAEL NOVAK

Michael Novak (b. 1933) is the author of numerous books, including Belief and Unbelief *(1965),* The Rise of the Unmeltable Ethnics *(1972), and* Human Rights and the New Realism *(1986). He has taught Philosophy, Religious Studies, and American Studies at a number of universities and is currently Professor of American Studies at the University of Notre Dame. An American of Slovak descent, Novak is sensitive to the needs of ethnic groups to understand themselves and be understood in their own historical and cultural contexts, particularly those white ethnic groups apparently so assimilable yet estranged by class and education from American intellectual life.*

The selection below is excerpted from Novak's essay "How American Are You If Your Grandparents Came from Serbia in 1888?" which is the first chapter in The Rediscovery of Ethnicity *(ed. Sallie TeSelle, 1973). In this essay, Novak argues for the "new ethnicity," a broad form of ethnic consciousness that he believes will lead to a genuine cultural pluralism, to reduced conflicts, and to effective coalitions among such groups as blacks and white ethnics.*

◆ FREEWRITING

In paragraph 35, Michael Novak asserts that "in America, every group is a minority." He goes on to emphasize that even America's "core culture," the Anglo-Saxon Protestant, is a minority. Freewrite for ten or fifteen minutes in response to Novak's assertions.

Now that the theme of "ethnicity" has blazed up again before public eyes, a number of important questions have been raised, a number of objections voiced. What is the meaning of ethnicity? What is the difference between the "old ethnicity" and the "new ethnicity"? Is *everybody* ethnic? What political implications follow?

One of the most interesting developments is the abrupt rejection of ethnic analysis altogether. This rejection is of three types. Those who have been trying all their lives to *get over* their ethnic origin and join the influential mainstream sometimes see the experience of ethnicity as regressive; sometimes don't even want the subject brought up, have vivid emotional reactions against it; sometimes experience a new sense of relaxation and liberation, in a kind of expanded and (at last) integrated self-consciousness.

A second type of rejection occurs among some who have for a time been living in "superculture," that is, in the influential mainstream of power, wealth, and ideas, apart from any ethnic "sub-culture." In the 1930's many intellectuals retained not only an ideological but also an experiential contact with lower-middle-class workers. Since the Second World War the population of superculture has expanded enormously, and now there are millions of educated suburban Americans who maintain almost no contact, ideological or experiential, with ordinary people who work for a living, in blue-collar or white-collar jobs. One sees this gap between cultures on university campuses between faculty and other staff members, or at newspaper offices between the city room and the press room.

It used to be that democracy meant faith in "the common man." But for some time now the common man has come to be perceived as the nation's greatest menace, a racist, a fascist, and—if one is pressed—a pig. All hope is placed in "a constituency of conscience," as opposed presumably to people without conscience. Needless to say, anyone who writes *in support of* the white ethnic is looked upon with puzzlement. What's a nice man like you doing with people like those? . . . This puzzlement sometimes changes to shock, horror, and indignation if the subject is seriously pursued.

5 Thus passionate intensity is frequently stirred by the theme of ethnicity, most remarkably among people who believe in the universality of reason or love and simultaneously bewail the blandness and mindless conformity of the suburbs. Perhaps this is because the theme of ethnicity intimately involves each participant. Each is challenged to examine his or her own life for its ethnic materials. Almost by definition, these are more unconscious than not, having been taught informally rather than in explicit words or deeds. Gratitude for being prompted to live the examined life is sometimes keen, but sometimes absent.

This invitation to self-examination, moreover, is not simply a use of the *ad hominem* argument. In a reasonably homogeneous culture, as in England or France, the terms of discourse are reasonably fixed. In a heterogeneous one like ours, the key terms themselves derive from our different historical experiences of America. Words like "moral" used in politics mean something different to a house mother in a dormitory in a small Ohio college, to Philip Roth, to John Courtney Murray, to Shirley MacLaine, to George Meany, to Jesse Jackson. When you see each speaker in his or her own historical context, the words make considerably more sense, even if one continues to disagree. The more sensitive to historical nuance one becomes, the more intelligible various classical arguments—between sectarian and mainline Protestants, for example—become. In the United States, our personal histories retain an influential ethnic and regional component, to which far too little note is methodologically paid. Thus many of our arguments result not in mutual understanding but in frustration and separation.

A third type of rejection occurs among some who are quite unconscious of any ethnicity on their part at all, either because they're simply white Anglo-Saxons who "don't make anything of it" or because they're "veritable living melting pots," nobody having traced the family's intermarriages for years. Anglo-Saxons who learn English in school, read English literature, have long learned the superiority of English political institutions, and unconsciously accept Anglo-Saxon rituals and traditions as normative (Thanksgiving dinner without *spaghetti* or *kolache,* for example) are not aware of being ethnic, because the mainstream supports their self-image. Only gradually is the perception dawning that, much as this nation owes the Anglo-Saxon heritage, it is *not* an Anglo-Saxon nation. It is a pluralistic nation. What do you do if your grandmother came to America from Serbia in 1888? The nation is by that increment also made to be Serbian. But when will the cultural impact finally be felt? So many things taken for granted by many in America are unconsciously but effectively ethnocentric. Even the "civil religion" is defined as Anglo-Saxon Protestant—not really even German or Scandinavian Protestant.

Values once highly developed in Anglo-Saxon culture, like those in other groups, are constantly under threat from superculture and its technology—not least that Anglo-Saxon quality par excellence, civility. University students were just yesterday attacking even highly civilized parents as "uptight," "effete," or "subservient." Shouting, for a time at least, was the moralists' vogue. The power of television, the cinema, and high mobility threaten every ethnic culture—which is to say, culture itself. Values and tastes are taught in families and families need, as well, public social supports. We have not yet counted the costs—in anomie, rage, and mindlessness—of allowing families, neighborhoods, and local cultures to bow to commercial forces.

As for those who claim to be "veritable melting pots," one usually finds that the more they talk about their families, the more the "significant others" in their family history come into focus. Certain sympathies, certain ways of looking at things, certain mannerisms of thought or behavior are found to have social antecedents. There is a widespread illusion in America that each individual is alone, entirely invents herself, or wholly creates his own style. Our proverbial historical blindness masks from us the ways in which the experience of past generations continues to live on in each of us, passed on in countless tacit ways in the earliest years of our rearing. The generations are amazingly repetitive in their unpredictable cycles.

In a nation as large and diverse as ours, accurate ethnic perception is crucial 10
for mutual understanding. Regionally, in social class, in race, in religion and in ethnic culture, we differ from one another. We use the same words but in the context of different historical experiences. Yet we, of all peoples, have been afraid of ethnicity! We have treated ethnicity as a dirty secret about which we should not speak, except softly, in hopes it would go away. Even our usage of the term "ethnic" reflects our emotional and intellectual confusion. The following dictionary sample, especially in usages 3 and 4, suggests amusing biases:

> Ethnic, adj. 1. *pertaining to or characteristic of a people, esp. to a speech or cultural group.* 2. *referring to the origin, classification, characteristics, etc. of such groups.* 3. *pertaining to non-Christians.* 4. *belonging to or deriving from the cultural, racial, religious or linguistic traditions of a people or a country, esp. a primitive one:* ethnic dances *(The Random House Dictionary).*

"Non-Christian" and "primitive"—these are the images in the background. Not so subtly, "ethnic" is being contrasted with "civilized," from a Western perspective, indeed, from an English perspective.

For good reasons, educated Americans have for a long time hoped that ethnic differences would weaken and disappear. Ethnic conflicts in Europe seem to antedate even the rise of nationalism. Sometimes for generations, nevertheless, ethnic differences seemed not to lead to conflict and a high degree of cosmopolitan interchange was reached. When religious division and nationalism were added to the mix, however, conflicts were brutal and fierce. So it must not be thought that ethnicity is a neutral, unambiguous, or safe part of human consciousness. No part is. . . .

There are several theses about white ethnics that are conventional but wrong. Let me state them and argue against them.

1. *Ethnic consciousness is regressive.* In every generation, ethnic consciousness is different. The second generation after immigration is not like the first, the third is not like the second. The native language begins to disappear; family and residential patterns alter; prosperity and education create new possibilities. The new ethnicity does not try to hold back the clock. There is no possibility of returning to the stage of our grandparents.

Nevertheless, emotional patterns that have been operative for a thousand years do not, for all that, cease to function. Those of white ethnic background do not usually react to persons, issues, or events like Blacks, or like Jews, or like

Unitarians. In a host of different ways, their instincts, judgments, and sense of reality are heirs to cultural experiences that are now largely unconscious. These intuitive leads, these echoes of yet another language, yet another rhythm, yet another vision of reality, are resources which they are able to recover, if they should so choose.

Jimmy Breslin, for example, has lamented the loss of language suffered by the American Irish. He urges Irish Americans to read Brendan Behan: "For a style is there to examine, and here and there you get these wonderful displays of the complete lock the Irish have on the art of using words to make people smile." Breslin loves "the motion and lilt that goes into words when they are written on paper by somebody who is Irish." He compares Behan's tongue to the language of the 100,000 Irishmen marching down Fifth Avenue on March 17: "You can take all of them and stand them on their heads to get some blood into the skull for thinking, and when you put them back on their feet you will not be able to get an original phrase out of the lot of them. They are Irish and they get the use of words while they take milk from their mothers, and they are residing in the word capital of the world and we find that listed below are the two fine passages representing some of the most important Irish writing being done in the City of New York today." He then lists business notices from Brady the Lawyer and Walsh the Insurance Man.

Jewish writers are strong by virtue of their closeness to the Jewish experience in America—e.g., their sense of story, and irony, and dissent. Mike Royko writes with a hard realism and a blend of humor that is distinctively Slavic; like *The Good Soldier Schweik.* Phil Berrigan refers to Liz MacAlister as "Irish," and shares a traditionally tough Irish priest's suspicion of liberal intellectuals.

Authenticity requires that one write and act out of one's own experience, images, subconscious. Such materials are not merely personal (although they *are* personal) but also social. We did not choose our grandfathers.

2. *Ethnic consciousness is only for the old; it is not shared by the young.* It is true that hardly anyone in America encourages ethnic consciousness. The church, the schools, the government, the media encourage "Americanization." So it is true that the young are less "conscious" of their ethnicity. This does not mean that they do not have it. It does not mean that they do not feel joy and release upon discovering it. Often, all one has to do is begin to speak of it and shortly they begin recollecting, begin raising questions, begin exploring—and begin recovering.

Consider the enormous psychic repression accepted by countless families—the repression required for learning a new language, a new style of life, new values and new emotional patterns, during a scant three or four generations of Americanization. Many descendants of the immigrants who do not think of themselves as "ethnic" experience a certain alienation from public discourse in America, from the schools, from literature, from the media, and even from themselves. Nowhere do they see representations of their precise feelings about sex, authority, realism, anger, irony, family, integrity, and the like. They try to follow traditional American models, of course: the classic Protestant idealism of

George McGovern, for example. They see a touch of their experience in *Portnoy's Complaint.* But nowhere at all, perhaps, will they see artistic or political models expressing exactly their state of soul. Nowhere do they find artists or political leaders putting into words what remains hidden in their hearts.

The young are more ripe for the new ethnicity than the old, for the new 20
ethnicity is an attempt to express the experience of *their* generation, not of an earlier generation. It treats past history only as a means of illuminating the present, not as an ideal to which they must return. The new ethnicity is oriented toward the future, not the past.

3. *Ethnic consciousness is illiberal and divisive, and breeds hostility.* The truth is the reverse. What is illiberal is homogenization enforced in the name of liberalism. What is divisive is an enforced and premature unity, especially a unity in which some groups are granted cultural superiority as models for the others. What breeds hostility is the quiet repression of diversity, the refusal to allow others to be culturally different, the enforcement of a single style of Americanism. Our nation suffers from enormous emotional repression. Our failure to legitimate a genuine cultural pluralism is one of the roots of this repression. Our rationalization is fear of disunity; and in the name of unity, uniformity is benignly enforced. (The weapon of enforcement is ordinarily shame and contempt.)

Countless young Italians were given lessons in school on how *not* to talk with their hands; Latin girls were induced to shave their lips and legs; Irish girls to hide their freckles; Poles to feel apologetic about their difficult names; Italians to dread association with criminal activity; Scandinavians and Poles to hate misinterpretations of their taciturnity and impassive facial expression; Catholics to harden themselves against the anti-Catholicism both of intellectual culture and nativist America.

The assumption that ethnic consciousness breeds prejudice and hostility suggests that Americanization frees one from them. The truth is that *every* ethnic culture—including mainstream America, and, yes, even intellectual America—has within it resources of compassion and vision as well as capacities for evil. Homogenized America is built on a foundation of psychic repression; it has not shown itself to be exempt from bitter prejudices and awful hostilities.

America announces itself as a nation of cultural pluralism. Let it become so, openly and with mutual trust.

4. *Ethnic consciousness will disappear.* The world will end, too. The question is 25
how to make the most fruitful, humanistic progress in the meantime. The preservation of ethnicity is a barrier against alienation and anomie, a resource of compassion and creativity and intergroup learning. If it *might* disappear in the future, it has *not* disappeared in the present. And there are reasons to work so that it never does. Who would want to live on a thoroughly homogenized planet?

5. *Intermarriage hopelessly confuses ethnicity.* Intermarriage gives children multiple ethnic models. The transmission of a cultural heritage is not a process clearly understood. But for any child a "significant other" on one side of the

family or another may unlock secrets of the psyche as no other does. The rhythm and intensity of emotional patterns in families are various, but significant links to particular cultural traditions almost always occur. One discovers these links best by full contact with ethnic materials. It is amazing how persons who claim themselves to have a "very mixed" ethnic background, and "no particular" ethnic consciousness, exhibit patterns of taste and appreciation that are very ethnic indeed: a delight in the self-restraint of Scotsmen, discomfort with the effusiveness of Sicilians—or, by contrast, a sense of release in encountering Sicilian emotions, a constriction of nervousness faced with the puzzling cues of the culture of the Scots.

Cues for interpreting emotion and meaning are subtly learned, in almost wholly unconscious, informal ways. These cues persist through intermarriage for an indeterminate period. Cues to pain, anger, intimacy and humor are involved. (Many of the passages of *The Rise of the Unmeltable Ethnics* were intended ironically and written in laughter; many reviewers, almost exclusively British-American ones, took them seriously, incredulously.)

6. *Intelligent, sensitive ethnics, proud of their heritage, do not go around thumping their chests in ethnic chauvinism.* Who would want chest-thumping or chauvinism? But be careful of the definition of "good" ethnics, "well-behaved" ethnics. Many successful businessmen, artists, and scholars of white ethnic background carry two sets of scars. On the one hand, they had to break from their families, neighborhoods, perhaps ghettoes, and they became painfully aware of the lack of education and experience among those less fortunate than they. On the other hand, they had to learn the new styles, new images, new values of the larger culture of "enlightenment." The most talented succeed rather easily; those of lesser rank have quietly repressed many all-too-painful memories of the period of their transition. As surely as their grandparents emigrated from the homeland, each generation has had to carry the emigration farther. Americanization is a process of bittersweet memory, and it lasts longer than a hundred years.

7. *The new ethnicity will divide group against group.* The most remarkable fact about the new ethnic consciousness is that it is cross-cultural. We do not speak only of "Polish" consciousness or "Italian" consciousness, but of "white ethnic" consciousness. The new ethnicity is not particularistic. It stresses the general contours of *all* ethnicity and notes analogies between the cultural history of the many groups. The stress is not only on what differentiates each group but also upon the similarities of *structure* and *process* in which all are involved. In coming to recognize the contours of his or her own unique cultural history, a person is better able to understand and to sympathize with the uniqueness of others'.

8. *Emphasis on white ethnics detracts from the first priority to be given Blacks.* On 30
the contrary, blindness to white ethnics is an almost guaranteed way of boxing Blacks into a hopeless corner. A group lowest on the ladder cannot advance *solely* at the expense of the next group. Any skillful statesman could discern that in an instant. The classic device of the affluent and the privileged is to pretend to a higher morality, while setting the lower classes in conflict with one another.

The most divisive force in America today is, ironically, precisely the "new class" of liberal and radical academics, media personnel, and social service professionals that thinks itself so moral. Perhaps out of guilt feelings—or for whatever reason—they have projected all guilt for "white racism" onto others. And, without undergoing any of the costs themselves, they take sides or plainly appear to take sides in the very sharp competition between lower-class people, white and black, for scarce jobs, scarce housing, scarce openings in colleges, scarce scholarship funds. They take sides not only with Blacks against whites but also with militant Blacks against other Blacks. For almost a decade they have made "white racism" the central motif of social analysis, and have clearly given the impression that vast resources were going for Blacks, nothing for others. The "Open Admissions" program in New York City schools, e.g., was trumpeted as a program for Blacks and Puerto Ricans. Not much realism would have been required to predict, as turned out to be the case, that 75% of the students taking advantage of the program were white ethnics previously unable to enter colleges.

It is easy for Blacks, at least militant Blacks, to voice their grievances on television and in the papers. It is extremely difficult to get coverage of white ethnic grievances. They are not supposed to *have* grievances, it seems, only prejudices. All problems are defined as black-white problems, even when there are obviously real economic issues for real families in straitened circumstances. With all good intentions, therefore, the desire of liberals to give Blacks highest priority has become exclusionary and divisive.

One can still give Blacks highest priority, but in an inclusionary way that aims at coalitions of whites and Blacks on the grievances they have in common. Newark is divided almost wholly between Blacks and Italians; Detroit between Poles and Blacks. Inadequate schools, the dangers of drugs, insufficient housing, the lack of support for families and neighborhoods—these grievances afflict white ethnics and Blacks alike. If these problems are, by definition, problems of race, what sort of practical coalition can possibly grow? If they are perceived as problems of *class* (with ethnic variables) there is at least a practical ground for effective coalition.

In order for a political coalition to work well, people do not have to love one another; they do not have to share the same life style or cherish the same values. They have to be realistic enough to pursue limited goals in line with their own self-interest. Lower-middle-class Blacks and white ethnics share more self-interests in common than either group does with any other. It is on the basis of shared self-interests that lasting political coalitions are built, and on no other.

9. *Ethnicity is all right for minorities, but not for the mainstream.* In America, 35
every group is a minority. Even among white Anglo-Saxon Protestants there are many traditions. What is often called "mainline Protestantism," centered in the Northeast: Episcopal, Congregational, Presbyterian, is only one tradition within a far larger and more complex Protestant reality. The father of Senator

George McGovern experienced prejudice in South Dakota because the kind of Methodist fundamentalism he represented was closer in style to the lower classes, not fashionable either among "mainline" Methodists nor among Germans and Scandinavians, who were mostly Lutheran. Each of these traditions affects the imagination in a different way. British-Americans from small towns in New England live and work in quite different emotional and imaginative worlds from British-Americans who are Brahmins in Boston and New York. Anglo-Saxon Protestants who are dirt-farmers in Georgia, Alabama, or East Tennessee feel just as much prejudice from Northeastern-style settlers as Polish or Italian Catholics: stereotypes of the Southern sheriff and the redneck function like those of the Irish cop and the dumb hard-hat. The Scotch-Irish and the Scots have a vivid ethnic consciousness, as a conversation with John Kenneth Galbraith and Carey McWilliams, Jr., would make plain.

There is no good reason why we do not all drop our pretensions of being *like* everyone else, and attempt instead to enlarge the range of our sympathies, so as to delight in every observed cultural difference and to understand each cultural cue correctly and in its own historical context. Styles of wit and understatement vary. Each culture has its own traditions of emotional repression and expressiveness. Our major politicians are often misunderstood, systematically, by one cultural group or another; the cues they depend on are absent, or mean something else. . . .

It is not necessary to idealize white ethnics in order to construct a social scheme within which it would be to their advantage to work for equality for Blacks in jobs, housing, and good schools. It is not even necessary to *like* white ethnics. But it does help to understand their history in various parts of America, their spiritual resources, and their chronic weaknesses. Fear of the new ethnicity is very like the early fear of "Black power." Even some Blacks sound, with regard to the new ethnicity, like some whites with regard to Black pride. Such fears must be proven groundless.

If we knew all we had to know about Poles, Italians, Greeks, and others in America, there would perhaps be no need for the almost desperate tones with which the new ethnicity is sometimes announced. But the fact is, we know very little about them. Our anthropologists know more about some tribes in New Guinea than about the Poles in Warren or Lackawanna. We have encouraged too few of the talented white ethnics to stay with their people and to give voice to their experience. Local political leadership is often at a very low level. Community organizers who spring from the community are all too few. Uncle Toms are many. If there is anomie, fear, or rage in such communities (often there is a great deal of bottled-up political energy and great good will), it is to no one's advantage.

The new ethnicity gives promise of *doing* something creative in such places. The new ethnicity is the best hope of all who live in our major urban centers. What we have without it is not promising at all.

QUESTIONS FOR DISCUSSION

1. Explain what a "superculture" is and why those who regard themselves as members of such a group often reject the importance of ethnic analysis altogether. Have you experienced a gap between supercultures and subcultures?

2. Why does Novak cite a dictionary entry in paragraph 10? Discuss the effectiveness of his strategy.

3. Comment on the following ideas on the basis of your own and your family's experience:
   a. "For some time now the common man has come to be perceived as the nation's greatest menace" (4).
   b. "Our personal histories retain an influential ethnic and regional component" (6).
   c. "It [America] is *not* an Anglo-Saxon nation. It is a pluralistic nation" (7).
   d. "So many things taken for granted by many in America are unconsciously but effectively ethnocentric" (7).
   e. "Many descendants of the immigrants who do not think of themselves as 'ethnic' experience a certain alienation from public discourse in America" (19).
   f. "What breeds hostility is the quiet repression of diversity, the refusal to allow others to be culturally different" (21).

4. Novak argues that "the desire of liberals to give Blacks highest priority has become exclusionary and divisive" (32). Explain what he means, and discuss how economic and political coalitions may help this problem.

WRITING ASSIGNMENTS

1. Reaction Journal: In his opening paragraph Novak asks, "What is the difference between the 'old ethnicity' and the 'new ethnicity'?" He concludes his essay by stating that "the new ethnicity is the best hope of all who live in our major urban centers." In your journal write a letter to Mr. Novak. Begin by defining what his notion of "new ethnicity" means to you. Focus on how clearly and convincingly he defined this term.

2. Much of Novak's essay is organized around the principle of classification and division. In paragraph 2, for example, he divides a concept into three types. In paragraph 12 he introduces a similar organizational principle. Following these examples, write a division and classification essay in which you discuss the following: "The power of television, the cinema, and high mobility threaten every ethnic culture—which is to say, culture itself" (8). If you prefer, you may write in response to one of the statements in Question 3 above.

3. Novak mentions that "in every generation, ethnic consciousness is different" (13). Use your own family, or a family you feel comfortable interviewing, and write an essay in which you discuss such generational differences.

4. Write your own cultural history. Discuss how an understanding of such a history helps you understand and sympathize with the uniqueness of others.

WHO AND WHAT IS AMERICAN?

LEWIS H. LAPHAM

Lewis H. Lapham (b. 1935) is Editor of Harper's *magazine. He has been a reporter and writer for the* New York Herald Tribune, *the* Saturday Evening Post, *and* Life *magazine, as well as a television host for the PBS weekly series* "Bookmark" *and the documentary series* "America's Century." *In the following essay, which appeared in* Harper's *in 1992, Lapham speaks of "the improvised character of the American experience" and identifies as the common elements uniting Americans a love of freedom and participation in building the future.*

◆ FREEWRITING

The subtitle of Lewis Lapham's essay is "The Things We Continue to Hold in Common." Before reading his essay, freewrite for ten or fifteen minutes on what you perceive to be the things that all American citizens hold in common.

> There may not be an American character, but there is the emotion of being American. It has many resemblances to the emotion of being Russian—that feeling of nostalgia for some undetermined future when man will have improved himself beyond recognition and when all will be well.
>
> —*V. S. Pritchett*

Were I to believe what I read in the papers, I would find it easy to think that I no longer can identify myself simply as an American. The noun apparently means nothing unless it is dressed up with at least one modifying adjective. As a plain American I have neither voice nor authentic proofs of existence. I acquire a presence only as an old American, a female American, a white American, a rich American, a black American, a gay American, a poor American, a native American, a dead American. The subordination of the noun to the adjectives makes a mockery of both the American premise and the democratic spirit, but it serves the purposes of the politicians as well as the news media, and throughout the rest of this election year I expect the political campaigns to pitch their tents and slogans on the frontiers of race and class. For every benign us, the candidates will find a malignant them; for every neighboring we (no matter how eccentric or small in number), a distant and devouring they. The strategies of division sell newspapers and summon votes, and to the man who would be king (or president or governor) the popular hatred of government matters less than the atmosphere of resentment in which the people fear and distrust one another.

Democratic politics trades in only two markets—the market in expectation and the market in blame. A collapse in the former engenders a boom in the latter. Something goes wrong in the news—a bank swindle of genuinely spectacular size, a series of killings in Milwaukee, another disastrous assessment of the nation's schools—and suddenly the air is loud with questions about the paradox of the American character or the Puritan subtexts of the American soul. The questions arise from every quarter of the political compass—from English professors and political consultants as well as from actors, corporate vice presidents, and advertising salesmen—and the conversation is seldom polite. Too many of the people present no longer can pay the bills, and a stray remark about acid rain or a third-grade textbook can escalate within a matter of minutes into an exchange of insults. Somebody calls Jesse Helms a fascist, and somebody else says that he is sick and tired of paying ransom money to a lot of welfare criminals. People drink too much and stay too late, their voices choked with anecdote and rage, their lexicons of historical reference so passionately confused that both Jefferson and Lincoln find themselves doing thirty-second commercials for racial quotas, a capital gains tax, and the Persian Gulf War.

The failures in the nation's economy have marked up the prices for obvious villains, and if I had a talent for merchandising I would go into the business of making dolls (black dolls, white dolls, red-necked dolls, feminist dolls, congressional dolls) that each of the candidates could distribute at fund-raising events with a supply of color-coordinated pins. Trying out their invective in the preseason campaigns, the politicians as early as last October were attributing the cause of all our sorrows to any faction, interest, or minority that could excite in its audiences the passions of a beloved prejudice. David Duke in Louisiana denounced the subsidized beggars (i.e., black people) who had robbed the state of its birthright. At a partisan theatrical staged by the Democratic Party in New Hampshire, Senator Tom Harkin reviled the conspiracy of Republican money. President Bush went to Houston, Texas, to point a trembling and petulant finger at the United States Congress. If the country's domestic affairs had been left to him, the President said, everybody would be as prosperous and smug as Senator Phil Gramm, but the liberals in Congress (blind as mollusks and selfish as eels) had wrecked the voyage of boundless opportunity.

The politicians follow the trends, and apparently they have been told by their handlers to practice the arts of the demagogue. Certainly I cannot remember an election year in which the political discourse—among newspaper editorialists and the single-issue lobbies as well as the candidates—relied so unashamedly on pitting rich against poor, black against white, male against female, city against suburb, young against old. Every public event in New York City—whether academic appointment, traffic delay, or homicide—lends itself to both a black and a white interpretation of the news. The arguments in the arenas of cultural opinion echo the same bitter refrain. The ceaseless quarrels about the canon of preferred texts (about Columbus the Bad and Columbus the Good, about the chosen company of the politically correct, about the ice people and the sun people) pick at the scab of the same questions, *Who and what is an American?* How and where do we find an identity that is something other than a fright mask? When using the collective national pronoun ("we the people," "we happy few," etc.) whom do we invite into the club of the we?

Maybe the confusion is a corollary to the end of the Cold War. The image 5
of the Soviet Union as monolithic evil held in place the image of the United States as monolithic virtue. Break the circuit of energy transferred between negative and positive poles, and the two empires dissolve into the waving of sectional or nationalist flags. Lacking the reassurance of a foreign demon, we search our own neighborhoods for fiends of convincing malevolence and size.

The search is a boon for the bearers of false witness and the builders of prisons. Because it's so easy to dwell on our differences, even a child of nine can write a Sunday newspaper sermon about the centrifugal forces that drive the society apart. The more difficult and urgent questions have to do with the centripetal forces that bind us together. What traits of character or temperament do we hold in common? Why is it that I can meet a black man in a street or a Hispanic woman on a train and imagine that he and I, or she and I, share an allied hope and a joint purpose? That last question is as American as it is rhetorical, and a Belgian would think it the work of a dreaming imbecile.

What we share is a unified field of emotion, but if we mistake the sources of our energy and courage (i.e., if we think that our uniqueness as Americans rests with the adjectives instead of the noun) then we can be rounded up in categories and sold the slogan of the week for the fear of the month. Political campaigns deal in the commodity of votes, and from now until November I expect that all of them will divide the American promise into its lesser but more marketable properties. For reasons of their own convenience, the sponsors of political campaigns (Democratic, environmental, racial, Republican, sexual, or military-industrial) promote more or less the same false constructions of the American purpose and identity. As follows:

That the American achieves visible and specific meaning only by reason of his or her association with the political guilds of race, gender, age, ancestry, or social class.

The assumption is as elitist as the view that only a woman endowed with an income of $1 million a year can truly appreciate the beauty of money and the music of Cole Porter. Comparable theories of grace encourage the belief that only black people can know or teach black history, that no white man can play jazz piano, that blonds have a better time, and that Jews can't play basketball.

America was founded on precisely the opposite premise. We were always 10 about becoming, not being; about the prospects for the future, not about the inheritance of the past. The man who rests his case on his color, like the woman who defines herself as a bright cloud of sensibility beyond the understanding of merely mortal men, makes a claim to special privilege not unlike the divine right of kings. The pretensions might buttress the cathedrals of our self-esteem, but they run counter to the lessons of our history.

We are a nation of parvenus, all bound to the hopes of tomorrow, or next week, or next year. John Quincy Adams put it plainly in a letter to a German correspondent in the 1820s who had written on behalf of several prospective émigrés to ask about the requirements for their success in the New World. "They must cast off the European skin, never to resume it," Adams said. "They must look forward to their posterity rather than backward to their ancestors."

We were always a mixed and piebald company, even on the seventeenth-century colonial seaboard, and we accepted our racial or cultural differences as the odds that we were obliged to overcome or correct. When John Charles Frémont (a.k.a. The Pathfinder) first descended into California from the East in 1843, he remarked on the polyglot character of the expedition accompanying him south into the San Joaquin Valley:

"Our cavalcade made a strange and grotesque appearance, and it was impossible to avoid reflecting upon our position and composition in this remote solitude . . . still forced on south by a desert on one hand and a mountain range on the other; guided by a civilized Indian, attended by two wild ones from the Sierra; a Chinook from the Columbia; and our own mixture of American, French, German—all armed; four or five languages heard at once; above a hundred horses and mules, half-wide; American, Spanish and Indian dresses and equipments intermingled—such was our composition."

The theme of metamorphosis recurs throughout the whole chronicle of American biography. Men and women start out in one place and end up in another never quite knowing how they got there, perpetually expecting the unexpected, drifting across the ocean or the plains until they lodge against a marriage, a land deal, a public office, or a jail. Speaking to the improvised character of the American experience, Daniel Boorstin, the historian and former Librarian of Congress, also summed up the case against the arithmetic of the political pollsters' zip codes: "No prudent man dared to be too certain of exactly who he was or what he was about; everyone had to be prepared to become someone else. To be ready for such perilous transmigrations was to become an American."

That the American people aspire to become more nearly alike. 15

The hope is that of the ad salesman and the prison warden, but it has become depressingly familiar among the managers of political campaigns. Apparently they think that no matter how different the native songs and dances in different parts of the country, all the tribes and factions want the same beads, the same trinkets, the same prizes. As I listen to operatives from Washington talk about their prospects in the Iowa or New Hampshire primary, I understand that they have in mind the figure of a perfect or ideal American whom everybody in the country would wish to resemble if only everybody could afford to dress like the dummies in the windows of Bloomingdale's or Saks Fifth Avenue. The public opinion polls frame questions in the alphabet of name recognitions and standard brands. The simplicity of the results supports the belief that the American citizen or the American family can be construed as a product, and that with only a little more time and a little more money for research and development all of us will conform to the preferred images seen in a commercial for Miller beer.

The apologists for the theory of the uniform American success sometimes present the example of Abraham Lincoln, and as I listen to their sentimental after-dinner speeches about the poor country grown to greatness, I often wonder what they would say if they had met the man instead of the statue. Throughout most of his life Lincoln displayed the character of a man destined for failure —a man who drank too much and told too many jokes (most of them in bad taste), who was habitually late for meetings and always borrowing money, who never seized a business opportunity and missed his own wedding.

The spirit of liberty is never far from anarchy, and the un-American is apt to look a good deal more like one of the contestants on "Let's Make a Deal" (i.e., somebody dressed like Madonna, or Wyatt Earp, or a giant iguana) than any of the yachtsmen standing around on the dock at Kennebunkport. If America is about nothing else, it is about the invention of the self. Because we have little use for history, and because we refuse the comforts of a society established on the blueprint of class privilege, we find ourselves set adrift at birth in an existential void, inheriting nothing except the obligation to construct a plausible self, to build a raft of identity on which (with a few grains of luck and a cheap bank loan) maybe we can float south to Memphis or the imaginary islands of the blessed. We set ourselves the tasks of making and remaking our destinies with whatever lumber we happen to find lying around on the banks of the Snake or Pecos River.

Who else is the American hero if not a wandering pilgrim who goes forth on a perpetual quest? Melville sent Ahab across the world's oceans in search of a fabulous beast, and Thoreau followed the unicorn of his conscience into the silence of the Maine woods. Between them they marked out the trail of American literature as well as the lines of speculation in American real estate. To a greater or a lesser extent, we are all confidence men, actors playing the characters of our own invention and hoping that the audience—fortunately consisting of impostors as fanciful or synthetic as ourselves—will accept the performance at par value and suspend the judgments of ridicule.

The settled peoples of the earth seldom recognize the American as both a 20
chronic revolutionary and a born pilgrim. The American is always on the way to someplace else (i.e., toward some undetermined future in which all will be well), and when he meets a stranger on the road he begins at once to recite the summary of the story so far—his youth and early sorrows, the sequence of his exits and entrances, his last divorce and his next marriage, the point of his financial

departure and the estimated time of his spiritual arrival, the bad news noted and accounted for, the good news still to come. Invariably it is a pilgrim's tale, and the narrator, being American, assumes that he is addressing a fellow pilgrim. He means to exchange notes and compare maps. His newfound companion might be bound toward a completely different dream of Eden (a boat marina in Naples, Florida, instead of a garden in Vermont; a career as a Broadway dancer as opposed to the vice presidency of the Wells Fargo bank), but the destination doesn't matter as much as the common hope of coming safely home to the land of the heart's desire. For the time being, and until something better turns up, we find ourselves embarked on the same voyage, gazing west into the same blue distance.

That the American people share a common code of moral behavior and subscribe to identical theories of the true, the good, and the beautiful.

Senator Jesse Helms would like to think so, and so would the enforcers of ideological discipline on the vocabulary of the doctrinaire left. The country swarms with people making rules about what we can say or read or study or smoke, and they imagine that we should be grateful for the moral guidelines (market-tested and government-inspected) imposed (for our own good) by a centralized bureau of temporal health and spiritual safety. The would-be reformers of the national character confuse the American sense of equality with the rule of conformity that governs a police state. It isn't that we believe that every American is as perceptive or as accomplished as any other, but we insist on the preservation of a decent and mutual respect across the lines of age, race, gender, and social class. No citizen is allowed to use another citizen as if he or she were a means to an end; no master can treat his servant as if he or she were only a servant; no government can deal with the governed as if they were nothing more than a mob of votes. The American loathing for the arrogant or self-important man follows from the belief that all present have bet their fortunes (some of them bigger than others, and some of them counterfeit or stolen) on the same hypothesis.

The American premise is an existential one, and our moral code is political, its object being to allow for the widest horizons of sight and the broadest range of expression. We protect the other person's liberty in the interest of protecting our own, and our virtues conform to the terms and conditions of an arduous and speculative journey. If we look into even so coarse a mirror as the one held up to us by the situation comedies on prime-time television, we see that we value the companionable virtues—helpfulness, forgiveness, kindliness, and, above all, tolerance.

The passenger standing next to me at the rail might be balancing a parrot on his head, but that doesn't mean that he has invented a theory of the self any less implausible then the one I ordered from a department-store catalogue or assembled with the tag lines of a two-year college course on the great books of Western civilization. If the traveler at the port rail can balance a parrot on his head, then I can continue my discussion with Madame Bovary and Mr. Pickwick, and the two gentlemen standing aft of the rum barrels can get on with the business of rigging the price of rifles or barbed wire. The American equation rests on the habit of holding our fellow citizens in thoughtful regard not because they are exceptional (or famous, or beautiful, or rich) but simply because they are our fellow citizens. If we abandon the sense of mutual respect, we abandon the premise as well as the machinery of the American enterprise.

That the triumph of America corresponds to its prowess as a nation-state. 25

The pretension serves the purposes of the people who talk about "the national security" and "the vital interest of the American people" when what they mean is the power and privilege of government. The oligarchy resident in Washington assumes that all Americans own the same property instead of taking part in the same idea, that we share a joint geopolitical program instead of a common temperament and habit of mind. Even so faithful a servant of the monied interests as Daniel Webster understood the distinction: "The public happiness is to be the aggregate of individuals. Our system begins with the individual man."

The Constitution was made for the uses of the individual (an implement on the order of a plow, an ax, or a surveyor's plumb line), and the institutions of American government were meant to support the liberties of the people, not the ambitions of the state. Given any ambiguity about the order of priority or precedence, it was the law that had to give way to the citizen's freedom of thought and action, not the citizen's freedom of thought and action that had to give way to the law. The Bill of Rights stresses the distinction in the two final amendments, the ninth ("The enumeration in the Constitution, of certain rights, shall not be construed to deny or disparage others retained by the people") and the tenth ("The powers not delegated to the United States by the Constitution, nor prohibited by it to the States, are reserved to the States, respectively, or to the people").

What joins the Americans one to another is not a common nationality, language, race, or ancestry (all of which testify to the burdens of the past) but rather their complicity in a shared work of the imagination. My love of country follows from my love of its freedoms, not from my pride in its fleets or its armies or its gross national product. Construed as a means and not an end, the Constitution stands as the premise for a narrative rather than a plan for an invasion or a monument. The narrative was always plural. Not one story but many stories.

That it is easy to be an American.

30 I can understand why the politicians like to pretend that America is mostly about going shopping, but I never know why anybody believes the ad copy. Grant the existential terms and conditions of the American enterprise (i.e., that we are all bound to invent ourselves), and the position is both solitary and probably lost. I know a good many people who would rather be British or Nigerian or Swiss.

Lately I've been reading the accounts of the nineteenth-century adventurers and pioneers who traveled west from Missouri under circumstances almost always adverse. Most of them didn't find whatever it was they expected to find behind the next range of mountains or around the next bend in the river. They were looking for a garden in a country that was mostly desert, and the record of their passage is largely one of sorrow and failure. Travelers making their way across the Great Plains in the 1850s reported great numbers of dead horses and abandoned wagons on the trail, the echo of the hopes that so recently preceded them lingering in an empty chair or in the scent of flowers on a new grave.

Reading the diaries and letters, especially those of the women in the caravans, I think of the would-be settlers lost in an immense wilderness, looking into the mirrors of their loneliness and measuring their capacity for self-knowledge against the vastness of the wide and indifferent sky.

Too often we forget the proofs of our courage. If we wish to live in the state of freedom that allows us to make and think and build, then we must accustom ourselves to the shadows on the walls and the wind in trees. The climate of anxiety is the cost of doing business. Just as a monarchy places far fewer burdens on its subjects than a democracy places on its citizens, so also bigotry is easier than tolerance. When something goes wrong with the currency or the schools, it's always comforting to know that the faults can be easily found in something as obvious as a color, or a number, or the sound of a strange language. The multiple adjectives qualifying the American noun enrich the vocabulary of blame, and if the election year continues as it has begun I expect that by next summer we will discover that it is not only middle-aged Protestant males who have been making a wreck of the culture but also (operating secretly and sometimes in disguise) adolescent, sallow, Buddhist females.

Among all the American political virtues, candor is probably the one most necessary to the success of our mutual enterprise. Unless we try to tell each other the truth about what we know and think and see (i.e., the story so far as it appears to the travelers on the voyage out) we might as well amuse ourselves (for as long as somebody else allows us to do so) with fairy tales. The vitality of the American democracy always has rested on the capacity of its citizens to speak and think without cant. As long ago as 1838, addressing the topic of *The American Democrat*, James Fenimore Cooper argued that the word "American" was synonymous with the habit of telling the truth: "By candor we are not to understand trifling and uncalled for expositions of truth; but a sentiment that proves a conviction of the necessity of speaking truth, when speaking at all; a contempt for all designing evasions of our real opinions.

"In all the general concerns, the public has a right to be treated with candor. 35
Without this manly and truly republican quality . . . the institutions are converted into a stupendous fraud."

If we indulge ourselves with evasions and the pleasure of telling lies, we speak to our fears and our weaknesses instead of to our courage and our strength. We can speak plainly about our differences only if we know and value what we hold in common. Like the weather and third-rate journalism, bigotry in all its declensions is likely to be with us for a long time (certainly as long as the next hundred years), but unless we can draw distinctions and make jokes about our racial or cultural baggage, the work of our shared imagination must vanish in the mist of lies. The lies might win elections (or sell newspapers and economic theories) but they bind us to the theaters of wish and dream. If I must like or admire a fellow citizen for his or her costume of modifying adjectives (because he or she is black or gay or rich), then I might as well believe that the lost continent of Atlantis will rise next summer from the sea and that the Japanese will continue to make the payments—now and forever, world without end—on all our mortgages and battleships.

Among all the nations of the earth, America is the one that has come most triumphantly to terms with the mixtures of blood and caste, and maybe it is another of history's ironic jokes that we should wish to repudiate our talent for assimilation at precisely the moment in time when so many other nations in the world (in Africa and Western Europe as well as the Soviet Union) look to the promise of the American example. The jumble of confused or mistaken identities that was the story of nineteenth-century America has become the story of a late-twentieth-century world defined by a vast migration of peoples across seven continents and as many oceans. Why, then, do we lose confidence in ourselves and grow fearful of our mongrel freedoms?

The politician who would lift us to a more courageous understanding of ourselves might begin by saying that we are all, each and every one of us, as much at fault as anybody else, that no matter whom we blame for our troubles (whether George Bush, or Al Sharpton, or David Duke) or how pleasant the invective (racist, sexist, imperialist pig), we still have to rebuild our cities and revise our laws. We can do the work together, or we can stand around making strong statements about each other's clothes.

QUESTIONS FOR DISCUSSION

1. One of several devices Lapham uses to unify his essay is the adjective/noun relationship that he discusses in his opening paragraph. Explain how the relationship works and trace its use throughout the essay. Lapham also uses metaphor to define the American character. For example, he uses a principle of electricity in paragraph 5 and the image of a wandering pilgrim in paragraph 19. Find other such figures, and discuss their rhetorical effectiveness.
2. Examine Lapham's organization strategy. What is the central principle upon which his essay is organized and developed?
3. Discuss the following assertions:
    a. "Maybe the confusion is a corollary to the end of the Cold War" (5).
    b. "Comparable theories of grace encourage the belief that only black people can know or teach black history" (9).
    c. "If America is about nothing else, it is about the invention of the self" (18).

d. "If we abandon the sense of mutual respect, we abandon the premise as well as the machinery of the American enterprise" (23).

e. "Unless we can draw distinctions and make jokes about our racial or cultural baggage, the work of our shared imagination must vanish in the mist of lies" (36).

4. Lapham concludes his essay with this sentence: "We can do the work together, or we can stand around making strong statements about each other's clothes." Discuss the intent and the rhetorical effectiveness of this closing.

WRITING ASSIGNMENTS

1. Reaction Journal: Now that you have read Lapham's essay, freewrite again for ten or fifteen minutes on what you perceive to be the qualities that all American citizens hold in common. Compare the contents of your two freewritings, and be prepared to discuss how Lapham's essay shaped your thinking.

2. In question 3e Lapham refers to racial and cultural humor. Collect examples of such humor from the media and your own experience. Write an essay in which you classify your examples according to type of humor and discuss the appropriateness and the inappropriateness of racial and ethnic humor in our heterogeneous society.

3. Write an essay that focuses on one of the assertions in Question 3. Draw from Lapham's essay as well as from other readings and your own experiences.

Suggestions for Discussion and Writing

1. Read (or reread) the Preface for Students, especially the paragraph on Student Audience. Make a list of your group identities. Consider age, race, gender, religion, residence, employment, ethnic background, citizenship, education, social and economic class, political views, professional, cultural, and recreational interests, and anything else that defines you as a member of a group. Which are the most significant in your life? Lewis Lapham speaks of the noun American "dressed up with at least one modifying adjective." Try dressing up your sense of self as an American with five or six adjectives in order of decreasing importance. Which group identity (-ies) are you most conscious of in your relationship with other people? How do special situations and relationships change the way you see yourself and others? Classify your group commitments as strong, moderate, or weak, or, if you prefer, rank them on a scale of one to five. If you are in a discussion group, compare your priorities and commitments with those of the other group members. Try to explain similarities and differences in your perspectives. If you are working alone, consider how people you know and writers you have read might describe and rank their group identities. Keep notes on your discussions and your reading. When you are ready to write a paper on group identity, make some reference to the Preface for Students and some of the ideas, attitudes, and experiences of the authors you have read in this and other units.

   At various points in the course, return to your notes or your paper and reevaluate and revise. Make additions and deletions, qualify, moderate, intensify, explain, justify, recant—whatever. Comment on your own revisions and, if you are in a group, on those of your classmates. Comment also on what you have *not* changed, what seem to you to be attitudes and commitments that will not or cannot be changed.

2. Ask Kopan, Novak, and Lapham to join Mead and Baldwin in a "rap" on National Identity and Cultural Pluralism. As moderator and commentator, raise three or four questions based on the readings in this unit and have the participants respond. Summarize their comments and tell the group which position comes closest to your own.

3. Some people are concerned that we are going too far in our cultural pluralism and point to the violent and disastrous "tribalism" that is rampant in the former Soviet Union, the former Yugoslavia, and other parts of the world. Others are confident that our pluralism is benign and that "it can't happen here." Collect a few relevant news reports, articles, editorials, or letters to the editor from newspapers and magazines and offer them as evidence to support either or both sides of the question. Write a paper based on these materials and the readings in this unit. If you wish to offer an opinion, do so. If you are not ready to take a posi-

tion, tell the reader why. In either case, come back to your paper from time to time and reevaluate and revise or make note of your new ideas in your journal.

4. Read (or reread) the paragraphs on Focus in the Preface for Students and the introduction to this unit. How would you describe our pluralistic society? What are the implications of the various terms? If you like, suggest your own metaphor and comment on its implications. How does the concept of Confrontation and Accommodation differ from the other descriptions? Reserve a section in your journal for entries on confrontations and accommodations that you find in the readings and encounter or have encountered in your experience. Keep adding to your entries from time to time. Make use of this information in your discussions and writing whenever you think appropriate.

PART

II

ETHNIC JOURNEYS

From England—The Charter Members

From North America—The Displaced Landlords

From Europe—The Huddled Masses

From Africa—The Dreamers and Liberators

From the Americas—The Cultural Rainbow

From Asia—"The Model Minorities"?

Not like the brazen giant of Greek fame,
With conquering limbs astride from land to land;
Here at our sea-washed, sunset gates shall stand
A mighty woman with a torch, whose flame
Is the imprisoned lightning, and her name
Mother of Exiles. From her beacon-hand
Glows world-wide welcome; her mild eyes command
The air-bridged harbor that twin cities frame.

"Keep, ancient lands, your storied pomp!" cries she
With silent lips. "Give me your tired, your poor,
Your huddled masses yearning to breathe free,
The wretched refuse of your teeming shore.
Send these, the homeless, tempest-tossed to me.
I lift my lamp beside the golden door!"

—THE NEW COLOSSUS—*Emma Lazarus, 1883*

From England—The Charter Members

THE NORTH AMERICAN SETTLEMENTS that immigrants from England began to establish in 1607 depended on England for trade and capital, for the training of many of their clergy, lawyers, and public officials, and for literary and artistic culture. Thus, in spite of the distance of the settlements from England, the differing reasons for their founding, and the strain of initially harsh frontier conditions, the predominantly white Anglo-Saxon Protestant culture that took root in the English colonies reflected in many ways the English society from which its people had come. Displacing rather quickly the native peoples they encountered, the English settlers were the only immigrants to the future United States who did not have to accommodate themselves to an already established culture. Rather, they set the standards for the society that future immigrants would find in place.

While sharing for the most part a white Anglo-Saxon Protestant heritage, the early colonists did not all espouse identical ideals, nor were they drawn to their new environments for the same reasons. During the period from 1628 to 1642, an estimated 2 percent of the entire British population emigrated from the British Isles, approximately 58,000 of them destined for North America and the Caribbean. Those arriving on the mainland went either to the colonies of Virginia (founded in 1607) and Maryland (the only Roman Catholic colony, founded in 1632) or to the New England colonies of Plymouth (1620), Massachusetts Bay (1632), Connecticut (1635–1636), and Rhode Island (1636). Although all the immigrants were British subjects and therefore shared certain basic cultural beliefs and traditions, they were a diverse group. Differences in the settlers' backgrounds and in their reasons for immigration, combined with the considerable differences in the natural features of their new environments, caused these regions to take on quite different characteristics, each contributing features that became either temporary or permanent characteristics of American life. The Jamestown (Virginia) and the Massachusetts Bay settlements were established by joint-stock companies in which men who brought their families and paid their own passage were stockholders and thus voting members of the settlements. An early link was thereby established between economics and politics. In addition, since land was readily available in North America, men who had been unable to vote in England because of high property requirements easily met the minimal property requirements in the colonies. Thus, accessibility to enfranchisement set the stage for a revolution in political thinking.

In Virginia, the tobacco export trade provided the colony with its chief means of support. The availability of land attracted self-financed entrepreneurs such as William Byrd, whose son William Byrd II recorded in his famous diary the activities and thoughts of a Virginia aristocrat. The establishment of large agricultural enterprises in the South created a severe labor shortage and led to increased efforts to encourage immigration to that region. Indentured service was one means of meeting the labor needs of the region while also providing immigrants with opportunities unavailable to them at home. One half of the settlers arriving in the Southern colonies after 1620 came as unfree laborers under the English system of indentured service. Among the indentured laborers were some blacks, but it was not until later in the century, when improvement in the English economy inclined fewer English and Irish to indenture themselves, that planters changed the law regarding black laborers. What had begun as temporary indenture of blacks became permanent enslavement of black Africans. For a century and a half thereafter slavery provided the constant cheap labor supply demanded by the plantation economy. Before that time, however, farm laborers, domestic servants, skilled laborers, and artisans from Britain and Ireland were able, under the indenture system, to obtain free passage in return for a term of service during which they received room and board but generally no wages. Most of the immigrants thus recruited were young, single males between the ages of fourteen and thirty whose chief motivation was economic betterment. While for the most part these settlers, like their kinsmen who settled in New England, had been religiously observant in England, the new environment separating them from ties of family and congregation did not actively support the continuance of these traditions. The diary of William Byrd of Westover reveals a relatively casual attitude toward prayers that are occasionally omitted from his daily routine without occasioning any of the soul searching such an unthinkable lapse would have brought among the Puritans in the Massachusetts Bay Colony. Similarly, the sexual escapades Byrd indulges in seem in no way to interfere with his maintaining a clear conscience and enjoying a good night's sleep.

After their indentures were complete, workmen were able to establish themselves on their own land with little difficulty. The richness of the land in the Southern colonies provided an easy living even for small landowners. On an expedition to survey the boundary between Virginia and North Carolina in 1728, William Byrd described the regions through which he traveled as close to "Lubberland," a mythical land of ease and plenty because of "the great felicity of its climate, the easiness of raising provisions, and the slothfulness of the people." While the women were busy with household tasks, the farmers themselves, according to Byrd, suffered from the "distemper of laziness" and often chose to "loiter away their lives."

The immigration to New England was of a different nature, made up largely of family groups and entire congregations. Women and children were represented in good numbers, and most of the men were middle-aged or older. Although only about 27 of the 100 persons aboard the *Mayflower* in 1620 were Separatists, a large number of the later settlers in this region were motivated by religious issues, with purposes beyond economic betterment. The tenacity with which they hung on in the inhospitable New England climate through winters of starvation and summers of infectious diseases and the determination with which they cultivated the rocky soil of the region have become part of the enduring national idea of the Yankee character.

Because the New England settlements tended to consist largely of transplanted social units, these colonies, unlike their Southern counterparts, were characterized by a high degree of social cohesiveness. Also contributing to this sense of community was the custom of first granting land to a group of town leaders who then allocated it to settlers, with prominent figures such as ministers and lawyers receiving the choicest parcels. There was thus in position a kind of social control and community planning absent in the South, where settlers claimed their lands individually.

Both the Pilgrims of the Plymouth Colony, Separatists who wished to break all ties with the Church of England, and the Puritans of the Massachusetts Bay Colony, who hoped to purify the Church of England from within, were religious reformers not satisfied with the degree to which the Church of England had differentiated itself from the Roman Catholic Church. They opposed practices which they felt distracted worshippers from the pure elements of their faith, objecting specifically to rituals and ambience reminiscent of Roman Catholicism. They advocated simplicity in both their personal lives and their religious practices, doing away with the set forms of prayer, ornamentation of services with choirs, bells, and organ music, and the elaborate priestly robes characteristic of the Anglican Church. The plain style of their religious buildings and observances extended as well to their literature, which consisted mostly of sermons, spiritual autobiographies, diaries, and religious poetry. In addition to seeking new forms for worship, the dissenters objected to the control of the church by the English monarchy, which politicized the church and sometimes resulted in the appointment of priests without what the reformers regarded as the proper spiritual credentials. Both Separatists and Puritans defended the right of congregations to choose their own religious leaders, thus establishing in the colonies important ideals of self-determination.

While religion was the primary concern of the Puritans, they were not, as the stereotype would have it, grim, joyless, sexually repressed, abstemious, superstitious, persecuting bigots. They danced, drank, begat many children, got into trouble with the law, and were more educated and enlightened than most people of the time and no more intolerant than most. If the literature of the period makes anything clear, it is that they were like any other group—populated by all kinds of human beings with all kinds of virtues and flaws, strengths and weaknesses. They certainly were not ascetics who withdrew from the world. Indeed, prospering in the world could be seen as a sign of God's favor. It was a Puritan's duty to achieve worldly success by properly using his God-given talents. As Carl N. Degler points out, Puritanism, in ways similar to Quakerism, which emphasized the virtues of frugality, hard work, and accumulation of wealth without ostentation, provided a moral justification for success in business. The Puritans were a practical and industrious people who applied their religious principles to everyday living. Everything was part of God's design, and every event was fraught with meaning. Adrienne Rich has observed that "seventeenth-century Puritan life was perhaps the most self-conscious ever lived in its requirements of the individual understanding: no event so trivial that it could not speak a divine message, no disappointment so heavy that it could not serve as a 'correction,' a disguised blessing." The intimate relationship between faith and daily routine is evident in Samuel Sewall's *Diary*. His conviction that his personal family tragedies resulted from his role as a judge in the Salem witchcraft trials illustrates the kind of divine purpose that meticulous self-scrutiny could uncover in daily events. The mass hysteria of 1692 that led to the deaths of twenty persons accused of witchcraft in Salem reveals a darker side of the search for signs of spiritual grace or depravity in oneself and others.

Since the religious doctrines of both Separatists and Puritans held that all believers had the obligation to read and study the Bible, not simply to hear it interpreted by religious leaders, New England Puritans placed great emphasis on education. Literate congregations and learned clergy were essential to their way of life. In fostering a literate population free as a group to choose their own ministers and establish their own doctrines, the Puritans helped set certain ideals of self-determination central to American ideology. Because of Puritan belief in the importance of access to education, the Massachusetts Bay Colony became the cultural center of the English colonies in North America. Harvard, the first college in the colonies, was founded in Cambridge in 1636, and the first American book published in English was printed in Cambridge in 1640. While education of women was approved and women were voting members of their congregations, the Puritans did not encourage them to engage in public literary, artistic, or intellectual pursuits. Intellectually inclined women were regarded as unnaturally egocentric with dangerous ambitions for self-fulfillment. It is remarkable that Sarah Kemble Knight, accomplished and intrepid proprietress of a writing school in Boston and chronicler of her travels through New England to New York in 1704–05, was able to lead an active life outside the home and still earn the respect of her fellow citizens.

In spite of their high regard for learning and their history of having suffered persecution in England for their religious beliefs, the Puritans were not tolerant of those who wished to practice other religions in their midst. The right to practice their own religion as they saw fit was a motivating force for many of the New England colonists, but those who differed from the Puritans in religious or social pursuits were not welcome in the Massachusetts Bay Colony. For religious and social toleration one must look to Rhode Island, founded by Roger Williams, who was banished from the Massachusetts Bay Colony in 1635 for preaching religious toleration, separation of church and state, and the rights of Indians to their land.

Such radical ideas were soon to be institutionalized in the Quaker colony of Pennsylvania, founded by William Penn in 1681, which not only practiced religious toleration but encouraged ethnic and religious diversity. Although the Quakers shared similar values with the Puritans—a strong work ethic, a rejection of ostentation and worldly vanity, and a life-encompassing religious commitment—they differed on how they applied their values in relations with outsiders. John Woolman exemplifies the Quaker doctrine of the "inner light," which taught that every human being is capable of direct communion with God. His humanitarianism, his belief that "liberty was the natural right of all men equally," led him, as it did many other reforming Quakers, to oppose slavery, exploitation of the poor, and mistreatment of the Indians. Indeed, as Lawrence H. Fuchs has pointed out, the "civic culture" of America is based on the Pennsylvania model, and it is this culture that unifies the diverse strains in American society to this day.

In 1690, 90 percent of the colonists in what would become the United States were of English birth or descent, but by the time of the American Revolution, English immigrants and their descendants made up only half of the colonies' population. Since then, the culture of the United States has been enriched by the diversity of its peoples and shaped by the nature of the land itself and by the events of almost three and a half centuries. Many of its basic values and traditions, however, including the linked virtues of work and success, self-determination, the inviolable sacredness of the individual, religious toleration, and a relatively fluid class structure based on merit rather than birth, can be found among those of the Anglo-Saxon settlers who established a culture that later immigrants and events have shaped and reshaped.

THE FORCES THAT SHAPED MODERN AMERICA

CARL N. DEGLER

Carl N. Degler (b. 1921) is Professor Emeritus of American History at Stanford University. He earned his A.B. at Upsala College and his Ph.D. at Columbia. Before joining the faculty at Stanford, Degler taught at Hunter College, New York University, Adelphi College, CCNY, and Vassar College. His books include Neither Black Nor White: Slavery and Race Relations in Brazil and the U.S. *(1971), which won the Pulitzer Prize in 1972, and* In Search of Human Nature: The Decline and Revival of Darwinism in American Social Thought *(1991), which won the Phi Beta Kappa Ralph Waldo Emerson Prize in 1992. In the following selection from* Out of Our Past: The Forces That Shaped America *(1959), Degler cites the roles of Puritanism and Quakerism in establishing the American virtues of work and wealth.*

◆ FREEWRITING

The introduction to this section suggests that the English settlers were the only immigrants to the future United States who did not have to accommodate themselves to an already established culture. "Rather, they set the standards for the society that future immigrants would find in place." Before reading Degler, freewrite for ten or fifteen minutes on some of the many ways the English have defined our culture.

In more ways than is often recognized, the one hundred years after the death of Elizabeth I in 1603 comprise the first century of the modern world. A number of developments peculiar to modern European thought cluster within these years: the true beginnings of modern science in the work of Galileo and Newton, Harvey and Boyle; the first expression of modern democratic ideas by the Levelers and in the Army Debates of the English Civil Wars; the decisive break in a millennium of religious dominance with the end of the wars of religion and the acceptance of the principle of religious tolerance; the achievement of lasting constitutional and representative government in England with the Glorious Revolution of 1688. It was also the time of the first permanent settlement of English colonists.

For America, its origin in this first century of the modern era was filled with meaning. In the New World, the future was still fluid. Europe's ways, both the new and the old, could be planted in America free of the choking weeds of outmoded habits. America would be a testing ground, but it would be difficult to predict what would happen. Some of the European ways would wither; some would strike root; still others would change and adapt to the new environment. For a good part of the century this plasticity was characteristic. But then, by the end of the century, the mold had hardened. In a number of ways what Americans would be for generations to come was settled in the course of those first hundred years.

To men coming from the "tight little isle" the vast land of America, though untamed and dense with forest, was remarkably like the old, both in the flora that covered it and in the crops that it would yield. Although in a region like England settlers would soon discover the soil to be thin and unfertile compared with that of the more southern colonies, it was not a desert, and from the beginning a well-organized group like the Massachusetts Bay people were able to wring a comfortable, if not opulent, living from the lean and rocky soil. The Chesapeake colonies had better soil and, as it turned out, a climate conducive to the production of a staple of world-wide appeal—the infamous weed, tobacco.

A land endowed with such promise could not fail to attract a continuous stream of men and women from the shops and farms of Europe. For centuries the problem in Europe had been that of securing enough land for the people, but in the New World the elements in the equation were reversed. "I hear . . . that servants would be more advantageous to you than any commodity," wrote a Londoner to a Virginian in 1648. For over three centuries, through wars and revolutions, through economic disaster and plague, the underlying, insistent theme of American history was the peopling of a continent.

Though the pervasive influence which Frederick Jackson Turner attributed 5
to the frontier in the shaping of the American character can be overestimated, the possibility of exaggeration should not hide the undeniable fact that in early America, and through most of the nineteenth century, too, land was available to an extent that could appear only fabulous to land-starved Europeans. From the outset, as a result, the American who worked with his hands had an advantage over his European counterpart. For persistent as employers and rulers in America might be in holding to Old World conceptions of the proper subordination of labor, such ideas were always being undercut by the fact that labor was scarcer than land.

The imagination of men was stretched by the availability of land in America. Though land was not free for the taking, it was nearly so. In seventeenth-century New England there were very few landless people, and in the Chesapeake colonies it was not unusual for an indentured servant, upon the completion of his term, to be granted a piece of land. Thus, thanks to the bounty of America, it was possible for an Englishman of the most constricted economic horizon to make successive jumps from servant to freeman, from freeman to freeholder, and, perhaps in a little more time, to wealthy speculator in lands farther west. Not all men were successful in America, to be sure, but as the emigration literature reveals, enough were to encourage most men in the new land to strive hard for wealth and success.

In America the availability of land rendered precarious, if not untenable, those European institutions which were dependent upon scarcity of land. Efforts to establish feudal or manorial reproductions in the New World came to nothing. The Dutch, for example, tried to set up an ambitious system of patroons, or great landowners, whose broad acres along the Hudson were intended to be worked by tenants. In keeping with the manorial practices common in Europe, the patroon was to dispense justice and administer in his own right the government of his little kingdom. But contrary to the popular tradition that sees these patroonships carrying over into the period of English rule after 1664, only two of the Dutch grants outlasted New Netherland, and of them, only one was in existence ten years later. . . .

Thus in those areas where an attempt was made to perpetuate the social system of Europe, it was frustrated almost from the beginning. Quite early in the colonial period, great disparities of wealth appeared in the agricultural South, as elsewhere, but this was stratification resting initially and finally upon wealth, not upon honorific or hereditary conceptions derived from Europe. As such, the upper class in America was one into which others might move when they had acquired the requisite wealth. And so long as wealth accumulation was open to all, the class structure would be correspondingly flexible.

In New England there was no experimentation with feudal or manorial trappings at all. The early history of that region is a deliberate repudiation of European social as well as religious practices. As early as 1623, for example, William Bradford wrote that communal property arrangements had failed in Plymouth and that as a consequence the governing officials divided the land on an individual basis. Individual ownership of land, so typical of American land tenure ever since, was thus symbolically begun. The larger colony of Massachusetts Bay, in its first codification of laws, the Body of Liberties of 1641, made explicit its departure from feudal and manorial incidents upon landholding. "All our lands and heritages shall be free from all fines and licenses upon Alienations, and from all hariotts, wardships, Liveries, Primerseisins, yeare day and wast, Escheates and forfeitures. . . ."[1]

In place of medieval and aristocratic notions about the degrading nature of 10
trade and business, seventeenth-century Englishmen brought to America two forms of that bourgeois spirit which Max Weber has called the Protestant ethic: Puritanism and Quakerism. It is possible to overemphasize the extent to which Puritanism departed from medieval conceptions of a just price, prohibitions on interest, and so forth, for such restrictions on unfettered capitalism also formed a part of Puritan economic practice in Massachusetts. But the general loosening of economic restraints which Puritanism unquestionably condoned, and its strong accent on work and wealth accumulation, bestowed religious sanction upon business enterprise. The backward-looking and forward-looking economic attitudes of Puritanism are both apparent in a Massachusetts statute of 1633. The first part of the law, in keeping with medieval practices, prescribed the proper wages for bricklayers, wheelwrights, and other skilled craftsmen, while the second part of the statute ordered "that noe person, hawseholder or other, shall spend his time idely or unprofflably, under paine of such punishment as the Court shall thinke meet to inflicte. . . ." The close connection the Puritans saw between godliness and worldly success is implied in a story told by Governor Winthrop in his *History.* The story concerns one Mansfield who arrived in Mas-

sachusetts poor but "godly." With the help of a local rich man, "this Mansfield grew suddenly rich, and then lost his godliness, and his wealth soon after."

The calling or occupation of a Christian was an important conception in Puritan thought; it also serves as an illuminating instance of the tight linkage between religion and economics. To the Puritan, a Christian's work was part of his offering to God. "As soon as ever a man begins to look toward God and the way of his Grace," the Reverend John Cotton taught, "he will not rest til he find out some warrantable calling and employment." No matter what the calling, "though it be but of a day laborer," yet he will make of it what he can, for "God would not have a man receive five talents and gain but two; He would have his best gifts improved to the best advantage." To work hard is to please God. As Cotton Mather, the grandson of Cotton, said at the end of the century, "Would a man *Rise* by his Business? I say, then let him Rise to his Business. . . . Let your *Business* ingross the most of your time."

Important, but often overlooked in the Puritan conception of the calling, was the idea of social obligation. For a calling to be "warrantable," John Cotton emphasized, a Christian "would see that his calling should tend to public good." Moreover, he continued, "we live by faith in our vocations, in that faith, in serving God, serves man, and in serving man, serves God." Cotton Mather at the end of the century put it even more succinctly. One should have a calling "so he may Glorify God by doing Good for *Others*, and getting of *Good* for himself." It was this cementing of social conscience to thoroughgoing individualism which saved Puritanism from degenerating into a mere defense of economic exploitation.

If the earliest New England divines, like John Cotton, had some doubts about the trader because—as the medieval schoolmen had contended—he bought cheap and sold dear, later Puritans easily accepted the new economic order. Cotton Mather, in good Calvinist fashion, argued that there "is every sort of law, except the Popish, to justify a regulated *usury*. 'Tis justified by the law of necessity and utility; humane society, as now circumstanced, would sink, if all *usury* were impracticable." By the end of the century the bulging warehouses, the numerous ships in Boston Harbor, and the well-appointed mansions of the merchants bore ample testimony to the compatibility of Puritanism and wealth-getting.

Widely recognized as the dominance of Puritan economic ideals may be in New England, it is less often acknowledged that the thriving commercial center of Philadelphia owed much of its drive to a similar ethic among the Quakers. It was William Penn, not John Winthrop, who advised his children to "cast up your income and live on half; if you can, one third; reserving the rest for casualties, charities portions." Simple living, as the bewigged Cotton Mather reminds us, was more a trait of Quakers in the seventeenth and eighteenth century than of Puritans. Indeed, so concerned were the Friends over the vices of ostentation and vanity that they would not permit portraits to be painted of themselves. The only concessions to the ego were black silhouettes. "Be plain in clothes, furniture and food, but clean," William Penn told his children, "and the coarser the better; the rest is folly and a snare." Furthermore, he counseled, diligence "is the Way to Wealth: *the diligent Hand makes Rich. . . . Frugality* is a Virtue too, and not of little Use in Life, the better Way to be Rich, for it has less Toil and Temptation."

As early as the seventeenth century, "the legend of the Quaker as Businessman" was widely accepted. This view, which was very close to the truth, pictured the Friends as shrewd, canny traders, "singularly industrious, sparing no Labour or Pains to increase their Wealth," as one seventeenth-century observer put it. Much like the Puritans, the Quakers were eminently successful in the counting-house, preaching and practicing that doctrine of the calling which united religion and bourgeois economic virtues in happy and fruitful marriage.

As New Englanders fanned out into the upper Middle West in the late eighteenth and early nineteenth centuries, the seed of Puritanism, now stripped of its theological skin, was planted across America. Furthermore, if one recognizes that the doctrine of the calling was Calvinist before it was Puritan, then the numbers of people imbibing that economic precept with their religious milk swells to impressive proportions. At the time of the Revolution, Ralph Barton Perry has calculated, one out of every two white Americans was a Calvinist of some persuasion.

Though no longer clothed in theological vestments, the virtue of work and wealth has remained with Americans. As Max Weber pointed out, the advice of Franklin's Poor Richard is but the Puritan ethic shorn of its theology; in Franklin the Puritan has become the Yankee. No longer anxious about unearthly salvation, but keenly concerned about a good bargain, the American still carries the telltale brand of Puritanism.

Notes

1. Not all the legal incidents and limitations on landholding then in practice in England were absent in America. Primogeniture, for example, obtained in the southern colonies and entail prevailed in all the English settlements. But it is also a fact that both institutions, all through the colonial period, were viewed as foreign to the tendency of American social development, to be abandoned completely by the end of the eighteenth century. "By the time of the Revolution, although much land throughout Colonial America was still held in fee tail estates, the practice of holding land in fee simple estates was widespread. Great strides had been made in barring fee tail estates by provisions in original grants to private parties, by private action in the making of wills, and by special acts of the colonial assemblies on behalf of individual cases." Marshall Harris, *Origin of the Land Tenure System in the United States* (Ames, Iowa, 1953), p. 373. By way of contrast, it might be recalled that primogeniture was not finally relinquished in England until 1926.

QUESTIONS FOR DISCUSSION

1. Degler begins this selection by asserting that "the one hundred years after the death of Elizabeth I in 1603 comprise the first century of the modern world" (1). What are some signals of this modern age? How did the settling of America help establish the modern era?

2. The Europeans were not used to the American dilemma that labor was scarcer than land. Discuss how this issue helped define the American character.

3. Explain why class structure became more flexible in America than it had been in Europe.

WRITING ASSIGNMENTS

1. Reaction Journal: Write a letter to an anonymous immigrant from a culture of your choosing. In your letter discuss how the immigrant would have to make cultural accommodations to adjust to the Anglo-Saxon Protestant value system.

2. Define the Protestant ethic, and write a summary of the different ways that Puritanism and Quakerism developed it. Write an essay in which you discuss how this ethic provides a moral justification of success in free enterprise.

FROM THE DIARY OF SAMUEL SEWALL

SAMUEL SEWALL

Samuel Sewall (1652–1730) was a very active and successful citizen of the Massachusetts Bay Colony, respected in many areas of endeavor. Born in England and brought to America by his parents in 1661, Sewall was raised in Newbury and studied for the ministry at Harvard College, where he received a bachelor's and a master's degree. Deciding against a career in the ministry, Sewall engaged in banking, publishing, international trading, politics, and the law. He was elected to thirty-three consecutive one-year terms as councillor and served as justice and later chief justice of the Superior Court of Judicature. His knowledge and conscientiousness were well regarded by his contemporaries.

In 1673 Sewall began to keep a diary in which he made entries for the next fifty-six years. Because he knew well all of the important people of his day and was himself a significant figure in colonial Massachusetts Bay, as well as a devoted record-keeper, Sewall has provided through his diaries one of the fullest accounts existing of daily life during this period. Diary-keeping was common among the Puritans, and diaries were often devoted largely to spiritual self-examination. Sewall's diary, however, is unique not only in the wealth of detail available to a writer who had experience in nearly all of the careers available in colonial America but also in the record it provides of a thoughtful and sensitive individual at a cultural crossroads. His diaries reveal Sewall as one of the last Puritans, devout in his faith, yet worldly and pragmatic in business and courtship.

Sewall is probably most often remembered as one of the judges at the witchcraft trials in Salem, Massachusetts, in 1692. As a man of his time, Sewall believed in witchcraft. He is, however, the only one of the Puritan judges involved in the trials to later question the wisdom or justice of the trials and to make a public statement of regret over his partici-

pation, confessing guilt, and begging forgiveness of God and men. A copy of this statement is recorded in his diary entry for January 15, 1696/7. The statement was read aloud at a church service on January 14, 1697, a day of fasting and repentance set aside to mark public recognition of the wrongs perpetrated by the trials.

◆ FREEWRITING

Prepare a personal journal in which you freewrite for ten or fifteen minutes each day for one week. Attempt to write so the journal entries tell your readers something about your own belief system and how it reflects your region and culture.

1674–1729

April 11th 1692. Went to Salem, where, in the Meeting-house, the persons accused of Witchcraft were examined; was a very great Assembly; 'twas awfull to see how the afflicted persons were agitated. Mr. Noyes pray'd at the beginning, and Mr. Higginson concluded. [*In the margin*], Væ, Væ, Væ, Witchcraft.

Augt. 19th 1692. This day the Lieut. Governour, Major Phillips, Mr. Russel, Capt. Lynde and myself went to Watertown. Advis'd the Inhabitants at their Town Meeting to settle a Minister; and if could not otherwise agree, should first have a Town-Meeting to decide where the Meetinghouse should be set. Many say Whitney's Hill would be a convenient place.

This day [*in the margin*, Dolefull! Witchcraft] George Burrough, John Willard, Jn° Procter, Martha Carrier and George Jacobs were executed at Salem, a very great number of Spectators being present. Mr. Cotton Mather was there, Mr. Sims, Hale, Noyes, Chiever, &c. All of them said they were innocent, Carrier and all. Mr. Mather says they all died by a Righteous Sentence. Mr. Burrough by his Speech, Prayer, protestation of his Innocence, did much move unthinking persons, which occasions their speaking hardly concerning his being executed.

Augt. 25. Fast at the old [*First*] Church, respecting the Witchcraft, Drought, &c.

Monday, Sept. 19, 1692. About noon, at Salem, Giles Corey was press'd to 5
death for standing Mute; much pains was used with him two days, one after another, by the Court and Capt. Gardner of Nantucket who had been of his acquaintance: but all in vain.*

* Giles Corey, approximately eighty years old, was pressed to death under heavy stones. This form of punishment was dictated by English law for those who refused to plead to an indictment. Corey, feeling he had little chance of escaping the charges of witchcraft brought against him, and knowing that were he found guilty his land holdings would be taken from him, chose to remain mute in order not to disinherit his heirs. Sewall's September 20, 1692, entry about the Corey case reveals the sort of "spectral evidence" that was allowed to be entered in the witchcraft trials. In this case, twelve-year-old Ann Putnam testified to having been visited by a ghostly apparition who claimed he had been murdered by Corey. Although Corey had been tried and acquitted of that crime, the spectral visitation convinced many people that his acquittal had been engineered by Corey's having made a compact with the Devil.

Sept. 20. Now I hear from Salem that about 18 years agoe, he was suspected to have stampd and press'd a man to death, but was cleared. Twas not remembred till Anne Putnam was told of it by said Corey's Spectre the Sabbath-day night before Execution.

Jan. 13, 1695/6. When I came in, past 7 at night, my wife met me in the Entry and told me Betty had surprised them.[1] I was surprised with the abruptness of the Relation. It seems Betty Sewall had given some signs of dejection and sorrow; but a little after dinner she burst out into an amazing cry, which caus'd all the family to cry too: Her Mother ask'd the reason; she gave none; at last said she was afraid she should goe to Hell, her Sins were not pardon'd. She was first wounded by my reading a Sermon of Mr. Norton's, about the 5th of Jan. Text Jno 7. 34. Ye shall seek me and shall not find me. And those words in the Sermon, Jno 8. 21. Ye shall seek me and shall die in your sins, ran in her mind, and terrified her greatly. And staying at home Jan. 12. she read out of Mr. Cotton Mather —Why hath Satan filled thy heart, which increas'd her Fear. Her Mother ask'd her whether she pray'd. She answer'd, Yes; but feared her prayers were not heard because her Sins not pardon'd. Mr. Willard though sent for timelyer, yet not being told of the message, till bruised Dindsdals [?][2] was given him; He came not till after I came home. He discoursed with Betty who could not give a distinct account, but was confused as his phrase was, and as had experienced in himself. Mr. Willard pray'd excellently. The Lord bring Light and Comfort out of this dark and dreadful Cloud, and Grant that Christ's being formed in my dear child, may be the issue of these painfull pangs.

Feb. 22. 1695/6. Betty comes into me almost as soon as I was up and tells me the disquiet she had when waked; told me was afraid should go to Hell, was like Spira, not Elected. Ask'd her what I should pray for, she said, that God would pardon her Sin and give her a new heart. I answer'd her Fears as well as I could, and pray'd with many Tears on either part; hope God heard us. I gave her solemnly to God.

Decr 21 [1696]. A very great Snow is on the Ground. I go in the morn to Mr. Willard, to entreat him to chuse his own time to come and pray with little Sarah: He comes a little before night, and prays very fully and well. Mr. Mather, the President, had pray^{d} with her in the time of the Courts sitting. *Decr 22.* being Catechising day, I give Mr. Willard a note to pray for my daughter publickly, which he did. . . .

The Lord take away my filthy garments, and give me change of Rayment. This day I remove poor little Sarah into my Bed-chamber, where about Break of Day Decr 23 she gives up the Ghost in Nurse Cowell's Arms. Born, Nov. 21, 1694. Neither I nor my wife were by: Nurse not expecting so sudden a change, and having promis'd to call us. I thought of Christ's Words, could you not watch with me one hour! and would fain have sat up with her: but fear of my wives illness, who is very valetudinarious, made me to lodge with her in the new Hall, where was call'd by Jane's Cry, to take notice of my dead daughter. Nurse did long and pathetically ask our pardon that she had not call'd us, and said she was surpriz^{d}. Thus this very fair day is rendered fowl to us by reason of the general

Sorrow and Tears in the family. Master Chiever was here the evening before, I desir'd him to pray for my daughter. The Chapt^{r} read in course on Decr 23. m. was Deut. 22. which made me sadly reflect that I had not been so thorowly tender of my daughter; nor so effectually carefull of her Defence and preservation as I should have been. The good Lord pity and pardon and help for the future as to those God has still left me.

Secund-day Jany 11, 1696/7 God helped me to pray more than ordinarily, that He would make up our Loss in the burial of our little daughter and other children, and that would give us a Child to Serve Him, pleading with Him as the Institutor of Marriage, and the Author of every good work. . . .

Jany 15. . . . Copy of the Bill I put up on the Fast day [January 14, 1696/7]; giving it to Mr. Willard as he pass'd by, and standing up at the reading of it, and bowing when finished; in the Afternoon.

Samuel Sewall, sensible of the reiterated strokes of God upon himself and family; and being sensible, that as to the Guilt contracted, upon the opening of the late Commission of Oyer and Terminer* at Salem (to which the order for this Day relates) he is, upon many accounts, more concerned than any that he knows of, Desires to take the Blame and Shame of it, Asking pardon of Men, And especially desiring prayers that God, who has an Unlimited Authority, would pardon that Sin and all other his Sins; personal and Relative: And according to his infinite Benignity, and Soveraignty, Not Visit the Sin of him, or of any other, upon himself or any of his, nor upon the Land: But that He would powerfully defend him against all Temptations to Sin, for the future; and vouchsafe him the Efficacious, Saving Conduct of his Word and Spirit.

Fourth-day, June, 19. 1700. Having been long and much dissatisfied with the Trade of fetching Negros from Guinea; at last I had a strong Inclination to Write something about it; but it wore off. At last reading Bayne, Ephes.[3] about servants, who mentions Blackamoors; I began to be uneasy that I had so long neglected doing any thing. When I was thus thinking, in came Bro^{r} Belknap to shew me a Petition he intended to present to the Genl Court for the freeing a Negro and his wife, who were unjustly held in Bondage. And there is a Motion by a Boston Committee to get a Law that all Importers of Negros shall pay 40^{s} *per* head, to discourage the bringing of them. And Mr. C. Mather resolves to publish a sheet to exhort Masters to labour their Conversion. Which makes me hope that I was call'd of God to Write this Apology for them; Let his Blessing accompany the same.[4]

[Sewall's first wife died after forty-one years of marriage. Two years later he married the Widow Tilley, who died six months later, in May 1720. He now begins his famous courtship of Madam Winthrop. When she turned down his proposal two months later, he gave up the courtship with the Hebrew exclamation "*Jehovah jireh!*" ("The Lord will provide!").]

* Oyer and Terminer" comes from the Middle English meaning "to hear and to determine"; thus, a Commission of Oyer and Determiner is a commission allowing a court to hear and judge criminal cases.

8^{r} [October 1720] 1. Satterday, I dine at Mr. Stoddard's: from thence I went to Madam Winthrop's just at 3.[5] Spake to her, saying, my loving wife died so soon and suddenly, 'twas hardly convenient for me to think of Marrying again; however I came to this Resolution, that I would not make my Court to any person without first Consulting with her. Had a pleasant discourse about 7 Single persons sitting in the Fore-seat 7^{r} 29th, viz. Mad^{m} Rebekah Dudley, Catharine Winthrop, Bridget Usher, Deliverance Legg, Rebekah Loyd, Lydia Colman, Elizabeth Bellingham. She propounded one and another for me; but none would do, said Mrs. Loyd was about her Age.

Octb^{r} 3. 2. Waited on Madam Winthrop again; 'twas a little while before she came in. Her daughter Noyes being there alone with me, I said, I hoped my Waiting on her Mother would not be disagreeable to her. She answer'd she should not be against that that might be for her Comfort. I Saluted her, and told her I perceiv'd I must shortly wish her a good Time; (her mother had told me, she was with Child, and within a Moneth or two of her Time). By and by in came Mr. Airs, Chaplain of the Castle,[6] and hang'd up his Hat, which I was a little startled at, it seeming as if he was to lodge there. At last Madam Winthrop came in. After a considerable time, I went up to her and said, if it might not be inconvenient I desired to speak with her. She assented, and spake of going into another Room; but Mr. Airs and Mrs. Noyes presently rose up, and went out, leaving us there alone. Then I usher'd in Discourse from the names in the Fore-seat; at last I pray'd that Katharine [*Mrs. Winthrop*] might be the person assign'd for me. She instantly took it up in way of Denyal, as if she had catch'd at an Opportunity to do it, saying she could not do it before she was asked. Said that was her mind unless she should Change it, which she believed she should not; could not leave her Children. I express'd my Sorrow that she should do it so Speedily, pray'd her Consideration, and ask'd her when I should wait on her agen. She setting no time, I mention'd that day Sennight. Gave her Mr. Willard's Fountain open'd with the little print and verses; saying, I hop'd if we did well read that book, we should meet together hereafter, if we did not now. She took the Book, and put it in her Pocket. Took Leave.

8^{r} 6th A little after 6. p. m. I went to Madam Winthrop's. She was not within. I gave Sarah Chickering the Maid 2^{s}, Juno, who brought in wood, 1^{s} Afterward the Nurse came in, I gave her 18^{d}, having no other small Bill. After awhile Dr. Noyes came in with his Mother; and quickly after his wife came in: They sat talking, I think, till eight a-clock. I said I fear'd I might be some Interruption to their Business: Dr. Noyes reply'd pleasantly: He fear'd they might be an Interruption to me, and went away. Madam seem'd to harp upon the same string. Must take care of her Children; could not leave that House and Neighbourhood where she had dwelt so long. I told her she might doe her children as much or more good by bestowing what she laid out in Hous-keeping, upon them. Said her Son would be of Age the 7th of August. I said it might be inconvenient for her to dwell with her Daughter-in-Law, who must be Mistress of the House. I gave her a piece of Mr. Belcher's Cake and Ginger-Bread wrapped up in a clean sheet of Paper.

Notes

1. Betty Sewall was fifteen. In the editor's opinion, this entry, the one of 10 January 1689/90 (when she was eight), and the entries of 22 February, 3 May, and 12 November of this year concerning her, reveal the real horrors of the Calvinist religion. The rationale is set forth in Sandford Fleming, *Children and Puritanism* (New Haven, 1933). It is pleasant to record that Betty survived these experiences, in due time married Grove Hirst, took her place in Boston society, and was the mother of eight children: Samuel was a Harvard graduate; Mary became Lady Pepperrell, Elizabeth married Rev. Charles Chauncy of the First Church, and Jane married Rev. Addington Davenport of Trinity Church.

2 These two words are not clear in the MS, though they resemble the words printed. We have not been able to make any more sense out of them than the earlier editors.

3 Paul Baynes, *A Commentarie Vpon The First Chapter of the Epistle of Saint Pavl, written to the Ephesians* (London, 1618).

4 Here Sewall is referring to his anti-slavery tract, "The Selling of Joseph," which was printed 24 June 1700.

5 Madam Winthrop was Katherine Brattle, daughter of Thomas Brattle and Elizabeth Tyng; she was born 26 September 1664, and was fifty-six years old at this time. She married first John Eyre, 20 May 1680. Of their children, three lived to maturity: Katharine, born 20 July 1694, who married David Jeffries (Harvard 1708), and, after his death at sea, Dr. Oliver Noyes (Harvard 1695); Bethiah, born 24 July 1695, who married John Walley; and John, a posthumous child, born 7 August 1700 (Harvard 1718). John Eyre Sr. died in June 1700. Katharine Brattle Eyre married, as her second husband, Major-General Wait Still Winthrop, 13 November 1707; he died 7 November 1717. She did not marry again, and died 2 August 1725 at Boston. *Sibley; Savage;* L. S. Mayo, *The Winthrop Family* (1948), 93, 107, 110.

6 Obadiah Ayers (Harvard 1710), chaplain of Castle William.

Note: For study questions, see page 71.

FROM THE PRIVATE JOURNAL OF A JOURNEY FROM BOSTON TO NEW YORK

SARAH KEMBLE KNIGHT

Born in Boston and married to a shipowner, Sarah Kemble Knight (1666–1727) was a woman respected in the Massachusetts Bay Colony for her writing and legal skills. Benjamin Franklin and Cotton Mather's son Samuel are thought to have attended the writing school which she operated in Boston from 1706 to 1713. The Journal of Madam Knight, *first published in 1825, records Knight's experiences on a journey by horseback from Boston to New York and back. She undertook this difficult wilderness trip with a series of guides between October 1704 and March 1705 in order to help a relative with legal documents in settling an estate in New Haven. Her* Journal *recounts the hardships and rewards of the journey, much of it through territory with few roads and bridges, as well as the local manners and customs she observed. After two months in New Haven, Knight accompanied a family member to New York City. The following excerpts from her* Journal *reveal Knight's fortitude and adventuresome spirit and her skill in recording the details of colonial American life.*

Friday, October the Sixth

I got up very early, in order to hire somebody to go with me to New Haven, being in great perplexity at the thoughts of proceeding alone; which my most hospitable entertainer observing, himself went, and soon returned with a young gentleman of the town, who he could confide in to go with me; and about eight this morning, with Mr. Joshua Wheeler my new guide, taking leave of this worthy gentleman, we advanced on towards Seabrook. The roads all along this way are very bad, encumbered with rocks and mountainous passages, which were very disagreeable to my tired carcass; but we went on with a moderate pace which made the journey more pleasant. But after about eight miles riding, in going over a bridge under which the river run very swift, my horse stumbled, and very narrowly escaped falling over into the water; which extremely frightened me. But through God's goodness I met with no harm, and mounting again, in about half a mile's riding, come to an ordinary,[1] were well entertained by a woman of about seventy and vantage,[2] but of as sound intellectuals as one of seventeen. She entertained Mr. Wheeler with some passages of a wedding awhile ago at a place hard by, the bride's-groom being about her age or something above, saying his children was dreadfully against their father's marrying, which she condemned them extremely for.

From hence we went pretty briskly forward, and arrived at Saybrook ferry about two of the clock afternoon; and crossing it, we called at an inn to bait[3] (foreseeing we should not have such another opportunity 'til we come to Killingsworth). Landlady come in, with her hair about her ears, and hands at full pay[4] scratching. She told us she had some mutton which she would broil, which I was glad to hear; but I suppose forgot to wash her scratches; in a little time she brought it in; but it being pickled, and my guide said it smelled strong of head sauce,[5] we left it, and paid sixpence a piece for our dinners, which was only smell.

So we put forward with all speed, and about seven at night come to Killingsworth, and were tolerably well with travelers' fare, and lodged there that night.

From December the Sixth

The city of New York is a pleasant, well-compacted place, situated on a commodious river which is a fine harbor for shipping. The buildings brick generally, very stately and high, though not altogether like ours in Boston. The bricks in some of the houses are of divers colors and laid in checkers, being glazed look very agreeable. The inside of them are neat to admiration, the wooden work, for only the walls are plastered, and the sumers and gist[6] are plained and kept very white scowered as so is all the partitions if made of boards. The fireplaces have no jambs (as ours have) but the backs run flush with the walls, and the hearth is of tiles and is as far out into the room at the ends as before the fire, which is generally five foot in the lower rooms, and the piece over where the mantle tree should be is made as ours with joiners' work,[7] and as I suppose is fastened to iron rods inside. The house where the vendue[8] was, had chimney corners like ours, and they and the hearths were laid with the finest tile that I ever see, and the staircases laid all with white tile which is ever clean, and so are the walls of the kitchen which had a brick floor. They were making great preparations to receive their governor, Lord Cornbury from the Jerseys,[9] and for that end raised the militia to guard him on shore to the fort.

They are generally of the Church of England and have a New England 5
gentleman for their minister, and a very fine church set out with all customary requisites. There are also a Dutch and divers conventicles as they call them, *viz.* Baptist, Quakers, &c. They are not strict in keeping the sabbath as in Boston and other places where I had been, but seem to deal with great exactness as far as I see or deal with. They are sociable to one another and courteous and civil to strangers and fare well in their houses. The English go very fashionable in their dress. But the Dutch, especially the middling sort, differ from our women, in their habit go loose, wear French muchets which are like a cap and a headband in one, leaving their ears bare, which are set out with jewels of a large size and many in number. And their fingers hooped with rings, some with large stones in them of many colors as were their pendants in their ears, which you should see very old women wear as well as young.

They have vendues very frequently and make their earnings very well by them, for they treat with good liquor liberally, and the customers drink as liberally and generally pay for't as well, by paying for that which they bid up briskly for, after the sack[10] has gone plentifully about, though sometimes good penny worths are got there. Their diversions in the winter is riding sleighs about three or four miles out of town, where they have houses of entertainment at a place called the Bowery, and some go to friends' houses who handsomely treat them. Mr. Burroughs carried his spouse and daughter and myself out to one Madame Dowes, a gentlewoman that lived at a farm house, who gave us a handsome entertainment of five or six dishes and choice beer and metheglin,[11] cider, &c. all which she said was the produce of her farm. I believe we met 50 or 60 sleighs that day—they fly with great swiftness and some are so furious that they'll turn out of the path for none except a loaden cart. Nor do they spare for any diversion the place affords, and sociable to a degree, they'r tables being as free to their neighbors as to themselves.

Having here transacted the affair I went upon and some other that fell in the way, after about a fortnight's stay there I left New York with no little regret[.]

Notes

1. An inn; a place where meals are served.
2. I.e., about 70 or more.
3. Refresh themselves and rest the horses.
4. I.e., busily.
5. Cheese sauce.
6. Main beams and joists.
7. Joiners were craftsmen who constructed things by joining pieces of wood together; their work was more finished than a carpenter's.
8. Auction.
9. Edward Hyde (1661–1723), royal Governor of New York and New Jersey from 1702 to 1708.
10. Wine; specifically, white wine imported from Spain or the Canaries.
11. A spiced drink rather like mead.

Note: For study questions, see page 71.

FROM THE SECRET DIARY OF WILLIAM BYRD OF WESTOVER, 1709–1712

WILLIAM BYRD

Born in Virginia, the son of a wealthy colonial aristocrat, William Byrd (1674–1744) spent most of his youth in England. He received an English public school education, learning to read Greek, Hebrew, Latin, Italian, Dutch, and French, studied law at the London Inns of Court, was admitted to the bar, and traveled to Holland to study business and trade. He associated with nobles and literary figures, living a life of elegance and privilege. When he returned to Virginia in 1705 to take over the Native American, colonial, and transatlantic trading enterprises established by his father and to manage the family lands, Byrd brought with him a level of learning unusual in the colonies, as well as a sophistication of taste well suited to the life of a Virginia aristocrat. An elected member of the House of Burgesses and an appointee to the Council of State, Byrd rebuilt the family home in Westover into one of the finest Georgian manor houses in the country and gathered a personal library of 3,600 volumes, second in size in the American colonies only to that of Cotton Mather's in Boston. The Enlightenment had shaped his values, tempering religion with rationalism and toleration.

In his Secret Diary, *which he began in 1709 and wrote in a shorthand code not decoded and published until the 1940s, Byrd recorded the intimate details of his private life. Like the diaries of Samuel Sewall, Byrd's diaries were not meant for publication and thus do not present a self-consciously prepared public image but rather an unedited glimpse of the activities and thoughts of an individual. It is interesting to compare the temperaments that emerge in these two very different records, one reflecting the mind and pursuits of a man who sat as judge on the witchcraft trials in Puritan Salem and the other the mind and pursuits of a Virginia aristocrat who took for the motto on his coat of arms Horace's phrase "No Guilt to Make One Pale."*

[February 1709]

21. I rose at 6 o'clock and read a chapter in Hebrew and 400 verses in Homer's *Odyssey*. I said my prayers with devotion. I ate milk for breakfast. The wind blew hard and it rained all the morning. I read law. I ate nothing for dinner but boiled pork and pie. In the afternoon the Doctor came from Williamsburg[1] and brought me a letter from the President[2], who informed me that Mr. Burwell was by the Council made naval officer of York River in the place of Colonel Cary deceased. In the evening I had a letter from Mr. Parker who sent me a fat steer for a present. I gave the man a crown that brought it. I said my prayers. I had good thoughts, good health, and good humor, thanks be to God Almighty.

22. I rose at 7 o'clock and read a chapter in Hebrew and 200 verses in Homer's *Odyssey*. I said my prayers, and ate milk for breakfast. I threatened Anaka with a whipping if she did not confess the intrigue between Daniel and Nurse, but she prevented by a confession. I chided Nurse severely about it, but she denied, with an impudent face, protesting that Daniel only lay on the bed for the sake of the child. I ate nothing but beef for dinner. The Doctor went to Mr. Dick Cocke who was very dangerously sick. I said my prayers. I had good health, good thoughts, and good humor, thanks be to God Almighty.

23. I rose at 6 o'clock and read a chapter in Hebrew and 100 verses in Homer's *Odyssey*. I said my prayers and ate milk for breakfast. Captain Worsham was here and Mr. Ligon about business. I ate battered eggs and then went to Will Randolph's, who was not at home. From thence I went to Colonel Randolph's, where I met Mr. C-s, a sensible man, who had fled from G-l-s W-l. The Colonel told me that two Nansemond Indians and two Meherrins were sent by the Tuscaroras to see if the English were alive. If they were, the Tuscaroras would send in the offenders. I went to visit Dick Cocke who was a little recovered of his gripes. I returned to Colonel Randolph's again where I ate milk. I said my prayers shortly. I had good thoughts, good health, and good humor, thanks be to God Almighty.

24. I rose at 6 o'clock. I ate milk for breakfast. I said my prayers. Then I went away and on the way called on Dick Cocke and found him better. From thence I went to Falling Creek, where I found all things well except the dam which had lost several of the stones but without any damage to the dam. In the afternoon I went to the Falls where I did not find things in so good order as I expected. Two of my negroes were sick. In the evening I returned to Falling Creek where I ate milk. I forgot to say my prayers. I had good health and good thoughts, but was out of humor with my affairs.

[October 1709]

6. I rose at 6 o'clock and said my prayers and ate milk for breakfast. Then I proceeded to Williamsburg, where I found all well. I went to the capitol where I sent for the wench to clean my room and when I came I kissed her and felt her, for which God forgive me. Then I went to see the President, whom I found indisposed in his ears. I dined with him on beef on beef [*sic*]. Then we went to his house and played at piquet[3] where Mr. Clayton came to us. We had much to do to get a bottle of French wine. About 10 o'clock I went to my lodgings. I had good health but wicked thoughts, God forgive me.

19. I rose at 6 o'clock and could not say my prayers because Colonel Bassett and Colonel Duke came to see me. For the same reason I could read nothing. I ate milk for breakfast. About ten o'clock we went to court where a man was tried for ravishing a very homely woman. There were abundance of women in the gallery. I recommended myself to God before I went into court. About one o'clock I went to my chambers for a little refreshment. The court rose about 4 o'clock and I dined with the Council. I ate boiled beef for dinner. I gave myself the liberty to talk very lewdly, for which God forgive me. I said my prayers and had good health, good thoughts, and good humor, thanks be to God Almighty.

[July 1710]

30. I rose at 5 o'clock and wrote a letter to Major Burwell about his boat which Captain Broadwater's people had brought round and sent Tom with it. I read two chapters in Hebrew and some Greek in Thucydides. I said my prayers and ate boiled milk for breakfast. I danced my dance.[4] I read a sermon in Dr. Tillotson and then took a little [nap]. I ate fish for dinner. In the afternoon my wife and I had a little quarrel which I reconciled with a flourish. Then she read a sermon in Dr. Tillotson to me. It is to be observed that the flourish was performed on the billiard table. I read a little Latin. In the evening we took a walk about the plantation. I neglected to say my prayers but had good health, good thoughts, and good humor, thanks be to God. This month there were many people sick of fever and pain in their heads; perhaps this might be caused by the cold weather which we had this month, which was indeed the coldest that ever was known in July in this country. Several of my people have been sick, but none died, thank God.

[December 1710]

31. I rose at 5 o'clock and read a chapter in Hebrew and four leaves[5] in Lucian. I said my prayers and ate boiled milk for breakfast. My daughter was very sick all night and vomited a great deal but was a little better this morning. All my sick people were better, thank God, and I had another girl come down sick from the quarters.[6] I danced my dance. Then I read a sermon in Dr. Tillotson[7] and after that walked in the garden till dinner. I ate roast venison. In the afternoon I looked over my sick people and then took a walk about the plantation. The weather was very warm still. My wife walked with me and when she came back she was very much indisposed and went to bed. In the evening I read another

sermon in Dr. Tillotson. About 8 o'clock the wind came to northwest and it began to be cold. I said my prayers and had good health, good thoughts, and good humor, thank God Almighty.

Some night this month I dreamed that I saw a flaming sword in the sky and called some company to see it but before they could come it was disappeared, and about a week after my wife and I were walking and we discovered in the clouds a shining cloud exactly in the shape of a dart and seemed to be over my plantation but it soon disappeared likewise. Both these appearances seemed to foretell some misfortune to me which afterwards came to pass in the death of several of my negroes after a very unusual manner. My wife about two months since dreamed she saw an angel in the shape of a big woman who told her the time was altered and the seasons were changed and that several calamities would follow that confusion. God avert his judgment from this poor country.

[October 1712]

21. I rose about 6 o'clock and we began to pack up our baggage in order to return. We drank chocolate with the Governor and about 10 o'clock we took leave of the Nottoway town and the Indian boys went away with us that were designed for the College. The Governor made three proposals to the Tuscaroras: that they would join with the English to cut off those Indians that had killed the people of Carolina, that they should have 40 shillings for every head they brought in of those guilty Indians and be paid the price of a slave for all they brought in alive, and that they should send one of the chief men's sons out of every town to the College. I waited on the Governor about ten miles and then took leave of him and he went to Mr. Cargill's and I with Colonel Hill, Mr. Platt, and John Hardiman went to Colonel Harrison's where we got about 3 o'clock in the afternoon. About 4 we dined and I ate some boiled beef. My man's horse was lame for which he was let blood. At night I asked a negro girl to kiss me, and when I went to bed I was very cold because I pulled off my clothes after lying in them so long. I neglected to say my prayers but had good health, good thoughts, and good humor, thank God Almighty.

[May 1712]

22. I rose about 6 o'clock and read two chapters in Hebrew and some Greek in Lucian. I said my prayers and ate boiled milk for breakfast. I danced my dance. It rained a little this morning. My wife caused Prue to be whipped violently notwithstanding I desired not, which provoked me to have Anaka whipped likewise who had deserved it much more, on which my wife flew into such a passion that she hoped she would be revenged of me. I was moved very much at this but only thanked her for the present lest I should say things foolish in my passion. I wrote more accounts to go to England. My wife was sorry for what she had said and came to ask my pardon and I forgave her in my heart but seemed to resent, that she might be the more sorry for her folly. She ate no dinner nor appeared the whole day. I ate some bacon for dinner. In the afternoon I wrote two more accounts till the evening and then took a walk in the garden. I

said my prayers and was reconciled to my wife and gave her a flourish in token of it. I had good health, good thoughts, but was a little out of humor, for which God forgive me.

Notes

1. Colonial capital of Virginia.
2. Of the Council of State.
3. A card game.
4. Did his calisthenics.
5. Pages.
6. Slave quarters.
7. Archbishop of Canterbury.

Note: For study questions, see page 71.

FROM THE JOURNAL OF JOHN WOOLMAN

JOHN WOOLMAN

The child of Quaker farmers who lived near Mount Holly, New Jersey, John Woolman (1720–1772) became a Quaker minister and worked as a shopkeeper, tailor, and orchard keeper. The Quaker sect (the Society of Friends) was founded in England in the 1650s, without the paid clergy, standardized liturgy, music, and hierarchy that characterized organized religion. Any person who felt inspired during their gatherings in simple meetinghouses could address the group, and those who were frequent and effective speakers were regarded as ministers. The Quakers in America settled in Pennsylvania and West Jersey in order to avoid persecution by the Puritans.

During his lifetime, Woolman was not widely known outside the Quaker community, but his Journal, *published posthumously in 1774, had considerable literary influence. The American transcendentalists and the English romantics, in particular, appreciated his clear unadorned style, his commitment to the abolition of slavery, and the Quaker virtues revealed in his writings: a devotion to the simple life, an intuitive belief in the natural goodness of human beings and a belief in the acceptability to God of all "sincere, upright-hearted people" regardless of their membership in a particular sect. Unlike the diaries of colonial Puritans, which were private records of soul-searching, Quaker journals were autobiographical reflections intended for publication. A careful stylist, Woolman prepared three successive drafts of his* Journal.

I have often felt a motion of love to leave some hints in writing of my experience of the goodness of God, and now, in the thirty-sixth year of my age, I begin this work.

I was born in Northampton, in Burlington County, West Jersey, in the year 1720. Before I was seven years old I began to be acquainted with the operations of Divine love. Through the care of my parents, I was taught to read nearly as soon as I was capable of it; and as I went from school one day, I remember that while my companions were playing by the way, I went forward out of sight, and, sitting down, I read the twenty-second chapter of Revelation: "He showed me a pure river of water of life, clear as crystal, proceeding out of the throne of God and of the Lamb, &c." In reading it, my mind was drawn to seek after that pure habitation which I then believed God had prepared for his servants. The place where I sat, and the sweetness that attended my mind, remain fresh in my memory. This, and the like gracious visitations, had such an effect upon me that when boys used ill language it troubled me; and, through the continued mercies of God, I was preserved from that evil.

The pious instructions of my parents were often fresh in my mind, when I happened to be among wicked children, and were of use to me. Having a large family of children, they used frequently, on first-days, after meeting,* to set us one after another to read the Holy Scriptures, or some religious books, the rest sitting by without much conversation; I have since often thought it was a good practice. From what I had read and heard, I believed there had been, in past ages, people who walked in uprightness before God in a degree exceeding any that I knew or heard of now living: and the apprehension of there being less steadiness and firmness amongst people in the present age often troubled me while I was a child.

I may here mention a remarkable circumstance that occurred in my childhood. On going to a neighbor's house, I saw on the way a robin sitting on her nest, and as I came near she went off; but having young ones, she flew about, and with many cries expressed her concern for them. I stood and threw stones at her, and one striking her she fell down dead. At first I was pleased with the exploit, but after a few minutes was seized with horror, as having in a sportive way, killed an innocent creature while she was careful for her young. I beheld her lying dead and thought those young ones, for which she was so careful, must now perish for want of their dam to nourish them. After some painful considerations on the subject, I climbed up the tree, took all the young birds, and killed them, supposing that better than to leave them to pine away and die miserably. In this case I believed that Scripture proverb was fulfilled, "The tender mercies of the wicked are cruel." I then went on my errand, and for some hours could think of little else but the cruelties I had committed, and was much troubled. Thus He

* Rather than attending church services, Quakers gather at "meetings" to pray together, generally doing so silently until one of those present is moved to speak. Woolman refers to "first-days" because Quakers numbered the days of the week rather than using the names associated with pagan gods.

whose tender mercies are over all his works hath placed a principle in the human mind, which incites to exercise goodness towards every living creature; and this being singly attended to, people become tender-hearted and sympathizing; but being frequently and totally rejected, the mind becomes shut up in a contrary disposition.

About the twelfth year of my age, my father being abroad, my mother reproved me for some misconduct, to which I made an undutiful reply. The next first-day, as I was with my father returning from meeting, he told me that he understood I had behaved amiss to my mother and advised me to be more careful in future. I knew myself blamable, and in shame and confusion remained silent. Being thus awakened to a sense of my wickedness, I felt remorse in my mind, and on getting home I retired and prayed to the Lord to forgive me, and I do not remember that I ever afterwards spoke unhandsomely to either of my parents, however foolish in some other things.

Having attained the age of sixteen years, I began to love wanton company; and though I was preserved from profane language or scandalous conduct, yet I perceived a plant in me which produced much wild grapes; my merciful Father did not, however, forsake me utterly, but at times, through his grace, I was brought seriously to consider my ways; and the sight of my backslidings affected me with sorrow, yet for want of rightly attending to the reproofs of instruction, vanity was added to vanity, and repentance to repentance. Upon the whole, my mind became more and more alienated from the truth, and I hastened toward destruction. While I meditate on the gulf towards which I travelled, and reflect on my youthful disobedience, for these things I weep, mine eye runneth down with water.

Advancing in age, the number of my acquaintance increased, and thereby my way grew more difficult. Though I had found comfort in reading the Holy Scriptures and thinking on heavenly things, I was now estranged therefrom. I knew I was going from the flock of Christ and had no resolution to return, hence serious reflections were uneasy to me, and youthful vanities and diversions were my greatest pleasure. In this road I found many like myself, and we associated in that which is adverse to true friendship.

In this swift race it pleased God to visit me with sickness, so that I doubted of recovery; then did darkness, horror, and amazement with full force seize me, even when my pain and distress of body were very great. I thought it would have been better for me never to have had being, than to see the day which I now saw. I was filled with confusion, and in great affliction, both of mind and body, I lay and bewailed myself. I had not confidence to lift up my cries to God, whom I had thus offended; but in a deep sense of my great folly I was humbled before him. At length that word which is as a fire and a hammer broke and dissolved my rebellious heart; my cries were put up in contrition; and in the multitude of his mercies I found inward relief, and a close engagement that if he was pleased to restore my health I might walk humbly before him. . . .

I kept steadily to meetings; spent first-day afternoons chiefly in reading the Scriptures and other good books, and was early convinced in my mind that true religion consisted in an inward life, wherein the heart doth love and reverence God the Creator, and learns to exercise true justice and goodness, not only toward all men, but also toward the brute creatures; that, as the mind was moved by an inward principle to love God as an invisible, incomprehensible Being, so, by the same principle, it was moved to love him in all his manifestations in the visible world; that, as by his breath the flame of life was kindled in all animal sensible creatures, to say we love God as unseen, and at the same time exercise cruelty toward the least creature moving by his life, or by life derived from him, was a contradiction in itself. I found no narrowness respecting sects and opinions, but believed that sincere, upright-hearted people in every society who truly love God, were accepted of him. . . .

About the twenty-third year of my age, I had many fresh and heavenly openings in respect to the care and providence of the Almighty over his creatures in general, and over man as the most noble amongst those which are visible. And being clearly convinced in my judgment that to place my whole trust in God was best for me, I felt renewed engagements that in all things I might act on an inward principle of virtue, and pursue worldly business no further than as truth opened my way.

About the time called Christmas I observed many people, both in town and from the country, resorting to public-houses, and spending their time in drinking and vain sports, tending to corrupt one another; on which account I was much troubled. At one house in particular there was much disorder; and I believed it was a duty incumbent on me to speak to the master of that house. I considered I was young, and that several elderly friends in town had opportunity to see these things; but though I would gladly have been excused, yet I could not feel my mind clear.

The exercise was heavy; and as I was reading what the Almighty said to Ezekiel,* respecting his duty as a watchman, the matter was set home more clearly. With prayers and tears I besought the Lord for his assistance, and He, in loving-kindness, gave me a resigned heart. At a suitable opportunity I went to the public-house; and seeing the man amongst much company, I called him aside, and in the fear and dread of the Almighty expressed to him what rested on my mind. He took it kindly, and afterwards showed more regard to me than before. In a few years afterwards he died, middle-aged; and I often thought that had I neglected my duty in that case it would have given me great trouble; and I was humbly thankful to my gracious Father, who had supported me herein.

My employer, having a negro woman, sold her, and desired me to write a bill of sale, the man being waiting who bought her. The thing was sudden; and though I felt uneasy at the thoughts of writing an instrument of slavery for one of my fellow creatures, yet I remembered that I was hired by the year, that it was my master who directed me to do it, and that it was an elderly man, a member of our Society, who bought her; so through weakness I gave way, and wrote it; but

* Ezekiel was a prophet who delivered warnings to the Israelites from God.

at the executing of it I was so afflicted in my mind, that I said before my master and the Friend that I believed slave-keeping to be a practice inconsistent with the Christian religion. This, in some degree, abated my uneasiness; yet as often as I reflected seriously upon it I thought I should have been clearer if I had desired to be excused from it, as a thing against my conscience; for such it was. Some time after this a young man of our Society spoke to me to write a conveyance of a slave to him, he having lately taken a negro into his house. I told him I was not easy to write it; for, though many of our meeting and in other places kept slaves, I still believed the practice was not right, and desired to be excused from the writing. I spoke to him in good-will; and he told me that keeping slaves was not altogether agreeable to his mind; but that the slave being a gift made to his wife, he had accepted her.

QUESTIONS FOR DISCUSSION

1. Discuss some of the major differences the journal entries reflect between the lives, beliefs, and values of the Virginia aristocrat (Byrd), the Quaker (Woolman), and the Puritan (Sewall).
2. Knight was a woman who led an active life outside the home and still earned the respect of her fellow citizens during the colonial period. Her journal points to some gender as well as regional differences. Discuss how her journal entries support this assertion.

WRITING ASSIGNMENTS

1. Reaction Journal: Write a letter to one of the four journal writers. Comment on how you feel this individual would respond to your time and your region.
2. Choose two of the journal writers and write an essay in which you compare and contrast their writing styles and their belief systems as reflected in the entries.

From North America—The Displaced Landlords

PRIOR TO THE ARRIVAL of the first Europeans in 1492, the Native American* peoples living north of the Rio Grande may have numbered as many as 12 to 14 million. Widely distributed throughout the United States, these peoples were diverse in language, architecture, religion, and life-style. Some lived in migratory bands as food gatherers, some in agricultural city states, and some united in sophisticated political confederacies. In spite of a rapid decline in population to a low point of 210,000 in 1920, much of the diversity still exists today in more than 300 tribal identity groups in the continental United States and about 200 in Alaska. Over the past seventy years the population has steadily increased to nearly 2 million.

Although Native American stock is now genetically mixed as a result of intermarriage between tribes and with blacks, Mexicans, and Europeans, there is both a strong sense of pan-Indian identity and a commitment to reclaiming distinctive historical identities. Tribal identity is very strong and can, as Mary Crow Dog admits, work against the establishment of Indian unity. Underlying obvious geographic, linguistic, and cultural differences among Native American groups, however, is a shared sense of the strength that comes from spiritual ties to the land and to nature. A kind of mystic tie to the land emerges repeatedly as Native Americans describe their cultural heritage. The Iroquois Creation Myth speaks powerfully of the relationship of the people to the land. The theme of

* With renewed pride in ethnic heritage, debates over terminology have arisen. There is some resistance to the use of the word "Indian," the term applied erroneously by subjugating explorers under the mistaken impression that they had arrived in India. Thus the term "Native American" has come into wide acceptance. Similar controversy surrounds the term "tribe," a word that carries some connotations of inferiority and that began to replace the original term "nation" in the early nineteenth century. By the middle of the twentieth century, many Native Americans rejected the word "tribe" in favor of "nation." The Bureau of Indian Affairs, however, continues to use the term "tribe" and has named the political bodies it has encouraged "tribal councils." Usage, as the following selections demonstrate, varies, depending on how politically charged a given writer finds these terms. Many contemporary Native American writers refer to themselves as "Indians." Paula Gunn Allen, for instance, identifies herself as an "American Indian woman" and refers to her "tribal identity."

harmony with nature also informs Luther Standing Bear's description of the main features of the Native American approach to life—"an intense and absorbing love for nature; a respect for life; enriching faith in a Supreme Power; and principles of truth, honesty, generosity, equity, and brotherhood as a guide to mundane relations."

These ideals of existing in harmony with the land and one's fellows and the democratic principles modeled by the Iroquois Confederacy* seems at odds with the fear and distrust with which European settlers often regarded Native Americans. Writing in the first half of the nineteenth century, in the climate of cultural relativism set in part by Rousseau's concept of the "noble savage," James Fenimore Cooper depicted the Mohican Chief Chingachgook with tolerance and respect: "There is a soul and a heart under that red skin . . . although they are a soul and a heart with gifts different from our own." But for the early settlers such a benign view did not predominate. Captain John Smith, of the settlement at Jamestown, refers to the native peoples as "savages" and "barbarians," perhaps not surprisingly considering that he had been held captive by the Algonquian chief Powhatan, his life saved only through the intervention of Powhatan's daughter Pocahontas. Mary Rowlandson, author of one of the well-known captivity narratives, refers to "the bloody heathen" who attacked the village of Lancaster, Massachusetts, in 1676, taking herself and others captive. Mary Eastman, who lived for seven years among the Sioux at Fort Snelling on the Michigan frontier during the first half of the nineteenth century, describes Sioux women who were warm and caring and yet wore necklaces made from the hands and feet of Chippewa children. On the other hand, government removal policies that resulted in the expulsion of the Cherokees from their lands in Georgia and their removal to Arkansas by forced march in midwinter of 1838 along a "trail of tears" demonstrate that cruelty was far from one-sided.

By and large, it was the desire of neither Native Americans nor settlers to pursue a route of assimilation or integration. The Seneca Chief Red Jacket said in 1805, "The Great Spirit has made us all, but he has made a difference between his red and white children." When at the first encounter between the Pawnees and Anglo-American settlers the whites proposed to exchange blankets, guns, and steel knives for land, the chief of the Pawnees replied, "Go back to the country from whence you came. We do not want your presents, and we do not want you to come into our country." As for the English settlers, they viewed the Native Americans primarily as an impediment to their acquisition of land. Between 1810 and 1821 more than half a million settlers had moved into Ken-

* A stable political union, the Iroquois Confederacy was known as the League of the Five Nations when it was founded in the sixteenth century by the Mohawk, Onondaga, Cayuga, Oneida, and Seneca tribes. When the Tuscaroras were admitted in the early eighteenth century, it became known as the League of Six Nations. Decisions relating to all the tribes were debated at common councils by elected delegates, each of whom represented both a tribe and a particular matrilinear clan within the tribe. Some revisionist historians suggest that this confederacy served as a model for the American representative form of government (see Ishmael Reed, "America: The Multinational Society," p. 514).

tucky, Tennessee, Alabama, Mississippi, and Louisiana, and almost half a million more arrived in Ohio, Indiana, Illinois, and Missouri.

A comparison of locations of American Indian groups in 1970 with their locations around 1600 indicates that the almost four hundred intervening years were marked by consolidation and removal of Native American populations westward. While in the early 1600s there were at least 75,000 American Indians, divided into forty groups, along the east coast from Maine to North Carolina, by 1970 the population of the same area was under 10,000, representing only sixteen distinct groups. A similar situation occurred in the midsection of the country when the settling of the fertile plains transformed lands that were traditional Indian hunting territory into American farmland.

In some respects the history of U.S. government policy toward Native Americans reflects the changing views on the place of ethnic groups within American society in general. An initial period of separation and removal, during which the objective was to remove Native Americans from lands settlers wanted and to draw boundaries between the two groups, resulted in such policies as the Indian Removal Act of 1830. This act gave President Andrew Jackson the power to move eastern Indians west of the Mississippi, which then marked the western line of frontier settlement, into Indian Territory, much of which is now Oklahoma. The notorious removal of the Cherokee, in the winter of 1838, from their lands in Georgia, North Carolina, and Tennessee—lands to which the Supreme Court had in 1832 affirmed their sovereign right—took the lives of 4,000 who died from hunger and exposure.

By the middle of the nineteenth century, it became obvious that U.S. expansion was going to continue west of the Mississippi. Thus, the policy of removal also began to include containment, as the government sought to define the large previously unspecified tracts of Indian territory as reservations and, during the Plains Indian Wars of the last half of the nineteenth century, to restrict forcibly Native American populations to these reservation lands. The fate of some of the Plains Indians who repeatedly sought peace yet were maneuvered into war is a shameful part of the achievement of U.S. Manifest Destiny. The massacre of 133 Cheyennes and Arapahos, 105 of them women and children, gathered peacefully at Sand Creek, Colorado, in 1851 caused chiefs who had held out for peace with the white men to ally themselves with the Sioux and turn to war for survival. Not until the bloody encounter between the Oglala Sioux and the U.S. Cavalry at Wounded Knee, South Dakota, in December 1890 did the Plains Wars finally end.

The declining population of Native Americans toward the end of the nineteenth century made it appear as if they were on the verge of extinction, a possibility that caused rethinking of government policies of separation and restriction. As an alternative, the government decided to absorb the native peoples into mainstream American society as quickly as possible. The Indian nations had previously functioned as sovereign nations negotiating treaties with the U.S. government, but in 1871 Congress abandoned the treaty process and began to legislate on behalf of Native Americans, thus effectively making them wards of the U.S. government. A period of coercive assimilation began, its goal the elimination of Indian cultural traditions. Government- or church-run boarding schools for Indian youngsters, often located hundreds of miles from their reservations, required use of the English language, taught Christianity, and devalued traditional ways. Luther Standing Bear attended the most famous of these schools, in Carlisle, Pennsylvania. Thomas "Bearhead" Swaney of the Salish tribe speaks of the way in which "boarding school Indians" were deprived of Native American culture, becoming "dark-skinned kids raised in white education, unable to speak their language, sing their songs, dance their dances, pray their religion." Paula Gunn Allen, reflecting on how little has changed in the ways Native American culture is presented in the curriculum in "Where I Come from Is like This," observes that still "no Indian can grow to any age without being informed that her people were 'savages' who interfered with the march of progress pursued by respectable, loving, civilized white people." The Dawes General Allotment Act of 1887 added to the loss of autonomy and culture a loss of land by granting lands to individuals in 160-acre allotments rather than to tribes and allowing speculators to purchase hundreds of thousands of acres of previously held tribal lands that remained after the allotments were made. Further loss of traditional lands occurred as Native Americans moved off the reservations and sold their allotments to outsiders. The climax of the assimilation movement came in 1924, when Congress granted citizenship to all Native Americans.

The effort at forced assimilation, during which approximately one half of the Indian languages were lost, ended in 1934 with the passage of the Indian Reorganization Act, which ended allotment and encouraged tribes to establish their own local governments on reservations. At the same time the Bureau of Indian Affairs reversed its former policies and encouraged freedom of choice in religion and other cultural matters and made a commitment to hiring more Native Americans for positions within the BIA. This period of official sanction of and support for maintaining distinctive cultural identities was interrupted by a brief termination period in the 1950s when a House resolution sought to end the special relationship between Native Americans and the federal government. The resolution proposed the withdrawal of federal support and responsibility for Indian affairs. Almost all Native Americans opposed this policy of termination, and there was strong opposition as well in Congress and among the general population. Since 1961 the trend in policy has been to reaffirm and develop the provisions of the IRA.

The 1970s were marked by the emergence of Indian activist groups and public protests such as the 1970 occupation of Alcatraz island in San Francisco Bay, the takeover of the Bureau of Indian Affairs in Washington, D.C., and the 1973 seventy-one-day armed siege at Wounded Knee, all of which Mary Crow Dog refers to in her essay about the American Indian Movement (AIM). The incident at Wounded Knee brought the goals of AIM's militant leadership into the national consciousness through daily news coverage. While representing a minority view, AIM's goals of separatism, political activism, rejection of white values, and the dismantling of existing tribal organizations brought renewed attention to the problems of Native Americans in contemporary society. The goal of regaining identity and pride continues, as tribes work through the courts in pressing claims for lost lands, winning settlements in many cases. Nonetheless, as Michael Dorris points out in "Crazy Horse Malt Liquor and Other Cultural Metaphors," in relation to the general population, Native Americans suffer disproportionately from unemployment, infant mortality, fetal alcohol syndrome and effect, and teenage suicide. Such social problems have created, in a portion of the Native American population, a sense of hopelessness that tends to perpetuate them. Alienated from their own traditions by policies of forced assimilation and from mainstream society by a history of violated land rights and broken promises, Native Americans grapple with economic and spiritual problems as they seek to redefine themselves in relation to their own and the general culture.

IROQUOIS CREATION MYTH

IROQUOIS

The following creation myth was published by Harriet Maxwell Converse in "Myths and Legends of the New York State Iroquois," in the New York State Museum Bulletin *in 1909. Like creation myths of many other cultures, it accounts not only for the creation and peopling of the earth but also for the existence of good and evil.*

◆ FREEWRITING

A myth is a traditional story that often originates in preliterate societies. Myths frequently deal with supernatural beings, ancestors, or heroes, who serve as fundamental types in a nonscientific view of the world. They appeal to the consciousness of a people because they usually embody and explain cultural ideals and phenomena. Many religions celebrate myths and beliefs that account for our origin. Freewrite for ten or fifteen minutes about the myths or religious beliefs with which you are familiar that focus on "origin." You may wish to look to your own religion or culture, perhaps the creation account in *Genesis* 1–2:3.

The Council Tree

In the faraway days of this floating island there grew one stately tree that branched beyond the range of vision. Perpetually laden with fruit and blossoms, the air was fragrant with its perfume, and the people gathered to its shade where councils were held.

One day the Great Ruler said to his people: "We will make a new place where another people may grow. Under our council tree is a great cloud sea which calls for our help. It is lonesome. It knows no rest and calls for light. We will talk to it. The roots of our council tree point to it and will show the way."

Having commanded that the tree be uprooted, the Great Ruler peered into the depths where the roots had guided, and summoning Ata-en-sic, who was with child, bade her look down. Ata-en-sic saw nothing, but the Great Ruler knew that the sea voice was calling, and bidding her carry its life, wrapped around her a great ray of light and sent her down to the cloud sea.

Hah-nu-nah, the Turtle

Dazzled by the descending light enveloping Ata-en-sic, there was great consternation among the animals and birds inhabiting the cloud sea, and they counseled in alarm.

"If it falls it may destroy us," they cried.

"Where can it rest?" asked the Duck.

"Only the oeh-da (earth) can hold it," said the Beaver, "the oeh-da which lies at the bottom of our waters, and I will bring it." The Beaver went down but never returned. Then the Duck ventured, but soon its dead body floated to the surface.

Many of the divers had tried and failed when the Muskrat, knowing the way, volunteered to obtain it and soon returned bearing a small portion in his paw. "But it is heavy," said he, "and will grow fast. Who will bear it?"

The Turtle was willing, and the oeh-da was placed on his hard shell.

Having received a resting place for the light, the water birds, guided by its glow, flew upward, and receiving the woman on their widespread wings, bore her down to the Turtle's back.

And Hah-nu-nah, the Turtle, became the Earth Bearer. When he stirs, the seas rise in great waves, and when restless and violent, earthquakes yawn and devour.

Ata-en-sic, the Sky Woman

The *oeh-da* grew rapidly and had become an island when Ata-en-sic, hearing voices under her heart, one soft and soothing, the other loud and contentious, knew that her mission to people the island was nearing.

To her solitude two lives were coming, one peaceful and patient, the other restless and vicious. The latter, discovering light under his mother's arms, thrust himself through, to contentions and strife, the right born entered life for freedom and peace.

These were the Do-ya-da-no, the twin brothers, Spirits of Good and Evil. Foreknowing their powers, each claimed dominion, and a struggle between them began, Hah-gweh-di-yu claiming the right to beautify the island, while Hah-gweh-da-ĕt-găh determined to destroy. Each went his way, and where peace had reigned discord and strife prevailed.

The Sun, Moon, and Stars

At the birth of Hah-gweh-di-yu his Sky Mother, Ata-en-sic, had died, and the island was still dim in the dawn of its new life when, grieving at his mother's death, he shaped the sky with the palm of his hand, and creating the Sun from her face, lifted it there, saying, "You shall rule here where your face will shine forever." But Hah-gweh-da-ĕt-găh set Darkness in the west sky, to drive the Sun down behind it.

Hah-gweh-di-yu then drew forth from the breast of his Mother, the Moon and the Stars, and led them to the Sun as his sisters who would guard his night sky. He gave to the Earth her body, its Great Mother, from whom was to spring all life.

All over the land Hah-gweh-di-yu planted towering mountains, and in the valleys set high hills to protect the straight rivers as they ran to the sea. But Hah-gweh-da-ĕt-găh wrathfully sundered the mountains, hurling them far apart, and drove the high hills into the wavering valleys, bending the rivers as he hunted them down.

Hah-gweh-di-yu set forests on the high hills, and on the low plains fruit-bearing trees and vines to wing their seeds to the scattering winds. But Hah-gweh-da-ĕt-găh gnarled the forests besetting the earth, and led monsters to dwell in the sea, and herded hurricanes in the sky which frowned with mad tempests that chased the Sun and the Stars.

The Animals and Birds

Hah-gweh-di-yu went across a great sea where he met a Being who told him he was his father. Said the Being, "How high can you reach?" Hah-gweh-di-yu touched the sky. Again he asked, "How much can you lift?" and Hah-gweh-di-yu grasped a stone mountain and tossed it far into space. Then said the Being, "You are worthy to be my son"; and lashing upon his back two burdens, bade him return to the earth.

Hah-gweh-di-yu swam for many days, and the Sun did not leave the sky until he had neared the earth. The burdens had grown heavy but Hah-gweh-di-yu was strong, and when he reached the shore they fell apart and opened.

From one of the burdens flew an eagle guiding the birds which followed, filling the skies with their song to the Sun as they winged to the forest. From the other there came animals led by the deer, and they sped quickly to the mountains. But Hah-gweh-da-ĕt-găh followed with wild beasts that devour, and grim flying creatures that steal life without sign, and creeping reptiles to poison the way.

Duel of Hah-gweh-di-yu and Hah-gweh-da-ĕt-găh

When the earth was completed and Hah-gweh-di-yu had bestowed a protecting Spirit upon each of his creation, he besought Hah-gweh-da-ĕt-găh to reconcile his vicious existence to the peacefulness of his own, but Hah-gweh-da-ĕt-găh refused, and challenged Hah-gweh-di-yu to combat, the victor to become the ruler of the earth.

Hah-gweh-da-ĕt-găh proposed weapons which he could control, poisonous roots strong as flint, monsters' teeth, and fangs of serpents. But these Hah-gweh-di-yu refused, selecting the thorns of the giant crab-apple tree, which were arrow pointed and strong.

With the thorns they fought. The battle continued many days, ending in the overthrow of Hah-gweh-da-ĕt-găh.

Hah-gweh-di-yu, having now become the ruler, banished his brother to a pit under the earth, whence he cannot return. But he still retains Servers, half human and half beasts, whom he sends to continue his destructive work. These Servers can assume any form Hah-gweh-da-ĕt-găh may command, and they wander all over the earth.

Hah-gweh-di-yu, faithful to the prophesy of the Great Ruler of the floating island, that the earth be peopled, is continually creating and protecting.

QUESTIONS FOR DISCUSSION

1. The introduction to this chapter states that "among Native American groups . . . is a shared sense of the strength that comes from spiritual ties to the land and to nature." Discuss the ways that the Iroquois Creation Myth supports that statement.
2. How does this myth explain such phenomena as natural disasters? What impression does it give you of the nature of human beings?

WRITING ASSIGNMENTS

1. Reaction Journal: Freewrite for ten or fifteen minutes on ways your own belief system about our origin may or may not accommodate scientific data.
2. Interview a member of a religious/cultural community different from your own. Focus your interview on the issue of origin. Write an essay in which you describe the interview. Do you see any commonality among the notions of origin as reflected in the Iroquois myth, in your interview, and in your own belief system?

WHAT THE INDIAN MEANS TO AMERICA

LUTHER STANDING BEAR

Raised in a Teton Sioux tribe during the period of rapid westward expansion when U.S. troops were forcibly relocating Native Americans onto reservations, Luther Standing Bear (1868–1947) experienced firsthand the encounter of two very different ways of life. After attending the government Indian school in Carlisle, Pennsylvania, Standing Bear served as clerk, storekeeper, rancher, and minister among his people on the Rosebud and later the Pine Ridge reservations in the Nebraska Territory. He was also a performer with Buffalo Bill's Wild West Show, an actor in silent films, and a lecturer on Native American culture.

Standing Bear found the government policies toward Native Americans demeaning and counterproductive and publicized his views in My People the Sioux *(1928),* My Indian Boyhood *(1931), and* Stories of the Sioux *(1934). The following essay is the final chapter in* Land of the Spotted Eagle *(1933), which through its emphasis on the positive values of Native American ways and the destructive effects of government policies helped bring about more benign policies toward Native Americans under Franklin D. Roosevelt.*

◆ FREEWRITING

In this selection Luther Standing Bear points out that "the feathered and blanketed figure of the American Indian has come to symbolize the American continent." Freewrite for ten or fifteen minutes on situations in which you have seen the Indian used as a national and/or commercial symbol.

The feathered and blanketed figure of the American Indian has come to symbolize the American continent. He is the man who through centuries has been moulded and sculpted by the same hand that shaped its mountains, forests, and plains, and marked the course of its rivers.

The American Indian is of the soil, whether it be the region of forests, plains, pueblos, or mesas. He fits into the landscape, for the hand that fashioned the continent also fashioned the man for his surroundings. He once grew as naturally as the wild sunflowers; he belongs just as the buffalo belonged.

With a physique that fitted, the man developed fitting skills—crafts which today are called American. And the body had a soul, also formed and moulded by the same master hand of harmony. Out of the Indian approach to existence there came a great freedom—an intense and absorbing love for nature; a respect for life; enriching faith in a Supreme Power; and principles of truth, honesty, generosity, equity, and brotherhood as a guide to mundane relations. . . .

The white man does not understand the Indian for the reason that he does not understand America. He is too far removed from its formative processes. The roots of the tree of his life have not yet grasped the rock and soil. The white man is still troubled with primitive fears; he still has in his consciousness the perils of this frontier continent, some of its fastnesses not yet having yielded to his questing footsteps and inquiring eyes. He shudders still with the memory of the loss of his forefathers upon its scorching deserts and forbidding mountain-tops. The man from Europe is still a foreigner and an alien. And he still hates the man who questioned his path across the continent.

But in the Indian the spirit of the land is still vested; it will be until other 5
men are able to divine and meet its rhythm. Men must be born and reborn to belong. Their bodies must be formed of the dust of their forefathers' bones.

The attempted transformation of the Indian by the white man and the chaos that has resulted are but the fruits of the white man's disobedience of a fundamental and spiritual law. The pressure that has been brought to bear upon the native people, since the cessation of armed conflict, in the attempt to force conformity of custom and habit has caused a reaction more destructive than war, and the injury has not only affected the Indian, but has extended to the white population as well. Tyranny, stupidity, and lack of vision have brought about the situation now alluded to as the "Indian Problem."

There is, I insist, no Indian problem as created by the Indian himself. Every problem that exists today in regard to the native population is due to the white man's cast of mind, which is unable, at least reluctant, to seek understanding and achieve adjustment in a new and a significant environment into which it has so recently come.

The white man excused his presence here by saying that he had been guided by the will of his God; and in so saying absolved himself of all responsibility for his appearance in a land occupied by other men.

Then, too, his law was a written law; his divine decalogue reposed in a book. And what better proof that his advent into this country and his subsequent acts were the result of divine will! He brought the Word! There ensued a blind worship of written history, of books, of the written word, that has denuded the spoken word of its power and sacredness. The written word became established as a criterion of the superior man—a symbol of emotional fineness. The man who could write his name on a piece of paper, whether or not he possessed the spiritual fineness to honor those words in speech, was by some miraculous formula a more highly developed and sensitized person than the one who had never had a pen in hand, but whose spoken word was inviolable and whose sense of honor and truth was paramount. With false reasoning was the quality of human character measured by man's ability to make with an implement a mark upon paper. But granting this mode of reasoning be correct and just, then where are to be placed the thousands of illiterate whites who are unable to read and write? Are they, too, 'savages'? Is not humanness a matter of heart and mind, and is it not evident in the form of relationship with men? Is not kindness more powerful than arrogance; and truth more powerful than the sword?

True, the white man brought great change. But the varied fruits of his civili- 10
zation, though highly colored and inviting, are sickening and deadening. And if it be the part of civilization to maim, rob, and thwart, then what is progress? . . .

After subjugation, after dispossession, there was cast the last abuse upon the people who so entirely resented their wrongs and punishments, and that was the stamping and the labeling of them as savages. To make this label stick has been the task of the white race and the greatest salve that it has been able to apply to its sore and troubled conscience now hardened through the habitual practice of injustice.

But all the years of calling the Indian a savage has never made him one; all the denial of his virtues has never taken them from him; and the very resistance he has made to save the things inalienably his has been his saving strength—that which will stand him in need when justice does make its belated appearance and he undertakes rehabilitation.

All sorts of feeble excuses are heard for the continued subjection of the Indian. One of the most common is that he is not yet ready to accept the society of the white man—that he is not yet ready to mingle as a social entity.

This, I maintain, is beside the question. The matter is not one of making over the external Indian into the likeness of the white race—a process detrimental to both races. Who can say that the white man's way is better for the Indian? Where resides the human judgment with the competence to weigh and value Indian ideals and spiritual concepts; or substitute for them other values?

Then, has the white man's social order been so harmonious and ideal as to 15
merit the respect of the Indian, and for that matter the thinking class of the white race? Is it wise to urge upon the Indian a foreign social form? Let none but the Indian answer!

Rather, let the white brother face about and cast his mental eye upon a new angle of vision. Let him look upon the Indian world as a human world; then let him see to it that human rights be accorded to the Indians. And this for the purpose of retaining for his own order of society a measure of humanity. . . .

The spiritual health and existence of the Indian was maintained by song, magic, ritual, dance, symbolism, oratory (or council), design, handicraft, and folk-story.

Manifestly, to check or thwart this expression is to bring about spiritual decline. And it is in this condition of decline that the Indian people are today. There is but a feeble effort among the Sioux to keep alive their traditional songs and dances, while among other tribes there is but a half-hearted attempt to offset the influence of the Government school and at the same time recover from the crushing and stifling régime of the Indian Bureau.

One has but to speak of Indian verse to receive uncomprehending and unbelieving glances. Yet the Indian loved verse and into this mode of expression went his deepest feelings. Only a few ardent and advanced students seem interested; nevertheless, they have given in book form enough Indian translations to set forth the character and quality of Indian verse.

Oratory receives a little better understanding on the part of the white pub- 20
lic, owing to the fact that oratorical compilations include those of Indian orators.

Hard as it seemingly is for the white man's ear to sense the differences, Indian songs are as varied as the many emotions which inspire them, for no two of them are alike. For instance, the Song of Victory is spirited and the notes high and remindful of an unrestrained hunter or warrior riding exultantly over the prairies. On the other hand, the song of the *Cano unye* is solemn and full of urge, for it is meant to inspire the young men to deeds of valor. Then there are the songs of death and the spiritual songs which are connected with the ceremony of initiation. These are full of the spirit of praise and worship, and so strong are some of these invocations that the very air seems as if surcharged with the presence of the Big Holy.

The Indian loved to worship. From birth to death he revered his surroundings. He considered himself born in the luxurious lap of Mother Earth and no place was to him humble. There was nothing between him and the Big Holy. The contact was immediate and personal, and the blessings of Wakan Tanka flowed over the Indian like rain showered from the sky. Wakan Tanka was not aloof, apart, and ever seeking to quell evil forces. He did not punish the animals and the birds, and likewise He did not punish man. He was not a punishing God. For there was never a question as to the supremacy of an evil power over and above the power of Good. There was but one ruling power, and that was *Good.*

Of course, none but an adoring one could dance for days with his face to the sacred sun, and that time is all but done. We cannot have back the days of the buffalo and beaver; we cannot win back our clean blood-stream and superb health, and we can never again expect that beautiful *rapport* we once had with Nature. The springs and lakes have dried and the mountains are bare of forests. The plow has changed the face of the world. Wi-wila is dead! No more may we heal our sick and comfort our dying with a strength founded on faith, for even the animals now fear us, and fear supplants faith.

And the Indian wants to dance! It is his way of expressing devotion, of communing with unseen power, and in keeping his tribal identity. When the Lakota heart was filled with high emotion, he danced. When he felt the benediction of the warming rays of the sun, he danced. When his blood ran hot with success of the hunt or chase, he danced. When his heart was filled with pity for the orphan, the lonely father, or bereaved mother, he danced. All the joys and exaltations of life, all his gratefulness and thankfulness, all his acknowledgments of the mysterious power that guided life, and all his aspirations for a better life, culminated in one great dance—the Sun Dance.

When the Indian has forgotten the music of his forefathers, when the sound of the tomtom is no more, when noisy jazz has drowned the melody of the flute, he will be a dead Indian. When the memory of his heroes are no longer told in story, and he forsakes the beautiful white buckskin for factory shoddy, he will be dead. When from him has been taken all that is his, all that he has visioned in nature, all that has come to him from infinite sources, he then, truly, will be a dead Indian. His spirit will be gone, and though he walk crowded streets, he will, in truth, be—*dead*!

But all this must not perish; it must live, to the end that America shall be educated no longer to regard native production of whatever tribe—folk-story, basketry, pottery, dance, song, poetry—as curios, and native artists as curiosities. For who but the man indigenous to the soil could produce its song, story, and folk-tale; who but the man who loved the dust beneath his feet could shape it and put it into undying, ceramic form; who but he who loved the reeds that grew beside still waters, and the damp roots of shrub and tree, could save it from seasonal death, and with almost superhuman patience weave it into enduring objects of beauty—into timeless art!

Regarding the "civilization" that has been thrust upon me since the days of reservation, it has not added one whit to my sense of justice; to my reverence for the rights of life; to my love for truth, honesty, and generosity; nor to my faith in Wakan Tanka—God of the Lakotas. For after all the great religions have been preached and expounded, or have been revealed by brilliant scholars, or have been written in books and embellished in fine language with finer covers, man—all man—is still confronted with the Great Mystery.

So if today I had a young mind to direct, to start on the journey of life, and I was faced with the duty of choosing between the natural way of my forefathers and that of the white man's present way of civilization, I would, for its welfare, unhesitatingly set that child's feet in the path of my forefathers. I would raise him to be an Indian!

QUESTIONS FOR DISCUSSION

1. What is the "fundamental and spiritual law" that Standing Bear says the white man has violated in his attempts to reshape Native American cultures? What, according to the author, is the importance of truly belonging to a land?
2. What is the white man's final abuse according to Standing Bear? What is the most common (and perhaps the most feeble) excuse for the continued subjugation of the Indian?
3. Discuss the importance of song and dance to the spiritual health and the existence of the Indian.
4. Discuss the effectiveness of Standing Bear's introductory and concluding paragraphs. Does he directly state a thesis, or is one implied? Why does he introduce the personal "I" so late in the selection? Comment on his use of parallel structure and of rhetorical questions throughout the selection.

QUESTIONS FOR WRITING

1. Reaction Journal: Standing Bear asserts that "the man from Europe is still a foreigner and an alien." Write a letter to the author in which you respond to this statement in the context of "What the Indian Means to America."
2. What does the Indian mean to America according to Standing Bear? Write an essay in which you present and respond to Standing Bear's position. Be certain to include an examination of how Standing Bear uses the word "natural" in his conclusion and how you respond to this usage.

INDIAN HUMOR

VINE DELORIA, JR.

Vine Deloria, Jr. (b. 1933), a Standing Rock Sioux, was born and raised on a South Dakota reservation. He has studied theology and law and has become a leading spokesman for

Native Americans and an advocate for political separatism. Among his works are We Talk, You Listen: New Tribes, New Turf *(1970), and* Behind the Trail of Broken Treaties: An Indian Declaration of Independence *(1974). In "Indian Humor," which appeared in* Custer Died for Your Sins: An Indian Manifesto *(1969), Deloria illustrates the prominent place humor plays in Indian society and points to the power of laughter to unify an ethnic group and to convey to outsiders the essential experience of the group.*

◆ FREEWRITING

Deloria's opening sentence reads, "One of the best ways to understand a people is to know what makes them laugh." This may well be just as true for a family unit or a group of friends as it is for larger ethnic and cultural groups. Freewrite for ten or fifteen minutes on the role of humor in your family, your group of friends, or your ethnic and/or cultural group.

One of the best ways to understand a people is to know what makes them laugh. Laughter encompasses the limits of the soul. In humor life is redefined and accepted. Irony and satire provide much keener insights into a group's collective psyche and values than do years of research.

It has always been a great disappointment to Indian people that the humorous side of Indian life has not been mentioned by professed experts on Indian Affairs. Rather the image of the granite-faced grunting redskin has been perpetuated by American mythology.

People have little sympathy with stolid groups. Dick Gregory did much more than is believed when he introduced humor into the Civil Rights struggle. He enabled non-blacks to enter into the thought world of the black community and experience the hurt it suffered. When all people shared the humorous but ironic situation of the black, the urgency and morality of Civil Rights was communicated.

The Indian people are exactly opposite of the popular stereotype. I sometimes wonder how anything is accomplished by Indians because of the apparent overemphasis on humor within the Indian world. Indians have found a humorous side of nearly every problem and the experiences of life have generally been so well defined through jokes and stories that they have become a thing in themselves.

For centuries before the white invasion, teasing was a method of control of 5
social situations by Indian people. Rather than embarrass members of the tribe publicly, people used to tease individuals they considered out of step with the consensus of tribal opinion. In this way egos were preserved and disputes within the tribe of a personal nature were held to a minimum.

Gradually people learned to anticipate teasing and began to tease themselves as a means of showing humility and at the same time advocating a course of action they deeply believed in. Men would depreciate their feats to show they were not trying to run roughshod over tribal desires. This method of behavior served to highlight their true virtues and gain them a place of influence in tribal policy-making circles.

Humor has come to occupy such a prominent place in national Indian affairs that any kind of movement is impossible without it. Tribes are being brought together by sharing humor of the past. Columbus jokes gain great sympathy among all tribes, yet there are no tribes extant who had anything to do with Columbus. But the fact of white invasion from which all tribes have suffered has created a common bond in relation to Columbus jokes that gives a solid feeling of unity and purpose to the tribes.

The more desperate the problem, the more humor is directed to describe it. Satirical remarks often circumscribe problems so that possible solutions are drawn from the circumstances that would not make sense if presented in other than a humorous form.

Often people are awakened and brought to a militant edge through funny remarks. I often counseled people to run for the Bureau of Indian Affairs in case of an earthquake because nothing could shake the BIA. And I would watch as younger Indians set their jaws, determined that they, if nobody else, would shake it. We also had a saying that in case of fire call the BIA and they would handle it because they put a wet blanket on everything. This also got a warm reception from people.

Columbus and Custer jokes are the best for penetration into the heart of the 10
matter, however. Rumor has it that Columbus began his journey with four ships. But one went over the edge so he arrived in the new world with only three. Another version states that Columbus didn't know where he was going, didn't know where he had been, and did it all on someone else's money. And the white man has been following Columbus ever since.

It is said that when Columbus landed, one Indian turned to another and said, "Well, there goes the neighborhood." Another version has two Indians watching Columbus and one saying to the other, "Maybe if we leave them alone they will go away." A favorite cartoon in Indian country a few years back showed a flying saucer landing while an Indian watched. The caption was "Oh, no, not again."

The most popular and enduring subject of Indian humor is, of course, General Custer. There are probably more jokes about Custer and the Indians than there were participants in the battle. All tribes, even those thousands of miles from Montana, feel a sense of accomplishment when thinking of Custer. Custer binds together implacable foes because he represented the Ugly American of the last century and he got what was coming to him.

Some years ago we put out a bumper sticker which read "Custer Died for Your Sins." It was originally meant as a dig at the National Council of Churches. But as it spread around the nation it took on additional meaning until everyone claimed to understand it and each interpretation was different.

Originally, the Custer bumper sticker referred to the Sioux Treaty of 1868 signed at Fort Laramie in which the United States pledged to give free and undisturbed use of the lands claimed by Red Cloud in return for peace. Under the covenants of the Old Testament, breaking a covenant called for a blood sacrifice for atonement. Custer was the blood sacrifice for the United States breaking the Sioux treaty. That, at least originally, was the meaning of the slogan.

Custer jokes, however, can barely be categorized, let alone sloganized. In- 15
dians say that Custer was well-dressed for the occasion. When the Sioux found his body after the battle, he had on an Arrow shirt.

Many stories are derived from the details of the battle itself. Custer is said to have boasted that he could ride through the entire Sioux nation with his Seventh Cavalry and he was half right. He got half-way through.

One story concerns the period immediately after Custer's contingent had been wiped out and the Sioux and Cheyennes were zeroing in on Major Reno and his troops several miles to the south of the Custer battlefield.

The Indians had Reno's troopers surrounded on a bluff. Water was scarce, ammunition was nearly exhausted, and it looked like the next attack would mean certain extinction.

One of the white soldiers quickly analyzed the situation and shed his clothes. He covered himself with mud, painted his face like an Indian, and began to creep toward the Indian lines.

A Cheyenne heard some rustling in the grass and was just about to shoot. 20

"Hey, chief," the soldier whispered, "don't shoot, I'm coming over to join you. I'm going to be on your side."

The warrior looked puzzled and asked the soldier why he wanted to change sides.

"Well," he replied, "better red than dead."

Custer's Last Words occupy a revered place in Indian humor. One source states that as he was falling mortally wounded he cried, "Take no prisoners!" Other versions, most of them off color, concentrate on where those **** Indians are coming from. My favorite last saying pictures Custer on top of the hill looking at a multitude of warriors charging up the slope at him. He turns resignedly to his aide and says, "Well, it's better than going back to North Dakota."

Since the battle it has been a favorite technique to boost the numbers on the 25
Indian side and reduce the numbers on the white side so that Custer stands out as a man fighting against insurmountable odds. One question no pseudo-historian has attempted to answer, when changing the odds to make the little boy in blue more heroic, is how what they say were twenty thousand Indians could be fed when gathered into one camp. What a tremendous pony herd must have been gathered there, what a fantastic herd of buffalo must have been nearby to feed that amount of Indians, what an incredible source of drinking water must have been available for fifty thousand animals and some twenty thousand Indians!

Just figuring water-needs to keep that many people and animals alive for a number of days must have been incredible. If you have estimated correctly, you will see that the Little Big Horn was the last great *naval* engagement of the Indian wars.

The Sioux tease other tribes a great deal for not having been at the Little Big Horn. The Crows, traditional enemies of the Sioux, explain their role as Custer's scouts as one of bringing Custer where the Sioux could get at him! Arapahos and Cheyennes, allies of the Sioux in that battle, refer to the time they "bailed the Sioux out" when they got in trouble with the cavalry.

Even today variations of the Custer legend are bywords in Indian country. When an Indian gets too old and becomes inactive, people say he is "too old to muss the Custer anymore." . . .

One-line retorts are common in Indian country. Popovi Da, the great Pueblo artist, was quizzed one day on why the Indians were the first ones on this continent. "We had reservations," was his reply. Another time, when questioned by an anthropologist on what the Indians called America before the white man came, an Indian said simply, "*Ours.*" A young Indian was asked one day at a conference what a peace treaty was. He replied, "That's when the white man wants a piece of your land."

The best example of Indian humor and militancy I have ever heard was 30
given by Clyde Warrior one day. He was talking with a group of people about the National Indian Youth Council, of which he was then president, and its program for a revitalization of Indian life. Several in the crowd were skeptical about the idea of rebuilding Indian communities along traditional Indian lines.

"Do you realize," he said, "that when the United States was founded, it was only 5 percent urban and 95 percent rural and now it is 70 percent urban and 30 percent rural?"

His listeners nodded solemnly but didn't seem to understand what he was driving at.

"Don't you realize what this means?" he rapidly continued. "It means we are pushing them into the cities. Soon we will have the country back again."

Whether Indian jokes will eventually come to have more significance than that, I cannot speculate. Humor, all Indians will agree, is the cement by which the coming Indian movement is held together. When a people can laugh at themselves and laugh at others and hold all aspects of life together without letting anybody drive them to extremes, then it seems to me that that people can survive.

QUESTIONS FOR DISCUSSION

1. Deloria points out different types of humor as well as common subjects for humor. Describe how the different categories give "a solid feeling of unity and purpose" to the Native American community.

2. With a group of three or four peers, discuss the types and subjects of humor in your lives. Give examples, and explain how they do or do not function as Deloria suggests.

3. Discuss Deloria's abundant use of examples. How does he organize them, and what do they add to the essay's overall effect?

WRITING ASSIGNMENTS

1. Reaction Journal: Write a letter to Deloria in which you respond to his analysis of the role of humor for Native Americans. Develop your letter with a discussion of the role of humor in your life, and provide examples.
2. Think about "Indian Humor" as you read your freewriting and reaction journal entry. Write an essay in which you exemplify and define the role of humor in a group to which you belong.

WE AIM NOT TO PLEASE

MARY CROW DOG

Mary Crow Dog, born Mary Brave Bird, grew up in a cabin without electricity or running water on a South Dakota reservation. Rebelling against the alcoholism and hopelessness of reservation life, she joined the new tribal movement that swept through Native American communities during the 1960s and 1970s. She married Leonard Crow Dog, the chief medicine man of the American Indian Movement (AIM), who revived the outlawed Ghost Dance. In the following excerpt from her autobiography,* Lakota Woman *(1990), Crow Dog describes the role AIM played in the revival of Native American traditions and turning some Native Americans into militant activists. In writing* Lakota Woman, *Crow Dog collaborated with Richard Erdoes, whose other books include* American Indian Myths and Legends *(with Alfonso Ortiz, 1985).*

◆ FREEWRITING

Mary Crow Dog quotes Bill Kunstler, lawyer for the American Indian Movement, as saying, "You hate those most whom you have injured most." Freewrite for ten or fifteen minutes on your response to Kunstler's remark. Try to relate it to prejudice and ethnocentric behavior

* The Ghost Dance, which became popular among the Dakotas in 1889, originated among the Paiutes. Wovoka, the Paiute messiah, claimed to be the returned Christ and preached that after new floods had come, drowning the white man, the Indian dead would return reunited, game would return, and protection would be granted to those who wore supposedly bulletproof "ghost shirts" and took part in a special dance. Alarmed by the spirited dancing, which they interpreted as a signal to attack whites, the Bureau of Indian Affairs undertook a number of actions against the Sioux, culminating in the massacre at Wounded Knee, South Dakota, on December 29, 1890.

throughout our culture. What does his remark have to do with the notion of confrontation and accommodation? Have you ever observed this phenomenon in a peer or family group?

> They call us the New Indians.
> Hell, we are the Old Indians,
> the landlords of this continent,
> coming to collect the rent.
>
> —*Dennis Banks*

The American Indian Movement hit our reservation like a tornado, like a new wind blowing out of nowhere, a drumbeat from far off getting louder and louder. It was almost like the Ghost Dance fever that had hit the tribes in 1890, old uncle Dick Fool Bull said, spreading like a prairie fire. It even was like the old Ghost Dance song Uncle Dick was humming:

> Maka sitomniya teca ukiye
> Oyate ukiye, oyate ukiye . . .
> A new world is coming,
> A nation is coming,
> The eagle brought the message.

I could feel this new thing, almost hear it, smell it, touch it. Meeting up with AIM for the first time loosened a sort of earthquake inside me. Old Black Elk in recounting his life often used the expression "As I look down from the high hill of my great old age . . ." Well, as I am looking from the hill of my old age—I am thirty-seven now but feel as if I have lived for a long time—I can see things in perspective, not subjectively, no, but in perspective. Old Black Elk had a good way of saying it. You really look back upon ten years gone past as from a hill—you have a sort of bird's-eye view. I recognize now that movements get used up and the leaders get burned out quickly. Some of our men and women got themselves killed and thereby avoided reaching the dangerous age of thirty and becoming "elder statesmen." Some leaders turned into college professors, founded alternative schools, or even took jobs as tribal officials. A few live on in the past, refusing to recognize that the dreams of the past must give way to the dreams of the future. I, that wild, rebellious teenager of ten years ago, am nursing a baby, changing diapers, and making breakfast for my somewhat extended family. And yet it was great while it lasted and I still feel that old excitement merely talking about it. Some people loved AIM, some hated it, but nobody ignored it.

I loved it. My first encounter with AIM was at a powwow held in 1971 at Crow Dog's place after the Sun Dance. Pointing at Leonard Crow Dog, I asked a young woman, "Who is that man?"

"That's Crow Dog," she said. I was looking at his long, shining braids. Wearing one's hair long at the time was still something of a novelty on the res. I asked, "Is that his real hair?"

"Yes, that's his real hair."

I noticed that almost all of the young men wore their hair long, some with eagle feathers tied to it. They all had on ribbon shirts. They had a new look about them, not that hangdog reservation look I was used to. They moved in a different way, too, confident and swaggering, the girls as well as the boys. Belonging to many tribes, they had come in a dilapidated truck covered with slogans and paintings. They had traveled to the Sun Dance all the way from California, where they had taken part in the occupation of Alcatraz Island.

One man, a Chippewa, stood up and made a speech. I had never heard anybody talk like that. He spoke about genocide and sovereignty, about tribal leaders selling out and kissing ass—white man's ass. He talked about giving up the necktie for the choker, the briefcase for the bedroll, the missionary's church for the sacred pipe. He talked about not celebrating Thanksgiving, because that would be celebrating one's own destruction. He said that white people, after stealing our land and massacring us for three hundred years, could not come to us now saying, "Celebrate Thanksgiving with us, drop in for a slice of turkey." He had himself wrapped up in an upside-down American flag, telling us that every star in this flag represented a state stolen from Indians.

Then Leonard Crow Dog spoke, saying that we had talked to the white man for generations with our lips, but that he had no ears to hear, no eyes to see, no heart to feel. Crow Dog said that now we must speak with our bodies and that he was not afraid to die for his people. It was a very emotional speech. Some people wept. An old man turned to me and said, "These are the words I always wanted to speak, but had kept shut up within me."

I asked one of the young men, "What kind of Indians are you?" "We are AIM," he told me, "American Indian Movement. We're going to change things."

AIM was born in 1968. Its fathers were mostly men doing time in Minnesota prisons, Ojibways. It got its start in the slums of St. Paul taking care of Indian ghetto problems. It was an Indian woman who gave it its name. She told me, "At first we called ourselves 'Concerned Indian Americans' until somebody discovered that the initials spelled CIA. That didn't sound so good. Then I spoke up: 'You guys all aim to do this, or you aim to do that. Why don't you call yourselves AIM, American Indian Movement?' And that was that."

In the beginning AIM was mainly confined to St. Paul and Minneapolis. The early AIM people were mostly ghetto Indians, often from tribes which had lost much of their language, traditions, and ceremonies. It was when they came to us on the Sioux reservations that they began to learn about the old ways. We had to learn from them, too. We Sioux had lived very isolated behind what some people called the "Buckskin Curtain." AIM opened a window for us through which the wind of the 1960s and early '70s could blow, and it was no gentle breeze but a hurricane that whirled us around. It was after the traditional reservation Indians and the ghetto kids had gotten together that AIM became a force nationwide. It was flint striking flint, lighting a spark which grew into a flame at which we could warm ourselves after a long, long winter.

After I joined AIM I stopped drinking. Others put away their roach clips and airplane glue bottles. There were a lot of things wrong with AIM. We did not see these things, or did not want to see them. At the time these things were unimportant. What was important was getting it on. We kids became AIM's spearheads and the Sioux set the style. The AIM uniform was Sioux all the way, the black "angry hats" with the feathers stuck in the hatband, the bone chokers, the medicine pouches worn on our breasts, the Levi's jackets on which we embroidered our battle honors—Alcatraz, Trail of Broken Treaties, Wounded Knee. Some dudes wore a third, extra-thin braid as a scalp lock. We made up our own songs—forty-niners, honoring songs, songs for a warrior behind bars in the slammer. The AIM song was made up by a fourteen-year-old Sioux boy. The Ojibways say it was made up by one of their own kids, but we know better.

We all had a good mouth, were good speakers and wrote a lot of poetry, though we were all dropouts who could not spell. We took some of our rhetoric from the blacks, who had started their movements before we did. Like them we were minorities, poor and discriminated against, but there were differences. I think it significant that in many Indian languages a black is called a "black white man." The blacks want what the whites have, which is understandable. They want *in*. We Indians want *out*! That is the main difference.

At first we hated all whites because we knew only one kind—the John Wayne kind. It took time before we met whites to whom we could relate and whose friendships we could accept. One of our young men met a pretty girl. She said she was Indian and looked it. She told him, "Sleep with me." In bed, in the middle of the night, he somehow found out that she was Puerto Rican. He got so mad that she was not a real skin that he beat up on her. He wanted to have to do only with Indian girls and felt tricked. He had run away from a real bad foster home, seeking refuge among his own kind. Later he felt ashamed for what he had done and apologized. Eventually we were joined by a number of Chicano brothers and sisters and learned to love and respect them, but it took time. We lived in a strange, narrow world of our own, suspicious of all outsiders. Later, we found ourselves making speeches on campuses, in churches, and on street corners talking to prominent supporters such as Marlon Brando, Dick Gregory, Rip Torn, Jane Fonda, and Angela Davis. It was a long-drawn-out process of learning and experiencing, this widening of our horizons.

15 We formed relationships among ourselves and with outsiders. We had girls who would go to bed with any warrior who had done something brave. Other girls loved one boy only. Usually a boy would say to a girl, "Be my old lady," and she might answer, "Ohan, you are my old man." They would go find a medicine man to feather and cedar them, to smoke the pipe with them, to put a red blanket around their shoulders. That made them man and wife Indian style. Then they slept under the same blanket. The white law did not recognize such a marriage, but we would respect it. It might last only a few days. Either of them could

have a run-in with the law and wind up in jail or be blown away by the goons. We did not exactly lead stable lives, but some of these marriages lasted for years. Short or long, it was good while it lasted. The girl had somebody to protect and take care of her; the boy had a wincincala to cook his beans or sew him a ribbon shirt. They inspired each other to the point where they would put their bodies on the line together. It gave them something precious to remember all their lives. One seventeen-year-old boy had a twenty-two-year-old girlfriend. He called her "grandma." He had a T-shirt made for her with the word GRANDMA on it, and one for himself with the legend I LOVE GRANDMA. He was heartbroken when she left him for an "older man." Some of the AIM leaders attracted quite a number of "wives." We called them "wives of the month."

I got into one of these marriages myself. It lasted just long enough for me to get pregnant. Birth control went against our beliefs. We felt that there were not enough Indians left to suit us. The more future warriors we brought into the world, the better. My older sister Barbara got pregnant too. She went to the BIA hospital where the doctors told her she needed a cesarean. When she came to, the doctors informed her that they had taken her womb out. In their opinion, at that time, there were already too many little red bastards for the taxpayers to take care of. No use to mollycoddle those happy-go-lucky, irresponsible, oversexed AIM women. Barb's child lived for two hours. With better care, it might have made it. For a number of years BIA doctors performed thousands of forced sterilizations on Indian and Chicano women without their knowledge or consent. For this reason I was happy at the thought of having a baby, not only for myself but for Barbara, too. I was determined not to have my child in a white hospital.

In the meantime I had nine months to move around, still going from confrontation to confrontation. Wherever anthros were digging up human remains from Indian sites, we were there threatening to dig up white graves to display white men's skulls and bones in glass cases. Wherever there was an Indian political trial, we showed up before the courthouse with our drums. Wherever we saw a bar with a sign NO INDIANS ALLOWED, we sensitized the owners, sometimes quite forcefully. Somehow we always found old jalopies to travel in, painted all over with Red Power slogans, and always found native people to take us in, treating us to meat soup, fry bread, and thick, black coffee. We existed entirely without money, yet we ate, traveled, and usually found a roof over our heads.

Something strange happened then. The traditional old, full-blood medicine men joined in with us kids. Not the middle-aged adults. They were of a lost generation which had given up all hope, necktie-wearers waiting for the Great White Father to do for them. It was the real old folks who had spirit and wisdom to give us. The grandfathers and grandmothers who still remembered a time when Indians were Indians, whose own grandparents or even parents had fought Custer gun in hand, people who for us were living links with a great past. They had a lot of strength and power, enough to give some of it to us. They still knew all the old legends and the right way to put on a ritual, and we were eager to learn from them. Soon they had us young girls making flesh offerings or piercing our wrists at the Sun Dance, while young warriors again put the skewers through their breast and found out the hard way where they came from. Even those who had grown up in cities, who had never been on a horse or heard an owl hoot, were suddenly getting it together. I am not bragging, but I am proud that we Lakotas started this.

The old grandmothers especially made a deep impression upon me. Women like Lizzy Fast Horse, a great-grandmother, who scrambled up all the way to the top of Mount Rushmore, standing right on the top of those gigantic bald pates, reclaiming the Black Hills for their rightful owners. Lizzy who was dragged down the mountain by the troopers, handcuffed to her nine-year-old great-granddaughter until their wrists were cut, their blood falling in drops on the snow. It is really true, the old Cheyenne saying: "A nation is not dead until the hearts of its women are on the ground." Well, the hearts of our old full-blood women were not on the ground. They were way up high and they could still encourage us with their trilling, spine-tingling brave-heart cry which always made the hairs on my back stand up and my flesh break out in goose pimples whenever I heard it, no matter how often.

We did freak out the honkies. We were feared throughout the Dakotas. I could never figure out why this should have been so. We were always the victims. We never maimed or killed. It was we who died or got crippled. Aside from ripping off a few trading posts, we were not really bad. We were loud-mouthed, made a lot of noise, and got on some people's nerves. We made Mr. White Man realize that there were other Indians besides the poor human wrecks who posed for him for a quarter—but that should not have made them kill us or hide from us under their beds. "The AIMs is coming, the AIMs is coming" was the cry that went up whenever a couple of fourteen-year-old skins in Uncle Joe hats showed up. The ranchers and the police spread the most fantastic rumors about us. The media said that we were about to stage bank robberies, storm prisons, set fire to the state capitol, blow up Mount Rushmore, and assassinate the governor. The least we were accused of was that we were planning to paint the noses of the giant Mount Rushmore heads red. Worst of all we were scaring the tourists away. The concessionaires at Rushmore and in all the Black Hills tourist traps were losing money. It was only right to kill us for that.

I think it was their bad conscience which made the local whites hate us so much. Bill Kunstler, the movement lawyer who defended us in a number of trials, once said: "You hate those most whom you have injured most." The whites near the reservations were all living on land stolen from us—stolen not in the distant past, but by their fathers and grandfathers. They all made their living in some way by exploiting us, by using Indians as cheap labor, by running their cattle on reservation land for a mere pittance in lease money, by using us as colorful props to attract the Eastern tourists. They could only relate to the stereotyped song-and-dance Indian, locking their doors and cowering behind their curtains whenever we came to town, crying: "The AIMs is coming, get the police." Always a day or two after we made our appearance all the gun shops in the place were sold out. White folks took to toting guns again. They carried revolvers wherever they went, slept with loaded .38s under their pillows, drove around with high-powered rifles in racks behind the seats of their pickups. It was rumored that the then governor of South Dakota, who once vowed to put every AIM member behind bars or six feet underground, had imported a special, quick-firing, newly invented type of machine gun from West Germany and installed it in the dome of the state capitol, where he spent hours, training the gun on Indians who happened to walk by, zeroing in, moving the gun silently back and forth, back and forth. It may be only a story, but knowing the man, I am prepared to believe it. I did not mind their being afraid of us. It was better than being given a quarter and asked to pose smilingly for their cameras.

We were not angels. Some things were done by AIM, or rather by people who *called* themselves AIM, that I am not proud of. But AIM gave us a lift badly needed at the time. It defined our goals and expressed our innermost yearnings. It set a style for Indians to imitate. Even those Native Americans who maintained that they wanted to have nothing to do with AIM, that it ran counter to their tribal ways of life, began to dress and talk in the AIM manner. I have had some conflicts with the American Indian Movement at some time or another. I don't know whether it will live or die. Some people say that a movement dies the moment it becomes acceptable. In this case there should be some life left in its body, at least in the Dakotas. But whatever happens, one can't take away from AIM that it fulfilled its function and did what had to be done at a time which was decisive in the development of Indian America.

The Sun Dance at Rosebud in the late summer of 1972 will forever remain in my memory. Many of the AIM leaders came to Crow Dog's place to dance, to make flesh offerings, to endure the self-torture of this, our most sacred rite, gazing at the sun, blowing on their eagle-bone whistles, praying with the pipe. It was like a rebirth, like some of the prophesies of the Ghost Dancers coming true. The strange thing was seeing men undergoing the ordeal of the Sun Dance who came from tribes which had never practiced this ritual. I felt it was their way of saying, "I am an Indian again."

This Sun Dance was also an occasion for getting to know each other, for a lot of serious talk. I was happy watching the women taking a big part in these discussions. One of the AIM men laughingly said, "For years we couldn't get the women to speak up, and now we can't get them to shut up." I just listened. I was still too shy and too young to do anything else but stay in the background.

The people were tensed up. Everything was in ferment. The mood was bit- 25
ter. News reached us after the Sun Dance that Richard Oaks, from the Mohawk tribe, a much loved and respected leader at Alcatraz, had been murdered by a white man. Not long before that a Sioux, Raymond Yellow Thunder, a humble, hard-working man, had been stripped naked and forced at gunpoint to dance in an American Legion hall at Gordon, Nebraska. Later he was beaten to death—just for the fun of it. Before that a millionaire rancher had shot and killed an unarmed Indian from Pine Ridge, Norman Little Brave, and gone unpunished. Norman had been a sober-minded churchgoer, but that had not saved him. It was open season on Indians again and the people were saying, "Enough of this

shit!" It was out of these feelings of anger, hope, and despair that the "Trail of Broken Treaties" was born.

I am still proud that it was born at Rosebud, among my people. That is probably bad. The feeling of pride in one's particular tribe is standing in the way of Indian unity. Still it is there and it is not all bad. The man who first thought of having caravans of Indians converging upon Washington from all directions was Bob Burnette. He had been tribal chairman at Rosebud and he was not an AIM member. Other Indian leaders of this caravan, such as Hank Adams, Reuben Snake, and Sid Mills—Sid and Hank from the Northwest, where they had been fighting for native fishing rights—were not AIM. Neither were the Six Nation people from upstate New York or the representatives of some Southwestern tribes, but though they had not started it, it was the AIM leaders who dominated this march in the end.

The Trail of Broken Treaties was the greatest action taken by Indians since the Battle of the Little Big Horn. As Eddie Benton, the Ojibway medicine man, told us: "There is a prophecy in our tribe's religion that one day we would all stand together. All tribes would hook arms in brotherhood and unite. I am elated because I lived to see this happen. Brothers and sisters from all over this continent united in a single cause. That is the greatest significance to Indian people . . . not what happened or what may yet happen as a result of our actions."

Each caravan was led by a spiritual leader or medicine man with his sacred pipe. The Oklahoma caravan followed the Cherokees' "Trail of Tears," retracing the steps of dying Indians driven from their homes by President Andrew Jackson. Our caravan started from Wounded Knee. This had a special symbolic meaning for us Sioux, making us feel as if the ghosts of all the women and children murdered there by the Seventh Cavalry were rising out of their mass grave to go with us.

I traveled among friends from Rosebud and Pine Ridge. My brother and my sister Barbara were among this group. I did not know what to expect. A huge protest march like this was new to me. When we arrived in Washington we got lost. We had been promised food and accommodation, but due to government pressure many church groups which had offered to put us up and feed us got scared and backed off. It was almost dawn and still we were stumbling around looking for a place to bed down. I could hardly keep my eyes open. One thing we did accomplish: in the predawn light we drove around the White House, honking our horns and beating our drums to let President Nixon know that we had arrived.

We were finally given a place to sleep in, an old, dilapidated, and abandoned 30
church. I had just crawled into my bedroll when I saw what I thought to be a fair-sized cat walking over it. I put my glasses on and discovered that it was a big rat, the biggest and ugliest I had ever seen. The church was in an uproar. Women screamed. Mine was not the only rat in the place, as it turned out. An old lady who had hitchhiked two thousand miles from Cheyenne River to get to Washington complained that the toilets were broken. It was the first week of

November and there was no heat. An elderly Canadian Indian dragged himself around on crutches. His legs were crippled and he could find no soft place to rest. A young girl shouted that there were not only rats but also millions of cockroaches. A young Ojibway man said that he had not left the slums of St. Paul for this kind of facility. I told him that I had expected nothing else. Did he think Nixon would put him up at the Holiday Inn with wall-to-wall carpeting and color TV? Everywhere groups were standing huddled together in their blankets. People were saying, "They promised us decent housing. Look how they're treating us. We ain't gonna stand for this."

Somebody suggested, "Let's all go to the BIA." It seemed the natural thing to do, to go to the Bureau of Indian Affairs building on Constitution Avenue. They would have to put us up. It was "our" building after all. Besides, that was what we had come for, to complain about the treatment the bureau was dishing out to us. Everybody suddenly seemed to be possessed by the urge to hurry to the BIA. Next thing I knew we were in it. We spilled into the building like a great avalanche. Some people put up a tipi on the front lawn. Security guards were appointed. They put on red armbands or fastened rainbow-colored bits of cloth to their ribbon shirts or denim jackets. They watched the doors. Tribal groups took over this or that room, the Iroquois on one floor, the Sioux on another. The Oklahoma Indians, the Northwest Coast people, all made themselves a place to stay. Children were playing while old ladies got comfortable on couches in the foyer. A drum was roaring. I could smell kinnikinnick—Indian tobacco. Someone put a sign over the front gate reading INDIAN COUNTRY. The building finally belonged to us and we lost no time turning it into a tribal village.

My little group settled down in one room on the second floor. It was nice—thick carpets, subdued light, soft couches, and easy chairs. The bureaucrats sure knew how to live. They had marble stairs, wrought-iron banisters, fine statues and paintings depicting the Noble Savage, valuable artifacts. I heard somebody speaking Sioux. I opened a door and there was Leonard Crow Dog talking to some young men, telling them why we were here, explaining what it all meant. Somebody motioned to me: "Quiet! Crow Dog is talking!" Young as I was, Crow Dog seemed an old man to me, old with responsibilities, but he was only thirty-two then. It did not occur to me that one day I would bear his children.

The takeover of the BIA building had not been planned. We honestly thought that arrangements for our stay had been made. When the promises turned out to be the same old buffalo shit, as one of the leaders put it, we simply occupied the BIA. It was a typical spontaneous Indian happening. Nobody had ordered us to do it. We were not very amenable to orders anyhow. It's not our style. The various tribal groups caucused in their rooms, deciding what proposals to make. From time to time everybody would go down into the great hall and thrash out the proposals. The assembly hall had a stage, many chairs, and loudspeakers. Always discussions opened with one of the medicine men performing a ceremony. I think it was a black civil rights organization which brought in the first truckload of food. Later various church groups and other sympathizers donated food and money. The building had a kitchen and cafeteria and we quickly organized cooking, dishwashing, and garbage details. Some women were appointed to watch the children, old people were cared for, and a medical team was set up. Contrary to what some white people believe, Indians are very good at improvising this sort of self-government with no one in particular telling them what to do. They don't wait to be told. I guess there were altogether six to eight hundred people crammed into the building, but it did not feel crowded.

The original caravan leaders had planned a peaceful and dignified protest. There had even been talk of singing and dancing for the senators and inviting the lawmakers to an Indian fry bread and corn soup feast. It might have worked out that way if somebody had been willing to listen to us. But the word had been passed to ignore us. The people who mattered, from the president down, would not talk to us. We were not wanted. It was said that we were hoodlums who did not speak for the Indian people. The half-blood tribal chairmen with their salaries and expense accounts condemned us almost to a man. Nixon sent some no-account underling to tell us that he had done more for the American Indian than any predecessor and that he saw no reason for our coming to Washington, that he had more important things to do than to talk with us—presumably surreptitiously taping his visitors and planning Watergate. We wondered what all these good things were that he had done for us.

We had planned to have Crow Dog conduct a ceremony at the grave of Ira 35
Hayes, the Pima Indian who had won the Congressional Medal of Honor at Iwo Jima, and who had died drunk and forgotten in a ditch. The army, which was in charge of Arlington Cemetery, forbade this ceremony "because it would be political, not religious." Slowly our mood changed. There was less talk of dancing and singing for the senators and more talk about getting it on. Dennis Banks said that AIM was against violence, but that it might take another Watts to bring home to the public the plight of Native Americans. Russel Means remarked to some reporters that the media were ignoring us: "What do we have to do to get some attention? Scalp somebody?" It was on this occasion that I learned that as long as we "behaved nicely" nobody gave a damn about us, but as soon as we became rowdy we got all the support and media coverage we could wish for.

We obliged them. We pushed the police and guards out of the building. Some did not wait to be pushed but jumped out of the ground-floor windows like so many frogs. We had formulated twenty Indian demands. These were all rejected by the few bureaucrats sent to negotiate with us. The most we got out of these talks was one white official holding up an Indian baby for a snapshot, saying, "Isn't she sweet?" We had not come for baby-kissing nor for kissing ass. The moderate leaders lost credibility. It was not their fault. Soon we listened to other voices as the occupation turned into a siege. I heard somebody yelling, "The pigs are here." I could see from the window that it was true. The whole building was surrounded by helmeted police armed with all kinds of guns. A fight broke out between the police and our security. Some of our young men got hit over the head with police clubs and we saw the blood streaming down their faces. There was a rumor, which turned out to be true, that we had received an ultimatum: "Clear out—or else!"

I felt the tension rise within the building, felt it rising within me, an ant heap somebody was plunging a stick into, stirring it up. I heard a woman screaming, "They are coming, they are going to kill us all!" Men started shouting, "Women and children upstairs! Get upstairs!" But I went downstairs. I saw the riot squad outside. They had just beaten up two Indians and were hauling them off to jail. We barricaded all doors and the lowest windows with document boxes, Xerox machines, tables, file cabinets, anything we could lay our hands on. Some brothers piled up heavy typewriters on windowsills to hurl down on the police in case they tried to storm the building. Young men were singing and yelling, "It's a good day to die!" We started making weapons for ourselves. Two or three guys discovered some archery sets and were ready to defend themselves with bow and arrows. Others were swinging golf clubs, getting the feel of them. Still others were tying pen knives to fishing rods. A letter opener taped to a table leg became a tomahawk. Floyd Young Horse, a Sioux from Cherry Creek, was the first to put war paint on his face in the ancient manner. Soon a lot of young men did the same. Many wrapped themselves in upside-down American flags—like the Ghost Dancers of old.

I took apart a pair of scissors and taped one half to a broken-off chair leg and went outside to join the security. My brother was one of the guards. He saw me and laughed. He had been four years in the marines and had taught me to take apart, clean, and fire a .38. Seeing me with my measly weapon broke him up. "What are you going to do with that thing?" "Get them in the balls before they can hit me!"

At last the police were withdrawn and we were told that they had given us another twenty-four hours to evacuate the building. This was not the end of the confrontation. From then on, every morning we were given a court order to get out by six P.M. Came six o'clock and we would be standing there ready to join battle. I think many brothers and sisters were prepared to die right on the steps of the BIA building. When one of the AIM leaders was asked by a reporter whether the Indians were not afraid that their women and children could get hurt, he said, "Our women and children have taken this risk for four hundred years and accept it," and we all shouted "Right on!" I don't think I slept more than five or six hours during the whole week I was inside the BIA.

Every morning and evening was crisis time. In between, the negotiations went on. Groups of supporters arrived, good people as well as weirdos. The Indian commissioner Lewis Bruce stayed one night in the building to show his sympathy. So did LaDonna Harris, a Kiowa-Comanche and a senator's wife. One guy who called himself Wavy Gravy, who came from a place in California called the Hog Farm and who wore a single enormous earring, arrived in a psychedelically decorated bus and set up a loudspeaker system for us. At the same time the police cut all our telephone wires except the one connecting us with the Department of the Interior. A certain Reverend McIntire came with a bunch of followers waving signs and singing Christian hymns. He was known to us as a racist and Vietnam War hawk. Why he wanted to support us was a big mystery. Cameramen and reporters swarmed through the building; tourists took snapshots of our guards. It was as if all these white people around the BIA were hoping for some sort of Buffalo Bill Wild West show.

For me the high point came not with our men arming themselves, but with Martha Grass, a simple middle-aged Cherokee woman from Oklahoma, standing up to Interior Secretary Morton and giving him a piece of her mind, speaking from the heart, speaking for all of us. She talked about everyday things, women's things, children's problems, getting down to the nitty-gritty. She shook her fists in Morton's face, saying, "Enough of your bullshit!" It was good to see an Indian mother stand up to one of Washington's highest officials. "This is our building!" she told him. Then she gave him the finger.

In the end a compromise was reached. The government said they could not go on negotiating during Election Week, but they would appoint two high administration officials to seriously consider our twenty demands. Our expenses to get home would be paid. Nobody would be prosecuted. Of course, our twenty points were never gone into afterward. From the practical point of view, nothing had been achieved. As usual we had bickered among ourselves. But morally it had been a great victory. We had faced White America collectively, not as individual tribes. We had stood up to the government and gone through our baptism of fire. We had not run. As Russel Means put it, it had been "a helluva smoke signal!"

QUESTIONS FOR DISCUSSION

1. From her title to her closing words, Mary Crow Dog's reflective narrative sustains a militant tone that has been tempered by her "bird's-eye view" of "ten years gone past." Think about the effectiveness of her tone, and locate specific examples of diction and syntax that exemplify her strident voice. Is her tone justified?
2. In paragraph 13 Crow Dog compares AIM with the African-American civil rights movement. Discuss the reasoning behind her comparison, and look for differences as well as similarities.
3. In paragraph 18 Crow Dog points to a close link between youth and the elderly. She suggests that the middle-aged adults were a "lost generation which had given up all hope." Explain the reasons for this generation gap. Have you observed similar generation gaps in your own experience with other ethnic groups?

WRITING ASSIGNMENTS

1. Reaction Journal: In her closing Crow Dog asserts that AIM achieved nothing from a practical point of view but that morally it achieved "a great victory." Reexamine her narrative, and write her a letter in which you respond to her attitude about victory.

2. Try to remember a confrontation in which you won a moral victory. (Victories over an unjust school policy or community regulation are among many possible topics.) Write an essay that presents the confrontation in a reflective narrative. Pay attention to Crow Dog's techniques as you develop your essay.

CRAZY HORSE MALT LIQUOR AND OTHER CULTURAL METAPHORS

MICHAEL DORRIS

A member of the Modoc tribe, Michael Dorris (b. 1945) has taught in the Department of Native American Studies at Dartmouth College. His published writings include the novel A Yellow Raft in Blue Water *(1987) and* The Broken Cord *(1987), an account of raising his adopted son, who suffers from fetal alcohol syndrome and effect. With his wife, Louise Erdrich, Dorris has coauthored* The Crown of Columbus *(1991). In the following piece, which appeared in the April 21, 1992,* New York Times, *Dorris points out the distorted reflection of Native Americans provided by the metaphors of popular culture.*

◆ FREEWRITING

Recently, Native American activists have protested the use of their heritage as popular culture symbols. Native American place-names, the names of athletic teams, and names of commercial products are a cause for concern. Recent demonstrations against the Washington Redskins football team or the tomahawk chop of the Atlanta Braves baseball fans are examples. Freewrite for ten or fifteen minutes on this issue. Do you feel the Native American objection is warranted, or do you (as many non–Native American Americans) simply view such symbolization as harmless fun?

People of proclaimed good will have the oddest ways of honoring American Indians. Sometimes they dress themselves in turkey feathers and paint—"cultural drag," my friend Duane Bird Bear calls it—and boogie on 50-yard lines.

Presumably they hope this exuberant if ethnographically questionable display will do their teams more good against opponents than those rituals they imitate and mock did for 19th century Cheyenne and Nez Perce men and women who tried, with desperation and ultimate futility, to defend their homelands from invasion.

Sometimes otherwise impeccably credentialed liberals get so swept up in honoring Indians that they beat fake tom-toms or fashion their forearms and hands into facsimiles of the axes European traders used for barter and attempt, unsuccessfully, to chop their way to victory.

Everywhere you look such respects are paid: the street names in woodsy, affluent subdivisions; mumbo-jumbo in ersatz male-bonding weekends and Boy Scout jamborees; geometric fashion statements, weepy anti-littering public service announcements. In the ever popular noble-savage spectrum, red is the hot, safe color.

5 For centuries, flesh and blood Indians have been assigned the role of a popular-culture metaphor for generations. Today, their evocation instantly connotes fuzzy images of Nature, the Past, Plight or Summer Camp. War-bonneted apparitions pasted to football helmets or baseball caps act as opaque, impermeable curtains, solid walls of white noise that for many citizens block or distort all vision of the nearly two million native Americans today.

And why not? Such honoring relegates Indians to the long-ago and thus makes them magically disappear from public consciousness and conscience. What do the 300 federally recognized tribes, with their various complicated treaties governing land rights and protections, their crippling unemployment, infant mortality and teen-age suicide rates, their manifold health problems have in common with jolly (or menacing) cartoon caricatures, wistful braves or ravenous Mazola girls?

Perhaps we should ask the Hornell Brewing Company of Baltimore, manufacturers of the Original Crazy Horse Malt Liquor, a product currently distributed in New York with packaging inspired by, according to the text on the back, "the Black Hills of Dakota, *steeped* [my italics] in the History of the American West, home of Proud Indian Nations, a land where imagination conjures up images of blue clad Pony Soldiers and magnificent Native American Warriors."

Whose imagination? Were these the same blue-clad lads who perpetrated the 1890 massacre of 200 captured, freezing Dakota at Wounded Knee? Are Pine Ridge and Rosebud, the two reservations closest to the Black Hills and, coincidentally, the two counties in the United States with the lowest per capita incomes, the Proud Nations?

Is the "steeping" a bald allusion to the fact that alcohol has long constituted the No. 1 health hazard to Indians? Virtually every other social ill plaguing native Americans—from disproportionately frequent traffic fatalities to arrest statistics—is related in some tragic respect to ethanol, and many tribes, from Alaska to New Mexico, record the highest percentage in the world of babies born disabled by fetal alcohol syndrome and effect. One need look no further than the Congressionally mandated warning to pregnant women printed in capital letters on every Crazy Horse label to make the connection.

10 The facts of history are not hard to ascertain: the Black Hills, the "paha sapa," the traditional holy place of the Dakota, were illegally seized by the Government, systematically stripped of their mineral wealth—and have still not been returned to their rightful owners. Crazy Horse, in addition to being a pa-

triot to his Oglala people, was a mystic and a religious leader murdered after he voluntarily gave himself up in 1887 to Pony Soldiers at Fort Robinson, Neb. What, then, is the pairing of his name with 40 ounces of malt liquor supposed to signify.

The Hornell brewers helpfully supply a clue. The detail of the logo is focused on the headdress and not the face; it's pomp without circumstance, form without content. Wear the hat, the illustration seems to offer, and in the process fantasize yourself more interesting (or potent or tough or noble) than you are. Play at being a "warrior" from the "land that truly speaks of the spirit that is America."

And if some humorless Indians object, just set them straight. Remind them what an honor it is to be used.

QUESTIONS FOR DISCUSSION

1. Discuss how Dorris uses such techniques as abrupt syntax and the rhetorical question to strengthen his argument. What is the thesis of this selection? At what point is the thesis clear? Comment on the effectiveness of the conclusion.
2. Explain in detail why Dorris objects to the Hornell Brewing Company and its Original Crazy Horse Malt Liquor.

WRITING ASSIGNMENTS

1. Reaction Journal: Now that you have read this selection, freewrite for another ten or fifteen minutes. Focus on whether Dorris affected your thinking as it appeared in your earlier freewriting.
2. Write an essay in which you discuss, using examples, how the majority culture continues to use popular cultural metaphors for Native Americans and other minorities. If you wish, focus on the ways cinema and television engage in this "cultural drag."

FROM WHERE I COME FROM IS LIKE THIS

PAULA GUNN ALLEN

Paula Gunn Allen (b. 1939), a Laguna Pueblo/Sioux, was born on the Cubero land grant in New Mexico. A poet, writer, and critic, Allen has taught Native American and Ethnic Studies at the Universities of New Mexico and California at Berkeley and Los Angeles. She has also been involved in the antiwar, antinuclear, and feminist movements. The fol-

lowing essay, from The Sacred Hoop: Recovering the Feminine in American Indian Traditions *(1986), reveals some of the ways in which women are viewed in traditional Native American culture and also suggests something of the bicultural bind in which Native American women find themselves in contemporary society.*

◆ FREEWRITING

Freewrite for ten or fifteen minutes about stories you were told in your childhood. Such stories could be fictional, or they could be about successful or unusual members of your family or community. Focus on the stories' content and how they may have been told to influence your behavior.

An American Indian woman is primarily defined by her tribal identity. In her eyes, her destiny is necessarily that of her people, and her sense of herself as a woman is first and foremost prescribed by her tribe. The definitions of woman's roles are as diverse as tribal cultures in the Americas. In some she is devalued, in others she wields considerable power. In some she is a familial/clan adjunct, in some she is as close to autonomous as her economic circumstances and psychological traits permit. But in no tribal definitions is she perceived in the same way as are women in western industrial and postindustrial cultures. . . .

The tribes see women variously, but they do not question the power of femininity. Sometimes they see women as fearful, sometimes peaceful, sometimes omnipotent and omniscient, but they never portray women as mindless, helpless, simple, or oppressed. And while the women in a given tribe, clan, or band may be all these things, the individual woman is provided with a variety of images of women from the interconnected supernatural, natural, and social worlds she lives in. . . .

My mother told me stories all the time, though I often did not recognize them as that. My mother told me stories about cooking and childbearing; she told me stories about menstruation and pregnancy; she told me stories about gods and heroes, about fairies and elves, about goddesses and spirits; she told me stories about the land and the sky, about cats and dogs, about snakes and spiders; she told me stories about climbing trees and exploring the mesas; she told me stories about going to dances and getting married; she told me stories about dressing and undressing, about sleeping and waking; she told me stories about herself, about her mother, about her grandmother. She told me stories about grieving and laughing, about thinking and doing; she told me stories about school and about people, about darning and mending; she told me stories about turquoise and about gold; she told me European stories and Laguna stories; she told me Catholic stories and Presbyterian stories; she told me city stories and country stories; she told me political stories and religious stories. She told me stories about living and stories about dying. And in all of those stories she told me who I was, who I was supposed to be, whom I came from, and who would follow me. In this way she taught me the meaning of the words she said, that all life is a circle and everything has a place within it. That's what she said and what she showed me in the things she did and the way she lives.

Of course, through my formal, white, Christian education, I discovered that other people had stories of their own—about women, about Indians, about fact, about reality—and I was amazed by a number of startling suppositions that others made about tribal customs and beliefs. According to the un-Indian, non-Indian view, for instance, Indians barred menstruating women from ceremonies and indeed segregated them from the rest of the people, consigning them to some space specially designed for them. This showed that Indians considered menstruating women unclean and not fit to enjoy the company of decent (non-menstruating) people, that is, men. I was surprised and confused to hear this because my mother had taught me that white people had strange attitudes toward menstruation: they thought something was bad about it, that it meant you were sick, cursed, sinful, and weak and that you had to be very careful during that time. She taught me that menstruation was a normal occurrence, that I could go swimming or hiking or whatever else I wanted to do during my period. She actively scorned women who took to their beds, who were incapacitated by cramps, who "got the blues."

5 As I struggled to reconcile these very contradictory interpretations of American Indians' traditional beliefs concerning menstruation, I realized that the menstrual taboos were about power, not about sin or filth. My conclusion was later borne out by some tribes' own explanations, which, as you may well imagine, came as quite a relief to me.

The truth of the matter as many Indians see it is that women who are at the peak of their fecundity are believed to possess power that throws male power totally out of kilter. They emit such force that, in their presence, any male-owned or -dominated ritual or sacred object cannot do its usual task. For instance, the Lakota say that a menstruating woman anywhere near a yuwipi man, who is a special sort of psychic, spirit-empowered healer, for a day or so before he is to do his ceremony will effectively disempower him. Conversely, among many if not most tribes, important ceremonies cannot be held without the presence of women. Sometimes the ritual woman who empowers the ceremony must be unmarried and virginal so that the power she channels is unalloyed, unweakened by sexual arousal and penetration by a male. Other ceremonies require tumescent women, others the presence of mature women who have borne children, and still others depend for empowerment on post-menopausal women. Women may be segregated from the company of the whole band or village on certain occasions, but on certain occasions men are also segregated. In short, each ritual depends on a certain balance of power, and the positions of women within the phases of womanhood are used by tribal people to empower certain rites. This does not derive from a male-dominant view; it is not a ritual observance imposed on women by men. It derives from a tribal view of reality that distinguishes tribal people from feudal and industrial people.

Among the tribes, the occult power of women, inextricably bound to our hormonal life, is thought to be very great; many hold that we possess innately the blood-given power to kill—with a glance, with a step, or with the judicious mixing of menstrual blood into somebody's soup. Medicine women among the Pomo of California cannot practice until they are sufficiently mature; when they are immature, their power is diffuse and is likely to interfere with their practice until time and experience have it under control. So women of the tribes are not especially inclined to see themselves as poor helpless victims of male domination. Even in those tribes where something akin to male domination was present, women are perceived as powerful, socially, physically, and metaphysically. In times past, as in times present, women carried enormous burdens with aplomb. We were far indeed from the "weaker sex," the designation that white aristocratic sisters unhappily earned for us all.

I remember my mother moving furniture all over the house when she wanted it changed. She didn't wait for my father to come home and help—she just went ahead and moved the piano, a huge upright from the old days, the couch, the refrigerator. Nobody had told her she was too weak to do such things. In imitation of her, I would delight in loading trucks at my father's store with cases of pop or fifty-pound sacks of flour. Even when I was quite small I could do it, and it gave me a belief in my own physical strength that advancing middle age can't quite erase. My mother used to tell me about the Acoma Pueblo women she had seen as a child carrying huge ollas (water pots) on their heads as they wound their way up the tortuous stairwell carved into the face of the "Sky City" mesa, a feat I tried to imitate with books and tin buckets. ("Sky City" is the term used by the Chamber of Commerce for the mother village of Acoma, which is situated atop a high sandstone table mountain.) I was never very successful, but even the attempt reminded me that I was supposed to be strong and balanced to be a proper girl.

Of course, my mother's Laguna people are Keres Indian, reputed to be the last extreme mother-right people on earth. So it is no wonder that I got notably nonwhite notions about the natural strength and prowess of women. Indeed, it is only when I am trying to get non-Indian approval, recognition, or acknowledgment that my "weak sister" emotional and intellectual ploys get the better of my tribal woman's good sense. At such times I forget that I just moved the piano or just wrote a competent paper or just completed a financial transaction satisfactorily or have supported myself and my children for most of my adult life.

Nor is my contradictory behavior atypical. Most Indian women I know are 10
in the same bicultural bind: we vacillate between being dependent and strong, self-reliant and powerless, strongly motivated and hopelessly insecure. We resolve the dilemma in various ways: some of us party all the time; some of us drink to excess; some of us travel and move around a lot; some of us land good jobs and then quit them; some of us engage in violent exchanges; some of us blow our brains out. We act in these destructive ways because we suffer from the societal conflicts caused by having to identify with two hopelessly opposed cultural definitions of women. Through this destructive dissonance we are un-

happy prey to the self-disparagement common to, indeed demanded of, Indians living in the United States today. Our situation is caused by the exigencies of a history of invasion, conquest, and colonization whose searing marks are probably ineradicable. A popular bumper sticker on many Indian cars proclaims: "If You're Indian You're In," to which I always find myself adding under my breath, "Trouble."

No Indian can grow to any age without being informed that her people were "savages" who interfered with the march of progress pursued by respectable, loving, civilized white people. We are the villains of the scenario when we are mentioned at all. We are absent from much of white history except when we are calmly, rationally, succinctly, and systematically dehumanized. On the few occasions we are noticed in any way other than as howling, bloodthirsty beings, we are acclaimed for our noble quaintness. In this definition, we are exotic curios. Our ancient arts and customs are used to draw tourist money to state coffers, into the pocketbooks and bank accounts of scholars, and into support of the American-in-Disneyland promoters' dream.

As a Roman Catholic child I was treated to bloody tales of how the savage Indians martyred the hapless priests and missionaries who went among them in an attempt to lead them to the one true path. By the time I was through high school I had the idea that Indians were people who had benefited mightily from the advanced knowledge and superior morality of the Anglo-Europeans. At least I had, perforce, that idea to lay beside the other one that derived from my daily experience of Indian life, an idea less dehumanizing and more accurate because it came from my mother and the other Indian people who raised me. That idea was that Indians are a people who don't tell lies, who care for their children and their old people. You never see an Indian orphan, they said. You always know when you're old that someone will take care of you—one of your children will. Then they'd list the old folks who were being taken care of by this child or that. No child is ever considered illegitimate among the Indians, they said. If a girl gets pregnant, the baby is still part of the family, and the mother is too. That's what they said, and they showed me real people who lived according to those principles.

Of course the ravages of colonization have taken their toll; there are orphans in Indian country now, and abandoned, brutalized old folks; there are even illegitimate children, though the very concept still strikes me as absurd. There are battered children and neglected children, and there are battered wives and women who have been raped by Indian men. Proximity to the "civilizing" effects of white Christians has not improved the moral quality of life in Indian country, though each group, Indian and white, explains the situation differently. Nor is there much yet in the oral tradition that can enable us to adapt to these inhuman changes. But a force is growing in that direction, and it is helping Indian women reclaim their lives. Their power, their sense of direction and of self will soon be visible. It is the force of the women who speak and work and write, and it is formidable.

QUESTIONS ON CONTENT

1. In another essay, Allen says that in Western culture, "few images of women form part of the cultural myths, and these are largely sexually charged." Do you agree? In what ways are Native American images different?
2. Allen asserts that Indian tribes do not question the power of femininity. What does she mean, and how does she use menstruation to demonstrate her point?
3. Paragraph 3 consists primarily of a catalogue of story types Allen's mother shared with her. What effect does the author achieve with such a catalogue? What is the function of the paragraph's final sentence? In what ways is the paragraph's structure similar to that of the opening paragraph?

WRITING ASSIGNMENTS

1. Reaction Journal: Write a letter to Allen in which you compare her views of the role of Indian women with your views of your own culture. Define what she means by the "bicultural bind" this conflict creates.
2. Allen suggests that Native as well as non-Native cultures squeeze women between conflicting views of the way they are perceived and what they really are. From your own experiences and/or observations, write an essay in which you discuss concretely the ways in which women are pulled in conflicting directions, If you prefer, write an essay in which you demonstrate the ways men are or are not torn by cultural stereotypes.

From Europe—The Huddled Masses

Emma Lazarus's poem "The New Colossus," (page 44) written in 1883, was inscribed on the base of the Statue of Liberty in 1886 during the peak years of European immigration, a time that coincided with the beginning of the era of federal regulation. While it is true that the United States has served as a haven for the "homeless, tempest-tossed" fleeing economic and political conditions in their native lands, there has also been a strong element of national self-interest in the welcoming of immigrants to the "golden door." Early leaders expected immigration to play an important role in the nation's growth and development. In passing the Northwest Ordinance of 1787, which guaranteed freedom of religion in the Northwest Territories, Congress hoped that this freedom would attract immigrants. James Madison observed that those parts of America which most welcomed foreigners had "advanced most rapidly in population, agriculture, and the arts." The degree to which the "golden door" has remained open at various points in our history reflects the extent to which immigration has been seen as beneficial to the nation as a whole.

From the time of the drafting of the Constitution through the first half of the nineteenth century, the federal government did little either to control or promote immigration. In fact, until 1820, no federal records of immigrants were kept. The business of attracting and settling immigrants was left to state and territorial governments and to entrepreneurs. By the 1870s, however, with more than 280,000 immigrants a year entering the United States and the numbers increasing, the need for a uniform system for dealing with immigration became evident. Accordingly, Congress enacted a number of statutes that brought immigration under the direct control of the federal government.

Federal records indicate that between 1820 and 1880 over 86 percent of the immigrants entering the United States came from northern and western Europe. Population growth, crop failures, and unemployment caused by the Industrial Revolution, combined with the lure of opportunity in the United States, caused substantial numbers of Western Europeans to undertake resettlement here. Catholic Irish and Germans accounted for the majority of this migration, though Scandinavians, Dutch, Swiss, French, and British also entered the United States in large numbers. Irish, fleeing the potato famine of 1845–1849, settled mainly in the cities of the Northeast and the mid-Atlantic region, Germans in the mid-Atlantic and Midwestern regions, and Scandinavians, Dutch, and Swiss in the Midwest. English and Scots were represented in all regions, and the Welsh were most strongly represented in the mid-Atlantic states. Latin European groups, with the exception of the Portuguese, large numbers of whom settled in the Northeast, were attracted to California and the area around the port of New Orleans.

The expanding frontier and newly industrialized cities demanded increasing numbers of settlers and laborers. Individual states mounted aggressive campaigns to attract immigrants. In 1845 Michigan appointed an agent to recruit immigrants at the docks in New York City, an example Wisconsin quickly followed. Minnesota hired a clerk to draw up mailing lists of settlers' friends and family still living in Europe and to send abroad recruitment leaflets (including essays by settlers describing the opportunities in the state) in English, Welsh, German, Dutch, Norwegian, and Swedish. Minnesota also had agents stationed in Sweden and Germany to promote immigration to the state. By the end of the nineteenth century, thirty-three states and territories had established their own immigration offices charged with the task of attracting newcomers. Their recruiting pamphlets extolled the virtues of their own areas as well as pointing out the lack of railroad services and threats posed by drought, blizzard, locusts, and Indians in competing territories.

Indeed, life for the German, Swedish, Norwegian, and other immigrant farmers on the plains of the Midwest during the mid-1800s was not easy. In "Swedish Exodus" Lars Ljungmark describes the hardships of the living conditions and the isolation settlers suffered on the Minnesota frontier. The lives these pioneers led have entered the national consciousness through the fiction of writers such as Ole Rölvaag and Willa Cather. Eugene Boe, speaking of the million Norwegians who emigrated to the United States in the nineteenth and early twentieth centuries, remarks that "the wonder is not that so many of these first settlers succumbed, but that so many survived," considering the grasshopper plagues, long Arctic winters, relentlessly hot summers, prairie fires, threats of Indian attacks, hailstorms, crop failures, tornadoes, epidemics of influenza, typhoid, diphtheria, "backbreaking labor without end, and the aching loneliness."

Newcomers arriving at the port of New York between 1855 and 1890 entered the country through Castle Garden, a former opera house at the southern tip of Manhattan that then served as the city's immigration depot. Staffed by volunteers, Castle Garden provided orientation and hospital services, free baths, inexpensive food, boardinghouse connections, and practical advice, all in an atmosphere of benevolence. Record keeping was casual, medical examinations cursory. The expanding country needed willing hands, and immigrants were welcomed and guided to their destinations by the staff.

During the late nineteenth century, the federal government began to establish its own bureaucracy for dealing with immigration. Pressure for federal regulation began to restrict Chinese immigration in California, and the resulting legislation set the precedent for an era of exclusionary policies. By the time of the Chinese Exclusion Act (1882), the nature of the European immigration had changed. Ninety-two percent of the immigrants who arrived during the last two decades of the nineteenth century were Europeans, but immigration from northern and western Europe began to be balanced by increasing numbers of Italians, Poles, Czechs, Russians, and Jews from all over the Continent. During this peak era of immigration, 1907 alone saw the admission of 1,285,349 immigrants, the largest number for any one year in U.S. history. One third of eastern European Jewry left their homes between 1880 and 1920, over 90 percent of them coming to the United States. This shift in origin from northern and western to eastern and southern Europe continued into the twentieth century, with Italians as the dominant group in the 8.8 million immigrants arriving between 1900 and 1910.

At the same time that the national origins of immigrants shifted, the nature of opportunities and living conditions in the United States were changing as well. Throughout Europe populations were moving from farms to cities. Conditions on both sides of the Atlantic colluded in bringing a new kind of immigrant to these shores, and it was in keeping with the natural migration pattern of the time that they chose to settle mostly in urban areas. Large tracts of farmland along the frontier were not so readily available, and expansion of the railroads brought the products of farm, field, forest, and mine into the urban areas. Large cities grew simultaneously with the phenomenon of mass production. The factory system, with its call for laborers to perform unskilled repetitive tasks and long-standing resistance to unionization, created unhealthy, dangerous, and degrading working conditions. New immigrants were often accused of creating the "un-American" conditions under which they labored and in which they had no choice but to live. Most of the southern and eastern Europeans settled in fewer regions than the earlier groups had, with the exception of the Irish. The highly industrialized cities of New England, the mid-Atlantic region, and the eastern Midwest were the main destinations for Italians and peoples from the Austro-Hungarian and Russian empires. The consequent visibility of large groups of unassimilated peoples from language and cultural backgrounds quite different from those of the dominant group—what Richard O'Connor refers to as the "Anglo-Teutonic amalgamation"—made immigrants easy marks on whom responsibility for the economic and social woes that beset U.S. cities could be pinned.

For the new immigrants flocking to American cities, the trials of the city were formidable. The human cost of overcrowded, airless tenement conditions in which immigrants were often forced to live were revealed at the turn of the century by Jacob Riis, a Danish-born journalist, photographer, and social reformer whose *How the Other Half Lives* (1890), *The Battle with the Slum* (1902), *Children of the Tenements* (1903), and many other writings exposed the misery of life in the tenement districts of New York City (see the Introduction to "Neighborhoods"). A Rumanian immigrant living in New York's Lower East Side described the "filth and garbage littering the sidewalks and the gutters . . . being kicked about by street urchins who screamed at each other in half a dozen European jargons seasoned with mangled Americanese." Mario Puzo, the son of Italian immigrants, describes the Hell's Kitchen area of New York along Tenth Avenue between 30th and 31st streets in similarly inhospitable terms: "Our tenements were the western wall of the city. Beneath our windows were the vast black iron gardens of the New York Central railroad, absolutely blooming with stinking boxcars freshly unloaded of cattle and pigs for the city slaughterhouses." Of the large American cities, New York had the largest and most congested immigrant neighborhoods. Five- or six-story walkup tenements packed tightly together were the unhealthy domain of immigrants. The overcrowded conditions and the threat of fire posed constant dangers to the inhabitants. In cities such as Chicago, St. Louis, and Philadelphia the tenements were generally only two or three stories, but flimsily constructed additions were often tacked onto their backs, filling up the scant open spaces between buildings and adding to the hazards of tenement living.

The notorious conditions in unregulated sweatshops, in which employees labored sixty-five to seventy-five hours a week, were occasionally brought to popular attention through disasters such as the fire at the ten-story Triangle Shirtwaist Factory in 1911 in which 147 women and 21 men were killed and some 200 more workers critically injured. The kinds of work available to women were largely confined to such sweatshops or to household work. As the source of immigration changed toward the end of the nineteenth century, providing a less-sophisticated and less-educated pool of female workers, unscrupulous "labor intelligence offices" sprang up to serve as middlemen in placing foreign-born girls as domestics. As Aleksandra Rembiénska's letters home in "A Polish Peasant Girl in America" indicate, the work schedules of domestic servants allowed no time to learn the language of their new country or to see anything of it beyond the confines of the houses in which they worked. "I am in America," wrote Rembiénska in 1911, "and I do not even know whether it is America, only it seems to me as if there were only a single house in the whole world and nothing more, only walls and very few people." Unlike many of the earlier immigrants who relied on the contacts made by family and close friends to find suitable domestic positions (see, for instance, the letter by Hans Mattson in "Swedish Exodus"), many of the new immigrants, lacking training, depended on agencies to find them work. Often, they ended up working long hours for low wages. Frances Kellor, an early advocate for the regulation and reform of female labor practices, pointed out in 1904 that because these "intelligence offices" knew the languages and customs of the immigrant girls, they frequently exploited their dependency, extorting money from them, lodging them in unsanitary, crowded tenements, and even sending many into prostitution.

Citizens eager to assign blame and find a simple solution for depressed wages, poor working conditions, and unhealthy slum conditions found in these new immigrants convenient scapegoats. They were attacked as being racially inferior, and, as Henry Pratt Fairchild stated in his 1926 defense of immigration quotas, as being the cause of the "mongrelization" of the "highly specialized" English and American genetic "types" and as compromising the "racial effectiveness of the American people." (See also the discussion of eugenics in the Introduction to "Confrontations.") Such thinking was informed by early applications of Darwinian principles of natural selection to social issues, by what John Higham in *Strangers in the Land: Patterns of American Nativism, 1860–1925* refers to as "the fusion—and confusion—of natural history with national history, of 'scientific' with social ideas." Such race-thinking and the concomitant fear of disturbing the racial and ethnic character that had prevailed throughout the building of the country had very specific effects on changes in the immigration laws as well as on the ruthless exploitation of labor. From 1891 to 1929 Congress passed a series of laws successively narrowing the range of immigrants qualifying for admission.

In 1891 Congress placed control of immigration in federal hands. The Bureau of Immigration and Naturalization, established in 1906, formulated minimum health qualifications for immigrants, required steamship companies to return all unacceptable passengers to their countries of origin, made illegal aliens and those who became public charges within one year of their arrival subject to deportation, and expanded the excluded categories to include polygamists and those suffering from "a loathsome or dangerous contagious disease." The excluded categories continued to grow. After the assassination of President William McKinley in 1901 by Leon Czolgosz (who, despite his foreign-sounding name, was American-born), fear of aliens as radicals resulted in the addition of saboteurs and anarchists to the list, along with epileptics and professional beggars.

Approximately three quarters of the new immigrants entered at the Port of New York through the new federal facility of Ellis Island, which opened in 1892. The impersonal, efficient (and sometimes officious) operation at Ellis Island was a contrast to the casual and personal atmosphere at Castle Garden. The huge numbers of immigrants to be processed and the new health regulations and exclusion clauses made the procedure more complex and time-consuming. Of the more than 16 million immigrants who passed through the Great Hall of the Ellis Island reception center, approximately 250,000 were denied entry to the United States. In "More than Just a Shrine: Paying Homage to the Ghosts of Ellis Island," Mary Gordon reflects on the frightening passage of immigrants through the examinations and interviews and the awful consequences for those who were turned away.

The movement to restrict the new immigration was lent an air of respectability by the Immigration Restriction League, which was influential in promulgating the idea that the new immigrants were fundamentally different from and inferior to the northern and western Europeans and thus hard to assimilate. The League waged a twenty-year campaign for an immigration literacy requirement, introducing legislation to this end on six occasions between 1896 and 1915, but none of their initiatives were successful.

Instrumental in restricting immigration from southern and eastern Europe were the findings of the congressionally appointed Dillingham Commission. When the Immigration Act of 1917, which imposed a literacy test, did not produce the desired result, a quota system was devised. The Quota Act of 1921 (the Johnson Act) limited the annual number of immigrants of admissible nationalities to 3 percent of the foreign-born population from each of these nationalities as recorded in the census of 1910. More restrictive was the Immigration Act of 1924 (the Johnson-Reid Act), which reduced the annual quota for each nation to 2 percent of the foreign-born of each nationality, as recorded in the 1890 census. Pushing the critical date back to 1890 was a further disadvantage to immigrants from southern and eastern Europe, few of whom had come to the United States that early. It also barred entrance to any nationalities ineligible for citizenship, thereby reaffirming the exclusion of the Chinese and adding to the excluded groups the Japanese who, by a 1922 Supreme Court decision, had been declared ineligible for citizenship. Furthermore, the Immigration Act of 1924 stated that a national origins system favoring groups from northern and western Europe would replace the quota system in 1927. Not surprisingly, the figures reserved 82 percent of the annual quota for northern and western Europe (including Britain), 16 percent for southern and eastern Europe, and 2 percent for all other areas.

In truth, the belief that earlier immigrants were more eager to assimilate linguistically and culturally is a myth. Between 1830 and 1890, 4.5 million Germans entered the United States. While they recognized the need for their children to master English in order to participate fully in mainstream American society, they (along with other groups such as Swedes, Dutch, and French) fought hard for the right to retain their native language in the public schools (see James Fallows, "Language," pp. 378–385). The process of becoming American has never been a simple matter. The eventual "success" of the German assimilation was no doubt facilitated by two world wars with Germany, which caused German-Americans to want to seem more American than German. As Richard O'Connor suggests, immigration was probably also made easier by the relative heterogeneity of the German immigrant population, representing as it did, a cross section of a modern society that could blend on different levels with existing American society. By contrast, many of the new immigrant groups contained a much larger percentage of peasants and unskilled laborers. It has taken some of these groups most of the twentieth century to feel that they are equal partners in American society.

In *The Rise of the Unmeltable Ethnics*, Michael Novak describes the ethnic experience of what he calls the PIGS—the Poles, Italians, Greeks, and Slovaks who came to number so greatly among the U.S. working classes. He describes the PIGS as "not particularly liberal or radical . . . : born outside what, in America, is considered the intellectual mainstream—and thus privy to neither power nor status nor intellectual voice." With bitter irony, Novak refers to these groups as "the great unwasped." He was "taught to be proud of being Slovak, but to recognize that others wouldn't know what it meant, or care." His statement that "we did not feel this country belonged to us" is echoed by Mary Gordon's feeling that "the country really belonged to the early settlers." In fact, though, the social distance between various European groups has diminished over the past sixty-five years. Sociological studies on stereotypes and willingness of racial and ethnic groups to interact with each other have indicated an overall decline in social distance between the top- and bottom-ranked groups. There are now, for instance, insignificant differences in the rankings of French, Italians, Swedes, and Irish and almost no difference in the relative rankings of Finns, Jews, and Greeks. Nonetheless, the prevalence of so-called ethnic jokes attests to the fact that some Europeans long suffered the effects of the race-thinking that characterized the exclusionary period in American immigration policy. Not until the Hart-Celler Act of 1965, which took effect in 1968, was the national origins quota system abolished. The act replaced it with numerical ceilings for the Western and Eastern Hemispheres, with preference categories based on relationship and occupation.

In spite of fears that the new immigrants would never become "real Americans," assimilation proceeded much as it had with other ethnic groups, and the mix of national origins in the American population as a whole has remained remarkably stable. The top three ancestry groups in the 1990 census are the same as in the 1790 census, though the English are no longer in first place. Out of a population of 248 million, 58 million claim whole or partial German ancestry, 38 million Irish, and 32 million English. Another 15 million claim Italian, 10 million claim French, 9 million Polish ancestry. The influx of immigrants during the periods of great migration from Europe profoundly influenced spiritually and materially the American way of life. In addition to acknowledging the contributions of the many notable artists, musicians, writers, industrialists, scientists, and innovators of every sort who came to this country from all over Europe, few would deny at least partial truth to Mary Gordon's description of American history as "a very classy party that was not much fun until they arrived, brought the good food, turned up the music, and taught everyone to dance."

FROM THE UPROOTED

OSCAR HANDLIN

Oscar Handlin (b. 1915), Harvard professor and social historian, was born in Brooklyn, New York, the son of immigrant parents. He studied at Brooklyn College and earned his Ph.D. at Harvard, where, under the guidance of Arthur M. Schlesinger, he became interested in American and social history. His first book, Boston's Immigrants, 1790–1865 *(1941), which won the Dunning Prize of the American Historical Association, was his doctoral dissertation. From the beginning, most of Handlin's research and writing has been concerned with the problems of first- and second-generation immigrants in American cities.* The Uprooted *(1951), a study of immigration to America after 1820, received the Pulitzer Prize in History. Among Handlin's other books are* Al Smith and His America *(1958) and* The Newcomers—Negroes and Americans in a Changing Metropolis *(1959). In the following selection from* The Uprooted, *Handlin describes some of the social and economic changes that led to the emigration of 35 million people from Europe to the United States.*

◆ FREEWRITING

Most families in the United States have kept alive stories that describe the arrival of the first family members to America's shores. Freewrite for ten or fifteen minutes on stories on this topic that have been kept alive in your family. If you don't know any such stories, write about stories you have heard through other sources.

The immigrant movement started in the peasant heart of Europe. Ponderously balanced in a solid equilibrium for centuries, the old structure of an old society began to crumble at the opening of the modern era. One by one, rude shocks weakened the aged foundations until some climactic blow suddenly tumbled the whole into ruins. The mighty collapse left without homes millions of helpless, bewildered people. These were the army of emigrants.

Disaster chained the peasant to his place. The harshness of these burdens immobilized those upon whom they fell, made the poor also poor in spirit. Revolt, escape, were not the stuff their dreams were made of as they paused in the sickle's swing or leaned back in the shadows of the long winter evening. It was for an end to all striving that their tired hearts longed.

While there was no surcease, they would hold on. Peasant wisdom knew well the fate of the rolling stone, knew that if it remained fixed, even a rock might share in growth. The unwillingness to move reflected, in part, a stubborn attachment to that fierce mistress, the land. It expressed also a lethargic passivity in which each man acquiesced in the condition of his life as it was.

Long habit, the seeming changelessness of things, stifled the impulse to self-improvement. In the country round (the parish, *okolica*) each village had a reputation, a pack of thieves, a crew of liars, a lot of drunkards, fools, or good husbandmen, thrifty, prosperous. Within the village, each family had its place, and in the family each individual. Precisely because the peasant thought only in terms of the whole, he defined his own station always by his status within the larger units. The virtue of one brought benefits, his sin, shame to the whole.

The efforts of man were directed not toward individual improvement but toward maintenance of status. It was fitting and proper to exact one's due rights, to fulfill one's due obligations. It was not fitting to thrust oneself ahead, to aspire to a life above one's rank, to rebel against one's status; that was to argue against the whole order of things.

The deep differences among peasants and between the peasants and the other groups were not a cause of envy. This was the accepted configuration of society. The lord was expected to be proud and luxurious, but humane and generous, just as the peasant was expected to be thrifty and respectful. Even bitterly burdensome privileges were not open to dispute. All knew that to him that can pay, the musicians play. The peasant did not begrudge the magnates the pleasures of their manor houses; let *them* at least draw enjoyment from life.

Acceptance of status stifled any inclination toward rebelliousness. There were occasional peasant outbursts when the nobility deviated from their expected role or when they tried to alter traditional modes of action. The Jacquerie then or Whiteboys, the followers of Wat Tyler or of Pugachev, savagely redressed their own grievances. But apart from such spasmodic acts of vengeance there were no uprisings against the order within which peasant and noble lived. The same docility blocked off the alternative of secession through emigration. If disaster befell the individual, that was not itself a cause for breaking away. It did not become so until some external blow destroyed the whole peasant order.

The seeds of ultimate change were not native to this stable society. They were implanted from without. For centuries the size of the population, the amount of available land, the quantity of productive surplus, and the pressure of family stability, achieved together a steady balance that preserved the village way of life. Only slowly and in a few places were there signs of unsteadiness in the seventeenth century; then more distinctly and in more places in the eighteenth. After 1800, everywhere, the elements of the old equilibrium disintegrated. The old social structure tottered; gathering momentum from its own fall, it was unable to right itself, and under the impact of successive shocks collapsed. Then the peasants could no longer hang on; when even to stay meant to change, they had to leave.

Earliest harbinger of the transformations to come was a radical new trend in the population of Europe. For a thousand years, the number of people on the continent had remained constant. From time to time there had been shifts in the areas of heaviest density. In some centuries famine, plague, and war had temporarily lowered the total; in others, freedom from famine, plague, and war had temporarily raised it. But taken all in all these fluctuations canceled each other out.

Then in the eighteenth century came a precipitous rise, unprecedented and, 10
as it proved, cataclysmic. For a hundred years growth continued unabated, if anything at an accelerating rate. Between 1750 and 1850 the population of the continent leaped from about one hundred and forty million to about two hundred and sixty, and by the time of the First World War to almost four hundred million. In addition, by 1915 some two hundred and fifty million Europeans and their descendants lived outside the continent. Even taking account of the relief from emigration, the pressure on social institutions of this increase was enormous. The reckoning is simple: where one man stood in 1750, one hundred and sixty-five years later there were three.

This revolutionary change came under the beneficent guise of a gradual decline in the death rate, particularly in that of children under the age of two. Why infants, everywhere in Europe, should now more often survive is not altogether clear. But the consequences were unmistakable; the happy facility with which the newborn lived to maturity put a totally unexpected strain upon the whole family system and upon the village organization. The new situation called into question the old peasant assumption that all sons would be able to find farms capable of maintaining them at the status their fathers had held. As events demonstrated the falsity of that assumption, stability disappeared from peasant life.

All now found themselves compelled to raise crops that could be offered for sale. Confined to their own few acres and burdened with obligations, the peasants had no other recourse. The necessity was cruel for they were in no position to compete on the traders' market with the old landlords whose great holdings operated with the efficiency of the new methods and ultimately of the new machinery. Steadily the chill of mounting debt blanketed the village. Like the chill of winter, it extinguished growth and hope, only worse, for there seemed no prospect of a spring ahead.

The change, which weakened all, desolated those whose situation was already marginal. The cottiers, the crop-sharers, the tenants on short-term leases of any kind could be edged out at any time. They had left only the slimmest hopes of remaining where they were.

Some early gave up and joined the drift to the towns, where, as in England, they supplied the proletariat that manned the factories of the Industrial Revolution. Others swelled the ranks of the agricultural labor force that wandered seasonally to the great estates in search of hire. Still others remained, working the land on less and less favorable terms, slaving to hold on.

A few emigrated. Those who still had some resources but feared a loss of 15
status learned with hope of the New World where land, so scarce in the Old, was abundantly available. Younger sons learned with hope that the portions which at home would not buy them the space for a garden, in America would make them owners of hundreds of acres. Tempted by the prospect of princely rewards for their efforts, they ventured to tear themselves away from the ancestral village, to

undertake the unknown risks of transplantation. The movement of such men was the first phase of what would be a cataclysmic transfer of population.

But this phase was limited, involved few peasants. A far greater number were still determined to hold on; mounting adversities only deepened that determination. In addition, the costs of emigration were high, the difficulties ominous; few had the energy and power of will to surmount such obstacles. And though the landlords were anxious to evict as many as possible, there was no point in doing so without the assurance that the evicted would depart. Otherwise the destitute would simply remain, supported by parish charity, in one way or another continue to be a drain upon the landlords' incomes.

Soon enough disaster resolved the dilemma. There was no slack to the peasant situation. Without reserves of any kind these people were helpless in the face of the first crisis. The year the crops failed there was famine. Then the alternative to flight was death by starvation. In awe the peasant saw his fields barren, yielding nothing to sell, nothing to eat. He looked up and saw the emptiness of his neighbors' lands, of the whole village. In all the country round his startled eyes fell upon the same desolation. Who would now help? The empty weeks went by, marked by the burial of the first victims; at the workhouse door the gentry began to ladle out the thin soup of charity; and a heartsick weariness settled down over the stricken cottages. So much striving had come to no end.

Now the count was mounting. The endless tolling of the sexton's bell, the narrowing family circle, were shaping an edge of resolution. The tumbled huts, no longer home to anyone were urging it. The empty road was pointing out its form. It was time.

He would leave now, escape; give up this abusive land his fathers had never really mastered. He would take up what remained and never see the sight of home again. He would become a stranger on the way, pack on back, lead wife and children toward some other destiny. For all about was evidence of the consequences of staying. Any alternative was better.

What sum the sale of goods and land would bring would pay the cost. And if 20
nothing remained, then aid would come from the gentry or the parish, now compassionate in the eagerness to rid the place of extra hands, now generous in the desire to ease the burden on local charity. So, in the hundreds of thousands, peasants came to migrate. This was the second phase in the transfer of a continent's population.

It was not the end. Years of discontent followed. The burdens of those who stayed grew no lighter with the going of those who went. Grievances fed on the letters from America of the departed. From outposts in the New World came advice and assistance. Across the Atlantic the accumulation of immigrants created a magnetic pole that would for decades continue to draw relatives and friends in a mighty procession. This was the third phase.

With the peasants went a host of other people who found their own lives disrupted by the dislocation of the village. The empty inn now rarely heard the joy of wedding celebrations. The lonely church ministered to a handful of communicants. The tavernkeeper and priest, and with them smith and miller, followed in the train of those they once had served. There was less need now for the petty trade of Jews, for the labor of wandering artisans, for the tinkering of gypsies. These too joined the migration.

And toward the end, the flow of peoples received additions as well from the factories and mines. Often these were peasants or the sons of peasants whose first remove had been to the nearby city, men who had not yet found security or stability and who, at last, thought it better to go the way their cousins had earlier gone.

So Europe watched them go—in less than a century and a half, well over thirty-five million of them from every part of the continent. In this common flow were gathered up people of the most diverse qualities, people whose rulers had for centuries been enemies, people who had not even known of each other's existence. Now they would share each other's future.

Westward from Ireland went four and a half million. On that crowded is- 25
land a remorselessly rising population, avaricious absentee landlords, and English policy that discouraged the growth of industry early stimulated emigration. Until 1846 this had been largely a movement of younger sons, of ambitious farmers and artisans. In that year rot destroyed the potato crop and left the cottiers without the means of subsistence. Half a million died and three million more lived on only with the aid of charity. No thought then of paying rent, of holding on to the land; the evicted saw their huts pulled down and with bitter gratitude accepted from calculating poor-law officials the price of passage away from home. For decades after, till the end of the nineteenth century and beyond, these peasants continued to leave, some victims of later agricultural disasters, some sent for by relatives already across, some simply unable to continue a way of life already thoroughly disrupted.

Westward from Great Britain went well over four million. There enclosure and displacement had begun back in the eighteenth century, although the first to move generally drifted to the factories of the expanding cities. By 1815, however, farmers and artisans in substantial numbers had emigration in mind; and after midcentury they were joined by a great mass of landless peasants, by operatives from the textile mills, by laborers from the potteries, and by miners from the coal fields. In this number were Scots, Welsh, and Englishmen, and also the sons of some Irishmen, sons whose parents had earlier moved across the Irish Sea.

From the heart of the continent, from the lands that in 1870 became the German Empire, went fully six million. First to leave were the free husbandmen of the southwest, then the emancipated peasants of the north and east. With them moved, in the earlier years, artisans dislocated by the rise of industry, and later some industrial workers.

From the north went two million Scandinavians. Crop failures, as in 1847 in Norway, impelled some to leave. Others found their lots made harsher by the decline in the fisheries and by the loss of the maritime market for timber. And for many more, the growth of commercial agriculture, as in Sweden, was the indication no room would remain for free peasants.

From the south went almost five million Italians. A terrible cholera epidemic in 1887 set them moving. But here, as elsewhere, the stream was fed by the deeper displacement of the peasantry.

From the east went some eight million others—Poles and Jews, Hungarians, Bohemians, Slovaks, Ukrainians, Ruthenians—as agriculture took new forms in the Austrian and Russian Empires after 1880. 30

And before the century was out perhaps three million more were on the way from the Balkans and Asia Minor: Greeks and Macedonians, Croatians and Albanians, Syrians and Armenians.

In all, thirty-five million for whom home had no place fled to Europe's shores and looked across the Atlantic.

What manner of refuge lay there?

QUESTIONS FOR DISCUSSION

1. Handlin discusses changes in the old structure of European society. What was the primary cause that tilted the balance against the preservation of peasant village life?
2. What were the three phases in the transplantation of the continent's population?

WRITING ASSIGNMENTS

1. Reaction Journal: Handlin suggests that one reason the peasants were unwilling to change until change was forced upon them was that "peasant wisdom knew well the fate of the rolling stone." Write a paragraph that clarifies the quotation and discuss whether it is relevant to any aspect of today's society.
2. Interview an elderly citizen whose family migrated from Europe or another foreign land. Write an essay based on the interview in which you discuss the migration and the adjustments to the New World.

MORE THAN JUST A SHRINE: PAYING HOMAGE TO THE GHOSTS OF ELLIS ISLAND

MARY GORDON

Mary Gordon (b. 1949), novelist and short story writer, was born on Long Island and educated at Barnard College and Syracuse University. She taught English at Dutchess Com-

munity College in Poughkeepsie, New York, from 1974 to 1978. Since then she has published several novels, including Final Payments *(1978),* The Company of Women *(1981), and* The Other Side *(1990), which explores relations between parents and children in three generations of Irish Americans, and contributed many articles and reviews to the* New York Times. *In the following essay, which appeared in the* Times *in 1985, Gordon explains why Ellis Island was the only American landmark she has ever visited as she reflects on the experiences of immigrants who passed through its Great Hall and on the spirit they contributed to America's character.*

◆ FREEWRITING

Gordon has this to say about American historical treasures such as Plymouth Rock and Gettysburg: "I am American, and those places purport to be my history. But they are not mine." To Gordon her history goes back to the European homes of her grandparents. Most people have a sense of history, a sense of place that is somehow their own. Freewrite for ten or fifteen minutes on your own sense of "historical place."

I once sat in a hotel in Bloomsbury trying to have breakfast alone. A Russian with a habit of compulsively licking his lips asked if he could join me. I was afraid to say no; I thought it might be bad for détente. He explained to me that he was a linguist, and that he always liked to talk to Americans to see if he could make any connection between their speech and their ethnic background. When I told him about my mixed ancestry—my mother is Irish and Italian, my father a Lithuanian Jew—he began jumping up and down in his seat, rubbing his hands together, and licking his lips even more frantically.

"Ah," he said, "so you are really somebody who comes from what is called the boiling pot of America." Yes, I told him, yes I was, but I quickly rose to leave. I thought it would be too hard to explain to him the relation of the boiling potters to the main course, and I wanted to get to the British Museum. I told him that the only thing I could think of that united people whose backgrounds, histories, and points of view were utterly diverse was that their people had landed at a place called Ellis Island.

I didn't tell him that Ellis Island was the only American landmark I'd ever visited. How could I describe to him the estrangement I'd always felt from the kind of traveler who visits shrines to America's past greatness, those rebuilt forts with muskets behind glass and sabers mounted on the walls and gift shops selling maple sugar candy in the shape of Indian headdresses, those reconstructed villages with tables set for fifty and the Paul Revere silver gleaming? All that Americana—Plymouth Rock, Gettysburg, Mount Vernon, Valley Forge—it all inhabits for me a zone of blurred abstraction with far less hold on my imagination than the Bastille or Hampton Court. I suppose I've always known that my uninterest in it contains a large component of the willed: I am American, and those places purport to be my history. But they are not mine.

Ellis Island is, though; it's the one place I can be sure my people are connected to. And so I made a journey there to find my history, like any Rotarian traveling in his Winnebago to Antietam to find his. I had become part of that humbling democracy of people looking in some site for a past that has grown unreal. The monument I traveled to was not, however, a tribute to some old glory. The minute I set foot upon the island I could feel all that it stood for: insecurity, obedience, anxiety, dehumanization, the terrified and careful deference of the displaced. I hadn't traveled to the Battery and boarded a ferry across from the Statue of Liberty to raise flags or breathe a richer, more triumphant air. I wanted to do homage to the ghosts.

I felt them everywhere, from the moment I disembarked and saw the build- 5
ing with its high-minded brick, its hopeful little lawn, its ornamental cornices. The place was derelict when I arrived; it had not functioned for more than thirty years—almost as long as the time it had operated at full capacity as a major immigration center. I was surprised to learn what a small part of history Ellis Island had occupied. The main building was constructed in 1892, then rebuilt between 1898 and 1900 after a fire. Most of the immigrants who arrived during the latter half of the nineteenth century, mainly northern and western Europeans, landed not at Ellis Island but on the western tip of the Battery at Castle Garden, which had opened as a receiving center for immigrants in 1855.

By the 1880s the facilities at Castle Garden had grown scandalously inadequate. Officials looked for an island on which to build a new immigration center because they thought that on an island immigrants could be more easily protected from swindlers and quickly transported to railroad terminals in New Jersey. Bedloe's Island was considered, but New Yorkers were aghast at the idea of a "Babel" ruining their beautiful new treasure, "Liberty Enlightening the World." The statue's sculptor, Frédéric Auguste Bartholdi, reacted to the prospect of immigrants landing near his masterpiece in horror; he called it a "monstrous plan." So much for Emma Lazarus.

Ellis Island was finally chosen because the citizens of New Jersey petitioned the federal government to remove from the island an old naval powder magazine that they thought dangerously close to the Jersey shore. The explosives were removed: no one wanted the island for anything. It was the perfect place to build an immigration center.

I thought about the island's history as I walked into the building and made my way to the room that was the center in my imagination of the Ellis Island experience: the Great Hall. It had been made real for me in the stark, accusing photographs of Louis Hine and others who took those pictures to make a point. It was in the Great Hall that everyone had waited—waiting, always, the great vocation of the dispossessed. The room was empty, except for me and a handful of other visitors and the park ranger who showed us around. I felt myself grow insignificant in that room, with its huge semicircular windows, its air, even in dereliction, of solid and official probity.

I walked in the deathlike expansiveness of the room's disuse and tried to think of what it might have been like, filled and swarming. More than sixteen million immigrants came through that room: approximately 250,000 were rejected. Not really a large proportion, but the implications for the rejected were dreadful. For some, there was nothing to go back to, or there was certain death; for others, who left as adventurers, to return would be to adopt in local memory the fool's role, and the failure's. No wonder that the island's history includes reports of three thousand suicides.

Sometimes immigrants could pass through Ellis Island in mere hours, though for some the process took days. The particulars of the experience in the Great Hall were often influenced by the political events and attitudes on the mainland. In the 1890s and the first years of the new century, when cheap labor was needed, the newly built receiving center took in its immigrants with comparatively little question. But as the century progressed, the economy worsened, eugenics became both scientifically respectable and popular, and World War I made American xenophobia seem rooted in fact.

Immigration acts were passed; newcomers had to prove, besides moral correctness and financial solvency, their ability to read. Quota laws came into effect, limiting the number of immigrants from southern and eastern Europe to less than 14 percent of the total quota. Intelligence tests were biased against all non-English-speaking persons and medical examinations became increasingly strict, until the machinery of immigration nearly collapsed under its own weight. The Second Quota Law of 1924 provided that all immigrants be inspected and issued visas at American consular offices in Europe, rendering the center almost obsolete.

On the day of my visit, my mind fastened upon the medical inspections, which had always seemed to me most emblematic of the ignominy and terror the immigrants endured. The medical inspectors, sometimes dressed in uniforms like soldiers, were particularly obsessed with a disease of the eyes called trachoma, which they checked for by flipping back the immigrants' top eyelids with a hook used for buttoning gloves—a method that sometimes resulted in the transmission of the disease to healthy people. Mothers feared that if their children cried too much, their red eyes would be mistaken for a symptom of the disease and the whole family would be sent home. Those immigrants suspected of some physical disability had initials chalked on their coats. I remembered the photographs I'd seen of people standing, dumbstruck and innocent as cattle, with their manifest numbers hung around their necks and initials marked in chalk upon their coats: "E" for eye trouble, "K" for hernia, "L" for lameness, "X" for mental defects, "H" for heart disease.

I thought of my grandparents as I stood in the room; my seventeen-year-old grandmother, coming alone from Ireland in 1896, vouched for by a stranger who had found her a place as a domestic servant to some Irish who had done well. I tried to imagine the assault it all must have been for her; I've been to her hometown, a collection of farms with a main street—smaller than the athletic field of my local public school. She must have watched the New York skyline as the first- and second-class passengers were whisked off the gangplank with the most cursory of inspections while she was made to board a ferry to the new immigration center.

What could she have made of it—this buff-painted wooden structure with its towers and its blue slate roof, a place *Harper's Weekly* described as "a latter-day watering place hotel"? It would have been the first time she'd have heard people speaking something other than English. She would have mingled with people carrying baskets on their heads and eating foods unlike any she had ever seen—dark-eyed people, like the Sicilian she would marry ten years later, who came over with his family, responsible even then for his mother and sister. I don't know what they thought, my grandparents, for they were not expansive people, nor romantic; they didn't like to think of what they called "the hard times," and their trip across the ocean was the single adventurous act of lives devoted after landing to security, respectability, and fitting in.

What is the potency of Ellis Island for someone like me—an American, ob- 15
viously, but one who has always felt that the country really belonged to the early settlers, that, as J. F. Powers wrote in "Morte D'Urban," it had been "handed down to them by the Pilgrims, George Washington and others, and that they were taking a risk in letting you live in it." I have never been the victim of overt discrimination; nothing I have wanted has been denied me because of the accidents of blood. But I suppose it is part of being an American to be engaged in a somewhat tiresome but always self-absorbing process of national definition. And in this process, I have found in traveling to Ellis Island an important piece of evidence that could remind me I was right to feel my differentness. Something had happened to my people on that island, a result of the eternal wrongheadedness of American protectionism and the predictabilities of simple greed. I came to the island, too, so I could tell the ghosts that I was one of them, and that I honored them—their stoicism, and their innocence, the fear that turned them inward, and their pride. I wanted to tell them that I liked them better than the Americans who made them pass through the Great Hall and stole their names and chalked their weaknesses in public on their clothing. And to tell the ghosts what I have always thought: that American history was a very classy party that was not much fun until they arrived, brought the good food, turned up the music, and taught everyone to dance.

QUESTIONS FOR DISCUSSION

1. Does your experience lead you to believe that Gordon's sense of historical place is typical of that of most Americans? Discuss what she means and how it may or may not be relevant to your family's sense of history.

2. Emma Lazarus's poem "The New Colossus" serves as an epigraph to this section. Reread the poem and discuss Gordon's reference to it.

WRITING ASSIGNMENTS

1. Reaction Journal: In a paragraph or two discuss the meaning of Gordon's closing words: "American history was a very classy party that was not much fun until they arrived, brought the good food, turned up the music, and taught everyone to dance."

2. Select an immigrant group with which you are familiar. Use your reaction from question 1 to help you write a concrete essay that illuminates Gordon's closing words.

FROM THE MELTING POT MISTAKE

HENRY PRATT FAIRCHILD

Until the 1880s, immigrants were for the most part welcomed in the United States. At this time, however, mounting opposition to immigration resulted in the passage of restrictive legislation. Informing this sentiment was a strong streak of racism, with opponents of the so-called new immigration claiming that the immigrants from southern and eastern Europe had racial characteristics inferior to those of the early colonists and immigrants from northern Europe. Such views, allegedly supported by scientific and sociological data, provided an ideological basis for the quota laws of the 1920s, which sought to maintain the existing racial and ethnic balance within the American population. Sociologist Henry Pratt Fairchild (1880–1956) contributed significantly to the literature in the field of immigration and ethnic relations within the United States. The Melting Pot Mistake *(1926), in which the following piece originally appeared, provides a notable example of the kind of race-thinking that influenced immigration policy during the 1920s. Fairchild here defends the post–World War I quota systems and voices his concern about the racial "mongrelization" that he felt threatened the "racial effectiveness of the American people."*

◆ FREEWRITING

Confrontation and subsequent accommodation has had a predictable pattern in U.S. immigration history. Cross-cultural encounters between newcomers and natives began when the first European settlers arrived, and the character of the country has been shaped by ethnic and racial interactions between new arrivals and established citizens ever since. Freewrite for ten or fifteen minutes on your awareness of the history of such confrontations and their impact on society today.

Beginning about 1882, the immigration problem in the United States has become increasingly a racial problem in two distinct ways, first by altering profoundly the Nordic predominance in the American population, and second, by introducing various new elements which, while of uncertain volume, are so radically different from any of the old ingredients that even small quantities are deeply significant. A somewhat vague, but widespread and rapidly growing popular appreciation of this fact contributed largely to the general support of the immigration law of 1924.

A new problem of group identification, therefore, was created by the typical immigration of the last generation. Instead of facing national complications alone, the United States was confronted with the additional problem of race mixture. To get even a partial idea of all that this involved it is necessary to consider in some detail what the nature of race mixture is, and what results may be expected to follow when numbers of persons representing two or more different racial stocks are put in close territorial contact with each other.

We have observed that the qualities of race are carried in the germ plasm; that in a given stream of germ plasm they remain constant and unchanged from generation to generation; and that the only way they are modified is by putting them together in different combinations. The basic elements are never changed. It follows that, no matter how closely associated representatives of different races may be, there will be no change in the racial characteristics of any of them unless physical matings take place. Social contacts and associations alone, even though continued over many generations, will produce no alteration in racial qualities. . . .

The question then is, under what conditions do matings take place among associated racial groups, and what is the character of the products of those matings? The answer to the first part of this question is that some matings will take place under almost any conceivable conditions. Doctor Harry H. Laughlin, in a statement before the House Committee on Immigration and Naturalization, summed the matter up in the following words: "The committee of the Eugenics Research Association has had the matter in hand, and has failed to find a case in history in which two races have lived side by side for a number of generations and have maintained racial purity. Indeed, you can almost lay it down as an essential principle that race mixture takes place whenever there is racial contact."[1] The reasons for this are obvious. As has been observed, the prevailing opinion among scientists is that all races of men are descended from a single original stock, and are still to be considered as belonging to a single species. At any rate, all existing data seem to indicate that fertile unions are possible among all human races, and that the sexual impulse knows no racial boundaries. . . .

It follows that a country receiving large contingencies of foreigners of dif- 5
ferent races, especially if they are not too widely separated, need have no doubt as to the processes of race mixture—they will go on spontaneously without encouragement, and in spite of impediments. To the extent to which they are retarded—which may, to be sure, be a very important extent—the causes are to be found more in national feeling than in racial feeling. This will be considered

later. What such a country really needs to concern itself about is the effects of race mixture. This is a profoundly important problem concerning which, unfortunately, it is as yet impossible to state conclusions with certainty. The difficulties of carrying on experiments with human beings, and the scanty information that exists with reference to the "natural experiments" which have taken place at various times and places, leave the question as to the final effect of the mixing of human races quite unsettled. For our tentative conclusions we are forced to rely very largely upon the analogies furnished by experiments and observations upon the lower animals and plants. Fortunately, these are analogies in which we may place a high degree of confidence. For, as already repeatedly emphasized, race mixture is strictly a biological process, and in his biological processes man is closely akin to other types of living organisms. This is particularly striking in matters pertaining to reproduction, in which certain general principles run through all species, down almost to the very lowest forms. It is reasonable to assume, therefore, that facts of heredity which are universal, at least in the higher forms of animal life, will be carried over into the human field.

The phrase "race mixture" then, unlike so many popular phrases, accurately describes the process to which it is commonly applied. The product of the mating of different racial stocks really is a mixture. It may be compared to pouring together various chemically inert liquids—water, milk, wine, ink, etc. If the resulting mixture is thoroughly stirred, it will have the appearance of a smooth homogeneous liquid. But every separate molecule remains just what it was before the mixing took place; there is just as much water, just as much milk, just as much wine, just as much ink, as there was at the beginning. The analogy with race mixture is particularly close if some of the ingredients—like milk, for instance—are themselves mixtures, corresponding to mixed races. . . .

But two great questions remain: What kind of substance are you going to have when the fusion is complete? And what are you going to do with it?

Taking the latter of these queries first, it has been aptly observed that a melting pot implies a mold. The object in fusing the various ingredients is to get them into a plastic state so that they may be cast into a predetermined form which they will thereafter retain permanently. In this respect the analogy of the melting pot as applied in America obviously breaks down completely. The assumption is that the mixture itself is the final goal; there is nothing even remotely corresponding to a mold into which it is to be poured.

Much more important than this, however, is the question as to the character of the mixture itself. On this point, the champions of racial amalgamation for the most part beg the question. They seem to assume that if it can be proved that racial fusion will eventually be complete, that settles the matter. Nothing more need be said. They ignore the consideration as to whether the molten mass will be good for anything. True, certain sweeping statements are made to the effect that mixed races are superior to either of the originals, especially if the latter are not too far apart, and some efforts are made to bolster up this assertion by reference to various of the great civilizations of history. But these are mostly *ex cathedra* pronouncements, without a semblance of support by any factual evidence. It is, indeed, as already stated, a matter about which we know very little. The various cases of race mixture about which information is available are so complicated by social and environmental factors, often of a very unfavorable kind—as, for instance, in the case of the racial nondescripts in the seaports of the world—that it is practically impossible to isolate the results of purely racial factors. Consequently, it is easy to assert that the environmental factors are the ones responsible for the poor results, and that if these racial crosses had been given half a chance they would have been at least the equals of either of their parents.

Here, again, biology fortunately comes to our aid. The mixing of races among plants and animals has been carried on to a very vast extent, and many definite principles and rules have been worked out. Only the simplest and most fundamental need concern us here. First of all it should be recognized that many of the most beautiful, most useful, and generally finest types of plants and animals are crosses. The crossing of races is not necessarily disastrous. But these desirable crosses are either the result of long experimentation with various combinations or else of the union of carefully selected varieties chosen deliberately for certain traits which they possess and which promise to blend to advantage. No breeder would expect to improve his stock by random crossing with any variety that chanced to present itself. In other words, the desirable crosses are just as definite in their racial composition as the pure varieties.

More than this, the plant or animal breeder knows that the indiscriminate mixing of a large number of varieties can be expected to produce just one result —the mongrel. This is true even though the different varieties themselves may each be of a high type. The reason for this is clear. As remarked above, the germ plasm carried by every individual contains two classes of genes, first, those that are common to all the members of his species and give him the characteristic features of his species, and second, those that are peculiar to his own variety or race, and mark him off as a member of that particular kin-group. The varieties of the various species have been produced by specialization in the germ plasm. In wild plants and animals this specialization is produced by the general processes of natural selection; in domesticated creatures it is the result of the manipulations of the breeder, usually with a definite type of program in mind; and in man it is the outcome of the processes of race formation which have already been discussed. Accordingly, when a large number of different varieties are bred together the tendency is for the specialized genes to neutralize or cancel each other, and for the common general genes to support each other and intensify the corresponding qualities. The result to be looked for in the offspring is therefore a primitive, generalized type—often spoken of as a "reversion," "atavism," or "throwback."

There is every reason to believe that these rules hold good for man in his biological aspects. Many mixtures of human races have taken place, and some of them seem to have not only definite traits, but desirable traits according to certain widely accepted criteria. The combination of a large amount of Nordic with smaller proportions of Mediterranean and Alpine has certainly produced a type with outstanding characteristics; in the judgment of many persons (specifically those who are members of it) it is a type of peculiar excellence. This is the English type and it is the American type. It remained the prevailing type of the immigrants to America up till nearly the close of the nineteenth century. It is certainly a notable type, with a remarkable record of achievement in the past and promise of achievement for the future. Whether one likes the type or not, it is at least a known quantity. And it is a highly specialized type.

The change in the character of immigration which developed within the past generation and a half signalized the beginning of the process of mongrelization of this type. This process was not nearly so extreme in degree or rapid in rate as it would have been if we had not definitely excluded, by various means, the Chinese, Japanese, and Hindus as soon as their respective numbers began to reach serious proportions, and if the immigration of Negroes and Malays had not been negligible in proportions for reasons which need not delay us here. Nevertheless, the new arrivals were sufficiently different, not only in their racial proportions but in their basic elements, to threaten the existing type with annihilation. What the resulting product would have been at the end of two centuries can not be definitely determined, nor can it be positively asserted that it would have been inferior to the present type. The latter is largely a matter of taste. It is almost certain that it would have been a much less specialized type, resembling much more closely a more primitive stage of human evolution. If any one, contemplating this probability, is led to deplore the check to such a development he is of course fully entitled to his own views. . . .

The outstanding feature of the post-War sentiment of the American people was the conviction that the mere exclusion of the non-white races did not go far enough in racial discrimination. It was more and more strongly felt that there must also be some definite measures to check any further dilution of the typical American mixture, any alteration in the basic proportions of the various sections of the white race. It was realized that while there is not in any accurate sense an "American race," the components of the American people are decidedly limited in variety, and combined in characteristic proportions, and that this racial composite must be held largely responsible for the development of an American culture distinctly agreeable at least to Americans. The destruction of this characteristic racial foundation held potentialities of change in American institutions and cultural values which the bulk of the citizens did not care to face. A detailed examination into the causes of this alteration in attitude would take us too far afield. The War itself doubtless has a great deal to do with it. The bright searchlight which the great conflict turned upon social relations threw into bold relief the truth of many obscure problems. Probably the continued insistence of the special students of the question had its effect upon public opinion, bringing, among other things, a better comprehension of the real nature of racial factors. Whatever the causes, the fact is that racial considerations played a wholly unprecedented part in the post-War agitation about immigration. The popular voice demanded not only a positive reduction in the total volume of immigration, but a reapportionment of such immigration as there was so as to bring the "old immigration" once more into predominance, that is, to provide that immigration, however voluminous, should leave the racial proportions of the American people intact.

In seeking to meet this demand, Congress, most of the influential members of which were already thoroughly persuaded, adopted a device which had been suggested many years before, and which has now become widely familiar as the "percentage" or "quota" plan. This idea, as embodied in temporary legislation which ran for three years, provided that the total immigration of persons of a given nationality in any fiscal year should be limited to three per cent of the foreign-born persons of that nationality who were resident in the United States in 1910, as reported by the census of that year. The question will probably at once arise, why, if this legislation was a response to a demand for racial discrimination, was it expressed in terms of nationality? The answer is simple. As has already been shown, our actual knowledge of the racial composition of the American people, to say nothing of the various foreign groups, is so utterly inadequate that the attempt to use it as a basis of legislation would have led to endless confusion and intolerable litigation. So Congress substituted the term nationality, and defined nationality as country of birth. It is clear, then, that "nationality," as used in this connection, does not conform exactly to the correct definition of either nationality or race. But in effect it affords a rough approximation of the racial character of the different immigrant streams. Certainly it had the result of drawing the great bulk of our immigration once more from those countries out of which our original population had been built up.

This discriminatory effect of the quota principle was due to the fact that the old immigration, though coming in only small numbers in recent years, had been coming for so long that it had built up large reservoirs of foreign-born population by 1910, while the new immigration, though of enormous volume in the two decades just before the census of 1910, had been coming for so short a time that its base numbers were small. Thus a three per cent quota admitted considerably more immigrants from northwestern Europe than had actually been coming in recent years, but only a fraction of those from southern and eastern Europe.

By the time Congress was ready to put the principle of restriction in permanent form in 1924, advanced thought on the question had reached the point where it was recognized that quotas based on foreign-born residents exclusively were illogical and themselves discriminatory against the old stock. It was realized that the native population had at least as good a right as foreigners to be considered in determining the composition of the immigration of the future. If the goal was to preserve the racial character of the American people, why not go at it directly? The proposal was therefore made that instead of quotas based on foreign-born residents there should be a flat total of one hundred fifty thousand set for the quota countries, and that this total should be distributed among the quota countries in the same proportions as persons deriving their origin from each country respectively were found among the residents of the United States by the census of 1920. This is called the principle of "national origins," nationality once more being defined as country of birth. The task, then, is to make an estimate of the foreign sources of the total population of the country, clear back to the first white settlements, and to express this estimate in terms of the proportions of the population of 1920 attributable to each foreign country respectively. The annual total of one hundred fifty thousand is to be apportioned pro rata. In order that time might be allowed for the making of this estimate it was provided that this plan should not go into effect for three years, that is until the fiscal year beginning July 1, 1927. In the meantime, the old quota plan is continued, the percentage, however, being reduced to two, and the census of 1910 being replaced by that of 1890, which obviously has the effect of prodigiously favoring the old immigration, as it was meant that it should.

All of these provisions apply only to the Eastern Hemisphere. The countries of both of the American continents and the adjacent islands are at present left without numerical restriction at all. This plainly leaves a large loophole for racial admixture in the future. It also seems to convey a peculiar implication as to the relative desirability of the peoples of Mexico and the West Indies, for instance, and those of Italy or Roumania. Of course the fact is that something more than racial considerations led to the decision to exempt our neighbor countries from quantitative regulation. Nevertheless, the possibilities of serious race mixture involved in a heavy migration from the regions to the south of us are so great that there has already developed a vigorous sentiment in favor of bringing all countries under some form of quota regulation, and it is wholly probable that the next few years will see a definite maximum fixed to the migration of persons of every nationality.

As far as we can look into the future, then, it appears that the race problem in the United States will be confined to the unification of the various elements already established here. Further additions represented by the immigration of the future will involve few complications of a truly racial character. With reference to the sections of the white race already included in the American population, there is little doubt that the process of unification by amalgamation will go on steadily and irresistibly, until at the end of a few generations racial differentiation will have been practically wiped out, and the population of the country will once more present a racially homogeneous aspect. And we may hope that, diverse as the present varieties may be, the proportions of the definitely esoteric elements are sufficiently small so that the degree of resulting mongrelization will not be enough to reduce seriously the racial effectiveness of the American people.

Notes

1 Biological Aspects of Immigration, Sixty-Sixth Congress, Second Session, April 16–17, 1920, page 15.

QUESTIONS FOR DISCUSSION

1. *The Melting Pot Mistake* is an example of "nativist" prejudice. Explain how Fairchild manages to reduce the immigration question to a biological question. Cite examples of such ethnocentric attitudes today, worldwide and nationally, and discuss their consequences.

2. An analogy is a comparison that clarifies one thing by likening it to something more familiar. Locate two examples of Fairchild's use of analogy. Does their use strengthen his position?

3. Why does Fairchild approve of the changes in the immigration laws?

WRITING ASSIGNMENTS

1. Reaction Journal: Respond to Fairchild's ideas, drawing on your knowledge of immigration history, citizenship, and ethnic relations in the seventy years since Fairchild was writing.

2. Draw on your freewriting, your reading, and your experience and write a letter to Fairchild.

THE GERMAN-AMERICANS: THE GREAT WHITE WHALE

RICHARD O'CONNOR

Richard O'Connor (1915–1975) was a newspaperman, biographer, novelist, and author of popular histories. The subjects of his biographies include Bret Harte, Ambrose Bierce, O. Henry, and Jack London. His numerous other books include The Irish: A Portrait of a People *(1971) and* The German-Americans: An Informal History *(1968), from which the following piece is excerpted. Here O'Connor describes the assimilation of the single largest ethnic group in American society.*

◆ FREEWRITING

Freewrite for ten or fifteen minutes about the epigraph below. What is the "conception that shrivels . . . all lesser loyalties"? Is Hagedorn's description of America applicable today?

America is the many-made-one, the children of feuding races, creeds and nations, united by a conception that shrivels in its glow all lesser loyalties.

— *Hermann Hagedorn,* The Hyphenated American

The visible and physical Germanic influences on American life have now all but disappeared or been homogenized—gone with the little German bands that played on street corners, the German butchers in their sawed-off straw hats and white aprons, the beer gardens, the summer-night festivals, the May wine parades. From each national migration American culture has taken much, adapted it to its own purposes, and left only the faintest individual stamp to be imprinted for more than a generation or two on the ethnic group itself. The Fourth Rome —ours—has discovered and perfected to an almost unimaginable degree the process of absorption which the earlier struggled and failed to formulate.

You can search the old German sections of American cities and find only the faintest traces of their former way of life. The Yorkville section of Manhattan is still the entry port for the slender stream of immigrants from West Germany, and on its main street, East Eighty-sixth between Lexington and First Avenues, you can actually hear German spoken and, if you're lucky, see a Steuben Day parade or a bock beer festival. The names emblazoned on neon signs suggest that the old country hasn't been entirely forgotten: Kleine Konditorei (with something called, significantly, Touristen-wurst in the window), Cafe Hindenburg, Lorelei Bar, Bremen House, Mozart Hall, Kreutzer Hall, 86th Street Brauhaus. But there are almost as many French and Italian restaurants on that stretch of Eighty-sixth Street; the accordion players blare out the strains of "Lili Marlene" for Ivy League college students learning to drink beer chug-a-lug, and a sign advertising a *sängerfest* is placed in the window of a Chinese restaurant. The late Fritz Lieber Kuhn would hardly recognize the place.

It's the same with other communities once heavily Germanic, only more so. Milwaukee can boast of the world-famous Mader's restaurant and the hospitable taprooms in which the breweries entertain their visitors, but its citizens are more likely to haul you off to its venturesome new repertory theater which has never echoed with the ponderous dialogue of Sudermann.

A score of miles northwest of Milwaukee is the old village of Freistadt, founded in 1839 by twenty families driven from Germany by religious persecution. The settlement's first log cabin and the old stone Lutheran church have been lovingly preserved, along with a graveyard in which the names on the stone tablets have been all but erased by a century of wind and weather, but a new house on the outskirts bears the rather irreverent name "Gesund Heights."

Not far away, on the Milwaukee River, is the almost equally old settlement 5
of a colony of freethinkers who for eighty-odd years stoutly resisted all Christianizing influences and repelled all missionary efforts. The original settlers had their children married without religious sanction of any kind. When a nonconforming newcomer tried to raise funds for a local church, he was offered twice as much to discontinue his efforts and build his church elsewhere. The place was known as "The Godforsaken Village" and by those who attributed everything godless to the French as "Little Paris." Now Cotton Mather himself wouldn't be able to catch a whiff of heresy around Thiensville. A Catholic Church was established in 1919, but its founders were so uncertain of their reception that they

brought in a portable altar on a freight car. Ten years later the Lutherans moved in, and Thiensville now is merely another quiet suburb of Milwaukee.

In the old German enclave of South St. Louis there are only a few German restaurants and taverns to remind the visitor of the times when tapping the bung out of the first barrel of bock beer caused dancing in the streets and, earlier, when its German immigrant population shouldered muskets and saved Missouri, and possibly the West, for the Union. It's the same in Cincinnati, Chicago, Baltimore, San Francisco, Cleveland. And the old communistic colony of Amana, Iowa, now admits nonmembers to work on the production lines of a highly capitalistic enterprise, the Amana Refrigerator Company, which is operated by a communal corporation; dancing is allowed in the local high school, and plain living is becoming unfashionable.

The ideas which Germans brought from their homeland—which lack nothing in diversity, ranging from Marxism and freethinking to religious colonization, separate ethnic states, the first glimmerings of a world government—have made little real impact on the commonalty. But there has been a constant fluttering in the national dovecote often caused by German-Americans, who contributed more than their share to what Professor Richard Hofstadter describes in his recent work as *The Paranoid Style in American Politics.* Certainly they have not remembered the advice of Holderlin against "making the state a school of morals" and his warning that "the state has always been made a hell by man's wanting to make it his heaven." The one point at which German-American opinion was measurably decisive, perhaps as much as that of the New England abolitionists, was in demanding an end to human slavery.

The ferment of the German-Americanism of the last century ended with the century. What had been politically volatile is now inert. No other minority stirred up so much trouble for the establishment of its time as the Germans, and no other, despite the wholesale infusion of German blood in the composite American, has subsided so gratefully, so wholeheartedly into the national consensus. If that makes them honorary Anglo-Saxons, they are more than content. An attempt to present the rough edges of any surviving Germanism would be buffed away, by common consent, overnight. Of that element, all that remains is a vague feeling of best wishes for the Federal German Republic of West Germany and an equally vague but lingering sense of guilt for what happened in Germany under the Nazis.

If assimilation is the goal of all minorities, the German-Americans have succeeded beyond all others, with the Scandinavians a close second. They have all but become invisible. In their study of the leading minorities in New York City, *Beyond the Melting Pot,* Nathan Glazer and Daniel P. Moynihan have taken note of the phenomenon and called it an ethnic "disappearance." They explain that "while German influence is to be seen in virtually every aspect of the city's life, the Germans *as a group* are vanished. No appeals are made to the German vote, there are no German politicians in the sense that there are Irish or Italian politicians and, generally speaking, no German component in the structure of the ethnic interests of the city. The logical explanation of this development, in terms of the presumed course of American social evolution, is simply that the Germans have been 'assimilated' by the Anglo-Saxon center. To some extent this has happened. The German immigrants of the nineteenth century were certainly much closer to the old Americans than were the Irish who arrived in the same period. Many were Protestants, many were skilled workers or even members of the professions, and their level of education in general was high."

The Germans, Glazer and Moynihan believe, lacked the "homogeneity" of 10
other minorities, they were "split between Catholics and Protestants, liberals and conservatives, craftsmen and businessmen and laborers. They reflected, as it were, an entire modern society, not simply an element of one."

In the sense that all traces of their origin have been rubbed away, the German-Americans can pride themselves on an exemplary success. The effect of this transference, this merging of what had been separate Anglo-Saxon and German entities into a new Anglo-Teutonic amalgamation, sealed and solidified in the years since World War II, will be of great social and political significance. No less so for having been accomplished quietly and subtly, without conscious effort or formal negotiation. Together the old breed of English, Welsh and Scotch-Irish and those of German origin are in a position of unassailable dominance; they are the lords of government, industry, business, science, agriculture, education and the military establishment. The change from an Anglo-Saxon to an Anglo-Teutonic majority will have effects ranging far into the future. It will bear on the racial situation, on the American response to the challenges of the Communist and neutralist worlds, and most particularly on whether the United States, under grinding internal and external pressure, will veer toward an authoritarian state or will attempt to solve its problems in a more liberal, flexible and permissive manner.

QUESTIONS FOR DISCUSSION

1. In their study *Beyond the Melting Pot,* Nathan Glazer and Daniel P. Moynihan point out that the successful German assimilation amounts to an ethnic "disappearance." Explain why this group was able to assimilate so completely.
2. Think of another group in your region that has successfully assimilated into the majority culture. Discuss the cultural traces that have survived.

WRITING ASSIGNMENTS

1. Reaction Journal: Write a letter to a classmate in which you describe the cultural and ethnic mix in your own family. Discuss how the groups have blended to form a "family" as well as how they have assimilated into our larger society.
2. Choose a group that is on its way to "ethnic disappearance." Write an essay in which you account for its successful assimilation into the larger culture as well as the ethnic traces it still retains.

FROM SWEDISH EXODUS

LARS LJUNGMARK

Lars Ljungmark (b. 1927) is a professor of history at Göthenburg University in Sweden. His book Swedish Exodus *(1979) is a revision and translation (by Kermit B. Westerberg) of* Den stora unvandringen, *which appeared in 1965 as a course book for a Swedish radio series dealing with the immigration of 1.25 million Swedes to the United States. Ljungmark's earlier book,* For Sale—Minnesota, *deals with Captain Hans Mattson's recruitment of Swedes for the state of Minnesota. In the following excerpt from* Swedish Exodus *Ljungmark describes the voyage of immigrants from Göthenburg to New York and their journey west to Chicago and Minnesota. He points out how the expense of setting up farms and the loneliness of life on the frontier were eased by collective efforts among the settlers.*

◆ FREEWRITING

You have probably heard tales of immigrant loneliness and hardship from older members of your family or from their friends. Assume the role of one of these immigrants and freewrite for ten or fifteen minutes about your experiences. Focus on the reason for your immigration as well as on the experience itself.

The Atlantic Crossing

> I advise you not to take a lot of linen cloth. Instead bring plenty of tinware. Pack down some food so that you have something to eat, in case you cannot stomach what they give you at sea. Hardtack is good; also some cheese and dried meat. Take along a food basket. When you arrive in America there will be many who will approach you and offer you help. But you must watch your step, for there are plenty of scoundrels around who are ready to cheat the emigrants.
>
> *The advice of Maria Helene Jönsdotter to her sister, in a letter written from Iowa in 1869.*[1]

The first emigrants who traveled in groups usually sailed directly to America from Sweden. Most of them left from Gothenburg, although others chose Gävle, Söderhamn, or Stockholm as ports of embarkation. Accommodations on board these sailing vessels were primitive to say the least. Passengers occupied the steerage section located directly above the cargo hold with its load of iron bars. Although there was no set time schedule, it usually took between one and a half to two months to reach America.

During the 1850s and 1860s English and American shipping lines acquired control of the emigrant traffic. By the 1860s nearly all emigrants were sailing an indirect route by way of England, and around the middle of the decade steamship travel was common. The standard route for Swedish emigrants was by sea from Gothenburg to the English port city of Hull; by railroad from Hull to Liverpool; and, after several days' delay, by sea from Liverpool to the major immigrant harbors of New York, Boston, and Quebec.

Passenger comfort still left much to be desired at this time, and the Swedish press was particularly critical of conditions on board the English steamships. All passengers supplied their own food for the two-day journey across the North Sea to England. During the Atlantic crossing, however, all meals were provided free of charge. A typical weekly menu for steamship passengers in 1859 contained the following items:

> Sunday: a half pound of beef, porridge or pudding, dried fruit;
> Monday: pork, pea soup or boiled cabbage;
> Tuesday: beef, gruel or peas;
> Wednesday: beef, rice and molasses;
> Thursday: beef, porridge or pudding, dried fruit;
> Friday: beef, pork, pea soup or dried fruit;
> Saturday: herring or fish, peas or brown beans.

Each passenger was also allotted five pounds of white rusk biscuits per week and five and a half pounds of butter. Coffee was served in the morning and tea in the evening. Male passengers were entitled to one glass of *snaps* during the morning hours.

Though powered by steam, the Atlantic liners of the 1860s and 1870s were equipped with sails that could be used for additional speed in brisk tail winds. As the century wore on and steam engines became more refined, sail cloth and canvas disappeared from the scene. By the late 1880s, only steamships were plying the transatlantic route, and in the process the voyage had been reduced to an average of ten to twelve days per crossing.

It may be hard for us to recapture the full panorama of impressions that 5
greeted the Swedish landlubber during the Atlantic crossing. Some insights into the lives of midship passengers, however, are provided by a Swedish-English handbook called "The Emigrant's Interpreter" *(Utvandrarens Tolk)* which was published in 1881. . . .

The hatches closed off the passenger quarters in the steerage section from the upper deck area. Passenger quarters were usually very primitive, both in appearance and function. They might best be described as large, communal sleeping areas, which gave little or no chance of privacy. Conditions improved somewhat as time went by, and an arrangement of small berths or alcoves became a standard feature on most ships. Up until the 1890s, however, when mass Swedish emigration reached its culmination, passenger comfort remained far from satisfactory.

Swedish emigrants complained less about these hardships than they did about the difficulties in dealing with fellow passengers from other countries. They had particularly negative impressions of the Irish and often referred to them in letters published in the Swedish press as "rough and uncivilized creatures." Their opinions must have had an impact in some shipping circles, for by the early 1870s Swedish emigrant agents began to insert in their advertising brochures special notices that advised Swedes that they "would not be thrown together with the Irish." The strange menus on board ship were also a sore point of contention, and certain emigrant agents specified the fact that all food was prepared "according to Swedish tastes and customs."

Up until World War I the vast majority of Swedish emigrants booked passage on English and American ships that sailed to America by way of Hull and Liverpool. It was not until 1915 that the Swedish American Line opened a direct service route between Gothenburg and New York. From that point on the liners *Stockholm*, *Kungsholm*, and *Gripsholm* assumed major control of the Swedish emigrant traffic.

Upon arrival in New York, Swedish emigrants caught their first glimpse of America at the eastern edge of Manhattan Island, the site of an imposing architectural structure called Castle Garden. This served as the clearing station for new arrivals during the greater part of the 1800s, and it was here that emigrants passed through customs and immigration control before making contacts with railroad company agents. During the 1890s the American immigration authorities moved their headquarters to Ellis Island, at the entrance to New York harbor. Through its portals streamed the new waves of southern and eastern European immigrants around the turn of the century.

The Journey West

A combination of canal boats, river steamers, and railroads carried the early im- 10
migrants from the East Coast to destinations farther west. A typical itinerary during the 1850s included the following connections: New York to Albany (river steamer); Albany to Buffalo (train); and Buffalo to Chicago (steamer across the Great Lakes). Swedes bound for northern Minnesota during the 1870s often took the train from New York to Oswego on Lake Ontario, where they boarded a Great Lakes steamer for Duluth. From the mid 1860s, however, the railroads dominated the westward travel offering direct connections between New York and Chicago by special emigrant trains. "The Emigrant's Interpreter" came to the aid of Swedish passengers with a set of instructional phrases for railroad travel. One conversation read as follows:

At the railroad.
Where are the emigrant-cars?
Here sir. Step in.
Is this line much trafficed?

Yes very much.
Does it belong to a company?
. . .
May I offer you a cigarr?
. . .
Shall we not open the window?
. . .
Your railroads seem not to be built so solid as that in Europe.
This may be, but our cars are much more convenient; you may walk about as you like, through the whole train during the passage, and you enjoy of all conveniences as on a steamer.
Yes, that is true.

At the station.
Passengers for the West change cars.
What shall we do?
Get out all of you!
We stop here till Monday.

It is easy to imagine how the average Swedish emigrant must have felt when confronted with this type of elevating conversation. The surprise was probably all his own if he never attempted to learn it by heart. He had time to practice, however, as the trip to Chicago from New York at that time took four to five days, with no less than three stops every day for meals. For most Swedes Chicago was the great transit station on the road west, but those who settled there soon transformed it into the world's third largest Swedish city.

Land agencies, railroad companies, and state interest groups were not the only ones who looked for new customers among immigrant arrivals. Some reception committees included members of the established immigrant community, who represented Chicago's boarding houses, express offices, and currency exchanges. They descended on their unsuspecting countrymen with a display of feigned understanding or paternalistic authority and literally convinced them to surrender their baggage receipts, climb aboard hired carriages, and spend the night at a boarding house. It made no difference whether the new arrivals had ever planned to stay in Chicago or were anxious to meet other train connections. Far less fortunate were the immigrants who arrived in Chicago with absolutely no idea of where they were headed. They fell the frequent victims of fly-by-night operators and their disreputable business practices. These circumstances made it all the more important that railroad representatives and travelers' aids were on hand to meet every emigrant train.

Many Swedes were forced to stay in Chicago for the simple reason that their money had run out. The May and June issues of Chicago's Swedish newspapers carried such familiar headlines as "The destitute have already arrived," "Our countrymen are starving." An article from 1868 described the situation in more detail:

> Between June 29 and July 6 a total of 1,570 Scandinavians arrived in Chicago. Departures during this same period were approximately 800. At present 16 destitute families have found places to stay at the Michigan Central Railroad warehouse. They are waiting to hear from relatives in Minnesota and Wisconsin who have promised to send them money. Several weeks have gone by now, and they are no longer able to provide for themselves. One day last week they received food donations worth thirteen dollars. This week, however, 5 children in these families have died of cholera.[2]

However disturbing such scenes may have been, the Chicago Swedes showed great concern for their needy countrymen. At the end of the 1860s two Scandinavian relief associations were founded to handle such crises.

Whether or not they experienced the hardships of being stranded in a large and unfamiliar city, most Swedish immigrants eventually pushed on from Chicago for points farther west, primarily the older Swedish settlements and the rising industrial cities of the Upper Northwest. Along the way some of them received help from Swedish benevolent societies and relief committees, while others found relatives and friends to take care of them for the time being. There were always those, however, who would not be satisfied until they had established themselves on the frontier, and after a while they moved on to homestead areas, railroad teams, and lumberjack camps.

"There at last!"

Once they had chosen a place to settle, immigrant farmers and their families 15
spent the first months clearing the land and felling timber for their first rude cabins. When winter approached, the head of the family was usually forced to find work with the railroads or lumber companies, leaving his wife and children to manage on their own for months on end. Though conditioned by necessity, this separation was particularly hard on immigrant women, who had little or no knowledge of English and were accustomed to the simple but secure surroundings of the Swedish countryside. Other families, who arrived in this country with sufficient savings, spared themselves many of these hardships by buying land in more populated areas.

It was not unusual for three or four families to join forces on the American frontier by establishing a closely knit farm community. For the first few years all work was performed on a collective basis, each family helping the others in purchasing farm equipment, building log cabins, and breaking the land. When money ran short after the harvest season, one family head would stay in the area while the others looked elsewhere for work. Their earnings supplied food for the winter months and seed for the new planting season. This collective arrangement was only temporary, lasting three or four years, by which time each family had become self-sufficient.

Deciding where to settle was an important step for Swedish farm families, and many of them sent one or two relatives ahead to scout out the possibilities and make arrangements for the rest to follow. In most cases the responsibility fell to the husband or eldest son, who went to work for the railroads or lumber companies to earn ticket money for the immediate family. In some cases, however, daughters had an equally important role to play. One example of this comes from a letter written in 1869 by Hans Mattson to his wife in Red Wing, Minnesota. Describing his visit to a close relative in Skåne Mattson wrote:

> They are a very large family, and almost all of them want to join us in Minnesota. Pehr Pehrsson also wants to come, and he is sending his two youngest daughters with me this spring to scout the possibilities. They are terribly nice girls and would like to find positions with good American families. I am therefore asking you, Chersti, and sister Anna, to keep them in mind when you hear of such positions. I have promised them that they will have no difficulties in finding homes and friends in our midst. It is likely that the rest of the family will come to Lake Ripley at some later date.[3]

Most emigrants from rural Sweden were accustomed to hard work, but the unfamiliar surroundings and the language difficulties often created hardships for them during their first years in America. The experiences of one Swedish immigrant in 1869 were probably shared by many others.

> I went to work for the railroad with a promise of $2 per day. It wasn't until that moment that I realized who I really was—an immigrant, and nothing better than a "greenhorn." To begin with, the weather was so unbearably warm that few of us newcomers could stand the work. Our camps were located in the woods, and there we were fed and lodged for $4 a week which was deducted from our pay. But the food was so bad that none of us could live on it. When pay day came and we figured we had some $20 to our credit, in addition to food, all we were left with was $7. There was nobody around who could speak a word of English, and so it was impossible to change things.[4]

Another immigrant characterized his life as a lumberjack and railroad worker in these terms: "We've all read about and admired the exploits of King Karl XII and his men, but I can tell you that I've stamped about in the same frost-biting cold and weathered the same hardships glorified in the history books."

As time wore on, more and more Swedish immigrants settled in American cities, where they usually found relatives and friends who could help them adjust to their new surroundings. Those skilled in a special trade or profession often had difficulties in finding the same kind of work in America. "My countrymen taught me never to admit that I didn't know how a certain job was to be done."[5] That was the comment of one Swede who immigrated during the 1890s. Others like him probably followed the same rule-of-thumb. It came almost as a shock to most emigrants that their first wages were well below the average for American workers. This was usually a result of language difficulties and misunderstandings connected with labor contracts. Under these circumstances one can easily understand why many immigrants became homesick. This feeling, however, rarely found its way into letters back home but, instead, was shared with friends in America or committed to memory. One example of this is found in the diary of a Halland emigrant, who summarized his first six months in America with the following tersely worded sentences:

> I began work and earned a little money in Colchester, Connecticut, on June 14, 1888. I was 26 years old. It was hard work, it was terribly hot, and I was incredibly homesick for Sweden.
>
> Things have gotten a little better now, as I write. Colchester, January 3, 1889.
>
> Emil A. Johansson.[6]

Notes:

1. George M. Stephenson, ed. and trans., "Typical American Letters," in the Swedish Historical Society *Yearbook* 7 (1921–22), 93–95. The translation used here has been supplied by Kermit B. Westerberg.
2. *Hemlandet* (Chicago), May 5, 1868.
3. Letter from Hans Mattson to Mrs. Mattson, dated January 27, 1869. Hans Mattson Papers, Manuscript Department, Minnesota Historical Society, St. Paul, MN.
4. *Emigrationsutredningen, Bilaga* VII, p. 138.
5. Ibid., p. 174.
6. Fritjof Bengtsson, ed., *Halländska emigrantöden*, p. 215.

QUESTIONS FOR DISCUSSION

1. During the Swedish immigration wave of the last three decades of the nineteenth century, what was the emigrants' greatest complaint? Discuss other ethnic conflicts you are familiar with or have read about.
2. Throughout this selection Ljungmark cites excerpts from personal letters and diaries. Discuss what they add to the essay. Are there differences in tone and purpose between the letters and the diaries?

WRITING ASSIGNMENTS

1. Reaction Journal: Look over your freewriting for this selection. Continue to assume the immigrant role, but this time compose a letter to a friend from your homeland.
2. Meet with a group of three or four peers and discuss some of the experiences and feelings that are reflected in your freewriting. Plan an essay in which you discuss similarities and differences you have discovered among the immigrant groups.

FROM THE RISE OF DAVID LEVINSKY

ABRAHAM CAHAN

As a struggling Russian immigrant, Abraham Cahan (1860–1951) was intimately acquainted with New York's Lower East Side. He worked in its tenements, taught in its schools, helped to organize its early Jewish unions, and took part in the labor conflicts in its clothing industry. He founded and edited until his death the Jewish Daily Forward, *which became the most widely read Yiddish newspaper in the world. His novels, short stories, and literary criticism were notable contributions to the cultural life of the Lower East Side. Cahan's major novel,* The Rise of David Levinsky *(1917), from which the following excerpt is taken, reveals both the conflict of values in American Jewish life and the problems of adjustment that faced all immigrants entering the unfamiliar environment of opportunity and exploitation presented by an American city.*

◆ FREEWRITING

Think of a trip that you have taken. It needn't have been to another country, but it could have been. Recall your feelings as you were traveling and upon your arrival. Freewrite for ten or fifteen minutes using concrete details to chronicle your anticipation and excitement.

I was one of a multitude of steerage passengers on a Bremen steamship on my way to New York. Who can depict the feeling of desolation, homesickness, uncertainty, and anxiety with which an emigrant makes his first voyage across the ocean? I proved to be a good sailor, but the sea frightened me. The thumping of the engines was drumming a ghastly accompaniment to the awesome whisper of the waves. I felt in the embrace of a vast, uncanny force. And echoing through it all were the heart-lashing words:

"Are you crazy? You forget your place, young man!"

When Columbus was crossing the Atlantic, on his first great voyage, his men doubted whether they would ever reach land. So does many an America-bound emigrant to this day. Such, at least, was the feeling that was lurking in my heart while the Bremen steamer was carrying me to New York. Day after day passes and all you see about you is an unbroken waste of water, an unrelieved, a hopeless monotony of water. You know that a change will come, but this knowledge is confined to your brain. Your senses are skeptical.

In my devotions, which I performed three times a day, without counting a benediction before every meal and every drink of water, grace after every meal and a prayer before going to sleep, I would mentally plead for the safety of the ship and for a speedy sight of land. My scanty luggage included a pair of phylacteries and a plump little prayer-book, with the Book of Psalms at the end. The prayers I knew by heart, but I now often said psalms, in addition, particularly when the sea looked angry and the pitching or rolling was unusually violent. I would read all kinds of psalms, but my favorite among them was the 104th, generally referred to by our people as "Bless the Lord, O my soul," its opening words in the original Hebrew. It is a poem on the power and wisdom of God as manifested in the wonders of nature, some of its verses dealing with the sea. It is said by the faithful every Saturday afternoon during the fall and winter; so I could have recited it from memory; but I preferred to read it in my prayer-book. For it seemed as though the familiar words had changed their identity and meaning, especially those concerned with the sea. Their divine inspiration was now something visible and audible. It was not I who was reading them. It was as though the waves and the clouds, the whole far-flung scene of restlessness and mystery, were whispering to me:

"Thou who coverest thyself with light as with a garment, who stretchest out 5
the heavens like a curtain: who layeth the beams of his chambers in the waters: who maketh the clouds his chariot: who walketh upon the wings of the wind. . . . So is this great and wide sea wherein are things creeping innumerable, both small and great beasts. There go the ships: there is that leviathan whom thou hast made to play therein. . . ."

The relentless presence of Matilda in my mind worried me immeasurably, for to think of a woman who is a stranger to you is a sin, and so there was the danger of the vessel coming to grief on my account. And, as though to spite me, the closing verse of Psalm 104 reads, "Let the sinners be consumed out of the earth and let the wicked be no more." I strained every nerve to keep Matilda out of my thoughts, but without avail.

When the discoverers of America saw land at last they fell on their knees and a hymn of thanksgiving burst from their souls. The scene, which is one of the most thrilling in history, repeats itself in the heart of every immigrant as he comes in sight of the American shores. I am at a loss to convey the peculiar state of mind that the experience created in me.

When the ship reached Sandy Hook I was literally overcome with the beauty of the landscape.

The immigrant's arrival in his new home is like a second birth to him. Imagine a new-born babe in possession of a fully developed intellect. Would it ever forget its entry into the world? Neither does the immigrant ever forget his entry into a country which is, to him, a new world in the profoundest sense of the term and in which he expects to pass the rest of his life. I conjure up the gorgeousness of the spectacle as it appeared to me on that clear June morning: the magnificent verdure of Staten Island, the tender blue of sea and sky, the dignified bustle of passing craft—above all, those floating, squatting, multitudinously windowed palaces which I subsequently learned to call ferries. It was all so utterly unlike anything I had ever seen or dreamed of before. It unfolded itself like a divine revelation. I was in a trance or in something closely resembling one.

"This, then, is America!" I exclaimed, mutely. The notion of something en- 10
chanted which the name had always evoked in me now seemed fully borne out.

In my ecstasy I could not help thinking of Psalm 104, and, opening my little prayer-book, I glanced over those of its verses that speak of hills and rocks, of grass and trees and birds.

My transport of admiration, however, only added to my sense of helplessness and awe. Here, on shipboard, I was sure of my shelter and food, at least. How was I going to procure my sustenance on those magic shores? I wished the remaining hour could be prolonged indefinitely.

Psalm 104 spoke reassuringly to me. It reminded me of the way God took care of man and beast: "Thou openest thine hand and they are filled with good." But then the very next verse warned me that "Thou hidest thy face, they are troubled: thou takest away their breath, they die." So I was praying God not to hide His face from me, but to open His hand to me; to remember that my mother had been murdered by Gentiles and that I was going to a strange land. When I reached the words, "I will sing unto the Lord as long as I live: I will sing praise to my God while I have my being," I uttered them in a fervent whisper.

My unhappy love never ceased to harrow me. The stern image of Matilda blended with the hostile glamour of America.

One of my fellow-passengers was a young Yiddish-speaking tailor named 15
Gitelson. He was about twenty-four years old, yet his forelock was gray, just his forelock, the rest of his hair being a fine, glossy brown. His own cap had been blown into the sea and the one he had obtained from the steerage steward was too small for him, so that gray tuft of his was always out like a plume. We had not been acquainted more than a few hours, in fact, for he had been seasick throughout the voyage and this was the first day he had been up and about. But then I had seen him on the day of our sailing and subsequently, many times, as he wretchedly lay in his berth. He was literally in tatters. He clung to me like a lover, but we spoke very little. Our hearts were too full for words.

As I thus stood at the railing, prayer-book in hand, he took a look at the page. The most ignorant "man of the earth" among our people can read holy tongue (Hebrew), though he may not understand the meaning of the words. This was the case with Gitelson.

"Saying, 'Bless the Lord, O my soul'?" he asked, reverently. "Why this chapter of all others?"

"Because— Why, just listen." With which I took to translating the Hebrew text into Yiddish for him.

He listened with devout mien. I was not sure that he understood it even in his native tongue, but, whether he did or not, his beaming, wistful look and the deep sigh he emitted indicated that he was in a state similar to mine.

When I say that my first view of New York Bay struck me as something not 20
of this earth it is not a mere figure of speech. I vividly recall the feeling, for example, with which I greeted the first cat I saw on American soil. It was on the Hoboken pier, while the steerage passengers were being marched to the ferry. A

large, black, well-fed feline stood in a corner, eying the crowd of new-comers. The sight of it gave me a thrill of joy. "Look! there is a cat!" I said to Gitelson. And in my heart I added, "Just like those at home!" For the moment the little animal made America real to me. At the same time it seemed unreal itself. I was tempted to feel its fur to ascertain whether it was actually the kind of creature I took it for.

We were ferried over to Castle Garden. One of the things that caught my eye as I entered the vast rotunda was an iron staircase rising diagonally against one of the inner walls. A uniformed man, with some papers in his hands, ascended it with brisk, resounding step till he disappeared through a door not many inches from the ceiling. It may seem odd, but I can never think of my arrival in this country without hearing the ringing footfalls of this official and beholding the yellow eyes of the black cat which stared at us at the Hoboken pier.

The harsh manner of the immigration officers was a grievous surprise to me. As contrasted with the officials of my despotic country, those of a republic had been portrayed in my mind as paragons of refinement and cordiality. My anticipations were rudely belied. "They are not a bit better than Cossacks," I remarked to Gitelson. But they neither looked nor spoke like Cossacks, so their gruff voices were part of the uncanny scheme of things that surrounded me. These unfriendly voices flavored all America with a spirit of icy inhospitality that sent a chill through my very soul.

The stringent immigration laws that were passed some years later had not yet come into existence. We had no difficulty in being admitted to the United States, and when I was I was loath to leave the Garden.

Many of the other immigrants were met by relatives, friends. There were cries of joy, tears, embraces, kisses. All of which intensified my sense of loneliness and dread of the New World. The agencies which two Jewish charity organizations now maintain at the Immigrant Station had not yet been established. Gitelson, who like myself had no friends in New York, never left my side. He was even more timid than I. It seemed as though he were holding on to me for dear life. This had the effect of putting me on my mettle.

"Cheer up, old man!" I said, with bravado. "America is not the place to be a ninny in. Come, pull yourself together."

In truth, I addressed these exhortations as much to myself as to him; and so far, at least, as I was concerned, my words had the desired effect.

I led the way out of the big Immigrant Station. As we reached the park outside we were pounced down upon by two evil-looking men, representatives of boarding-houses for immigrants. They pulled us so roughly and their general appearance and manner were so uninviting that we struggled and protested until they let us go—not without some parting curses. Then I led the way across Battery Park and under the Elevated railway to State Street. A train hurtling and panting along overhead produced a bewildering, a daunting effect on me. The active life of the great strange city made me feel like one abandoned in the midst of a jungle. Where were we to go? What were we to do? But the presence of

Gitelson continued to act as a spur on me. I mustered courage to approach a policeman, something I should never have been bold enough to do at home. As a matter of fact, I scarcely had an idea what his function was. To me he looked like some uniformed nobleman—an impression that in itself was enough to intimidate me. With his coat of blue cloth, starched linen collar, and white gloves, he reminded me of anything but the policemen of my town. I addressed him in Yiddish, making it as near an approach to German as I knew how, but my efforts were lost on him. He shook his head. With a witheringly dignified grimace he then pointed his club in the direction of Broadway and strutted off majestically.

"He's not better than a Cossack, either," was my verdict.

At this moment a voice hailed us in Yiddish. Facing about, we beheld a middle-aged man with huge, round, perpendicular nostrils and a huge, round, deep dimple in his chin that looked like a third nostril. Prosperity was written all over his smooth-shaven face and broad-shouldered, stocky figure. He was literally aglow with diamonds and self-satisfaction. But he was unmistakably one of our people. It was like coming across a human being in the jungle. Moreover, his very diamonds somehow told a tale of former want, of a time when he had landed, an impecunious immigrant like myself; and this made him a living source of encouragement to me.

"God Himself has sent you to us," I began, acting as the spokesman; but he gave no heed to me. His eyes were eagerly fixed on Gitelson and his tatters.

"You're a tailor, aren't you?" he questioned him.

My steerage companion nodded. "I'm a ladies' tailor, but I have worked on men's clothing, too," he said.

"A ladies' tailor?" the well-dressed stranger echoed, with ill-concealed delight. "Very well; come along. I have work for you."

That he should have been able to read Gitelson's trade in his face and figure scarcely surprised me. In my native place it seemed to be a matter of course that one could tell a tailor by his general appearance and walk. Besides, had I not divined the occupation of my fellow-passenger the moment I saw him on deck?

As I learned subsequently, the man who accosted us on State Street was a cloak contractor, and his presence in the neighborhood of Castle Garden was anything but a matter of chance. He came there quite often, in fact, his purpose being to angle for cheap labor among the newly arrived immigrants.

We paused near Bowling Green. The contractor and my fellow-passenger were absorbed in a conversation full of sartorial technicalities which were Greek to me, but which brought a gleam of joy into Gitelson's eye. My former companion seemed to have become oblivious of my existence.

As we resumed our walk up Broadway the bejeweled man turned to me.

"And what was your occupation? You have no trade, have you?"

"I read Talmud," I said, confusedly.

"I see, but that's no business in America," he declared. "Any relatives here?"

"No."

"Well, don't worry. You will be all right. If a fellow isn't lazy nor a fool he has no reason to be sorry he came to America. It'll be all right."

"All right" he said in English, and I conjectured what it meant from the context. In the course of the minute or two which he bestowed upon me he uttered it so many times that the phrase engraved itself upon my memory. It was the first bit of English I ever acquired.

The well-dressed, trim-looking crowds of lower Broadway impressed me as a multitude of counts, barons, princes. I was puzzled by their preoccupied faces and hurried step. It seemed to comport ill with their baronial dress and general high-born appearance.

In a vague way all this helped to confirm my conception of America as a unique country, unlike the rest of the world.

When we reached the General Post-Office, at the end of the Third Avenue surface line, our guide bade us stop.

"Walk straight ahead," he said to me, waving his hand toward Park Row. "Just keep walking until you see a lot of Jewish people. It isn't far from here." With which he slipped a silver quarter into my hand and made Gitelson bid me good-by.

The two then boarded a big red horse-car.

I was left with a sickening sense of having been tricked, cast off, and abandoned. I stood watching the receding public vehicle, as though its scarlet hue were my last gleam of hope in the world. When it finally disappeared from view, my heart sank within me. I may safely say that the half-hour that followed is one of the worst I experienced in all the thirty-odd years of my life in this country.

The big, round nostrils of the contractor and the gray forelock of my young steerage-fellow haunted my brain as hideous symbols of treachery.

With twenty-nine cents in my pocket (four cents was all that was left of the sum which I had received from Matilda and her mother) I set forth in the direction of East Broadway.

QUESTIONS FOR DISCUSSION

1. Few writers have matched Cahan in the ability to convey the anticipation, excitement, and bewilderment of the immigrant's arrival in America. Point out specific techniques and details that bring out these feelings.

2. Cahan makes recurring references to Psalm 104. Discuss its significance. Discuss the importance of religious belief to Cahan and, in the next selection, Rembiénska.

WRITING ASSIGNMENTS

1. Reaction Journal: Think once again of the journey you focused on in your freewriting. This time write about the disillusionment and bewilderment you may have experienced after the excitement of the arrival had subsided.

2. Assume the role of Cahan and write a letter of less than five hundred words to Matilda in which you describe your crossing and your arrival. Try to include experiences and feelings similar to those Cahan uses in his narrative.

A POLISH PEASANT GIRL IN AMERICA

ALEKSANDRA REMBIÉNSKA

As part of the new immigration from eastern and southern Europe after the turn of the century, more than three and one quarter million men and women came to the United States from Poland. Most of these people were from peasant origins and had little or no English and few marketable skills. The women generally sought work as domestic help, often among their own nationality. The following letter from one peasant girl in America, Aleksandra Rembiénska, describes the extremely circumscribed life and long hours of labor that characterized the lives of immigrants in domestic service in the early twentieth century.

◆ FREEWRITING

Recall a time when you were away from home for an extended period or when a loved one was away from you. Freewrite for ten or fifteen minutes about the memories you had of your home and about your new circumstances. What, for example, did you remember most about your family and friends?

Brooklyn, N.Y.
October 14th [1911]

My dear Family,

In the first words "Praised be Jesus Christus" . . .

And now, dear parents, I inform you that I am in good health. Thanks to God, which I wish you also with my truest heart. And now I am on duty and I do well, I have fine food, only I must work from 6 o'clock in the morning to 10 o'clock at night and I have $13 a month. And now, dear parents, I implore you don't grieve about me, thinking that I am without money. . . . As it is I have spent more than 50 rubles on myself for the coming winter, and nevertheless I am not so beautifully dressed as all the others. Only I regret to spend money, I prefer to put it away rather than buy luxurious dresses like Olcia Kubaczónna [her cousin] who buys herself a new dress every week and doesn't look at money and doesn't think what can happen. She thinks only how to dress and says she does not need to think about anything more. But I am not of the same opinion, I think about my home. I have brothers and sisters and I intend to help them all to come to America. First I will take Stasia, let her hope to come in the early spring about Easter, and let her be patient and wait. I would take her now, but in winter there is no such work as in spring. And now, dear parents, you may hope that I will send you for Christmas 10 rubles. I would not send them, but thanks to God, I have some, and I have work, so every month money comes to me, I only ask our Lord Jesus for health, and then no bad fortune will overtake me. I go dressed like a lady only I am sad, because I must remain at home and cannot go outside at all. I am not far away from Uncle and Auntie Kubacz, but I cannot see them more than twice a month.

And now I have nothing more to write, and bow to you, dear family, and I wish you every good. May God grant that this letter finds you in good health, and I ask for a quick answer.

Aleksandra Rembiénska

And I request you, dear parents, send letters with stamps, because I have great difficulties. A letter with stamps arrives sooner.

O dear Family, I write this letter to you on November 20, and I got 5
your letter on November 20. And now, dear family, I inform you that I am in good health, thanks to our Lord God, and I wish to you also happiness, health, and good success. And now, dear family, I let you know that in October I did not work for two weeks, because I did not like to work for nothing, and I left this place because they wouldn't pay me more than $12. And now I am in another place, only far away from Uncle, for it is necessary to travel an hour to Uncle; but Uncle comes to meet me every second Sunday. I am well enough, I receive now $16 for this month. I don't feel lonesome, because there are two of us girls in this household. The master and mistress are Polish. We are near a Church and they send us every Sunday at 6 o'clock in the morning to the mass. We have every day 18 rooms to clean, and to cook and to wash linen. It is myself who washes every week about 300 pieces of linen, and iron it. But I have easy washing because I don't wash with my hands; the machine washes alone, I only cover the linen with soap and put 5 pieces in the machine at once. After 15 minutes I take them out and put in new ones, and so by noon I wash all the 300 pieces. I iron 4 days, from 6 A.M. to 8 P.M. I do nothing but iron those 4 days. Dear parents, you admonish me so severely to be on my guard. But I cannot and do not walk about the city. I cannot even go out before the house for a while. I am in America and I do not even know whether it is America, only it seems to me as if there were only a single house in the whole world and nothing more, only walls and very few people.

And now, dear family, I have nothing more to write, but only I send you low bows and wish you every good.

I have received the photograph for which I thank you very heartily.

QUESTIONS FOR DISCUSSION

1. Imagine that you had the opportunity to meet Rembiénska twenty years after the experiences she describes in her letters to her family. Make a list of five questions you would ask her.
2. What one word best describes the mood of Rembiénska's letter? Be prepared to defend your choice in class discussion.

WRITING ASSIGNMENTS

1. Reaction Journal: Assume the role of one of Rembiénska's parents. Write a letter in response to the two letters in this selection. Address some of the immigrant's problems that the letters raise.
2. Borrow from your freewriting as you write a letter of your own to a family member or loved one. Make the content appropriate to your own experiences, but imitate the style of Rembiénska as you write.

From Africa—The Dreamers and Liberators

JEAN-PAUL SARTRE DESCRIBED African Americans as the "true existential people." Separated from a truly African identity by acculturation and from a purely American identity by race, American blacks have had to search for ways in which to identify themselves. In his 1903 collection of essays, *The Souls of Black Folk*, W. E. B. Du Bois observed that "it is a peculiar sensation, this double-consciousness, this sense of always looking at one's self through the eyes of others. . . . One ever feels his twoness—an American, a Negro, two souls, two thoughts, two unreconciled strivings." This "double consciousness" has continued to inform black experience even to the present day. One finds it in Stokely Carmichael's explanation of the Black Power movement as an effort at self-definition, an attempt to proclaim from within the black experience a black identity that is "energetic, determined, intelligent" to counter the ascribed qualities of "lazy, apathetic, dumb." It appears as well in Shelby Steele's admission that he wears a tie and carries a briefcase on the first day of class so that his students will know he is the teacher.

The position of blacks in the American ethnic spectrum is marked by a history of enslavement and a painfully slow progress toward social justice. The first African slaves were brought to the West Indies in 1501, and the permanent settlement of Africans in North America began when a Dutch ship sold twenty blacks to the English colonists at Jamestown in 1619. The majority of slaves brought to British North America and French Louisiana, approximately 427,000 in all, arrived during the seventy-year period between 1741 and 1810. During the peak years of the slave trade, 1741–1760, over 5,000 slaves per year were brought into territories that would become the United States. The last legal slave was brought into the country in 1807, nearly sixty years before the abolition of slavery in 1865. Because of this lag between the closing of the slave trade and the emancipation, the first generation of blacks to live in freedom in the United States was composed almost entirely of individuals three and four generations removed from their African roots.

Most of the slaves brought to British North America came from the West African coast between Senegal and southern Nigeria. The shock of enslavement and the brutality of the middle passage across the Atlantic from West Africa to America have been described in slave narratives such as that by the Ibo Olaudah Equiano. Since the slave population represented many different groups who identified themselves with such tribes as the Ibo, the Malinké, and the Yoruba and since their primary social unit was the small rural village, the notion of a primary unified African or black identity took years to emerge. Kinship ties were the essential social and psychological element and defined economic, political, and social behaviors. The significance of these kinship ties magnified the horror of slavery that routinely caused the separation of families.

Early frontier conditions permitted a lack of strict racial segregation and afforded many opportunities for cultural interchange as black and Indian slaves and indentured white servants labored together, and the conditions and terms of enslavement varied considerably from place to place. Some blacks were held as indentured servants instead of slaves and were permitted a degree of economic freedom that allowed them to amass property after serving their terms. Gradually, however, the black slave's status was distinguished from that of Indian slaves and indentured servants as colonies passed laws making the black's term of slavery lifelong and hereditary through the mother. The lives of plantation slaves were marked by deprivation in the basic needs of shelter, clothing, and food, as well as by exhausting labor. Nor were conditions much better for the approximately 5 percent of black slaves who worked in mines and factories. In the first half of the nineteenth century, the average life expectancy for black slaves was 12 percent below that of white Americans.

Antislavery sentiment, which had always existed in the North, became stronger following the War of Independence, and several New England states incorporated the principles of human equality into their constitutions. Pennsylvania began to abolish slavery in 1783, followed by New York and New Jersey in 1799 and 1804. Freedom, however, when it finally came, even when achieved nationally and unconditionally through the Thirteenth Amendment, did not bring immediate relief to the plight of African-Americans. For many blacks, physical bondage was replaced by economic restrictions as they became sharecroppers with little chance of escaping a state of permanent indebtedness. Thus began a steady migration from the countryside to the cities, where blacks faced rigorous job competition from immigrants as well as laws and ordinances that served to make racial discrimination legal.

Economic problems were not the only difficulties confronting black Americans. Although black citizenship had been guaranteed by the Fourteenth Amendment in 1868 and the right to vote by the Fifteenth Amendment in 1869, blacks still found their freedoms severely curtailed. The late nineteenth century saw in the South the passage of Jim Crow laws, which enforced the segregation of public places and discriminatory literacy tests and poll taxes, which, in effect, rescinded the right of most blacks to vote. By 1910 eleven southern states had passed laws disenfranchising blacks, and the Supreme Court's narrow interpretations relentlessly weakened the civil rights of black Americans. The *Plessy* v. *Ferguson* decision of 1896, which allowed for "separate but equal" schools for blacks and whites, gave official sanction to segregation, a policy that was not successfully challenged until 1954, when the decision in *Brown* v. *Board of Education of Topeka, Kansas* declared the concept of separate but equal inherently unequal and hence unconstitutional.

Continued lack of opportunity in the South made migration an attractive option for blacks in the early nineteenth century. When World War I put a virtual end to European immigration in 1914, jobs opened up in northern cities and the Great Northern Migration commenced. This migration continued through the 1920s and resumed again during World War II, changing the economic, social, and political fabric of American society, as more than one million blacks left the South between the wars to seek fuller citizenship in the North. Between 1910 and 1920 the black population of New York increased by 61,400 (67 percent), Chicago by 65,000 (147 percent), and Detroit by 36,240 (611 percent). Most blacks ended up in low-paying unskilled jobs in foundries and meatpacking companies, on the railroads, and as servants, porters, and janitors. The higher wages in northern cities were often consumed by the higher cost of living. Like the immigrants before and after them, urban blacks often paid high rents for overcrowded, unsanitary housing. Economic gain was not, however, the only motivation for moving north. Better educational opportunities and greater personal freedom were powerful motivators as well. In Chicago the schools, formally integrated since 1874 and subject to Illinois compulsory education law, epitomized northern opportunity. This access to education was a critical factor in the development of black consciousness and in the creation of a literate black audience for the 1920s "Renaissance generation" of black writers who wrote for their own people rather than as interpreters and apologists for their culture to whites. Although there was racially motivated violence in northern as well as southern cities—eighty people were killed during rioting in East St. Louis in 1917 and the summer of 1919 saw violent racial confrontations in twenty-five northern cities and towns—conditions and opportunities were better than those prevailing in the South, and the vast majority of blacks who came north stayed.

De facto segregation in the cities of the North resulted in the emergence of black ghettos. One historian of Detroit's black community has observed that the "push of discrimination" and the "pull of ethnocentrism" combined to keep blacks in ghettos. This concentration and isolation proved to be a source of vitality and self-consciousness as blacks were forced to take business and professional initiatives in their own communities. In *The New Negro*, published in 1925, Alain Locke observed that "in Harlem, Negro life is seizing upon its first chances for group expression and self-determination." In the new northern urban environments, black media expanded significantly. The Pittsburgh *Courier*, the Chicago *Defender*, the NAACP's *Crisis* magazine, and the National Urban League's *Opportunity* achieved national circulation. The Harlem Renaissance of the 1920s was a creative celebration of the vitality and traditions of the African-

American community. More novels and volumes of black poetry were published during the 1920s than in the fifty years before the First World War. Writers such as Countée Cullen, Jean Toomer, Zora Neale Hurston, Langston Hughes, and Claude McKay established a tradition of strong black voices speaking to both black and white audiences. Black theater came to Broadway with Willis Richardson's *The Chip Woman's Fortune* (1923), Garland Anderson's *Appearances* (1925), and Wallace Thurman's *Harlem* (1929).

Although the Renaissance was short-lived, business enterprise and cultural activity alike suffering from the Great Depression, it signaled the existence of a serious black presence within American society, an independent presence less interested than previous generations in making accommodations to white society. A black professional elite had arisen and continued to expand its leadership in the black community. By the 1950s the achievements of black leaders, the solidarity of the black community, and the considerable political and economic power it represented could not be denied. Between 1937 and 1954 the Supreme Court expanded its previously narrow interpretations of the fourteenth amendment. President Truman's Civil Rights Commission declared the doctrine of separate but equal invalid in 1947, an initiative that received the sanction of the Supreme Court decision in *Brown* v. *Board of Education.*

Even after the reversal of the separate but equal doctrine, segregation in schools continued to be supported by the governors of several southern states. Their refusal to comply with the new national standards increased racial tensions and led to renewed determination on the part of blacks to secure their civil rights. Ten years after the *Brown* decision, less than 2 percent of southern black students attended integrated schools. Riots accompanying the enrollment of James Meredith at the University of Mississippi in 1962 required the dispatch of federal troops, and the intervention of the Justice Department was necessary to insure registration of two black students at the University of Alabama in 1963.

Education was not the only arena of confrontation. The yearlong Montgomery (Alabama) bus boycott, sparked by Rosa Parks's refusal to give up her seat to a white man on a Montgomery city bus in 1955, brought the effective use of direct action to national attention and initiated an era of increasing civil rights protests. The success of the boycott in bringing about a Supreme Court ban on segregated public transportation led to the founding of the Southern Christian Leadership Conference (SCLC) under the leadership of the Reverend Martin Luther King, Jr., in 1957. Direct action spread, highlighted by sit-ins and street demonstrations, such as the protest in Birmingham, Alabama, that occasioned King's "Letter from Birmingham Jail," which characterized the civil disobedience practiced by civil rights activists in the early 1960s. The anticipated changes in the political balance of power in the South, sparked by voter registration and school desegregation and resistance to them, brought about increased racial violence. Other racial tensions erupted in riots in Harlem in 1964, Watts in 1965, Cleveland in 1967, and Detroit in 1968. The intervention of 70,000 troops was required to quell the rioting that erupted in 125 cities following the assassination of Martin Luther King, Jr., on April 4, 1968.

As resistance to progress continued, guaranteeing the rights of black citizens repeatedly required special legislation. While the right to use public facilities belongs to all citizens, the Civil Rights Bill of 1964 was necessary in order for blacks to exercise that right. Similarly, the Voting Rights Act of 1965 was necessary to guarantee that right to blacks, and only through the 1968 Open Housing Act were blacks guaranteed equal access to housing.

There were factions in the black community that felt that what Martin Luther King, Jr., called the "horse and buggy pace" at which American blacks were proceeding toward attaining their civil rights was not being sufficiently challenged by the moderate position represented by King's SCLC and the more conservative NAACP and National Urban League. CORE (Congress of Racial Equality), which had emerged in 1942 as a result of direct-action campaigns in the North and upper South, began to shed its original commitment to pacifism in the 1960s under the leadership of young black activists who advocated militant direct action. Elijah Muhammad's Nation of Islam, for whom Malcolm X was a prominent spokesperson, spread an aggressive message which portrayed whites as the natural enemies of black advancement. At a mass meeting in Selma, Alabama, in 1965, Malcolm X, then one of the most outspoken opponents of nonviolence, announced that "whites better be glad Martin Luther King is rallying the people because other forces are waiting to take over if he fails." After breaking with Elijah Muhammad's Nation of Islam, Malcolm founded the Organization of Afro-American Unity, a group whose aim was the attainment of human rights and whose stance was that of militant black nationalism. OAAU sought to convert blacks from nonviolence, which Malcolm X consistently disparaged, to active self-defense. He pledged to send "armed guerrillas" anywhere that "black people's lives are threatened by white bigots." In an interview with the Pittsburgh *Courier*, Malcolm proclaimed, "Anyone who wants to follow me and my movement has got to be ready to go to jail, to the hospital, and to the cemetery before he can be truly free." Toward the end of his life, Malcolm moderated his denunciation of white Americans and attempted to revise his image as "a fomentor of violence." In clarifying his "new position" he remarked, "I don't speak against the sincere, well-meaning, good white people. I have learned that there *are* some." While declaring that he did not condone "wanton violence," however, he still maintained that violence is an appropriate response to "being brutalized."

Stokely Carmichael and Charles V. Hamilton saw the politics of Black Power as the only hope for the United States to resolve its racial problems and avoid prolonged guerrilla warfare. In their book *Black Power: The Politics of Liberation in America* (1967), Carmichael and Hamilton spoke of the necessity for blacks to build the unified political and ideological base that would allow them to operate from a position of power rather than weakness. They defined Black Power as "black self-determination and self-identity" and identified its goals as the full participation of black people in the making of policies that affect them and recognition and affirmation by blacks of the virtues inherent in themselves and in their culture. Today the movement toward full participation frequently has a broader base, expanding to accommodate the concerns of other groups that have struggled for recognition and acceptance. In his speech before the Democratic National Convention in 1992, the Reverend Jesse Jackson reminded the nation that "we are more interdependent than we realize. . . . Red, yellow, brown, black and white" and pledged that his Rainbow Coalition "will continue to build a movement for economic justice in this land."

What is the most appropriate and productive relationship between the black community and the white community is still a matter of heated debate. Some urge separation, group solidarity, and confrontation; others advocate integration, individual initiative, and accommodation. Among the latter is Shelby Steele, who remarks in "Individualism and Black Identity" that he believes "it is time for blacks to begin the shift from a wartime to a peacetime identity." Achieving such "peacetime identities" for all its citizens, an admirable goal for society as a whole, will involve the creation of a climate in which individual initiative does not threaten the integrity of group identity and the desire to maintain group solidarity does not restrict individual achievement. As they seek ways of maintaining their black identity while taking advantage of their expanding opportunities in contemporary society, African-Americans still struggle with the "double consciousness" Du Bois articulated at the turn of the century.

FROM INCIDENTS IN THE LIFE OF A SLAVE GIRL

HARRIET JACOBS

Harriet Ann Jacobs (1813–1897) was born into slavery in North Carolina. After the death of her first mistress, who had treated her with gentleness and taught her to read and write, fifteen-year-old Jacobs found herself harassed by her master, who continually made sexual advances to her. In order to protect herself, Jacobs began a liaison with a white lawyer, by whom she had two children. Hounded by her master, Jacobs went into hiding in 1835, first in a swamp and then, for seven years, in the attic of her grandmother's shed. Although she escaped to the North in 1842, Jacobs's freedom remained in jeopardy with the strengthening of the Fugitive Slave Law in 1850. In Boston, Jacobs became acquainted with members of the antislavery movement, one of whom encouraged her to write her life's story. When Incidents in the Life of a Slave Girl: Written by Herself *appeared in 1861, it was under the pseudonym Linda Brent. The book was advertised as having been edited by a famous white author of the time, the abolitionist Lydia Maria Child. In the preface, the author explains that she had used fictitious names for people and places in her narrative and that its purpose was "to arouse the women of the North to a realizing sense of the condition of two million of women at the South, still in bondage, suffering what [she] suffered, and most of them far worse." The following excerpt describes Jacobs's efforts to escape both the sexual advances of her master and the jealous temper of his second wife.*

◆ FREEWRITING

In "Harlem," African-American poet Langston Hughes asks: "What happens to a dream deferred?" Freewrite for ten or fifteen minutes about the question and how it may apply to the subtitle of this chapter, "The Dreamers and Liberators." Try to find the poem in your library and comment on the several possible answers Hughes offers in response to his question.

I would ten thousand times rather that my children should be the half-starved paupers of Ireland than to be the most pampered among the slaves of America. I would rather drudge out my life on a cotton plantation, till the grave opened to give me rest, than to live with an unprincipled master and a jealous mistress. The felon's home in a penitentiary is preferable. He may repent, and turn from the error of his ways, and so find peace; but it is not so with a favorite slave. She is not allowed to have any pride of character. It is deemed a crime in her to wish to be virtuous.

Mrs. Flint possessed the key to her husband's character before I was born. She might have used this knowledge to counsel and to screen the young and the innocent among her slaves; but for them she had no sympathy. They were the objects of her constant suspicion and malevolence. She watched her husband with unceasing vigilance; but he was well practised in means to evade it. What he could not find opportunity to say in words he manifested in signs. He invented more than were ever thought of in a deaf and dumb asylum. I let them pass, as if I did not understand what he meant; and many were the curses and threats bestowed on me for my stupidity. One day he caught me teaching myself to write. He frowned, as if he was not well pleased; but I suppose he came to the conclusion that such an accomplishment might help to advance his favorite scheme. Before long, notes were often slipped into my hand. I would return them, saying, "I can't read them, sir." "Can't you?" he replied; "then I must read them to you." He always finished the reading by asking, "Do you understand?" Sometimes he would complain of the heat of the tea room, and order his supper to be placed on a small table in the piazza. He would seat himself there with a well-satisfied smile, and tell me to stand by and brush away the flies. He would eat very slowly, pausing between the mouthfuls. These intervals were employed in describing the happiness I was so foolishly throwing away, and in threatening me with the penalty that finally awaited my stubborn disobedience. He boasted much of the forbearance he had exercised towards me, and reminded me that there was a limit to his patience. When I succeeded in avoiding opportunities for him to talk to me at home, I was ordered to come to his office, to do some errand. When there, I was obliged to stand and listen to such language as he saw fit to address to me. Sometimes I so openly expressed my contempt for him that he would become violently enraged, and I wondered why he did not strike me. Circumstanced as he was, he probably thought it was better policy to be forbearing. But the state of things grew worse and worse daily. In desperation I told him that I must and would apply to my grandmother for protection. He threatened me with death, and worse than death, if I made any complaint to her. Strange to say, I did not despair. I was naturally of a buoyant disposition, and always I had a hope of somehow getting out of his clutches. Like many a poor, simple slave before me, I trusted that some threads of joy would yet be woven into my dark destiny.

I had entered by sixteenth year, and every day it became more apparent that my presence was intolerable to Mrs. Flint. Angry words frequently passed between her and her husband. He had never punished me himself, and he would not allow any body else to punish me. In that respect, she was never satisfied; but, in her angry moods, no terms were too vile for her to bestow upon me. Yet I, whom she detested so bitterly, had far more pity for her than he had, whose duty it was to make her life happy. I never wronged her, or wished to wrong her; and one word of kindness from her would have brought me to her feet.

After repeated quarrels between the doctor and his wife, he announced his intention to take his youngest daughter, then four years old, to sleep in his apartment. It was necessary that a servant should sleep in the same room, to be on hand if the child stirred. I was selected for that office, and informed for what purpose that arrangement had been made. By managing to keep within sight of people, as much as possible, during the day time, I had hitherto succeeded in eluding my master, though a razor was often held to my throat to force me to change this line of policy. At night I slept by the side of my great aunt, where I felt safe. He was too prudent to come into her room. She was an old woman, and had been in the family many years. Moreover, as a married man, and a professional man, he deemed it necessary to save appearances in some degree. But he resolved to remove the obstacle in the way of his scheme; and he thought he had planned it so that he should evade suspicion. He was well aware of how much I prized my refuge by the side of my old aunt, and he determined to dispossess me of it. The first night the doctor had the little child in his room alone. The next morning, I was ordered to take my station as nurse the following night. A kind Providence interposed in my favor. During the day Mrs. Flint heard of this new arrangement, and a storm followed. I rejoiced to hear it rage.

After a while my mistress sent for me to come to her room. Her first question was, "Did you know you were to sleep in the doctor's room?"

"Yes, ma'am."

"Who told you?"

"My master."

"Will you answer truly all the questions I ask?"

"Yes, ma'am."

"Tell me, then, as you hope to be forgiven, are you innocent of what I have accused you?"

"I am."

She handed me a Bible, and said, "Lay your hand on your heart, kiss this holy book, and swear before God that you tell me the truth."

I took the oath she required, and I did it with a clear conscience.

"You have taken God's holy word to testify your innocence," said she. "If you have deceived me, beware! Now take this stool, sit down, look me directly in the face, and tell me all that has passed between your master and you."

I did as she ordered. As I went on with my account her color changed frequently, she wept, and sometimes groaned. She spoke in tones so sad, that I was touched by her grief. The tears came to my eyes; but I was soon convinced that her emotions arose from anger and wounded pride. She felt that her marriage vows were desecrated, her dignity insulted; but she had no compassion for the poor victim of her husband's perfidy. She pitied herself as a martyr; but she was incapable of feeling for the condition of shame and misery in which her unfortunate, helpless slave was placed.

Yet perhaps she had some touch of feeling for me; for when the conference was ended, she spoke kindly, and promised to protect me. I should have been much comforted by this assurance if I could have had confidence in it; but my experiences in slavery had filled me with distrust. She was not a very refined woman, and had not much control over her passions. I was an object of her jealousy, and, consequently, of her hatred; and I knew I could not expect kindness or confidence from her under the circumstances in which I was placed. I could not blame her. Slaveholders' wives feel as other women would under similar circumstances. The fire of her temper kindled from small sparks, and now the flame became so intense that the doctor was obliged to give up his intended arrangement.

I knew I had ignited the torch, and I expected to suffer for it afterwards; but I felt too thankful to my mistress for the timely aid she rendered me to care much about that. She now took me to sleep in a room adjoining her own. There I was an object of her especial care, though not of her especial comfort, for she spent many a sleepless night to watch over me. Sometimes I woke up, and found her bending over me. At other times she whispered in my ear, as though it was her husband who was speaking to me, and listened to hear what I would answer. If she startled me, on such occasions, she would glide stealthily away; and the next morning she would tell me I had been talking in my sleep, and ask who I was talking to. At last, I began to be fearful for my life. It had been often threatened; and you can imagine, better than I can describe, what an unpleasant sensation it must produce to wake up in the dead of night and find a jealous woman bending over you. Terrible as this experience was, I had fears that it would give place to one more terrible.

My mistress grew weary of her vigils; they did not prove satisfactory. She changed her tactics. She now tried the trick of accusing my master of crime, in my presence, and gave my name as the author of the accusation. To my utter astonishment, he replied, "I don't believe it; but if she did acknowledge it, you tortured her into exposing me." Tortured into exposing him! Truly, Satan had no difficulty in distinguishing the color of his soul! I understood his object in making this false representation. It was to show me that I gained nothing by seeking the protection of my mistress; that the power was still all in his own hands. I pitied Mrs. Flint. She was a second wife, many years the junior of her husband; and the hoary-headed miscreant was enough to try the patience of a wiser and better woman. She was completely foiled, and knew not how to proceed. She would gladly have had me flogged for my supposed false oath; but, as I have already stated, the doctor never allowed any one to whip me. The old sinner was politic. The application of the lash might have led to remarks that would have exposed him in the eyes of his children and grandchildren. How often did I rejoice that I lived in a town where all the inhabitants knew each other? If I had been on a remote plantation, or lost among the multitude of a crowded city, I should not be a living woman at this day.

The secrets of slavery are concealed like those of the Inquisition. My master 20
was, to my knowledge, the father of eleven slaves. But did the mothers dare to tell who was the father of their children? Did the other slaves dare to allude to it, except in whispers among themselves? No, indeed! They knew too well the terrible consequences.

My grandmother could not avoid seeing things which excited her suspicions. She was uneasy about me, and tried various ways to buy me; but the never-changing answer was always repeated: "Linda does not belong to *me*. She is my daughter's property, and I have no legal right to sell her." The conscientious man! He was too scrupulous to *sell* me; but he had no scruples whatever about committing a much greater wrong against the helpless young girl placed under his guardianship, as his daughter's property. Sometimes my persecutor would ask me whether I would like to be sold. I told him I would rather be sold to any body than to lead such a life as I did. On such occasions he would assume the air of a very injured individual, and reproach me for my ingratitude. "Did I not take you into the house, and make you the companion of my own children?" he would say. "Have I ever treated you like a negro? I have never allowed you to be punished, not even to please your mistress. And this is the recompense I get, you ungrateful girl!" I answered that he had reasons of his own for screening me from punishment, and that the course he pursued made my mistress hate me and persecute me. If I wept, he would say, "Poor child! Don't cry! don't cry! I will make peace for you with your mistress. Only let me arrange matters in my own way. Poor, foolish girl! you don't know what is for your own good. I would cherish you. I would make a lady of you. Now go, and think of all I have promised you."

I did think of it.

Reader, I draw no imaginary pictures of southern homes. I am telling you the plain truth. Yet when victims make their escape from this wild beast of Slavery, northerners consent to act the part of bloodhounds, and hunt the poor fugitive back into his den, "full of dead men's bones, and all uncleanness." Nay, more, they are not only willing, but proud, to give their daughters in marriage to slaveholders. The poor girls have romantic notions of a sunny clime, and of flowering vines that all the year round shade a happy home. To what disappointments are they destined! The young wife soon learns that the husband in whose hands she has placed her happiness pays no regard to his marriage vows. Children of every shade of complexion play with her own fair babies, and too well she knows that they are born unto him of his own household. Jealousy and hatred enter the flowery home, and it is ravaged of its loveliness.

Southern women often marry a man knowing that he is the father of many little slaves. They do not trouble themselves about it. They regard such children as property, as marketable as the pigs on the plantation; and it is seldom that they do not make them aware of this by passing them into the slave-trader's hands as soon as possible, and thus getting them out of their sight. I am glad to say there are some honorable exceptions.

I have myself known two southern wives who exhorted their husbands to free those slaves toward whom they stood in a "parental relation;" and their request was granted. These husbands blushed before the superior nobleness of their wives' natures. Though they had only counselled them to do that which it was their duty to do, it commanded their respect, and rendered their conduct more exemplary. Concealment was at an end, and confidence took the place of distrust.

Though this bad institution deadens the moral sense, even in white women, to a fearful extent, it is not altogether extinct. I have heard southern ladies say of

Mr. Such a one, "He not only thinks it no disgrace to be the father of those little niggers, but he is not ashamed to call himself their master. I declare, such things ought not to be tolerated in any decent society!"

QUESTIONS FOR DISCUSSION

1. What did Jacobs feel was the single most reprehensible thing about being a slave, even the so-called favorite slave?

2. Examine the tone of this selection. Use evidence from the text to illustrate the audience Jacobs had in mind.

3. Explain the complexity of the relationship between Jacobs and her master's second wife, Mrs. Flint. Why, for example, did Jacobs pity the woman who detested her?

WRITING ASSIGNMENTS

1. Reaction Journal: Harriet Jacobs writes that starvation and imprisonment are preferable to enslavement. Write two or three paragraphs about the special horrors inflicted on enslaved women. Make specific references to the experience of Harriet Jacobs.

2. In the introduction we point out that African-Americans, "separated from a truly African identity by acculturation and from a purely American identity by race . . . have had to search for ways in which to identify themselves." W. E. B. Du Bois called this "peculiar sensation," this "double-consciousness . . . this sense of always looking at one's self through the eyes of others." Demonstrate how this sense is reflected in Jacobs's narrative.

LETTER FROM BIRMINGHAM JAIL*

MARTIN LUTHER KING, JR.

Martin Luther King, Jr. (1929–1968), was born in Atlanta, Georgia. He did his undergraduate work at Morehouse College and received a B.D. from the Crozer Theological

* Author's Note: This response to a published statement by eight fellow clergymen from Alabama (Bishop C. C. J. Carpenter, Bishop Joseph A. Durick, Rabbi Hilton L. Grafman, Bishop Paul Hardin, Bishop Holan B. Harmon, the Reverend George M. Murray, the Reverend Edward V. Ramage and the Reverend Earl Stallings) was composed under somewhat constricting circumstances. Begun on the margins of the newspaper in which the statement appeared while I was in jail, the letter was continued on scraps of writing paper supplied by a friendly Negro trusty, and concluded on a pad my attorneys were eventually permitted to leave me. Although the text remains in substance unaltered, I have indulged in the author's prerogative of polishing it for publication.

Seminary in Chester, Pennsylvania, and his doctorate in systematic theology from Boston University. Shortly after becoming pastor of the Drexel Avenue Baptist Church in Montgomery, Alabama, King led a 382-day bus boycott there that led to the 1956 Supreme Court decision declaring segregation on public transportation illegal. In 1963, as leader of SCLC (Southern Christian Leadership Conference), King organized a campaign against segregation in Birmingham, Alabama. The nonviolent direct action protests that characterized King's actions throughout his career as a civil rights leader were strongly opposed by the city's police and administration as well as by white moderates who condemned King's actions because, although his actions were nonviolent, they incited violence. King was one of the leaders of the August 1963 March on Washington, where he delivered his famous "I Have a Dream" speech. In 1964 he was awarded the Nobel Peace Prize, the youngest person ever to receive this honor. King was assassinated in April 1968 in Memphis, Tennessee, where he had gone to support a strike by municipal workers. His books include Stride Toward Freedom *(1958) and* Where Do We Go from Here: Chaos or Community? *(1967).* A Testament of Hope *(1968), and* The Words of Martin Luther King *(1983) are collections of his shorter writing. In "Letter from Birmingham Jail," King defends his actions of civil disobedience in Birmingham and maintains that people have "a moral responsibility to disobey unjust laws." The letter is addressed to a group of white clergymen who had written a letter to a local newspaper praising the actions of the Birmingham police force and urging King to call off the demonstrations.*

◆ FREEWRITING

In his famous defense of civil disobedience, King argues that "injustice anywhere is a threat to justice everywhere." Before reading this selection, freewrite for ten or fifteen minutes in response to this assertion. Draw concrete illustrations from your own experiences and observations about injustices.

April 16, 1963

My Dear Fellow Clergymen:

While confined here in the Birmingham city jail, I came across your recent statement calling my present activities "unwise and untimely." Seldom do I pause to answer criticism of my work and ideas. If I sought to answer all the criticisms that cross my desk, my secretaries would have little time for anything other than such correspondence in the course of the day, and I would have no time for constructive work. But since I feel that you are men of genuine good will and that your criticisms are sincerely set forth, I want to try to answer your statement in what I hope will be patient and reasonable terms.

I think I should indicate why I am here in Birmingham, since you have been influenced by the view which argues against "outsiders coming in." I have the honor of serving as president of the Southern Christian Leadership Conference, an organization operating in every southern state, with headquarters in Atlanta, Georgia. We have some eighty-five affiliated organizations across the South, and one of them is the Alabama Christian Movement for Human Rights. Frequently we share staff, educational and financial resources with our affiliates. Several months ago the affiliate here in Birmingham asked us to be on call to engage in a nonviolent direct-action program if such were deemed necessary. We readily consented, and when the hour came we lived up to our promise. So I, along with several members of my staff, am here because I was invited here. I am here because I have organizational ties here.

But more basically, I am in Birmingham because injustice is here. Just as the prophets of the eighth century B.C. left their villages and carried their "thus saith the Lord" far beyond the boundaries of their home towns, and just as the Apostle Paul left his village of Tarsus and carried the gospel of Jesus Christ to the far corners of the Greco-Roman world, so am I compelled to carry the gospel of freedom beyond my own home town. Like Paul, I must constantly respond to the Macedonian call for aid.

Moreover, I am cognizant of the interrelatedness of all communities and states. I cannot sit idly by in Atlanta and not be concerned about what happens in Birmingham. Injustice anywhere is a threat to justice everywhere. We are caught in an inescapable network of mutuality, tied in a single garment of destiny. Whatever affects one directly, affects all indirectly. Never again can we afford to live with the narrow, provincial "outside agitator" idea. Anyone who lives inside the United States can never be considered an outsider anywhere within its bounds.

You deplore the demonstrations taking place in Birmingham. But your 5
statement, I am sorry to say, fails to express a similar concern for the conditions that brought about the demonstrations. I am sure that none of you would want to rest content with the superficial kind of social analysis that deals merely with effects and does not grapple with underlying causes. It is unfortunate that demonstrations are taking place in Birmingham, but it is even more unfortunate that the city's white power structure left the Negro community with no alternative.

In any nonviolent campaign there are four basic steps: collection of the facts to determine whether injustices exist; negotiation; self-purification; and direct action. We have gone through all these steps in Birmingham. There can be no gainsaying the fact that racial injustice engulfs this community. Birmingham is probably the most thoroughly segregated city in the United States. Its ugly record of brutality is widely known. Negroes have experienced grossly unjust treatment in the courts. There have been more unsolved bombings of Negro homes and churches in Birmingham than in any other city in the nation. These are the hard, brutal facts of the case. On the basis of these conditions, Negro leaders sought to negotiate with the city fathers. But the latter consistently refused to engage in good-faith negotiation.

Then, last September, came the opportunity to talk with leaders of Birmingham's economic community. In the course of the negotiations, certain promises were made by the merchants—for example, to remove the stores' humiliating racial signs. On the basis of these promises, the Reverend Fred Shuttlesworth and the leaders of the Alabama Christian Movement for Human

Rights agreed to a moratorium on all demonstrations. As the weeks and months went by, we realized that we were the victims of a broken promise. A few signs, briefly removed, returned; the others remained.

As in so many past experiences, our hopes had been blasted, and the shadow of deep disappointment settled upon us. We had no alternative except to prepare for direct action, whereby we would present our very bodies as a means of laying our case before the conscience of the local and the national community. Mindful of the difficulties involved, we decided to undertake a process of self-purification. We began a series of workshops on nonviolence, and we repeatedly asked ourselves: "Are you able to accept blows without retaliating?" "Are you able to endure the ordeal of jail?" We decided to schedule our direct-action program for the Easter season, realizing that except for Christmas, this is the main shopping period of the year. Knowing that a strong economic-withdrawal program would be the by-product of direct action, we felt that this would be the best time to bring pressure to bear on the merchants for the needed change.

Then it occurred to us that Birmingham's mayoral election was coming up in March, and we speedily decided to postpone action until after election day. When we discovered that the Commissioner of Public Safety, Eugene "Bull" Connor, had piled up enough votes to be in the run-off, we decided again to postpone action until the day after the run-off so that the demonstrations could not be used to cloud the issues. Like many others, we waited to see Mr. Connor defeated, and to this end we endured postponement after postponement. Having aided in the community need, we felt that our direct-action program could be delayed no longer.

You may well ask: "Why direct action? Why sit-ins, marches and so forth? 10
Isn't negotiation a better path?" You are quite right in calling for negotiation. Indeed, this is the very purpose of direct action. Nonviolent direct action seeks to create such a crisis and foster such a tension that a community which has constantly refused to negotiate is forced to confront the issue. It seeks so to dramatize the issue that it can no longer be ignored. My citing the creation of tension as part of the work of the nonviolent-resister may sound rather shocking. But I must confess that I am not afraid of the word "tension." I have earnestly opposed violent tension, but there is a type of constructive, nonviolent tension which is necessary for growth. Just as Socrates felt that it was necessary to create a tension in the mind so that individuals could rise from the bondage of myths and half-truths to the unfettered realm of creative analysis and objective appraisal, so must we see the need for nonviolent gadflies to create the kind of tension in society that will help men rise from the dark depths of prejudice and racism to the majestic heights of understanding and brotherhood.

The purpose of our direct-action program is to create a situation so crisis-packed that it will inevitably open the door to negotiation. I therefore concur with you in your call for negotiation. Too long has our beloved Southland been bogged down in a tragic effort to live in monologue rather than dialogue.

One of the basic points in your statement is that the action that I and my associates have taken in Birmingham is untimely. Some have asked: "Why didn't you give the new city administration time to act?" The only answer that I can give to this query is that the new Birmingham administration must be prodded about as much as the outgoing one, before it will act. We are sadly mistaken if we feel that the election of Albert Boutwell as mayor will bring the millennium to Birmingham. While Mr. Boutwell is a much more gentle person than Mr. Connor, they are both segregationists, dedicated to maintenance of the status quo. I have hope that Mr. Boutwell will be reasonable enough to see the futility of massive resistance to desegregation. But he will not see this without pressure from devotees of civil rights. My friends, I must say to you that we have not made a single gain in civil rights without determined legal and nonviolent pressure. Lamentably, it is an historical fact that privileged groups seldom give up their privileges voluntarily. Individuals may see the moral light and voluntarily give up their unjust posture; but, as Reinhold Niebuhr has reminded us, groups tend to be more immoral than individuals.

We know through painful experience that freedom is never voluntarily given by the oppressor; it must be demanded by the oppressed. Frankly, I have yet to engage in a direct-action campaign that was "well timed" in the view of those who have not suffered unduly from the disease of segregation. For years now I have heard the word "Wait!" It rings in the ear of every Negro with piercing familiarity. This "Wait" has almost always meant "Never." We must come to see, with one of our distinguished jurists, that "justice too long delayed is justice denied."

We have waited for more than 340 years for our constitutional and God-given rights. The nations of Asia and Africa are moving with jetlike speed toward gaining political independence, but we still creep at horse-and-buggy pace toward gaining a cup of coffee at a lunch counter. Perhaps it is easy for those who have never felt the stinging darts of segregation to say, "Wait." But when you have seen vicious mobs lynch your mothers and fathers at will and drown your sisters and brothers at whim; when you have seen hate-filled policemen curse, kick and even kill your black brothers and sisters; when you see the vast majority of your twenty million Negro brothers smothering in an airtight cage of poverty in the midst of an affluent society; when you suddenly find your tongue twisted and your speech stammering as you seek to explain to your six-year-old daughter why she can't go to the public amusement park that has just been advertised on television, and see tears welling up in her eyes when she is told that Funtown is closed to colored children, and see ominous clouds of inferiority beginning to form in her little mental sky, and see her beginning to distort her personality by developing an unconscious bitterness toward white people; when you have to concoct an answer for a five-year-old son who is asking: "Daddy, why do white people treat colored people so mean?"; when you take a cross-country drive and find it necessary to sleep night after night in the uncomfortable corners of your automobile because no motel will accept you; when you are humiliated day in and day out by nagging signs reading "white" and "colored"; when your first name becomes "nigger," your middle name becomes "boy" (however old you are) and your last name becomes "John," and your wife and mother are never given the respected title "Mrs."; when you are harried by day and haunted by night by the fact that you are a Negro, living constantly at tiptoe stance, never quite knowing what to expect next, and are plagued with inner fears and outer resentments; when you are forever fighting a degenerating sense of "nobodiness"—then you will understand why we find it difficult to wait. There comes a time when the cup of endurance runs over, and men are no longer willing to be plunged into the abyss of despair. I hope, sirs, you can understand our legitimate and unavoidable impatience.

You express a great deal of anxiety over our willingness to break laws. This is 15
certainly a legitimate concern. Since we so diligently urge people to obey the Supreme Court's decision of 1954 outlawing segregation in the public schools, at first glance it may seem rather paradoxical for us consciously to break laws. One may well ask: "How can you advocate breaking some laws and obeying others?" The answer lies in the fact that there are two types of laws: just and unjust. I would be the first to advocate obeying just laws. One has not only a legal but a moral responsibility to obey just laws. Conversely, one has a moral responsibility to disobey unjust laws. I would agree with St. Augustine that "an unjust law is no law at all."

Now, what is the difference between the two? How does one determine whether a law is just or unjust? A just law is a man-made code that squares with the moral law or the law of God. An unjust law is a code that is out of harmony with the moral law. To put it in the terms of St. Thomas Aquinas: An unjust law is a human law that is not rooted in eternal law and natural law. Any law that uplifts human personality is just. Any law that degrades human personality is unjust. All segregation statutes are unjust because segregation distorts the soul and damages the personality. It gives the segregator a false sense of superiority and the segregated a false sense of inferiority. Segregation, to use the terminology of the Jewish philosopher Martin Buber, substitutes an "I–it" relationship for an "I–thou" relationship and ends up relegating persons to the status of things. Hence segregation is not only politically, economically and sociologically unsound, it is morally wrong and sinful. Paul Tillich has said that sin is separation. Is not segregation an existential expression of man's tragic separation, his awful estrangement, his terrible sinfulness? Thus it is that I can urge men to obey the 1954 decision of the Supreme Court, for it is morally right; and I can urge them to disobey segregation ordinances, for they are morally wrong.

Let us consider a more concrete example of just and unjust laws. An unjust law is a code that a numerical or power majority group compels a minority group to obey but does not make binding on itself. This is *difference* made legal. By the same token, a just law is a code that a majority compels a minority to follow and that it is willing to follow itself. This is *sameness* made legal.

Let me give another explanation. A law is unjust if it is inflicted on a minority that, as a result of being denied the right to vote, had no part in enacting or devising the law. Who can say that the legislature of Alabama which set up that state's segregation laws was democratically elected? Throughout Alabama all sorts of devious methods are used to prevent Negroes from becoming registered voters, and there are some counties in which, even though Negroes constitute a majority of the population, not a single Negro is registered. Can any law enacted under such circumstances be considered democratically structured?

Sometimes a law is just on its face and unjust in its application. For instance, I have been arrested on a charge of parading without a permit. Now, there is nothing wrong in having an ordinance which requires a permit for a parade. But such an ordinance becomes unjust when it is used to maintain segregation and to deny citizens the First-Amendment privilege of peaceful assembly and protest.

I hope you are able to see the distinction I am trying to point out. In no 20
sense do I advocate evading or defying the law, as would the rabid segregationist. That would lead to anarchy. One who breaks an unjust law must do so openly, lovingly, and with a willingness to accept the penalty. I submit that an individual who breaks a law that conscience tells him is unjust, and who willingly accepts the penalty of imprisonment in order to arouse the conscience of the community over its injustice, is in reality expressing the highest respect for law.

Of course, there is nothing new about this kind of civil disobedience. It was evidenced sublimely in the refusal of Shadrach, Meshach and Abednego* to obey the laws of Nebuchadnezzar, on the ground that a higher moral law was at stake. It was practiced superbly by the early Christians, who were willing to face hungry lions and the excruciating pain of chopping blocks rather than submit to certain unjust laws of the Roman Empire. To a degree, academic freedom is a reality today because Socrates practiced civil disobedience. In our own nation, the Boston Tea Party represented a massive act of civil disobedience.

We should never forget that everything Adolf Hitler did in Germany was "legal" and everything the Hungarian freedom fighters** did in Hungary was "illegal." It was "illegal" to aid and comfort a Jew in Hitler's Germany. Even so, I am sure that, had I lived in Germany at the time, I would have aided and comforted my Jewish brothers. If today I lived in a Communist country where certain principles dear to the Christian faith are suppressed, I would openly advocate disobeying that country's antireligious laws.

I must make two honest confessions to you, my Christian and Jewish brothers. First, I must confess that over the past few years I have been gravely disappointed with the white moderate. I have almost reached the regrettable conclusion that the Negro's great stumbling block in his stride toward freedom is not the White Citizen's Councilor or the Ku Klux Klanner, but the white moderate, who is more devoted to "order" than to justice; who prefers a negative peace which is the absence of tension to a positive peace which is the presence of justice; who constantly says: "I agree with you in the goal you seek, but I cannot agree with your methods of direct action"; who paternalistically believes he can set the timetable for another man's freedom; who lives by a mythical concept of

* *The Book of Daniel* records that they refused to bow down to a golden image set up by Nebuchadnezzar.

** In 1956, Hungarians who wanted to end Soviet power revolted in the streets and were suppressed by Soviet armed forces.

time and who constantly advises the Negro to wait for a "more convenient season." Shallow understanding from people of good will is more frustrating than absolute misunderstanding from people of ill will. Lukewarm acceptance is much more bewildering than outright rejection.

I had hoped that the white moderate would understand that law and order exist for the purpose of establishing justice and that when they fail in this purpose they become the dangerously structured dams that block the flow of social progress. I had hoped that the white moderate would understand that the present tension in the South is a necessary phase of the transition from an obnoxious negative peace, in which the Negro passively accepted his unjust plight, to a substantive and positive peace, in which all men will respect the dignity and worth of human personality. Actually, we who engage in nonviolent direct action are not the creators of tension. We merely bring to the surface the hidden tension that is already alive. We bring it out in the open, where it can be seen and dealt with. Like a boil that can never be cured so long as it is covered up but must be opened with all its ugliness to the natural medicines of air and light, injustice must be exposed, with all the tension its exposure creates, to the light of human conscience and the air of national opinion before it can be cured.

In your statement you assert that our actions, even though peaceful, must be 25
condemned because they precipitate violence. But is this a logical assertion? Isn't this like condemning a robbed man because his possession of money precipitated the evil act of robbery? Isn't this like condemning Socrates because his unswerving commitment to truth and his philosophical inquiries precipitated the act by the misguided populace in which they made him drink hemlock? Isn't this like condemning Jesus because his unique God-consciousness and never-ceasing devotion to God's will precipitated the evil act of crucifixion? We must come to see that, as the federal courts have consistently affirmed, it is wrong to urge an individual to cease his efforts to gain his basic constitutional rights because the quest may precipitate violence. Society must protect the robbed and punish the robber.

I had also hoped that the white moderate would reject the myth concerning time in relation to the struggle for freedom. I have just received a letter from a white brother in Texas. He writes: "All Christians know that the colored people will receive equal rights eventually, but it is possible that you are in too great a religious hurry. It has taken Christianity almost two thousand years to accomplish what it has. The teachings of Christ take time to come to earth." Such an attitude stems from a tragic misconception of time, from the strangely irrational notion that there is something in the very flow of time that will inevitably cure all ills. Actually, time itself is neutral; it can be used either destructively or constructively. More and more I feel that the people of ill will have used time much more effectively than have the people of good will. We will have to repent in this generation not merely for the hateful words and actions of the bad people but for the appalling silence of the good people. Human progress never rolls in on wheels of inevitability; it comes through the tireless efforts of men willing to be co-workers with God, and without this hard work, time itself becomes an ally of the forces of social stagnation. We must use time creatively, in the knowledge that the time is always ripe to do right. Now is the time to make real the promise of democracy and transform our pending national elegy into a creative psalm of brotherhood. Now is the time to lift our national policy from the quicksand of racial injustice to the solid rock of human dignity.

You speak of our activity in Birmingham as extreme. At first I was rather disappointed that fellow clergymen would see my nonviolent efforts as those of an extremist. I began thinking about the fact that I stand in the middle of two opposing forces in the Negro community. One is a force of complacency, made up in part of Negroes who, as a result of long years of oppression, are so drained of self-respect and a sense of "somebodiness" that they have adjusted to segregation; and in part of a few middle-class Negroes who, because of a degree of academic and economic security and because in some ways they profit by segregation, have become insensitive to the problems of the masses. The other force is one of bitterness and hatred, and it comes perilously close to advocating violence. It is expressed in the various black nationalist groups that are springing up across the nation, the largest and best-known being Elijah Muhammad's Muslim movement. Nourished by the Negro's frustration over the continued existence of racial discrimination, this movement is made up of people who have lost faith in America, who have absolutely repudiated Christianity, and who have concluded that the white man is an incorrigible "devil."

I have tried to stand between these two forces, saying that we need emulate neither the "do-nothingism" of the complacent nor the hatred and despair of the black nationalist. For there is the more excellent way of love and nonviolent protest. I am grateful to God that, through the influence of the Negro church, the way of nonviolence became an integral part of our struggle.

If this philosophy had not emerged, by now many streets of the South would, I am convinced, be flowing with blood. And I am further convinced that if our white brothers dismiss as "rabble-rousers" and "outside agitators" those of us who employ nonviolent direct action, and if they refuse to support our nonviolent efforts, millions of Negroes will, out of frustration and despair, seek solace and security in black-nationalist ideologies—a development that would inevitably lead to a frightening racial nightmare.

Oppressed people cannot remain oppressed forever. The yearning for free- 30
dom eventually manifests itself, and that is what has happened to the American Negro. Something within has reminded him of his birthright of freedom, and something without has reminded him that it can be gained. Consciously or unconsciously, he has been caught up by the *Zeitgeist*, and with his black brothers of Africa and his brown and yellow brothers of Asia, South America and the Caribbean, the United States Negro is moving with a sense of great urgency toward the promised land of racial justice. If one recognizes this vital urge that has engulfed the Negro community, one should readily understand why public demonstrations are taking place. The Negro has many pent-up resentments and latent frustrations, and he must release them. So let him march; let him make prayer pilgrimages to the city hall; let him go on freedom rides—and try to un-

derstand why he must do so. If his repressed emotions are not released in nonviolent ways, they will seek expression through violence; this is not a threat but a fact of history. So I have not said to my people: "Get rid of your discontent." Rather, I have tried to say that this normal and healthy discontent can be channeled into the creative outlet of nonviolent direct action. And now this approach is being termed extremist.

But though I was initially disappointed at being categorized as an extremist, as I continued to think about the matter I gradually gained a measure of satisfaction from the label. Was not Jesus an extremist for love: "Love your enemies, bless them that curse you, do good to them that hate you, and pray for them which despitefully use you, and persecute you." Was not Amos an extremist for justice: "Let justice roll down like waters and righteousness like an ever-flowing stream." Was not Paul an extremist for the Christian gospel: "I bear in my body the marks of the Lord Jesus." Was not Martin Luther an extremist: "Here I stand; I cannot do otherwise, so help me God." And John Bunyan: "I will stay in jail to the end of my days before I make a butchery of my conscience." And Abraham Lincoln: "This nation cannot survive half slave and half free." And Thomas Jefferson: "We hold these truths to be self-evident, that all men are created equal . . ." So the question is not whether we will be extremists, but what kind of extremists we will be. Will we be extremists for hate or for love? Will we be extremists for the preservation of injustice or for the extension of justice? In that dramatic scene on Calvary's hill three men were crucified. We must never forget that all three were crucified for the same crime—the crime of extremism. Two were extremists for immorality, and thus fell below their environment. The other, Jesus Christ, was an extremist for love, truth and goodness, and thereby rose above his environment. Perhaps the South, the nation and the world are in dire need of creative extremists.

I had hoped that the white moderate would see this need. Perhaps I was too optimistic; perhaps I expected too much. I suppose I should have realized that few members of the oppressor race can understand the deep groans and passionate yearnings of the oppressed race, and still fewer have the vision to see that injustice must be rooted out by strong, persistent and determined action. I am thankful, however, that some of our white brothers in the South have grasped the meaning of this social revolution and committed themselves to it. They are still all too few in quantity, but they are big in quality. Some—such as Ralph McGill, Lillian Smith, Harry Golden, James McBride Dabbs, Ann Braden and Sarah Patton Boyle—have written about our struggle in eloquent and prophetic terms. Others have marched with us down nameless streets of the South. They have languished in filthy, roach-infested jails, suffering the abuse and brutality of policemen who view them as "dirty nigger-lovers." Unlike so many of their moderate brothers and sisters, they have recognized the urgency of the moment and sensed the need for powerful "action" antidotes to combat the disease of segregation.

Let me take note of my other major disappointment. I have been so greatly disappointed with the white church and its leadership. Of course, there are some notable exceptions. I am not unmindful of the fact that each of you has taken some significant stands on this issue. I commend you, Reverend Stallings, for your Christian stand on this past Sunday, in welcoming Negroes to your worship service on a nonsegregated basis. I commend the Catholic leaders of this state for integrating Spring Hill College several years ago.

But despite these notable exceptions, I must honestly reiterate that I have been disappointed with the church. I do not say this as one of those negative critics who can always find something wrong with the church. I say this as a minister of the gospel, who loves the church; who was nurtured in its bosom; who has been sustained by its spiritual blessings and who will remain true to it as long as the cord of life shall lengthen.

35 When I was suddenly catapulted into the leadership of the bus protest in Montgomery, Alabama, a few years ago, I felt we would be supported by the white church. I felt that the white ministers, priests and rabbis of the South would be among our strongest allies. Instead, some have been outright opponents, refusing to understand the freedom movement and misrepresenting its leaders; all too many others have been more cautious than courageous and have remained silent behind the anesthetizing security of stained-glass windows.

In spite of my shattered dreams, I came to Birmingham with the hope that the white religious leadership of this community would see the justice of our cause and, with deep moral concern, would serve as the channel through which our just grievances could reach the power structure. I had hoped that each of you would understand. But again I have been disappointed.

I have heard numerous southern religious leaders admonish their worshipers to comply with a desegregation decision because it is the law, but I have longed to hear white ministers declare: "Follow this decree because integration is morally right and because the Negro is your brother." In the midst of blatant injustices inflicted upon the Negro, I have watched white churchmen stand on the sideline and mouth pious irrelevancies and sanctimonious trivialities. In the midst of a mighty struggle to rid our nation of racial and economic injustice, I have heard many ministers say: "Those are social issues, with which the gospel has no real concern." And I have watched many churches commit themselves to a completely otherworldly religion which makes a strange, un-Biblical distinction between body and soul, between the sacred and the secular.

I have traveled the length and breadth of Alabama, Mississippi and all the other southern states. On sweltering summer days and crisp autumn mornings I have looked at the South's beautiful churches with their lofty spires pointing heavenward. I have beheld the impressive outlines of her massive religious-education buildings. Over and over I have found myself asking: "What kind of people worship here? Who is their God? Where were their voices when the lips of Governor Barnett dripped with words of interposition and nullification? Where were they when Governor Wallace gave a clarion call for defiance and hatred? Where were their voices of support when bruised and weary Negro men and women decided to rise from the dark dungeons of complacency to the bright hills of creative protest?"

Yes, these questions are still in my mind. In deep disappointment I have wept over the laxity of the church. But be assured that my tears have been tears of love. There can be no deep disappointment where there is not deep love. Yes, I love the church. How could I do otherwise? I am in the rather unique position of being the son, the grandson and the great-grandson of preachers. Yes, I see the church as the body of Christ. But, oh! How we have blemished and scarred that body through social neglect and through fear of being nonconformists.

There was a time when the church was very powerful—in the time when 40
the early Christians rejoiced at being deemed worthy to suffer for what they believed. In those days the church was not merely a thermometer that recorded the ideas and principles of popular opinion; it was a thermostat that transformed the mores of society. Whenever the early Christians entered a town, the people in power became disturbed and immediately sought to convict the Christians for being "disturbers of the peace" and "outside agitators." But the Christians pressed on, in the conviction that they were "a colony of heaven," called to obey God rather than man. Small in number, they were big in commitment. They were too God-intoxicated to be "astronomically intimidated." By their effort and example they brought an end to such ancient evils as infanticide and gladiatorial contests.

Things are different now. So often the contemporary church is a weak, ineffectual voice with an uncertain sound. So often it is an archdefender of the status quo. Far from being disturbed by the presence of the church, the power structure of the average community is consoled by the church's silent—and often even vocal—sanction of things as they are.

But the judgment of God is upon the church as never before. If today's church does not recapture the sacrificial spirit of the early church, it will lose its authenticity, forfeit the loyalty of millions, and be dismissed as an irrelevant social club with no meaning for the twentieth century. Every day I meet young people whose disappointment with the church has turned into outright disgust.

Perhaps I have once again been too optimistic. Is organized religion too inextricably bound to the status quo to save our nation and the world? Perhaps I must turn my faith to the inner spiritual church, the church within the church, as the true *ekklesia* and the hope of he world. But again I am thankful to God that some noble souls from the ranks of organized religion have broken loose from the paralyzing chains of conformity and joined us as active partners in the struggle for freedom. They have left their secure congregations and walked the streets of Albany, Georgia, with us. They have gone down the highways of the South on tortuous rides for freedom. Yes, they have gone to jail with us. Some have been dismissed from their churches, have lost the support of their bishops and fellow ministers. But they have acted in the faith that right defeated is stronger than evil triumphant. Their witness has been the spiritual salt that has preserved the true meaning of the gospel in these troubled times. They have carved a tunnel of hope through the dark mountain of disappointment.

I hope the church as a whole will meet the challenge of this decisive hour. But even if the church does not come to the aid of justice, I have no despair about the future. I have no fear about the outcome of our struggle in Birmingham, even if our motives are at present misunderstood. We will reach the goal of freedom in Birmingham and all over the nation, because the goal of America is freedom. Abused and scorned though we may be, our destiny is tied up with America's destiny. Before the pilgrims landed at Plymouth, we were here. Before the pen of Jefferson etched the majestic words of the Declaration of Independence across the pages of history, we were here. For more than two centuries our forebears labored in this country without wages; they made cotton king; they built the homes of their masters while suffering gross injustice and shameful humiliation—and yet out of a bottomless vitality they continued to thrive and develop. If the inexpressible cruelties of slavery could not stop us, the opposition we now face will surely fail. We will win our freedom because the sacred heritage of our nation and the eternal will of God are embodied in our echoing demands.

Before closing I feel impelled to mention one other point in your statement 45
that has troubled me profoundly. You warmly commended the Birmingham police force for keeping "order" and "preventing violence." I doubt that you would have so warmly commended the police force if you had seen its dogs sinking their teeth into unarmed, nonviolent Negroes. I doubt that you would so quickly commend the policemen if you were to observe their ugly and inhumane treatment of Negroes here in the city jail; if you were to watch them push and curse old Negro women and young Negro girls; if you were to see them slap and kick old Negro men and young boys; if you were to observe them, as they did on two occasions, refuse to give us food because we wanted to sing our grace together. I cannot join you in your praise of the Birmingham police department.

It is true that the police have exercised a degree of discipline in handling the demonstrators. In this sense they have conducted themselves rather "nonviolently" in public. But for what purpose? To preserve the evil system of segregation. Over the past few years I have consistently preached that nonviolence demands that the means we use must be as pure as the ends we seek. I have tried to make clear that it is wrong to use immoral means to attain moral ends. But now I must affirm that it is just as wrong, or perhaps even more so, to use moral means to preserve immoral ends. Perhaps Mr. Connor and his policemen have been rather nonviolent in public, as was Chief Pritchett in Albany, Georgia, but they have used the moral means of nonviolence to maintain the immoral end of racial injustice. As T. S. Eliot has said: "The last temptation is the greatest treason: To do the right deed for the wrong reason."

I wish you had commended the Negro sit-inners and demonstrators of Birmingham for their sublime courage, their willingness to suffer and their amazing discipline in the midst of great provocation. One day the South will recognize its real heroes. They will be the James Merediths,* with the noble sense of purpose that enables them to face jeering and hostile mobs, and with the agonizing lone-

* The first black man to be admitted to the all-white University of Mississippi.

liness that characterizes the life of the pioneer. They will be old, oppressed, battered Negro women, symbolized in a seventy-two-year-old woman in Montgomery, Alabama,* who rose up with a sense of dignity and with her people decided not to ride segregated buses, and who responded with ungrammatical profundity to one who inquired about her weariness: "My feets is tired, but my soul is at rest." They will be the young high school and college students, the young ministers of the gospel and a host of their elders, courageously and nonviolently sitting in at lunch counters and willingly going to jail for conscience' sake. One day the South will know that when these disinherited children of God sat down at lunch counters, they were in reality standing up for what is best in the American dream and for the most sacred values in our Judaeo-Christian heritage, thereby bringing our nation back to those great wells of democracy which were dug deep by the founding fathers in their formulation of the Constitution and the Declaration of Independence.

Never before have I written so long a letter. I'm afraid it is much too long to take your precious time. I can assure you that it would have been much shorter if I had been writing from a comfortable desk, but what else can one do when he is alone in a narrow jail cell, other than write long letters, think long thoughts and pray long prayers?

If I have said anything in this letter that overstates the truth and indicates an unreasonable impatience, I beg you to forgive me. If I have said anything that understates the truth and indicates my having a patience that allows me to settle for anything less than brotherhood, I beg God to forgive me.

50 I hope this letter finds you strong in the faith. I also hope that circumstances will soon make it possible for me to meet each of you, not as an integrationist or a civil-rights leader but as a fellow clergyman and a Christian brother. Let us all hope that the dark clouds of racial prejudice will soon pass away and the deep fog of misunderstanding will be lifted from our fear-drenched communities, and in some not too distant tomorrow the radiant stars of love and brotherhood will shine over our great nation with all their scintillating beauty.

Yours for the cause of Peace and Brotherhood,

Martin Luther King, Jr.

QUESTIONS FOR DISCUSSION

1. Analyze the tactics that King employs to persuade his clergymen audience. Comment on the nature of his evidence and how the relationship he establishes with his audience influences the presentation of that evidence.

2. Can you observe evidence in your own experience that supports King's assertion that "privileged groups seldom give up their privileges voluntarily"?

* Rosa Parks, who in 1955 refused to ride in the back of a segregated Montgomery, Alabama, bus, thus provoking massive civil rights demonstrations.

3. Describe the distinction that King draws between just and unjust laws. As you think about the distinction, try to identify examples of unjust laws with which you are familiar.

WRITING ASSIGNMENTS

1. Reaction Journal: Assume the role of a "white moderate" and write a letter to King in which you defend yourself against his charges of complacency.
2. Write a summary of the major arguments King presents in defense of civil disobedience. In your summary discuss the evidence he uses to support each of his arguments.
3. Write an argument of your own that invites people to "get involved" with a local or campus situation or policy that you believe is unfair. Begin with King's position that "the time is always ripe to do right."

FROM THE AUTOBIOGRAPHY OF MALCOLM X

MALCOLM X

Malcolm X (1925–1965) was born Malcolm Little in Omaha, Nebraska. He left school in the eighth grade and became involved in crime. While serving a six-year jail term for burglary and larceny, he began studying the teachings of Muhammad, became a Black Muslim minister, and changed his name to Malcolm X. Many black activists adopted new names in order to reject identities associated with the legacy of slavery. When he was released from prison in 1952, Malcolm X became an evangelist with Elijah Muhammad's Nation of Islam and preached a message of aggressive response to white racism. His view of the relationship between blacks and whites during that period is clear in the following excerpt from his Autobiography, *in which he refers to whites as the "Caucasian devil slavemaster" and proclaims, "Our* enemy *is the* white man!*" While on a pilgrimage to Mecca during the last year of his life, he arrived at what he called a "new position regarding white people." He learned, he said, that not all white people are racists. After breaking with the Nation of Islam, Malcolm X founded the Organization of Afro-American Unity, a militant black nationalist group dedicated to the attainment of human rights. He was assassinated in 1965.*

The Autobiography of Malcolm X *(1964) was written with the collaboration of Alex Haley.*

◆ FREEWRITING

In this selection Malcolm X asserts that "*no* one will know *who* we are . . . until *we* know who we are!" Before reading this selection freewrite for ten or fifteen minutes on this issue of group and personal identity.

The public mind fixed on "Black Muslims." From Mr. Muhammad on down, the name "Black Muslims" distressed everyone in the Nation of Islam. I tried for at least two years to kill off that "*Black* Muslims." Every newspaper and magazine writer and microphone I got close to: "*No!* We are black *people* here in America. Our *religion* is Islam. We are properly called 'Muslims'!" But that "Black Muslims" name never got dislodged.

Our mass rallies, from their very beginning, were astounding successes. Where once Detroit's struggling little Temple One proudly sent a ten-automobile caravan to Chicago to hear Mr. Muhammad, now, from East Coast Temples —the older Temples as well as the new ones that all of the massive publicity had helped to bring into being—as many as 150, 200 and even as many as 300 big, chartered buses rolled the highways to wherever Mr. Muhammad was going to speak. On each bus, two Fruit of Islam men were in charge. Big three-by-nine-foot painted canvas banners hung on the buses' sides, to be read by the highway traffic and thousands of people at home and on the sidewalks of the towns the buses passed through.

Hundreds more Muslims and curious Negroes drove their own cars. And Mr. Muhammad with his personal jet plane from Chicago. From the airport to the rally hall, Mr. Muhammad's motorcade had a siren-screaming police escort. Law agencies once had scoffed at our Nation as "black crackpots"; now they took special pains to safeguard against some "white crackpots" causing any "incidents" or "accidents."

America had never seen such fantastic all-black meetings! To hear Elijah Muhammad, up to ten thousand and more black people poured from public and private transportation to overflow the big halls we rented, such as the St. Nicholas Arena in New York City, Chicago's Coliseum, and Washington, D.C.'s Uline Arena.

The white man was barred from attendance—the first time the American 5
black man had ever dreamed of such a thing. And that brought us new attacks from the white man and his black puppets. "Black segregationists . . . racists!" Accusing *us* of segregation! Across America, whites barring blacks was standard.

Many hundreds arrived too late for us to seat them. We always had to wire up outside loudspeakers. An electric atmosphere excited the great, shifting masses of black people. The long lines, three and four abreast, funneling to the meeting hall, were kept in strict order by Fruit of Islam men communicating by walkie-talkie. In anterooms just inside the halls, more Fruit of Islam men and white-gowned, veiled mature Muslim sisters thoroughly searched every man, woman, and child seeking to enter. Any alcohol and tobacco had to be checked, and any objects which could possibly be used to attempt to harm Mr. Muhammad. He always seemed deathly afraid that some one would harm him, and he insisted that everyone be searched to forestall this. Today I understand better, why.

The hundreds of Fruit of Islam men represented contingents which had arrived early that morning, from their Temples in the nearest cities. Some were detailed as ushers, who seated the people by designated sections. The balconies and the rear half of the main floor were filled with black people of the general public. Ahead of them were the all-Muslim seating sections—the white-garbed beautiful black sisters, and the dark-suited, white-shirted brothers. A special section near the front was for black so-called "dignitaries." Many of these had been invited. Among them were our black puppet and parrot attackers, the intellectuals and professional Negroes over whom Mr. Muhammad grieved so much, for these were the educated ones who should have been foremost in leading their poor black brothers out of the maze of misery and want. We wanted them to miss not a single syllable of the truths from Mr. Muhammad in person.

The front two or three press rows were filled with the black reporters and cameramen representing the Negro press, or those who had been hired by the white man's newspapers, magazines, radio and television. America's black writers should hold a banquet for Mr. Muhammad. Writing about the Nation of Islam was the path to success for most of the black writers who now are recognized.

Up on the speaker's platform, we ministers and other officials of the Nation, entering from backstage, found ourselves chairs in the five or six rows behind the big chair reserved for Mr. Muhammad. Some of the ministers had come hundreds of miles to be present. We would be turning about in our chairs, beaming with smiles, wringing each other's hands, and exchanging "As-Salaam-Alaikum" and "Wa-Alaikum-Salaam" in our genuine deep rejoicing to see each other again.

Always, meeting us older hands in Mr. Muhammad's service for the first 10
time, there were several new ministers of small new Temples. My brothers Wilfred and Philbert were respectively now the ministers of the Detroit and Lansing Temples. Minister Jeremiah X headed Atlanta's Temple. Minister John X had Los Angeles' Temple. The Messenger's son, Minister Wallace Muhammad, had the Philadelphia Temple. Minister Woodrow X had the Atlantic City Temple. Some of our ministers had unusual backgrounds. The Washington, D.C., Temple Minister Lucius X was previously a Seventh Day Adventist and a 32nd degree Mason. Minister George X of the Camden, New Jersey, Temple, was a pathologist. Minister David X was previously the minister of a Richmond, Virginia, Christian church; he and enough of his congregation had become Muslims so that the congregation split and the majority turned the church into our Richmond Temple. The Boston Temple's outstanding young Minister Louis X, previously a well-known and rising popular singer called "The Charmer," had written our Nation's popular first song, titled "White Man's Heaven Is

Black Man's Hell." Minister Louis X had also authored our first play, "Orgena" ("A Negro" spelled backwards); its theme was the all-black trial of a symbolic white man for his world crimes against non-whites; found guilty, sentenced to death, he was dragged off shouting about all he had done "for the nigra people."

Younger even than our talented Louis X were some newer ministers, Minister Thomas J. X of the Hartford Temple being one example, and another the Buffalo Temple's Minister Robert J. X.

I had either originally established or organized for Mr. Muhammad most of the represented temples. Greeting each of these Temples' brother ministers would bring back into my mind images of "fishing" for converts along the streets and from door-to-door wherever the black people were congregated. I remembered the countless meetings in living rooms where maybe seven would be a crowd; the gradually building, building—on up to renting folding chairs for dingy little storefronts which Muslims scrubbed to spotlessness.

We together on a huge hall's speaking platform, and that vast audience before us, miraculously manifested, as far as I was concerned, the incomprehensible power of Allah. For the first time, I truly understood something Mr. Muhammad had told me: he claimed that when he was going through the sacrificial trials of fleeing the black hypocrites from city to city, Allah had often sent him visions of great audiences who would one day hear the teachings; and Mr. Muhammad said the visions also buoyed him when he was locked up for years in the white man's prison.

The great audience's restless whisperings would cease. . . .

15 At the microphone would be the Nation's National Secretary John Ali, or the Boston Temple Minister Louis X. They enlivened the all-black atmosphere, speaking of the new world open to the black man through the Nation of Islam. Sister Tynetta Dynear would speak beautifully of the Muslim women's powerful, vital contributions, of the Muslim women's roles in our Nation's efforts to raise the physical, mental, moral, social, and political condition of America's black people.

Next, I would come to the microphone, specifically to condition the audience to hear Mr. Muhammad who had flown from Chicago to teach us all in person.

I would raise up my hand, "*As-Salaikum-Salaam*—"

"*Wa-Alaikum-Salaam!*" It was a roared response from the great audience's Muslim seating section.

There was a general pattern that I would follow on these occasions:

20 "My black brothers and sisters—of all religious beliefs, or of no religious beliefs—we have in common the greatest binding tie we could have . . . we all are *black* people!

"I'm not going to take all day telling you some of the greatnesses of The Honorable Elijah Muhammad. I'm just going to tell you now his *greatest* greatness! He is the *first*, the *only* black leader to identify, to you and me, *who* is our enemy!

"The Honorable Elijah Muhammad is the first black leader among us with the *courage* to tell us—out here in public—something which when you begin to think of it back in your homes, you will realize we black people have been *living* with, we have been *seeing*, we have been *suffering*, all of our lives!

"Our *enemy* is the *white man*!

"And why is Mr. Muhammad's teaching us this such a great thing? Because when you know *who* your enemy is, he can no longer keep you divided, and fighting, one brother against the other! Because when you *recognize* who your enemy is, he can no longer use trickery, promises, lies, hypocrisy, and his evil acts to keep you deaf, dumb, and blinded!

"When you recognize *who* your enemy is, he can no longer brainwash you, 25
he can no longer pull wool over your eyes so that you never stop to see that you are living in pure *hell* on this earth, while *he* lives in pure *heaven* right on this same earth!—This enemy who tells you that you are both supposed to be worshiping the same white Christian God that—you are told—stands for the *same* things for *all* men!

"Oh, *yes*, that devil is our enemy. I'll *prove* it! Pick up any daily newspaper! Read the false charges leveled against our beloved religious leader. It only points up the fact that the Caucasian race never wants any black man who is not their puppet or parrot to speak for our people. This Caucasian devil slavemaster does not want or trust us to leave him—yet when we stay here among him, he continues to keep us at the very *lowest level* of his society!

"The white man has always *loved* it when he could keep us black men tucked away somewhere, always out of sight, around the corner! The white man has always *loved* the kind of black leaders whom he could ask, 'Well, how's things with your people up there?' But because Mr. Elijah Muhammad takes an uncompromising stand with the white man, the white man *hates* him! When you hear the *white man* hate him, you, too, because you don't understand Biblical prophecy, wrongly label Mr. Muhammad—as a racist, a hate-teacher, or of being anti-white and teaching black supremacy—"

The audience suddenly would begin a rustling of turning. . . .

Mr. Muhammad would be rapidly moving along up a center aisle from the rear—as once he had entered our humble little mosques—this man whom we regarded as Islam's gentle, meek, brown-skinned Lamb. Stalwart, striding, close-cropped, handpicked Fruit of Islam guards were a circle surrounding him. He carried his Holy Bible, his holy Quran. The small, dark pillbox atop his head was gold-embroidered with Islam's flag, the sun, moon, and stars. The Muslims were crying out their adoration and their welcome. "Little lamb!" "As-Salaikum-Salaam!" "Praise be to Allah!"

Tears would be in more eyes than mine. He had rescued me when I was a 30
convict; Mr. Muhammad had trained me in his home, as if I was his son. I think that my life's peaks of emotion, until recently, at least, were when, suddenly, the Fruit of Islam guards would stop stiffly at attention, and the platform's several steps would be mounted alone by Mr. Muhammad, and his ministers, including me, sprang around him, embracing him, wringing his both hands. . . .

I would turn right back to the microphone, not to keep waiting those world's biggest black audiences who had come to hear him.

"My black brothers and sisters—*no* one will know *who* we are . . . until *we* know who we are! We never will be able to *go* anywhere until we know *where* we are! The Honorable Elijah Muhammad is giving us a true identity, and a true position—the first time they have ever been *known* to the American black man!

"You can be around this man and never *dream* from his actions the power and the authority he has—" (Behind me, believe me when I tell you, I could *feel* Mr. Muhammad's *power*.)

"He does not *display*, and *parade*, his *power*! But no other black leader in America has followers who will lay down their lives if he says so! And I don't mean all of this non-violent, begging-the-white-man kind of dying . . . all of this sitting-in, sliding-in, wading-in, eating-in, diving-in, and all the rest—

"My black brothers and sisters, you have come from your homes to hear—now you are *going* to hear—America's *wisest* black man! America's *boldest* black man! America's most *fearless* black man! This wilderness of North America's most *powerful* black man!"

Mr. Muhammad would come quickly to the stand, looking out over the vacuum-quiet audience, his gentle-looking face set, for just a fleeting moment. Then, "As-Salaikum-Salaam—"

"WA-ALAIKUM-SALAAM!"

The Muslims roared it, as they settled to listen.

QUESTIONS FOR DISCUSSION

1. Noted African-American scholar Gerald Early says that Malcolm X is more popular today than he has been at any time since his assassination in 1965. Because he died "this tragic death of a political martyr . . . [he] remains forever young." Discuss this point in the context of this selection. Can the same be said about Martin Luther King? About John F. Kennedy?

2. Malcolm X suggests that one of Mr. Muhammad's central messages is that "when you know *who* your enemy is, he can no longer keep you divided." Has your experience and knowledge of human relations led you to a similar conclusion?

WRITING ASSIGNMENTS

1. Reaction Journal: Assume the role of a follower of Martin Luther King, Jr. After reading "Letter from Birmingham Jail," write a letter to a follower of Elijah Muhammad in which you defend your more moderate position. (If you prefer, you may assume the role of a follower of Mr. Muhammad.)

2. The focus of this selection is on Malcolm X's fiery introduction of Mr. Muhammad to a throng of followers and invited guests. Choose a controversial and politically divisive historical figure and take the role of a supporter who has been asked to introduce him or her to a similar gathering. Write your introduction after carefully considering Malcolm X's strategy in his introduction.

BLACK POWER

STOKELY CARMICHAEL AND
CHARLES V. HAMILTON

Stokely Carmichael (Kwame Toure) (b. 1941) was born in Trinidad. He earned his B.A. from Howard University and became an organizer for the Student Nonviolent Coordinating Committee (SNCC) before taking leadership roles in the Black Panthers and the All-Afrikan People's Revolutionary Party. He is the author of Stokely Speaks: Black Power Back to Pan-Africanism *(1971) and, with Charles V. Hamilton,* Black Power: The Politics of Liberation in America *(1967). Charles V. Hamilton (b. 1929) is a professor of political science at Columbia University. He holds a B.A. from Roosevelt University in Chicago, a law degree from Loyola University, and a doctorate from the University of Chicago. In addition to teaching at several universities before joining the faculty at Columbia, Hamilton has participated in and advised civil rights organizations in several states. In the following selection from their book* Black Power, *Carmichael and Hamilton define the goal of Black Power and assert the need for black people to unite and to "redefine themselves" as a "vibrant, valiant people" in order to gain a position of strength in American society.*

◆ FREEWRITING

Freewrite for ten or fifteen minutes on your ideas about group power and individual power. As you write, define each concept and discuss your sense of its importance in our pluralistic society.

"To carve out a place for itself in the politico-social order," V. O. Key, Jr., wrote in *Politics, Parties and Pressure Groups*, "a new group may have to fight for reorientation of many of the values of the old order." This is especially true when that group is composed of black people in the American society—a society that has for centuries deliberately and systematically excluded them from political participation. Black people in the United States must raise hard questions, questions which challenge the very nature of the society itself: its long-standing values, beliefs and institutions.

To do this, we must first redefine ourselves. Our basic need is to reclaim our history and our identity from what must be called cultural terrorism from the depredation of self-justifying white guilt. We shall have to struggle for the right to create our own terms through which to define ourselves and our relationship to the society, and to have these terms recognized. This is the first necessity of a free people, and the first right that any oppressor must suspend.

Black people must redefine themselves, and only *they* can do that. Throughout this country, vast segments of the black communities are beginning to recognize the need to assert their own definitions, to reclaim their history, their culture; to create their own sense of community and togetherness. There is a growing resentment of the word "Negro," for example, because this term is the invention of our oppressor; it is *his* image of us that he describes. Many blacks are now calling themselves African-Americans, Afro-Americans or black people because that is *our* image of ourselves. When we begin to define our own image, the stereotypes—that is, lies—that our oppressor has developed will begin in the white community and end there. The black community will have a positive image of itself that *it* has created. This means we will no longer call ourselves lazy, apathetic, dumb, good-timers, shiftless, etc. Those are words used by white America to define us. If we accept these adjectives, as some of us have in the past, then we see ourselves only in a negative way, precisely the way white America wants us to see ourselves. Our incentive is broken and our will to fight is surrendered. From now on we shall view ourselves as African-Americans and as black people who are in fact energetic, determined, intelligent, beautiful and peace-loving.

There is a terminology and ethos peculiar to the black community of which black people are beginning to be no longer ashamed. Black communities are the only large segments of this society where people refer to each other as brother—soul-brother, soul-sister. Some people may look upon this as *ersatz*, as make-believe, but it is not that. It is real. It is a growing sense of community. It is a growing realization that black Americans have a common bond not only among themselves, but with their African brothers. In *Black Man's Burden*, John O. Killens described his trip to ten African countries as follows:

> Everywhere I went people called me brother. . . . "Welcome, American brother." It was a good feeling for me, to be in Africa. To walk in a land for the first time in your entire life knowing within yourself that your color would not be held against you. No black man ever knows this in America.

5 More and more black Americans are developing this feeling. They are becoming aware that they have a history which pre-dates their forced introduction to this country. African-American history means a long history beginning on the continent of Africa, a history not taught in the standard textbooks of this country. It is absolutely essential that black people know this history, that they know their roots, that they develop an awareness of their cultural heritage. Too long have they been kept in submission by being told that they had no culture, no manifest heritage, before they landed on the slave auction blocks in this country. If black people are to know themselves as a vibrant, valiant people, they must

know their roots. And they will soon learn that the Hollywood image of man-eating cannibals waiting for, and waiting on, the Great White Hunter is a lie.

With redefinition will come a clearer notion of the role black Americans can play in this world. This role will emerge clearly out of the unique, common experiences of Afro-Asians. Killens concludes:

> I believe furthermore that the American Negro can be the bridge between the West and Africa-Asia. We black Americans can serve as a bridge to mutual understanding. The one thing we black Americans have in common with the other colored peoples of the world is that we have all felt the cruel and ruthless heel of white supremacy. We have all been "niggerized" on one level or another. And all of us are determined to "deniggerize" the earth. To rid the world of "niggers" is the Black Man's Burden, human reconstruction is the grand objective.

Only when black people fully develop this sense of community, of themselves, can they begin to deal effectively with the problems of racism in *this* country. This is what we mean by a new consciousness; this is the vital first step.

The next step is what we shall call the process of political modernization—a process which must take place if the society is to be rid of racism. "Political modernization" includes many things, but we mean by it three major concepts: (1) questioning old values and institutions of the society; (2) searching for new and different forms of political structure to solve political and economic problems; and (3) broadening the base of political participation to include more people in the decision-making process. These notions (we shall take up each in turn) are central to our thinking throughout this book and to contemporary American history as a whole. As David Apter wrote in *The Politics of Modernization*, ". . . the struggle to modernize is what has given meaning to our generation. It tests our cherished institutions and our beliefs. . . . So compelling a force has it become that we are forced to ask new questions of our own institutions. Each country, whether modernized or modernizing, stands in both judgment and fear of the results. Our own society is no exception."

The values of this society support a racist system; we find it incongruous to ask black people to adopt and support most of those values. We also reject the assumption that the basic institutions of this society must be preserved. The goal of black people must *not* be to assimilate into middle-class America, for that class—as a whole—is without a viable conscience as regards humanity. The values of the middle class permit the perpetuation of the ravages of the black community. The values of that class are based on material aggrandizement, not the expansion of humanity. The values of that class ultimately support cloistered little closed societies tucked away neatly in tree-lined suburbia. The values of that class do *not* lead to the creation of an open society. That class *mouths* its preference for a free, competitive society, while at the same time forcefully and even viciously denying to black people as a group the opportunity to compete.

We are not unmindful of other descriptions of the social utility of the middle class. Banfield and Wilson, in *City Politics*, concluded:

> The departure of the middle class from the central city is important in other ways. . . . The middle class supplies a social and political leavening in the life of a city. Middle-class people demand good schools and integrity in government. They support churches, lodges, parent-teacher associations, scout troops, better-housing committees, art galleries, and operas. It is the middle class, in short, that asserts a conception of the public interest. Now its activity is increasingly concentrated in the suburbs.

But this same middle class manifests a sense of superior group position in regard to race. This class wants "good government" *for themselves;* it wants good schools *for its children.* At the same time, many of its members sneak into the black community by day, exploit it, and take the money home to their middle-class communities at night to support their operas and art galleries and comfortable homes. When not actually robbing, they will fight off the handful of more affluent black people who seek to move in; when they approve or even seek token integration, it applies only to black people like themselves—as "white" as possible. *This class is the backbone of institutional racism in this country.*

The adoption of the concept of Black Power is one of the most legitimate 10
and healthy developments in American politics and race relations in our time. The concept of Black Power speaks to all the needs mentioned in this chapter. It is a call for black people in this country to unite, to recognize their heritage, to build a sense of community. It is a call for black people to begin to define their own goals, to lead their own organizations and to support those organizations. It is a call to reject the racist institutions and values of this society.

The concept of Black Power rests on a fundamental premise: *Before a group can enter the open society, it must first close ranks.* By this we mean that group solidarity is necessary before a group can operate effectively from a bargaining position of strength in a pluralistic society. Traditionally, each new ethnic group in this society has found the route to social and political viability through the organization of its own institutions with which to represent its needs within the larger society. Studies in voting behavior specifically, and political behavior generally, have made it clear that politically the American pot has not melted. Italians vote for Rubino over O'Brien; Irish for Murphy over Goldberg, etc. This phenomenon may seem distasteful to some, but it has been and remains today a central fact of the American political system. There are other examples of ways in which groups in the society have remembered their roots and used this effectively in the political arena. Theodore Sorensen describes the politics of foreign aid during the Kennedy Administration in his book *Kennedy:*

> No powerful constituencies or interest groups backed foreign aid. The Marshall Plan at least had appealed to Americans who traced their roots to the Western European nations aided. But there were few voters who identified with India, Colombia or Tanganyika.

The extent to which black Americans can and do "trace their roots" to Africa, to that extent will they be able to be more effective on the political scene.

A white reporter set forth this point in other terms when he made the following observation about white Mississippi's manipulation of the anti-poverty program:

> The war on poverty has been predicated on the notion that there is such a thing as a community which can be defined geographically and mobilized for a collective effort to help the poor. This theory has no relationship to reality in the deep South. In every Mississippi county there are two communities. Despite all the pious platitudes of the moderates on both sides, these two communities habitually see their interests in terms of conflict rather than cooperation. Only when the Negro community can muster enough political, economic and professional strength to compete on somewhat equal terms, will Negroes believe in the possibility of true cooperation and whites accept its necessity. En route to integration, the Negro community needs to develop a greater independence—a chance to run its own affairs and not cave in whenever "the man" barks—or so it seems to me, and to most of the knowledgeable people with whom I talked in Mississippi. To OEO, this judgment may sound like black nationalism. . . .[1]

The point is obvious: black people must lead and run their own organizations. Only black people can convey the revolutionary idea—and it is a revolutionary idea—that black people are able to do things themselves. Only they can help create in the community an aroused and continuing black consciousness that will provide the basis for political strength. In the past, white allies have often furthered white supremacy without the whites involved realizing it, or even wanting to do so. Black people must come together and do things for themselves. They must achieve self-identity and self-determination in order to have their daily needs met.

Black Power means, for example, that in Lowndes County, Alabama, a black sheriff can end police brutality. A black tax assessor and tax collector and county board of revenue can lay, collect, and channel tax monies for the building of better roads and schools serving black people. In such areas of Lowndes, where black people have a majority, they will attempt to use power to exercise control. This is what they seek: control. When black people lack a majority, Black Power means proper representation and sharing of control. It means the creation of power bases, of strength, from which black people can press to change local or nation-wide patterns of oppression—instead of from weakness.

It does not mean *merely* putting black faces into office. Black visibility is not Black Power. Most of the black politicians around the country today are not examples of Black Power. The power must be that of a community, and emanate from there. The black politicians must start from there. The black politicians must stop being representatives of "downtown" machines, whatever the cost might be in terms of lost patronage and holiday handouts.

Black Power recognizes—it must recognize—the ethnic basis of American politics as well as the power-oriented nature of American politics. Black Power therefore calls for black people to consolidate behind their own, so that they can bargain from a position of strength. But while we endorse the *procedure* of group solidarity and identity for the purpose of attaining certain goals in the body politic, this does not mean that black people should strive for the same kind of rewards (i.e., end results) obtained by the white society. The ultimate values and goals are not domination or exploitation of other groups, but rather an effective share in the total power of the society.

Nevertheless, some observers have labeled those who advocate Black Power as racists; they have said that the call for self-identification and self-determination is "racism in reverse" or "black supremacy." This is a deliberate and absurd lie. There is no analogy—by any stretch of definition or imagination—between the advocates of Black Power and white racists. Racism is not merely exclusion on the basis of race but exclusion for the purpose of subjugating or maintaining subjugation. The goal of the racists is to keep black people on the bottom, arbitrarily and dictatorially, as they have done in this country for over three hundred years. The goal of black self-determination and black self-identity—Black Power—is full participation in the decision-making processes affecting the lives of black people, and recognition of the virtues in themselves as black people. The black people of this country have not lynched whites, bombed their churches, murdered their children and manipulated laws and institutions to maintain oppression. White racists have. Congressional laws, one after the other, have not been necessary to stop black people from oppressing others and denying others the full enjoyment of their rights. White racists have made such laws necessary. The goal of Black Power is positive and functional to a free and viable society. No white racist can make this claim.

A great deal of public attention and press space was devoted to the hysterical accusation of "black racism" when the call for Black Power was first sounded. A national committee of influential black churchmen affiliated with the National Council of Churches, despite their obvious respectability and responsibility, had to resort to a paid advertisement to articulate their position, while anyone yapping "black racism" made front-page news. In their statement, published in the *New York Times* of July 31, 1966, the churchmen said:

> We, an informal group of Negro churchmen in America, are deeply disturbed about the crisis brought upon our country by historic distortions of important human realities in the controversy about "black power." What we see shining through the variety of rhetoric is not anything new but the same old problem of power and race which has faced our beloved country since 1619.
>
> . . . The conscience of black men is corrupted because having no power to implement the demands of conscience, the concern for justice in the absence of justice becomes a chaotic self-surrender. Powerlessness breeds a race of beggars. We are faced with a situation where pow-

> erless conscience meets conscienceless power, threatening the very foundations of our Nation.
>
> We deplore the overt violence of riots, but we feel it is more important to focus on the real sources of these eruptions. These sources may be abetted inside the Ghetto, but their basic cause lies in the silent and covert violence which white middle class America inflicts upon the victims of the inner city.
>
> . . . In short, the failure of American leaders to use American power to create equal opportunity *in life* as well as *law*, this is the real problem and not the anguished cry for black power.
>
> . . . Without the capacity to participate with power, i.e., to have some organized political and economic strength to really influence people with whom one interacts, integration is not meaningful.
>
> . . . America has asked its Negro citizens to fight for opportunity as *individuals*, whereas at certain points in our history what we have needed most has been opportunity for the *whole group*, not just for selected and approved Negroes.
>
> . . . We must not apologize for the existence of this form of group power, for we have been oppressed as a group and not as individuals. We will not find our way out of that oppression until both we and America accept the need for Negro Americans, as well as for Jews, Italians, Poles, and white Anglo-Saxon Protestants, among others, to have and to wield group power.

It is a commentary on the fundamentally racist nature of this society that the concept of group strength for black people must be articulated—not to mention defended. No other group would submit to being led by others. Italians do not run the Anti-Defamation League of B'nai B'rith. Irish do not chair Christopher Columbus Societies. Yet when black people call for black-run and all-black organizations, they are immediately classed in a category with the Ku Klux Klan. This is interesting and ironic, but by no means surprising: the society does not expect black people to be able to take care of their business, and there are many who prefer it precisely that way.

In the end, we cannot and shall not offer any guarantees that Black Power, if 20
achieved, would be non-racist. No one can predict human behavior. Social change always has unanticipated consequences. If black racism is what the larger society fears, we cannot help them. We can only state what we hope will be the result, given the fact that the present situation is unacceptable and that we have no real alternative but to work for Black Power. The final truth is that the white society is not entitled to reassurances, even if it were possible to offer them.

Notes

1. Christopher Jencks, "Accommodating Whites: A New Look at Mississippi," *The New Republic* (April 16, 1966).

QUESTIONS FOR DISCUSSION

1. Carmichael and Hamilton argue that it is absolutely essential for black people to know African-American history and to develop an awareness of their cultural heritage. They refer to such an awareness as "new consciousness." How important is a knowledge of your cultural heritage to you and your family? To your cultural community?
2. The authors suggest that the middle class is *"the backbone of institutional racism in this country."* Does this surprise you?
3. Before reading this selection, what was your impression of the meaning of "Black Power"? Have Carmichael and Hamilton altered your earlier opinions?

WRITING ASSIGNMENTS

1. Reaction Journal: In a nation that places so much emphasis on the worth and power of the individual, why do Carmichael and Hamilton emphasize the role of group power? Reread your freewriting, then write a few paragraphs in which you discuss group and individual power.
2. Carmichael and Hamilton assert that white America's definition of African-American people is based on lies and stereotypes. Write about the manner in which stereotyping affects the way our greater society defines other ethnic groups.
3. Carmichael and Hamilton contend that "politically the American pot has not melted." Write an essay in which you demonstrate your agreement or disagreement with this assertion. Develop your essay with illustrations from your readings as well as from your own experiences and observations.

INDIVIDUALISM AND BLACK IDENTITY

SHELBY STEELE

Shelby Steele (b. 1946), a professor of English at San Jose State University in California, has written a number of controversial essays criticizing what he sees as the debilitating effects of affirmative action policies. He urges African-Americans to rely on their own efforts rather than to harbor the "illusion of deliverance by others." In the following excerpt from the epilogue to his book The Content of Our Character: A New Vision of Race in America *(1990), Steele speaks of the need for a new definition of black identity that draws its strength not from victimization but from achievement through individual initiative in mainstream American society.*

◆ FREEWRITING

Steele says, "I have been more in charge of my fate than I always wanted to believe." Freewrite for ten or fifteen minutes on how much you feel in charge of your fate. Do you believe that race and cultural identity interfere with people's ability to control their destinies?

I have mentioned in several places in this book that I was caught up in the new spirit of black power and pride that swept over black America in the late sixties like one of those storms that changes the landscape. I will always believe this storm was inevitable and, therefore, positive in many ways. What I gained from it was the power to be racially unapologetic, no mean benefit considering the long trial of patience that the civil rights movement subjected blacks to. But after awhile, by the early seventies, it became clear that black power did not offer much of a blueprint on how to move my life forward. Despite the strong feeling that it had given me a crucial part of myself, it told me virtually nothing about who I was as an individual or how I might live in the world as myself. Of course, it was my mistake to think it could. But in the late sixties, "blackness" was an invasive form of collective identity that cut so deeply into one's individual space that it seemed also to be an individual identity. It came as something of a disappointment to realize that the two could not be the same, that being "black" in no way spared me the necessity of being myself.

In the early seventies, without realizing it, I made a sort of bargain with the prevailing black identity—I subscribed in a general way to its point of view so that I could be free to get on with my life. Many other blacks I knew made this same bargain, got on with their lives and fellow-traveled with black power. I don't believe this subscription was insincere, but it was convenient since it opened the individual space out of which we could make our lives.

And what were we subscribing to? Generally, I think it was a form of black identity grounded in the spirit of black power. It carried a righteous anger at and mistrust of American society. It believed that blacks continued to be the victims of institutional racism, that we would have to maintain an adversarial stance toward society, and that a tight racial unity was necessary both for survival and advancement. This identity was, and is, predicated on the notion that those who burned you once will burn you again, and it presupposes a deep racist reflex in American life that will forever try to limit black possibility.

I think it was the space I cleared for myself by loosely subscribing to this identity that ultimately put me in conflict with it. It is in the day-to-day struggle of living on the floor of a society, so to speak, that one gains a measure of what is possible in that society. And by simply living as an individual in America—with my racial identity struggle suspended by my subscription to the black power identity—I discovered that American society offered me and blacks in general a remarkable range of opportunity if we were willing to pursue it.

In my daily life I continue to experience racial indignities and slights. This 5
morning I was told that blacks had too much musical feeling (soul, I suppose) to

be good classical musicians; yesterday I passed two houses with gnomish little black lawn jockeys on the front porch; my children have been called "nigger," not to mention myself; I wear a tie and carry a professorial briefcase so my students on the first day of class will know I'm the teacher; and so on. I also know that actual racial discrimination persists in many areas of American life. I have been the victor in one housing-discrimination suit, as were my parents before me. And, certainly, garden variety racism is still a tonic for the inadequate white. In my daily life I have no immunity from any of this. What is more, I do not like it, nor will I ever endure it with élan. Yet I have also come to realize that in this same society, I have been more in charge of my fate than I always wanted to believe, and that though I have been limited by many things, my race was not foremost among them.

The point is that both realities are true. There is still racial insensitivity and some racial discrimination against blacks in this society, but there is also much opportunity. What brought me into conflict with the prevailing black identity was that it was almost entirely preoccupied with the former to the exclusion of the latter. The black identity I was subscribing to in the seventies—and that still prevails today—was essentially a "wartime" identity shaped in the confrontational sixties. It presumed that black opportunity was sharply limited by racism and that blacks had to "win" more "victories" "against" society before real opportunity would open up. This was an identity that still saw blacks as victims and that kept them at war with society even as new possibilities for advancement opened all around. Worse, by focusing so exclusively on white racism and black victimization, it implied that our fate was in society's control rather than our own, and that opportunity itself was something that was given rather than taken. This identity robs us of the very self-determination we have sought for so long, and deepens our dependency on the benevolence of others.

Why do we cling to an adversarial, victim-focused identity that preoccupies us with white racism? I think because of fear, self-doubt, and simple inexperience. As I've discussed elsewhere in this book, I believe we carry an inferiority anxiety that makes the seizing of opportunity more risky for us, since setbacks and failures may seem to confirm inferiority. To avoid this risk we may hold a victim-focused identity that tells us there is less opportunity than there really is. Our culture was formed in oppression rather than in freedom, which means we are somewhat inexperienced in the full use of freedom, in seeing possibilities and developing them. In oppression we were punished for having initiative and thereby conditioned away from it. Also, our victimization itself has been our primary source of power in society—the basis of our demands for redress—and the paradoxical result of relying on this source of power is that it rewards us for continuing to see ourselves as victims of a racist society. So our victim-focused identity serves us by preserving our main source of power and by shielding us from our fear of inferiority and our relative inexperience with the challenges of freedom.

And yet this leaves us with an identity that is at war with our own best interests, that magnifies our oppression and diminishes our sense of possibility. I think this identity is a weight on blacks because it is built around our collective insecurity rather than our faith in our human capacity to seize opportunity as individuals. It amounts to a self-protective collectivism that obsesses us with black unity instead of individual initiative. To be "black" in this identity, one need only manifest the symbols, postures, and rhetoric of black unity. Not only is personal initiative unnecessary for being "black," but the successful exercise of initiative—working one's way into the middle class, becoming well-off, gaining an important position—may in fact jeopardize one's "blackness," make one somehow less black. The poor black is the true black; the successful black is more marginally black unless he (or she) frequently announces his solidarity with the race in the way politicians declare their patriotism. This sort of identity never works, never translates into the actual uplift of black people. It confuses racial unity with initiative by relying on unity to do what only individual initiative can do. Uplift can only come when many millions of blacks seize the possibilities inside the sphere of their personal lives and use them to take themselves forward. Collectively, we can resist oppression, but racial development will always be, as Ralph Ellison once put it, "the gift of its individuals."

The collective black identity fogs up the sacred line between the individual and the collective. To find my own individuality, I had to do what many blacks in fact do—push the collective out of my individual space by subscribing to an identity I wasn't living by. Many blacks maintain their "blackness" as a sort of union card while actually living by principles and values that are classically American and universal to the middle class everywhere: hard work, self-reliance, initiative, property ownership, family ties, and so on. In pushing the collective identity out of our individual space, we are also pushing back the diminished sense of possibility that it carries in order to take advantage of the broader field of possibility that our actual experience shows us is there. To retrieve our individuality and find opportunity, blacks today must—consciously or unconsciously—disregard the prevailing victim-focused black identity. Though it espouses black pride, it is actually a repressive identity that generates a victimized self-image, curbs individualism and initiative, diminishes our sense of possibility, and contributes to our demoralization and inertia. It is a skin that needs shedding.

There are many profound problems facing black America today—a swelling 10
black underclass, a black middle class that declined slightly in the eighties, a declining number of black college students, an epidemic of teenage pregnancy, drug use, and gang violence, continuing chronic unemployment, astoundingly high college and high school dropout rates, an increasing number of single-parent families, a disproportionately high infant mortality rate, and so on. Against all this it seems almost esoteric to talk about identity and possibility. Yet, in this book, I have tried to look at the underlying network of attitudes, pressures, and anxieties that have deepened our problems even as more opportunity has opened up to us. Without understanding these intangibles, I don't think we can easily know what to do.

Many remedies have been tried. Here and there various social programs, "interventions," have worked. Many more programs and policies have not worked. Clearly we should find the ones that do work and have more of them. But my deepest feeling is that, in a society of increasingly limited resources, there will never be enough programs to meet the need. What I really believe is that we black Americans will never be saved or even assisted terribly much by others, never be repaid for our suffering, and never find that symmetrical, historical justice that we cannot help but long for. These things will never happen. Jean-Paul Sartre once said that we were the true "existential people," and certainly we have always had to create ourselves out of whole cloth and find our own means for survival. Nothing has really changed.

I think the most cursory glance at the list of problems that blacks now face reveals that we are in a kind of despair. The evidence of this is everywhere, from the college campuses—where black students are five times more likely than whites to drop out—to the black underclass where a miasma of drug addiction, violence, and hopelessness has already transformed many inner cities into hearts of darkness. I have written in this book about some of the sources of this despair, but I also believe that they all pressure us into a single overriding mistake: a hesitation before the challenges of self-interested, individual action. It is at the point of taking self-interested action in the American mainstream that all the unresolved wounds of oppression manifest themselves and become a wall. Here is where inferiority anxiety, a victim-focused identity, that peculiar mix of personal and racial self-doubt, fear of failure, and even self-hate all combine to make for a fear of self-interested action. And without such action, there can only be despair and inertia.

There will be no end to despair and no lasting solution to any of our problems until we rely on individual effort within the American mainstream—rather than collective action against the mainstream—as our means of advancement. We need a collective identity that encourages diversity within the race, that does not make black unity a form of repression, that does not imply that the least among us are the most black, and that makes the highest challenge of "blackness" personal development. This identity must be grounded also in the reality that I and many other blacks have discovered in the space of our individual lives: that there is today, despite America's residual racism, an enormous range of opportunity open to blacks in this society. The nexus of this new identity must be a meeting of black individual initiative and American possibility.

I believe black leadership must make this nexus its primary focus. They must preach it, tell it, sell it, and demand it. Our leadership has looked at government and white society very critically. Now they must help us look at ourselves. We need our real problems named and explained; otherwise, we have no chance to overcome them. Their impulse is to be "political," to keep the larger society on edge, to keep them feeling as though they have not done enough for blacks. And, clearly, they have not. But the price they pay for this form of "politics" is to keep blacks focused on an illusion of deliverance by others, and no illusion weakens us more. Our leaders must take a risk. They must tell us the truth, tell us of the freedom and opportunity they have discovered in their own lives. They must tell us what they tell their own children when they go home at night: to study hard, pursue their dreams with discipline and effort, to be responsible for themselves, to have concern for others, to cherish their race and at the same time make their own lives as Americans. When our leaders put a spotlight on our victimization and seize upon our suffering to gain us ineffectual concessions, they inadvertently turn themselves into enemies of the truth, not to mention enemies of their own people.

I believe that black Americans are infinitely freer today than ever before. 15
This is not a hope; this is a reality, an extremely hard-won reality. Many of our great leaders, and countless foot soldiers with them, died for this reality. Racial hatred has not yet left the American landscape. Who knows how or when this deliverance will occur? Yet the American black, supported by a massive body of law and the not inconsiderable goodwill of his fellow citizens, is basically as free as he or she wants to be. For every white I have met who is a racist, I have met twenty more who have seen me as an equal. And of those twenty, ten have only wished me the best as an individual. This I say, as opposed to confessing, has been my actual reality. I believe it is time for blacks to begin the shift from a wartime to a peacetime identity, from fighting for opportunity to the seizing of it. The immutable fact of late twentieth-century life is that it *is* there for blacks to seize. Martin Luther King did not live to experience this. But, of course, on the night before he died he seemed to know he would not. From the mountaintop he had looked over and seen the promised land, but then he said, "I may not get there with you . . ." I won't say we are snuggled deep in the promised valley he saw beyond the mountain. Every day things remind me that we are not. But I also know that we have it over our greatest leader. We are on the other side of his mountaintop, on the downward slope toward the valley he saw. This is something we ought to know. But what we must know even more than this is that nothing on this earth can be promised but a chance. The promised land guarantees nothing. It is only an opportunity, not a deliverance.

QUESTIONS FOR DISCUSSION

1. Steele contends that his efforts to find his "black identity grounded in the spirit of black power" is what put him in conflict with Black Power. Is this a response that you can relate to your experience? Does Steele's response surprise you?
2. What does Steele mean by "inferiority anxiety"? How does it relate to race? Does it relate only to minority populations?
3. Steele applauds author and critic Ralph Ellison, who argued that racial development is "the gift of its individuals" as opposed to groups. What is your response to Ellison's comment?
4. Steele refers to many black political and social leaders as "enemies of the truth"? Does his description also apply to political and social leaders in general?

WRITING ASSIGNMENTS

1. Reaction Journal: Assume the role of Shelby Steele and write a letter to Stokely Carmichael about the potential failures that underlie the Black Power movement. (Half the class may assume Carmichael's role and write a response to Steele.) Discuss the results.

2. Write a balanced and logical essay in which you compare and contrast Carmichael's view of the importance of group power and individual power to Steele's.

SPEECH BEFORE THE DEMOCRATIC NATIONAL CONVENTION

REVEREND JESSE L. JACKSON

Jesse Jackson (b. 1941), an ordained Baptist minister and an eloquent orator, had by the 1980s become the nation's best-known civil rights activist. From 1966 to 1971, Jackson directed Operation Breadbasket, the arm of the Southern Christian Leadership Conference under the leadership of Martin Luther King, Jr., which exerted economic pressure on companies to end racial discrimination in hiring. In Chicago in 1971 he founded Operation PUSH (People United to Serve Humanity), a civil rights and self-help organization. Jackson's campaigns for the Democratic nomination for the presidency in 1984 and 1988 played an important role in increasing the number of African-Americans registered to vote. In conjunction with his candidacy, he formed the National Rainbow Coalition, a Washington-based political organization representing racial and other minorities. His speeches and papers from the 1988 presidential campaign are published in Keep Hope Alive *(1989). He has also published* Straight from the Heart *(1978), a collection of speeches, and* A Time to Speak: The Autobiography of Jesse Jackson *(1988). In the following excerpt from his speech before the 1992 Democratic Convention, Jackson urges unity—"partnership, not . . . polarization"—and moral vision in seeking to solve persistent social problems.*

◆ FREEWRITING

In the opening to his nationally televised speech Jackson says, "The great temptation in these difficult days of racial polarization and economic injustice is to make political arguments black and white, and miss the moral imperative of wrong and right." Before reading the rest of his address, freewrite for ten or fifteen minutes in response to this remark.

July 14, 1992
Madison Square Garden
New York City

We stand as witnesses to a pregnant moment in history. Across the globe, we feel the pain that comes with new birth. Here, in our country pain abounds. We must be certain that it too leads to new birth, and not a tragic miscarriage of opportunity.

We must turn pain to power, pain into partnership, not pain into polarization.

The great temptation in these difficult days of racial polarization and economic injustice is to make political arguments black and white, and miss the moral imperative of wrong and right. Vanity asks—is it popular? Politics asks—will it win? Morality and conscience ask—is it right?

We are part of a continuing struggle for justice and decency, links in a chain that began long before we were born and will extend long after we are gone. History will remember us not for our positioning, but for our principles. Not by our move to the political center, left or right, but rather by our grasp on the moral and ethical center of wrong and right.

We who stand with working people and poor have a special burden. We must 5
stand for what is right, stand up to those who have the might. We do so grounded in the faith, that that which is morally wrong will never be politically right. But if it is morally sound, it will eventually be politically right.

The Long Path to Progress

When I look at you gathered here today, I hear the pain and see the struggles that prepared the ground that you stand on. We have come a long way from where we started.

A generation ago—in 1964—Fanny Lou Hamer had to fight even to sit in this convention. Tonight, 28 years later, the chair of the Party is Ron Brown from Harlem; the manager is Alexis Herman, an African American woman from Mobile, Alabama. We have come a long way from where we started.

We are more interdependent than we realize. Not only African Americans benefitted from the movement for justice. It was only when African Americans were free to win and sit in these seats, that Bill Clinton and Al Gore from the new South could be able to stand on this rostrum. We are inextricably bound together in a single garment of destiny. Red, yellow, brown, black and white, we are all precious in God's sight. We have come a long way from where we started.

Tonight we face another challenge. Ten million Americans are unemployed, 25 million on food stamps, 35 million in poverty, 40 million have no health care. From the coal miners in Bigstone Gap, West Virginia, to the loggers and environmentalists in Roseburg, Oregon, from displaced textile workers in my home town of Greenville, South Carolina, to plants closing in Van Nuys, California, pain abounds. Plants are closing, jobs leaving on a fast track, more are working for less, trapped by repressive anti-labor laws. The homeless are a source of national shame and disgrace.

The Moral Center

Politics cannot be reduced to a matter of money and ambition. We must stay true to our values, or lose our way.

- In 1939—900 Jews were turned away from the shores of Miami by the U.S. government, sent back to Germany haunted by Hitler.
- In 1942—120,000 Japanese Americans were rounded up and put in American concentration camps.
- In 1992—the U.S. government is turning Haitians away, back into the arms of death, and relaxing sanctions on South Africa.

It was anti-Semitic and wrong in 1939 to lock the Jews out. It was racist and wrong in 1942 to lock the Japanese Americans up. And it is racist and wrong in 1992 to lock the Haitians out and abandon Nelson Mandela in South Africa. South Africa remains a terrorist state. Sanctions should be reimposed until the interim government is established.

Valuing the Family

We hear a lot of talk about family values, even as we spurn the homeless on the street. Remember, Jesus was born to a homeless couple, outdoors in a stable, in the winter. He was the child of a single mother. When Mary said Joseph was not the father, she was abused. If she had aborted the baby, she would have been called immoral. If she had the baby, she would have been called unfit, without family values. But Mary had family values. It was Herod—the Quayle of his day—who put no value on the family.

We who would be leaders must feel and be touched by people's pain. How can you be a doctor and not touch the sick? How can you be a leader and not touch the hurt? Gandhi adopted the untouchables. Dr. King marched with violent gang members, hoping to turn them to the discipline of non-violence.

Above all, we must reach out and touch our children. Our children are embittered and hurt, but it is not a congenital disease. They were not born that way. They live amidst violence and rejection, in broken streets, broken glass, broken sidewalks, broken families, broken hearts. Their music, their rap, their video, their art reflects their broken world. We must reach out and touch them.

Before the riots in Los Angeles, Rep. Maxine Waters and I visited the Imperial Courts and Nickerson Gardens housing projects in Watts, where we spent the night with our children, and then visited the youth detention center with Arsenio Hall and James Almos. We listened to the youth describe their busted and deferred dreams. They suffer 50% unemployment, with no prospects of a job or going to college. It costs $5,000 to send them to high school, $34,000 to send them downtown to the youth detention center.

For many of them, jail is a step up. In jail, they are safe from drive-by shootings. 15
In jail, it's warm in the winter, cool in the summer. In jail they get three balanced meals, access to health care, education and vocational training. Everything they should have on the outside they only get on the inside.

Too many of our children see jail as a relief station, and death as a land beyond pain. We must reach out and touch them. Surely, it is better to have dirty hands and clean hearts than clean hands and a dirty heart.

If we reach out, we can win—and deserve to win. We have heard many different arguments about a winning strategy—whether to rally the base or appeal to those who have strayed. But these are not choices. We will win only if we put forth a vision that corresponds with the size of our problems and the scope of our opportunity, if we reach out to those in despair and those who care, reach across the lines that divide by race, region or religion.

As for the Rainbow Coalition, we will continue to build a movement for economic justice in this land. We will work to mobilize working and poor people to change the course of this country. We will join in defeating George Bush in the fall—that is a necessary first step.

We must continue to build. When Roosevelt came to office, a movement of working people made a new deal possible. When Kennedy came to office, he did not teach Dr. King about civil rights; Dr. King led a movement that made civil rights unavoidable. When Bill Clinton comes to office, we must build a movement that keeps economic justice at the forefront of the agenda.

I know it's dark. But in the dark the flame of hope still burns. 20

In L.A., they focused on Rodney King beaten by white officers, who were acquitted by an all-white jury. But it was a white man who had the instinct and the outrage to film it and make it public. The media focus was on the white truck driver beaten by black youth. But it was four young black youth who stepped in and saved his life, good samaritans.

In the final analysis it comes down to a question of character. On a small Southern college campus, I once observed a lesson never to be forgotten. I saw a dwarf and a giant walking together—they were an odd couple. He was six feet three, she was three feet tall. When they reached the parting paths, they embraced. He handed her her books and she skipped down the path. It looked to be romantic. I asked the president—what is this I am seeing? He said, I thought you would ask. You see, that is his sister, in fact his twin sister. By a twist of fate he came out a giant, she a dwarf. All the big schools offered him athletic scholarships. The pros offered him money. But he said I can only go where my sister can go. And so he ended up here with us.

Somewhere that young man learned ethics, caring for others. Few of us are driven by a tailwind. Most of us struggle with headwinds. Not all of us can be born tall, some are born short, motherless, abandoned, hungry, orphaned. Somebody has to care. It must be us. And if we do, we will win, and deserve to win.

Keep hope alive.

QUESTIONS FOR DISCUSSION

1. Jackson's address abounds with rhetorical strategy appropriate to oratory. His attention to sound and rhythm as well as his use of rhetorical questions, figurative language, and parallel structure attest to his oratorical skill. Read the speech aloud and listen carefully as you collect examples of such techniques.
2. Early in his address Jackson says that "history will remember us not for our positioning, but for our principles." History is important to Jackson, and he uses it frequently in his speeches. Comment on how he uses history and why his usage of it is so appropriate to oratory.

WRITING ASSIGNMENTS

1. Reaction Journal: Reread the quotation and your response in your freewriting for this selection. After examining your initial response, freewrite once again for ten or fifteen minutes, this time with your awareness of the content and strategy of Jackson's speech in mind.
2. Write a short address to a local audience about campus and/or community issues. Consider Jackson's oratorical strategy carefully as you model your own speech after his. Be prepared to read your address to a group of your classmates.

From the Americas—
The Cultural Rainbow

THE HISPANIC POPULATION OF the United States (approximately 23 million) is made up of a number of Spanish-speaking ethnic groups, mainly Mexican-Americans but also Cubans, Puerto Ricans, Dominicans, Colombians, Salvadorans, Nicaraguans, and immigrants from other Latin American countries. Common though not identical features of language, culture, religion, and history unite what is in many ways a diverse and not always compatible group. As George J. Church points out in "A Melding of Cultures," the term Hispanic is a catchall term used to describe Spanish-speaking peoples of white, black, native, and mixed ancestry; as such, it is as imprecise as the term "Anglo," which includes all non-Hispanic whites. The term "Latino" is favored by some groups from Central and South America because it focuses on the idea of indigenous Latin American culture rather than on the colonial connection with Spain.

The sheer magnitude of the Spanish-speaking immigration and the appearance of insularity in the Hispanic community have raised concern about the ability of the United States to absorb what has become the largest number of newcomers from a single-language background in the history of U.S. immigration. Between the census of 1980 and 1990, the Hispanic population increased by 53 percent while the overall population of the United States increased by only 9.8 percent. Clara Rodriguez, in "Salsa in the Melting Pot," believes that the country will be "invigorated" by the influences of these new immigrants. Her optimism, however, is not shared by those who worry that its national identity is threatened by large groups of Spanish-speaking immigrants who, as Church observes, have been able to "colonize bigger chunks of bigger cities than previous waves of immigrants could" and who do not appear to be following historical patterns of linguistic and cultural assimilation.

The largest group of Hispanics—just over 60 percent—is Chicano (Mexican-American). As Luis Valdez and Stan Steiner point out in *Aztlan*, Chicanos are mestizos, racially a "blend of Indigenous America with European-Arabian Spain." The term "La Raza" (La Raza de Bronce) is an ethnic-pride term describing this bronze race, which was a presence in the Southwest before the first English settlement at Jamestown and which became a "minority" when in 1848 half of the national territory of Mexico was ceded to the United States by the Treaty of Guadalupe Hidalgo following the Mexican-American War. Article X of this treaty, included in the original draft but later eliminated by the United States government, promised that within the annexed territories all grants of land made by the Mexican government would be respected as valid. Elimination of this article and changes in others did not help build a relationship of trust and respect between the Mexican-Americans and their new government. In 1853 a financially pressured Mexican government sold an additional 30,000-square-mile strip of land, the Mesilla Valley (now in southern Arizona and New Mexico) in the Gadsden Treaty.

With this purchase, some 2,000 Mexicans who had moved into this area after the ceding of their original lands found themselves again annexed by the United States. The subsequent history of U.S. expansion in California and the Southwest involved further loss of lands for holders of Spanish and Mexican land grants. Since land had been the basis of the northern Mexican socioeconomic system, these losses contributed to the lower social and economic status of Mexican-Americans. Displaced small farmers and ranch workers frequently became migratory workers or moved to cities where they found low-paying, semiskilled jobs in areas such as construction, automobile manufacture, and food processing. Increasing immigration of Anglos into the Southwest reinforced social segregation of the Chicanos, with traditional Mexican towns becoming barrios within the newly expanded Anglo cities.

Because of the high proportion of agricultural workers, many of whom migrate with their families to follow seasonal crops, the Mexican-Americans have the lowest educational level among Hispanics. They have encountered educational segregation and have frequently been assigned to schools with low per-pupil expenditures. While many have experienced socioeconomic gains, the percentages of Mexican-Americans in professional, technical, and managerial positions is far short of being proportionate to their representation in the general population, and Mexican-Americans are still overrepresented in unskilled and farm labor. During the 1960s the Chicano movement became a force for social change. Dedicated to improving the Chicano socioeconomic position and supporting Chicano culture, the movement has been successful in organizing agricultural workers, increasing voter registration and the number of Chicanos running for public office, improving educational levels, and developing bilingual-bicultural programs in the schools. Perhaps the most visible effort of the Chicano movement has been the organization of the United Farm Workers by Cesar Chavez. Working to improve wages and working conditions for agricultural workers, Chavez and the UFW have increased public awareness of the problems many Chicanos face.

The 2,000 mile U.S.-Mexican border has been a significant factor in distinguishing Mexican immigration from that of many other groups. Since movement in both directions is easy, there has always been continuous cultural and linguistic reinforcement through travel and family visits and even through reception of Mexican radio and television broadcasts in border areas. Consequently, Chicano ties to Mexico remain strong. As a result of both legal and illegal immigration from Mexico, the Chicano population grew by 93 percent between 1970 and 1980. This dramatic rate of increase has given rise to fears of a separatist movement in the Southwest, where there are conflicts between Chicanos and Anglos over such issues as employment, schools, social programs, and where loyalty to La Raza is often associated with groups such as the Mexican-American Youth Organization (MAYO), a radical group militant in its antiassimilationist stance. Their activities in the late 1960s were regarded by some Mexican-American leaders as counterproductive. In a 1969 speech before the U.S. House of Representatives, Congressman Henry Gonzalez ("Reverse Racism") suggested that the MAYO leaders stand to do "great harm to themselves and the cause they supposedly are trying to advance" by fanning the flames of hatred and fear. Like the members of other ethnic groups, Mexican-Americans find themselves in different positions on the political spectrum.

After the Chicanos, the Puerto Ricans are the next largest group of Hispanics (approximately 12 percent). Unlike other Hispanics, Puerto Ricans are not, strictly speaking, immigrants, having been granted citizenship in 1917 after the Spanish-American War when the island became a U.S. territory. Between then and the Second World War, U.S. sugar companies established large plantations in Puerto Rico, and the island underwent an economic and agricultural transformation. Thousands of subsistence farmers moved down to the coastal lowlands, lived in shantytowns, and became virtual serfs of the large corporations, their living conditions characterized by extreme poverty and overpopulation. The era after the war saw great improvement in the economic, political, and educational systems of the island, but economic prospects for the large displaced peasantry were not bright. The continued problems of poverty and overpopulation, combined with the institution of cheap air travel between San Juan and New York City, resulted in heavy immigration from Puerto Rico to New York, a strangely nonagricultural destination for a basically rural people.

In 1940, New York had 70,000 Puerto Rican residents. In 1950 the population had increased to 250,000 and in 1960 to 613,000. One third of all Puerto Ricans in the United States live in New York City. The original center of settlement was East Harlem. By the end of the 1950s it had shifted to the South Bronx, where it remains today. With economic progress on the island, fear that New York would be inundated by a continual immigration of destitute Puerto Ricans abated. Concerns continue, however, that the Puerto Rican population in this country has not as a whole followed the typical American immigrant group pattern of rising out of poverty. Slow progress was made during the 1950s and 1960s, but in the 1970s family income dropped and family structure underwent a dramatic change, as the percentage of Puerto Ricans living in families headed by a single unemployed parent more than doubled. For a time in the 1980s nearly half of all Puerto Rican families were living in poverty. Compared with other Hispanics, Puerto Ricans have a higher poverty rate, higher health risks, higher rate of female-headed families, and higher rate of "labor force nonparticipation," a measure of the percentage of people who have not looked for a job in the previous month.

There seems to be no one explanation of why poverty is so widespread and persistent among Puerto Ricans. Some of the explanations advanced are related to the nature of the immigration itself and some to the conditions encountered in the new environment. Compared to immigrants from Cuba and the Dominican Republic, for instance, the Puerto Ricans who came to the United States during the peak years of immigration were not the best prepared to make a successful transition. Largely destitute former peasants, they were unequipped to compete in an industrial economy. Also, they were unlucky in their choice of destination. There was a general decline in unskilled labor opportunities in the large eastern cities where Puerto Ricans, without the skills necessary for white-collar jobs, tend to migrate. New York lost thousands of jobs during the 1970s, and the movement of much of the garment industry to the South was a particular hardship for Puerto Ricans. (Since 1970 there has been a change in this pattern, with better-educated immigrants coming to the United States because of a shortage of middle-income jobs in Puerto Rico.) The traditional island ethic that women should not work outside the home also contributes to the low income of Puerto Rican families. In "Profound Changes" Elena Padilla mentions working outside the home as one of the criteria that distinguish "bad" women from "good" women; when interviewed, some Puerto Rican women who have jobs deny that they work because of the social stigma that employment carries. There is therefore a higher percentage of Puerto Rican women out of the labor force than black or white women. An additional factor, as George J. Church points out, is that the freedom of Puerto Ricans to come and go as they please between the island and the United States may weaken motivation to succeed in the new environment, and because of improvements in the island economy many remain ambivalent about where their future lies. These and other factors such as racial discrimination and cultural insensitivity contribute to keeping Puerto Ricans at the bottom of the socioeconomic scale. Progress is being made, but at a slow pace.

Much of the data on the Puerto Rican population in the United States is drawn from the experience of the first and second generations. In the literature of immigration experience, the second generation—those growing up in homes reflecting the culture of their parents while at the same time being socialized in an American environment—has been identified as "the difficult generation." Typically, a certain number of individuals in this generation become lost between the two cultures, and it is easy to overemphasize their problems. In spite of a disturbingly high dropout rate, the overall educational achievement of second-generation Puerto Ricans is considerably higher than that of their parents, and culturally these children of two cultures—the "Nuyoricans"—have established a vibrant presence. Books such as Piri Thomas's *Down These Mean Streets*, the poetry of writers such as Pedro Pietri and Tato Laviera, the music of Charlie Palmieri and Tito Puente, the performances of the Puerto Rican Traveling Theatre and the Ballet Hispánico all bear witness to the vitality of the Puerto Rican presence in what Laviera calls this "you-name-it-we-got-it-society."

The experience of Cuban immigrants has for the most part been quite different from that of the Puerto Ricans. Cuban-Americans have the highest education and income levels among the U.S. Hispanic population, of which they comprise approximately 5 percent. Over 17 percent have completed four or more years of college. Their success derives largely from the socioeconomic characteristics of the Cubans who arrived in the United States as political refugees after the 1959 Castro-led Communist revolution.

From the beginning of the twentieth century until the revolution, Cubans migrated to the United States at the rate of 10,000 to 15,000 annually. Those migrating during that period represented various backgrounds, from members of the elite who happened to be socially or politically out of favor to unemployed workers seeking a better standard of living. But the more than 155,000 refugees arriving between 1959 and 1962, when Castro established a Communist system on the island, were largely upper- and upper-middle-class professional and commercial people and landowners. While the group was not homogeneous, these immigrants were disproportionately wealthy, well educated, and, since class and race in prerevolutionary Cuba were closely related, fair-skinned.

During the period between 1962 and 1965, when there were no diplomatic relations between the United States and Cuba and hence no direct flights, an additional 30,000 Cubans arrived, having escaped Cuba on small boats or through a third country. Typically, the first wave of political refugees to flee a country after a Communist takeover are the wealthiest, most ambitious, and most highly skilled. In contrast, the approximately 257,000 arriving via a special airlift from Varadero to Miami between 1965 and 1972 came mostly from lower-middle-class and blue-collar backgrounds, and the more than 120,000 coming on the Mariel boatlift of 1980 (some of whom had been incarcerated in Cuban prisons and mental hospitals) were among the least advantaged of the Cuban refugees. Oscar Hijuelos's "Visitors, 1965" offers a glimpse of the contrast that often existed between the social adjustment and upward mobility of those arriving during the pre- and post-revolutionary eras.

While New York is the center for the U.S. Puerto Rican population, Miami is the center for the Cuban-American population, with over 40 percent of all the Cubans in this country living in metropolitan Miami. They have been for the most part intent on maintaining their culture. Those living in the greater Miami area, now officially a bilingual city, have created an environment in which all aspects of their lives can be fulfilled within the ethnic community through establishments owned or managed by other Cubans. A flourishing number of private schools teach most of their classes in Spanish, emphasize Cuban history and culture, and serve as transmitters of traditional values and culture.

The very strong determination of the Cuban community to maintain its separate linguistic and cultural identity has to some extent added to Miami's tourist attractions. But it has also raised concerns among some Anglos about the potential loss of mainstream "American" identity in South Florida and the development of parallel cultures rather than a unified one. These concerns are echoed in other areas of the country, where the increasing presence of Spanish-speaking minorities is forcing American society to come to grips with basic issues regarding the relationship of language and ethnicity to national identity. Cultural pluralism has occasioned controversies over public education, where curricula are responding in various ways to the demand for multicultural education (see "Casebook on Multicultural Education") and over language policies in general, with English Only proponents attempting to hold the line against de facto bilingualism (see "Language"). In addition to these important and frequently divisive issues, the large numbers of immigrants and refugees exert critical pressures on local governments and social welfare programs. In Florida, for instance, there is rising concern that an influx of refugees that may result from deteriorating conditions in Cuba and Haiti could cause a crisis in housing, law enforcement, social services, and education. Officials cite statistics from the 1980 Mariel boat lift following which 90,000 Cuban refugees settled in southern Florida. One year after the boat lift food-stamp participation had increased by 36,000, school enrollment in Dade County had risen by 14,362, and unemployment in the county had risen from 6.7 percent to 13 percent. Thus many Florida residents—including Cubans—fear the consequences of the new wave of refugees.

Although the arrival in recent years of large numbers of Hispanics, many of them from Central America, has in some instances resulted in Anglo-Hispanic and, in other instances, Black-Hispanic confrontation, the increasingly significant Hispanic presence may have positive effects on Americans' perception of race. Clara Rodriguez and others have observed that while Euro-Americans think of race in physical terms, Latinos regard it as more a cultural than a physical phenomenon. Race in Latin America denotes a group of people who are essentially similar to one another across a wide range of variables, including class, manners, education, and appearance. One's "cultural identity" is more important than one's biologically determined race. The racial mixtures represented among Hispanics defy easy classification into the usual Black/White/Asian/Native American categories. Perhaps in the long run, the influence of Hispanic-American ways of seeing oneself and others will influence American society to place less emphasis on noting immutable biological differences and more emphasis on identifying shared values and beliefs.

SALSA IN THE MELTING POT

CLARA E. RODRIGUEZ

Clara E. Rodriguez (b. 1944) is a professor of sociology at Fordham University. A Puerto Rican, Rodriguez was born in New York and earned a bachelor's degree at City College and a Ph.D. at Washington University, Saint Louis. She has written Puerto Ricans, Born in the U.S.A. *(1989) and edited (with Virginia Sanche Vorroi and Oscar Alers)* The Puerto Rican Struggle *(1980). In this article, which appeared in the* Boston Globe *in 1991, Rodriguez points to the difference between the largely biologically based definition of race in the United States and its more culturally based definition among Latinos. She argues that the rapidly growing Latino population may effect an important change in the way race has traditionally been thought of in the United States.*

◆ FREEWRITING

Rodriguez points out that Latinos are changing and invigorating U.S. food, music, language, literature, visual arts, and personal behavior. Before reading this selection, freewrite for ten or fifteen minutes on ways Latinos have influenced your daily life.

Predictions proliferate about the impact that the fast-growing Latino population will have on the United States. Latinos, those citizens who trace their roots to Puerto Rico, Mexico and other Spanish-speaking Caribbean and South and Central American countries, will constitute the largest single "minority" group by the turn of the century. (Indeed, some argue this is already the case but that Latinos who are here illegally have not been counted by the census.) As a result, US food, music, language, literature, visual arts, family values and personal warmth will all be invigorated by Latino influences. The old U.S. melting pot—what some Latinos call the *sancocho*, after the lusty Caribbean stew—will be flavored with a big splash of salsa.

That is good news, but it is old news. There is another area, critical and unrecognized, where Latinos may have their greatest impact, and this is the way race is viewed and understood. Although there is general acceptance of the fact that there is only one human race with infinite variation and some population clusters, "race," as people experience it, is a cultural construct. How "races" or racial paradigms are determined varies from culture to culture, as does the meaning of the term "race." Each system of racial classification is seen to be—by those who utilize it—the only correct way of viewing individuals.

Latinos perceive race and react to it in ways that are fundamentally different from those of Euro-Americans. To Latinos, race is more cultural than physical. And while physical or "racial" characteristics may distinguish people from one another, they are not, in themselves, the basis for sub-group segregation. This is not to say that race is unimportant in Latin America or among Latinos; rather, it is different. The enslavement of both Africans and indigenous peoples was widespread, and it was often accompanied by cruel and harsh treatment. The emphasis on the racial superiority of white Europeans is an inherent part of the colonial legacy in Latin America. This legacy is often subtly manifested, e.g., in common parlance, kinky hair is referred to as *pelo malo* (bad hair), and standards of beauty seldom deviate from the European model.

The Traditional U.S. View of Race

In the United States, race has historically been seen as a black-white dichotomy. There were essentially two races: white and not white, which most often meant black. The white race was defined by the absence of any nonwhite blood, and the black race was defined by the presence of any black blood. Thus, the offspring of Native American Indians, Asians or whites who intermarried with blacks became black. Race was genetically or biologically defined, and it could not change over a person's lifetime, or as a person moved from one part of the United States to another.

The 1896 decision of the US Supreme Court in the *Plessy* vs. *Ferguson* case 5
legitimated this dualistic view of race. In this case, the petitioner averred that since he was "... seven eighths Caucasian and one eighth African blood; and that the mixture of colored blood was not discernible in him ..." that he was entitled to the rights and privileges of citizens of the white race. The Supreme Court decided against the plaintiff, thus further legitimizing the genetic or blood-quantum definition of race and sanctioning Jim Crow legislation.

This U.S. view of race, as an either/or condition where the basis for racial distinctions is biological, is in contrast to the Latin-American view, where race is conceived of as a continuum, with one's place along the continuum determined partly by social factors. In Latin America, race refers to a group of people who are felt to be somehow similar in their essential nature. That essential nature depends on biology but also on physical appearance, class, education, manners and other "social" variables. Thus, while in the United States race has been an ascribed characteristic that does not change after birth, or from country to country, in Latin America, race can change over time or from place to place. Consequently, a man can go from being white in Puerto Rico to mulatto in Mexico to black in the United States.

This more "ambiguous" concept of race has been a strong theme in Latin-American literature and political thought. It had its antecedents in Spain and Portugal and was redefined in the New World, the Amerindian colonies. In Brazil, for example, up to 40 racial categories have been enumerated, while in the Spanish Caribbean, race ranges along a continuum of racial categories. Latinos have a number of intermediate categories, e.g., *mestizo*, *triguano*, *indio*, *moreno*, etc., not known in the United States. But most important, for many Latinos, cultural identity often supersedes racial identity; while for other Latinos, racial identity is often fused with their cultural identity. By contrast, in the United States, non-Hispanic whites, when identifying themselves or others racially, tend to use the "traditional" racial categories, i.e., white, black, Asian and Native American Indian. These categories are used regardless of the ethnic or cultural identity of the individuals being racially classified.

The Census and U.S. Latinos

The fact that Latinos and Euro-Americans have different ways of racial identification has become more critical with the rapid growth of Hispanics in the United States. In the 1980 census, 40 percent of all the Latinos in the United States responded they were "other-Spanish" to the race question, while less than 2 percent of the non-Hispanic population in any state responded they were "other." The 1990 census showed a dramatic surge in the "other" category—10 million people listed their race as "other." This category increased by 45.1 percent since 1980, making it the second fastest-growing of all the racial categories, right behind Asian.

While some observers see this as indicating confusion, I see it as a clear rejection of the US biracial categorization, in favor of a category that indicates one is not culturally, socially or politically white or black, that one is something else, perhaps another "social race." Thus, for example, one may appear to be physically white or black but identify in terms of one's national origin or as a multiracial person. For many of these "others," there may be a physical component to race, but racial identity is ultimately a subjective sense of what one is (culturally), not what one looks like to others.

Physical and Cultural Identities

Because of its emphasis on biological descent, the U.S. race perspective tends to 10
utilize physical characteristics to determine cultural identities. Thus, Asian-appearing people are considered Asian even though they may never have been to Asia, i.e., they may be from the Andes, the Philippines or from Mexico. Within this U.S. racial perspective, cultural distinctions, such as the fact that while growing up some may speak (or spoke) Korean, while others spoke Tibetan, are irrelevant. Ironically, what are perhaps prime identifiers, i.e., national origin, culture or language, are ignored. Similarly, Panamanians who are Spanish-speaking but appear to be African-Americans are also asked to shed their unique culture and language and become "black and not Hispanic." Lastly, Latin Americans of Scandinavian appearance are seen to be non-Hispanic and sometimes placed into the position of having to prove their Hispanicity.

This tendency to classify individuals according to their race and not their culture continues the assimilationist thrust of the melting-pot theorists, while it preserves the inequities attendant on the dualistic race order in the United States. The long experience of African-Americans and Native American Indians from different tribes—which are really different nations, with unique cultures—exemplifies this dual process of homogenization and minoritization.

The Latino view of race—as a social, not biological phenomenon—turns all this on its head. For Latinos, culture is the more important aspect of who someone is.

The Challenge to U.S. Society

This Latino view of race, as cultural first and physical second, poses a fundamental challenge to the historic place of race in US society. Moreover, the influx of increasing numbers of other racially and ethnically diverse peoples to these shores is bound to force a reexamination of the US view of race. As minorities become the "emerging majority," and as whites become a "minority" in some urban areas, the dichotomous view of race in the United States, wherein one is white or nonwhite, will become less and less useful as a means of distinguishing groups and individuals.

We can only hope that this process of growing racial and cultural diversity in America will be seen and appreciated as a positive, enriching force. Then, and only then, when the American dream is framed as a cultural rainbow, can America fulfill its pluralistic heritage and promise.

QUESTIONS FOR DISCUSSION

1. Rodriguez contends that Latino perception of race could (and perhaps should) alter the U.S. black-white dichotomy. Explain how Latinos and non-Latinos regard race and how a new social perception might alter race relations. Why does Rodriguez argue that social factors are more important to Latinos than biological factors?
2. How might a cultural perception of racial differences address the central issue of confrontation and accommodation?

WRITING ASSIGNMENTS

1. Reaction Journal: Write a letter to a friend in which you explain the central point of "Salsa in the Melting Pot." After a personal opening paragraph, limit your summary to one paragraph of about one hundred words, then move to your closing.
2. Rodriguez suggests that race will be less dichotomous in urban areas as whites become a "minority." Write a brief essay in which you compare the biological and social perceptions of race. Do you agree that a social view of race is essential if America is to "fulfill its pluralistic heritage and promise"?

FROM AZTLAN

LUIS VALDEZ AND STAN STEINER

Dramatist Luis Valdez (b. 1940) founded Teatro Campesino in 1965 as a cultural outgrowth of Cesar Chavez's United Farm Workers. The teatro, of which Valdez's is the most famous, is a distinctive form of Chicano expression, emphasizing themes of Anglo discrimination, Chicano resistance, and Mexican heritage and features interaction between players and audience. As the company's director, Valdez has helped foster the growth of Mexican-American literature. In addition to a collection of short plays, Valdez has published Pensamiento Serpentino: A Chicano Approach to the Theater of Reality *(1973). Together with Stan Steiner he edited* Aztlan: An Anthology of Mexican American Literature *(1972).*

Among Stan Steiner's (1925–1987) many books on Native Americans and Mexican-Americans and the cultures of the American West are La Raza *(1969),* The Vanishing of the White Man *(1987), and* The Waning of the West *(1990). In the following excerpt from their introduction to* Aztlan, *Valdez and Steiner sketch the history of La Raza, the bronze race, and describe the emergence of its energy and spirit in the Chicano.*

◆ FREEWRITING

Read the first paragraph of "Aztlan" carefully. Before reading the rest of the selection, freewrite for ten or fifteen minutes on what you predict will be the tone and content of this selection. After reading the selection, discuss your freewriting with the class as you consider such issues as tone and opening paragraphs.

Man has been in the Americas for more than 38,000 years. White men have been around for less than five hundred. It is presumptuous, even dangerous, for anyone to pretend that the Chicano, the "Mexican-American," is only one more in the long line of hyphenated-immigrants to the New World. *We are the New World.*

Our insistence on calling ourselves Chicanos stems from a realization that we are not just one more minority group in the United States. We reject the semantic games of sociologists and whitewashed Mexicans who frantically identify us as Mexican-Americans, Spanish-Americans, Latin-Americans, Spanish-speaking, Spanish-surname, Americans of Mexican descent, etc. We further reject efforts to make us disappear into the white melting pot, only to be hauled out again when it is convenient or profitable for *gabacho** *(gringo)* politicians. Some of us are as dark as *zapote*,** but we are casually labeled Caucasian.

We are, to begin with, *Mestizos*—a powerful blend of Indigenous America with European-Arabian Spain, usually recognizable for the natural bronze tone it lends to human skin. Having no specific race of our own, we used poetry and labeled ourselves centuries ago as La Raza, the Race, albeit a race of half-breeds, misfits, and mongrels. Centuries of interbreeding further obfuscated our lineage, and La Raza gave itself other labels—*la plebe, el vulgo, la palomía*.*** Such is the natural poetry of our people. One thing, however, was never obscured: that the Raza was basically Indio, for that was borne out by our acts rather than mere words, beginning with the act of birth.

During the three hundred years of Nueva España, only 300,000 *gachupines*† settled in the New World. And most of these were men. There were so few white people at first, that ten years after the Conquest in 1531, there were more black men in Mexico than white. Negroes were brought in as slaves, but they soon intermarried and "disappeared." Intermarriage resulted in an incredible *mestizaje*, a true melting pot. Whites with Indios produced *mestizos*. Indios with blacks produced *zambos*. Blacks with whites produced mulattoes. *Pardos, cambujos, tercernones, salta atrases*,†† and other types were born out of mestizos with zambos and mulattoes with Indios, and vice versa. Miscegenation went joyously wild, creating the many shapes, sizes, and hues of La Raza. But the predominant strain of the mestizaje remained Indio. By the turn of the nineteenth century, most of the people in Mexico were mestizos with a great deal of Indian blood.

The presence of the Indio in La Raza is as real as the barrio. Tortillas, ta- 5
males, chile, marijuana, *la curandera, el empacho, el molcajete, atole*,††† La Virgen de Guadalupe—these are hard-core realities for our people. These and thousands of other little human customs and traditions are interwoven into the fiber of our daily life. América Indigena is not ancient history. It exists today in the barrio, having survived even the subversive onslaught of the twentieth-century neon gabacho commercialism that passes for American culture.

Yet the barrio is a colony of the white man's world. Our life there is second hand, full of *chingaderas*§ imitating the way of the *patrón*.§§ The used cars, rented houses, old radio and TV sets, stale grocery stores, plastic flowers—all the trash of the white man's world mixes with the bits and pieces of that other life, the Indio life, to create the barrio. Frijoles and tortillas remain, but the totality of

* Other, foreign, non-Hispanic.

** Type of plum.

*** Common people, masses, and the place where they gather.

† Originally, Capuchin monks; used by Mexicans to mean Spaniard.

†† indicate various degrees of racial mixture. *Salta atrases* = throwbacks.

††† *La curandera*—healer; *el empacho*—indigestion; figuratively, embarrassment; *el molcajete*—stone mortar; *atole*—a drink made from corn flour.

§ Stupidities.

§§ Boss, master.

the Indio's vision is gone. Curanderas make use of plants and herbs as popular cures, without knowing that their knowledge is what remains of a great medical science. Devout Catholics pray to the Virgen de Guadalupe, without realizing that they are worshipping an Aztec goddess, Tonatzin.

The barrio came into being with the birth of the first mestizo. Before we imitated the gringo, we imitated the *hacendado*†; before the hacendado, the gachupin. Before we lived in the Westside, Chinatown, the Flats, Dogtown, Sal Si Puedes, and El Hoyo, we lived in Camargo, Reynosa, Guamuchil, Cuautla, Tepoztlán. Before the Southwest, there was México; before México, Nueva España. The barrio goes all the way back to 1521, and the Conquest.

> We are Indian, blood and soul; the language and civilization are Spanish.
>
> —José Vasconcelos

Imagine the Conquistadores looking upon this continent for the first time. Imagine Pedro de Alvarado, Hernando Cortes! Fifty-foot caballeros with golden *huevos*,†† bringing the greed of little Europe to our jungle-ridden, god-haunted world. They saw the land and with a sweep of an arm and a solemn prayer claimed this earth for the Spanish crown, pronouncing it with Catholic inflection and Siglo de Oro* majesty, Nueva España. *New* Spain. Imagine now a fine white Spanish veil falling over the cactus mountains, volcanoes, valleys, deserts, and jungles; over the chirimoya, quetzal, ocelotl, nopal.** Imagine, finally, white men marching into the light and darkness of a very old world and calling it new.

This was not a new world at all. It was an ancient world civilization based on a distinct concept of the universe. Tula, Teotihuacan, Monte Alban, Uxmal, Chichen Itzá, México-Tenochtitlan were all great centers of learning, having shared the wisdom of thousands of generations of pre-Columbian man. The Mayans had discovered the concept of zero a thousand years before the Hebrews, and so could calculate to infinity, a profound basis of their religious concepts. They had operated on the human brain, and had evolved a mathematical system which allowed them to chart the stars. That system was vigesimal, meaning it was based on a root of twenty rather than ten, because they had started by counting on their fingers and toes instead of just their fingers as in the decimal system. . . .

None of the achievements of Indigenous America meant very much to the Conquistador. Nor was he content to merely exploit its physical strength. He

† landowner.

†† Eggs; here, balls.

* Golden Age (from the sixteenth to the seventeenth century).

** *Chirimoya*—a fruit called the custard apple; *quetzal*—a green bird of Central America known for its bright plumage; *ocelotl*—ocelot; *nopal*—prickly pear cactus.

sought to possess its mind, heart, and soul. He stuck his bloody fingers into the Indian brain, and at the point of the sword, gun, and cross ripped away a vision of human existence. He forced the Indio to accept his world, his reality, his scheme of things, in which the Indio and his descendants would forever be something less than men in Nueva España's hierarchy of living things. Murder and Christianity worked hand in hand to destroy the ancient cities, temples, clothes, music, language, poetry. The women were raped, and the universe, el Quinto Sol, the world of the Earthquake Sun, was shattered.

> Desgraciada raza mexicana, obedecer no quieres, gobernar no puedes.*
>
> —Amado Nervo

In the twilight of the Conquest, the Mestizo was born into colonization. Rejected as a bastard by his Spanish father, he clung to his Indian mother and shared the misery of her people, the overwhelming sense of loss:

> Nothing but flowers and songs of sorrow are left in Mexico and Tlaltelolco, where once we saw warriors and wise men.

Soon there was not even that. Death overtook all who remembered what it had been like, and colonization set in for three hundred years.

Our dark people looked into one another's eyes. The image reflected there was one the white man had given us. We were savage, Indio, Mestizo, half-breed: always something less than simple men. Men, after all, have a tendency to create God in their own image. No, men we could never be, because only the *patrón* could be a god. We were born to be his instrument, his peon, his child, his whore—this he told us again and again through his religion, literature, science, politics, economics. He taught us that his approach to the world, his logical disciplines of human knowledge, was truth itself. That everything else was barbaric superstition. Even our belief in God. In time there was nothing left in our hearts but an empty desire, a longing for something we could no longer define.

Still, for all the ferocity of the Conquest, the Mestizo cannot totally condemn the Spaniard. He might as well condemn his own blood. Anglos particularly are very fond of alluding to the black legend of the Conquistador in Mexico, perhaps to mask the even more inhuman treatment of the Indian in the United States. The gachupin offered the Indio colonization; the Anglo, annihilation. There is no question that Nueva España was more human to América Indigena than New England.

Some white men, such as Fray Bartolomé de las Casas, saw the evils of New Spain and denounced them:

* Unfortunate Mexican race, obey, you wish not, govern, you cannot.

> All the wars called conquests were and are most unjust and truly tyrannical. We have usurped all the kingdoms and lordships of the Indies.

Others, like Sahagun and Motolinia, saved what they could of ancient chronicles, *los codices de la tinta negra y roja*,* the life thought of a dispossessed world civilization.

It is doubtful, however, that any white man in colonial Mexico or New England was aware of the ultimate importance of the Mestizo. As the real new man of the Americas, he was the least likely candidate to be called an American. The reason may be that the name *America* was an imported European title, and reserved therefore only for European types. By right of discovery, the honor afforded to Amerigo Vespucci should have gone to Christopher Columbus. Yet *Columbia* would have been just as alien to the native people of this land as *America*. The naming of the continent had nothing to do with the Indios or their Mestizo children. It was strictly an amusement of white, western European man.

Once America was named, Europe yawned and went on with the dull but profitable business of exploitation and colonization. Wherever possible, North and South America were built or rebuilt in the image of Europe. Spain gorged itself on the gold of New Spain; and England did a brisk trade on the tobacco of New England. Aside from mercantile ventures, the Old World was so uninterested in the New that even white colonists felt neglected.

It took a revolution in the thirteen colonies of New England to again raise 15
the issue of America. Once again the Indios and Mestizos were forgotten. In 1776 the United States of America usurped the name of a continental people for a basically white, English-speaking, middle-class minority. It revealed, perhaps, the continental ambitions of that minority. But an American was henceforth defined as a white citizen of the U.S.A. The numerous brown Quiche, Nahuatl, and Spanish-speaking peoples to the south were given secondary status as Latin Americans, Spanish Americans, and South Americans. It was a historical snow job. The descendants of América Indigena were now foreigners in the continent of their birth.

Gabacho America, however, was not to touch the Mestizo for at least another half century. While the Monroe Doctrine and Manifest Destiny were being hatched in Washington, D.C., the Mestizo was still living in Nueva España. During the colonial period, he easily achieved numerical superiority over the white man. But the dominant culture remained Spanish. So the Mestizo stood at a cultural crossroads, not unlike the one he later encountered in the United States: choose the way of Mexico Indio and share degradation; or go the way of the white man and become Hispanicized.

The choice was given as early as 1598, when Don Juan de Oñate arrived in the Southwest to settle and claim New Mexico, "from the edge of the mountains to the stones and sand in the rivers, and the leaves of trees." With him came four

* The codexes of black and white.

hundred Mestizos and Indios as soldiers. Many of the Hispanos, or Spanish Americans living in New Mexico today, are descended directly from those first settlers. Their regional name reveals the cultural choice their ancestors made; but it also reveals a reluctance to choose, for Hispano to some New Mexicans also means Indiohispano. In 1598 there was not, of course, national status for Mestizos as Mexicanos. Even so, after Independence, Hispanos refused to identify with the racial, cultural, and political confusions of Mexico.

The internal conflicts of nineteenth-century Mexico resulted from a clash of races as well as classes. Conservative Criollos and the clergy usurped the War of Independence against Spain; after 1810, the bronze mass of Indios and Mestizos continued to be exploited by a white minority. Avarice and individual ambition superseded the importance of national unity. Coups and *pronunciamentos** became commonplace, and further weakened the new nation. Mexico did not belong to her people.

Watching the internal struggles south of the border, the United States circled around Texas and hovered above California like a buzzard. Mexico was ill-equipped to defend either state. When rebels struck at the Alamo, President Antonio López de Santa Ana unfortunately decided to rout them out personally. Leaving General don José Maria Tornel in charge of the government, he drafted an army of six thousand. Through forced loans from businessmen, he equipped them poorly, and with promises of land in Texas won their allegiance. The long march to Texas was painful and costly. Supplies, animals, ammunition, and hundreds of soldiers were lost due to the rigors of winter. Inept as a general, Santa Ana despotically ordered the worst routes for his convoys. He almost accomplished the failure of the expedition before even reaching Texas.

The rest is "American" history. The rebels lost the Alamo, but regrouped 20
under Samuel Houston to finally defeat Santa Ana at San Jacinto. Some important historical facts, however, are never mentioned in U.S. classrooms. After the fall of the Alamo and San Antonio Bejar, the rebels resorted to guerrilla warfare. They destroyed crops and burned towns, so that the Mexican troops would have no place to get supplies. They in turn received weapons, food, and men from the United States. The South particularly was interested in Texas as a future slave state. Mexico had outlawed slavery in 1824, but some of the defenders of freedom at the Alamo died for the freedom of holding black slaves.

Slavery was foremost in the minds of the Mexican signers of the Treaty of Guadalupe Hidalgo in 1848. Ceding fully half of the national territory of Mexico to the United States, they were concerned about the 75,000 Mexican citizens about to be absorbed into an alien country. They feared that the dark Mexican Mestizo would share the fate of the black man in America. They asked for guarantees that Mexican families would not lose their ancestral lands, that civil and

* Political uprisings, insurrections.

cultural rights would be respected. But the United States, still hot from its first major imperialistic venture, was not ready to guarantee anything.

Witness the memoirs of Ulysses S. Grant, who was with General Zachary Taylor at the Rio Grande, which admit that the United States had goaded Mexico into "attacking first." No stretch of the imagination can explain why Mexico, bleeding from internal conflict, would want to provoke war with the U.S. Known as *la invasion norte-americana* in Mexico, the Mexican War polluted the moral climate of America. Abraham Lincoln debated with Stephen Douglas over the ultimate wisdom and morality of the war. It was an early-day version of Vietnam. Manifest Destiny won the day, however, and the U.S. acquired the Southwest. When the Treaty of Guadalupe Hidalgo came before Congress for ratification, Article Nine was replaced and Article Ten was stricken out. The two Articles dealt, respectively, with civil rights and land guarantees.

The no-nonsense attitude of American politics merged with white racism to create the stereotype of the Mexican greaser. Carrying the added stigma of defeat in battle, the Mestizo was considered cowardly, lazy, and treacherous. Anglo America was barely willing to recognize his basic humanity, much less the nobility of his pre-Columbian origins. He was a Mexican, and that was it. But contrary to the myth of the Sleeping Giant, the Mexican in the Southwest did not suffer the abuses of the gringo by remaining inert.

In 1859, Juan N. Cortina declared war on the gringos in Texas. On November 23 from his camp in the Rancho del Carmen, County of Cameron, he released a proclamation:

> Mexicans! When the State of Texas began to receive the new organization which its sovereignty required as an integrant part of the Union, flocks of vampires, in the guise of men, came and scattered themselves in the settlements . . . many of you have been robbed of your property, incarcerated, chased, murdered, and hunted like wild beasts, because your labor was fruitful, and because your industry excited the vile avarice which led them. A voice infernal said, from the bottom of their soul, "kill them; the greater will be our gain!"

The document was intense but despairing for a real solution to the problem of gringo domination. Cortina proposed to fight to the death if need be, and offered La Raza in Texas the protection of a secret society sworn to defend them. He addressed his people as Mexicanos, but the fact remains that they were no longer citizens of Mexico. They were Mestizos cast adrift in the hellish limbo of Anglo America. Cortina got his war, and lost.

25 There were others, before and after Cortina, who waged guerrilla warfare from the mountains of the Southwest. In California, from 1850 to 1875, Joaquín Murieta and Tiburcio Vásquez span a period of unmitigated struggle. History dismissed them as bandits; asinine romanticized accounts of their "exploits" have totally distorted the underlying political significance of their rebellion.

Bandits in Mexico, meanwhile, were on the verge of creating the first major revolution of the twentieth century. The Revolution of 1910. The revolution of Emiliano Zapata and Pancho Villa. *El indio y el mestizo.* At Independence, only one fifth of Mexico's population had been white. A century later, it was less than one thirteenth. In the hundred years between Independence and the Revolution, the number of Mestizos had *quadrupled.* In 1910 they numbered fifty-three percent of the total population, while the Indios had remained fairly stable at close to forty percent. Yet white men ruled, while the blood and flesh of Mexico went hungry.

A new motivating force was behind the Revolution of 1910, and that force was La Raza, la plebe, *los de abajo.** Indigenous Mexico discovered itself and so arose with all the fury that four hundred years of oppression can create. The bloodroot of la patria exploded, and Mestizos and Indios fought to the death to make Mexico what it had not been since Cuauhtemoc: a unique creation of native will. La plebe burst into the private halls and dining rooms of the rich; it broke down the great walls of the haciendas and smashed the giant doors of holy cathedrals, shouting obscenities and laughing, crying, yelling, sweating, loving, killing, and singing:

La Cucaracha, La Cucaracha
Ya no puede caminar
Porque le falta, porque no tiene
Marijuana que fumar!**

It was a revolution with few restraints, and La Raza expressed itself as never before. A half-breed cultural maelstrom swept across Mexico in the form of *corridos,*† bad language, vulgar topics, disrespectful gestures, *pleberías.* It was all a glorious affront to the aristocracy, which, wrapped in their crucifixes and fine Spanish laces, had been licking the boots of American and British speculators for a lifetime. In 1916, when Woodrow Wilson sent Pershing into Mexican territory on a "punitive" expedition, looking for Pancho Villa, U.S. intervention had already seriously crippled the Revolution. Pershing failed to find Villa, but la plebe launched a corrido against the gringo:

Que pensarían esos gringos tan patones que nuestro suelo pretenden conquistar. Si ellos tienen cañones de amontones aquí tenemos lo mero principal!††

* The underdogs: Mariano Azuela used this expression as the title of his 1916 novel *Los de abajo.*

** The cockroach, the cockroach
Can no longer walk
Because he lacks, because he doesn't have
Marijuana to smoke.

† A ballad.

†† What would those big-footed gringos think, those who seek to conquer our land. If they have piles of cannon, we have the real treasure, the will to live.

Three years later Emiliano Zapata was dead in Chinameca, and the terrible reality of a dying Revolution began to settle on the people. In 1923 Pancho Villa was assassinated by a savage hail of bullets in the dusty streets of Parral, Chihuahua. That same year, almost 64,000 Mexicans crossed the fictitious border into the United States. During the following years 89,000 poured across, and the U.S., alarmed by the sudden influx, organized the border patrol. This was the first time the boundary between Mexico and the Southwest had ever been drawn, but now it was set, firmly and unequivocally. Even so, ten percent of Mexico's population made it across, *pa' este lado.** La plebe crossed the border, and their remembrance of the patria was forever stained by memories of bloody violence, festering poverty, and hopeless misery. For all their hopes of material gain, their migration (and it was only a short migration into the Southwest) meant a spiritual regression, for them and for their sons—a legacy of shame for being of Mexican descent in the land of the gringo.

Yet the *Revolución* would persist, in memory, in song, in cuentos. It would 30
reach into the barrio, through two generations of Mexicanos, to create the Chicano.

QUESTIONS FOR DISCUSSION

1. Think about the tone of this selection. Is it academic, ironic, accommodating, or confrontational? Locate specific examples of diction, figurative language, and style to illustrate your sense of Valdez and Steiner's tone.

2. The authors assert that *La Raza* is a product of a true melting pot. Explain. How does their view compare with the traditional U.S. view of a melting pot?

3. Why do Valdez and Steiner feel that "the barrio is a colony of the white man's world"? Can the same be said about other urban minority population centers?

WRITING ASSIGNMENTS

1. Reaction Journal: Assume that Valdez and Steiner are visiting your class. Prepare eight to ten questions that would help you understand their intent in "Aztlan." You may focus your questions on both content and rhetorical techniques.

2. If you had to choose one word from this selection as the most important in terms of what Valdez and Steiner are saying, what would it be? Make that word the title of an essay that you prepare in defense of your choice.

* To this side.

REVERSE RACISM

CONGRESSMAN HENRY GONZALEZ

Henry Gonzalez (b. 1916), a member of the U.S. Congress since 1961, holds an engineering degree from the University of Texas at Austin and law degrees from St. Mary's University School of Law in San Antonio. He began his career of public service in San Antonio as a member of the Housing Authority and the City Council. He served as a state senator in Texas from 1956 to 1961, when he was elected to the U.S. House of Representatives. In the following speech to Congress in 1969, Gonzalez records his opposition to the confrontational stance of the Mexican-American Youth Organization (MAYO) and warns against the logic of pursuing "a just cause with unjust tactics."

◆ FREEWRITING

Gonzalez offers this definition of racism: "It is fear, hatred and prejudice combined into a poison that divides men who under their skin are identical; it causes some to believe that they are superior to others, simply because they are one thing and others are not." Freewrite for ten or fifteen minutes on racism. Think of concrete examples you have observed or that have been related to you.

It is virtually impossible for any man of reason, intelligence and sensitivity not to see every day the destructive and corrosive effects of racism. It is virtually impossible for any man who has seen and acknowledges the existence of racism and its terrible results not to fight against it.

Racism is based on feelings that are beyond my power to fathom; it is fear, hatred and prejudice combined into a poison that divides men who under their skin are identical; it causes some to believe that they are superior to others, simply because they are one thing and others are not; and racism has given us all a burden of dishonor, guilt and grief.

The passions of racial hatred have been fanned high by fanatics and demagogues long since gone, but the poisons they disseminated remain with us still. Who can forget the contorted, hateful faces of people attacking innocent children who sought nothing more than to obtain equal educational opportunity, to enter schools freely without regard to the color of their skin? And who can forget the shameful defiance of law by George Wallace's stand in the doors of a great university, or the deadly riots at the University of Mississippi? And who can forget the fire hoses of Birmingham? Who among us did not feel shame on the day of the incident at Selma bridge? The passions that fueled those incidents, and that have bombed schools and churches, and that have created night riders and slick demagogues are with us still. The fears that created Jim Crow are still around, and we are burdened yet with the disaster that frightened *Plessy* vs. *Ferguson;* dozens of court decisions and hundreds of judicial orders have yet to erase the stain the decision placed on our legal system.

There is in physics a series of laws having to do with motion. There is a law of inertia which states that a mass that is headed in a given direction is inclined to continue in that direction until its force is spent or some superior force deflects or overcomes it. There is another law that states that for a given force there is an equal and opposite force; for every action there is an equal and opposite reaction. In the laws of civilizations gone by we can observe these same kinds of phenomena; and injustice will continue until its force is spent or until society rectifies it; and an injustice on one side may lead to another injustice on the other. Even as the poisons of racism are with us still, though its legal foundations be destroyed and gone for all time to come, so too can racism produce an equally deadly, opposite poison that can be called reverse racism. I say it can produce that opposite effect, for the laws of politics are not so precise as the laws of physics; in social interaction there are no immutable laws. It is true that inertia exists in political and social systems, much as it does in physics, but an opposite action, a reaction, will occur only when the force of inertia is so great that only legitimate force can change it.

I believe that we are attacking the forces of hate and bigotry, and I believe 5
that however slowly and painfully we may be doing it, our country is overcoming the forces of racism. I believe that the impetus of racism is spent, or very nearly so, and that it is possible that justice in this land can be achieved within legitimate means.

I do not believe that violence is necessary to obtain justice, and I do not believe that hatred is necessary either; I do not believe that there is any reason why despair should be so great that reverse racism can be justified. Yet reverse racism, and reverse racists exist and their voices are loud, if largely unheard.

No man ought to either practice or condone racism; every man ought to condemn it. Neither should any man practice or condone reverse racism.

Those who would divide our country along racial lines because they are fearful and filled with hatred are wrong, but those who would divide the races out of desire for revenge, or out of some hidden fear, are equally wrong. Any man, regardless of his ambitions, regardless of his aims, is committing an error and a crime against humanity if he resorts to the tactics of racism. If Bilbo's* racism was wrong—and I believe that it was—then so are the brown Bilbos of today.

Fifteen years ago as a member of the City Council of the city of San Antonio, Texas, I asked my fellow Council members to strike down ordinances and regulations that segregated the public facilities of the city, so as to end an evil

* Theodore G. Bilbo (1877–1947), Governor of Mississippi and U.S. Senator, proponent of segregation and white supremacy.

that ought never to have existed to begin with. That Council complied, because it agreed with me that it was time for reason to at long last have its day. Eleven years ago I stood almost alone in the Senate of the State of Texas to ask my colleagues to vote against a series of bills that were designed to perpetuate segregation, contrary to the law of the land. I saw the beginnings then of a powerful reaction to racist politics, and I begged my colleagues to remember: "If we fear long enough, we hate. And if we hate long enough, we fight." I still believe this to be true. Since then there has been vast progress in Texas. I did not know how to describe to you the oppression that I felt then; but I can tell you that the atmosphere today is like a different world. Injustices we still have aplenty, but no longer is there a spirit of blatant resistance to just redress of just grievance. Yet despite this change in the general atmosphere, despite the far healthier tenor of public debate and public action today, I felt compelled almost exactly a year ago to address the United States House of Representatives on the continuing and alarming practice of race politics, and what I chose to call the politics of desperation.

There are those in Texas today—and I suppose elsewhere as well—who be- 10
lieve that the only way that the problems of the poor, and the problems of ethnic minorities, will be solved, is by forcing some kind of confrontation. This confrontation can be economic, or it can be direct and personal, but whatever form it may take, the object is to state in the most forceful possible terms what is wrong, and to demand immediate and complete corrective action. This tactic leaves no room for debate and often no room for negotiation, however reasonable that might be. It is the tactic of drawing a line and saying that it is the point where one system ends and another begins. This may not sound unreasonable in itself, and in fact the tactics of confrontation may have a place in political life. But the problem is that this deliberate and very often sudden confrontation might or might not be reasonable, and the demands presented might or might not be legitimate. The fact is that the tactic deliberately attempts to eliminate alternatives to violence, and it is therefore risky at best and at worst it can lead to disaster. This sort of politics is only one step removed from rebellion.

When the politics of race are added to the politics of confrontation, the makings of tragedy are abundantly clear. Race politics is itself highly unstable, and the same is true of the politics of confrontation. When the potent mixtures of long held passions are met on a hard line, but with justice obscured or perhaps lost in the midst of empty slogans, then great and perhaps irreparable damage can result.

There are those in Texas who believe that reverse racism can be mixed with the politics of confrontation, and that the result will be justice—or if not justice at least revenge. One cannot be certain whether the new racists want justice or revenge; only one thing is certain and that is that you cannot have both.

Probably the leading exponent of the new racism in Texas is the current president of the Mexican-American Youth Organization. This young man is filled with passions that may be obscure even to himself; he is ready to accuse anyone who does not help him of being a "turncoat" and anyone who opposes him of having "gringo tendencies" and concludes that most of the citizens of Texas are racists. Indeed, if he is opposed, he says, ". . . within a few years I will no longer try to work with anybody." He is not certain of what he wants, except that he does not want to "assimilate into this gringo society in Texas." He wants to be "Mexicano" but not "Mexican." He wants to expose and eliminate "gringos," and by that he means killing if "it doesn't work." Of course, I am told that this young man never meant to make such threats, though he clearly uttered them. But those who utter threats and who clearly mean them, must be prepared to be challenged. And I do not believe that anyone who claims any position of responsibility, or anyone who pretends to leadership can make threats of killing and still be expected to be called responsible.

This young man and his followers have attempted to find settings in Texas to practice their militance, and in particular to test out their theory of confrontation.

They distribute literature that is replete with hatred, and which builds on 15
the supposed romance of revolution; too often one finds a photo of Juarez running alongside a photo of Che Guevara in MAYO literature. It would be hard to find a broader appeal than that to build a myth based on Guevara. They print such patent nonsense as "there is no bad luck, just bad gringos." They like to label enemies: "If you label yourself a gringo then you're one of the enemy." They give the overall impression that anyone the MAYO leadership disapproves of is either a gringo or has "gringo tendencies" or is a "turncoat." Only one thing counts to them: loyalty to *la raza* above all else, and MAYO next. Of course they reserve the right to judge who is loyal and who is not.

Filling people with the bright phrases of revolution and the ugly phrases of race hate, MAYO seeks to find a confrontation. They sought it at Del Rio, Texas, on Palm Sunday, but did not find it. Some of them sought it at Denver that same weekend, but did not find it. When they do, they have every likelihood of doing great harm to themselves and the cause they supposedly are trying to advance. The fuel of tension and the flame of passion make a dangerous mix.

I do not favor repression, because I do not believe that order is something that can be forced, at least not in an open and free society. I believe that there is enough good will and enough determination in this country that justice will prevail, and without resort to violence on one side or the other.

The young racists want to promote and exacerbate fears that already exist; they want to destroy what they perceive as an equilibrium, or a stalemate, that militates against their perception of justice. I do not think they will succeed. I believe that most Americans believe, as I do, and as Sandburg did, that:

Across the bitter years and howling winters
The deathless dream will be the strongest
The dream of equity will win.

This is no land of cynics, and it is no land of demagogues; it is a land wherein I believe reason can prevail; if it cannot succeed here, it can succeed nowhere.

20 I oppose this new racism because it is wrong, and because it threatens to destroy that good will, that sense of justice that alone can bring ultimate and lasting justice for all of us. This new racism threatens divisions that cannot be soon healed, and threatens to end whatever hope there may be—and I think that hope is considerable—of peaceful progress toward one country, indivisible, with liberty and justice for all.

I do not want to see Texas riots and burned buildings; and I do not want to see men beaten, men killed, and fear rampant. I have seen it happen in other cities; I have seen fear and hate and violence destroy that essential impetus toward full justice. I have seen the ugliness of division and violence. I do not want to see it again, and I do not want again to have to fight against blind unreasoning intolerance. It is not necessary and it is not inevitable.

But the fruit of racism is prejudice, fear and distrust. There can be no benefit from it, no matter how you color it with romance, or the new techniques of confrontation. There can only be tragedy from it. If MAYO gets its confrontation, it will not "crush any gringo who gets in (the) way"—"squashing him like a beetle"—and it will not "kick the door down." It will only find itself beaten in the end, and with it, the hopes of many innocent people who follow their false banner.

The new racists, if they succeed in their divisive efforts, will in the end only unloose destructive forces that may take generations to control, for those who plumb the well-springs of hate and break the dams of passion always learn too late that passions and hatreds are far easier to open than they are to close. It is not possible to pursue a just cause with unjust tactics, and it is not possible to justify cruel and deceitful actions by the end hoped for. It is not possible to expect sympathy or justice from those whom you threaten with hatred and destruction and it is self-deluding to think that there is no alternative to inviting violence.

I stand for justice, and I stand for classless, raceless politics. I stand for action, and I stand for freedom. I stand against violence, racism, and anyone or anything that threatens our ability in this land to govern ourselves as a free people.

QUESTIONS FOR DISCUSSION

1. Comment on the audience Gonzalez had in mind when he made this speech in 1969. How does paragraph 4 indicate his awareness of his audience?

2. Define reverse racism and discuss in small groups how it may have affected your lives. What are the effects of reverse racism in a pluralistic society such as our own?

WRITING ASSIGNMENTS

1. Reaction Journal: Imagine yourself as a leader of MAYO. Write a letter to Congressman Gonzalez in response to his speech.

2. Write an essay in which you develop your own definition of racism. Select concrete examples from your reading as well as from your experiences.

VISITORS, 1965

OSCAR HIJUELOS

Oscar Hijuelos (b. 1951), a native New Yorker with undergraduate and graduate degrees from City College, teaches writing at Hofstra University in New York. His writings about the Cuban-American community have been praised for their lively and sensitive portrayals of the lives of individuals living in two cultures. His second novel, The Mambo Kings Play Songs of Love *(1989), was awarded the 1990 Pulitzer Prize. "Visitors, 1965" is a chapter from Hijuelos' first novel,* Our House in the Last World *(1983), which tells the story of Hector Santinios, born in New York to parents who had immigrated from rural Cuba to New York during the 1940s. The following selection reveals Hector's struggle to understand his cultural identity, to reconcile his dreamy memories of a beautiful and idealized Cuba with the "cheap decorative art, plaster statues, and mass-produced paintings" that surround him in his family home in New York.*

◆ FREEWRITING

Read the opening paragraph of this story and stop. Think carefully about its content and freewrite for ten or fifteen minutes on what you expect from the rest of the story. Discuss your expectations with the class.

For Hector the prospect of Aunt Luisa's arrival stirred up memories. He began to make a conscious effort to be "Cuban," and yet the very idea of *Cubanness* inspired fear in him as if he would grow ill from it, as if *micróbios** would be transmitted by the very mention of the word *Cuba.* He was a little perplexed because he also loved the notion of Cuba to an extreme. In Cuba there were so many pleasant fragrances, like the smell of Luisa's hair and the damp clay ground of the early morning. Cuba was where Mercedes had once lived a life of style and

* Microbes, cooties.

dignity and happiness. And it was the land of happy courtship with Alejo and the land where men did not fall down. Hector was tired of seeing Mercedes cry and yell. He was tired of her moroseness and wanted the sadness to go away. He wanted the apartment to be filled with beams of sunlight, like in the dream house of Cuba.

He was sick at heart for being so Americanized, which he equated with being fearful and lonely. His Spanish was unpracticed, practically nonexistent. He had a stutter, and saying a Spanish word made him think of drunkenness. A Spanish sentence wrapped around his face, threatened to peel off his skin and send him falling to the floor like Alejo. He avoided Spanish even though that was all he heard at home. He read it, understood it, but he grew paralyzed by the prospect of the slightest conversation.

"*¡Hablame en español!*"** Alejo's drunken friends would challenge him. But Hector always refused and got lost in his bedroom, read *Flash* comic books. And when he was around the street Ricans, they didn't want to talk Spanish with Whitey anyway, especially since he was not getting high with them, just getting drunk now and then, and did not look like a hood but more like a goody-goody, round-faced, mama's boy: a dark dude, as they used to say in those days.

Even Horacio had contempt for Hector. Knowing that Hector was nervous in the company of visitors, he would instigate long conversations in Spanish. When visiting men would sit in the kitchen speaking about politics, family, and Cuba, Horacio would play the patrón and join them, relegating Hector to the side, with the women. He had disdain for his brother and for the ignorance Hector represented. He was now interested in "culture." He had returned from England a complete European who listened to Mozart instead of diddy-bop music. His hair was styled as carefully as Beau Brummell's. His wardrobe consisted of English tweed jackets and fine Spanish shoes; his jewelry, his watches, his cologne, everything was very European and very far from the gutter and the insecurity he had left behind. As he put it, "I'm never going to be fuckin' poor again."

He went around criticizing the way Mercedes kept house and cooked, the 5
way Alejo managed his money (buying everything with cash and never on credit) and the amounts of booze Alejo drank. But mostly he criticized Hector. The day he arrived home from the Air Force and saw Hector for the first time in years, his face turned red. He could not believe his eyes. Hector was so fat that his clothes were bursting at the seams, and when Hector embraced him, Horacio shook his head and said, "Man, I can't believe this is my brother."

And now the real Cubans, Luisa and her daughters and son-in-law, were coming to find out what a false life Hector led. Hector could not sleep at night, thinking of it. He tried to remember his Spanish, but instead of sentences, pictures of Cuba entered into his mind. But he did not fight this. He fantasized

** "Speak to me in Spanish!"

about Cuba. He wanted the pictures to enter him, as if memory and imagination would make him more of a man, a Cuban man.

The day before Luisa arrived he suddenly remembered his trip to Cuba with Mercedes and Horacio in 1954. He remembered looking out the window of the plane and seeing fire spewing from the engines on the wing. To Cuba. To Cuba. Mercedes was telling him a story when the plane abruptly plunged down through some clouds and came out into the night air again. Looking out the window he saw pearls in the ocean and the reflection of the moon in the water. For a moment he saw a line of three ships, caravels with big white sails like Columbus's ships, and he tugged at Mercedes's arm. She looked but did not see them. And when he looked again, they were gone.

Hector tried again for a genuine memory. Now he saw Luisa's house on Arachoa Street, the sun a haze bursting through the trees.

"Do you remember a cat with one eye in Cuba?" he asked Horacio, who was across the room reading *Playboy* magazine.

"What?" he said with annoyance. 10

"In Cuba, wasn't there a little cat who used to go in and out of the shadows and bump into things? You know, into the steps and into the walls, because it only had one eye. And then Luisa would come out and feed it bits of meat?"

"You can't remember anything. Don't fool yourself," he replied.

But Hector could not stop himself. He remembered bulldozers tearing up the street and that sunlight again, filtering through the flower heads, and flamingos of light on the walls of the house. He remembered the dog with the pathetic red dick running across the yard. Then he remembered holding an enormous, trembling white sunhat. His grandmother, Doña Maria, was sitting nearby in a blue-and-white dotted dress, and he took the sunhat to show her. But it wasn't a sunhat. It was an immense white butterfly. "*¡Ai, que linda!*"* Doña Maria said. "It's so pretty, but maybe we should let the poor thing go." And so Hector released the butterfly and watched it rise over the house and float silently away.

Then he saw Doña Maria, now dead, framed by a wreath of orchids in the yard, kissing him—so many kisses, squirming kisses—and giving advice. She never got over leaving Spain for Cuba and would always remain a proud Spaniard. "Remember," she had told Hector. "You're Spanish first and then Cuban."

He remembered sitting on the cool steps to Luisa's kitchen and watching 15
the road where the bulldozers worked. A turtle was crawling across the yard, and iguanas were licking up the sticky juice on the kitchen steps. Then he heard Luisa's voice: "Come along, child," she called. "I have something for you." And he could see her face again through the screen door, long and wistful.

Inside, she had patted Hector's head and poured him a glass of milk. Cuban milk alone was sour on the tongues of children, but with the Cuban magic po-

* "Oh, how beautiful!"

tion, which she added, it was the most delicious drink Hector ever tasted. With deep chocolate and nut flavors and traces of orange and mango, the bitter with the sweet, the liquid went down his throat, so delicious. "No child, drink that milk," Luisa said. "Don't forget your *tia.** She loves you."

Then a bam! bam! came from the television and Hector could hear voices of neighbors out in the hallway. No, he wasn't used to hearing Luisa's niceties anymore, and he couldn't remember what was in the milk, except that it was Cuban, and then he wondered what he would say to his aunt and cousins, whether he would smile and nod his head or hide as much as possible, like a turtle on a hot day.

It was late night when a van pulled up to the building and its four exhausted passengers stepped onto the sidewalk. Seeing the arrival from the window, Mercedes was in a trance for a moment and then removed her apron and ran out, almost falling down the front steps, waving her arms and calling, "Aaaaiiii, aaaaiiii, aaaaiiii! Oh my God! My God! My God," and giving many kisses. Alejo followed and hugged Pedro. The female cousins waited humbly, and then they began kissing Mercedes and Alejo and Hector and Horacio, their hats coming off and teeth chattering and hair getting all snarled like ivy on an old church . . . kisses, kisses, kisses . . . into the warm lobby with its deep, endless mirrors and the mailbox marked *Delgado/Santinio.* The female cousins, like china dolls, were incredibly beautiful, but struck dumb by the snow and the new world, silent because there was something dreary about the surroundings. They were thinking Alejo had been in this country for twenty years, and yet what did he have? But no one said this. They just put hands on hands and gave many kisses and said, "I can't believe I'm seeing you here." They were all so skinny and exhausted-looking, Luisa, Virginia, Maria, and Pedro. They came holding cloth bags with all their worldly possessions: a few crucifixes, a change of clothing, aspirins given to them at the airport, an album of old photographs, prayer medals, a Bible, a few Cuban coins from the old days, and a throat-lozenge tin filled with some soil from Holguín, Oriente province, Cuba.

After kissing and hugging them Alejo took them into the kitchen where they almost died: There was so much of everything! Milk and wine and beer, steaks and rice and chicken and sausages and ham and plantains and ice cream and black bean soup and Pepsi-Cola and Hershey chocolate bars and almond nougat, and popcorn and Wise potato chips and Jiffy peanut butter, and rum and whiskey, marshmallows, spaghetti, flan and pasteles and chocolate cake and pie, more than enough to make them delirious. And even though the walls were cracked and it was dark, there was a television set and a radio and lightbulbs and toilet paper and pictures of the family and crucifixes and toothpaste and soap and more.

It was "Thank God for freedom and bless my family" from Luisa's mouth, 20
but her daughters were more cautious. Distrusting the world, they approached

* Aunt.

everything timidly. In the food-filled kitchen Alejo told them how happy he was to have them in his house, and they were happy because the old misery was over, but they were still without a home and in a strange world. Uncertainty showed in their faces.

Pedro, Virginia's husband, managed to be the most cheerful. He smoked and talked up a storm about the conditions in Cuba and the few choices the Castro government had left to them. Smoking thick, black cigars, Horacio and Alejo nodded and agreed, and the conversation went back and forth and always ended with "What are you going to do?"

"Work until I have something," was Pedro's simple answer.

It was such a strong thing to say that Hector, watching from the doorway, wanted to be like Pedro. And from time to time, Pedro would look over and wink and flash his Victor Mature teeth.

Pedro was about thirty years old and had been through very bad times, including the struggle in 1957 and 1958 to get Castro into power. But wanting to impress Hector with his cheeriness, Pedro kept saying things in English to Hector like, "I remember Elvis Presley records. Do you know *You're My Angel Baby*?" And Hector would not even answer that. But Pedro would speak on, about the brave Cubans who got out of Cuba in the strangest ways. His buddy back in Holguín stole a small airplane with a few friends and flew west to Mexico, where they crash-landed their plane on a dirt road in the Yucatán. He ended up in Mexico City, where he found work in the construction business. He was due in America soon and would one day marry Maria, who wanted a brave man. These stories only made Hector more and more silent.

As for his female cousins, all they said to him was: "Do you want to eat?" or "Why are you so quiet?" And sometimes Horacio answered for him, saying: "He's just dumb when it comes to being Cuban."

Aunt Luisa, with her good heart, really didn't care what Hector said or didn't say. Each time she encountered him in the morning or the afternoons, she would take his face between her hands and say, "Give me a kiss and say 'Tia, I love you.'" And not in the way Alejo used to, falling off a chair and with his eyes desperate, but sweetly. Hector liked to be near Luisa with her sweet angelic face.

He felt comfortable enough around Aunt Luisa to begin speaking to her. He wasn't afraid because she overflowed with warmth. One day while Aunt Luisa was washing dishes, Hector started to think of her kitchen in Cuba. He remembered the magic Cuban drink.

"Auntie," he asked her. "Do you remember a drink that you used to make for me in the afternoons in Cuba? What was it? It was the most delicious chocolate but with Cuban spices."

She thought about it. "Chocolate drink in the afternoon? Let me see . . ." She wiped a plate clean in the sink. She seemed perplexed and asked, "And it was chocolate?"

"It was Cuban chocolate. What was it?"

She thought on it again and her eyes grew big and she laughed, slapping her knee. "Ai, bobo. It was Hershey syrup and milk!"

After that he didn't ask her any more questions. He just sat in the living room listening to her tell Mercedes about her impressions of the United States. For example, after she had sat out on the stoop or gazed out the window for a time, she would make a blunt declaration: "There are a lot of airplanes in the sky." But usually when Mercedes and Luisa got to talking, they drifted toward the subject of spirits and ghosts. When they were little girls spiritualism was very popular in Cuba. All the little girls were half mediums, in those days. And remembering this with great laughter, Luisa would say, "If only we could have seen what would happen to Papa! Or that Castro would turn out to be so bad!"

"Yes, Papa, that would have been something," Mercedes answered with wide hopeful eyes. "But Castro is something else. What could a few people do about him?"

"Imagine if you're dead in Cuba," said Luisa, "and you wake up to that mess. What would you do?"

"I would go to Miami, or somewhere like that."

"Yes, and you would go on angel wings."

It was Luisa's ambition to ignore America and the reality of her situation completely. So she kept taking Mercedes back to the old days: "You were such a prankster, so mischievous! You couldn't sit down for a moment without being up to something. Poor Papa! What he had to do with you!" And then, turning to Hector, she would add, "Look at your Mama. This innocent over here was the fright of us all. She was always imagining things. Iguanas, even little baby iguanas, were dragons. A rustle in the bushes were ghosts of fierce Indians looking for their bones!" She laughed. "There are ghosts, but not as many as she saw. She was always in trouble with Papa. He was very good to her but also strict. But his punishments never stopped your mother. My, but she was a fresh girl!"

When she wasn't talking to Mercedes, Luisa watched the Spanish channel on the television, or ate, or prayed. Pedro went out with Alejo and Horacio, looking for work. Maria and Virginia helped with the housecleaning and the cooking, and then they studied their books. They were very quiet, like felines, moving from one spot to another without a sound. Sometimes everyone went out to the movies; Alejo paid for it. Or they all went downtown to the department stores to buy clothing and other things they needed. Again, Alejo paid for everything, angering Mercedes, for whom he bought nothing.

"I know you're trying to be nice to my family, but remember we don't have money."

Still, he was generous with them, as if desperate to keep Luisa and her daughters in the apartment. Their company made him as calm and happy as a mouse. Nothing pleased Alejo more than sitting at the head of the dinner table, relishing the obvious affection that Luisa and her daughters and son-in-law felt for him. At meals Alejo would make toast after toast to their good health and long life, drink down his glass of rum or whiskey quickly, and then fill another and drink that and more. Mercedes always sat quietly wondering, "What does my sister really think of me for marrying him?" while Hector waited for Alejo suddenly to fall off his chair, finally showing his aunt and cousins just who the Santinios really were.

One night Alejo fell against the table and knocked down a big stack of plates. The plates smashed all around Alejo, who was on the floor. Hector scrambled to correct everything before Virginia and Maria and Pedro came to look. He scrambled to get Alejo up before they saw him. He pulled with all his strength, the way he and Horacio used to, but Alejo weighed nearly three hundred pounds. As the cousins watched in silence, Hector wished he could walk through the walls and fly away. He thought that now they would know one of his secrets, that the son is like the father. He tried again to pull Alejo up and had nearly succeeded when Pedro appeared and, with amazing strength, wrapped his arms around Alejo's torso and heaved him onto a chair with one pull.

Hector hadn't wanted them to see this, because then they might want to leave and the apartment would be empty of Pedro and Luisa and her daughters, those fabulous beings. He didn't want them to see the dingy furniture and the cracking walls and the cheap decorative art, plaster statues, and mass-produced paintings. He didn't want them to see that he was an element in this world, only as good as the things around him. He wanted to be somewhere else, be someone else, a Cuban . . . And he didn't want the family perceived as the poor relations with the drunk father. So he tried to laugh about Alejo and eventually went to bed, leaving Luisa and Pedro and his cousins still standing in the hall. Eventually, they did move away. Virginia and Maria found work in a factory in Jersey City, and Pedro came home one evening with news that he had landed a freight dispatcher's job in an airport. Just like that. He had brought home a big box of pastries, sweet cakes with super-sweet cream, chocolate eclairs, honey-drenched cookies with maraschino cherries in their centers.

As Alejo devoured some of these, he said to Pedro, "Well, that's good. You're lucky to have such good friends here. Does it pay you well?"

Pedro nodded slightly and said, "I don't know, it starts out at seven thousand dollars a year, but it will get better."

Alejo also nodded, but he was sick because after twenty years in the same job he did not make that much, and this brought down his head and made him yawn. He got up and went to his bedroom where he fell asleep.

A few months later, they were ready to rent a house in a nice neighborhood in Jersey. The government had helped them out with some emergency funds. ("We never asked the government for even a penny," Mercedes kept saying to Alejo.) Everyone but Luisa was bringing home money. They used that money to buy furniture and to send Virginia to night computer school taught by Spanish instructors. Instead of being cramped up in someone else's apartment with rattling pipes and damp plaster walls that seemed ready to fall in, they had a three-story house with a little yard and lived near many Cubans who kept the sidewalks clean and worked hard, so their sick hearts would have an easier time of it.

Hector was bereft at their leaving, but more than that he was astounded by how easily they established themselves. One day Pedro said, "I just bought a car." On another, "I just got a color TV." In time they would be able to buy an even larger house. The house would be filled with possessions: a dishwasher, a washing machine, radios, a big stereo console, plastic-covered velour couches and chairs, electric clocks, fans, air conditioners, hair dryers, statues, crucifixes, lamps and electric-candle chandeliers, and more. One day they would have enough money to move again, to sell the house at a huge profit and travel down to Miami to buy another house there. They would work like dogs, raise children, prosper. They did not allow the old world, the past, to hinder them. They did not cry but walked straight ahead. They drank but did not fall down. Pedro even started a candy and cigarette business to keep him busy in the evenings, earning enough money to buy himself a truck.

"*Qué bueno*,"* Alejo would say.

"This country's wonderful to new Cubans," Mercedes kept repeating. But then she added, "They're going to have everything, and we . . . what will we have?" And she would go about sweeping the floor or preparing chicken for dinner. She would say to Alejo, "Doesn't it hurt you inside?"

Alejo shrugged. "No, because they have suffered in Cuba."

He never backed off from that position and always remained generous to them, even after their visits became less frequent, even when they came only once a year. And when Pedro tried to repay the loans, Alejo always waved the money away. By this time Virginia was pregnant, so Alejo said, "Keep it for the baby."

"You don't want the money?"

"Only when you don't need it. It's important for you to have certain things now."

But Mercedes stalked around the apartment, screaming, "What about the pennies I saved? What about us?"

QUESTIONS FOR DISCUSSION

1. How do you account for the different responses of Alejo and Mercedes to the material and cultural successes of Pedro and Luisa?

2. Discuss what Hector does as he struggles to understand his cultural identity. Does his cultural awareness change throughout the selection, or does it remain static?

WRITING ASSIGNMENTS

1. Reaction Journal: Imagine that you are a young man or woman of Cuban ancestry living in New York City. Write about how your responses to Hijuelos's story might differ from the ones you have experienced in reading it yourself.

* "How good."

2. Write an essay in which you compare and contrast the American life-style of Alejo and Mercedes with that of Pedro and Luisa. To what extent are the contrasts based on personal characteristics, and to what extent are they based on cultural identity?

PROFOUND CHANGES

ELENA PADILLA

In the following excerpt from her 1958 book Up from Puerto Rico, *sociologist Elena Padilla (b. 1923) examines the ways in which interpersonal relationships change when Puerto Ricans come to the United States. She finds that how they view the new ways and values they encountered in the United States depends to a large extent on whether they think of themselves as settlers or transients.*

◆ FREEWRITING

Freewrite for ten or fifteen minutes on "home." Think beyond the physical structure (although that's certainly important) and focus on issues of extended neighborhood, personal and cultural identity, and personal and family relationships.

Many Hispanos see their lives and those of their children as unfolding in this country. To them, Puerto Rico is something of the past, and for many of the children who are growing up or have grown up in the United States, Puerto Rico is less than an echo; it is a land they have never visited, a "foreign country." Some migrants consciously decide at some point or other to make their homes here, to stay in this country permanently, never again turning back to look at Puerto Rico. These are to be found even among recent migrants. They are the people who view their future as being tied up with whatever life in New York may offer. We can call these Hispanos settlers, and can distinguish them from transients or those who regard their future life as gravitating toward Puerto Rico and who hope to return to live there later on, after their children have grown up or when they have enough savings to buy a house or start a business.

Settlers who have migrated to New York as adults are those who have lost or who give little importance to their relationships with their home towns, their friends and relatives who are still in Puerto Rico or are recent migrants to New York. They have cut off their emotional ties with the homeland, but they may still have significant interpersonal relationships with their kin and within cliques that may consist largely of persons from their own home town who are residents of New York. The settler fulfills or expects to fulfill his social needs in relation to living in New York.

One sort of settler has in his formative years moved away from his home town, rural or urban, in Puerto Rico to another town or city in the island itself. He started to break away from the primary relations and bonds of his home town then. By the time he comes to New York, he has already experienced life situations in which primary groups derived from his home town contexts have no longer operated for him, in which he has developed new social bonds, wherever he may have been. The primary group relationships of this kind of settler lack the continuity and history of those of the settler who, throughout his life, whether in Puerto Rico or New York, has been able to continue depending and relying on persons known to him for many years.

The consequent social adjustments that the settlers here have made are the outcome of a gradual process of adaptation to living in New York, and of recognizing that home, friends, and other interests are here and not in Puerto Rico. The settler may be oriented within the ethnic group of Puerto Ricans in New York, partially by his participation in the cliques and other small groups of people from his home town and in those of his New York neighbors. But the one who has lost his primary ties with a home town and has been exposed to a greater variety of group experiences in Puerto Rico through moving about there is likely to become involved in New York in groups and cliques that are not derived from any particular home town context. The kinds of adjustments he can make to these changing group situations is related to his own background experiences as a migrant in Puerto Rico itself. There he may have reacted to and resolved the social stresses of the uprooting he underwent as a migrant, acquiring as a result the social techniques for making it easier to establish satisfactory social relationships outside of home town and family settings.

The migrant who is essentially a transient, on the other hand, still maintains 5
ties with the homeland: he has a strong feeling of having a country in Puerto Rico, a national identity there, and there he has friends and relatives whom he writes, visits, and can rely upon. "If things get bad" *(si las cosas se ponen malas)*, he can go back to Puerto Rico and get sympathy and help from those he grew up with. The transient migrants can be expected to feel obligated to their Puerto Rican friends and relatives, should these come to New York. The settler, on the other hand, is likely to say that he will "not return to Puerto Rico even if I have to eat stones in New York," and he will feel less bound to friends and relatives left in the island.

But becoming a settler does not necessarily involve a conscious decision. Transients may change into settlers as life orientations and social relations that are satisfactory and meaningful to them become part of their life in New York. The fundamental difference between settlers and transients is that the settler's life is organized in New York, while that of the transient is both in New York and in Puerto Rico.

In New York the lives of Puerto Ricans must, obviously, undergo profound changes. For those who learn American life in a slum like Eastville, the experience is one thing. For Puerto Ricans who were in better circumstances and had better life-chances in the island, it is another: they can begin life in New York as members of the middle class and avoid the particular cultural and social difficulties that beset the residents of Eastville. Yet all have their difficulties. Many overcome them. Many Eastvillers have made their way out of the slum into satisfactory fulfillment of their aspirations for themselves and their children. Others have returned to Puerto Rico.

One of the matters that concern Eastville Puerto Ricans is what has happened and is happening to Puerto Ricans in New York. Among migrants, social and cultural changes among Hispanos are a conscious preoccupation. They see the results of change in their own lives and in those of their friends. It is on this basis that they evaluate social behavior. Their awareness also reflects the conflicting values, orientations, and ambivalence of New York Hispanos.

True, old migrants and Hispanos who have grown up in New York regard recent migrants as representing a departure from their culture and as being socially inferior; on the other hand, recent migrants, in turn, express discontent with the ways Hispanos "are"—behave—in this country. George Espino, a New York-born man of Puerto Rican parents voiced a sentiment frequently heard from others who like himself have grown up in New York: "The Puerto Ricans that are coming over today, well, they're the most hated people . . . the most hated people." Migrants, particularly those who have come as adults, contrast and evaluate the changes they experienced in their lives in Puerto Rico with those they are experiencing in New York. To them, changes here in family life, in the expectancies of what family members can demand of each other, in the ways children are brought up, in marital behavior, and in the behavior of men, women, and children—all these factors that govern daily life—are of concern. Migrants are conscious of these changes and speak of how they have something to do both with modern life and with living in New York. Some of these changes are acceptable and "good," while others are disapproved of and considered "bad."

Migrants write of their experiences in New York, tell of them on visits to 10
Puerto Rico, or show in their behavior the new ways they have adopted. In Puerto Rico some of these types of behavior are considered to be for the best, others for the worst. Potential migrants in the island know their future life in New York is going to be different from their life in Puerto Rico. How, and to what extent, however, is part of the adventure and "changing environment" they will find in New York.

The impact of New York life on Puerto Rican migrants is described in fact and popular fancy, but whether it is described glowingly, soberly, or depressingly, depends on the aspirations, frustrations, hopes, and anxieties of the one who is speaking. Men, women, and children change in New York, it is said. How?

Clara Fredes, now a mother of three, who migrated after the Second World War when she was a teen-ager, replied to a member of the field team when asked if there were any differences between “the way people act here and in Puerto Rico,” that “when women get here they act too free. They go out and stand in the street and don’t cook dinner or anything. Puerto Rican women in New York City are bad. They talk to other men beside their husband, and just aren’t nice. They boss the men. In Puerto Rico a wife obeys her husband, and keeps house, and takes care of her children. But here they run wild. [They are] all day long in the candy store talking and forgetting about their houses. Men here don’t always support their wives and children. They are too free too. They think they can get away with everything, but I think it’s the woman’s fault. They are so bad. They don’t take care of the children right. The children [are] out on the streets at all hours of the night.”

Another informant, Gina Ortiz, said that Puerto Rican women in New York like to go dancing the mambo and drinking and that “they don’t do it in Puerto Rico. In Puerto Rico the woman who smokes and drinks is a bad woman.”

Rosa Burgos also explained changes in the behavior of women migrants. “[It is] because they work and they have too much freedom. In Puerto Rico the wife is always in the house. Here they go out, they go to work, get together with another girl, drink beer, and so on. In Puerto Rico they don’t do that.”

15 Women who want to be rated as “good” do not admit to having changed in these directions. They would claim that they do not drink, smoke, or work outside the home, though they may acknowledge having changed in such areas as child-rearing, including giving greater freedom to their children.

Among changes that men undergo in New York, Dolores Miro mentioned that “some of them take friends. The friends like to drink and has women in the street. They change. They like to do same thing the friends do. . . . In Puerto Rico they have the same friends always, but here they have friends from other places, other towns. Some of them are good friends, some bad.”

Good men are expected not to change in New York, but to continue recognizing their obligations to their wives and children. They may say they do not have friends in New York because friends get a man in trouble.

A couple that consider themselves good and as having a satisfactory relationship with each other and their children may deny changes in their lives in New York. Manuel and Sophia Tres, in telling a fieldworker about themselves, said, “We don’t have any change. We still the same.” Manuel continued, “Some of them [Hispanos] when they come here they want to go to the bar and drink, are drunk people and have plenty girl friends,” to which Sophia added, “because they make more money to spend. We are not changed, we have the same customs.”

In New York children also change, in a variety of ways. It is more difficult to make them respect their parents and elders, and one must keep them upstairs in order to prevent their becoming too uncontrollable and bad. For Juana Roman: “In Puerto Rico the father’s don’t want the children to do what they want. They are strict; is better there. In Puerto Rico if your kids do anything wrong, the father punishes. Here you can't punish a big boy. . . . One day my boy went with another boy and they took a train and got lost, and when I got to the Children's Shelter, the lady said, 'Don't punish the boy' and I said, 'Oh yes [I will punish him], I don't want him to do it again.' I see many kids that they do what they want."

Antonia Velez, now in her mid-thirties, finds that in this country people 20
are nice to old people, but says that in Puerto Rico old people are more respected. Her children do not respect in the same way she respected her father and mother in Puerto Rico when she was a child. Yet she is acceptant to some of the changes in patterns of respect she finds among her children. Says she, "Everybody is nice with the old people here in this country. They take care better of the old people and the children. I didn't pay too much attention to it in Puerto Rico. They are nice too. Everybody respects old people. The children are more respectful to old people in Puerto Rico than here . . . I know. I never used to argue with my mother in Puerto Rico. If she had a reason or no, I keep quiet. And with my father too. The word that he said was the only word to me. If he said not to go to a movie, I didn't discute [argue] that with him. I didn't go. No here. The children are more free here. Tommy, when I say, do that, and he don't want to and he explains me why, I don't mind that. I think it is better for him. You know, we didn't do that but it was not good inside. I think so, because they are human beings too. I love my father and mother because they are so good to me. If I didn't go to movies they may have the reason to say no, but I don't know it. Maybe that way, if I know it, I would have been better."

Children who have migrated recently at ages when they had friends and were allowed to play in the yards and streets in their home towns and now are being reared "upstairs in the home" speak of their past life in Puerto Rico with nostalgia. Lydia Rios, age twelve, says that "here one cannot do anything," referring to having to remain at home, sitting and watching from a window the play of other children, except when she goes to church or school.

Advantages listed of living in New York are the higher wages and income, better opportunities to educate the children, better medical care, more and better food, more and better clothes, furniture, and material things here than in Puerto Rico. In New York one can even save money to go back to Puerto Rico and purchase a house. Which place is better to live in is contingent on whether the migrant has realized or is on his way to realizing the aspirations and hopes connected with his coming to New York.

For Emilio Cruz it is better to live in New York than in Puerto Rico. "I think life in New York is better. We have better living in New York and can give the children the food they want and need. When we work we have more money. We spend more here but we earn more so we can live better. In Puerto Rico we rent a house [for] $10.00 or $12.00 a month, and here we [pay] so much [more] money and [must have] a lease too, [of] two or three years in New York."

Migrants speak of the future with reference to a good life, and a good life can be realized either in New York or in Puerto Rico, though one must search for it. As Rafael Dorcas put it, "A good life is when we work and we has the things we need for all the family. I think that's a good life."

QUESTIONS FOR DISCUSSION

1. In her title Padilla suggests that Puerto Rican immigrants will experience "Profound Changes" when they settle in the United States. What are some of these changes? Explain how she demonstrates such changes in her discussion of the differences between a settler and a transient.

2. Discuss why Puerto Rican women who migrate to New York are less likely to be "good." Whose concept of "good" does Padilla use?

WRITING ASSIGNMENTS

1. Prepare a topic outline of this selection and be prepared to describe the effectiveness of Padilla's organizational plan and transitional devices.

2. Meet with a small group of your peers and discuss the concept of "home" that you developed in your freewriting. Did you find, for example, a difference in attitudes between students who have moved frequently as opposed to those who have not? Write an essay in which you define "home." Use examples and ideas from your freewriting, your group discussion, and Padilla's essay as you develop your essay.

A MELDING OF CULTURES

GEORGE J. CHURCH

In the following essay, George J. Church (b. 1931), a writer for Time, *in which the essay originally appeared, explores the cultural, linguistic, and economic impact of the rapidly expanding population of American Hispanics. Church responds to some Anglos' fear of cultural inundation by citing the diversity within the Hispanic communities and examining the progress of "the Americanization of Hispanics."*

◆ FREEWRITING

Choose a neighborhood or a cultural, ethnic, or even social or generation group. Freewrite for ten or fifteen minutes on customs, goals, and life-styles that define the group. Try to emphasize generalities that apply to most members.

The Yakima Valley of southern Washington is 1,000 miles from the Mexican border. But so many former migrants have settled there after coming north to pick the valley's apples, pears, and cherries that no one thought it odd when the governor of the Mexican state of Michoacán made a speech to them last spring over the local Spanish-language radio station. The governor, or so went the local joke, was only trying to stay in touch with his constituents.

Union City, N.J., is 1,300 miles from Cuba. But refugees from Fidel Castro's island so dominate the community that a service organization posts the days when the "Cuban Lions" meet. A children's shop does a brisk business in *mosquiteros*, lace mosquito nets for cribs that are a necessity in Cuba but only a nostalgic and expensive decoration in Union City.

Chicago is far from any entry point for Hispanics into the U.S. But it has drawn such a diverse Latin population that the Spanish language alone is no guide as to what kind of neighborhood a visitor has wandered into. Says Democratic Ward Committeeman Jesús Garcia: "You can tell where you are from the sounds and the smell of the cooking. In Mexican areas people are doing the taco thing with beans and rice; in Puerto Rican areas it's roast pork and fried rice. If you walk around Pilsen [a Mexican enclave] you'll hear mariachi music; in [Puerto Rican] Humboldt Park you'll hear salsa and conga drums."

An Anglo's nose and ears, to be sure, might be unable to tell the difference today. But that is likely to change. Already the growth of the U.S. Hispanic population is one of the most startling phenomena in American social history, and if anything it is likely to speed up.

As recently as 1950, the census counted fewer than 4 million residents on 5
the U.S. mainland who would today fall under the category Hispanic, the majority of Mexican descent. Last year there were an estimated 17.6 million, with roughly 60% tracing their ancestry to Mexico and the rest to Puerto Rico, Cuba, El Salvador, the Dominican Republic, Colombia, Venezuela and about two dozen other countries of Central and South America. Fully two-thirds were immigrants, according to a study by Yankelovich, Skelly & White Inc., a New York market-research and polling firm, that was commissioned by the SIN Television Network, a national grouping of Spanish-language stations. Some 24% had entered during the previous ten years alone. These figures are open to argument, since they include Puerto Ricans on the mainland, who legally are not immigrants but citizens from birth. Even so, never before has the U.S. absorbed so many newcomers speaking the same foreign language.

Shortly after World War II, three-quarters of all Hispanics on the U.S. mainland lived in Texas or California. As of 1980, those two states still accounted for 51% of the total Hispanic population. But large numbers have also settled in Arizona (16% Hispanic) and New Mexico (36%) and in such inland and Northern cities as Denver (19%) and Hartford, Conn. (20%). In South Florida, nearly a million Hispanics (78% Cuban) have spread so rapidly beyond Miami (64% Hispanic) that they sometimes refer to the entire 25-mile-or-so stretch from Miami to the Everglades as Calle Ocho (Eighth Street), after the main drag of Miami's Little Havana.

Moreover, American Hispanics are a predominantly young (median age: 23) and highly fertile population. Yankelovich found that 54% of all Hispanic households consist of four or more people, vs. only 28% of all U.S. families. They keep coming too in such numbers that even if all illegal immigration could be stopped, the Hispanic population would still grow. Some 42% of legal immigrants are Hispanic, and they follow the classic pattern of sending for spouses, children, and parents once the first family member has established a home in the U.S.

Some analysts think that Hispanic Americans by the year 2000 will total 30 million to 35 million, or 11% to 12% of all U.S. residents, vs. 6.4% in 1980. If so, they would constitute the largest American minority, outnumbering blacks and, indeed, people of English, Irish, German, Italian or any other single ethnic background.

It is no wonder, then, that frightened Anglos sometimes whisper about a "silent invasion from the south" that will transform parts of the U.S. into annexed territories. But this fear is much more mythology than fact, in part because the Hispanics are anything but a unified force.

The word Hispanic, to begin with, is a catchall term embracing new immi- 10
grants and some families that have been living in what is now the Southwestern U.S. for 300 years or more. It applies to people of white, black, Indian and, frequently, thoroughly mixed ancestry who hail from countries that sometimes seem to have little in common except historical traditions and the Spanish language itself, and even that gets a little confused at times. For example, the translation by someone from a country bordering the Caribbean for "I am waiting for the bus" might be taken by a native of South America's Andes region to signify "I am waiting for the small child." Many use the word Hispanic only when distinguishing themselves from Anglos (another catchall term meaning all non-Hispanic whites; it applies to people of German, Italian, Jewish and other non-English ancestries).

When they meet in the U.S., Hispanics feel as much rivalry as camaraderie. Many of the first Cubans who fled from Castro were middle class or even wealthy. Other Hispanics call them "the hads" *(los tenía)* because so many of their sentences supposedly begin "In Cuba, I had . . ." These Cubans in turn contrast themselves with others who fled in the 1980 boatlift from the port of Mariel, a minority of whom had been inmates of prisons or mental hospitals. The word Marielito, flung by one Cuban American at another, can be a fighting insult.

For all their diversity, Hispanics share some common characteristics. Though many immigrate from rural areas, in the U.S. they have overwhelmingly become an urban population. As many as 90% live in cities or suburban towns. Seeking companionship, and in response to discrimination, they cluster together in communities where they can preserve their language, customs, and tastes.

In Miami's Calle Ocho district, open-air markets sell plantains, mangoes, and *boniatos* (sweet potatoes); old men play excitedly at dominoes in the main park. Little but Spanish is heard on the streets and indeed in many offices and shops. A Hispanic in need of a haircut, a pair of eyeglasses or legal advice can visit a Spanish-speaking barber, optometrist or lawyer. In the barrios of Los Angeles, an Argentine can watch the latest movies from his homeland at any of a dozen theaters, while a Guatemalan can find a soccer league composed entirely of players from the country he left. In Chicago, says Ariel Zapata, a journalist who emigrated from Colombia last year, "it is possible to live, work and play without speaking any English at all."

Immigrants to the U.S. and their children have always tended to live together, of course. But the trend seems stronger, or at least more visible, among Hispanics. For one thing, their sheer numbers enable Hispanics to colonize bigger chunks of bigger cities than previous waves of immigrants could. Perhaps more important, coming from countries that can be reached by an inexpensive plane ride or even a short foot trip across the Mexican border, many Hispanics have thought of themselves as being in the U.S. only long enough to earn a little money. Most, of course, eventually change their minds as they come to realize that jobs in their home countries still pay next to nothing when available at all. Still, the process of deciding to stay can take years, and meanwhile, the immigrants have little incentive to put down roots outside the barrio.

To many Anglos, Hispanic insularity seems to be, to put it bluntly, un- 15
American. This feeling not infrequently is reinforced by straightforward, ugly racism. Neil Rogers, who conducts a talk show on Miami radio station WINZ, last December broadcast a prediction of continued heavy Cuban immigration into South Florida and invited his listeners to comment. "Shoot them before they land," suggested one caller. More often, Anglos simply avoid contact with Hispanics. Bob Lansing, who runs a collection agency in Beverly Hills, grew up in the Boyle Heights neighborhood of East Los Angeles when it was predominantly Jewish. Now that it has become a Mexican-American neighborhood, he tries to stay as far away as possible, even though he frequently vacations in Mexico and speaks some Spanish. Says Lansing of Boyle Heights: "I think it is pretty dangerous, a real barrio with a lot of gang activity."

If Anglos looked closer, they would find some of their suspicions unfounded. Though many narcotics enter the U.S. from Central and South America, addiction among Hispanic Americans, according to drug-enforcement agencies, appears to be less common than in black ghettos and indeed in many poor and middle-class Anglo districts. Youth gangs are a problem in some areas, but police generally report that barrio crime rates at worst are no higher than in poor black and white areas. Illegal immigrants in particular seem to be less the perpetrators than the victims of crimes, which they often are reluctant to report for fear of being deported. Says Police Chief John Swan of Beaumont, Texas, with no conscious irony: "Our experience is that illegals are very law-abiding members of our community."

Hispanics also frequently display what U.S. Anglos have come to regard as old-fashioned virtues: devotion to God, to family and, despite Anglo misconceptions about siesta and mañana, to work. Even the concept of machismo has a different ring in Hispanic than in Anglo ears. Asked to define the essence of masculinity, 54% of Hispanics responding to the 1984 Yankelovich survey answered that the ideal man above all else "is a good provider to his wife and family," vs. 34% of all Americans who defined that as the primal male trait.

Economically, Hispanics occupy a middle ground. According to the Census Bureau, the 1983 median income for Hispanic families was $16,960. That was $2,450 higher than the figure for blacks but still well below the non-Hispanic white median of $25,760. The Hispanic figure probably was held down by the initially low earnings of recent immigrants. Barry Chiswick, a visiting economist at Stanford's Hoover Institution, calculates that Hispanic immigrants generally work their way up to national-average incomes eleven to 16 years after entering the U.S.

Oddly, Puerto Ricans, who are Hispanic by language and culture though they were granted citizenship in 1917, have been the least successful. "Any indicator of well-being shows that we're at the bottom of society," says José Hernández, professor of Puerto Rican and black studies at New York's Hunter College. Family incomes of the roughly 2 million Puerto Ricans living on the mainland, about half of whom are crowded into Greater New York, averaged a mere $11,300 in 1981. More than 40% live below the official 1983 poverty line of $10,778 for a family of four.

One paradoxical reason is the very fact that Puerto Ricans are free to come 20
and go as they please; many indeed do travel back and forth between the mainland and Puerto Rico. Says Robert Martínez, a sales executive who was born in Brooklyn but now lives on the island: "Puerto Ricans always dream of coming back, and that dream has prevented them from settling down and their offspring from progressing." Some Puerto Ricans also believe they have encountered more discrimination than other Hispanics. "Our special status does us no good," says Teresa Rivera, director of Miami's Puerto Rican Opportunity, a city-funded social service agency. "We are regarded neither as Hispanics nor as Americans. We are Puerto Ricans, outsiders."

Cubans generally have done the best. In Dade County, which encompasses Miami, their family incomes average $25,000. As political refugees they knew they could not go home soon, and from 1960 to 1979 the Federal Government provided over $1.3 billion in financial assistance to the refugees and state and local governments. Perhaps more important, it was precisely the most ambitious spirits who found Communist uniformity intolerable and fled to the U.S.

Juan and Carmencita Rodríguez, who left Cuba in 1969, are reasonably typical. They settled in New Jersey, where Carmencita had a sister. Juan, 49, a former storekeeper, got a job in an embroidery shop by saying that he could cut lace left-handed. In fact he is right-handed and had never cut lace. Carmencita, 47, a former teacher, worked in a handbag factory and cut insignia for uniforms on a piece-work basis at home. "See this finger, see the callus I still have on it," she says proudly. The couple saved enough money to open two gift shops in Union City, living in an apartment over one. Like many Hispanic-owned businesses, the stores are a family enterprise: Daughter Alina, 20, who is studying at St. Peter's College to become a teacher, helps to manage them, and Yesinia, 12, clerks after school.

Other Hispanics came to the U.S. primarily to escape the poverty of many of their homelands and frequently had to resolve serious doubts as to whether to stay. But they, too, follow the immigrant pattern of hard work and an uphill struggle. Some varied examples:

- Wilson Brandao Giono, a Panamanian painter and sculptor, came to New York City in 1978 following his German girlfriend (now his wife) and, he says, "ran out of money. I was nervous and ready to go back three times; once I even had my suitcase packed. Eventually I found a job as a dishwasher." He began to sell a few art works. One, a geometric illustration of a woman, was chosen as the cover for a New York Spanish telephone directory. He still works two to three days a week as a carpenter and elevator operator but has exhibited paintings and sculptures in several galleries, learned reasonably fluent though still accented English and for the moment has given up all thought of leaving. Says Brandao Giono: "I like it here because there is more competition. I can prove myself better."
- César Dovalina, 53, followed a brother to Chicago in 1947 after the crops failed on his family's farm in Mexico. He worked in factories making ladders and road-construction equipment, sold tacos in his off-hours, and saved enough to open his own taco stand in 1952. He now is a millionaire who owns three restaurants, five apartment buildings and a construction company. Says Dovalina: "I came to work a year or two and return, but you get used to the comforts of life here."
- Guillermo, 41, a furniture repairman, asked that his family name not be revealed because he is in the U.S. illegally. He entered in 1975 from a village in Michoacán, Mexico, and drifted north to Seattle, hoping to earn enough to start his own business back home ("upholstery or construction, señor, it would not matter"). But by 1979 his wife Guadelupe advised him that prospects for founding a business or even earning a living wage in Michoacán were nil, so Guillermo brought Guadelupe and their four children to join

him in Seattle. Today he earns $400 a month from a boss who deducts $250 for rent on a ramshackle apartment that the boss owns. Somehow, though, Guillermo is saving money to buy a sewing machine and once more dreams of going into business for himself. Marvels Guillermo: "Me, a businessman in America!"

What are the prospects that the immigrants, and eventually their children, will be fully integrated into American life? The process so far has been slow. Politically, Hispanics have yet to wield anything like the clout of the blacks that they are rapidly overtaking in numbers, primarily because voter registration among Hispanics has remained low. Many either are not citizens or are too young to vote, but estimates in Los Angeles are that only half of those who are eligible to register do so. Many Hispanics are too busy earning a living to vote, and some come from countries where elections, if held at all, are rigged and meaningless.

In Texas, however, determined sign-up campaigns by both parties and the 25
Southwest Voter Registration Education Project nearly tripled the number of registered Hispanics, from 488,000 to 1,132,000, between the 1976 and 1984 elections. Their votes supplied the margin of victory for Democratic Governor Mark White in his 1982 upset of incumbent Republican William Clements. Nationally, Hispanic registration is increasing more slowly: the census counted a rise of 800,000, to a total of 3 million, between the 1980 and 1984 elections. Hispanics generally are liberal on economic issues, and as late as 1976 they gave Jimmy Carter 81% of their votes. But as many as 35% pulled the lever last year for Ronald Reagan, partly because they admired his leadership qualities and emphasis on conservative social values. Cuban and Nicaraguan refugees, in addition, often express an anti-Communism as vehement as the most right-wing Republicans.

Social assimilation may lag behind political participation, since it is easier to vote than face possible backlash by moving into an Anglo neighborhood. Moreover, Hispanics can remain in ethnic enclaves even as they move up economically. The bigger communities in fact have begun to spawn middle-class suburbs. Sweetwater, Fla., in Dade County, is a city of solid ranch-style homes with red tiled roofs and, frequently, Buicks and Cadillacs parked in the driveways; it is populated primarily by Hispanics.

Some Hispanics question whether full assimilation, at least in the sense of giving up the Spanish language and Hispanic cultural traditions, is even desirable. Says Daniel Villanueva, a former field-goal kicker for the Dallas Cowboys and Los Angeles Rams who is now general manager of KMEX in Los Angeles, a Spanish-language TV station: "I bought hook, line and sinker the myth that said you had to give up your culture to assimilate." Now, he says, he shares "a new mentality that says you can take the beautiful parts of the Hispanic culture and you can take the drive and aggressiveness from the Anglo culture."

Nonetheless, social assimilation of a sort is coming, led as usual among immigrant groups by the children. At the Loyola School in the Miami suburb of Westchester, both the Cuban and American flags are raised each morning, but nearly all the students gulp Big Macs and admire Madonna. In Miami proper, Josefina Fraga, assistant principal of Auburndale Elementary School, who immigrated in 1962, reminisces: "As soon as my kids got here they wanted to get rid of their embroidered dresses. They were more American than George Washington."

The impact of Hispanics on the larger culture is growing imperceptibly. The most noticeable change is culinary. In Chicago, for example, the Yellow Pages list 36 Latin restaurants, one with the hybrid name of Guadalaharry's; some have appeared in the fashionable Lincoln Park and Old Town areas. In the Long Island suburbs of New York City, packaged taco mixes are appearing in many supermarkets whose customers are nearly all Anglo.

Latin rhythms have long influenced American jazz and pop tunes, and 30
vibrate today at many rock concerts. In sports, Hispanics have been most conspicuous—and successful—in boxing and baseball. They make up a sizable proportion of the crowds at boxing matches in New York and Los Angeles, cheering for the many Hispanic fighters who are ranking contenders (Cruiserweight Carlos "Sugar" DeLeon, from Puerto Rico, is world champion). Almost 100 of the roughly 1,000 players in major league baseball at the beginning of the season were born in Latin America. A Hispanic All-Star team might include Pitchers Fernando Valenzuela, Joaquin Andujar and Willie Hernandez; Infielders Rod Carew, Damaso García and Dave Concepción; Outfielders Tony Armas and Pedro Guerrero.

In business, the number of companies interested in selling to Hispanics "is growing by leaps and bounds," says Howell Boyd, executive vice president of Sosa & Associates, a Hispanic-owned ad agency in San Antonio that has picked up such major accounts as Anheuser-Busch and Westinghouse. In Los Angeles, Villanueva reports that more than 30% of KMEX's advertising revenue comes from national-brand companies. Says he: "No longer is the attitude among advertisers 'Why don't you learn English?'"

Sheer numbers are not the only reason for this interest. Hispanic consumers have a reputation for seeking high quality in the products they can afford and, once sold, showing more loyalty to their favorite brands than Anglos do. But selling to them, experts warn, requires more than translating ads into Spanish. Attention must be paid to cultural and linguistic nuances. Example: the slogan "Catch That Pepsi Spirit," translated into Spanish, had an overly physical intonation. The company accordingly urged Hispanics to "*Vive el Sentir de Pepsi*" ("Live the Pepsi Feeling").

In all probability, though, the Americanization of Hispanics will be far more rapid and thorough than any Hispanicization of Anglo culture. Businessmen, Roman Catholic clergymen and politicians in Hispanic areas find it useful and sometimes essential to learn Spanish. But an Anglo lawyer in Coral Gables, Fla., who took the trouble to learn some limited Spanish now finds that most of his Hispanic clients prefer to speak to him in English. Says the lawyer: "America triumphs over these immigrants as it has over others." A survey of Midwestern Hispanic voters by the Midwest Voter Education Project probably is unrepresentative, since many Hispanics do not register, but nonetheless suggestive. Of the 1,346 people questioned, 9.4% spoke no English—but almost twice as many, 17.9%, could not speak Spanish.

QUESTIONS FOR DISCUSSION

1. Church doesn't present his thesis until the fourth paragraph. What are the rhetorical functions of the first three paragraphs, and how do they prepare the readers for the rest of the article?
2. Church points out that many Anglos fear the rapid growth in our Latino population, the "silent invasion from the south." He goes on to suggest that this fear is based more on myth than fact. Do you feel an understanding of such issues will help us accommodate the values of our Latino neighbors? Explain.

WRITING ASSIGNMENTS

1. Reaction Journal: Certainly one of Church's important points is that many Hispanics question whether full assimilation is desirable. Assume the role of a Latino community leader and write an open letter to your community in which you discuss the issue of full and partial assimilation.
2. In paragraphs 24 through 26 Church uses personal interviews to illustrate the generalization about Hispanics that he posits in paragraph 23. Look over your freewriting and write a paragraph that makes a generalization about defining "your group." Arrange for three or four personal interviews with group members. Write an essay modeled after Church's paragraphs in which you use your interviews to support your generalization.

From Asia—The Model Minorities?

To speak of Asian-Americans is to speak of an incredibly diverse group of people. Although they are often considered as one demographic ethnic group, Asians and Pacific Islanders come from over two dozen countries and represent a variety of languages, religions, and cultures. Since the 1980s, when the A/PI population went from 3.8 to 6.9 million, they have been the fastest-growing minority group in the United States (measured by birthrate and legal immigration). The widely publicized economic and educational achievements of Asians in the United States has created an image of them as a "model minority." Such a perception, however, overlooks the fact that, as in any group, some Asians and Pacific Islanders are educationally and economically mobile while others are unprepared to compete. It tends to overlook as well the many restrictions that had been placed on Asians and Pacific Islanders in the United States through exclusionary immigration policies and discriminatory state laws and local ordinances from the mid-1800s until the late 1960s.

The first Asians to arrive in the United States in large numbers were the Chinese. Drawn by the discovery of gold in California, a shortage of labor in the United States, and economic chaos in China, 322,000 Chinese (some of whom were reentrants) entered this country between 1850 and 1882. The great majority of these immigrants were unskilled laborers from Kwangtung province in southern China. The initial immigration was almost entirely made up of many who regarded themselves as sojourners rather than immigrants, men who intended to return to China after making money here. Perhaps the most visible contribution of Chinese to the developing prosperity of the American West was the employment of 12,000 to 14,000 Chinese laborers in the construction of the Central Pacific link in the transcontinental railroad, which was completed in 1869.

From the beginning, Chinese immigrants, nonwhite and non-Christian, faced difficult lives in the United States. In his book *Ethnic America*, Thomas Sowell points out that the Chinese "were both non-white and non-Christian, at a time when either trait alone was a serious handicap." Their willingness to work long hours for low pay at jobs that white Americans were unwilling to do eventually made them feared as economic competitors. To limit the profits these industrious workers accrued, economic sanctions were imposed. Reaction to increasing numbers of Chinese staking claims in the gold fields of California brought the 1852 reenactment of the Foreign Miners' Tax Law, initially used against Mexicans in 1850. In addition, the city of San Francisco enacted restricting and harassing ordinances, for example, the Sidewalk Ordinance of 1870, which made it a misdemeanor to use poles to carry laundry on the sidewalks in the fashion of the Chinese laundries. Depressed economic conditions in the 1870s led to increased anti-Chinese discrimination, culminating in the anti-Chinese riots described by Betty Lee Sung in "The Chinese Must Go" (see "Confrontations" section) and the Chinese Exclusion Act of 1882, which barred entry to Chinese laborers for ten years and marked the end of U.S. free-immigration policy. This act was only one of many pieces of legislation enacted to limit Chinese immigration. Not until 1930 were these immigration laws modified to allow some Chinese wives to join their husbands in the United States.

As a result of these exclusionary measures, the early immigrant generation of Chinese endured a greater imbalance between the sexes than any other ethnic group. Betty Lee Sung reports that in 1890 the ratio of Chinese men to women was about 27:1, and in 1930 the ratio had improved only to 4:1. This imbalance resulted in a very small American-born second generation, a phenomenon that slowed assimilation since the important acculturating roles of school and children were not a part of the lives of the group as a whole. In addition, the preponderance of men stranded in this country without their families or unable to begin families of their own because of laws prohibiting intermarriage contributed to a subculture of vice within Chinatowns during the last quarter of the nineteenth century, with white as well as Chinese frequenting these areas for prostitution, drugs, and gambling. Sporadic outbreaks of violence among the secret societies (tongs) controlling these illegal activities sometimes escalated to Tong Wars in Chinatowns in the late nineteenth and early twentieth centuries.

The repeal of the Chinese Exclusion Act in 1943 and new legislation that allowed for limited immigration from China helped to restore normal family life to a people for whom dedication to family is among the chief values. Strong family and regional ties within the Chinese community helped people make the most of limited opportunities. Rotating credit pools helped fellow villagers or kinsmen amass the capital necessary to start a business, and during difficult financial times or disasters such as the San Francisco earthquake of 1906, Chinese-American organizations collected money in Chinese communities across the country to help those in need. At the height of the Depression in the early 1930s, few Chinese applied for federal aid. In 1933 only 4 percent of the Chinese population of Chicago and 1 percent of the Chinese population of New York received federal unemployment relief, while the percentages of the white population receiving such relief in the same cities was 10 percent and 9 percent respectively.

The Chinese fought the discriminatory exclusion laws by legal and illegal means. Cases argued before the Supreme Court resulted in the right of Chinese merchants to bring their wives and minor children into the United States and the right of American-born Chinese to citizenship and hence to readmission. In addition, the court ruled that foreign-born minor children of American-born Chinese had the right of "derivative citizenship" and were therefore eligible to immigrate to the United States. This right of derivative citizenship opened the possibility of admission through falsified relationship. Chinese-Americans returning from visits to China often falsely reported the birth of children whose positions could be filled by unrelated persons seeking entry to the United States. Such efforts to circumvent the law resulted in extended detention, isolation, and interrogation of immigrants in an effort to determine the legitimacy of their claims for admission. Their frustration and homesickness was recorded on the barrack walls of the Angel Island immigration station in San Francisco Bay. One inmate wrote of his first impression of the United States, "The Western styles and buildings are lofty; but I have not the luck to live in them. How was anyone to know that my dwelling place would be a prison?"

The shortage of workers during World War II was helpful to the social and economic growth of the Chinese in America. Job opportunities opened up for minorities both in war-related industries and in the professions. Whereas the traditional Chinese-American community was made up largely of people from one region and culture, the new refugees from the Communist takeover in China came from all over China. In general, these new immigrants were better educated and wealthier than the earlier immigrants. Members of the intelligentsia and former officials of the deposed Kuomintang were among those arriving after World War II. More recent immigration has followed a similar pattern. Only 3 percent of the almost 16,000 Taiwanese students in the United States between 1962 and 1969 ever returned to Taiwan. The Cultural Revolution of the 1970s resulted in application for political asylum from Chinese students studying here, and the crushing of the rebellion in Tiananmen Square in 1989 has had similar results.

Like the Chinese, many of the early Japanese arrivals regarded their move to the United States not as a migration but as a sojourn. Attracted by the need for inexpensive labor on the railroads and in canneries, fishing, and agriculture in California, nearly 300,000 Japanese entered this country between 1891 and 1924. Characteristic of sojourners, most of those arriving were male—with a male-female ratio of 7:1 in 1890 and 24:1 in 1900—and most came from farming backgrounds. Most of these first-generation Japanese-Americans—the Issei—were distinguished from many of the immigrants from other nations in being educated people, literate in their native language, and selected by their government for their ambition, good character, and health. While not wealthy, they were a select group who valued reading, hard work, and careful saving. Although almost all performed manual tasks in industry or agriculture, they possessed character traits that contributed to their success in a not always welcoming environment. In addition, Japan during the Meiji Era (1868–1912) admired the American way of life. English-language study had been incorporated into the secondary school curriculum in Japan in 1876, and Japanese textbooks presented Benjamin Franklin and Abraham Lincoln as role models. Thus, Japanese immigrants to the United States were relatively westernized and predisposed to accommodate to the social, cultural, and economic features of their new environment.

The success of the Japanese in California's rapidly developing agriculture and their ability to move up to entrepreneurship made them, like the Chinese, targets of anti-Asian legislation. They were specifically excluded from citizenship by the 1922 Takao Ozawa Supreme Court decision, which interpreted the standing law that only white immigrants and those of African descent were eligible for citizenship as meaning that foreign-born Japanese would remain permanent aliens. Under California's 1913 Alien Land Act (amended and made more restrictive in 1920), aliens who were ineligible for citizenship were also barred from owning agricultural land. Nonetheless, many who had initially come as sojourners chose to stay, and the Japanese community began to achieve stability and permanency between 1910 and 1924. Because the American government allowed wives of Japanese in this country to join their husbands here, the Japanese did not suffer the degree of gender imbalance that plagued other Asian groups in California well into the twentieth century. By 1920 the ratio of Japanese men to women was reduced to less than 2:1. Some of the wives who joined their husbands here were so-called picture brides, who, never having met their husbands, were chosen by the husband's family in Japan, approved via photograph, and married by proxy in Japan.

At the beginning of World War II there were approximately 127,000 Japanese in the United States, with the population concentrated on the West Coast. Two thirds of these Japanese had been born in the States and were therefore citizens. This second generation, the Nisei, were eligible to own land and participate in mainstream social and economic life in ways unavailable to their parents, the Issei or immigrant generation. In addition to owning small businesses, Japanese-Americans were very successful in gardening and agriculture, producing by 1940 approximately one third of the commercial truck crops grown in California.

The surprise attack on Pearl Harbor on December 7, 1941, had devastating financial and psychological consequences for the Japanese-American community. The Japanese Relocation Order (February 1942), conceived as a military necessity in light of widespread fears of sabotage, resulted in the removal of more than 110,000 West Coast Japanese from their homes to relocation camps. Sixty-four percent of those removed were American citizens. Not all Japanese-Americans spent the duration of the war in internment. There were opportunities for those who passed government tests of loyalty to relocate outside the restricted zones for the purpose of work or study. In addition, when the prohibition against military service was rescinded in 1943, thousands of Japanese-Americans joined the armed forces. But for those interned, businesses had to be liquidated on short notice, homes and belongings sold in haste. Inside the barbed-wire bounded internment camps in isolated regions of Utah, Arizona, California, Idaho, Wyoming, Colorado, and Arkansas, Japanese-Americans were housed in barracks where they shared communal mess halls, bathing and toilet facilities and were paid $16 per month for manual labor, $19 for professional work. Ted Nakashima, who experienced the relocation, describes the indignities suffered by the internees in "Why Won't America Let Us Be Americans?" Not until 1944 did the Supreme Court declare the Evacuation Order unconstitutional. In October 1990, in accordance with the Civil Liberties Act of 1988, the U.S. government officially apologized to the Japanese-Americans interned during the war and began distributing reparation checks totaling $1.25 billion to the 60,000 living former internees.

Postwar national prosperity provided opportunities for young Japanese-Americans beginning their careers. The Nisei were well educated and English speaking and thus prepared to fill many kinds of professional positions. Although discrimination did not disappear, progress in ensuring equal rights was made. In the years since World War II, Japanese-Americans have experienced increasing rates of intermarriage and upward social mobility, accommodating to American values and behavior while maintaining their cultural identity.

For most of the twentieth century Japanese-Americans were the largest Asian group in the United States. Recent immigration from Indochina, Korea, the Philippines, Hong Kong, Taiwan, and India, however, has put Japanese-Americans demographically third behind Chinese- and Filipino-Americans. This shift in population is due largely to the 1965 Immigration and Nationality Act, which took effect in July 1968 and allowed entry to Asian groups excluded by previous immigration laws.

These recent arrivals from Asia are a diverse group. The fall of the South Vietnamese government in 1975 and political upheavals in Laos and Cambodia have brought hundreds of thousands of Indochinese refugees to the United States. In "A Tragic Voyage," Dang Hong Loan tells of her own danger-ridden escape from Vietnam. Among those arriving early were wives and children of U.S. servicemen and those who worked for the U.S. government or military in Southeast Asia. Voluntary agencies accepted responsibility for sponsoring refugees after they left the resettlement camps. Although at least 20 percent of those over the age of eighteen had had some university education, the low-paying jobs available resulted in many of them going on public assistance. While the government plan had involved relocating refugees in scattered, often rural, settlements, most of those placed in such locations subsequently moved to urban centers with support networks of already established Indochinese communities. These communities have provided opportunities for the reuniting of extended families broken up because of the limited capabilities of sponsoring agencies and individuals.

The resettlement camps, closed within a year, were established to handle only the first wave of immigrants after the fall of Saigon. The second wave of refugees escaping from Communist governments, for the most part less well educated than those arriving earlier, had to rely on private voluntary agencies with minimal support from the government.

Of course, not all Asians who have benefited from the 1965 reform in the immigration laws are political refugees. The Korean population of the United States is also expanding rapidly. Like their Chinese counterparts, recent Korean immigrants tend to be well educated, approximately half having arrived with college educations. Although many teachers and other professionals among them must take lower-level jobs when they arrive, they often view these jobs as temporary necessities while they hone their language skills and fulfill certification requirements in their fields. Entrepreneurship is also high among Korean-Americans, with small business ownership a major source of employment.

Another rapidly growing ethnic group are Filipino-Americans. Like the Chinese and Japanese before them, most of the early immigrants from the Philippines were recruited as cheap contract laborers for low-skilled work in agriculture, fishing, canneries, and domestic services. From 1898, when the United States acquired the Philippines from Spain in the Treaty of Paris, until 1935, when its status was changed from colony to commonwealth, there was no restriction on Filipino immigration. Less than one third of the early arrivals were women, as many of the workers thought of themselves as sojourners who planned to return home to rejoin their families or to begin families. Because many of them moved from place to place pursuing seasonal occupations, there were few permanent Filipino settlements. Carlos Bulosan relates in *America Is in the Heart* the migratory and often dangerous lives of the Pinoy who suffered during the Depression the same sort of discrimination and violence visited upon the Chinese of an earlier generation. However, while most of the earlier immigrants were recruited from uneducated farm laborers, many of those arriving after the 1965 revision of the immigration laws have been technicians and professionals, including large numbers of doctors, nurses, and health-related professionals.

The preponderance of professionals among recent Filipino immigrants mirrors a similar situation in Chinese- and Korean-American communities. The preference system, established as part of the quota system for immigrants from the Eastern Hemisphere under the 1965 Immigration and Naturalization Act, places immigrants in the professions (along with their spouses and children) in the preference category right after unmarried adult children of U.S. citizens (First Preference) and spouses, unmarried adult children of resident aliens, and their children (Second Preference), while refugees are assigned to the Seventh Preference category. Because unused slots in each preference category are allowed to spill over into the category below, an enormous number of immigration slots are available to people in the professions. Thus, the new immigration laws have favored professionals, who enter the work force at higher levels and are therefore able to improve their socioeconomic standing much more rapidly than their predecessors. The very obvious upward mobility of many recently arrived Asians is a direct result of the structure of the current immigration laws.

The economic and educational successes of Asians have created a public image of Asian-Americans as a "model minority." But as Richard T. Schaefer points out in "Model Minority?" reports of socioeconomic successes of Asian-Americans are somewhat misleading, since figures are often based on household income, and the number of Asian-American households with two and more wage earners is greater than that of the general population. Futhermore, many Asian-Americans work in family-owned businesses in which they put in far more than the forty hours that make up the normal American work week. In spite of the large number of Asian-Americans in high-paying professional positions, the income of most A/PIs is below the national average and the community as a whole tends to be polarized economically with some achieving at a high level and others unable to break out of low-income and low-status jobs. The "model minority" label, then, while seemingly a positive title, can have negative repercussions, including resentment from other groups and even guilt among those A/PIs who do not measure up to this image. When the phenomenon of exaggerated expectations gives rise to frustration and confrontation, it can be a burden as well as an incentive as a minority seeks to define itself within the society as a whole.

"MODEL MINORITY?"

RICHARD T. SCHAEFER

Richard T. Schaefer (b. 1946) is Dean of Arts and Sciences at Western Illinois University, where he has taught a course in race and ethnicity not only to undergraduates but also to older students through independent home study and to inmates at a maximum security prison. In Racial and Ethnic Groups, *Schaefer examines relations among racial and ethnic groups in America, comparing tensions here with those arising in several other countries. The following excerpt considers the realities behind and the effects of the positive ethnic stereotype of Asian-Americans.*

◆ FREEWRITING

In his opening paragraph Schaefer suggests that a common perception of Asian-American groups is that they are the model minority. Before reading the selection, freewrite for ten or fifteen minutes on your sense of whether such a label is an asset or a liability for Asian-Americans. Use concrete examples from your observation and reading to develop your freewriting.

President Ronald Reagan called Asian Americans "our exemplars of hope and inspiration." *Time* and *Newsweek* articles have featured headlines such as "A Formula for Success" and "The Drive to Excel." There seems to be no end to the praise (Commission on Civil Rights, 1980d; McLeod, 1986; Oxnam, 1986; Ramirez, 1986).

A common view of many Asian American groups is that they constitute the model or ideal minority, supposedly because, despite past sufferings from prejudice and discrimination, they have succeeded economically, socially, and educationally without resorting to political and violent confrontations with Whites. Some observers see the existence of a model minority as reaffirmation that anyone can get ahead in the United States. Proponents of the model minority view declare that because Asian Americans have achieved success, they have ceased to be a minority, and are no longer disadvantaged. As we will see, we have a variation of "blaming the victim"; with Asian Americans, it is "praising the victim." Let us examine some areas of socioeconomic status to explore this view more thoroughly (Kim and Hurh, 1983; Wong, 1985).

Education

There is some truth to the belief that Asian Americans have succeeded. As shown in Table 1, every Asian-American group has impressive school enrollment rates in relation to Whites as well as to Black and Hispanic minorities. Al-

TABLE 1 Asian American School Enrollment, 1980

Compared to White, Black, and Hispanic American youths, Asian Americans display high levels of enrollment in high school and college.

Population	Percentage enrolled in school	
	Aged 16–17	Aged 20–24
White	89.0	23.9
Black	87.9	21.1
Hispanic	80.2	18.2
Japanese	96.2	48.0
Chinese	96.0	59.8
Filipino	92.8	27.1
Korean	94.9	40.1
Asian Indian	92.2	44.5
Vietnamese	90.2	41.8

Source: Bureau of the Census, 1981b; Gardner et al., 1985, p. 27.

though these data do include Asians who come to the United States in order to study, enrollment rates for native-born Asian Americans are also generally higher than for Whites of the same age.

Asian-American youths are also more likely to be at work as well as in school, as is evident from the very low *inactivity rate* for Asian Americans. The inactivity rate is the proportion of people neither in school nor in the labor force. In 1980, 8 percent of Whites aged 16–19 were inactive, compared to 3 percent for Korean Americans. The pattern was similar for other groups. Only recently arrived Vietnamese-born youths had inactivity rates higher than those of Whites (Gardner et al., 1985, p. 32; Hirschman and Wong, 1986).

This positive picture does carry some qualifications for the optimistic 5
model-minority view. Asian Americans maintain that at some universities they must have better records than other applicants to gain admission, and even when they do, they are turned down. Some observers therefore claim that some institutions adopt unofficial quotas to reduce Asian Americans' disproportionately high representation among college students. At the very least, many colleges fail to even consider that some Asian Americans deserve some of the same consideration given to talented members of other minorities (Bell, 1985, pp. 28–29; Biemiller, 1986; Butterfield, 1986; Lindsey, 1987; Salholz, 1987; Sue, 1985).

The Work Force

Although Asian Americans as a group work in the same occupations as Whites, which seems to convey the image of success, the pattern shows some differences (see Figure 1). Asian immigrants, like other minorities and immigrants before them, are found disproportionately in the low-paying service occupations. Even among these immigrants, though, substantial proportions are also concentrated at the top in professional, managerial, and executive positions.

As we compare in Figure 1 the occupational profiles of Asian American groups with those of Whites, Blacks, and Hispanics, we notice that the middle or "other" category is smaller for most Asian American groups, particularly the Chinese Americans. Wen Lang Li describes the *bipolar occupational structure* of Chinese Americans (which also applies to other Asian American groups), referring to the clustering of workers in both high-paying professional occupations and low-paying service jobs with relatively few in between (1982, pp. 318–329; also see Sung, 1976, pp. 66–89). Figure 1 shows the bipolarity for native-born Chinese Americans, 45 percent of whom are employed in these extreme categories. The large numbers of service workers reflect the type of employment Asian Americans were restricted to in the past. The strong representation at the other end of the occupational ladder partly results from upward mobility but also from selective immigration. Many Asian Americans still find themselves in service occupations, just as their ancestors did.

Success is not complete, however, as indicated by the lack of Asian American executives in firms. Asian Americans have become middlemen in the economy, doing well in small businesses and modest agricultural ventures. Asian Americans are therefore typical of the minorities sociologists refer to as *middlemen minorities*—groups that occupy middle positions rather than positions at the bottom of the social scale, where racial and ethnic minorities are typically located. Asian Americans involved in small businesses of course tend to maintain their ties more with the other Asian Americans than do individuals who join larger corporations. The present disproportionality of Asian Americans as middlemen, however, is the result of exclusion from other work, not of success (Blalock, 1967, pp. 79–84; Bonacich, 1981; Bonacich and Modell, 1981; Kim and Hurh, 1983; Sue et al., 1985; for a different view, see Wong, 1985).

Income

Wide publicity was given to the 1980 census figure of $23,600—the median family income of the six largest Asian American groups. This income exceeded the comparable figure for Whites by nearly $3,000. Once again, success for the model racial minority. Yet these family income figures are misleading. Asian Americans live almost exclusively in urban areas, where incomes are higher. They are also concentrated in parts of the nation where the prevailing wages are higher. We have also seen that they are better educated than Whites, which adds to their earning power. They approach parity with Whites because of their greater achievement compared to Whites in formal schooling. In fact, sociologist Morrison G. Wong shows that with their higher level of education, Asian Americans are actually $1,000 below where they should be compared to simi-

FIGURE 1 Occupational Status of Asian Americans Compared to Whites, Blacks, and Hispanics

Asian Americans are more likely to be found at either the top or bottom occupationally, compared with Whites and other minorities.

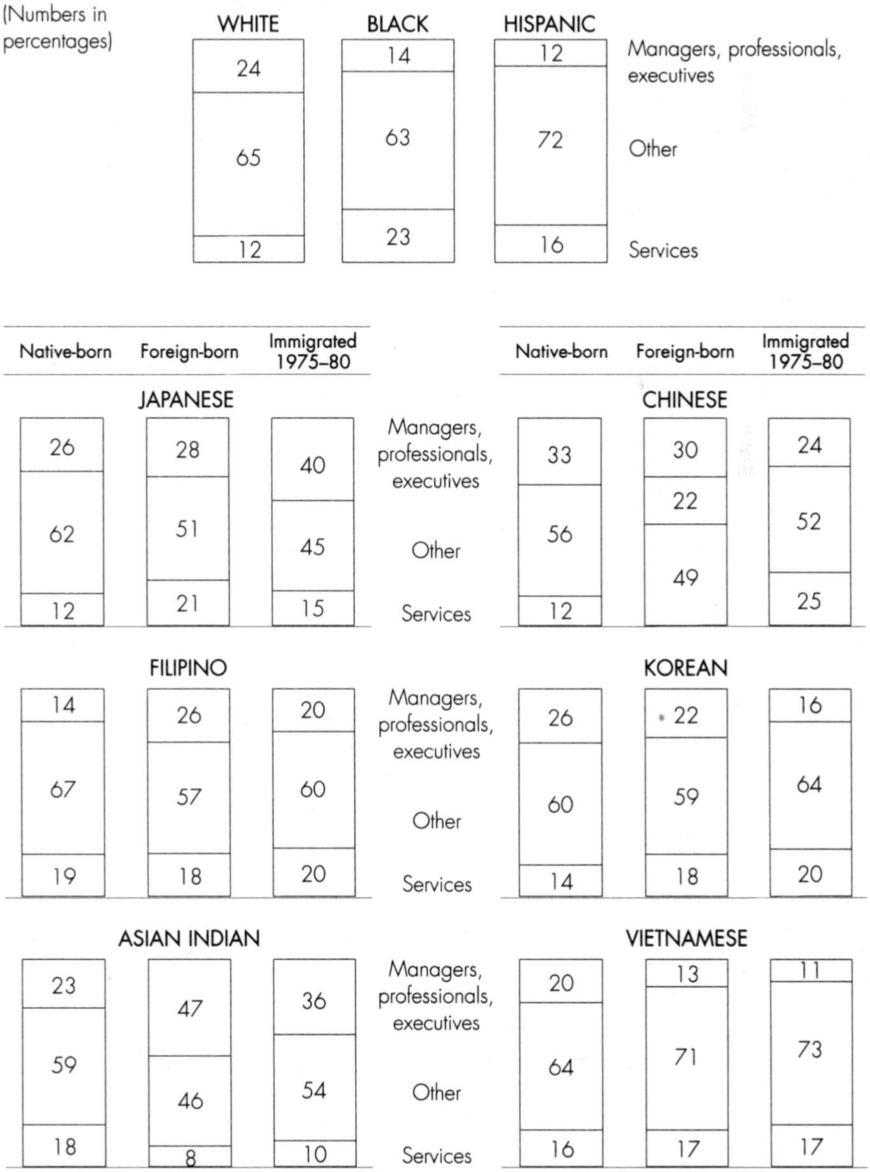

(Numbers in percentages)

	WHITE	BLACK	HISPANIC
Managers, professionals, executives	24	14	12
Other	65	63	72
Services	12	23	16

	Native-born	Foreign-born	Immigrated 1975–80
JAPANESE			
Managers, professionals, executives	26	28	40
Other	62	51	45
Services	12	21	15
CHINESE			
Managers, professionals, executives	33	30	24
Other	56	22	52
Services	12	49	25
FILIPINO			
Managers, professionals, executives	14	26	20
Other	67	57	60
Services	19	18	20
KOREAN			
Managers, professionals, executives	26	22	16
Other	60	59	64
Services	14	18	20
ASIAN INDIAN			
Managers, professionals, executives	23	47	36
Other	59	46	54
Services	18	8	10
VIETNAMESE			
Managers, professionals, executives	20	13	11
Other	64	71	73
Services	16	17	17

Sources: Bureau of the Census, 1981b; Gardner, Robey, and Smith. 1985, p. 31.

larly trained Whites. If Asian Americans received the same return for their educational credentials as do Whites, the so-called successful minority would have substantially higher occupational levels as well as higher earnings. A good education has not consistently led to a high-paying job equal to that of comparably educated Whites (Commission on Civil Rights, 1980d; Hirschman and Wong, 1984, pp. 598–600; Hurh and Kim, 1986; McLeod, 1986, p. 51; Sue et al., 1985; Woo, 1985).

Even more than in their income, Asian Americans differ in their way of mo- 10
bilizing their households. In 1980, 63 percent of Asian American families had two or more paid workers, compared to 55 percent for whites. Rates per worker show comparable earning power, though figures for recent arrivals show low incomes, but these reflect only paid labor. A significant number of Asian Americans operate family businesses (the proportion of Korean Americans is three times that of Whites), in which all family members pitch in with long hours to make them a success. The talk of "model minority" ignores the diversity among Asian Americans. There are rich and poor Japanese, rich and poor Filipinos, and rich and poor immigrants (Bell, 1985, pp. 28, 39; Gardner et al., 1985, pp. 33–35, 38–39).

The Door Half Open

On June 19, 1982, in a Detroit lounge two White males began arguing with a Chinese American, Vincent Chin. They mistook him for being of Japanese descent and blamed Chin for the dire straits of the American automobile industry. They chased Chin into the parking lot, where they beat him with a baseball bat numerous times. He died four days later. Through plea-bargaining, the two laid-off automobile workers were found guilty of manslaughter. Much to the shock of the Asian American community, the accused killers of Vincent Chin were sentenced to three years' probation and fined $3,700 each. Subsequently they were tried in federal courts for interfering with Chin's civil rights. One not directly involved in beating Chin was acquitted, and the other was sentenced to twenty-five years in prison (Commission on Civil Rights, 1986).

The Chin case is an extraordinary example, but Asian Americans have not enjoyed a successful welcome into society. The major problem with the model-minority image is that social acceptance by the dominant group has been incomplete: they are still Asian, not quite 100 percent Americans, to their fellow citizens. That a model minority has a positive stereotype does not necessarily indicate either that the group is assimilated into American society or that cultural pluralism will henceforth be tolerated. Racial slurs, job tension, and sporadic acts of violence continue. In 1984, the United States Commission on Civil Rights began investigating the growing acts of violence, particularly those directed at refugees. These occur in urban areas and are not limited to the Gulf Coast tensions that we have considered. Reviewing these and other evidence,

U.S. Civil Rights Commissioner John Bunzel declared in 1987 that such incidents are "pernicious and disturbing"—part of "the resurgence of an ugly anti-Asian sentiment in the United States" (McBee, 1986, p. 30). Violence attracts the headlines, but subtler forms of reminding Asian Americans of their "place" persist, such as asking a fourth-generation American of American descent "how I learned to speak English so well" (Butterfield, 1985; Commission on Civil Rights, 1986; McBee, 1984).

A poignant incident shows how easily both prejudice and discrimination can surface. In northern Nevada the army arranged with a civilian contractor to handle the tricky business of clearing a 743-acre dump site that for thirty years had received defective or leftover bombs. A Vietnam War veteran got the contract but could find no one locally to do the hot and sometimes dangerous work. Drawing upon his positive war experiences with Indochinese, the contractor brought in nineteen strong young Vietnamese and Laotians. Trouble soon began and escalated when some of the youths tried to attend a dance. Fights and attacks by Whites on their homes forced many of the Asian Americans to leave. Still faced with a job to be done, the contractor completed the project with a few remaining Asian Americans supplemented by Blacks and American Indians (Stanley, 1986).

At first glance, one might be puzzled to see a positive generalization such as "model minority" being held in disrepute. Why should the stereotype of being problem-free be a disservice to Asian Americans? As we have seen, this incorrect view serves to exclude Asian Americans from social programs and conceals unemployment and other social ills. When representatives of their groups do seek assistance for those in need, they are resented by those who totally subscribe to the model-minority view. If a minority group is viewed as successful, it is unlikely that its members will be included in programs designed to alleviate problems they encounter as minorities. We have seen how important small businesses are in Asian Americans' economic life. Yet laws related to small businesses often fail to include Asian Americans as an eligible minority. The stereotype means that the special needs of recent immigrants may be ignored. Although few foreign-born Asian Americans have yet succeeded, the positive stereotype reaffirms the American system of mobility; other minorities can achieve more merely by working the system. We find in this [conflict perspective] yet another instance of "blaming the victims," for Blacks and Hispanics must be irresponsible if Asian Americans have succeeded (Commission on Civil Rights, 1980d; Hurh and Kim, 1986; Ryan, 1976).

Asian American Identity

Despite the diversity among groups of Native Americans, they have spent gen- 15
erations being treated as a monolithic group. Out of the experience has come a pan-Indian identity in which self-image as an Indian is shared with one's tribal identity.

Are Asian Americans finding a panethnic identity? It is true that in the United States extremely different Asian nationalities have been lumped together in past discrimination and present stereotyping. One may contend that Asian Americans have called upon unifying principles that are clearly products of contact with Whites. After centuries of animosity between ethnic groups in Asia, any feelings of community among Asian Americans must develop anew here; none are brought with them. We find some structural signs of a unitary identity: Asian studies programs in various colleges and organizations meant to represent all Asian Americans, such as the Asian Law Collective in Los Angeles (Trottier, 1981).

Despite these signs of a panethnic identity, the evidence is compelling that identity for Americans of Asian descent is defined by their status as a racial minority, their ancestry, and their participation in American society as contributing members. Asian American minorities came at very different stages in United States history, so that their patterns of work, settlement, and family life have varied greatly. Even though all have been subjected to many of the same policies and laws, those denying cultural differences have not been in effect for at least thirty years. Most can rejuvenate their ethnic culture because the traditions live on in the home countries—China, Japan, Korea, and the Philippines. Although at least the people of Indochina in the United States have trouble keeping in close contact with homelands, continuing immigration revives distinctive traditions that separate rather than unite Asian American groups.

Glancing Back and Looking Ahead

For some people, it is simple to say that Asian Americans are one, a cohesive group that is easy to understand; like other subordinate groups, though, Americans of Asian descent represent varied life-styles. They immigrated to the United States at different times, leaving behind a bewildering array of cultural experiences.

Today Asian Americans are a rapidly growing group, well over five million. Despite striking differences among them, they are frequently viewed as if they came from one culture, all at once. They are characterized too as being a successful or model minority. Individual cases of success and some impressive group data do not imply, though, that the diverse group of peoples who make up the Asian American community are uniformly successful. Indeed, despite significantly high levels of formal schooling, Asian Americans earn far less than Whites with comparable education and continue to be victims of discriminatory employment practices (Commission on Civil Rights, 1980d, p. 24).

The ties of the United States with the Korean Americans, the Filipino 20
Americans, and the Indochinese Americans . . . came out of warfare, but today their descendants work to succeed in civilian society. Hawaii is interesting because of its relatively harmonious social relationships crossing racial lines. Though not an interracial paradise, Hawaii does illustrate that, given proper

historical and economic conditions, continuing conflict is not inevitable. Chinese and Japanese Americans . . . have experienced problems in American society despite their striving to achieve economic and social equality with the dominant majority.

References

Bell, David A. "The Triumph of Asian-Americans." *The New Republic* 193 (July 15, 1985), pp. 24–26, 28–31.

Biemiller, Lawrence. "Asian Students Fear Top Colleges Use Quota Systems." *The Chronicle of Higher Education* 23 (November 19, 1986), pp. 1, 34–35, 37.

Blalock, Hubert M., Jr. *Toward a Theory of Minority Group Relations.* New York: Capricorn Books, 1967.

Bonacich, Edna, and Modell, John. *The Economic Basis of Ethnic Solidarity.* Berkeley: University of California Press, 1981.

Bureau of Census. *Statistical Abstract, 1981.* Washington, D.C.: U.S. Government Printing Office, 1981b.

Butterfield, Fox. "Why Asians Are Going to the Head of the Class." *New York Times* (August 3, 1986), Sect. 12, pp. 18–23.

Commission on Civil Rights. *Success of Asian Americans: Fact or Fiction?* Washington, D.C.: U.S. Government Printing Office, 1980d.

———. *Recent Activity Against Citizens and Residents of Asian Descent.* Washington, D.C.: U.S. Government Printing Office, 1986.

Gardner, Robert W.; Roky, Bryant; and Smith, Peter C. "Asian Americans: Growth, Change, and Diversity." *Population Bulletin* 40 (October, 1985).

Hirschman, Charles, and Wong, Morrison G. "The Extraordinary Educational Attainment of Asian-Americans: A Search for Historical Evidence and Explanations." *Social Forces* 65 (September, 1986), 1–27.

Hurh, Won Moo, and Kim, Kwang Chung. "The Success Image of Asian Americans: Its Validity, Practical and Theoretical Implications." Paper presented at the annual meeting of American Sociological Association, New York City, 1986.

Kim, Kwang Chung, and Hurh, Won Moo. "Korean Americans and the Success Image: A Critique." *Amerasia* 10 (No. 2), pp. 3–21, 1983.

Li, Wen Lang. "Chinese Americans: Exclusion from the Melting Pot." In Anthony Gary Dworkin and Rosalind J. Dworkin, eds., *The Minority Report: An Introduction to Racial, Ethnic, and Gender Relations*, 2nd ed., pp. 303–328. New York: Holt, Rinehart and Winston, 1982.

Lindsey, Robert. "Colleges Accused of Bias to Stem Asians' Gains." *New York Times* (January 19, 1987), p. A10.

McBee, Susanna. "Are They Making the Grade?" *U.S. News and World Report* 96 (April 2, 1984), pp. 41–43, 46–47.

———. Asian Merchants Find Ghettos Full of Peril. *U.S. News and World Report* 101 (November 24, 1986), pp. 30, 31.

McLeod, Beverly. "The Oriental Express." *Psychology Today* 20 (July, 1986), pp. 48–52.

Oxnam, Robert B. "Why Asians Succeed Here," *New York Times Magazine* (November 30, 1986), pp. 72, 74–75, 88–89, 92.

Ramirez, Anthony. "America's Super Minority." *Fortune* 114 (November 24, 1986), pp. 148–149, 152, 156, 160.

Ryan, William. *Blaming the Victim*, rev. ed. New York: Random House, 1976.

Salholz, Eloise. "Do Colleges Set Asian Quotas?" *Newsweek* 109 (February 9, 1987), p. 60.

Stanley, Alessandra. "Scraphogs Invade Hawthorne." *Time* 127 (June 30, 1986), p. 41.

Sue, Stanley. "Asian Americans and Educational Pursuits: Are the Doors Beginning to Close?" *P/AAMHRC Review* 4 (July/October, 1985), p. 25.

Sue, Stanley; Zane, Nolan W. S.; and Sue, Derald. "Where Are the Asian American Leaders and Top Executives?" *P/AAMHRC Review* 4 (January/April, 1985), pp. 13–15.

Sung, Betty Lee. "Mountains of Gold: The Story of the Chinese in America." New York: Macmillan, 1967.

———. *A Survey of Chinese-American Manpower and Employment.* New York: Praeger, 1976.

Trottier, Richard W. "Charters of Panethnic Identity: Indigenous American Indians and Immigrant Asian-Americans." In Charles F. Keyes, ed., *Ethnic Change*, pp. 272–305. Seattle: University of Washington Press, 1981.

Wong, Eugene F. "Asian American Middleman Minority Theory: The Framework of an American Myth." *The Journal of Ethnic Studies* 13 (Spring, 1985), pp. 51–88.

Woo, Deborah. "The Socioeconomic Status of Asian American Women in the Labor Force." *Sociological Perspectives* 28 (July, 1985) pp. 307–338.

QUESTIONS FOR DISCUSSION

1. Schaefer argues that figures showing Asian-American incomes exceeding comparable figures for whites are deceptive. Explain.
2. Discuss the rich diversity that exists among Asian-American groups.

WRITING ASSIGNMENTS

1. Reaction Journal: Reread your freewriting now that you have read this selection. Freewrite once again for ten or fifteen minutes on whether or not the label "model minority" is in actuality an asset or a liability.
2. List what you feel are the three most important issues that Schaefer raises about the Asian-American experience. If you are able to arrange an interview with a member of the Asian-American community, do so, and write an essay about the relationships you found between Schaefer's essay and your interview.

ASIAN PACIFIC AMERICAN WOMEN AND FEMINISM

MITSUYE YAMADA

Mitsuye Yamada (b. 1923) is a second-generation Japanese-American poet and teacher of creative writing and children's literature. Her Camp Notes and Other Poems *(1976) includes poems written while she was in a detention camp in Idaho during World*

War II. Her later writings focus on issues concerning Asian-Pacific women in the United States. In the following essay, which was published in the collection This Bridge Called My Back: Writings by Radical Women of Color *(1981), Yamada speaks of what she feels is the false dilemma confronting women of color who are frequently expected to choose either an ethnic or a feminist identity when both racism and sexism are intertwined in their lives.*

◆ FREEWRITING

In her essay Yamada says she has "come to know who [she is] through understanding the nature of [her] mother's experience." Freewrite for ten or fifteen minutes on how the life of one or both of your parents has helped you understand your own life.

Most of the Asian Pacific American women I know agree that we need to make ourselves more visible by speaking out on the condition of our sex and race and on certain political issues which concern us. Some of us feel that visibility through the feminist perspective is the only logical step for us. However, this path is fraught with problems which we are unable to solve among us, because in order to do so, we need the help and cooperation of the white feminist leaders, the women who coordinate programs, direct women's buildings, and edit women's publications throughout the country. Women's organizations tell us they would like to have us "join" them and give them "input." These are the better ones; at least they know we exist and feel we might possibly have something to say of interest to them, but every time I read or speak to a group of people about the condition of my life as an Asian Pacific woman, it is as if I had never spoken before, as if I were speaking to a brand new audience of people who had never known an Asian Pacific woman who is other than the passive, sweet, etc. stereotype of the "Oriental" woman.

When Third World women are asked to speak representing our racial or ethnic group, we are expected to move, charm or entertain, but not to educate in ways that are threatening to our audiences. We speak to audiences that sift out those parts of our speech (if what we say does not fit the image they have of us), come up to shake our hands with "That was lovely my dear, just lovely," and go home with the same mind set they come in with. No matter what we say or do, the stereotype still hangs on. I am weary of starting from scratch each time I speak or write, as if there were no history behind us, of hearing that among the women of color, Asian women are the least political, or the least oppressed, or the most polite. It is too bad not many people remember that one of the two persons in Seattle who stood up to contest the constitutionality of the Evacuation Order in 1942 was a young Japanese American woman. As individuals and in groups, we Asian Pacific women have been (more intensively than ever in the past few years) active in community affairs and speaking and writing about our activities. From the highly political writings published in *Asian Women* in 1971 (incisive and trenchant articles, poems and articles), to more recent voices from the Basement Workshop in New York City to Unbound Feet in San Francisco, as well as those Asian Pacific women showcased at the Asian Pacific Women's Conferences in New York, Hawaii and California this year, these all tell us we *have* been active and vocal. And yet, we continue to hear, "Asian women are of course traditionally not attuned to being political," as if most other women are; or that Asian women are too happily bound to their traditional roles as mothers and wives, as if the same cannot be said of a great number of white American women among us.

When I read in *Plexus* recently that at a Workshop for Third World women in San Francisco, Cherríe Moraga exploded with "What each of us needs to do about what we don't know is to go look for it," I felt like standing up and cheering her. She was speaking at the Women's Building to a group of white sisters who were saying, in essence, "it is *your* responsibility as Third World women to teach *us*." If the majority culture know so little about us, it must be *our* problem, they seem to be telling us; the burden of teaching is on us. I do not want to be unfair; I know individual women and some women's groups that have taken on the responsibility of teaching themselves through reaching out to women of color, but such gestures by the majority of women's groups are still tentatively made because of the sometimes touchy reaction of women who are always being asked to be "tokens" at readings and workshops.

Earlier this year, when a group of Asian Pacific American women gathered together in San Francisco poet Nellie Wong's home to talk about feminism, I was struck by our general agreement on the subject of feminism *as an ideal.* We all believed in equality for women. We agreed that it is important for each of us to know what it means to be a woman in our society, to know the historical and psychological forces that have shaped and are shaping our thoughts which in turn determine the directions of our lives. We agreed that feminism means a commitment to making changes in our own lives and a conviction that as women we have the equipment to do so. One by one, as we sat around the table and talked (we women of all ages ranging from our early twenties to the mid-fifties, single and married, mothers and lovers, straight women and lesbians), we knew what it was we wanted out of feminism, and what it was supposed to mean to us. For women to achieve equality in our society, we agreed, we must continue to work for a common goal.

But there was a feeling of disappointment in that living room toward the 5
women's movement as it stands today. One young woman said she had made an effort to join some women's groups with high expectations but came away disillusioned because these groups were not receptive to the issues that were important to her as an Asian woman. Women in these groups, were, she said "into pushing their own issues" and were no different from the other organizations that imposed opinions and goals on their members rather than having them shaped by the needs of the members in the organizations. Some of the other women present said that they felt the women's organizations with feminist goals are still "a middle-class women's thing." This pervasive feeling of mistrust to-

ward the women in the movement is fairly representative of a large group of women who live in the psychological place we now call Asian Pacific America. A movement that fights sexism in the social structure must deal with racism, and we had hoped the leaders in the women's movement would be able to see the parallels in the lives of the women of color and themselves, and would "join" *us* in our struggle and give *us* "input."

It should not be difficult to see that Asian Pacific women need to affirm our own culture while working within it to change it. Many of the leaders in the women's organizations today had moved naturally from the civil rights politics of the '60's to sexual politics, while very few of the Asian Pacific women who were involved in radical politics during the same period have emerged as leaders in these same women's organizations. Instead they have become active in groups promoting ethnic identity, most notably ethnic studies in universities, ethnic theater groups or ethnic community agencies. This doesn't mean that we have placed our loyalties on the side of ethnicity over womanhood. The two are not at war with one another; we shouldn't have to sign a "loyalty oath" favoring one over the other. However, women of color are often made to feel that we must make a choice between the two.

If I have more recently put my energies into the Pacific Asian American Center (a job center for Asians established in 1975, the only one of its kind in Orange County, California) and the Asian Pacific Women's Conferences (the first of its kind in our history), it is because the needs in these areas are so great. I have thought of myself as a feminist first, but my ethnicity cannot be separated from my feminism.

Through the women's movement, I have come to truly appreciate the meaning of my mother's life and the lives of immigrant women like her. My mother, at nineteen years of age, uprooted from her large extended family, was brought to this country to bear and raise four children alone. Once here, she found that her new husband who had been here as a student for several years prior to their marriage was a bachelor-at-heart and had no intention of changing his lifestyle. Stripped of the protection and support of her family, she found the responsibilities of raising us alone in a strange country almost intolerable during those early years. I thought for many years that my mother did not love us because she often spoke of suicide as an easy way out of her miseries. I know now that for her to have survived "just for the sake" of her children took great strength and determination.

If I digress it is because I, a second generation Asian American woman who grew up believing in the American Dream, have come to know who I am through understanding the nature of my mother's experience; I have come to see connections in our lives as well as the lives of many women like us, and through her I have become more sensitive to the needs of Third World women throughout the world. We need not repeat our past histories; my daughters and I need not merely survive with strength and determination. We can, through collective struggle, live fuller and richer lives. My politics as a woman are deeply rooted in my immigrant parents' and my own past.

Not long ago at one of my readings a woman in the audience said she was 10
deeply moved by my "beautifully tragic but not bitter camp poems which were apparently written long ago,"[1] but she was distressed to hear my poem "To A Lady." "Why are you, at this late date, so angry, and why are you taking it so personally?" she said. "We need to look to the future and stop wallowing in the past so much." I responded that this poem *is not* at all about the past. I am talking about what is happening to us right now, about our nonsupport of each other, about our noncaring about each other, about not seeing connections between racism and sexism in our lives. As a child of immigrant parents, as a woman of color in a white society and as a woman in a patriarchical society, what is personal to me *is* political.

These are the connections we expected our white sisters to see. It should not be too difficult, we feel, for them to see why being a feminist activist is more dangerous for women of color. They should be able to see that political views held by women of color are often misconstrued as being personal rather than ideological. Views critical of the system held by a person in an "out group" are often seen as expressions of personal angers against the dominant society. (If they hate it so much here, why don't they go back?) Many lesbians I know have felt the same kind of frustration when they supported unpopular causes regarded by their critics as vindictive expressions to "get back" at the patriarchical system. They too know the disappointments of having their intentions misinterpreted.

In the 1960's when my family and I belonged to a neighborhood church, I became active in promoting the Fair Housing Bill, and one of my church friends said to me, "Why are you doing this to us? Haven't you and your family been happy with us in our church? Haven't we treated you well?" I knew then that I was not really part of the church at all in the eyes of this person, but only a guest who was being told I should have the good manners to behave like one.

Remembering the blatant acts of selective racism in the past three decades in our country, our white sisters should be able to see how tenuous our position in this country is. Many of us are now third and fourth generation Americans, but this makes no difference; periodic conflicts involving Third World peoples can abruptly change white Americans' attitudes towards us. This was clearly demonstrated in 1941 to the Japanese Americans who were in hot pursuit of the great American Dream, who went around saying, "Of course I don't eat Japanese food, I'm an American." We found our status as true-blooded Americans was only an illusion in 1942 when we were singled out to be imprisoned for the duration of the war by our own government. The recent outcry against the Iranians because of the holding of American hostages tells me that the situation has not changed since 1941. When I hear my students say "We're not against the Iranians here who are minding their own business. We're just against those ungrateful ones who overstep our hospitality by demonstrating and badmouthing our government," I know they speak about me.

Asian Pacific American women will not speak out to say what we have on our minds until we feel secure within ourselves that this is our home too; and until our white sisters indicate by their actions that they want to join us in our struggle because it is theirs also. This means a commitment to a truly communal education where we learn from each other because we want to learn from each other, the kind of commitment we do not seem to have at the present time. I am still hopeful that the women of color in our country will be the link to Third World women throughout the world, and that we can help each other broaden our visions.

Note

1. *Camp Notes and Other Poems* by Mitsuye Yamada (San Francisco: Shameless Hussy Press), 1976.

QUESTIONS FOR DISCUSSION

1. Yamada believes that this culture's stereotype of the "Oriental" woman makes attempts to achieve visibility from the feminine perspective very difficult. Discuss the stereotype as you know it and explain the difficulties Yamada cites.
2. In paragraph 13 Yamada makes a point about her students' response to the Iranian hostage situation. Explain why she concludes, "I know they speak about me."

WRITING ASSIGNMENTS

1. Reaction Journal: Assume the role of a white feminist and write a letter to Yamada in which you try to address her concerns about stereotyping, misunderstanding key issues, and compromising between ethnicity and womanhood.
2. Reread your freewriting, and continue to focus your thoughts on how the lives of your parents have helped you define your own life. Organize your freewriting and prepare an essay in which you develop this topic with illustrations from your parents' lives and from your own.

WHY WON'T AMERICA LET US BE AMERICANS?

TED NAKASHIMA

Japanese-American Ted Nakashima was interned at a resettlement camp during World War II. In the following piece, which appeared in The New Republic *in 1942, Nakashima describes the conditions under which the residents of these camps lived, their losses of material possessions, privacy, and dignity, and their frustration at having their Americanism held suspect.*

◆ FREEWRITING

In the previous selection Mitsuye Yamada points out that white Americans often judge immigrant groups by the problems and conflicts that exist in the immigrants' homeland. Such a judgment forces one to disregard the loyalty and status of the immigrants themselves. The outcry against Americans from the Middle East during the Iranian hostage crisis is one example. Freewrite for ten or fifteen minutes on such problems that you have observed in the media or in your own experience.

Unfortunately in this land of liberty, I was born of Japanese parents; born in Seattle of a mother and father who have been in this country since 1901. Fine parents, who brought up their children in the best American way of life. My mother served with the Volunteer Red Cross Service in the last war—my father, an editor, has spoken and written Americanism for forty years.

Our family is almost typical of the other unfortunates here at the camp. The oldest son, a licensed architect, was educated at the University of Washington, has a master's degree from the Massachusetts Institute of Technology, and is a scholarship graduate of the American School of Fine Arts in Fontainebleau, France. He is now in camp in Oregon with his wife and three-months-old child. He had just completed designing a much-needed defense housing project at Vancouver, Washington.

The second son is an M.D. He served his internship in a New York hospital, is married, and has two fine sons. The folks banked on him, because he was the smartest of us three boys. The army took him a month after he opened his office. He is now a lieutenant in the Medical Corps, somewhere in the South.

I am the third son, the dumbest of the lot, but still smart enough to hold down a job as an architectural draftsman. I have just finished building a new home and had lived in it three weeks. My desk was just cleared of work done for the Army Engineers, another stack of 391 defense houses was waiting (a rush job), when the order came to pack up and leave for this resettlement center called "Camp Harmony."

Mary, the only girl in the family, and her year-old son, "Butch," are with our 5
parents—interned in the stables of the Livestock Exposition Buildings in Portland.

Now that you can picture our thoroughly American background, let me describe our new home.

The resettlement center is actually a penitentiary—armed guards in towers with spotlights and deadly tommy guns, fifteen feet of barbed-wire fences, everyone confined to quarters at nine, lights out at ten o'clock. The guards are ordered to shoot anyone who approaches within twenty feet of the fences. No one is allowed to take the two-block-long hike to the latrines after nine, under any circumstances.

The apartments, as the army calls them, are two-block-long stables, with windows on one side. Floors are . . . two-by-fours laid directly on the mud, which is everywhere. The stalls are about eighteen by twenty-one feet; some contain families of six or seven persons. Partitions are seven feet high, leaving a four-foot opening above. The rooms aren't too bad, almost fit to live in for a short while.

The food and sanitation problems are the worst. We have had absolutely no fresh meat, vegetables or butter since we came here. Mealtime queues extend for blocks; standing in a rainswept line, feet in the mud, waiting for the scant portions of canned wieners and boiled potatoes, hash for breakfast or canned wieners and beans for dinner. Milk only for the kids. Coffee or tea dosed with saltpeter and stale bread are the adults' staples. Dirty, unwiped dishes, greasy silver, a starchy diet, no butter, no milk, bawling kids, mud, wet mud that stinks when it dries, no vegetables—a sad thing for the people who raised them in such abundance. Memories of a crisp head of lettuce with our special olive oil, vinegar, garlic and cheese dressing.

10 Today one of the surface sewage-disposal pipes broke and the sewage flowed down the streets. Kids play in the water. Shower baths without hot water. Stinking mud and slops everywhere.

Can this be the same America we left a few weeks ago?

As I write, I can remember our little bathroom—light coral walls. My wife painting them, and the spilled paint in her hair. The open towel shelving and the pretty shower curtains which we put up the day before we left. How sanitary and clean we left it for the airlines pilot and his young wife who are now enjoying the fruits of our labor.

It all seems so futile, struggling, trying to live our old lives under this useless, regimented life. The senselessness of all the inactive manpower. Electricians, plumbers, draftsmen, mechanics, carpenters, painters, farmers—every trade—men who are able and willing to do all they can to lick the Axis. Thousands of men and women in these camps, energetic, quick, alert, eager for hard, constructive work, waiting for the army to do something for us, an army that won't give us butter.

I can't take it! I have 391 defense houses to be drawn. I left a fine American home which we built with our own hands. I left . . . good friends, friends who would swear by us. I don't have enough of that Japanese heritage *ga-man*—a code of silent suffering and ability to stand pain.

15 Oddly enough I still have a bit of faith in army promises of good treatment and Mrs. Roosevelt's pledge of a future worthy of good American citizens. I'm banking another $67 of income tax on the future. Sometimes I want to spend the money I have set aside for income tax on a bit of butter or ice cream or something good that I might have smuggled through the gates, but I can't do it when I think that every dollar I can put into "the fight to lick the Japs," the sooner I will be home again. I must forget my stomach.

What really hurts most is the constant reference to us evacués as "Japs." "Japs" are the guys we are fighting. We're on this side and we want to help.

Why won't America let us?

QUESTIONS FOR DISCUSSION

1. Comment on how Nakashima's rhetorical strategy, including his tone and rhetorical questions, serve his purpose.
2. Even though this selection was written in 1942, it illustrates America's shifting attitudes toward its immigrant groups in the context of global events. Discuss these attitudes and give current examples.

WRITING ASSIGNMENTS

1. Reaction Journal: Imagine that you are a Japanese-American university student who has few or no direct family ties to the internment camps of the World War II era. Freewrite for ten or fifteen minutes on how this role change might have affected your reading.
2. Select what you consider to be the most important single word in this selection. Write a well-developed paragraph defending your choice.

FILIPINO FRUIT PICKERS

CARLOS BULOSAN

Carlos Bulosan (1913–1956) was born in Binalonan Pangasinan, in Luzon, in the central Philippines. The son of a small farmer, Bulosan had completed only three years of schooling and spoke virtually no English when he traveled by steerage to Seattle at the age of seventeen. He never returned to the Philippines and never became a U.S. citizen. Arriving on the West Coast during the Depression and at the height of discrimination against Filipinos, Bulosan worked as a casual laborer in agriculture and canning. Acquainted with loneliness, hunger, and fear, he learned about American society from the lowest economic and social vantage point. Bulosan became one of the first influential Filipino writers to write in English in this country. America Is in the Heart *(1943), from which the following selection is taken, recounts his early experiences in this country and declares his continuing faith in human beings and in the promise of America.*

◆ FREEWRITING

Read Bulosan's narrative and think of a time when someone helped you find a sense of hope when you were filled with anger and despair. Freewrite for ten or fifteen minutes as you remember the details of this experience.

After a day and a night of driving we arrived in a little town called Moxee City. The apple trees were heavy with fruit and the branches drooped to the ground. It was late afternoon when we passed through the town; the hard light of the sun punctuated the ugliness of the buildings. I was struck dumb by its isolation and the dry air that hung oppressively over the place. The heart-shaped valley was walled by high treeless mountains, and the hot breeze that blew in from a distant sea was injurious to the apple trees.

The leader of our crew was called Cornelio Paez; but most of the oldtimers suspected that it was not his real name. There was something shifty about him, and his so-called bookkeeper, a pockmarked man we simply called Pinoy (which is a term generally applied to all Filipino immigrant workers), had a strange trick of squinting sideways when he looked at you. There seemed to be an old animosity between Paez and his bookkeeper.

But we were drawn together because the white people of Yakima Valley were suspicious of us. Years before, in the town of Toppenish, two Filipino apple pickers had been found murdered on the road to Sunnyside. At that time, there was ruthless persecution of the Filipinos throughout the Pacific Coast, instigated by orchardists who feared the unity of white and Filipino workers. A small farmer in Wapato who had tried to protect his Filipino workers had had his house burned. So however much we distrusted each other under Paez, we knew that beyond the walls of our bunkhouse were our real enemies, waiting to drive us out of Yakima Valley.

I had become acquainted with an oldtimer who had had considerable experience in the United States. His name was Julio, and it seemed that he was hiding from some trouble in Chicago. At night, when the men gambled in the kitchen, I would stand silently behind him and watch him cheat the other players. He was very deft, and his eyes were sharp and trained. Sometimes when there was no game, Julio would teach me tricks.

Mr. Malraux, our employer, had three daughters who used to work with us 5
after school hours. He was a Frenchman who had gone to Moxee City when it consisted of only a few houses. At that time the valley was still a haven for Indians, but they had been gradually driven out when farming had been started on a large scale. Malraux had married an American woman in Spokane and begun farming; the girls came one by one, helping him on the farm as they grew. When I arrived in Moxee City they were already in their teens.

The oldest girl was called Estelle; she had just finished high school. She had a delightful disposition and her industry was something that men talked about with approval. The other girls, Maria and Diane, were still too young to be going about so freely; but whenever Estelle came to our bunkhouse they were always with her.

It was now the end of summer and there was a bright moon in the sky. Not far from Moxee City was a wide grassland where cottontails and jack rabbits roamed at night. Estelle used to drive her father's old car and would pick up some of us at the bunkhouse; then we would go hunting with their dogs and a few antiquated shotguns.

When we came back from hunting we would go to the Malraux house with some of the men who had musical instruments. We would sit on the lawn for hours singing American songs. But when they started singing Philippine songs their voices were so sad, so full of yesterday and the haunting presence of familiar seas, as if they had reached the end of creation, that life seemed ended and no bright spark was left in the world.

But one afternoon toward the end of the season, Paez went to the bank to get our paychecks and did not come back. The pockmarked bookkeeper was furious.

"I'll get him this time!" he said, running up and down the house. "He did that last year in California and I didn't get a cent. I know where to find the bastard!"

Julio grabbed him by the neck. "You'd better tell me where to find him if you know what is good for you," he said angrily, pushing the frightened bookkeeper toward the stove.

"Let me alone!" he shouted.

Julio hit him between the eyes, and the bookkeeper struggled violently. Julio hit him again. The bookkeeper rolled on the floor like a baby. Julio picked him up and threw him outside the house. I thought he was dead, but his legs began to move. Then he opened his eyes and got up quickly, staggering like a drunken stevedore toward the highway. Julio came out of the house with brass knuckles, but the bookkeeper was already disappearing behind the apple orchard. Julio came back and began hitting the door of the kitchen with all his force, in futile anger.

I had not seen this sort of brutality in the Philippines, but my first contact with it in America made me brave. My bravery was still nameless, and waiting to express itself. I was not shocked when I saw that my countrymen had become ruthless toward one another, and this sudden impact of cruelty made me insensate to pain and kindness, so that it took me a long time to wholly trust other men. As time went by I became as ruthless as the worst of them, and I became afraid that I would never feel like a human being again. Yet no matter what bestiality encompassed my life, I felt sure that somewhere, sometime, I would break free. This faith kept me from completely succumbing to the degradation into which many of my countrymen had fallen. It finally paved my way out of our small, harsh life, painfully but cleanly, into a world of strange intellectual adventures and self-fulfillment.

The apples were nearly picked when Paez disappeared with our money. We lost interest in our work. We sat on the lawn of the Malrauxs and sang. They came out of the house and joined us. The moonlight shimmered like a large diamond on the land around the farm. The men in the bunkhouse came with their violins and guitars. Julio grabbed Diane and started dancing with her; then the two younger girls were grabbed by other men.

It was while Estelle was singing that we heard a gun crack from the dirt road not far from the house. Malraux saw them first, saw the clubs and the iron bars in their hands, and yelled at us in warning. But it was too late. They had taken us by surprise.

I saw Malraux run into the house for his gun. I jumped to the nearest apple tree. I wanted a weapon—anything to hit back at these white men who had leaped upon us from the dark. Three or four guns banged all at once, and I turned to see Maria falling to the ground. A streak of red light flashed from the window into the crowd. Estelle was screaming and shouting to her father. Diane was already climbing the stairs, her long black hair shining in the moonlight.

I saw Julio motioning to me to follow him. Run away from our friends and companions? No! *Goddamn you, Julio!* I jumped into the thick of fight, dark with fury. Then I felt Julio's hands pulling me away, screaming into my ears:

"Come on, you crazy punk! Come on before I kill you myself!"

He was hurting me. Blinded with anger and tears, I ran after him toward our 20
bunkhouse. We stopped behind a pear tree when we saw that our house was burning. Julio whispered to me to follow him.

We groped our way through the pear trees and came out, after what seemed like hours of running, on a wide grass plain traversed by a roaring irrigation ditch. Once when we thought we were being followed, we jumped into the water and waited. The night was silent and the stars in the sky were as far away as home. Was there peace somewhere in the world? The silence was broken only by the rushing water and the startled cry of little birds that stirred in the night.

Julio led the way. We came to a dirt road that led to some farmhouses. We decided to stay away from it. We turned off the road and walked silently between the trees. Then we came to a wide desert land. We followed a narrow footpath and, to our surprise, came to the low, uninhabited, wide desert of the Rattlesnake Mountains. The stars were our only guide.

We walked on and on. Toward dawn, when a strong wind came, we jumped into the dunes and covered our heads with dry bushes until it had passed by. We were no longer afraid of pursuit. We were in another land, on another planet. The desert was wide and flat. There were rabbits in the bushes, and once we came upon a herd of small deer. We ran after them with a burning bush, but they just stood nonchalantly and waited for us. When we were near enough for them to recognize our scent, they turned about and galloped down the sand dunes.

When morning came we were still in the desert. We walked until about noon. Then we came to a narrow grassland. We stood on a rise and looked around to see the edge of the desert. Julio started running crazily and jumping into the air. I ran after him. At last we came to the beginning of a wide plain.

The town of Toppenish was behind us now, and the cool wind from the 25
valley swept the plain. We rested under a tree. Julio was different from other oldtimers; he did not talk much. I felt that he had many stories within him, and I longed to know America through him. His patience and nameless kindness had led me away from Moxee City into a new life.

After a while we crossed the plain again, hiding behind the trees whenever we saw anyone approaching us. I was too exhausted to continue when we reached Zillah, where some children stoned us. We hid in an orange grove and rested. At sunset we started again. When we were nearing the town of Granger, I heard the sudden tumult of the Yakima River. Julio started running again, and I followed him. Suddenly we saw the clear, cool water of the river. We sat in the tall grass, cooling our tired bodies beside the bright stream.

I was the first to enter the water. I washed my shirt and spread it to dry on the grass. Sunnyside was not far off. I could hear the loud whistle of trains running seaward.

"This is the beginning of your life in America," Julio said. "We'll take a freight train from Sunnyside and go to nowhere."

"I would like to go to California," I said. "I have two brothers there—but I don't know if I could find them."

"All roads go to California and all travelers wind up in Los Angeles," Julio said. "But not this traveler. I have lived there too long. I know that state too damn well. . . ."

"What do you mean?" I asked.

Suddenly he became sad and said: "It is hard to be a Filipino in California."

Not comprehending what he meant, I began to dream of going to California. Then we started for Sunnyside, listening eagerly to the train whistle piercing the summer sky. It was nearly ten in the evening when we reached Sunnyside. We circled the town, and then we saw the trains—every car bursting with fruit—screaming fiercely and chugging like beetles up and down the tracks. The voices of the trainmen came clearly through the night.

We stopped in the shadow of a water tower. Julio disappeared for a moment and came back.

"Our train leaves in an hour," he said. "I'll go around for something to eat. Wait for me here."

I waited for him to come back for several hours. The train left. Then I began to worry. I went to town and walked in the shadows, looking into the darkened windows of wooden houses. Julio had disappeared like a wind.

I returned to our rendezvous and waited all night. Early the next morning another train was ready to go; I ran behind the boxcars and climbed inside one. When the train began to move, I opened the door and looked sadly toward Sunnyside. Julio was there somewhere, friendless and alone in a strange town.

"Good-bye, Julio," I said. "And thanks for everything, Julio. I hope I will meet you again somewhere in America."

Then the train screamed and the thought of Julio hurt me. I stood peering outside and listening to the monotonous chugging of the engine. I knew that I could never be unkind to any Filipino, because Julio had left me a token of friendship, a seed of trust, that ached to grow to fruition as I rushed toward another city.

QUESTIONS FOR DISCUSSION

1. Discuss Bulosan's use of setting to emphasize this narrative account of a young man's movement from despair to faith in the promise of America.

2. Discuss how Bulosan's narrative might well serve as a microcosm for the immigrant experience in America as groups typically move from a period of conflict to one of accommodation.

WRITING ASSIGNMENTS

1. Reaction Journal: Assume that a group of your classmates has the opportunity to interview one of Bulosan's children—let's say a daughter. Now that fifty years have passed since the experience Bulosan narrates, prepare a list of questions you might ask her to help you come to a more complete understanding of the adult life of this immigrant from the Philippines.

2. Continue to work with your freewriting for this selection. Prepare a narrative of your own that describes a time when someone helped you find hope in the midst of anger and despair. Pay attention to setting and dialogue, using Bulosan's story as a model.

ARABS IN AMERICA

ALIXA NAFF

Alixa Naff (b. 1919) of the National Center for Urban Ethnic Affairs in Washington, D.C., is the author of Becoming American: The Early Arab Immigrant Experience *(1985). She has also produced an educational film on Arab-Americans and written the section on Arab-Americans in the* Harvard Encyclopedia of American Ethnic Groups *(1980). In the following essay, Naff focuses on the experiences of Arab-Americans from the Middle East. Describing the experiences of the early Christian Syrian immigrants and the later Muslim Arabs, Naff observes that were it not for renewed immigration and consequent ethnic awareness brought on by political and economic events, the "Syrian-Americans might have Americanized themselves out of existence."*

◆ FREEWRITING

Freewrite for ten or fifteen minutes on how your family values and customs have been influenced by your ethnic and cultural heritage. Compare your family with the family of a friend of a different cultural background.

Arabs had been in America for more than three quarters of a century before the general American public became aware of their existence.[1] In fact, it was not until the series of Middle East crises immediately following World War II that attention was focused on Arab–Americans and their homeland. This is not surprising, since American Arabs, one of the smaller groups in America's mosaic of ethnic peoples, had assimilated relatively rapidly and smoothly.

There are today roughly two million[2] Arabs in the United States—90 percent of them Christian and 10 percent Muslim, and over half of them well-assimilated third- and fourth-generation descendants of immigrants who arrived between 1875 and 1940.

Most of the original Arab immigrants were Christians from the Syrian province of the Ottoman Empire that included the semiautonomous administrative district of Mt. Lebanon, the coastal mountain range between the Syrian port cities of Beirut and Tripoli. They were likely to call themselves Syrians (the independent parliamentary Republic of Lebanon was not established until 1946) and tended to identify themselves in terms of their region, village of origin, or religious preference. They were not called Arabs, a term that has become familiar only in recent years. Most of the more recent Arab immigrants are Muslims from independent and often rival Arab states; in contrast to the earlier immigrants, they are frequently ardent Arab nationalists. Perhaps as many as 175,000 have come to the United States since 1948.

Christian and Muslim Arabs share a common heritage, but they are far from unified. Deeply rooted religious and sectarian beliefs as well as politics divide them in the United States as they do in their homelands, but at the same time an overarching Arab-American identity has begun to take shape. The Arab-American movement is little more than a decade old. Before the mid-1960s, and even now in some households, pre-World War II immigrants and their descendants were more comfortable with the designation Syrian or Lebanese-American. Interest in their Arab heritage has been awakened by the presence of Arab nationalists, indignation over U.S. foreign policy in the Middle East, objections to the unfavorable Arab image in the U.S. press, and the general contemporary interest in ethnicity.

Nomenclature is one problem; statistics is another. Official statistics are 5
clearly distorted. In immigration records until 1899 and in census records until 1920, all Arabs were recorded, together with Turks, Armenians, and others, under "Turkey in Asia." After 1920 the increase in their numbers warranted the separate classification "Syria," but religious differences were not noted. Official records have been slow to keep up with political changes; until relatively recently, for example, non-Syrian Arabs might be counted as "other Asian" and North African Arabs as "other African." Since 1948 the Palestinians, who account for much of the post-World War II Arab immigration, have been designated simply as refugees, or as from Palestine or Israel, or as nationals of the country of their last residence.

The first Arabs to discover the economic opportunities in the United States were probably the Christian tradesmen who, encouraged by the Ottoman sultan, came to exhibit Syrian wares at the Philadelphia International Exposition in 1876. Their enthusiastic reports, the activities of steamship agents recruiting labor from all over the world for American industry, and the efforts of native brokers and moneylenders combined to begin a chain emigration from the Mt. Lebanon area, the source of most pre–World War II Syrian migration. The overwhelming majority of these mountain-village emigrants were Christians in pursuit of economic interests.

In the late 19th century, Mt. Lebanon was an autonomous administrative district of the Ottoman Empire under the protection and influence of Western Christian powers and governed by a Christian Ottoman official. This district, according to historian Philip Hitti, was acknowledged to be "the best governed, most prosperous, peaceful and contented country in the Near East." Some residents migrated to escape military service which after 1908 became mandatory for Christians as well as Muslims under the new Turkish revolutionary government. Fear that they would be unable to maintain their Islamic traditions in a Western Christian society discouraged a mass migration of Muslims to the United States. Fragmentary data suggest that only a few thousand young Muslim men joined the Christian emigrants between 1900 and 1914, most of them after 1908.

The pioneers reported their success in letters home and demonstrated it in the amount of money they sent or in their ostentatious behavior if they went back to visit. The evidence attracted so many emigrants that before the turn of the century an entrepreneurial network of independent services developed to assist villagers along the stages of their journey. The operation of the network throughout most of the early period encouraged still more migration.

Adventurous bachelors were soon followed by married men and families. Some were small tradesmen, artisans, and skilled laborers, but most were off the land—owners of small, scattered holdings, tenant farmers, or laborers. Only a handful were intellectuals or professionals. With few exceptions, they came hoping to make a quick profit and return home to enjoy the status and privileges that money would bring; they were not leaving to escape religious or political persecution or economic oppression. Most of them were poor but not destitute. Emigration was generally a family venture and was financed by family resources. It was considered an investment whose return would be both wealth and prestige when the emigrant returned to his native village. Later, relatives already in the United States often paid for the trip.

Despite their unreliability, official immigration records are useful in reveal- 10
ing trends and characteristics of the Syrian migration. Immigration increased dramatically each year, from a few hundred in 1887 to over 4,000 in 1898; it rose to over 9,000 in 1913, but dropped sharply as result of World War I. Immigration rose again briefly, partly in anticipation of the restrictive Immigration Act of 1924; the threat of restriction hastened the migration or reentry of Syrians with their families and relatives, of émigrés dissatisfied with British and French League of Nations mandate governments that had been established after the war instead of promised Arab independence, and of Palestinians migrating as a result

of bitter struggles with the British authority over the influx of Jews from Europe who had been promised a Jewish homeland in Palestinian territory. Restrictions, the Depression, and World War II severely curbed immigration between 1925 and 1948. Arab immigration after 1945 included a few from Iraq, Egypt, and Morocco. Immigration records show that 107,593 Syrians and 8,425 Palestinians arrived in the United States before World War II. Census figures to 1940 reveal 206,128 Americans of Syrian and Palestinian origin and descent. But the figures are only a rough approximation resulting from inaccurate record-keeping, illegal entries, and other sources of error.

Few Syrians returned to their villages permanently. Family commitments, economic failures, and temporary dissatisfactions produced a continual two-way traffic, though villagers sometimes remained several years before reemigrating with their families. Figures for 1908–1910 show a 25 percent return rate, mostly of single males, suggesting individual restlessness rather than discontent with life in the United States. During the depressed 1930s over 60 percent of the approximately 1,500 arrivals left for home or elsewhere.

From 1899 to 1915, women composed about 47 percent of the Arab total; they, too, came to acquire wealth, join spouses, or increase their chances of marriage as villages emptied of single men. Despite their arrival, family, sect, and village traditions still compelled many men to seek wives in the homeland. In the twenties, when a sense of permanence set in, the women immigrants outnumbered the men. Throughout the period of immigration, up to 75 percent of the Syrian immigrants were between the ages of 15 and 45. The 44 percent illiteracy rate before 1910 reflected their humble origins; by the twenties it had dropped to 21 percent, an indication both of better reporting and the development of education at home.

Arab traits and values hinge on the central position held by the extended family in Arab society. The enhancement of family honor and status is an inviolable trust for its members; in return for protection, identity, and status, the family demands conformity and the subordination of individual will and interests. The honor or dishonor of an individual reflects on the entire family.

Noble ancestry, a claim few families can credibly make, has been supplanted in the United States by wealth as the basis for status and honor. Although money alone does not confer distinction on a family, it increases the ability of family members to manifest values—magnanimity, munificence, generosity, and hospitality—which even the poorest families cherish. Since in the structure of Arab society family honor is intricately entwined with loyalty to religion, sect, village, and even quarter, individual loyalty must extend to those as well. This system of values breeds family and group ties with strong clannish and factional tendencies. The determination to elevate and defend family honor and status produces a competitive spirit and an ethic of hard work, thrift, perseverance, shrewdness, and conservatism. The fear of shame restrains crime and indigence. Given the economic opportunities and the system of values in the United States, Syrians readily became success-oriented free-enterprisers. No two more dissimilar molds could have produced more similar products.

The Syrian immigrant occupation was peddling; no other immigrant group, 15
with the exception of the German Jews, so completely identified with it. Although the form of peddling as conducted in the United States was a departure from Levantine traditional forms, selling and bartering the products of their labor from village to village and door to door was common to petty farmers, artisans, and tradesmen in the homeland.

Before 1914 at least 90 percent of the immigrants, including women and children, took up the trade in the United States, if only for a short time. Peddling yielded good profits and required little training, capital, or English. The immigrants were not deluded about its hardships, but they preferred its independence to the drudgery of the factory and the isolation of the farm. Peddling drew young men and women from villages in groups of up to sixty or more, allowing the network of transit services to be formed and stimulating a Syrian industry of manufacturers, importers, and wholesalers to supply their needs. Those who did not peddle, or who tried and found its hardships intolerable, turned to work in mills and factories. A very few farmed or homesteaded in the West.

The transit network began in the homeland, but had its base in the new country in a peddling settlement clustered around a supplier, usually an enterprising veteran peddler. The port community of New York was the mother of peddling communities and their major supplier, but by 1900 Syrian peddlers had penetrated the remotest parts of the nation, from where suppliers, sometimes two or more in a town, recruited fellow villagers or attracted others. This proliferation of peddling settlements distributed Syrians throughout the United States; it also spared new arrivals the anxiety of finding work, since they could immediately be absorbed somewhere in the constantly expanding system.

Peddling was initially a trade in rosaries, jewelry, and notions that would fit into a small case. It soon expanded into suitcases filled with a wide range of dry goods from bed linens to lace—almost anything that an isolated farmer's wife or housebound city dweller might want to buy. Horses, wagons, and later automobiles allowed some peddlers to sell imported rugs and linens supplied by international traders in New York's Syrian community. By frugality, resourcefulness, long hours of work, and charging all that the market would bear, peddlers commonly calculated earnings into the thousands annually. Relatively few failed.

Syrian peddlers developed a network of routes from New York to California and from Maine to Texas. The more enterprising and determined, including a few women, remained on the road for weeks or months at a time, covering several states. Others concentrated on a single area. Most women, children, and old people remained within range of the settlement to which they returned in the evening. In addition to peddling, many women crocheted, embroidered, and sewed goods at home for their menfolk to sell, or worked in kimono or garment factories, sometimes also owned by Syrians. They generally continued this economic partnership through the various stages along the family's route to prosperity.

Peddling hastened acculturation and in the process contributed to its own 20
obsolescence. Peddlers accumulated capital, learned English quickly, and through constant contact with native-born Americans acquired new values, including the notion of settling permanently in the United States. When Syrians settled down, the majority opened family businesses in cities or smaller towns. Dry goods and grocery stores were the most common, but businesses ran the gamut. Numerous Syrian publications reflect the pride Syrians still take in "being in business."

Meanwhile, Muslim Arabs were also arriving, though in far smaller numbers. Higher industrial wages in the United States after 1910 attracted them to such industrial cities as Chicago, Toledo, and Dearborn, Michigan, although industrial labor usually proved to be a transitory occupation for the Muslims as well as for the Christians. When adjustment and capital were sufficient they generally turned to other pursuits.

Defending their traditions against acculturation pressures was much more difficult for the Muslims than for the Christians. Although Muslims have no priesthood and can pray in any ritually uncontaminated space, the mosque and its prayer leader (imam) are central to Muslim religious practice and a symbol of community unity. A Muslim working and living in a non-Muslim society has to make essential religious compromises: it is not usually possible to observe the Sabbath on Friday, pray five times a day, and fast during the sunlight hours of the holy month of Ramadan. Clues to the effect of American society on a Muslim group are provided by a small community established near Ross, North Dakota, around 1900. Before a mosque was built in the 1920s, prayer and ritual were conducted in private houses and led by the best informed among the group. Without a mosque for almost thirty years and without any cultural reinforcement from newcomers, the Muslims rapidly lost the use of Arabic, assumed Christian names, and married non-Muslims. The community dwindled as children moved away, and the mosque was abandoned by 1948. Elsewhere the sparse and scattered Muslim communities rarely even built mosques; only three are known to have been constructed in the twenties.

The breakdown of the patriarchal, extended family into nuclear units and the reduction in the father's authority were the first effects of immigration on Arab family life. Long hours, even days, away from home, peddling or minding the store, and the participation of wives in the family business weakened the paternal authority. The father lost ground as a disciplinarian, although he retained the respect due him as head of the family. American influence, education, and economic opportunities might impel sons to establish their own households when they married, but sentimental attachments and concern for the welfare of the family still tied the various units together.

The energy that women devoted to the economic goals of the family gradually freed them from some Old World customs. Muslim women usually abandoned the veil when they emigrated. Covering the head, a custom common to both Christian and Muslim women, was also soon abandoned except by the most traditional-minded. Working wives, and mothers did not relinquish their domestic roles, but they adjusted to necessity by having fewer children, cooking fewer time-consuming Arabic meals, and gradually adopting the custom of prearranged social visits.

Their labors helped build and support churches and kept the youth within the group. Their independence ended some time-honored traditions: by World War II the segregation of sexes at social gatherings in homes and churches had vanished except in mosques and among the most traditional Muslims. Only after the war did later marriages and unarranged ones become the rule; daughters were allowed to remain single if they wished, and the preference for male children lost much of its force.

Any hope for keeping marriage within the ethnic, religious, sectarian, or regional group was thwarted in the earliest years by a shortage of Syrian women, attendance at non-Syrian churches, and desire for acceptance in the larger American society. Interethnic, though not interreligious, marriages were sufficiently common to elicit admonitions against them in the Arabic press before 1914. An increase in the number of immigrant Syrian women, churches, and associations slowed the trend but did not entirely reverse it. Both convention and religion allowed men greater latitude than women in the choice of spouses. Until World War II unmarried women usually remained under the surveillance of the family, and their choices were carefully controlled and arranged to serve its interests. Women were expected to adhere to the faith of their husbands; if they married outside the sect, they and their children would be lost to it. Marriage was consequently a frequent source of conflict between the immigrant and the next generation. The children yearned for the aspects of American middle-class life that they had been exposed to through school, movies, radio, and military service. Marriage was for many an escape from parental authority; a non-Arab marriage presented itself as a solution to the dilemma of living in two cultures. Only occasionally did interethnic marriage result in permanent rupture in family relationships, however, and by the 1950s it was in any case so commonplace, especially among returning servicemen, that it ceased to be a major source of contention.

Marriage for the few Muslim Arabs posed more serious problems. In the early years women were few, and departure from custom, which had the force of holy law behind it, was attended with greater concern. The traditional-minded initially sought spouses in the homeland, but eventually the rate of interethnic (which for Muslims also meant interfaith) marriages among them increased as well. Beginning in the mid-sixties it soared among the professional and educated classes of both religious groups.

The attempts of the immigrant generation to maintain Arab culture ran afoul of their eagerness to succeed in the United States; the requirements of success relegated tradition to second place. Immigration restrictions after 1924 encouraged assimilation and prepared the way for the gap that developed between the descendants of the early immigrants and the culture-conscious Arabs of more recent times. The participation of the early immigrants in American life was somewhat cursory; coupled with their prosperity, however, it was nevertheless sufficient to allow their children to enter the larger American society with relatively little psychological stress.

The family, the keystone of Arab identity and social organization, had already been modified in the first generation to a degree determined by the family's economic status, the number of Syrians in the community, and the family's own inclinations regarding its cultural heritage. Hardly a family was unaffected at least to some extent by the assimilation process. The second generation maintained those elements of their parents' culture that were not incompatible with an American household. They raised their children according to local practices; they still relished ethnic food, but usually only on special occasions; if they did not attend church regularly, they at least observed religious holidays. They maintained family bonds but also developed relations with non-Syrian Americans of their own class.

The third and fourth generations are considerably more remote from the 30
culture of the first. A recent awakening to their ethnicity has caused them to turn to their parents for cultural pegs on which to hang their identity; but parental knowledge is often superficial, based only on being Syrians of one religious sect or another. Grandparents add little more than nostalgic reminiscences of an outdated past. If political and economic events had not reactivated Arab immigration and an interest in Arab culture, Syrian-Americans might have Americanized themselves out of existence.

For more than a century the West altered both social relations and political boundaries within the Arab world. By 1920 France ruled Morocco, Algeria, Tunisia, and Syria, including Mt. Lebanon. England governed Egypt, Sudan, Palestine, Transjordan, Iraq, and the eastern and southern shores of the Arabian peninsula, and exerted considerable influence in Libya. Only Saudi Arabia and Yemen remained independent. Greater Syria, which was supposed to be the basis for an independent, unified Arab nation promised by the West in return for Arab military aid to the Allies in World War I, was artificially divided in 1920 into a truncated Syria, a Maronite-dominated Greater Lebanon (incorporating the Syrian port cities of Sidon, Tyre, Beirut, and Tripoli), Transjordan, and a promised homeland in Palestine for the Jews. Lingering separatist feelings hardened and new ones developed. Arab nationalist ideology was born out of resentment and frustration over broken promises and thwarted aspirations. Arab nationalists set about building up Arab self-esteem and encouraging unity to counter foreign rule. The Arab nations gradually won their independence after World War II, but Arab unity foundered on separatist nationalist ideologies and sentiments that were reinforced by religious differences.

Between the wars, Western influence had led the upper and middle classes to send their sons, and some daughters, to be educated in Europe. After independence, governments committed to modernization subsidized education abroad, particularly in the United States. The rate of modernization lagged well behind the rate of education, however, as competing revolutionary ideologies, military coups, and wars with Israel sapped economies and career opportunities. As a result, despite the emigration restrictions imposed by several Arab governments and the dedication to the development of their countries of the individuals involved, hundreds of Muslim and Christian students sent to the United States for training simply remained there. Many professionals also emigrated, entering the United States under the terms of the professional-preference clause in the Immigration and Nationality Act of 1965. This Arab "brain drain" reached its highest point between 1968 and 1971, but from 1965 through 1976 "professional, technical, and kindred workers" averaged about fifteen percent of Arab immigrants—Egypt alone lost nearly seven thousand. A high percentage of immigrants from Jordan, Lebanon, and Syria are undoubtedly Palestinians; other Palestinians were admitted as refugees or under Israeli passports.

This immigration wave began in 1948, but it accelerated greatly after the Arab defeat in the Arab-Israeli war of 1967. From 1948 through 1979 arrivals totaled approximately 216,000; about 142,000 came during and after 1967. More than 44,000 came from Egypt; Jordan, Lebanon, Iraq, and Syria together provided about 126,000, most of them Palestinians; about 9,200 were listed as Palestinians; the rest came from North African countries, aside from a few thousand from the Arabian Peninsula. Some, like the stateless Palestinians, were pushed by political events; some by economic uncertainties. But most of them came to improve their prospects. In this group Muslims exceeded Christians by about 60 percent. About 45 percent were women, and over 50 percent were between 20 and 49 years old. From 1965 to 1976 skilled workers averaged 15 percent and unskilled workers 10 percent of Arab immigration; wives, children, and others reporting "no occupation" averaged over 50 percent. Recent arrivals under these classifications include Palestinians and Lebanese displaced by civil war in Lebanon.

Settlement and adjustment have been considerably easier for these Arabs. They have the advantages of education, language, special skills, and the communities and precedents already established by the Syrians. Most of them intended to return home eventually, and were simply awaiting a change in the circumstances that had precipitated their migration. Few actually go back. Some, like the unskilled Yemeni farmers and factory laborers, travel back and forth several times before finally deciding to settle.

The recent immigrants are considerably less sectarian, a trend that parallels declining sectarian allegiance among the American-born. Wherever they settle, postwar immigrants find American-born Arabs. Before the Arab-Israeli war of 1967, the two groups had difficulty understanding each other's concerns and tended to associate mainly with those Arabs who did not seriously challenge their views on Arab issues. After 1967 what they perceived as general American hostility toward Arabs drew the two groups closer together.

Arabs of the recent immigration are nationalistic and are eager to maintain their traditions. Their efforts harmonize with those of the newly ethnicized American-born Arabs. One result has been a sharp increase in the number of mosques in the United States. Since its use is essential to the Muslim faith, Arabic is also being revived. Mostly immigrant imams are trying to revive religious discipline and knowledge both of Arabic and modern Islamic thought.

Many Christian Arab churches have also begun to offer classes in Arabic language, history, and culture. Social events feature modern Arab food, songs, and dances; discussions at the parish level consider ways of encouraging a sense of community.

Outside the religious institutions a growing number of Syrian-Americans are also showing an interest in their ethnicity, learning about their culture, and taking at least some colloquial Arabic at college or doing research on Arabs and Arab-Americans in graduate school. One group, in concert with the recent arrivals, is trying to improve the quality of the teaching of Arab history and culture in high school. The long-term effects of all this activity remain to be seen, for in the meantime the children of the immigrants again experience the temptations of assimilation.

Notes

1. This article is a revised version of an earlier work which appeared in the *Harvard Encyclopedia of American Ethnic Groups* (1980: 128–136). It is reprinted here with permission of the author and publisher.

This article relies on primary data collected from in-depth interviews conducted by the author with first- and second-generation Arab-Americans in numerous communities in the United States. Other data sources included primary books, journals, memoirs, and documents from the author's private collection on Arab-Americans, which is to be housed in the Smithsonian Institute in Washington, D.C.

2. It is difficult to ascertain the exact number of Arab-Americans, given the lack of sound and reliable statistical data. Informed observers and experts generally agree that after more than a century of migration and growth, the total Arab-American population ranges from a low of 2 million to a high of 3 million.—The Editors

QUESTIONS FOR DISCUSSION

1. Why did Arabs arriving in the United States before World War II assimilate with less difficulty than postwar Arab immigrants? Discuss the issues of confrontation and accommodation as they apply to these two groups of Arab-Americans.
2. Discuss the role of the extended family in Arab society. What values were compromised during acculturation?

WRITING ASSIGNMENTS

1. Reaction Journal: Make a list of customs and values of Arab-Americans and show how "attempts of the immigrant generation to maintain Arab culture ran afoul of their eagerness to succeed in the United States." Do you feel that similar experiences can be associated with other immigrant groups?
2. Think about your freewriting as you prepare to write an essay discussing how values and customs in your own family have been compromised to accommodate a broader culture. (You may wish to interview older family members.) If you prefer, describe another family with which you are familiar.

A TRAGIC VOYAGE

DANG HONG LOAN

Dang Hong Loan (b. 1961) was born in Saigon. The daughter of an army officer, she attended a Catholic high school in a neighboring town. In 1975 Loan left Vietnam with her grandmother and her aunt's family and resettled in Houston, Texas. Her mother and two younger brothers had left earlier and settled in the Philippines. Her father remained in Vietnam. Loan graduated from the University of Massachusetts in 1985 with a degree in electrical engineering. She and her husband live in Dallas, Texas. "A Tragic Voyage" recounts the dangerous and haunting journey that she made when she was twelve years old from Vietnam to a refugee camp in Thailand. The essay appeared in The Far East Comes Near: Autobiographical Accounts of Southeast Asian Students in America, *edited by Lucy Nguyen-Hong-Nhiem and Joel Martin Halpern (1989).*

◆ FREEWRITING

After reading Dang Hong Loan's account of Ly's tragic story, freewrite for ten or fifteen minutes on what host countries for such involuntary emigrants can do to help these refugees come to terms with the horrors of their past and to adjust to their present.

I met with a young girl Ly whom I interviewed. In disbelief I learned of her tragic journey from Vietnam to Thailand which has left her with a painful scar.

Before the fall of Saigon in 1975 Ly was the happiest girl. She was the only daughter of a respected physician. Being a well-known physician, her father had been able to provide her with a good life, a life that many girls her age wished for. In school she always wore the nicest clothes. At home she had the cutest dolls of all her friends. But when the North Vietnamese took the south, her father, like many other high-ranking officials, including those who had been associated with the American government, were sent to the north (to camps). She and her mother had to move in with one of her aunts. Access to education was denied her because of her father's past. Life for her became a shattered dream. Now she could only watch in tears as her friends walked to school. She had to stay home helping her mother bake cakes to sell at a nearby market so that they could have money to buy clothes and medicine to send to her sick father in the "reeducation" camp. Her clothes which used to be the prettiest were now faded and mended in several places.

Ly's father was allowed to return home after three long years in the camp. Ly cried a lot at the sight of her father's condition. Once a strong, healthy, and confident man, he was now just a very sick old man who had suffered malnutrition and bad treatment. For him, three years in the reeducation camp had been like thirty. Most of his hair had turned gray, which made him look very old. After his recovery, he and his wife, who worried for their daughter's future, planned an escape for her to a foreign country where they hoped she would have a better chance for a future. After several attempts and failures, one rainy night her single uncle took her on a small boat with about sixty other people and they headed for freedom. Ly was used to many good-byes by now, but this time she had the feeling that this was going to be the last she would ever see her parents. Her parents must have felt the same way because her mother held Ly back for a long time. Finally, her father had to pull her away and gave her the last embrace before she went with her uncle. She was then twelve years old.

They had been at sea two days and they had been lucky because there were no high waves or strong winds, even though it was September. They had enough food and water for a week. Their stomachs would not go hungry and their throats would not go dry from the heat of the sun. They could only eat and drink a small amount. Ly had never cried as much as she did on the first day. She felt homesick, she felt lost in the big sea, she felt tiny and scared. The next day, there were some problems with the engine, but her uncle and two other men were able to fix it. Then it broke again the next day. This time they were helpless as they waited for someone to pass by. As night grew darker, some of the women and Ly started to cry for fear. The men just sat there looking into the dark, hoping to see some lights or something moving so they could have something to hope for.

The next morning, they saw a larger boat moving with high speed toward 5
them. Everybody cried out for joy. Some of them even stood up on the boat and waved and that caused the boat to rock back and forth vigorously. Ly was also happy, but as she looked at her uncle she sensed something was terribly wrong. The smile on his face quickly disappeared and was replaced by a look of fear. She followed his eyes to the other boat that came near to her little boat and sent strong waves to one side of it. Her uncle recognized the strange boat as belonging to pirates. He warned everyone on the boat about pirates. She saw the men on the other boat were armed with knives, and they yelled to the people on her boat in a strange language. A loud thud brought everybody back to reality as the large boat pulled over and hit her boat on one side. Water started to pour in through the big hole caused by the impact. With unfriendly gestures, the men on the other boat forced everybody into the corner of the boat. Two men from the strange boat jumped on her boat and started to search for valuable items. At the same time those men began to personally search the victims. A man fought back and was killed immediately. His body was thrown to the sea as others looked on in terror. Those wicked men laughed at each other as they attacked the women. After the search, they forced everybody but six girls and Ly onto their boat. That was the last she saw of her uncle. She was kept separate in the

cabin, away from the other six girls. An older man, probably the captain, brought her food every day. At night she slept in terror as she heard the screams and begging for mercies from the other girls and the lustful laughs of the wicked men. She did not know what was going on, but in her young mind she knew that it must have been something very terrible. The third night after watching her finish her meal, the old man attacked and raped her. She fought with all her might, but what could a twelve-year-old girl do to stop a grown man from attacking her? After raping her several times, he left her lying unconscious. The next day she had a high fever. The old man tried to feed her some food but she could not eat anything and was scared by his touches. Even the shadow of him sent her quivering into the corner of the bed. The fifth day, after attacking another refugee boat and ransacking it for valuable belongings, the pirates let the men, the children, and the elderly back into their old boat. The old man forced one of the victims to take Ly back with him into the refugee boat. Two days later, they landed in Thailand and arrived at Songkla refugee camp the same day. Ly was admitted to the hospital and stayed there for more than two weeks. In her case, she was lucky; nobody ever heard of what had happened to the other six girls that were captured at the same time with Ly.

Eight months after her discharge from the hospital, through a program to help single children resettle, Ly was adopted by an American couple and came to the United States in 1982. Now Ly is a straight A student but she rarely smiles. Behind her sad eyes is a memory of a tragic journey that changed her life. Occasionally, one finds her staring blankly at nothing in particular as tears come rolling down from her eyes. Is she thinking about her parents or about her sad experiences? Nobody seems to know.

QUESTIONS FOR DISCUSSION

1. Regrettably, Ly's tragic story is not unlike that of many other Southeast Asians who experienced forced emigration after years of turmoil in Vietnam and Cambodia. If possible, invite such a refugee to speak to your class about his or her struggle and eventual period of adjustment to a new culture.

WRITING ASSIGNMENTS

1. Reaction Journal: Assume that you know Ly's story and that she is coming to live as a foster child in your neighborhood. She will be attending the school that you attended, and her new foster parents are good friends with your family. Freewrite for ten or fifteen minutes on what you might say in a letter welcoming her to the school you attended and to your neighborhood.
2. After writing the letter in the Reaction Journal, share its contents with a group of your classmates. Discuss what your class, your university, and your community could do to help such refugees.

Suggestions for Discussion and Writing

1. H. L. Mencken defines Puritanism as "the haunting fear that someone, somewhere, may be happy." Puritans have long been stereotyped as prudish, joyless, abstemious, witch-hunting, avaricious bigots. Scholars have amassed much evidence from histories, documents, diaries (such as Samuel Sewall's), and other records of the time to prove these charges false. As in any other group, there were all kinds of individuals, ranging from saints to sinners. Discuss stereotyping you have encountered, read about, or witnessed, and then write an essay in which you provide evidence from your experience and general knowledge of the falsity or limited truth of such stereotyping.
2. Write an essay on the significance of ritual in the life of many Native Americans. Make specific reference to the writings of Luther Standing Bear, Mary Crow Dog, and Paula Gunn Allen. You may wish to expand this topic by writing about ritual in your own experience. Consider such matters as family traditions, religious ceremonies, and institutional and organizational practices.
3. Paula Gunn Allen writes about the special situation and problems of Native American women. Discuss the relationship of gender and ethnicity with your classmates. Do the men in your discussion group have the same perspectives on gender-related confrontations and accommodations as the women? You may also wish to raise this question outside of the classroom with acquaintances who are members of particular ethnic groups. Write an essay based on your discussion and reading. You will make your task easier if you make specific reference to some of the other women writers in this book, especially Harriet Jacobs, Elena Padilla, and Mitsuye Yamada.
4. The introduction to "From Europe—The Huddled Masses" summarizes some of the hardships and struggles of the European immigrants. Compare their problems with those of two other groups in the "Ethnic Journeys" unit. Make specific reference to at least four authors as well as to some statistical and historical information in the chapter introductions.
5. The following is a suggestion for a major writing project on cultural accommodation and assimilation. "The Huddled Masses" provides information about the immigration experiences of Swedes, a Russian Jew, and a Polish Roman Catholic. Discuss their experiences and those of some recent immigrants from the Americas and Asia. Consider what happened, according to Richard O'Connor, to the immigrant Germans and what Alixa Naff says nearly happened to the Syrian-Americans. In your experience, which groups have traveled the assimilationist path? If you consider yourself a member of an ethnic group (other than "American"), write about the degree of ethnic consciousness of your family. If you are not conscious of any specific ethnic identity, explain why. What do you think are the assimilationist prospects for recent immigrants, especially from the

Americas and Asia? You may wish to refer to readings in the "Living in Multicultural America" unit and do some additional research for this question.

6. Martin Luther King, Jr., Malcolm X, and Stokely Carmichael were all committed to the struggle for black liberation and equality, but they took different paths to reach this goal. Write an essay in which you discuss their philosophies as revealed in the selections in this unit. Your essay should make direct reference to their writings and consider their use of language and persuasive tactics as well as their ideas.
7. Militant leaders of other racial and ethnic groups often attribute their own militancy to the inspiration of the black civil rights movement. Construct a roundtable discussion in which King or Carmichael joins Mary Crow Dog and Luis Valdez to talk about the similarities and differences in their relationship with "white America" and their political and sociocultural agendas. If you wish, have Shelby Steele and Henry Gonzalez join them.
8. Research some aspect of the music, art, or literature of the Latino/Chicano groups in the United States. What issues, attitudes, and values are presented in the work of the artist(s), musician(s), and writer(s) you have chosen? Whenever possible make connections with readings in this unit and in "Living in Multicultural America."
9. Richard Schaefer considers the realities and effects of the stereotype of Asian-Americans as a "model minority." How one defines "model minority" depends to a great extent on how one views ethnicity and the goals of a particular group vis-à-vis the general culture. After explaining Schaefer's definition, choose two or three other writers from this unit and speculate on how they would define "model minority," Would, for instance, Shelby Steele and Stokely Carmichael agree with each other or with Schaefer? What about Ted Nakashima? Mitsuye Yamada? Mary Crow Dog? Luis Valdez? Henry Pratt Fairchild? Think carefully about the writers you select in order to present an interesting spectrum of opinion.

Return to assignment 1 at the end of "National Identity and Cultural Pluralism." Reevaluate and refine your initial thoughts on group identity.

Return to assignment 3 at the end of "National Identity and Cultural Pluralism" and continue to update your collection of news and opinion items on the pluralism-tribalism controversy.

Return to assignment 4 at the end of "National Identity and Cultural Pluralism." Make additional entries in your journal on the theme of Confrontation and Accommodation.

PART

III

LIVING IN MULTICULTURAL AMERICA

Neighborhoods

Family

Language

Education

Confrontations

Oh, the white folks hate the black folks, And the black folks hate the white folks.
To hate all the right folks is an old established rule.
But during National Brotherhood Week, National Brotherhood Week,
Lena Horne and Sheriff Clark are dancing cheek to cheek.
It's fun to eulogize the people you despise,
As long as you don't let 'em in your school.

Oh, the poor folks hate the rich folks, And the rich folks hate the poor folks.
All of my folks hate all of your folks, it's American as apple pie.
But during National Brotherhood Week, National Brotherhood Week,
New Yorkers love the Puerto Ricans 'cause it's very chic.
Step up and shake the hand of someone you can't stand,
You can tolerate him if you try.

Oh, the Protestants hate the Catholics, And the Catholics hate the Protestants,
And the Hindus hate the Moslems, and everybody hates the Jews.
But during National Brotherhood Week, National Brotherhood Week,
It's National Every-one-smile-at-one-another-hood Week.
Be nice to people who are inferior to you.
It's only for a week, so have no fear—
Be grateful that it doesn't last all year.

—NATIONAL BROTHERHOOD WEEK, *TOM LEHRER*

Neighborhoods

As Andrew Greeley observes, people are often "passionately committed" to their neighborhoods, bound by attachments that are both geographic and interactional. The ties are especially strong when the population of the neighborhood shares a common ethnic, linguistic, and religious background. While for immigrants the strength of these attachments may lessen with acculturation, the pleasure that people derive from familiar places and practices and the influence these places and practices have on their outlooks are undeniable. The survival of ethnic neighborhoods for generations after immigration attests both to the psychological comfort provided by a continued ethnic presence and, on a darker note, to unequal access to the larger society afforded to various groups.

Faced with the challenge of beginning a new life in an unfamiliar land, immigrants naturally seek out familiar faces, language, shared memories and customs and thereby re-create to some extent their native villages in the midst of an alien society. This clinging together has served to combat both loneliness and helplessness, as immigrants create institutions such as mutual-benefit societies to offer newcomers the support of extended families. So insulated can these ethnic enclaves become that Harry Mark Petrakis, speaking of his childhood in a Greek neighborhood in Chicago, remarks that "our neighborhood was a city within a city bounded by the walls of our streets. We knew there was an area called 'downtown,' made infrequent trips there with one of our parents, knew there was a North Side (home of the ritzy Cub fans) and a West Side, but for all the relevance these sections had for us, they might have been cities in Europe." The ethnic makeup of such city neighborhoods can change within a few blocks. Indeed, crossing these neighborhood boundaries can be difficult, dangerous, and, as our television news reports remind us nightly, even deadly. The streets are often regarded as belonging to "the neighborhood," and anything that is regarded as different on those streets is unacceptable.

The area of original settlement for an immigrant group is generally located near the edge of a city's business district, a congested area that offers inexpensive housing. New waves of immigrants from the same country are attracted to this core area by its familiar culture and language and affordable housing. After adapting to the new ways of life and achieving some financial security, immigrants tend to move outward into less densely populated, less homogeneous, more prosperous, and safer areas. The population of inner-city ethnic neighborhoods tends to be poorer and less upwardly mobile than members of the group who have moved on. Residents of these core areas are thus characterized not only by degree of ethnic identity but by class as well. The isolation of the urban poor, particularly before the television era, was such that in "We Who Came After" Ronald Fair can remark about his childhood in a black Chicago ghetto, "We had not yet learned we were the ones who were supposed to be deprived."

Large cities are not, of course, the only places where one can find ethnically or racially segregated neighborhoods. Nicholas Lemann, for instance, describes the lives of blacks in the rural southern community of Clarksdale, Mississippi, before the great mid-twentieth-century immigration to the northern cities. Other rural ethnic concentrations can be found in the Norwegian, Swedish, German, and Slavic settlements in the Plains states, such as described in Elise Amalie Waerenskjold's letters in "Four-Mile Prairie . . .," and the communities of Chicano farmworkers in the southwest and in California. The large cities, however, have been the traditional first home for most immigrants recently arrived in the United States, and it is such large population centers that afford the most opportunity for development of semi-independent linguistic and cultural communities within their boundaries. The term *"ghetto"* originally referred to the areas populated by eastern European Jews arriving in the United States near the end of the nineteenth century, but the term has now come to denote the segregated residential areas of any minority group in the inner-city slums, while a *"barrio"* is a Spanish-speaking ghetto.

The complex relationships of poverty, ethnicity, and urban environment began to be an object of study and an issue of widespread public concern during the middle of the nineteenth century. The great waves of migration during that period resulted in severely overcrowded and unhygienic conditions in the tenement districts of New York. Fear of a cholera epidemic in 1866 led to the formation of the Citizens' Council of Hygiene. Composed of sixteen distinguished physicians, this council reported that the lack of ventilation, lighting, and sanitary regulations, the dampness, and the building of tenements back to back with those on parallel streets (resulting in narrow, airless, unhealthy alleyways crowded with shanties) were factors contributing to the very high death rates in the tenement districts. It was the council's opinion that supervised sanitary controls should reduce the city's death rate by 30 percent. In fact, in the thirty-five years following the report, the death rate was reduced by over 50 percent. Citizens' commissions and a Department of Health, established to see that housing regulations and building codes were enforced, advocated the demolition of some of the worst slums. Prominent among those seeking reform was Jacob Riis. An immigrant himself, Riis became a photographer and reformer-journalist whose writings, such as *How the Other Half Lives* (1890), revealed to middle-class Americans the realities of slum conditions.

In spite of the degradation and the dangers associated with living in the ghetto, hardship conditions sometimes foster a sense of belonging, cooperation, and solidarity. The pluses and minuses of barrio life are related by Mario Suárez in his description of El Hoyo, a Spanish-speaking district in Tucson. Although El Hoyo is neither safe nor beautiful—a place were the "main things known to grow . . . are weeds, garbage piles, dogs, and kids"—it possesses a compelling spirit of its own. It is a neighborhood that "laughs and cries with the same amount of passion in times of plenty and of want," a place where "anything calls for a celebration." Ronald Fair, again speaking of his childhood, has his narrator recall the game of rat hunting he engaged in as a child, pursuing the rodents hated and feared from infancy since he and his friends all "had relatives who had either been bitten by rats or frightened out of their wits by them." Yet the detail in which the narrator relates the comradeship of the streets and his memory that "the coolness of sitting inside an ice truck on a hot summer day as Sampson allowed us to think we were helping him" provided "the warmest feeling of [his] childhood" leave a sense of a neighborhood intact, where fellow feeling and good memories provide a sense of belonging. The society outside the boundaries of the neighborhood, however, at times impinges on the consciousness even of children, forcing them to see themselves through others' eyes. Fair remembers the day he and his friends became aware that the radio-broadcast "God bless yous" of Christmas day "were not meant for [them]."

For some groups the forced concentration in inner-city neighborhoods became a source of political power, a means for economic advancement, and a prideful symbol of ethnic identity, while other groups have found transcending the class restrictions of ghetto life and "moving on" difficult if not impossible goals. The ways in which cultural resources interact with the environment either to alleviate or exacerbate the conditions of ghetto living vary from group to group, and surely racially stigmatized groups are not as easily integrated into mainstream society as groups whose ethnic identity is less apparent.

One finds a significant range of responses to the experiences of living within an ethnically or racially segregated neighborhood. Mixed with what is often the pleasure of feeling perfectly at home are questions about freedom, social justice, and mobility. Thus, the community with which one either chooses or is forced to identify can occasion complicated emotional responses.

SOCIAL TURF

ANDREW M. GREELEY

Andrew M. Greeley (b. 1928) is Director of the Center for the Study of American Pluralism at the National Opinion Research Center, University of Chicago, and professor of sociology at the University of Arizona, Tucson. He is also editor of the journal Ethnicity *and has written a syndicated column, "People and Values," for the* Chicago Sun Times *since 1985. Greeley has published widely on the history of Catholicism and Catholic education in the United States and in the fields of sociology, education, and religion, and he has also written a number of popular novels such as* Thy Brother's Wife. *Among his many nonfiction titles are* Unsecular Man *(1972),* Ethnicity in the United States *(1975), and* Andrew Greeley's Chicago *(1989). In "Social Turf," an excerpt from* Why Can't They Be Like Us? *(1971), Greeley describes human territoriality as "interactional" as well as "geographic" and suggests that people's commitment to the relationships and customs of their ethnic neighborhoods and their consequent determination to preserve these neighborhoods is "strongly rooted in the human condition."*

◆ FREEWRITING

In the introduction to this section we write that "the pleasure that people derive from familiar places [neighborhoods] and practices and the influence these places and practices have on their outlooks are undeniable." Freewrite for ten or fifteen minutes on your neighborhood. What makes it unique? How has it affected the way you view your world?

A number of zoologists and social scientists of whom the most famous is Konrad Lorenz have written of the "territoriality" of man. They argue that man, like most other animals, has a biological inclination to stamp out a certain amount of physical space as "his own" and to resent to the point of physical resistance any transgressions across the boundary of that territory. Some research evidence indicates that for specific individuals the boundaries of this territoriality can be determined with some accuracy. The amount of territory different individuals need seems to differ considerably; you can come closer to some than to others without violating the boundaries of their turf.

These writers make an interesting and plausible case, although any comparison of human behavior to the behavior of other animals has a certain amount of metaphor about it because of the vast complexity of human cultural and personality systems compared with the rather rudimentary nature of these systems in other animals. If there is a biological instinct which inclines us to define a certain piece of space as our own, the instinct operates together with cultural and personality dimensions that are quite different from anything to be found in other animals. Thus man's territoriality, even if it has biological roots, is also profoundly affected by his social structure and culture.

But whether the urge for one's "turf" has biological roots or not, no student of human behavior can doubt that it exists. Daniel Boone "moving out" to find more "elbow room," street gangs fighting over their own segment of the slums, border guards nervously eyeing each other across the line, the interminable petty boundary disputes between even countries that are supposedly friendly, children's definitions of which parts of a playroom are their own, personalizing of our hotel room by placing a picture on one table and a transistor radio on another—all of these are signs that we try to impress our personality on the area which we claim to be ours. The urge (whether cultural or biological or psychological) for territoriality may be greater in some than in others; indeed, in some it may even be vestigial, but it surely is part of the human condition.

Furthermore, it seems that our urge is not merely for turf but for "social turf." While the research data are thin to the point of being practically non-existent there does seem to be some reason to believe that man's turf is not only geographic but interactional. That is to say, his affiliation to his "place" includes a commitment not only to a segment of geography but also to the interaction network and the institutions which fill up that geographic space. Perhaps one of the principal reasons for the poor communication between the members of America's intellectual elite and the rest of the country is that intellectuals rarely are able to understand the concept of social turf. They do not understand why other Americans and particularly Americans of ethnic background are so committed to that segment of social turf that they call their *neighborhood.*

To a large segment of American society no explanation is necessary for the 5
concept of neighborhood. They have spent their whole lives inside one or more, likely many different, neighborhoods. They may be hard put to define in formal terms what a neighborhood is, but they know one when they see one. They understand the difference between their neighborhood and other neighborhoods and they are astonished to find that there are people in the land who have never lived in a neighborhood and do not understand what it is. They are even more astonished to find that these same people cannot understand the need to defend one's neighborhood and that they dismiss loyalty to one's neighborhood as immoral or racist. There may well be an element of racism involved in much of the defense of one's neighborhood, though a fear of any strange outsider "who will not be like us" is probably more important than truly racial bigotry. But there is far more involved in a neighborhood and affection for it than fear or bigotry. . . .

Similarly, I do not think that the controversy over neighborhood schools and the busing question can really be understood unless those who, for what they think to be reasons of social morality, insist on busing can come to understand that not all opposition to it is rooted solely in bigotry. Bigotry there certainly is and also fear, some of it well grounded and some of it foolish. But the overwhelming negative reaction to busing in the United States calls into play other emotions, one of the most important of which is strong personal identification with the school in one's own neighborhood, an identification which, be it noted, is by no means limited only to white ethnic groups.

Perhaps one of the reasons that social scientists are incapable of coping with the factor of neighborhood or social turf is that they have taken too literally the theories of "mass society" and have believed too literally that *gesellschaft* ("contractual") relationships have replaced *gemeinschaft* ("communitarian") relationships in most human reactions beyond the family level. The neighborhood should have been left behind in the peasant village where our ancestors lived in Europe; certainly it should have been relinquished when we moved out of the "old neighborhood" immigrant ghetto. Because they are so rootless and mobile themselves, most social analysts are astonished to discover that there can be upper middle-class and suburban neighborhoods. Even if they are forced to admit the neighborhood still exists, there seems to be an implicit conviction that the forces of urbanization, rationalization, bureaucratization and now computerization will slowly eliminate the neighborhood from American society. Neighborhoods were all right in William F. Whyte's *Street Corner Society*, but one can hardly expect them to be around in the year 2000.

Perhaps the reason that there is so much suspicion about the neighborhood is that its continuing existence runs contrary to important contemporary myths: the myth of "rapid social change" and the myth of "technological man." The first myth argues that because of the fantastic change in human life styles, and because of the population explosion and the various scientific revolutions of the last two hundred years, a situation has been created in which the only thing that is permanent is change itself. The second myth contends that because of the pace of change a new kind of man has evolved, a man who lives in Professor Harvey Cox's *Secular City* and is part of Professor Warren Bennis's *The Temporary Society*. Such men literally do not have permanent roots and do not need them; such men not only do not need but are incapable of creating myths; such men not only do not belong to tribes but have passed beyond the stage where tribalism is conceivable; such men are at home—and in Professor Bennis's view of things can even establish intimate relationships—in any part of the world and can move from one part of the world to another with physical and psychological ease.

The basic assumption of these two myths is that a change in technology almost inevitably generates (though perhaps with some "culture lag") new values, new personalities, new human needs, new patterns of basic behavior while at the same time eliminating the values, needs, aspirations and behavior patterns of the past. Such an assumption, however, is not an axiom but, at best, a testable hypothesis. I am always amused, for example, when I hear people talk today about the "sexual revolution" as though promiscuity was absent in the past. Our society, we are assured, is a permissive society, but I find myself wondering "permissive" with regard to what? Permissive compared to Herculaneum, to the Rome of Nero, to the Versailles of Louis XIV, to the London of the Restoration, of the Regency or even of Victoria? For a sensible social analysis to take place, the analyst must abandon the myth that his generation is the hinge of history and resist the quite modern temptation to label behavior as "revolutionary" when it is merely part of the human condition. . . .

I suspect that the reader who wants to investigate carefully the existence of ethnic neighborhoods and even the existence of ethnic groups will have to suspend temporarily, at least, his conviction that both these two myths are beyond challenge . . . [and] accept as a tentative hypothesis the notion that while there are some secular and technological men living in a temporary society, moving about the planet with the same ease their ancestors moved about the village (even though their biological systems revolt in the form of "jet lag"), these men are relatively few in number and do not necessarily represent the wave of the future. Considerable numbers of human beings continue to live in neighborhoods and continue to be deeply attached to their social turf, to view the geography and the interaction network of their local communities as an extension of themselves and to take any threat to the neighborhood as a threat to the very core of their being. When neighborhood loyalty, already something quite primordial, is reinforced by a common religion and a sense of common ethnic origins, the commitment to the neighborhood can become fierce and passionate indeed. Its streets, its markets, its meeting places, its friendships, its accepted patterns of behavior, its customs, its divisions, even its factional feuds provide a context for life that many of its citizens are most reluctant to give up. It is curious that in a world in which the "quest for community" has become so conscious, so explicit and so intense there is such little awareness of the existence of such primordial community ties. It would be an exaggeration to say that the "urban villages" which many neighborhoods seem to be are exactly the same as the peasant communes in the eighteenth and nineteenth centuries or the medieval manors or the Teutonic tribes (or the Celtic clans) or even the Neolithic communities along the river banks of southern France. Obviously many things have changed. The social control of the neighborhood, while frequently strong, is not nearly so strong as that of the communities of the past. There are more options available, more variety to be experienced, more opportunities to leave the community permanently or temporarily, and more intimate relationships with people beyond the boundaries of the community. Work, amusement, frequently education and sometimes even worship, take place elsewhere and yet anyone who has lived in a neighborhood knows how powerful and even seductive its attractions can be.

I do not wish to canonize neighborhoods. I do not wish to argue that the instinct for social turf is always benign. Having lived most of my life in various neighborhoods, I can easily resist any temptation to romanticize them. Both the University of Chicago ethnic neighborhood called Hyde Park and the South Side Irish ethnic neighborhood called Beverly Hills can be narrow, provincial, repressive places. Like all ethnics, the inhabitants of these two neighborhoods can be so concerned about their own welfare as to ignore the needs and aspirations of others. The preservation of a neighborhood, while strongly rooted in the human condition, is not an absolute value. My principal point, however, is not that social turf is always benign or that neighborhoods represent the ultimate in human values. My point is rather that one will simply not understand ethnic groups unless one knows that neighborhoods are the places in which they live, places to which many of their members are passionately committed. Any attempt to analyze American urban society, much less to reform it, which is not based on a prior attempt to understand, from the "inside," the part that a neighborhood plays in the lives of many people is doomed to frustration.

QUESTIONS FOR DISCUSSION

1. Greeley suggests that the human desire for territoriality is affected by social structure, culture, and biological instinct. What does he mean by "biological instinct" in this context, and how much importance does he give it?
2. Greeley makes a distinction between turf and social turf. What is the distinction, and what does it have to do with the human need for territory?
3. The author points out that there are social scientists who suggest there are people who have never lived in a neighborhood and that the power of the neighborhood is decreasing in this modern era. Explain why Greeley disagrees with much of this assumption.

WRITING ASSIGNMENTS

1. Reaction Journal: Reduce Greeley's essay to a one-paragraph definition of neighborhood.
2. Greeley implies that most of us live in neighborhoods. To be sure, ties are stronger when they are reinforced by common religion and ethnic origins, but he argues there can even be upper-middle-class and suburban neighborhoods. Write an essay in which you provide concrete examples that describe your own neighborhood and what holds it together. Use your freewriting for this selection as a starting point for your essay.
3. After you have written the essay for writing assignment 2, meet with several classmates and discuss the personality of your own neighborhood. Discuss how attached each of you is to your own social turf.

CLARKSDALE

NICHOLAS LEMANN

Nicholas Lemann (b. 1954), a native of New Orleans, was a reporter for the Washington Post *and is currently a national correspondent for* The Atlantic. *For his book* The Promised Land: The Great Black Migration and How It Changed America *(1991), from which the following excerpt is taken, Lemann won the 1991* New York Times *Book Prize and the Helen B. Bernstein Award for Excellence in Journalism, given annually by the New York Public Library.* The Promised Land, *which explores the impact of the migration of 5 million blacks from the South to large northern cities during the 1940s and 1950s, focuses on two cities on the migration route: Clarksdale in the Mississippi Delta, and Chicago.*

◆ FREEWRITING

Focus on one individual whose life-style and habits are representative of life in your neighborhood or town. Freewrite for ten or fifteen minutes as you generate concrete illustrations of that life.

When Ruby and her husband moved to Clarksdale at the end of 1938, she got a job as a cook and housekeeper for a white lady, at $2.50 a week. Ruby's education was pretty good for someone of her generation—eighth grade, with some time spent in one of the country schools endowed by Julius Rosenwald, the Sears Roebuck tycoon in Chicago, which were much better than the ordinary plantation schools. Still, there weren't any careers open to her except the cotton fields and domestic work. The pay was so low that every respectable white family in the Delta—even schoolteachers' and mail carriers' families—had at least one full-time servant.

Ruby got by. In those days you could buy salt pork, or beans, or black-eyed peas, for five cents a pound. You could make a batch of biscuits with a nickel's worth of flour. A dress cost $1.98 at the shops on Issaqueena Street. When money ran short, people shared what little they had. Ruby could go out on the trucks and pick cotton on Saturdays if she needed to. Sometimes at work she used to think: "This white woman thinks I'm good enough to nurse her baby and to make the meals that her family eats. Why am I not good enough to go in her house by the front door?" But such thoughts were not to be given free rein, even in one's own mind. When Ruby was growing up, she was taught to look up to white people, not to hate them. White people ran everything. They lived well. If you were black, you had to get things from white people. Rebellion against segregation was fruitless, so it was for Ruby a subject dealt with in whispers and private feelings. She had only one childhood memory of a protest against the system, and it was a hidden protest: a group of old folks walking down a country road in the 1920s when there weren't any white people around, quietly singing the old folk song "We Shall Overcome."

Black people in Clarksdale passed around stories, which were gradually burnished into legend, about the worst excesses of the system—stories involving sex and bloodshed. One day a black boy in Clarksdale who was working in a white family's yard was called into the house by the white woman. When he got inside, he saw that she had her blouse off. She asked him to fasten her in back. What could he do? Everybody knew that if a black man refused a white woman's advances, it was quite likely that she would accuse him of rape and he would be lynched. If he didn't refuse, and an affair began, and it was found out, an accusation of rape followed by a lynching was, again, the likely result. The woman could hardly afford to admit the truth, because if she did she would be banished from the community.

In this case there was no chance for the boy to make his decision, because the woman's husband walked in. She screamed, to indicate that she was being assaulted. The boy went on trial for rape, but the woman's husband had figured out the real story by then, and he stood up in court and said the boy should be set free. The freedom lasted only a few minutes. A gang of white boys waylaid the black boy as he was walking home from the courthouse, tied his feet to the back of a car, and drove all the way from Clarksdale to Marks with the black boy's crushed, bloody head bouncing along the roadbed.

Another story was about a crazy black man who got a gun, holed up in a 5
cotton warehouse, and started firing shots out. The county sheriff, A. H. "Brick" Gotcher, arrived at the scene and went inside the warehouse to talk the black man into surrendering. The black man shot and killed Gotcher; Gotcher's deputies shot and killed the black man. In white memory, the story was completely nonracial because the black man had no grievance, and its lesson was that Gotcher was heroically brave. In black memory, the story was absolutely racial —the black man had probably been set up in some way, and after he was killed his body was dragged down the black commercial strip on Fourth Street in broad daylight to impress in the minds of the blacks of Clarksdale that nobody else ever better try anything like that again.

Black Clarksdale was full of rumors and secrets, because there was so much that couldn't be expressed openly or that blacks were in no position to investigate. Everybody black in Clarksdale knew, though there was no hard proof of it, that Bessie Smith, the great singer who died after a car accident outside Clarksdale in 1937, had been refused admission to the county hospital on grounds of her race, at a time when she could still have been saved. Shortly after that, the same hospital refused admission to the wife of one of Clarksdale's two or three most prominent black citizens, a dentist named P. W. Hill, when she was in severe distress during childbirth. She and her baby died on the road to Memphis, or so the story went; it was so shrouded in mystery that even Dr. Hill's son and namesake doesn't know what really happened, because he never dared to ask his father about it.

White society as a whole looked corrupt to black people, because the corrupt side of it was most of what black people (especially black men, who rarely entered white people's homes) saw. Black people knew things about white people's secret lives that weren't known in the white part of town. When a light-skinned baby was born in the black part of Clarksdale, gossip would circulate as to which respectable white citizen was the father. Sometimes a black family would live inexplicably well, and the reason was that a conscience-stricken white man was sending remittances for the support of his officially unacknowledged children. White men's cars would be seen parked in the black section, in front of the houses of prostitutes or mistresses or bootleggers. White policemen could chase women or gamble or beat people up in black neighborhoods without anyone in authority finding out about it. A lot went on in the county jail that never saw the light of day.

In addition to keeping white people's secrets, black people kept their own. In daily life, any resentment that blacks felt for whites was usually kept hidden under a mask of slightly uncomprehending servility that black people knew fit whites' basic picture of them. Involvement in a civil rights organization had to be kept quiet too, of course. At the time, most of the high school- and college-educated black people in Clarksdale were in teaching—"preach, teach, or farm" was the slogan that summarized the black career options—and the state required black teachers to sign an affidavit that they weren't members of the National Association for the Advancement of Colored People. The NAACP was a middle-class organization that without teachers on the rolls would barely have existed, so black teachers joined it secretly. Any black people who had managed to accumulate some money took pains not to put it on display, because it was easy enough for someone deemed a rich, uppity nigger to have his bank credit denied, to find his white clientele (if he did construction work, or hauled labor to the plantations) abruptly taking its business elsewhere, or to lose his land through a trumped-up title dispute. There was an old tradition in the Delta of blacks gaining some temporary advantage by informing on their own people, tipping off the white folks about an errant black person's inclinations and intentions—to slip off a plantation, say. The resentment of the snitches, the "white man's niggers," was so intense that keeping your mouth shut was considered not merely a matter of prudence with regard to whites, but also of honor within black society.

For the black middle class of Clarksdale—a group that made up about 15 percent of the black population and was defined more by education and attitude than by money—the most important secret of all was not anything specific; it was the family life of the black poor. The catechism of the defenders of segregation ran this way: illegitimate childbearing, the short duration of romantic liaisons, and the constant domestic violence among the sharecroppers and poor blacks in town clearly demonstrated that blacks were sexually uncontrollable. This made social segregation a necessity. Social segregation led to legal segregation in education, government, and the economy. The main losers from legal segregation were not the black poor but the black middle class, whose members were educated enough to get good jobs but were denied them by law and by custom. The poor blacks' way of life, in other words, caused the middle-class blacks to suffer the humiliation and economic loss that went with second-class citizenship.

Outsiders who came down to study the South often mentioned how hard it 10
was to get middle-class blacks to talk about the black lower class. "It is difficult to get the truth about the lower-class patterns from middle-class Negro people," John Dollard complained. There was a code of silence on the subject. A scene in

Ralph Ellison's *Invisible Man* has the hero giving the rich white Northern benefactor of a black college in the South a tour of sharecropper cabins in the outlying rural area. They meet a sharecropper who tells the benefactor, in great detail, the story of how he impregnated his own daughter. The narrator reacts with horror: "How can he tell this to white men, I thought, when he knows they'll say that all Negroes do such things? I looked at the floor, a red mist of anguish before my eyes."

In Clarksdale, all blacks lived on the east side of the railroad tracks, and all whites on the west side, but there were distinct neighborhoods within the black area. Most of the poor blacks lived in an area called the Roundyard, which runs along the bank of the Sunflower River; all of the black middle class lived in the Brickyard, a little farther north. Families in the Brickyard went to the more middle-class churches, such as Friendship African Methodist Episcopal and First Baptist. Their social life revolved around church circles and associations like the Masons and the Knights and Daughters of Tabor, a venerable black mutual-aid society that operated a hospital in the all-black Delta town of Mound Bayou, twenty-five miles south of Clarksdale. Their children attended the county agricultural high school outside of town, which was the only secondary education available to blacks in Coahoma County, since Clarksdale didn't build a black high school until the 1950s. On Saturday night, most teenagers in the Brickyard were not allowed to go down to the clubs on Issaqueena Street, because they would be full of poor folks from the Roundyard and the plantations. If there was a shooting at the Red Top Inn, you were supposed to hear about it on the radio, not be an eyewitness. There were block clubs in the Brickyard; whenever a poor family, especially a poor family from the country, happened to move into the neighborhood, the block club quickly made contact and began the process of indoctrination into middle-class standards of household maintenance. The transition from plantation to town was supposed to be a step up in the world.

QUESTIONS FOR DISCUSSION

1. Why were stories so important to the African-Americans in Clarksdale?
2. What was the most important secret of the African-American middle class in Clarksdale? What were its consequences?

WRITING ASSIGNMENTS

1. Reaction Journal: *The Promised Land* addresses the largest internal migration in U.S. history. Lemann received critical praise for his ability to give a human face to history by looking at individuals. Now that you have read "Clarksdale," continue to freewrite as you describe the life-style of your own town or neighborhood by "zooming in" on select individuals like Ruby Lee Daniels.
2. Convert your two freewritings into an essay in which you give a human face to your neighborhood by looking at select individuals.

EL HOYO

MARIO SUÁREZ

Mario Suárez (b. 1925) has taught Chicano Studies at California State Polytechnic College in Pomona. In 1957 he received a John Hay Whitney Foundation Fellowship for creative writing. His stories frequently tell of barrio life in his childhood neighborhood in Tucson, Arizona. In "El Hoyo," Suárez describes the diversity and special sense of community that prevail among the district's Chicano inhabitants.

◆ FREEWRITING

You will discover from Suárez's description of El Hoyo that he is still intimately familiar with his childhood neighborhood and its residents. Freewrite for ten or fifteen minutes on specific advantages and disadvantages of living in your own neighborhood.

From the center of downtown Tucson the ground slopes gently away to Main Street, drops a few feet, and then rolls to the banks of the Santa Cruz River. Here lies the sprawling section of the city known as El Hoyo. Why it is called El Hoyo is not clear.

It is not a hole as its name would imply; it is simply the river's immediate valley. Its inhabitants are Chicanos who raise hell on Saturday night, listen to Padre Estanislao on Sunday morning, and then raise more hell on Sunday night. While the term "Chicano" is the short way of saying "Mexicano," it is the long way of referring to everybody. Pablo Gutierrez married the Chinese grocer's daughter and acquired a store; his sons are Chicanos. So are the sons of Killer Jones who threw a fight in Harlem and fled to El Hoyo to marry Cristina Mendez. And so are all of them—the assortment of harlequins, bandits, oppressors, oppressed, gentlemen, and bums who came from Old Mexico to work for the Southern Pacific, pick cotton, clerk, labor, sing, and go on relief. It is doubtful that all of these spiritual sons of Mexico live in El Hoyo because they love each other—many fight and bicker constantly. It is doubtful that the Chicanos live in El Hoyo because of its scenic beauty—it is everything but beautiful. Its houses are built of unplastered adobe, wood, license plates, and abandoned car parts. Its narrow streets are mostly clearings which have, in time, acquired names. Except for the tall trees which nobody has ever cared to identify, nurse, or destroy, the main things known to grow in the general area are weeds, garbage piles, dogs, and kids. And it is doubtful that the Chicanos live in El Hoyo because it is safe —many times the Santa Cruz River has risen and inundated the area.

In other respects, living in El Hoyo has its advantages. If one is born with the habit of acquiring bills, El Hoyo is where the bill collectors are less likely to find you. If one has acquired the habit of listening to Señor Perea's Mexican Hour in the wee hours of the morning with the radio on at full blast, El Hoyo is where you are less likely to be reported to the authorities. Besides, Perea is very popular, and to everybody sooner or later is dedicated "The Mexican Hat Dance." If one has inherited a bad taste for work but inherited also the habit of eating, where, if not in El Hoyo, are the neighbors more willing to lend you a cup of flour or beans? When Señora Garcia's house burned to the ground with all her belongings and two kids, a benevolent gentleman conceived the gesture that put her on the road to solvency. He took five hundred names and solicited from each a dollar. At the end of the week he turned over to the heartbroken but grateful señora three hundred and fifty dollars in cold cash and pocketed his recompense. When the new manager of a local business decided that no more Mexican girls were to work behind his counters, it was the Chicanos of El Hoyo who acted as pickets and, on taking their individually small but collectively great buying power elsewhere, drove the manager out, and the girls returned to their jobs. When the Mexican Army was enroute to Baja California and the Chicanos found out that the enlisted men ate only at infrequent intervals, they crusaded across town with pots of beans, trays of tortillas, boxes of candy, and bottles of wine to meet the train. When someone gets married, celebrating is not restricted to the immediate families and friends of the couple. The public is invited. Anything calls for a celebration, and in turn a celebration calls for anything. On Armistice Day there are no fewer than half a dozen fights at the Tira-Chancla Dance Hall. On Mexican Independence Day more than one flag is sworn allegiance to and toasted with gallon after gallon of Tumba Yaqui.

And El Hoyo is something more. It is this something more which brought Felipe Ternero back from the wars after having killed a score of Germans, with his body resembling a patchwork quilt. It helped him to marry a fine girl named Julia. It brought Joe Zepeda back without a leg from Luzon and helps him hold more liquor than most men can hold with two. It brought Jorge Casillas, a gunner flying B-24's over Germany, back to compose boleros. Perhaps El Hoyo is the proof that those people exist who, while not being against anything, have as yet failed to observe the more popular modes of human conduct. Perhaps the humble appearance of El Hoyo justifies the discerning shrugs of more than a few people only vaguely aware of its existence. Perhaps El Hoyo's simplicity motivates many a Chicano to move far away from its intoxicating *frenesi*, its dark narrow streets, and its shrieking children, to deny the blood-well from which he springs, to claim the blood of a conquistador while his hair is straight and his face beardless. Yet El Hoyo is not the desperate outpost of a few families against the world. It fights for no causes except those which soothe its immediate angers. It laughs and cries with the same amount of passion in times of plenty and of want.

Perhaps El Hoyo, its inhabitants, and its essence can best be explained by 5
telling you a little bit about a dish called *capirotada*. Its origin is uncertain. But it

is made of old, new, stale, and hard bread. It is sprinkled with water, and then it is cooked with raisins, olives, onions, tomatoes, peanuts, cheese, and general leftovers of that which is good and bad. It is seasoned with salt, sugar, pepper, and sometimes chili or tomato sauce. It is fired with tequila or sherry wine. It is served hot, cold, or just "on the weather," as they say in El Hoyo. The Garcias like it one way, the Quevedos another, the Trilos another, and the Ortegas still another. While in general appearance it does not differ much from one home to another, it tastes different everywhere. Nevertheless, it is still *capirotada.* And so it is with El Hoyo's Chicanos. While many seem to the undiscerning eye to be alike, it is only because collectively they are referred to as Chicanos. But like *capirotada*, fixed in a thousand ways and served on a thousand tables, which can only be evaluated by individual taste, the Chicanos must be so distinguished.

QUESTIONS FOR DISCUSSION

1. How does Suárez explain the meaning of the name "*Chicano*"? What is the dish "*capirotada,*" and how does the author use it as a metaphor for the residents of El Hoyo?
2. Suárez lists the advantages and disadvantages of living in El Hoyo. What are they?

WRITING ASSIGNMENTS

1. Reaction Journal: This description of El Hoyo serves as an introduction to a longer work that describes several characters who live there. Show how Suárez has prepared the reader for such character sketches. What sorts of characters might you expect to be described in the longer work?
2. Assume the role of a member of the Tucson, Arizona, City Council. A meeting has been scheduled to clear away the city slums, including El Hoyo, to create a new urban riverfront shopping area and promenade. Argue for the preservation of El Hoyo.
3. Use your freewriting as a resource and write an essay in which you discuss the advantages of living in your neighborhood. Model your writing after Suárez's essay.

BURDEN OF ARRIVAL IS FELT BY ALL

TOM COAKLEY

In the following article from a 1989 issue of the Boston Globe, *staff writer Tom Coakley examines the impact on Massachusetts communities of the arrival of tens of thousands of Southeast Asians. The need to provide housing, schooling, health care, and other services for large numbers of refugees places strains on local and state budgets, and new arrivals often face the suspicion and hostility in addition to the inevitable difficulties of relocation.*

◆ FREEWRITING

Imagine that a civil war somewhere in eastern Europe has forced hundreds of thousands of refugees to flee their homes and their country. Imagine also that many have been granted asylum in the United States and that a large group of refugees has been assigned to settle near you. Freewrite for ten or fifteen minutes on what your town or city can do to make the best of such a serious situation. Try to find accommodations that will minimize potential conflict.

Nam Koeun lives in a trash-strewn apartment building in Lynn, Massachusetts. Five of her children are in foster homes because she cannot care for them. In the United States since 1983, she does not have a job or speak English or understand the land in which she now lives.

The illiterate daughter of Cambodian farmers, she is lost. "I don't have any hope," she says through an interpreter.

Nam Koeun is one of the tens of thousands of Southeast Asian refugees and immigrants who have poured into communities such as Lynn, Lowell, Revere and Quincy in the past 13 years. Official estimates put their number in Massachusetts at 35,000, but experts say the real figure is much higher. Lowell officials say there are at least 25,000 refugees in their city alone.

The newcomers, many of them migrants from other places in the United States, are having a profound impact on the communities in which they have settled. Special needs in education, health care, housing and social services are taxing cities and towns that were largely unprepared for the population explosion.

5 The strain on municipal services does not begin to equal the burden on the refugees themselves, who fled war, oppression and genocide only to find themselves too often the victims of suspicion and racial hatred in their new homeland.

It is in the schools that the impact of the new arrivals is most evident. In 17 school systems in Massachusetts at least one in 20 students were Asian in 1987. In Lowell, the figure was one in five; in Revere, one in 10.

But the impact is being felt in many other areas as well.

ITEM: In Lowell—where one in five residents is Asian—the housing shortage is nothing short of a crisis. Overcrowding in dilapidated apartments prompted the creation of a housing court, which the state has yet to fund.

ITEM: In Quincy—where the number of Asians has risen from 600 three years ago to more the 8,500—doctors and nurses who speak Asian languages are in demand. English-as-a-second-language classes are jammed.

10 ITEM: In Lynn and Revere—where refugees are settling by the thousands on the North Shore—police departments now have Asian language translators on call.

The migration began with the arrival of refugees from Vietnam in the 1970s and has swelled to include Cambodians, Laotians and Chinese from Hong Kong and the mainland. As word spreads of job opportunities here, secondary migrants are drawn to cities such as Lowell, known among refugees as "a Cambodian town" for boasting the second-largest per capita population of Southeast Asians in the country after Long Beach, California.

Myriad federal and state programs are assisting refugees, but it is the localities that must deal with new pressures on the schools and racial tension in the neighborhoods. The need to provide services for these new residents comes at a time when state funds—given Massachusetts' budget woes—are at a premium. Gateway Cities, a state program that has provided money for everything from population surveys to Asian health care professionals, was cut this year from $11 million to $3 million.

Still, like generations of immigrants before them, Southeast Asians are writing their own stories, stories of contrast.

Nam Koeun's story is a sad one. She drifts through a world of despair. The floors of her three-room place are dirty; the wallpaper peeling. Stains mark the ceiling. Beds stand in the living room with family photographs of happier times.

The refrigerator provided by the landlord does not work. A friend bought the one that does. For months she cooked on a hot plate because the gas had been shut off. She longs for her children, placed in foster care by court order after their father left and she was unable to care for them.

Other immigrants are on their way to secure lives—learning English, getting good jobs, sending their children to college, opening shops, planting the seeds of political self-sufficiency on urban turf broken so often before by newcomers.

A few minutes walk from Nam Koeun's home, Cambodian Meng Kouch runs his Lynn Market, a prosperous neighborhood enterprise where most of the customers are Cambodian or Lao.

Kouch and his family have been here since 1980, settled by a local church. He and his wife saved money from their jobs, got a bank loan and opened the business about 2½ years ago.

Their sons and daughters have progressed successfully through the public schools. The children help at the supermarket, where carry-out rice in banana leaf, fresh tamarin and bamboo, Thai rice steamers and Buddhist altar alcoves are sold.

"We don't want to depend on welfare," said Low Kouch, 18, a high school senior who speaks English far better than his parents. "It doesn't go anywhere."

According to the latest available breakdowns, Cambodians are the single biggest refugee group in the state, while Vietnamese are second and Laotians, third.

When resettlement began in the mid-70s in the aftermath of the Vietnam War, most of the refugees were brought to the Boston area by sponsoring agencies. But in recent years, with the establishment of Asian communities and the lure of work in job-rich Massachusetts, word has spread to the refugee camps and to Asian settlements in Minnesota, Texas and New York.

New refugees arriving in the United States are helped with federal cash benefits for a year or two, and by a wide range of employment, medical and educational services. Dozens of federal- and state-funded programs offer refugees assistance with child care, health and mental health care, job training and education.

Daniel Lam, who heads the state Office of Refugees and Immigrants, said about 27 percent of Asian refugees never take any government aid. One state study found that only 14 percent of Massachusetts refugees from Southeast Asia went on welfare after exhausting their federal benefits. Ninety percent of those refugees were women who were single parents.

25 "Massachusetts does have a very successful refugee resettlement. The majority of our refugees actually go on to be independent," said Lam.

The transition is not always easy, however.

In Lowell, a critical housing shortage brought on by the arrival of Southeast Asians in the past five years led to the creation of a city task force to help deal with housing code violations, apartment overcrowding and rent gouging.

"We're at a point were I think we have a housing crisis," said city manager James Campbell. The vacancy rate in the city is 2 percent.

"We've had cases where there have been 10 or 12 mattresses on the floor and when you ask [the refugees], they deny people are sleeping on them. They are very fearful of losing their houses. That's why landlords can take advantage of the situation."

30 City officials and local activists helped push through state legislation last year establishing a badly needed housing court. But the state has not provided money to fund it.

Ravuth Yin, a housing counselor for the Cambodian Mutual Assistance Association of Greater Lowell, said about 40 families a month contact him. It is not unusual, he said, to encounter landlords who discriminate against Cambodians or against people on welfare.

Discrimination and overcrowding in apartments occupied by Southeast Asians is hardly limited to Lowell.

In Lynn, where about 3,000 Asians live, a fire just after Thanksgiving in a Commercial Street apartment house left several Cambodian families homeless, including the Longs—who had just moved to Lynn from Rochester, Minn.

When the fire struck, 11 persons were living in a three-bedroom apartment, which rented for $600 a month.

35 A lawsuit is pending in U.S. District Court alleging that an East Boston and Chelsea landlord violated the civil rights of his Southeast Asian tenants by providing substandard housing.

The language barrier has been a particular challenge in most communities. In Quincy, a local hospital and a community health center are seeking the services of doctors and nurses who speak Asian languages. An Asian ombudsman helps refugees with problems.

Many of the new settlers in Quincy are Chinese or ethnic Chinese-Cambodians or Vietnamese. Often better educated than other Asian groups, the Chinese choose Quincy because of the easy access to Boston—especially to Chinatown, where many work and do business.

In Revere—where 2,500 Southeast Asians live, mostly in the Shirley Avenue area—a satellite health care facility and a counseling center now have practitioners who speak various Asian languages.

The city has established an Office of Southeast Asian Affairs with a full-time coordinator, who is a liaison between the Cambodian community and public and private agencies.

Violence and arson in the mid-80s established Revere's reputation as a city inhospitable to Asians. Although conditions have improved, Cambodians said harassment continues there and in other communities where they have settled.

"Right now, maybe the American kids see the new neighbors. Asian or Oriental. They swear. They break into the car. Tires slashed. They say all the bad things—'Cambodians go back,' " said Kou Chandaravy, a 24-year-old Cambodian from Revere.

He talks in the doorway of the Pnom Penh restaurant in his Shirley Avenue neighborhood, where squares bear the names of Jewish heroes and a synagogue and kosher food shop are shuttered.

"But right now it really doesn't happen that often. Maybe sometimes," he said.

Cambodian leaders are especially concerned about a specific group of refugees, those who were uneducated in their homelands. "These people are facing very serious problems," said Rithipol Yem, chairman of the Chelsea-based Cambodian Community of Massachusetts. "They were farmers or uneducated people. I think they are very unfortunate. Their problems will not go away easily."

As they settle into working-class and poor neighborhoods, these Asians and their neighbors struggle with differences in language and culture.

"This place was beautiful before they moved in," said William Mitchell, who has owned a home in West Lynn for 42 years. "They've knocked down everything. I'm not opposed to them because they are Cambodian. We have had colored people over here."

But, he said, "I think the government if they want to bring them over here . . . why don't they pick an area and build houses for them. Decent houses. And let them come out into our culture slowly. Let them come out when they are ready. I don't care how slow or how fast."

QUESTIONS FOR DISCUSSION

1. Coakley discusses two burdens: those felt by large numbers of refugees and those felt by communities. Describe the nature of these burdens and some measures that are being employed to help.

2. What are "secondary migrants"? How have they contributed to the problems that Coakley describes? What group of refugees are Cambodian leaders particularly concerned about? What can be done to help this group adjust?

3. Explain why Meng Kouch is an appropriate illustration to follow Nam Koeun.

WRITING ASSIGNMENTS

1. Reaction Journal: A précis is a concise summary of the essential facts or statements of a book or article or other text. Write a one-paragraph précis that accurately reflects Coakley's article.

2. Assume you have to write a letter to the city council in Lowell, Massachusetts. The council has asked students studying multiculturalism and ethnicity to make suggestions that address the needs of the city's rapidly expanding Southeast Asian population. Try to make specific recommendations that will eliminate conflict and accommodate the needs of the refugees as well as Lowell's citizens. Base your response on your freewriting, Coakley's article, and your developing awareness of the problems.

FOUR-MILE PRAIRIE—FOUR LETTERS FROM TEXAS

ELISE AMALIE WAERENSKJOLD

Elise Amalie Waerenskjold (1814–1893), a native of Norway, was a woman of courage and cultivation. When only nineteen years old she established and ran for three years a private school for children in Tönsberg, Norway. After three years of marriage to the man who built up the modern whaling industry in Norway, she took the initiative in the amicable dissolution of the marriage, an act of courage at a time when divorce carried a serious social stigma. Waerenskjold went on to establish a handicraft training school for girls in the village of Lillesand over the objections of the mayor, who resisted the idea of a woman taking on such an entrepreneurial role. She was also active in the temperance movement in Norway, publishing a pamphlet on the evils of alcohol. Her continued interest in this cause after her move to the United States is evidenced in the following letters that she wrote home from the Norwegian settlement at Four-Mile Prairie, Texas.

◆ FREEWRITING

For ten or fifteen minutes, freewrite a letter to a distant relative who is unfamiliar with your neighborhood. Describe your life there by making specific references to such things as lifestyle and values.

January 6, 1857. You no doubt know that cattle-breeding is our principal means of livelihood. We do not plan to sell the cows, but only the steers until we can acquire about two hundred calves a year. This spring we can expect about seventy. Cows and calves are now $15 each, and a three-year-old untrained ox costs the same. When it is trained for work, it costs much more. We have four mares, a horse, and a mule. The latter is unusually gentle and sure-footed. It is the children's and my riding horse. Niels sits in my lap and Otto behind me. We do have a four-wheeled carriage but very seldom use it.

We have sixty-two sheep, and this month and next we are expecting many lambs. I help clip the sheep, but I am not very good at it. I can clip only one sheep while the others clip two. Wilhelm can keep up with anyone. He is very quick at all kinds of work. I do not know how many pigs we have, not because we have so many, but because pigs are so difficult to keep track of.

Since I hate liquor, it is a great joy to me that Wilhelm never tastes it. He has organized a temperance society in our settlement, and since that time the community has become so respectable and sober that it is a real pleasure.

All of us Norwegians, about eighty persons counting young and old, can come together for a social gathering without having strong drink, but we do have coffee, ale, milk, and mead, and food in abundance at our gatherings.

In the older Norwegian settlement there is a disgusting amount of drinking, 5
among both the Norwegians and the Americans. A young Norwegian boy shot himself as a result of his addiction to drink, and recently an American was stabbed to death by another American, likewise because of drunkenness. Drinking, quarreling, and fighting are common there. Yes, liquor destroys both body and soul.

February 26, 1858. Even though we Norwegians find ourselves content and happy in our new home, which is thousands of miles away from our mother country, we still cherish in our loving hearts the memory of old Norway and our countrymen over there. Every possible link with the beloved land of our birth is important and precious to us. For that reason, we Norwegians, Swedish, and Danish immigrants of this little settlement of Four-Mile Prairie have organized a reading club. As the group comprises only sixteen families, the total fund for the purchase of books is very small ($22). We are presuming, therefore, to ask our countrymen who may be interested in their distant brothers and sisters in Texas, for a gift of some books, to be delivered to the publisher, Jacob Dybwad, of Christiania. We should appreciate it if the kind donors would write their names in the book or books which they are good enough to donate. We shall gratefully welcome each book whether it is new or old. Because I am personally acquainted with several of the publishers, I am taking the liberty of appealing to them for a small donation. They must have many volumes that will not be sold out.

Many good books of the older authors have perhaps now little or no value in Norway as they are supplanted by the more recent writers. That is not the case here, where we so rarely have the opportunity to procure Norwegian books, as very few had the forethought to take books with them when they left Norway. The various editors would do us a great service if they would reprint these lines in their respective newspapers.

In 1854, a theological candidate, A. E. Fredrichson, was called as pastor to Four-Mile Prairie. That same year, a small, simple church was begun in the settlement and was dedicated immediately after the pastor's arrival the following year. Each member paid from $3 to $8 yearly toward his salary, not including the festal offerings and fees for baptisms, funerals, and the like. Some widows and spinsters subscribed $1 or $2. As Pastor Fredrichson plans to return this winter, it would be very desirable if a Christian-minded theologian would come to us. He assuredly must not come for any temporal gain, because he could not count on more than $300 annually and a simple house, from all three settlements.

October 16, 1858. You probably heard from your brother, to whom I have written a couple of times this summer, that I again expected a little boy, and now I can tell you, God be praised, that the baby arrived happy and well the fourth of this month. I cannot express to you how glad I was that everything went well because, after all, I am no longer young and, therefore, I was worried for fear I might have to leave my beloved children. Neither Wilhelm nor I have a single relative in this country, so it isn't easy to say what Wilhelm would have done with the children if I had died, because it is absolutely against the custom in this country for a white girl to keep house for a widower—and as to a stepmother, well, they are seldom good.

But, thank God, I am entirely well again and hope that the Almighty will 10
grant me yet a few years with my sweet little boys. The little one shall be named Thorvald August after your dear Thorvald and a little German friend I had on the emigrant ship. I can truly say that the neighbors here are very kind to one another on occasions such as this, for they look after and provide one another with food. That is to say, our neighbors in the country; the city women, on the other hand, follow the American customs.

March 24, 1860. This winter we had a visit from a minister, Elling Eielsen, who was ordained in Wisconsin, where he and his family live. He is a Haugean, to be sure, but a particularly capable man who is an untiring worker, although he is an old man. He visited all the Norwegians and preached every day and nearly all day. Thus, the day we had communion, he preached an especially good sermon first, then gave a long talk to the communicants. In the afternoon he first talked with the people about organizing a religious school and managed to arrange for us to have a Sunday school. Following that, he took up the temperance question, in which he is keenly interested.

He spent the most time in the Norwegian settlement at Brownsboro, where the Norwegians are great lovers of intoxicating drinks. He and my husband have again organized a temperance society there, since the one which my husband started five years ago died out almost immediately, partly because they had completely misunderstood the rules and thought that one might drink liquor if only one did not become intoxicated, and partly because there was no one who took charge of promoting the cause. This time we hope that with God's help it may fare better, as they seemed to be deeply moved by the minister's presentation and admonitions.

He confirmed four adults who had not wanted to be confirmed when Frederichson was the minister here. One of these was a married woman.

Eielsen undertook this long and difficult journey without arranging any guarantee of compensation for his expenses and his time, in fact, without the slightest indication that he expected that anyone should pay him. He does not accept offerings. Of course, they paid him something, but I very much doubt that his expenses were covered. I presume that he received about a hundred dollars in the three settlements. It was the general wish that he would move down here to be our minister, and I think we could not find anyone better fitted to work here.

We had snow four times this winter, and three times it lasted for several days. The poor starving cattle, which had nothing to eat, were nearly covered with ice. A great many cattle, swine, and sheep died this winter, and people have had a very costly lesson not to be so completely unconcerned about winter. I do not know a single person who had so much as stacked his straw. We had all left it on the ground, where it spoiled. We still do not know for sure how much we have lost, for we have not yet collected our livestock. Spring is very late this year, and the old saying "While the grass grows, the cows die" has been literally fulfilled, for most of the cattle have died after the grass began to grow.

Many who had no work in Norway are doing fairly well here. There are nineteen Norwegian families in our settlement. They are all satisfied, and I know of no one here who wishes he were back again. They are all prospering. My husband recently had a letter from a man who moved away from here to Wisconsin. He says that he often calls himself a fool because he sold his land and moved away from Texas. There is scarcely any doubt that it is now more profitable to come to Texas than to go to the northern states, according to what all those who come from them say.

QUESTIONS FOR DISCUSSION

1. In what ways were the rural Norwegian settlers in Texas different from their urban counterparts? How did the settlers at Brownsboro differ from those at Four-Mile Prairie?
2. Why was Waerenskjold so impressed with Reverend Elling Eielsen?
3. Identify as precisely as possible the audience for these letters. Is it safe to assume that the audience is the same for each of the four letters? Why or why not?

WRITING ASSIGNMENTS

1. Reaction Journal: Using the contents of your freewriting, write a letter to Waerenskjold's audience. Make a conscious effort to imitate Waerenskjold's writing style.

2. Write a character sketch of Elise Amalie Waerenskjold. Focus your writing on the style and the contents of her four letters. Be certain to address such issues as life-style, values, and attitudes.

A CITY WITHIN A CITY

HARRY MARK PETRAKIS

Writer, teacher, and lecturer Harry Mark Petrakis (b. 1923) has twice been nominated for the National Book Award and has won the O. Henry Award for short fiction. Among his many books are Pericles on 31st Street *(1965),* A Dream of Kings *(1966), and* Ghost of the Sun *(1990). In the following excerpt from* Stelmark: A Family Recollection *(1970), Petrakis describes the insular life created by language, food, school, and church that defined his ethnic Greek neighborhood in Chicago during the 1920s and 30s.*

◆ FREEWRITING

Before you read this selection, freewrite for ten or fifteen minutes. Pretend you are taking a visitor on a walking tour through a section of the town or city where you spent your childhood. After you read the essay, compare your organizational strategies with those of Petrakis.

I seem to forever remember streets of matching brick three-story apartment buildings, all with cramped-as-kangaroo-pouch entrances, and the windows veiled by flimsy, gossamer curtains. Separating the buildings were narrow gangways the sun never touched, leading into grassless back yards littered with scraps of old newspapers. A maze of porches with paint peeling from the wood hung in tiers above the yards. At dawn, the milkmen jingled and clinked their bottles on the stairs, and in the twilight the janitors lumbered up and down carrying the huge containers strapped to their backs into which they emptied the waste from the garbage cans. Standing like ragged kings on the landings of the porches, we surveyed the landscape of our domain, numerous identical porches and below them desolate, crumbling garages flanking the oil-soaked and turd-spattered alleys.

These were the reservations of the city where we lived wedged together, Poles and Lithuanians, Irish and Germans, Greeks and Jews. We had no common bond except that which we shared as the sons and daughters of parents who had forsaken their homelands and through successive years sought to retain what they feared they might lose when they became the uprooted. For each of us, as children, the city existed only as a province of the land from which our parents journeyed.

My earliest memories, tangled and ambulatory, had to do with what was almost totally Greek. Greek parents, Greek language, Greek food, Greek school, and Greek church. There were artifacts that belonged to the new land—candy and baseball, ice cream and movies. For the most part these existed as a kind of exotic bazaar outside the gates of the real city in which I lived. . . .

Our neighborhood was a city within a city bounded by the walls of our streets. We knew there was an area called "downtown," made infrequent trips there with one of our parents, knew there was a North Side (home of the ritzy Cub fans) and a West Side, but for all the relevance these sections had for us, they might have been cities in Europe.

There was a tangible smell to our neighborhood, a warmth and reassurance 5
in recognizable faces and sociable friends. I walked delightedly along our street at twilight, watching the lights from the windows throw their misted gleam across the walks. I knew who lived in each of the apartments. There was a basement flat where the husky German janitor lived, a curtained sanctuary of bacchanalian revels with the janitor and his friends singing boisterous drinking songs. Late at night their voices grew low and husky with nostalgia for the Black Forest and the Rhine. In a first-floor apartment a few doors from our own building lived my friend Marvin Salant, our friendship begun years before in an argument over our tricycles. In the middle of the block was the two-flat where the Asher sisters lived. Bernice and Florence, names that will forever connote for me those dark-eyed and black-haired beauties who graced our block with a basaltic elegance.

There were the storekeepers in the shops along the street that my sister, my father, and I walked on our way to church. Sometimes, after school was out, I visited them with my mother.

There was Belson's grocery, a neat, clean store with the fruits and vegetables stacked in careful tiers. Max Belson himself came to wait on my mother, the wife of the respected Greek priest.

"How much for this lettuce, Mr. Belson?" my mother would ask. This question she accompanied by holding the lettuce gingerly in her hand, involving it precariously on the scales of her decision. Max Belson would look at her with the suffering visage of a man who heard too many similar questions too many times.

Whatever the daily price he quoted my mother, her response was always the same. With the fervor of a tragic chorus she'd emit a low moan and drop the lettuce back on the pile where it seemed to shrivel in shame. Max Belson calmly smoothed the ruffled leaf.

"Your price, Mrs. Petrakis, you tell me. You tell Belson what you think it's 10
worth."

But my mother would not be drawn into that artful game and had already swept on to the tomatoes, to do battle over still another patch of produce, until the fortifications were breached by a dozen deployments and the defender so distracted he could not be sure where or on what item the final major assault would come.

There was a delicatessen run by a man with the euphonious name of Morris Satin. I can remember the pungent kosher scents when I stepped inside, the trays of glistening scarlet and pearl corned beef, pepper-riddled pastrami, and great swarthy pickles soaking in barrels of brine.

There was a magazine store with long racks of pulp magazines (before the days of the pocket book and TV) and the tall, thin dark-haired owner whose name escapes me now. At an early age I sought to expand my libidinal horizons by purchasing an occasional copy of *Spicy Western* stories. (That was the real West.) When I had selected the magazine from one of his racks and carried it to the register where he waited for me to pay him the quarter, our dialogue never varied.

"Does your father know you're buying magazines like this?" he asked.

"They're for my older brother," I said, looking at the tips of my scuffed 15
shoes.

That was not true and he knew it, but the identical question and answer each time satisfied the moral proprieties and assuaged whatever slight proddings of conscience he felt.

Farther along the street was a tiny candy store, the narrow space inside the door filled by a counter of jelly beans, spice drops, and a few varieties of hand-made chocolates. Almost filling the area between the counter and the door was a popcorn and caramel corn stand. The owner, a gentle, mild-voiced little Greek who lavished as much courtesy on a penny customer as he did on the dollar purchaser of his chocolates, drew almost all his trade from people attending the small neighborhood show next door.

During the Depression the show was sold to a pair of enterprising men, strangers from the North Side, and they quickly installed a candy counter and popcorn machine of their own. After that, the candy store closed down. For a long time, when I passed the abandoned store, the Coke placard in the window faded more deeply into the dust.

But remorse did not prevent me from going to work for those same ruthless violators of small business. I joined fifteen other ten- and eleven-year-olds an hour after school, two afternoons a week, stuffing the show's prevue handbills into neighborhood mailboxes. Because the owners were suspicious men, we were regularly pursued by a half-dozen older boys, hired as finks, to assure we did not dump our handbills into the first convenient garbage can.

Our salary came in the form of one free admission apiece to a regular showing. On Saturday afternoons, pursuers and pursued would be grouped together in a roped-off area in the lobby of the theater, while the prosperous children who paid cash for their admission tickets walked briskly past us. Only after the film, a Tim Holt or Buck Jones Western, or a Laurel and Hardy comedy, had run about ten minutes were we allowed to file quietly to our assigned rows in the back of the theater. Those ten minutes that we waited after the picture started and we could hear the sounds from within the darkened theater were among the most agonizing moments of my childhood. 20

If one traveled west from our neighborhood, across Cottage Grove Avenue, to the location of my father's church, the district was almost completely Negro, Cottage Grove being the dividing line. The church included our parish school, which taught English subjects from 9 to 12:30 and, after a break for lunch, Greek grammar and history from 1 until 3.

Our teachers were both Greek and American, and achieved a common ethnic denominator by their reliance upon the stick. Hardly a class passed without someone getting walloped. As a rule, the American teachers struck without any great conviction, but the Greek teachers struck with a rampant fervor.

We had boys in our class who, for continued infractions, received most of the punishment. There was one swift classmate of mine who when threatened with a beating would sprint to a rear window, open it, and leap through a second before the outraged teacher reached him. He was called "The Racer." We had another boy called, for obvious reasons, "The Howler." At the first blow, however light, he would begin to howl and shriek in unremitting agony, rolling his eyes, clutching his head. There was still another boy called "The Dodger," for his gymnastic ability. As supple as a snake, he would twist and coil his body, neatly evading most of the violent flailings of the stick. We watched these bouts with rapt admiration until the exhausted teacher gave up, having failed to land more than two or three blows out of thirty.

My own experience with the stick included a period when for some reason I was never struck. "You never get hit 'cause your father's the priest," classmates told me resentfully. There was another interminable period when I suffered the cursed stick for the most trivial infraction. "You always get hit 'cause your father's the priest," classmates told me consolingly.

Across the street from our church and school was a Roman Catholic church and parish school. That was a foreign country ruled by long-black-skirted, white-cowled sisters with the awesome capability to deliver bare-handed blows that equaled the force of the ones struck by our teachers with sticks. I once witnessed a boy pulled out of line by an irate sister who held him by the scruff of his jacket and then delivered a short, fierce blow to the side of his head. The boy landed crumpled against the fence, apparently out cold. It was a knockout Jack Dempsey would have envied. 25

Reflecting the neighborhood, most of the students in the Catholic school were Negroes. We came as interlopers from the white neighborhood across Cottage Grove. Black and white, we were mortal enemies, constantly at war. Our assaults and forays against one another ranged from curses and stone-throwing to full-scale battles with fists and sticks. I cannot remember anyone getting killed, which was a wonder considering the number of broken teeth and bloody heads. After such encounters our teachers pulled us inside and beat us, much as the Negro boys were being beaten across the street. The punishment served only to intensify our fury.

There was a Negro boy I will never forget, tall and strong, although he was no more than fourteen, with the speed and body of a superb athlete, who spread terror among us. The sight of his flashing eyes and great white teeth bared in a scream of battle struck us with panic. One ignominious day he hurtled the fence to enter our playground, and a hundred of us, boys and girls caught in some mob fear, fled frantically for the protection of our school buildings. The spectacle of that boy, all alone, chasing a hundred of us into the school remains with me to this day.

But our most disgraceful battles, organized and led by older boys, were reserved for Halloween. By twilight on that day we would have armed ourselves with overripe tomatoes, bottles, and sticks, and after dark, in gangs of fifty or more, we'd move into the alleys across Cottage Grove. Meanwhile, gangs of black youths would be foraging through our alleys, searching us out. Sometimes there were brief, preliminary skirmishes by patrols of a few boys, but ultimately the main forces were joined, the battle becoming a massive, tangled melee of bodies and missiles flying in the darkness. I was one of the younger boys, fighting in the rear ranks, and since it was impossible to distinguish friend or foe, we threw our tomatoes and bottles at random. We must have struck our own boys as often as we hit those of the other side. But this dereliction was equaled by the fact that our antagonists were doing the same thing.

In the basements afterwards where we retired to wash and dress our bruises before returning to our homes, a wound was a wound, whether inflicted by friend or foe. Shamefully, ignorantly, we felt a primal pride in the scars of battle.

Where are they now? The boys I played with, the girls I walked beside? Where 30
are the young Negroes we fought in the senseless, dupable bigotry of our youth? Where is the black Achilles who struck such terror in my heart? Where are "The Racer," "The Howler," "The Dodger"? Do they still meet the assaults of life as they once met the attacks of angry teachers?

Where is Belson, who suffered with patience and fortitude the daily assault of a hundred determined women? Where are the cruel men (invaders from the far North Side) who made us wait those frantic ten minutes on Saturday afternoons? Where are the store-keepers who greeted us each morning as my sister and I walked proudly beside my father on our way to school?

I know where my father is. He is dead now and lies straight and still beneath a flowered patch of cemetery sod. How many of the others must be dead, too, their sons and daughters scattered across the country and the world, remembering even as I remember now?

If I could I would say to them, this is the way it was on those crisp mornings in autumn when we scuffed our sneakers through the brown, wrinkled leaves; those afternoons in early spring, the windows of our classrooms open to the scent of new buds; those twilights in the summer with the mothers calling plaintively as we crouched hidden in the shadows.

For we shared this kingdom of our childhood, lived there as sprinters and fools, first learned of joy and sorrow, played against time in games we always won, and felt no dread of age and death.

And thought the sun would remain young forever. . . . 35

QUESTIONS FOR DISCUSSION

1. Petrakis concludes his second paragraph by saying, "The city existed only as a province of the land from which our parents journeyed." Explain what he means. Is this notion consistent with other immigrant experiences with which you are familiar?

2. Petrakis mentions the sense of smell in the opening sentence of paragraph 5. Find other examples in which he attempts to include senses other than sight. Go on to comment on the author's diligent attention to concrete detail.

3. Locate examples of humor in this selection. How does Petrakis use humor to help represent the childhood he remembers so concretely?

WRITING ASSIGNMENTS

1. Reaction Journal: Study Petrakis's opening paragraph very carefully. Using the same techniques he uses, write a paragraph in which you describe a neighborhood with which you are familiar. (The content will obviously differ; the technique should be much the same.)

2. Use your freewriting as a starting point and write an essay in which you take a visitor on a tour of the town or city where you grew up. Pay attention to Petrakis's use of parallel structure and other organizational devices that suggest motion.

3. Write an essay that portrays the "essence" of your childhood. Use a few carefully chosen concrete examples to develop your essay.

WE WHO CAME AFTER

RONALD L. FAIR

Ronald L. Fair (b. 1932) was born and raised in Chicago. He says that he began writing as a teenager because of his "anger with the life [he] knew and the inability of anyone [he] knew to explain why things were the way they were." Educated at Chicago high schools and for two years at a local business college, Fair worked for eleven years as a court reporter in Chicago before devoting himself entirely to his writing and doing occasional college teaching. During his years as a court reporter, he wrote and published his first two novels. He has published a number of books, among which are Many Thousand Gone, An American Fable *(1965) and* Hog Butcher *(1965), and his stories have appeared in various anthologies. The following piece appeared under a different title in the anthology* 19 Necromancers from Now *before becoming the prologue to* We Can't Breathe *(1972). It describes the world of children whose parents had come to Chicago during the Great Migration, children who the narrator says were "so young and excited with the life [they] knew that [they] had not yet learned [they] were the ones who were supposed to be deprived." "We Who Came After" is not an autobiographical sketch; the story is told by a first-person fictional narrator.*

◆ FREEWRITING

Before you read this selection, freewrite for ten or fifteen minutes on games you played in your neighborhood as a child. Bring your focus to one particular game.

This is a narrative of what it was like for those of us born in the Thirties. Our parents had come from Mississippi, Louisiana, Tennessee, Georgia, Alabama and many other southern states where the whites were so perverse and inhuman in their treatment of blacks, but mostly they came from Mississippi. They came to the big cities armed only with glorious fantasies about a new and better world, hoping to find the dignity that had been denied them, hoping to find the self-respect that had been cut out of them. They came north, and we were the children born in the place they had escaped to—Chicago.

You know, we were so young that we didn't know we were supposed to be poor. We were so young and excited with the life we knew that we had not yet learned we were the ones who were supposed to be deprived. We were even so young that sometimes we forgot we were supposed to be hungry, because we were just too busy living.

I can remember one spring, after the snow had finally seeped into the earth, and the mud in the vacant lots had become dirt again, how we would move over those lots cautiously, like the old rag man, our eyes sparkling with enthusiasm, our minds pulsating with the thrill of finds we surely knew would be there because there had been a whole winter of snow covering up the treasures that grownups had discarded—unknowingly, to our advantage. Things that we needed because they were treasures and were of value to us.

There would be razor blades, some broken in half, some whole, all rusty; a new metal.

"Careful, Sam. Don't cut yourself, man. If you do, man, your whole hand'll rot off."

A bottle! God, a bottle like we had never seen.

"I bet some ole rich white lady came along here and threw it away."

"Naw."

"I bet she did. Bet it was full of some rich perfume or somethin. Let's see if we can find the top?"

"Here's a top."

"Naw. Too big."

"I bet she kept the top."

"Ain't no rich lady been by here."

"She was."

"She wasn't."

"Well, I don't care. I know what I'm gonna do with it anyway so it don't matter. I'm gonna take it home to mama. She'll like it. She ain't never had no bottle like this before."

Maybe we would find a bullet, half of a scissors, the standard, big-name pop bottles which we would hoard to be returned to the school store or the grocery store or the drugstore only one or two at a time because the store owners never seemed to like giving up the deposit and the fewer the bottles, the less they would grumble. And always, reminding us of the problems of the grownups, there would be the wine bottles. Having the wine bottles available to us at that time, when we were very young, when we were young enough for vacant lots and alleys to be places of joy, was really a blessing because we could smash them against the side of the brick buildings that helped protect our lot. Sometimes we smashed them with such force that little slivers of glass sprang back in our direction. We dodged them, laughingly, saying, "Ain't no wine bottle fast enough to catch me."

The thought of the slivers of glass striking back at us excited us no end, and we moved closer to the wall and smashed them with even more force. Once, though, a wine bottle got even with me as a fragment of it ripped through my trousers and imbedded itself in my thigh. But I did not cry out. I just went on smashing the damn things against the wall because I hated them.

I didn't cry until later in the day when, safely hidden behind the locked bathroom door of our apartment, I dug it out with one of my mother's needles.

I could not have let the others know that I hadn't moved quickly enough to dodge the glass. Many years later I learned that each of us at one time or another had lost the battle with the flying glass. But those admissions came many years later when we were secure in our manhood. . . .

"Hey," somebody would say, "let's go kill rats."

A unanimous roar of approval would go up and we would begin searching 20
for sticks and bricks. Once sufficiently armed, we would leave our land of treasures and move down the alley toward one of the very best games we knew.

Each of us had relatives who had either been bitten by rats or frightened out of their wits by them. There was the story of the friend who used to live in the neighborhood but whose parents moved out when his baby sister had her right ear eaten away by one of them. There was also the story we whispered among ourselves about one of the group whose grandmother was said to have cooked her very best stew from rats she trapped in her pantry.

Almost from infancy we had been fighting them; in our sleep, fighting the noise they made in the walls as they chewed their way through the plaster to get at what few provisions we had; in our alleys, our Black Boulevards, fighting to get them out of the garbage and into their holes so we could play a game of stick ball with no fear of being bitten while standing on second or third base. Outside of the white insurance men who made their rounds daily collecting quarters and half dollars for the burial policies our parents paid for over and over, making the insurance companies richer and ending with our parents in their old age having almost enough money to pay the price of a pine-box funeral, outside of those strange little white peddlers who came into the neighborhood every week and trapped our mothers with flashy dresses, petticoats, slips and shoes supposedly half-priced ("No-money-down, lady." But the records were kept by the salesmen in their payment books, and the payments never ended.), outside of the white men from the telephone company who came far too often to take away someone's telephone, outside of these *strangers* who moved among us with all the arrogance and authority of giants, we hated the rats most.

We didn't always win against them, but we kept fighting because we knew if we didn't continue killing them they would soon make the alleys unsafe even for us. Once a new boy moved into the neighborhood with a BB gun, and with the large supply of ammunition he had, we killed two hundred rats in one day. We made bows and used umbrella staves for arrows and got so good with them that we only missed about two-thirds of the time.

But the best way to kill them was with bricks and clubs. We'd walk quietly down the alley, our little platoon advancing on the army of rats, plowing, in the summertime, through mounds of junk piled against the fences (always there because the garbage trucks came through so seldom), until we reached a mound that gave off sounds of their activity. We would surround it, leaving only the fence as their escape route, look at each other, nervous, excited, our blood blasting away inside of our temples, then one of us would poke a stick into the pile of garbage, and, with our anxiety mounting, we would wait for them to react.

The rats had already sensed our presence and had grown silent, waiting for the danger to pass. The stick would go in again and then, quickly, they would frantically dig their way farther into the garbage. They would not come out. Another stick, and finally a gray thing, its teeth sparkling like daggers in the early morning sun, would spring from the pile and charge one of us with all the rage and hostility of the killer it was. A brick would miss him, but a club would catch him in mid-air just as he was about to dig his teeth into someone's leg. His insides would explode out of him and blood would shoot into the air like a spurt from a fountain. Another one was out. A brick would stun him and then the clubs would beat him to death. Two others began climbing the fence and we left the fence stained with their blood. And then, as often happened, the biggest and oldest of them dashed between us and quickly disappeared into another pile of garbage. Including his tail, he was at least two feet long and as fat as any cat in the neighborhood, and even though we chased him, and spread the pile he had hidden in all over the alley, he was able to escape by squeezing through a small hole in the fence. It seemed to us we had been trying to kill that one rat for years, but there were so many that were two feet long that we could never be sure.

We were often victorious, but once in a while the rats would get the better of us; a child would be bitten by one of them. Sometimes we would club the rat away from his leg. Sometimes we would all run home crying, afraid of them all over again and thankful that it was someone else who had felt the needle-like teeth, and sometimes we would carry our crying friend home to his mother, hoping that he would not have to go through the torture of the shots.

Then, after our parents finally let us out again, we would group around a light pole on the street, or a fire hydrant, propping our feet on it pretending to be grown-up waiting for the news from the hospital about our wounded comrade.

But sometimes, even in the midst of the hunt, we would hear the call of the merchants, or the youth on the corner selling papers:

"Chi-cog-oo De-feen-da."

"I got em green. I got em ripe."

"Ice . . . Ice man."

"Waa-ta-mel-lons."

"Egg man . . . Chickens."

"I got em green. I got em ripe."

It would be a hot summer day. It was always another hot summer day with the heat seeming to rise up from the sidewalks, from the tarred streets, from foods fermenting in the garbage, from the grassless yards and weed-filled vacant lots. . . .

The excitement of the arrival of the merchants gave us another game as we ran through the debris in much the same way as one might run through shallow water at the beach. It wasn't so bad in winter, but in the summer one had to fight the gnats and flies and mosquitoes and rats and cats and dogs. The flies would take wing as we passed through their feeding ground and the noise was so horrendous that it was like a low-flying airplane. I sometimes think we were the breeding place of flies and rats for the entire city.

In school we had read stories about children in the country, but they had nothing on us. They could run through their tall grass, playing where nature was kindest, and we could run through our garbage, and since we had all been immunized naturally, we were totally unaffected by those little microscopic fellows that so terrified the white people who had clean alleys—alleys that were even paved! We could run through our tall garbage-grass where mother nature, in a negative sort of way, was kind to us too.

And when we heard the deep voice of Sampson calling "Ice . . . Ice man," we would run even faster because he was the man we all wanted to be like. We'd cut through yards, across streets, in front of traffic, through other alleys until we found him. We'd meet the ice truck and ride through our Black Boulevards as honored guests, snatching little chips of ice whenever Sampson would cut off a block with the ice pick. We all shared the same admiration for the giant in our lives. And I guess worshipping him as we did was a bit strange when one realizes that Sampson had to work harder than anyone else. Sometimes he'd let us help. He'd say, "Y'all gotta work for your ride." Four or five of us would scramble into the truck and push and strain for what seemed like an hour just to get it close enough to the edge of the truck so he could lean in, snag the block of ice with his tongs—one hundred pounds of ice—run his pick down the seams, tick-tick-tick, and a fifty-pound block would slide over to the side of the truck. He'd swing his tongs again, clamp them down on the ice and sling it over his shoulder like it was only a loaf of bread, all so effortlessly that his breathing didn't alter in the slightest.

His muscles would rise up like swells and little beads of perspiration, giving the effect of liquid silver, rolled over those black swells. He could do anything with his muscles. He used to make his biceps dance while we provided the musical accompaniment with our clapping hands.

Sampson also let us take our punching exercises on his muscular abdomen. He'd line us up and let us hit him in the stomach as hard as we could. And with each earth-shattering blow he'd rear back and laugh his deep warm laugh.

But one day when we were trying to crash his abdominal wall one of the smaller guys wanted to have his turn. He stepped up, took careful aim and swung as hard as he could. Sampson had already started laughing long before the blow landed, but his loud, husky laugh changed to a soprano's scream as he grabbed his groin and fell to the ground.

We were shocked, so shocked that we could not move for all of one minute. We just knew that even his testicles were made of solid muscle.

"I got Sampson. I knocked Sampson down!" the little guy screamed as he ran down the alley, the victory just too overwhelming for his young years.

Sampson remained our hero, though, even though he no longer let us take punching exercises on his abdomen. I think, as I look back now on those years, that the warmest feeling of my childhood there in that strange city that I still call home, surely must have been the coolness of sitting inside an ice truck on a hot summer day as Sampson allowed us to think we were helping him. . . .

45 But of all the seasons, winter was the most impressive. It was always beautiful in the winter. Everything was clean and smelled even better than it did after a spring rain. The temperature was often zero or below, and with holes in our shoes and no rubbers, our feet were always wet and cold, but it was a good time of year. Most of us carried pieces of newspaper in our pockets and when the paper in our shoes became too wet we would step inside someone's doorway and change the expendable linings. There was snow everywhere and the half dozen or so sleds on the block were enough to accommodate the thirty or forty children.

Snowplows never came through our neighborhood. It was good they didn't because the snow was a wedge against a reality we were glad not to face. I thank God it snowed as much as it did when we were young. I thank God we were freed from everything that was familiar.

Sometimes it seemed to snow for days; as if the elements had contrived to free us by transforming ugliness into beauty. There were other parts of the city that hated to see the snow come, and their snowplows worked almost daily trying to set the calendar back. But we prayed for it in our neighborhood. There were no landscaped gardens for us. There had been no year of fun on the golf course. There was no grass to be covered up, only broken glass and pages of old newspapers dancing in the wind with the leaves from the big cottonwoods that were always shedding something. There were no rose bushes that had to be protected against the subzero temperature, only weeds that were more than strong enough to fend for themselves. There was really not much beauty at all, only a gray, dirty, sad world we had lived in for nine months and we were delighted to see it changed.

In the alleys the snow packed down hard on the mounds of garbage and provided us with hills for sliding. It leveled the uneven sidewalks. It even painted the buildings and filled the holes in the streets and in yards and laid lawns, for once, over all the neighborhood. It was clean. It was pure. It was good.

With the coming of the snow, life became gentler as sounds became muffled. The snow was so special that all the children in the neighborhood respected its holiness and played more quietly.

50 Sampson would still come through three days a week, but he didn't sell much ice now. Who needed ice when every window sill was a refrigerator? The other four days of the week he would deliver coal. But there was one very cold winter when he figured out a way to sell both at the same time. He built wooden platforms on both sides of his truck and he lined them with ice and then covered the ice with canvas so it didn't get coal dust on it. And then, inside the truck, he dumped two or three tons of coal. He still didn't sell much ice, but at least he was able to travel the alleys in good conscience that year.

When we were very young we ate the snow. As we grew a little older, we washed girls' faces in it. And as we became of age, we rolled it up in little balls and threw them at shiny new cars driven by white people passing through our neighborhood on their way to work.

It was indeed beautiful in the winter. I remember one year the snow was so high that as we ran down the wavy path that led in front of the buildings we had to jump up to see over the top. And it was always clean! An empty wine bottle was swallowed up by it, and tucked away so we wouldn't have to see it for a while. Old Jesse, who was always vomiting his insides up early in the morning so that we'd see it on the way to school, was temporarily forgotten because the snow covered over his chili-mack and sweetened the air again. Inside the doorways of the buildings the urine smell was still there, but not outside in the gangways like it was the rest of the year. Outside it smelled like it did everywhere else in the city; like it smelled where people had jobs and money. Outside it was like a dream and it was a pleasure to get soaked with it; chilled and shivering until we could stand it no longer. And even then we didn't want to go in, for inside was a reality that no climatic conditions could change. Even on Christmas day with snow everywhere and a few toys under the trees and the radio playing Christmas music, and people saying "God bless you" everywhere in the world, even on *Christmas day* when it grew late and we stepped inside our dungeons we realized that those God-bless-yous were not meant for us.

QUESTIONS FOR DISCUSSION

1. White people seldom appeared in this Chicago neighborhood. When they did, however, their presence was predictable and resented. Explain. Why did the children appreciate the presence of Sampson so much?
2. This narrative is dominated by the voice of childhood. Little attention is given to the lives of the parents of the neighborhood children. What are you able to infer about the adult lives from reading about the lives of the children?
3. What does Fair reveal about the neighborhood children in the dialogue that begins with paragraph 5? Explain how such dialogue helps strengthen the narrative.

WRITING ASSIGNMENTS

1. Reaction Journal: During the Great Migration of African-Americans of the 1950s and '60s, tens of thousands of families moved from southern towns like Clarksdale, Mississippi. Assume the role of one of the narrator's parents in "We Who Came After" and write a letter to your sister, who you pretend is Ruby Lee Daniels, the focus of Nicholas Lemann's "Clarksdale."
2. Near the end of this selection, the persona tells us that winter transformed "ugliness into beauty." In a way, the very survival of the youth of such neighborhoods was defined by their ability to make such a transformation within their own environment. Write an essay in which you explain how such children as Fair's young personae were able to find beauty in the midst of their poverty.
3. Write a narrative in which you describe one of the games from your own childhood. Use some ideas from your freewriting as you describe a specific game. Pay attention to Fair's description of breaking bottles or hunting rats.

Family

DURING A TRIP TO THE UNITED STATES in the first half of the nineteenth century, Alexis de Tocqueville noted with approval many differences between the "democratic" American family and the aristocratic families of his native Europe. In *Democracy in America* (1835), he observed that "new relationships have sprung up in the bosom of the family . . . the austere, the conventional and the legal part of parental authority vanishes, and a species of equality prevails around the domestic hearth." In Tocqueville's analysis, family relationships in the United States reflected the democratic ideology on which the nation was based. But not all newcomers have viewed the apparent independence of family members in a positive light. Many have found puzzling and even threatening such cultural features as the relative equality of relationships within the family, the less authoritarian role played by parents, the freedom of children to make their own choices, the openness of discussion and affection between generations, and the increased opportunities for marrying outside of one's ethnic or racial group. The resulting conflicts between inherited family traditions and values and those of the new general culture have been frequent themes in the lives of immigrants.

Lawrence H. Fuchs points out that the family both reflects and transmits cultural values, and it is thus not surprising that family relationships become a focal point in the give-and-take of acculturation. The parent-child relationship in the immigrant generation often feels the most intense strain of this cultural conflict. Because of their exposure to public schools, their more ready acquisition of English, and their access to entertainment media, children are likely to be the first members of an immigrant family to come into intimate contact with the new culture. Intergenerational differences in expected behavioral norms can be intensified by cultural differences. The Vietnamese narrator of "Undisciplined Children" in James M. Freeman's *Hearts of Sorrow* laments the distance between parents and children and the heartache caused by children who "don't pay attention to what their parents say." Although he admits that a lack of parental control existed even in Vietnam, the problems seem to be compounded by a move from one cultural tradition to another. "In America," he concludes, "the problem is that we emphasize control of children, while Americans emphasize their freedom."

Mistaken interpretations based on observation of surface behavior alone are a peril of any cross-cultural experience. Accordingly, conclusions about what the freedom allowed many American children means with regard to their respect for their parents require careful examination. Confusion and disappointment can result from applying behavioral patterns of freedom when these behaviors are not informed by an understanding of the cultural context that has given rise to them. Similar problems arise from demanding adherence to standards of control outside of a cultural context that supports them. Arriving at a compromise that respects the expectations of both old and new cultures is a process that causes friction between many second-generation children and their parents. In "Profound Changes," in the chapter "From the Americas—The Cultural Rainbow," Elena Padilla speaks of Puerto Rican children in New York whose parents keep them inside their apartments during their free time lest they pick up on the street patterns of behavior characterized by lack of control and respect. She explains that the respect in Puerto Rico of children for parents and young people for old people generally is difficult to sustain in the youth-oriented culture of the United States, where parental restraints are as likely to be resisted as respected.

One of the chief roles in any family structure is to transmit culture, and to this end respect for tradition on the part of both parent and child is essential. Intermarriage is perhaps the major threat to this cultural continuity, and the fear of having one's children marry outside one's own racial/ethnic/religious group has always been a concern for those who see their group's continued existence threatened by acculturation. In "Secrets and Anger," David Mura, a Nisei, speaks of the decisions he and his Caucasian wife have had to make about how to raise their daughter. The decision not to give her a Japanese name because it "might mark her as too different" sometimes makes Mura "feel guilty about having given in to the dominant culture once again." The question of how to talk to her about the complicated issues of sexuality and race makes Mura realize how much easier it is to ignore the tough issues confronting biracial families and to "pretend multiculturalism means teaching her *kanji* and how to conjugate Japanese verbs."

The American style of partaking in many traditions while being defined by none exclusively is a concept at odds with the cause of ethnic unity. The fear of an end to cultural continuity is often expressed as a struggle between a controlling parent and an independence-seeking child, when in fact what is at stake is really something other than personal control or power. Monica McGoldrick explains, in "Ethnicity and Families," that intergenerational conflicts can be exacerbated by the stress parents feel about not being able to honor their own parents by passing their culture along intact to the next generation. She feels that "coming to terms with our ethnicity is necessary to gain a perspective on the relativity of our belief systems" and thus arrive at some sort of accommodation between the values of family and contemporary American culture. Because family members have to live with each other, the occasions for confrontation are multiplied—but so also are the opportunities for accommodation.

Since outmarriage is one of the last steps in cultural assimilation, it is not surprising that it increases with each generation removed from the immigrant experience. There are, however, as Paul Spickard points out in his study *Mixed Blood*, considerable differences in the rate for different groups within the United States. Intermarriage has been resisted not only by ethnic and racial minority groups but by the dominant white Protestant ethnic group as well. Those groups who differ most in appearance from this dominant group have lower rates of intermarriage with it. Not until 1967 were all state laws forbidding interracial marriage nullified. Twenty-nine states at one time or another imposed prison sentences on interracial couples. Resistance to intermarriage has both caused and been exacerbated by the need of couples in mixed marriages to identify exclusively with one group or the other, often because of a minority group's refusal to accept such marriages. The increased acceptance of mixed ethnic/racial marriages after the late 1960s has made it possible for the children of such unions to identify with and participate in the cultural lives of both halves of their heritage. Thus, contrary to expectations, accepting mixed marriages can help prevent the very sort of death of a tradition which, under a less accommodating mind-set, the marriages themselves appeared to augur. The possibility of such "voluntary ethnicity," which perhaps reflects the qualities of freedom and equality within family relationships, can reduce the fear of loss of identity that often accompanies the idea of intermarriage.

Being faced with questions of to what extent they will maintain their ethnic identity affects the relationship between husband and wife as well as that between parents and children. The couple in G. S. Sharat Chandra's "Saree of the Gods" find the fabric of their marriage threatened by the husband's eagerness to embrace what he perceives as American culture just as the fabric of his wife's wedding saree is literally eaten away by a spill of foreign brandy. The new freedom, too, is manifest not only in intergenerational conflicts. The unaccustomed freedom of Puerto Rican women to speak to men other than their husbands, to work outside of the home, to go out drinking and dancing causes one of the women interviewed by Padilla to remark, "In Puerto Rico, a wife obeys her husband, and keeps house, and takes care of her children. But here they run wild."

Categories of relationships are not easily translatable from one culture to another. Americans at family gatherings may loosely refer to all the people in their age range as "cousins." Few are genealogically sophisticated enough to negotiate the terminology of whether one is a "first" or a "second" cousin or whether one is once or twice "removed." Nor are many Americans inclined to make such distinctions in relationship outside the nuclear family. A Chinese extended family, on the other hand, is a complex and highly structured unit with an extensive vocabulary to denote relationship—"older brother," "aunt on the father's side," "senior uncle," and so forth. Such a family is bound by culturally determined ties of mutual obligation. In contrast, the American family may seem an untidy bundle of individuals who define themselves primarily by personal accomplishment rather than in terms of family relationships. Yet family ties endure, accommodating to changes in traditions and differences in the political perspectives of family members. Remarking on this phenomenon, Ellen Goodman has suggested that the family "may be the one social glue strong enough to withstand the centrifuge of special interests which send us spinning away from each other." The family provides a context for intergenerational caring and understanding while many other relationships dissolve as individuals move further apart in their pursuits of self-interest. We are reminded of Tocqueville's hypothesis that "democracy loosens social ties, but tightens natural ones; it brings kindred more closely together, whilst it throws citizens more apart."

Notions of what constitutes a family, how family members relate to each other, and what values are transmitted through the family continue to evolve. Increasing numbers of interracial and inter-ethnic marriages, single-parent families, and lesbian/gay households raise new issues in family relationships. Nevertheless, the motifs of freedom, independence, and affection that Tocqueville observed continue to characterize the American family. In spite of the freedom of individuals within these families to seek their own ways and espouse their own causes and the increased mobility of Americans, which often puts huge physical distances between family members, the important psychological reality of the family and its centrality to the wholeness of the social fabric holds.

The narrator of Shirley Ann Grau's "The Beginning" grew up in a world created by her single-parent mother, a world in which the narrator was "the queen of the world, the jewel of the lotus, the pearl without price, [her mother's] secret treasure." So consistent was this message that it survived numerous moves and hardships and oftentimes transcended sordid surroundings, taking root in the narrator's psyche so that when she was grown and faced the realities of her position in the world, she did so with strength and confidence. The family provides occasions for harmony and shared purpose, draws people together in spite of the many opportunities for discord and disillusionment. It plays a central role in defining the quality of one's life. As Raphael Dorcas, a Puerto Rican immigrant interviewed by Elena Padilla, explains, "A good life is when we work and we has [sic] the things we need for all the family. I think that's a good life."

THE AMERICAN WAY OF FAMILIES

LAWRENCE H. FUCHS

Lawrence H. Fuchs (b. 1927) is the Meyer and Walter Jaffe Professor of American Civilization and Politics at Brandeis University. He earned his undergraduate degree at New York University and his Ph.D. at Harvard. From 1961 to 1963 he was director of the Peace Corps in the Philippines, and he served from 1979 to 1981 as executive director of the U.S. Select Commission on Immigration and Refugee Policy. The report of this commission became the basis for the Immigration Reform and Control Act of 1986 and the Immigration Reform Act of 1990. Among his books are Those Peculiar Americans: The Peace Corps and American National Character *(1967),* American Ethnic Politics *(1968), and* The American Kaleidoscope: Race, Ethnicity, and the Civic Culture *(1990). In the following selection from* Family Matters *(1972), Fuchs points to the role the values of independence and equality have played in the evolution of the American family system.*

◆ FREEWRITING

Before reading this selection, freewrite for ten or fifteen minutes on what you perceive to be some of the defining characteristics of American families. If you are familiar with family values from other cultures, feel free to mention those.

The evolution of human families took hundreds of thousands of years, the development of an American family system less than one hundred. The forces which gave birth to the American family system were strikingly different in combination from those which appeared elsewhere: dissident Protestants who founded the nation stressed personal faith through a direct encounter with God as the road to salvation, an emphasis which ultimately encouraged individualism for all against patriarchal rule; immigrants to the New World were already somewhat independent of the patriarchal families they left behind, and in America they found a relative abundance of land and resources where labor and women were in short supply, making both women and children more valuable than they had ever been in the old country. As a result, women and children sought and achieved a degree of independence from patriarchal authority which they never had before. Experiencing some, they wanted more. Thus began a family system noted for its dispersive, competitive characteristics. When seen from a cross-cultural point of view—Latin-Catholic, Hindu, Chinese, Moslem, East European, or even North European—the early and continuing emphasis on personal independence and equality stands out. . . .

Who have been the American folk heroes? The independent pioneer always on the move, performing feats of daring; the lonesome cowboy, altogether unencumbered with family ties; the Horatio Algers who rise by their own bootstraps to great business success; and the gargantuan mythic heroes, such as Paul Bunyan and John Henry, who are ready for action and to make decisions from the moment they are born. Perhaps the greatest of all American folk heroes, John Henry, burst into the world without any need of his parents at all. On his first day, after ordering his mother and father to get him four ham bones, a potful of cabbage, corn bread, pot liquor, biscuits and a big jug full of cane molasses, he walked out of the house and away from them and Black River country forever.

The prophets of American values—from Jefferson to Ralph Waldo Emerson and Henry David Thoreau to William James and John Dewey—have insisted that the individual should trust no one but himself. The ideal man is one who is ready to confront the challenges of life depending only on his unique abilities. He lives and achieves apart from his historical and cultural inheritance. Emerson, whose influence on American education, philosophy and psychology has probably been larger than that of any other American, never tired of urging the individual, "trust thyself . . . nothing is at last sacred but the integrity of your own mind; . . . the only right is what is after my constitution; the wrong is against it." He never asked how man learned to trust himself (if not through being trusted and loved by others) or how he developed his own voice or manner without trustworthy, loving models to follow. For Emerson, not only is every man unique (a banality on which all could agree), but presumably he is sprung full-blown from the head of Zeus and, like John Henry, ready to manage for himself. . . .

Although the assertion of the independent self has been the common response of Americans to man's search for identity, most people of the world answer the question "Who are you?" by saying, "I am of Y family and village X." For them the individual grows up through an unending series of dependency relationships within a family. Recognition is given to the unequal capacities and responsibilities of small children, youths and adults. What most Americans would see as unwanted dependency feelings are viewed favorably. In India, for example, where there is no word for dependency, the terms *bandha*, *sambandha* and *bandhavy* (bond, bondship and kinship) are positive. There and in much of the world the ideal of human maturity is not independence from and within relationships but the maintenance of satisfying, pleasurable and continuous binding relationships. In the United States, by contrast, there evolved the first culture in human history where an increasing number of people drew little psychological strength from roles or relationships, from being able to say, "I am a woman," "I am a mother," "I am a man," "I am a father," "I am the son of L," "My grandfather is of the house of Y," "My ancestors were teachers," and so on.

The family not only exemplifies the dominant values of the culture but it 5
carries and impresses them on the young. There is the dilemma. With its emphasis on personal independence and equality, American ideology is at war with the very nature of family life, at least as it has been known through the ages. For thousands of years men, women and children in families understood to the

depths of their beings how totally dependent they were on each other. When resources were scarce and the family had to be defended against hostile outsiders, the young and the women always needed protection by dominant males, who usually were given positions of command. Biologically, it made sense. Only women became pregnant, suckled and warmed the young. Males were physically stronger. Roles and functions were assigned along hierarchical lines by age and sex. In America a new kind of family system emerged, based on the search of individual members for personal independence.

While I see anxiety, loneliness and new kinds of conflicts as the price Americans have paid for independence and equality in families, I believe there have been enormous benefits, too. One has only to see the envy of many European and Asian girls of the freedom which American young men and women have to appreciate that the American idea of independence holds something of real value. Love shared through an adult lifetime of conflict-and-reconciliation between a man and a woman who chose each other is an ideal which is becoming increasingly attractive in many parts of the world at the very time that Americans are raising questions about it. The liberation of women and children from the subjugation characteristic of many patriarchal and rigidly double-standard societies has brought happiness to them and has released creative talent for society. The American family system is good *and* bad in human terms. What is bad or good depends on your opinion of the emotional and spiritual needs of men and women. It is a question of your version of the good life. What is important is not that American families are better or worse than others. It is that they are different.

QUESTIONS FOR DISCUSSION

1. Fuchs provides a historical explanation for the fact that the American family system is so strikingly different from those of other cultures. What role does competition play in the difference?
2. Explain why, according to Fuchs, Emerson was such an influential voice in defining the values of the American family. What are some of the particular problems these values create?

WRITING ASSIGNMENTS

1. Reaction Journal: Fuchs suggests that "American ideology is at war with the very nature of family life." Write a letter to Fuchs in which you respond to his assertion. Feel free to provide concrete examples from your experience that support or contradict him.
2. Fuchs suggests that American families are characterized by the independence of individual members rather than by mutual dependence on one another. Write an essay about your own family (and/or other families with which you may be familiar) in which you respond to Fuchs's assertions. Remember that your response will be most meaningful if you are concrete.

ETHNICITY AND FAMILIES

MONICA MCGOLDRICK

Monica McGoldrick (b. 1943) is director of Family Training in the Psychiatric Department at Rutgers Medical School. A fourth-generation Irish-American, McGoldrick found that her husband, who emigrated from Greece at age twenty-one, and his family taught her a "great cultural lesson." She was surprised to find that their interpersonal relationships were governed by a set of cultural rules quite different from those according to which she had been raised. Keeping up appearances, muffling hostilities, and avoiding making a scene—rules always obeyed by her family—did not operate within theirs. In this selection from Ethnicity and Family Therapy, *McGoldrick describes how ethnicity affects family relationships.*

◆ FREEWRITING

Before reading this selection, freewrite for ten or fifteen minutes,. In your writing, try to come to terms with a definition of family. Show how the values of your family and other families you are familiar with are affected by ethnic origin.

Ethnicity relates family process to the broader context in which it evolves. Just as individuation requires that we come to terms with our families of origin, coming to terms with our ethnicity is necessary to gain a perspective on the relativity of our belief systems. For example, if young people experience their parents as cold, distant, and unfeeling, it may be hard for them, even with the appreciation that their grandparents were the same, to feel sympathetic to their life-styles. However, if we recognize in that "distance" the determined individualism on which the pioneers forged ahead in this country, we become connected with a fuller, more complex and accurate picture of our heritage, which may be easier to appreciate and to renegotiate.

Even the definition of "family" differs greatly from group to group. The dominant American (WASP) definition focuses on the intact nuclear family. Black families focus on a wide network of kin and community. For Italians there is no such thing as the "nuclear" family. To them family means a strong, tightly knit three- or four-generational family, which also includes godparents and old friends. The Chinese go beyond this and include in their definition of family all their ancestors and all their descendants. [Their conception of time is very different, and death does not create the same distinction it does for Westerners.]

The family life cycle phases also vary for different groups. For example, Mexican Americans have a longer courtship period and see early and middle childhood as extending longer than the dominant American pattern (Falicov and Karrer, 1980). Adolescence is shorter and leads more quickly into adulthood than in the dominant American structure, while middle age extends longer going into what Americans generally think of as older age.

Cultural groups vary also in the emphasis they place on different transitions. The Irish have always placed most emphasis on the wake, viewing death as the most important life cycle transition. Italians, in contrast, emphasize the wedding, while Jews often give particular attention to the Bar Mitzvah, a transition most groups hardly mark at all. Families' ways of celebrating these events differ also. As Greeley has noted, the Irish tend to celebrate weddings (and every other occasion) by drinking, the Poles by dancing, the Italians by eating, and the Jews by eating and talking.

Some groups celebrate Christmas most elaborately (e.g., Poles, Germans, 5
Scandinavians, WASPs), where others emphasize Easter (Greeks and Slavs), and others the Jewish New Year, the Chinese New Year, and so forth. These customs evoke deep feelings in people that relate to the continuity of the rituals over generations and centuries.

Every culture generates characteristic problems for itself. These problems are often consequences of cultural traits that are conspicuous strengths in other contexts. For example, WASP optimism leads to confidence and flexibility in taking initiative, an obvious strength when there are opportunities to do so. But the one-sided preference for cheerfulness also leads to the inability to cope with tragedy or to engage in mourning. Historically, WASPs have perhaps had less misfortune than most other peoples. But optimism becomes a vulnerability when they must contend with tragedy. They have few philosophical or expressive ways to deal with situations in which optimism, rationality, and belief in the efficacy of individuality are insufficient. The WASP strengths of independence and individual initiative work well in some situations, but WASPs may feel lost when dependence on the group is the only way to ensure survival.

Naturally, what behavior groups see as problematic will differ as well. WASPs may be concerned about dependency and emotionality, the Irish about "making a scene," Italians about disloyalty to the family, Greeks about any insult to their pride, or *filotimo*, Jews about their children not being "successful," or Puerto Ricans about their children not showing respect. . . .

Cultural differences are often ascribed to class rather than ethnicity. Class is also a major aspect of family life experience, but all differences cannot be ascribed to this factor alone. For example, Puerto Ricans, Italians, and Greeks all have similar rural, peasant backgrounds, and yet there are important ethnic differences among these groups. Puerto Ricans tend to have flexible boundaries between the family and the surrounding community, so that child lending is a common and accepted practice. Italians tend to have much more clear boundaries between the family and the surrounding community and extremely tight boundaries against outsiders. You can be taken in as a member of the extended family by long and close association, but the boundaries remain quite rigid between insiders and outsiders. Greeks have very definite family boundaries, are disinclined to adopt children, having deep feelings about the "blood line." Greeks are also nationalistic—a value that relates to a nostalgic vision of ancient Greece and to the country they lost under hundreds of years of Ottoman oppression. (Poles and Irish, who experienced similar foreign domination after a period of nationhood, also have intense nationalistic feelings.) By contrast, Italians, until coming to this country, defined themselves primarily by family ties, second, by their village, and, third, if at all, by the region of Italy from which they came. Puerto Ricans as a group have coalesced only within the past century or so and have developed their awareness of their group identity primarily in reaction to experiences with the United States.

Migration

Families that migrate with young children are perhaps strengthened by having each other, but they are vulnerable to the parental reversal of hierarchies. If the family migrates with small children (even more so with teenagers), there is a likelihood that the parents will acculturate more slowly than their children, creating a problematic power reversal in the family. If the children must take on the task of interpreting the new culture for the parents, parental leadership may be so threatened that children are left without effective adult authority to support them and without the positive identification with their ethnic background to ease their struggle with life in this new culture. If the parents have support in their cultural adjustment—through their work place or extended family and friends—the children's adjustment will be facilitated and may go more easily since children generally adapt well to new situations, even when it involves learning a new language. Problems may surface, however, in adolescence, when the children move out toward their peer culture. Coaching the younger generation to show respect for the values of the older generation is usually the first step in negotiating such conflicts.

Families migrating when their children are adolescents may have more diffi- 10
culty because they will have less time together as a unit before the children move out on their own. Thus the family must struggle with multiple transitions and generational conflicts at once. In addition, the distance from the grandparental generation in the old country may be particularly distressing as grandparents become ill, dependent, or die. The parents may experience severe stress in not being able to fulfill their obligations to their parents in the country of origin. It is not uncommon for symptoms to develop in adolescents in reaction to their parents' unexpressed distress. For example:

> John was admitted to an adolescent psychiatric unit in an acute psychotic state at age 17, two weeks after a visit to Greece with his parents and younger sister. He had begun acting strangely while in Greece,

> where the paternal grandfather had died two months previously. John's grandmother was in good health, but according to John, was severely depressed and lonely. In his psychotic talking he spoke often of taking care of her and of bridging the two worlds of Greece and the United States. John's father had begun a successful restaurant business in the United States, into which he had brought his younger brother, brother-in-law, and two cousins. John's mother had no immediate family in the United States, and missed her own parents and sisters a great deal. However, her husband had told her before they came to this country that she must never think of returning, and she obeyed.

John's dilemma, reflected, at least partially, his concern that his parents were in an impossible dilemma—cut off from their families in Greece, unable to give up the strivings they had in the United States or to reconcile themselves with what they had left behind. He felt that his paternal grandfather's death symbolized for his mother that her own parents would die without her support. He worried about her almost continuously. Therapy involved helping the family sort through their cultural conflicts. The worry and concern for the family in Greece was reframed as a sign of their loving sensitivity, while their struggle to achieve in this country was also for the family's benefit. The mother was encouraged to stay in close touch with her parents and sisters in Greece but also to develop contacts with the Greek women in her church, which she had been avoiding in her preoccupation with her own family members in Greece.

When families migrate in the launching phase, it is less often because they seek a better way of life and more often because circumstances in the country of origin make remaining there impossible. This phase causes particular difficulties for families because it is much more difficult for the middle generation to break into new work and friendship networks at this phase. Again, if aging parents are left behind, the stresses will be intensified.

The launching phase may be made more complex when children date or marry spouses from other backgrounds. This is naturally perceived as a threat by many, if not most, parents since it means a loss of the cultural heritage in the next generation. One cannot underestimate the stress it creates for parents, who themselves have had to give up their country of origin, to fear the loss of their traditions when their children intermarry.

Migration in later life is often especially difficult because families are leaving so very much behind. There is evidence that even those who migrate at a young age have a strong need to reclaim their ethnic roots at this phase, particularly because they are losing other supports around them (Gelfand and Kutzik, 1979). For those who have not mastered English, life can be extremely isolating at this phase. The need to depend on others may be particularly frustrating, as when one is forced to be in a nursing home where one cannot communicate easily.

Sometimes if the first generation is older at the time of immigration and 15
lives in an ethnic neighborhood in the new country, its conflicts of acculturation may be postponed. The next generation, particularly in adolescence, is likely to

reject the ethnic values of their parents and strive to become "Americanized" (Sluzki, 1979). Intergenerational conflicts often reflect the value struggles of families in adapting to the United States.

The third or fourth generations are usually freer to reclaim aspects of their identities that were sacrificed in the previous generations because of the need to assimilate.

Families from different ethnic groups may have very different kinds of intergenerational struggles. WASP families are likely to feel they have failed if their children do not move away from the family and become independent, while Italian families are likely to feel they have failed if their children do move away. Jewish families will expect a relatively democratic atmosphere to exist in the family, with children free to challenge parents and to discuss their feelings openly. Greek families, in contrast, do not expect or desire open communication between generations and would not appreciate the therapist getting everyone together to discuss and "resolve" their conflicts. Children are expected to respect parental authority, which is maintained by the distance parents preserve from their children. Irish families will be embarrassed to share feelings and conflicts across generations and cannot be expected to do so to any great extent.

Intermarriage

Obviously intermarriage complicates geometrically the picture presented by a family of a single ethnic group. Generally, the greater the difference between spouses in cultural background, the more difficulty they will have in adjusting to marriage.

For example, a WASP/Italian couple might run into conflicts because the WASP takes literally the dramatic expressiveness of the Italian, while the Italian finds the WASP's emotional distancing intolerable. The WASP may label the Italian "hysterical" or "crazy" and be labeled in return "cold" or "catatonic." Knowledge about differences in cultural belief systems can be helpful to spouses who take each other's behavior personally. In the extreme, of course, it may also be used as an excuse for not taking responsibility in a relationship: "I'm Italian, I can't help it" (i.e., the yelling, abusive language, impulsiveness). Or, "I'm a WASP. It is just the way I am" (the lack of emotional response, the rationalization and workaholism). Or, "I can't help being late, we Puerto Ricans have a different conception of time."

Cultural and religious groups have always had prohibitions against inter- 20
marriage. Until 1967 when the laws were declared unconstitutional, 19 states had laws prohibiting racial intermarriage. Until 1970 the Catholic Church prohibited intermarriage with non-Catholics unless the latter promised to raise all children as Catholic. Intermarriage is feared because it threatens the survival of the group.

References

Falicov, C., and Karrer, B. Cultural Variations in the Family Life Cycle. In E. A. Carter and M. McGoldrick (Eds.), *The Family Life Cycle: A Framework for Family Therapy.* New York: Gardner Press, 1980.

Gelfand, D. E., and Kutzik, A. J. (Eds.). *Ethnicity and Aging.* New York: Springer, 1979.

Sluzki, C. Migration and Family Conflict. *Family Process, 18* (4), 379–390, 1979.

QUESTIONS FOR DISCUSSION

1. Discuss the following with a group of your peers:
   a. "The family life cycle phases also vary for different groups."
   b. "But WASPs may feel lost when dependence on the group is the only way to ensure survival."
   c. "Class is also a major aspect of family life experience but all differences cannot be ascribed to this factor alone."
2. What are some of the difficulties associated with families who migrate with adolescents? Discuss some of the relationships between age and acculturation.

WRITING ASSIGNMENTS

1. Reaction Journal: Write a paragraph or two in which you discuss the relationships between your freewriting and the selection itself.
2. Look closely at the values of your family or those of a family you are close to. Write an essay in which you examine how such issues as cultural traits, behavior groups, class, and belief systems define this family.

OLD MAN LONIGAN

JAMES T. FARRELL

James T. Farrell (1904–1979) was a prolific novelist and short story writer whose works present the world of the working-class Irish-Catholics on Chicago's South Side. The author of over twenty-five novels, Farrell was born in Chicago and attended De Paul University and the University of Chicago. He did not, however, earn degrees at either institution, receiving instead much of his education through his many jobs in such varied places as a shoe store, a gas station, a cigar store, a newspaper office, and an express office. Farrell's works include several cycles of novels that follow the lives of characters such as Studs Lonigan, Danny O'Neill, and Eddie Ryan over many years. The most famous of these cycles is com-

posed of Young Lonigan: A Boyhood on the Chicago Streets *(1932),* The Young Manhood of Studs Lonigan *(1934), and* Judgment Day *(1935), which were published together as* Studs Lonigan: A Trilogy *(1935). In the following excerpt from* Young Lonigan, *family patriarch Patrick J. Lonigan reflects with satisfaction on his own accomplishments and dreams and on the example he has provided for his children by being a "good Catholic, a good American, a good father, and a good husband."*

◆ FREEWRITING

Freewrite for ten or fifteen minutes on the role of religion in shaping the value system of your family or of a family you know well.

Old man Lonigan, his feet planted on the back porch railing, sat tilted back in his chair enjoying his stogy. His red, well-fed-looking face was wrapped in a dreamy expression; and his innards made slight noises as they diligently furthered the process of digesting a juicy beefsteak. He puffed away, exuding burgher comfort, while from inside the kitchen came the rattle of dishes being washed. Now and then he heard Frances preparing for the evening. 1

He gazed, with reverie-lost eyes, over the gravel spread of Carter Playground, which was a few doors south of his own building. A six-o'clock sun was imperceptibly burning down over the scene. On the walk, in the shadow of and circling the low, rambling public school building, some noisy little girls, the size and age of his own Loretta, were playing hop-scotch. Lonigan puffed at his cigar, ran his thick paw through his brown-gray hair, and watched the kids. He laughed when he heard one of the little girls shout that the others could go to hell. It was funny and they were tough little ones all right. It sounded damn funny. They must be poor little girls with fathers and mothers who didn't look after them or bring them up in the right home atmosphere; and if they were Catholic girls, they probably weren't sent to the sisters' school; parents ought to send their children to the sisters' school even if it did take some sacrifice; after all, it only cost a dollar a month, and even poor people could afford that when their children's education was at stake. He wouldn't have his Loretta using such rowdy language, and, of course, she wouldn't, because her mother had always taught her to be a little lady. His attention wandered to a boy, no older than his own Martin, but dirty and less well-cared-for, who, with the intent and dreamy seriousness of childhood, played on the ladders and slides which paralleled his own back fence. He watched the youngster scramble up, slide down, scramble up, slide down. It stirred in him a vague series of impulses, wishes and nostalgias. He puffed his stogy and watched. He said to himself:

Golly, it would be great to be a kid again!

He said to himself:

Yes, sir, it would be great to be a kid! 5

He tried to remember those ragged days when he was only a shaver and his old man was a pauperized greenhorn. Golly, them were the days! Often there had not been enough to eat in the house. Many's the winter day he and his brother had to stay home from school because they had no shoes. The old house, it was more like a barn or a shack than a home, was so cold they had to sleep in their clothes; sometimes in those zero Chicago winters his old man had slept in his overcoat. Golly, even with all that privation, them was the days. And now that they were over, there was something missing, something gone from a fellow's life. He'd give anything to live back a day of those times around Blue Island, and Archer Avenue. Old man Dooley always called it Archey Avenue, and Dooley was one comical turkey, funnier than anything you'd find in real life. And then those days when he was a young buck in Canaryville. And things were cheaper in them days. The boys that hung out at Kieley's saloon, and later around the saloon that Padney Flaherty ran, and Luke O'Toole's place on Halsted. Old Luke was some boy. Well, the Lord have mercy on his soul, and on the soul of old Padney Flaherty. Padney was a comical duck, good-hearted as they make them, but crabby. Was he a first-rate crab! And the jokes the boys played on him. They were always calling him names, pigpen Irish, shanty Irish, Padney, ain't you the kind of an Irishman that slept with the pigs back in the old country.

He took a long puff. He gazed out, and watched a group of kids, thirteen, fourteen, fifteen, boys like Bill, who sat in the gravel near the backstop close to the Michigan Avenue fence. What do kids talk about? He wondered, because a person's own childhood got so far away from him he forgot most of it, and sometimes it seemed as if he'd never been a kid himself, he forgot the way a kid felt, the thoughts of a kid. He sometimes wondered about Bill. Bill was a fine boy. You couldn't find a better one up on the graduating stage at St. Patrick's tonight, no more than you would see a finer girl than Frances. But sometimes he wondered just what Bill thought about.

He puffed. It was nice sitting there. He would like to sit there, and watch it slowly get dark, because when it was just getting dark things were quiet and soft-like, and a fellow liked to sit in all the quiet and well, just sit, and let any old thoughts go through his mind; just sit and dream, and realize that life was a funny thing, but that he'd fought his way up to a station where there weren't no real serious problems like poverty, and he sits there, and is comfortable and content and patient, because he knows that he has put his shoulder to the wheel, and he has been a good Catholic, and a good American, a good father, and a good husband. He just sits there with Mary, and smokes his cigar, and has his thoughts, and then, after it gets dark, he can send one of the kids for ice cream, or maybe sneak down to the saloon at Fifty-eighth and State and have a glass of beer. But there was many another evening for that, and tonight he'd have to go and see the kids get a good sendoff; otherwise he wouldn't be much of a father. When you're a father you got duties, and Patrick J. Lonigan well knew that.

While Lonigan's attention had been sunk inwards, the kids had all left the playground. Now he looked about, and the scene was swallowed in a hush, broken only by occasional automobiles and by the noise from the State Street cars that seemed to be more than a block away. Suddenly, he experienced, like an unexpected blow, a sharp fear of growing old and dying, and he knew a moment of terror. Then it slipped away, greased by the thickness of his content. Where in hell should he get the idea that he was getting so old? Sure, he was a little gray in the top story, and a little fat around the belly, but, well, the fat was a healthy fat, and there was lots of stuff left in the old boy. And he was not any fatter than old man O'Brien who owned the coal yards at Sixty-second and Wabash.

He puffed at his stogy and flicked the ashes over the railing. He thought 10
about his own family. Bill would get himself some more education, and then learn the business, starting as a painter's apprentice, and when he got the hang of things and had worked on the job long enough, he would step in and run the works; and then the old man and Mary would take a trip to the old sod and see where John McCormack was born, take a squint at the Lakes of Killarney, kiss the blarney stone, and look up all his relatives.

Now, he'd have to be going inside, putting on his tie, and going up with Mary and the kids for the doings. He sat there, comfortable, puffing away. Life was a good thing if you were Patrick J. Lonigan and had worked hard to win out in the grim battle, and God had been good to you. But then, he had earned the good things he had. Yes, sir, let God call him to the Heavenly throne this very minute, and he could look God square in the eye and say he had done his duty, and he had been, and was, a good father. They had given the kids a good home, fed and clothed them, set the right example for them, sent them to Catholic schools to be educated, seen that they performed their religious duties, hustled them off to confession regularly, given them money for the collection, never allowed them to miss mass, even in winter, let them play properly so they'd be healthy, given them money for good clean amusements like the movies because they were also educational, done everything a parent can do for a child.

QUESTIONS FOR DISCUSSION

1. Imagine what prompts Lonigan to reflect on his own childhood. What are some of the differences and similarities he notes between his youth and the youth of Martin and Loretta?

2. Discuss how religion helps define Lonigan's view of his neighborhood and his world.

3. In this excerpt from *Young Lonigan*, a study of an Irish adolescent coming of age in a squalid Chicago neighborhood, we see Lonigan responding to his children's adolescence and remembering his own. How would you describe Lonigan's attitude toward his present? His past?

WRITING ASSIGNMENTS

1. Writing Journal: Imagine that your neighborhood (or a neighborhood you're familiar with) had an equivalent to old man Lonigan—someone who has spent most of a lifetime in the same neighborhood. Try to discover as much as

you can about the neighborhood's history, and write a few paragraphs of imagined reflection from this elderly person's point of view.

2. Interview an individual whose children are now adults. Try to focus on their childhood, their neighborhood, and their education. Then move on to discuss their children's growing up. Write an essay in which you discuss some different experiences the two generations have had. Gather concrete information.

SAREE OF THE GODS

G. S. SHARAT CHANDRA

G. S. Sharat Chandra (b. 1935) was trained as a lawyer, but he gave up the practice of law in 1967 to devote himself to writing. His short stories and poetry have appeared in several publications in the United States and abroad. "Saree of the Gods," with its vivid central image of the silver-bordered wedding saree, comments poignantly on the losses that accompany acculturation.

◆ FREEWRITING

Most families and cultures have traditions and customs that they hold on to over the years. Think of such customs in your household (or a household of a friend), and think of times you (or your family) have entertained guests who don't understand or perhaps misunderstand the tradition. Freewrite for ten or fifteen minutes on such experiences.

One of the things that Prapulla had insisted was to have a place waiting for them in New York where other Indian immigrants lived. She had worried a great deal over this sudden change in her life. First, there was her fear of flying over Mount Everest, a certain intrusion over Lord Shiva's territory which he did not approve of for any believing Hindu. Then the abrupt severance of a generation of relationships and life in a joint family. She had spent many a restless night. In daylight, she'd dismiss her nightmares as mere confusions of a troubled mind and set herself to conquer her problems as she faced them, like the educated and practical woman that she was. If anything happened to the transgressing jet, she would clutch her husband and child to her breasts and plummet with at least a partial sense of wholeness, to whatever ocean the wrath of the god would cast her. She would go down like those brave, legendary sea captains in the history 1 books and movies. But moving over to the West, where you lived half the year like a monk in a cave because of the weather, was something she was unable to visualize. Besides, how was she going to manage her household without the maid-servant and her stalwart mother-in-law? To be left alone in a strange apartment all day while Shekar went to work was a recurring fear. She had heard that in New York City, even married women wore mini-skirts or leather slacks and thought nothing of being drunk or footloose, not to mention their sexual escapades in summer in parks or parked automobiles. But cousin Manjula who had returned from the States was most reassuring:

"All that is nonsense! Women there are just like women here! Only they have habits and customs quite different from ours. There are hundreds of Indian families in New York. Once you've acclimatized yourself to the country, you'll find it hard to sit and brood. You may run into families from Bangalore in the same apartment house, who knows!"

Prapulla liked the apartment house as soon as she saw some sareed women in the lobby. It was Shekar who looked distraught at the Indian faces. In the time it took for them to arrive from the airport to the apartment, he had seen many of his brown brethren on the city streets, looking strange and out of place. Now he dreaded being surrounded by his kind, ending up like them building little Indias in the obscure corners of New York. He wasn't certain what Prapulla thought about it. She was always quiet on such subjects. Back in India, she was a recluse when it came to socializing and on the few occasions they had entertained foreigners at the firm, she would seek the nearest sofa as a refuge and drop her seven yards of brocade at anchor. She left the impression of being a proper Hindu wife, shy, courteous and traditional.

En route to New York on the jumbo, Shekar had discreetly opened up the conversation about what she'd wear once they were in America. At the mention of skirts she had flared up so defiantly he had to leave the seat. For Prapulla, it was not convenience but convention that made the difference. She had always prized her sarees, especially the occasions she wore her wedding saree with its blue handspun silk and its silver border of gods. There were times she had walked into a crowded room where others were dressed differently and had relished the sudden flush of embarrassment on their faces at her exquisite choice of wear.

The first day of their new life went quite smoothly. When Shekar returned 5
from the office, she was relieved to hear that all had gone well and he had made friends with two of his American colleagues. Shekar described them. Don Dellow was in the firm for fifteen years and was extremely pleasant and helpful. Jim Dorsen and his wife Shirley had always wanted to visit India and shared great interest in the country and its culture.

"I bought them lunch at the corner deli, you know, and you should've seen their faces when I asked for corned beef on rye!" Shekar chuckled. It was during that weekend that Shekar suggested they ought to invite the Dellows and the Dorsens for dinner so she could meet and get to know the wives. Prapulla shrugged her shoulders. It was so soon. She was still unaccustomed to walking into the sterilized supermarkets where you shopped like a robot with a pushcart, led on to the products by where they lay waiting like cheese in a trap, rather than having them beseech you like the vendors and merchants in the bazaars and markets in her country. Besides, everything had a fixed price tag. The frozen vegetables, the canned fruits and spices, the chicken chopped into shapes that were not its own but of the plastic, all bothered her. But Shekar had not complained about her cooking yet. He was so busy gabbing and gulping, she wasn't even sure he knew what was on the plate. Then Shekar walked in from the office Thursday and announced he had invited his friends for dinner on Saturday.

"They both accepted with great delight. It's rather important I develop a strong bond with them."

Prapulla pulled out a pad and started making the shopping list. Shekar was about to ask her what she'd wear but changed his mind.

The Dorsens arrived first. Shirley Dorsen introduced herself and immediately took a liking to Prapulla. The Dellows, caught in traffic, came late. Judy Dellow was a lean Spanish woman in her late twenties. She wore a velvet dress with lace cuffs and asked for bourbon. The living room filled with the aroma of spices. In the background, Subbalakshmi recited on the stereo.

"What sort of music is this?" Jim asked, looking somewhat sullen. He had just finished his drink. Shirley was on her fourth.

"Karnatak music," explained Prapulla. "Subbalakshmi is the soprano of South Indian music. She sings mostly devotional songs and lyrics."

"Sounds rather strange and off key to me," said Jim nodding his head in dismay. He sang for the church choir on Sundays.

Shekar announced dinner. He had set the wine glasses next to the handloomed napkins like he had seen in *Good Housekeeping*. As soon as everyone was seated, he abruptly got up. "Gee! I forgot to pour the wine!" he despaired. When he returned, he held an opaque bottle with a long German name.

"What kind of wine is it?" asked Jim.

"The best German riesling there is!" replied Shekar with authority.

"My, you do know your liquor!" said Shirley, impressed.

"Like a book!" quipped Prapulla.

"It's a misconception," Shekar continued hastily, "that French wines are the best. Germans actually mastered the art of wine making long before the French. Besides, you can't beat a German riesling to go with Indian food."

"Excellent!" said Jim. Shekar filled the glasses apologizing again for not having filled them beforehand. "You see, good wine has to be chilled right," he added avoiding Prapulla's unflinching stare. They began to eat. Shirley attacked everything, mumbling superlatives between mouthfuls. Shekar kept a benevolent eye on the plates and filled them as soon as they were empty. Prapulla sat beaming an appropriate smile. When everyone had their fill, Prapulla got up for dessert.

"Is it going to be one of the exotic Indian sweets?" Shirley asked.

"Of course," butted Shekar.

Prapulla returned from the kitchen with Pepperidge Farm turnovers. "Sorry, I had an accident with the jamoons," she said meekly.

"Don't worry dear. Turnovers do perfectly well," said Shirley, giving her an understanding look.

Shekar had placed a box of cigars on the coffee table. As they all sat, he offered it to his guests who waved it away in preference to their own crumpled packages of Salem. Don and Jim talked about a contract the firm had lost. A junior engineer from Bombay who used to work for the firm had bungled it. They asked Shekar if he knew the man. Shekar had already stiffened in the chair but he pressed for details. But they veered the conversation away from the topic to compliment him on his choice of brandy.

Prapulla entered with a tray of coffee mixed with cream and sugar, just like back home. Subbalakshmi coughed, cleared her throat and strummed the veena in prayer.

Judy raved about Prapulla's saree. Prapulla, momentarily saved from embarrassment over the coffee, began to explain the ritual importance of the wedding saree. She pulled the upper part from her shoulder and spread it on the table. The silver border with the embroidered legend of the creation of the universe, the different avatars of Lord Shiva and the demons he killed while on earthly mission gleamed under the light. Her favorite one depicted Shiva drinking the poison emitted by the sea serpent with which the universe was churned from the ocean. The craftsman had even put a knot of gold at Shiva's neck to indicate the poison the god had held in his throat. A sheer triumph of skill.

"With the exception of Shiva as the begging ascetic, the saree-maker has woven all the other avatars. This blank space on the border perhaps is the space left to challenge our imagination!" mused Prapulla. Shirley, with a snifterful of brandy leaned from her chair for a closer look. The brandy tipped. "Oh no!" screamed everyone. Judy ran into the kitchen for a towel but the alcohol hissed like a magical serpent over the saree spreading its poisonous hood. The silver corroded fast and the avatars, disfigured or mutilated, almost merged. Prapulla sat dazed, just staring at her saree. The silence was unbearable. Jim puffed on his pipe like a condemned man. Judy, after trying valiantly to wipe the brandy, bent her head over her hand. Shirley looked red, like she was either going to scream or giggle. Shekar came to the rescue:

"Don't worry. I know a way I can lift the smudges. It's nothing!"

No one believed him. Prapulla abruptly got up and excused herself.

"I guess we should better be leaving," said Don looking at his watch. "I've to drive the babysitter home and she lives three traffic jams away!"

Shekar hurried to the closet for their coats. "I hope you enjoyed the dinner!" he said meekly, piling up the coats over his shoulder. Prapulla appeared at the door in a different saree. She seemed to have recollected herself and felt bad about everyone leaving so soon. "You know, my husband is right. I've already dipped the saree border in the lotion. It'll be as good as new by morning," she said. They shook hands and Shirley hugged Prapulla and rocked her. "I'll call you, dear, let me know how it comes off!" she whispered drunkenly and backed into her coat like an animal perfectly trained.

Prapulla stood at the door with one hand on her stomach, and as the guests disappeared down the elevator, she banged the door shut and ran into the bedroom. She remembered the day she had shopped for the saree. It was a week before her wedding. The entire family had gone to the silk bazaar and spent the day looking for the perfect one. They had at last found it in the only hand-spun saree shop in the market. The merchant had explained that the weaver who had knitted the god into its border had died soon after, taking his craft with him. This was his last saree, his parting gift to some lucky bride. "You modern young people may not believe in old wives' tales, but I know that he was a devotee of Shiva. People say the Lord used to appear for him!" the merchant had said.

She sobbed into her shoulders. Where was she going to find a replacement? How was she ever going to explain the tragedy to her family? A wedding saree, selected by the bride became her second self, the sail of her destiny, the roof that protected her and her offspring from evil. She rushed to Ratri's room to make sure that no mythical serpent or scorpion had already appeared over her daughter's head.

She could hear Shekar washing the dishes in the kitchen and turning the sinkerator that gurgled like a demon with its gulletful of leftovers. She found the impulse to make sure that Shekar had not fallen into it. It was not really Shirley's fault. It was the brandy that her "Americanized" husband kept pouring into her glass. He was imitative and flippant, lavishing food and liquor that they could scarcely afford on people that were yet to be called friends. He had drunk more than he should have as if to prove that he held his liquor well enough to win points for promotion! Who really discovered brandy? Shekar had brackishly turned the picture of Napoleon on the bottle toward his guests, but surely it must have been a demon who despised her or was sent to convey the god's displeasure at her mixed company, her expatriatism.

She grew tired of her mind's hauntings. There was no way to change the events or turn back now. When Ratri grew up, she would cut the saree and make a dress for her. She'd write to her mother-in-law and send money for a special puja at the temple.

In her dream, it was her funeral. Four priests carried her on bamboo. The family walked behind. Shekar, dressed in traditional dhoti, walked ahead with the clay vessel of hot coals with which he'd kindle the first spark of fire. The procession moved briskly to the crematory grounds. A pyre was built and her corpse decked with her favorite flowers was laid on top. Someone tied the border of the saree firmly to a log. The bereaved went around chanting the necessary hymns and the priests sprinkled holy water over her. Suddenly she was ablaze. She felt nothing but an intense heat around her. The flames did not seem to touch her. She pinched herself. She was not on the pyre but was standing with her family. It was her wedding saree wrapped around a giant bottle of brandy that was burning! Inside the bottle a demon danced, spitting fire. The avatars slowly uncurled from the silver border like an inflated raft and ascended the smoke. They were all in miniature, fragile in their postures and luminous. The brandy in the bottle foamed and swirled like an ocean. The demon raved in its ring of fire. Prapulla screamed. One of the uncles gently touched her on the arm and said:

"Do not be alarmed. The demon points its tongue upwards. The gods have flown to their proper heaven."

When she woke herself from the nightmare, Shekar was soundly snoring on the bedside. The sky outside hung in a spent, listless grayness. She could see a haze of light back of a skyscraper. Dawn would soon brim the horizon of her new world with neither birds nor the song of priests in the air. She sat in the dark of the living room with the saree on her lap, caressing its border absent-mindedly. A brittled piece broke and fell.

QUESTIONS FOR DISCUSSION

1. Before her move to the United States, Prapulla was worried about several things. What were they? How did her cousin Manjula try to reassure her? Shekar wished to avoid other Asian-Indian immigrants. Why? Do you feel such concerns and responses are typical of new immigrants?
2. Discuss the importance of Prapulla's saree as a symbol in this narrative. What does it represent?
3. Why is point of view so crucial to the impact of this story? How would the story be different if it were written from the point of view of Shekar or one of the American dinner guests?

WRITING ASSIGNMENTS

1. Reaction Journal: Assume the role of one of the American dinner guests and write a concrete description of your evening with Prapulla and Shekar.
2. Write an essay in which you analyze the function of Prapulla's saree in this story. Discuss what it suggests and why it is so appropriate as a central symbol.

UNDISCIPLINED CHILDREN

JAMES M. FREEMAN

In his 1989 book Hearts of Sorrow: Vietnamese-American Lives, *James M. Freeman (b. 1936) has collected narratives from Vietnamese refugees who speak of their adjustment strategies, their successes and failures, in learning to live within a new culture. Common themes run through the narratives—difficulties in finding work appropriate to their training, dislike of American food, difficulties with their more acculturated children, loneliness stemming from linguistic and cultural isolation. The following excerpt from the narrative of an elderly civil servant whose sons have achieved success in education and employment in the United States reveals the toll that even apparently successful transitions can exact.*

◆ FREEWRITING

Freewrite for ten or fifteen minutes on how your values differ from the family values of your parents. Discuss how you and your parents addressed these differences during your adolescence.

The behavior of Vietnamese children in America is just beginning to change to the American direction. In Vietnam, children must listen to their parents and must not argue against them. They see the freedom of teenagers here, so they tend to imitate them. One of my good friends from Vietnam is really disturbed by the behavior of his five children here. One day, they did something wrong, I don't know what, but he got so mad! He threatened them with a kitchen knife. His wife called the police. Later, the man complained to me and other friends, "In Vietnam, my children listened to me, but over here they are not afraid of me anymore. They call the police." He was depressed.

With my family, too, my children, and their children, do not obey strictly. One of my sons has children who disobey and argue against him. He is afraid that they have too much freedom going to school; they associate too freely with girls, and they might run away together. So my son prohibited his sons from using the telephone, and as a result there is much disappointment in that family.

These things are very difficult and I don't know what to do because of the loss of traditional custom. Other people also complain that their children living in the United States imitate the new life and distort our old Vietnamese ways. They have freedom to be promiscuous. I know that in Vietnam some girls are not good, too. But because of the strict control of the parents, that really helped the children. Both boys and girls need to be controlled. If boys have lots of freedom, if they are let loose, that is not good. They will do anything they want, pay no respect to their parents, lie to them, and fool around while pretending to take money for school.

When I was young, I did not have a father, but I listened to my mother. She told me to go to town; I couldn't do anything besides that. I listened to her. Every year I tried to study and go back home after the semester was over.

5 Girls here have parents who cannot control them. They will grow up and marry anyone they want. Our old way was good in Vietnam, but it won't work here. My eldest son has two daughters about 15 and 20 years of age who told their father that he is too strict. They wanted to move out and live with their friends. My son consulted a counselor, saying, "My daughters are really stubborn ones. What shall I do?"

The counselor, an American female teacher, said, “You cannot beat your children in America; that is against the law. Since the eldest daughter wants to move out, let her go; you cannot do anything about it. The other one is too young and cannot go. Try to control her, but not the older one.”

I agree that if the eldest child is out of control, we have to let him or her go, but often I do not think it is good. Such a child is inexperienced and will make many mistakes. With regard to the Confucian rule, a girl should never escape the control of her parents until she gets married. Over here, females are as free as males.

In my college class, a young German woman asked me, “According to the customs of Vietnam, boys and girls are not allowed to kiss publicly, in front of everybody. But here it happens everywhere. What do you think of that?”

I felt embarrassed! In Vietnam, it would be the couples who would be embarrassed. If they were talking in an intimate way and I passed them by, they would look in different directions, the boy to the right, the girl to the left. A woman who kissed publicly lost the respect of young men; they would call her a prostitute and would refuse to marry her. But here in America, I saw boys and girls all over the place, holding hands and kissing.

10 Then the German woman asked, “What do you prefer, the American custom or the Vietnamese custom?”

I replied, “I like it here!”

She laughed.

Many people say that the difficulties with the Vietnamese family are a result of living in America, but that is not entirely true. Even in Vietnam, our children did not always follow our wishes.

In Vietnam we try to select a wife for our son who relates well to the family, so the selection should be done very carefully. In America, it is not the same way. Here children are very free; they marry whomever they choose, and they don’t pay attention to what their parents say.

15 That happened to me in Vietnam. I had a friend who wanted to marry one of his daughters with one of my older sons. On the eve of the lunar New Year, that man and his wife brought gifts to us, so I had to do the same in turn. But my son kept silent. He took a girl in Saigon city, married her, and had two children by her. He misled me. Although he had been married for a long time, he never told me. He just kept quiet and avoided our attempts to arrange his wedding. Finally in 1968 my wife told him, “If you will not have a wedding, I will delay the wedding of your younger sister because the elder must marry first.”

His mother was absent when he told me the truth. “I already have a wife. Not only that, but we already have two girls.” It was a real embarrassment. The wife we had selected for him was well educated; the woman he took for a wife had a very low education. My wife and I were very upset, for our son had made us lose face. On the eve of the New Year, I had to go for the last time to my friend’s house and offer him the last gift and confess that my son had already become married behind my back. I got so mad that I said to my son, "From now on, I never want to see you again! Please leave the family forever!" For about four years I did not see him.

In 1975, like us, my son and his family escaped by boat to the United States. He now lives in another part of the country, where he has a successful professional career. He and his family have visited us only once, when we lived in another state.

The behavior of this son affected our next two sons and several of our other children. His behavior was the key, because he set a bad example for the others. In Vietnam, when I mentioned how displeased my wife and I were about his choosing a girl whom we had never known, my next two sons would reply, "We are now adults. Why are you worried about who our wives might be? Let us be free about that matter." From that time, my wife and I connived to choose the right girls for them.

One day the second son roared up to our house in his Honda motorcycle accompanied by a girl sitting in back. "This is my friend," he said to his mother. He said nothing to me. My wife was silent. The woman came to the sitting room and stayed there alone. No one chatted with her. After an hour my son left with her. We never saw her again.

The third son also refused to listen to his mother. He knew many girls. And he refused the offer of a marriage set up for him by one of our relatives. One day in 1973 he came to us and said he wanted to marry a girl he had met in Saigon. We did not know that girl, but he insisted many times. He said he loved her and she loved him; no matter what, they would be married. So I consulted a fortune-teller who lived in my hamlet.

After reading the fortune-telling book, that man said, "The couple are not well matched. Their ages are against each other. Their future life will not be good."

I told my son what the fortune-teller had told me, and he in turn told his prospective father-in-law. That man, however, was a Christian who did not believe in fortune-telling. He said, "It's okay; I agree to marry my girl to you." He didn't care about bad fortune; he didn't care that the parents had not arranged the wedding, as long as his daughter had a husband. So I could not do anything else. We did not organize a big wedding; we just went through the formality.

The fortune-teller was right; it has not worked out well. In America, they live in the same city as we do, but we have no contact with them at all. We do not even know their telephone number or address.

A fourth son also does not obey us. He was for a while involved with a girlfriend of his own choice of whom the family was a troublemaker. We fear that he will follow the direction of his eldest brother.

Our eldest daughter married a man whom we did not think was a good match. Her husband has now left her.

Still another son, who lives at home with us and has seen all this, says, "You, Father and Mother, are always serious. After my wedding we will live apart."

Another of our daughters is married happily and has a small child. We gave her complete freedom to choose her husband here in America. I do not know much about her husband's behavior, but I gave permission, first, because she wanted him; second, because her brothers and sisters accepted him; and finally, because we also liked him when he came to visit us. We also write frequently to his parents in Vietnam. That marriage has worked out well. Even so, when I think back on it, I do not have any happy memories of our children.

In Vietnam, if a son refused to obey his parents, they might throw him out and say that he should never see them again. When they died, he would not be allowed to come back for the ceremonies, nor would he be allowed to wear symbols of mourning. In any family, most children are obedient, but I know many people who have been disowned. Sometimes parents relent when it is a son they have dismissed; for girls, disobedience is unforgivable.

These rules were strictly enforced in Vietnam. In America, the problem is that we emphasize control of children, while Americans emphasize their freedom.

QUESTIONS FOR DISCUSSION

1. Mention some of the differences in standards Vietnamese parents have for their sons and for their daughters. What is the source of most of the difficulty that the narrator had with his children? What advice did his eldest son receive from an American counselor?
2. The narrator has experienced difficulty in one way or another with all but one of his children's choices for marriage partners. Does he feel the American value system is totally responsible for these difficulties? Explain.
3. This memoir is not without humor. Try to find examples of the author's sense of humor. (One such example appears in his response to a German woman in paragraph 11.)

WRITING ASSIGNMENTS

1. Reaction Journal: Review some of the ideas you mentioned in your freewriting. Write an essay about conflict in generational values you may have experienced with your own parents. Discuss this issue with your parents. Were their values different from those of their parents?
2. Interview a peer whose parents are immigrants. Then write an essay discussing how cultural values may or may not complicate the conflict in values between generations. Feel free to borrow from this selection as you develop your essay.
3. The narrator concedes that parental standards in his Vietnamese culture are different for sons than they are for daughters. In effect, he admits to a cultural double standard based on gender. Write an essay in which you discuss your own family's attitudes toward gender.

THE BEGINNING

SHIRLEY ANN GRAU

Shirley Ann Grau (b. 1929), born in New Orleans and educated at Tulane, is a novelist and short story writer whose writing has won praise for its presentation of Louisiana local color and for its treatment of the problems of race. She has published several novels, including The Keepers of the House *(1964),* The Hard Blue Sky *(1960), and* The Condor Passes *(1971), and three collections of short stories,* The Black Prince *(1955),* The Wind Shifting West *(1973), and* Nine Women *(1986). "The Beginning" tells the story of a young black girl of illegitimate birth raised by a single mother whose talent, resilience, and strength of character foster in the girl an abiding sense of self-worth.*

◆ FREEWRITING

Imagine yourself back in your preschool or early elementary school years. Try to assume the voice of that young child. Freewrite for ten or fifteen minutes on the relationship you remember you had with one of your parents or with a care-giver. Include specific incidents that help to explain the relationship.

In the beginning there was just my mother and me.

"You are," my mother would say, "the queen of the world, the jewel of the lotus, the pearl without price, my secret treasure."

She whispered words like that, singsonging them in her soft high voice that had a little tiny crackle in it like a scratched record, to comfort me when I was a baby. Her light high whisper threaded through all my days, linking them tightly together, from the day of my birth, from that first moment when I slid from her body to lie in the softness of her bed, the same bed she slept in now. The one we took with us from place to place. And there were many different places. We were wanderers, my mother and I. I even had a wicker basket for my toys; I would pack and carry them myself.

It mattered little to me where we lived. I did not go outside. I did not go for walks, nor play on park swings. On the one day my mother was home, on Sunday, we worked together, all the while she sang her murmured song to me. Secret treasure. Lotus flower. And in her murmuring way she told me all she knew about my father, a Hindu from Calcutta, a salesman of Worthington pumps. Of all the many men my mother had known, he was the only one she had loved. She told me about his thin face and his large eyes black as oil, and his skin that was only slightly lighter than her own.

"You have his eyes and his skin," she said as, after my bath, she rubbed me 5
with oil. (It was baby oil, its vanilla scent soon lost in her heavier perfume.) "And you have his hair," she said, combing in more oil.

And there is, to be sure, a certain look of India about me. Even now, in the grown woman.

"You are a little queen," my mother would say, turning me around and around. "You are exquisite, a princess of all the world. You must have a lovely new dress."

And so I would. She made all my clothes, made and designed. Summer dresses of handkerchief linen and soft smooth voile, winter dresses of dark rich velvets, and monk's-cloth coats so heavily smocked across the shoulders they were almost waterproof.

Of course we couldn't afford to buy fabrics like that, not in those days. My mother worked as a stock girl for Lambert Brothers Department Store. She had worked there for years, even before I was born. Ever since she'd come out of the country. (That was the way she put it, as if it were the bottom of a well or a deep hole.) And Lambert Brothers provided our material, quite a lot of it over the years. It all began on a city bus when my mother met a clerk from the Perfection Cloth Shoppe. They began talking, casually at first and then with purpose. My mother exchanged a bottle of perfume or a box of dusting powder or some Lancôme lipsticks from Lambert Brothers for small lengths of expensive material from the Perfection Cloth Shoppe.

My mother never told me how she smuggled the cosmetics out of the store. 10
I suppose she'd been there so long and so faithfully that they half-trusted her. She did tell me how she and her friend robbed the Perfection Cloth Shoppe—a simple plan that worked for years.

My mother's friend collected the fabrics over a period of weeks, hiding them among the hundreds of stacked bolts. When she saw her chance, she bundled the pieces tightly and dropped them in a box of trash, making a small red check on the outside. My mother had only to pass along the service drive at the back of the building, look for the mark, remove the package. That evening we spread out the material on our kitchen table (the only table we had) and admired it together. Only once did something go wrong. Once the trash was collected an hour earlier than usual and my beautiful dress went to the city incinerator. My mother and I managed to laugh about that.

During those early years, during the long dull hours checking stock in dusty rooms, my mother began planning a business of her own, as dressmaker. My stolen clothes were the beginning. I was her model, the body on which her work came to life, the living sketchbook. Too small to see above the knees of adults, but perfectly quiet and perfectly composed, I displayed her clothes. My mother did not need to teach me how to walk or to act. Remember your father is an Indian prince and you are his only daughter, she would say to me. And so we made our rounds, peddling our wares, much like my father and his Worthington pumps. If he had traveled farther, half a world, our merchandise was far more beautiful. My mother and I went to talent shows and beauty contests, to church services and choir rehearsals. Wherever ladies gathered and the admission was free, there we were. My mother sold her clothes, as it were, from off my back.

"We are selling very well in the Afro-American community," my mother would say. "Soon I will open a small showroom. The walls will be painted white and the only thing on them will be pictures of you. On every wall, the entire way around."

And eventually she did just that. I remember it very clearly, the white room, quite bare and businesslike and lined with pictures of me. They were color photographs, very expensive for a woman just starting in business, but they showed the details of the clothes beautifully. My face, I remember, was rather blurred, but the light always seemed to catch the smooth line of my long dark hair. When I modeled for the customers (seated in creaking folding chairs and reeking with conflicting perfumes), my hair was always swept forward over one shoulder. My mother ironed it carefully in the dressing room at the very last moment. I remember the glare of the naked light bulbs around the mirror and the smell of singeing as my mother pressed my hair on her ironing board.

I don't remember saying a single word at any time. I have since noticed that people usually speak to a child, but no one spoke to me. Perhaps they did not think I was quite real.

Twice a month, in the evenings, my mother did her books. For years these were my favorite times. I sat, in my nightgown (always ankle length, always with a drawn-lace yoke), in the corner of the sofa, its red velvet worn and prickling on the sides of my arms, and watched my mother with her checkbooks and her account books and her order books. I watched her pencil picking away at the pages, flicking, stabbing, moving. She was a very good bookkeeper. In different circumstances I suppose she would have gone to college and earned a CPA to put behind her name. But she didn't. She just remained somebody who was very quick with numbers. And there was another strange thing about her, though I didn't notice it until many years later. She was so good with figures, she spoke so very well in soft tones as soothing as a cough lozenge—but she could hardly read at all. She wasn't illiterate, but she read street signs and phone books, business forms and contracts all the same way: carefully, taking a very long time, sounding out the words. As a child, I thought that muttering was the way everyone read. (The nuns at school soon corrected me.) Eventually I just fell asleep on the old sofa with that comforting whispering lullaby in my ears.

When my mother picked me up to carry me to bed, which was next to hers, she would always be smiling. "The figures dance so beautifully for me, my little love. The Afro-American community is contributing devotedly to the treasure of the mahal. The daughters saw her and blessed her, also the queens and the concubines." (Someone had once read the Bible to my mother; bits and pieces kept appearing in her talk.)

In the morning when I woke, she was gone. At first, when I was very small, when I first remember things, like wet diapers and throwing up in my bed, there was someone who stayed with me, an old old woman who sat in a rocker all day long and listened to the radio. Her name was Miss Beauty. I don't remember her ever feeding me, but I suppose she must have. She died one day, in her rocking chair. I thought she was asleep so I went on playing with my doll. My cat—we kept one to kill the mice that played all over the old house—jumped on Miss Beauty's lap, then jumped down again quickly, coming to sit next to me in the window. "You heard her snore," I whispered to the cat, very severely. "Don't wake her, she won't like that at all." At the usual time I heard my mother's key in the lock and the funny little nine-note tune she whistled every evening just inside the door. (It was from *Lucia di Lammermoor*, I discovered years later in a college music appreciation class, and I rose in my seat with the impact of memory.) I put my finger to my lips and pointed silently to Miss Beauty. My mother hesitated, eyes flicking between us, nose wrinkling like an animal. Without moving, she bent forward toward Miss Beauty. Then quickly, so quickly, with a clatter of feet across the linoleum floor, she snatched me up and ran outside.

After Miss Beauty's death, there was no one. I stayed by myself. We moved to a nicer neighborhood, a street with trees and double cottages behind small front gardens. (The landlord had paved over our garden with pale green cement.) I never felt afraid. If I got lonely, I could sit in the big front window and watch the neighborhood children play in the street. I never joined them.

During these years I do not remember my mother having any friends. I re- 20
member only one visitor. He was short and wore a plaid coat and a wide-brimmed hat, and the ring on his left hand flashed colored lights. He was waiting for my mother when she came home after work. They talked briefly, standing at the curb next to his big white car, then the two of them came into the house. He smiled at me, saying, "Well, well, now, is that your little girl? Hello there, little girl." My mother went straight to the red sofa, reached inside the top cushion. When she turned around, there was a gun in her hand. She just stood there, her long fingers wrapped around that small dull-blue gun, both hands holding it firm and steady. The man stopped smiling and backed out the door. He never said another word. Nor did my mother.

We moved again then, away from the house with the front yard of green-tinted cement. This time we packed and moved quickly, far away across town. My mother rented a truck and she hired two men to load it for us. She hurried them too. Our beds, the red velvet sofa, the two folding bridge chairs, the refrigerator and the gas stove, the enamel-topped kitchen table, the armoire with the cracked mirrored doors—they fitted neatly into the truck along with the boxes of clothes and dishes and my mother's sewing machine, which was the only new thing we owned.

"Hurry," my mother said, carrying some of the smaller things herself, "we haven't got all day. I am paying you to be quick."

Grumbling and complaining, the men finished the loading and took their money and stood on the sidewalk to watch us leave.

"Get in," my mother said to me. "Be quick."

We drove down highways lined with withered brown palm trees, past endless intersections where traffic lights stabbed out their signals like lighthouses. We waited, part of an impatient horn-blowing crowd, while canal bridges opened to let gravel-filled barges glide past through oily water.

And my mother said nothing at all. When I could wait no longer, when the silence between us seemed more dangerous and frightening than any nightmare, I asked, "Why are we running away?"

"To be safe," she said.

"Is it far?"

"It is far enough to be safe," she said.

When we finally reached the place where we would live, she hired two more neighborhood men to take our things up the stairs. She had moved without leaving a trace behind.

I guessed it had something to do with her visitor, but I did not worry. In all the stories my mother had told me, there were always threats and pursuits and enemies to be avoided. It was the way a princess lived. And my mother was always there, to bring me to safety at last.

When we sat in our new home, in the clutter of boxes and furniture, when we were safely inside, the door locked behind us, my mother smiled at me, a great slow smile that showed square strong teeth in the smooth darkness of her face. "My hidden princess," she said, "my lotus flower. . ."

The accustomed endearments tumbled from her lips, the expected exotic song of love and praise. I, young as I was, noted the change. For the past few days, and on the drive across town, she had spoken rarely, and then only in the crisp blunt language of everyday.

Now, by the smooth soft flow of her words, I knew that we were indeed safe. We had passed through a series of lodgings—I think I remember them all, even the one where I was born, the one with a chinaberry tree outside the window—but we had finally gained our castle, the one we had been searching for. There was even a turret, to command the approaches and to defend against enemies.

The house stood on a corner. Its old clapboard walls rose directly from the sidewalk through two stories of flaking gray paint to a roof decorated with fancy wooden scallops; in the dark spaces under the eaves generations of pigeons nested and fluttered. At the second-floor corner, jutting over the sidewalk, was a small turret or tower, capped with a high pointed roof like a clown's hat.

Inside the tower was a hinged seat of varnished wood entirely covered by scratch drawings: flowers and initials and hearts, dancing stick figures and even a face or two. Here we stored odd bits of things: old shoes, an umbrella with a broken rib, a doll in a pink and blue gingham dress, an Easter bunny of purple and yellow plush, a black patent purse. Roaches lived there too; they ate the stuffing from the doll and the feather from her hat, and they ate spots of fur from the Easter bunny so that it looked burned. I thought they had also nibbled the edge of the patent leather purse, but my mother said no, it was just useworn.

Day after day, I sat on top that jumble of things, above the secret workings of insects, and I watched through the windows, three panes of glass on the three sides of my tower, which my mother washed every month, so that I might see clearly.

Most of the floor below us was occupied by a drugstore, a small dark place that smelled of disinfectant and sugar candy, of brown paper and cough medicine. On two of the other corners were small houses, one room wide, perched off the ground on low brick foundations and edged by foot-wide runners of grass. On the third corner, directly across from my window was Providence Manor, a home for the old. A tall iron fence enclosed an entire block of grass and trees and even occasional blooming flowers, a wilderness that stretched out of my sight. Just inside the fence was a gravel path where, on good days, the old people walked, some slowly on canes, some with arms flexing rapidly in a military march, some in chairs wheeled by nuns in black habits and white headdresses. They rotated past the spear points of the fence, every good day taking their quota of sun and exhaust-laden air. After dark, on rainy nights, the flashing sign in the drugstore window beat against those railings, broke and ran off down the shiny black street.

Downstairs too, directly below, in our small slice of the old house, were the two rooms that were my mother's workshop and showroom. On our front door—up two wooden steps from the uneven brick sidewalk—was a small neat sign: MODISTE. My mother had lettered that herself; she had always been very clever with her hands. It was the first real shop she had.

I spent my days either at my window or in my mother's workrooms. The rest of the house, the other two rooms, I don't remember at all. I was either a princess in my tower or a mannequin in my mother's clothes.

Not until years later did I realize that all the faces I saw were black. (To me they had no color, no color at all.) The people walking on the street, the old on their therapeutic rounds, the Sisters of the Holy Family, the drivers impatiently threading their way through the heavy street traffic, my mother and her customers—they all wore black skin.

As did the children in school. Eventually I had to go to school. My mother did not send me when I was six, as the law said she must. For one extra year I dreamed and flaunted my beautiful dresses. I doubt that the authorities would have noticed had I not gone to school at all. I think it was my mother's new friend who finally persuaded her. For my mother at last had a friend, a good friend whose visits were regular and predictable. For him my mother bathed and did her hair and cooked specially and smiled when the doorbell rang.

My mother's friend was a tall, heavy man who came to church with us every Sunday and afterwards held my hand as I walked along the top of the low wall that bordered the churchyard. He owned a small cab company—he drove one himself—whose insignia was a lightning bolt across a bright blue circle. His name was David Clark, and he took me to school and picked me up every day of my first year.

I went to parochial school. Navy skirts and white blouses and black and white saddle oxfords, all of us. All of us, rows of little black raisins, waiting to be taught to read and to count and to love Lord Jesus. But I was the only one picked up by taxi every day at three o'clock. The children stared at me as I rode away, the Indian princess in her palanquin, the treasure of the mahal above Leconte's Drugstore.

On the first day of school my mother went with me. I remember very lit- 45
tle about that day—I was nauseated with excitement, gripped with fear—but I remember the dress she wore. She had made it herself of course, just as she had made my school uniform; it was brown linen, a long-sleeved blouse and an eight-gore skirt. I saw the nuns' eyes flick over us in brief appraisal: we passed with honors. (I took it as my due. I wonder now how my mother felt.)

The school smelled of peanuts and garlic bologna. The floor of my classroom was spotted with puddles of slimy liquid. Oddly enough, the other children's panic quieted me. In the reek of their nervousness, my own stomach settled, and when the harried janitor arrived with a bucket of sawdust to sprinkle on the vomit, I helped him by pushing aside the desks.

That first day was the longest I have ever known. And the hottest. It was early September and the afternoon sun burned through the window shades to polish our faces with sweat—all except the teaching sister. Her face remained dry and dull as if coated with a film of dust.

I never grew used to the noise and rush of children leaving class. When the bell sounded, I always waited while the room emptied. Then, in a pause disturbed only by the soft sounds of the teacher gathering her papers, I walked slowly through the door, last and alone. Always alone, except for once, years later when I was at boarding school at St. Mary's, mine the only dark face in a sea of Irish skin. (The other girls simply ignored me, saw through me as if I were invisible or transparent.) By the time I had gathered my books and reached the door, their departing backs were far down the hall. But at St. Mary's I was not alone. My companion was a moonfaced child of my own age who had rheumatoid arthritis, took massive doses of cortisone, and moved with the slow painful dignity of an ancient woman. She died in our second year of high school. I, along with every other girl in the school, wrote a letter of condolence to her parents. Mine was never acknowledged.

But that was in the future, in the time when I was no longer a child, a good many years away.

For first grade, I had two skirts, made by my mother according to the uni- 50
form dress code of the parochial school system, and two blouses. Every second day, when I came home, I was expected to wash my blouse carefully, using the kitchen sink and a small scrubbing board that my mother kept underneath, propped against the pipes. I then hung it on the back porch inside the screen, where no bird could soil it. Every so often my mother was dissatisfied with its whiteness and she would wash it again in bleach. The next time I wore that

blouse I was certain to have a rash across my neck and shoulders where the fabric rubbed my skin.

Later on, when my growing required new blouses (the skirts had deep hems to let down), my mother made them slightly different. She added small tucks down the front, two tiny rows on each side of the buttons. I noticed the nuns looking at me—they were very strict about uniforms in those days—and they must have written to my mother. My next blouses were perfectly plain. What the nuns couldn't know about were my slips. My mother made my slips too, and they had all the elaborate decorations that my blouses lacked. They were tucked, with drawn lace and wide bands of crochet at the shoulders, and a deep flounce of lace at the hem. Only one nun ever saw them and she wasn't really a nun. She was a novice: very young, shorter even than I was. She was cleaning the bathrooms and I, not noticing her, was fanning myself with my skirt against the heat. She stopped and fingered my slip. "What lovely work, what exquisite work." Then she looked shocked and ashamed—perhaps she had made a vow of silence —and she went hastily back to her pail and mop.

After the first year at school, I took the city bus home. The stop was at our corner. All I had to do was cross the street and open the door. Once inside, I rushed to bathe, to brush my hair, to put on the dresses that my mother would sell. Wearing her clothes and her dreams, I would move carefully among her customers, gracefully, as only a princess can.

The lotus blossom. The treasure of the mahal. In the women's faces I saw greed and covetousness. My mother's order books rustled busily. I myself drew spirit and sustenance from the flickering eyes and the fingers stretched out to touch. In the small crowded room, I had come into my castle and my kingdom.

And so I passed my childhood disguised to myself as a princess. I thrived, grew strong and resilient. When the kingdom at last fell and the castle was conquered, and I lost my crown and my birthright, when I stood naked and revealed as a young black female of illegitimate birth, it hardly mattered. By then the castle and the kingdom were within me and I carried them away.

QUESTIONS FOR DISCUSSION

1. Who was the persona's father? What do we learn about the relationship between the mother and father? What do we learn about the friendships and relationships the persona had with people other than her mother?

2. Most of the child's memories reflect a happy childhood. What clues do we have that all was not so happy? What does the narrative point of view have to do with this discrepancy?

3. When does the persona become aware of the color of her skin? Describe the circumstances that led to the discovery.

WRITING ASSIGNMENTS

1. Reaction Journal: Grau separates her final paragraph from the story by chronology and tone as well as by visual spacing. Write a paragraph or two explaining why you feel the closing strengthens or weakens the story.

2. The voice of the child in this story is typical of early childhood in that it looks at the world with a positive if limited vision. Write an essay in which you discuss the clues in the story that suggest all is not as pleasant as the child's voice suggests.

SECRETS AND ANGER

DAVID MURA

David Mura (b. 1952) is a third-generation Japanese-American who grew up near Chicago and now lives in St. Paul, Minnesota. He has published a collection of poetry, After We Lost Our Way *(1989), and two nonfiction works,* A Male Grief: Notes on Pornography and Addiction *(1987) and* Turning Japanese: Memoirs of a Sansei *(1991). He is working on an autobiographical book about Asian-Americans and race. In the following essay, Mura, who is married to a white woman, explains how having to decide how to raise his daughter has forced him to face questions of race and identity. "Secrets and Anger" appeared in* Mother Jones *in 1992.*

◆ FREEWRITING

Mura, a Japanese-American married to a white woman, wrote this essay on the occasion of the birth of their daughter. Early in the essay he says, "I sense that the world Samantha's inheriting won't be dominated by the melting-pot model, that multiculturalism is not a project but a reality." Respond to this assertion as you freewrite for ten or fifteen minutes.

On the day our daughter was born, as my wife, Susie, and I waited for the doctor to do a cesarean section, we talked about names. Standing at the window, I looked out and said, "Samantha, the day you were born was a gray and blustery day." We decided on Samantha Lyn, after my sisters, Susan Lynn and Lynda. I felt to give the baby a Japanese name might mark her as too different, especially since we live in St. Paul, where Asian Americans are a small minority. I had insisted that her last name be hyphenated, Sencer-Mura. My wife had argued that such a name was unwieldy. "What happens when Samantha Sencer-Mura marries Bob Rodriguez-Stein?" she asked. "That's her generation's problem," I said, laughing.

I sometimes wish now we'd given her a Japanese middle name, as Susie had wanted. Perhaps it's because I sense that the world Samantha's inheriting won't be dominated by the melting-pot model, that multiculturalism is not a project but a reality, that in the next century there will no longer be a white majority in this country. Or perhaps I simply feel guilty about having given in to the dominant culture once again.

I am working on a poem about my daughter, about trying to take in her presence, her life, about trying to link her with my sense of the past—my father and mother, the internment camps, my grandparents. I picture myself serving her sukiyaki, a dish I shunned as a child, and her shouting for more rice, brandishing her *hashi* (a word for chopsticks, which I never used as a child and only began to use after my trip to Japan). As I describe Samantha running through the garden, scattering petals, squashing tomatoes, I suddenly think of how someone someday will call her a "gook," that I know this with more certainty than I know she'll find happiness in love.

I speak to my wife about moving out to the West Coast or to Hawaii, where there would be more Asian Americans. In Hawaii, more than a third of the children are *happa* (mixed race); Samantha would be the norm, not the minority. I need to spend more time living in an Asian-American community: I can't tell its stories if I'm not a part of it. As I talk about moving one evening, Susie starts to feel uneasy. "I'm afraid you'll cross this bridge and take Sam with you, and leave me here," she says.

"But I've lived all my life on your side of the bridge. At most social gatherings, I'm the only person of color in the room. What's wrong with living awhile on my side of the bridge? What keeps you from crossing?" 5

Susie, a pediatric oncologist, works with families of all colors. Still, having a hybrid daughter is changing her experience. Often when she's in the grocery with Sam, someone will come up to her and say: "Oh, she's such a beautiful little girl. Where did you get her?" This has happened so often Susie swears she's going to teach Sam to say: "Fuck you. My genes came all the way over on the *Mayflower*, thank you."

These incidents mark ways Susie has experienced something negative over race that I have not. No one asks me where Sam came from: they assume I'm her father. For Susie, the encounters are a challenge to her position as Samantha's biological mother, the negation of an arduous pregnancy and the physical work of birth and motherhood. For me, they stir an old wound. The people who mistake Sam for an adopted child can't picture a white woman married to an Asian man.

Six ways of viewing identity: Identity is a social and historical construction. Identity is formed by political and economic and cultural exigencies. Identity is a fiction. Identity is a choice. Identity may appear unitary but is always fragmentary. Identity is deciding to acknowledge or not acknowledge political and economic and cultural exigencies.

When I address the question of raising my daughter, I address the question of her identity, which means I address the question of my identity, her mother's, our parents', and so on. But this multiplication of the self takes place along many lines. Who knows where it stops? At my grandparents? At the woman in the grocery store? At you, the imagined reader of this piece?

In the matrix of race and color in our society, there is the binary opposition 10
of black and white. And then there are the various Others, determined by race or culture or gender or sexual preference—Native Americans, Hispanic Americans, Asian Americans, Japanese Americans, women, men, heterosexuals, homosexuals. None of these definitions stands alone; together they form an intricate, mazelike weave that's impossible to disentangle.

I wrote my memoir, *Turning Japanese*, to explore the cultural amnesia of Japanese Americans, particularly those of the third generation, like myself, who speak little or no Japanese. When I give readings, people often ask if I'm going to raise Samantha with a greater awareness of Japanese culture than I received as a child. The obvious answer is yes. I also acknowledge that the prospects of teaching her about Japanese culture feel to me rather daunting, and I now have more sympathy for my nisei parents, whom I used to criticize for forgetting the past.

And yet, near the end of my stay in Japan, I decided that I was not Japanese, that I was never going to be Japanese, and that I was not even going to be an expert on Japanese culture. My identity was as a Japanese American. That meant claiming the particularities of Japanese-American history; it meant coming to terms with how the dominant culture had formed me; it meant realizing my identity would always be partially occluded. Finally, it meant that the issues of race were central to me, that I would see myself as a person of color.

Can I teach these things to my daughter? My Japanese-American identity comes from my own experience. But I am still trying to understand that experience and still struggling to find language to talk about the issues of race. My failures are caused by more than a lack of knowledge; there's the powerful wish not to know. How, for instance, can I talk to my daughter about sexuality and race? My own life is so filled with shame and regret, so filled with experiences I would rather not discuss, that it seems much easier to opt for silence. It's simpler to pretend multiculturalism means teaching her *kanji* and how to conjugate Japanese verbs.

I know that every day Samantha will be exposed to images telling her that Asian bodies are marginalized, that the women are exotic or sensual or submissive, that the men are houseboys or Chinatown punks, kung fu warriors or Japanese businessmen—robotlike and powerful or robotlike and comic. I know that she will face constant pressure to forget that she is part Japanese American, to assume a basically white middle-class identity. When she reaches adolescence, there will be strong messages for her to dissociate herself from other people of color, perhaps from the children of recent Asian immigrants. She may find herself wanting to assume a privilege and status that come from not calling attention to her identity or from playing into the stereotype that makes Asian women seem so desirable to certain white men. And I know I will have no power over these forces.

Should I tell her of how, when I look at her mother, I know my desire for her cannot be separated from the way the culture has inculcated me with standards of white beauty? Should I tell her of my own desire for a "hallucinatory whiteness," of how in my twenties such a desire fueled a rampant promiscuity and addiction to pornography, to the "beautiful" bodies of white women? It's all too much to expect Samantha to take in. It should not even be written down. It should be kept hidden, unspoken. These forces should not exist.

Samantha's presence has made me more willing to speak out on issues of race, to challenge the status quo. I suppose I want her to inherit a different world than the one I grew up in.

One day last year, I was talking with two white friends about the landmark controversy over the Broadway production of *Miss Saigon.* Like many Asian Americans, I agreed with the protest by Actor's Equity against the producer's casting. I felt disturbed that again a white actor, the British Jonathan Pryce, was playing a Eurasian and that no Asian-American actor had been given a chance to audition for that role. Beyond that, I was upset by the Madame Butterfly plot of *Miss Saigon,* where an Asian woman pines for her white male lover.

Both my friends—Paula, a painter, and Mark, a writer—consider themselves liberals; Mark was active in the antiwar movement during the sixties. He was part of my wedding and, at the time, perhaps my closest male friend. But neither agreed with me about *Miss Saigon.* They argued that art represented freedom of the imagination, that it meant trying to get inside other people's skin. Isn't color-blind casting what we're striving for? they said.

"Why is it everyone gets so upset when a white actor may be denied a role?" I asked. "What about every time an Asian-American actor tries out for a part that says 'lawyer' or 'doctor' and is turned down?"

But reverse discrimination isn't the answer, they replied.

I don't recall exactly what happened after this. I think the argument trailed off into some safer topic, as such arguments often do. But afterward, I felt angrier and angrier and, at the same time, more despairing. I realized that for me the fact that Warner Oland, a Swede, played Charlie Chan was humiliating. It did not show me that art was a democracy of the imagination. But for Paula and Mark, my sense of shame was secondary to their belief in "freedom" in the arts.

When I talked to my wife about my anger and despair, she felt uncomfortable. These were her friends, too. She said I'd argued before with them about the role of politics in art. Mark had always looked ruefully at his political involvement in the sixties, when he felt he had gone overboard with his zealous self-righteousness. "He's threatened by your increasing political involvement," Susie said. She felt I should take our disagreement as just another incident in a long friendly dialogue.

But when I talked with a black friend, Garth, who's a writer, he replied: "Yeah, I was surprised too at the reaction of some of my white artist friends to *Miss Saigon.* It really told me where they were. It marked a dividing line."

For a while, I avoided talking about my feelings when Paula and Mark came by. Susie urged me to talk to them, to work it out. "You're trying to get me to have sympathy with how difficult this is for them or for you, how this creates tensions between you and them," I said. "But I have to have this conversation about *Miss Saigon* with every white friend I have. Each of you only has to have it with me." My wife said that I was taking my anger out on her—which, in part, I was.

Finally, in a series of telephone calls, I told Paula and Mark I not only felt that their views about *Miss Saigon* were wrong but that they were racially based. In the emotionally charged conversations, I don't think I used the word "racist," but I know my friends objected to my lumping them together with other whites. Paula said I was stereotyping them, that she wasn't like other whites. She told me of her friendships with a few blacks when she lived back East, of the history of her mother's involvement in supporting civil rights. "It's not like I don't know what discrimination is," she said. "Women get discriminated against, so do artists." Her tone moved back and forth between self-righteousness and resentment to distress and tears about losing our friendship.

Mark talked of his shame about being a WASP. "Do you know that I don't have a single male friend who is a WASP?" he said. I decided not to point out that, within the context of color, the difference between a WASP male and, say, an Irish Catholic, isn't much of a difference. And I also didn't remark that he had no friends of color, other than myself. I suppose I felt such remarks would hurt him too much. I also didn't feel it was safe to say them.

A few months later, I had calmer talks with Mark, but they always ended with this distance between us. I needed some acknowledgment from him that, when we began talking about race I knew more about it than he did, that our arguing about race was not the same as our arguing about free verse versus formal verse. That my experience gave me insights he didn't have.

"Of course, that's true," he said. "I know you've had different experiences." But for him, we had to meet on an equal basis, where his views on race were considered at the start as just as valid as mine. Otherwise, he felt he was compromising himself, giving away his soul. He likened it to the way he gave away his self in his alcoholic family, where he denied his own feelings. He would be making himself a "victim" again.

At one point, I suggested we do some sessions with a therapist who was counseling him and whom I had also gone to. "No," said Mark. "I can't do that now. I need him on my side."

I can still see us sitting there on my front steps, on a warm early-spring day. 30
I looked at this man with whom I'd shared my writing and my most intimate secrets, with whom I'd shared the process of undergoing therapy and recovery, and I realized we were now no longer intimates. I felt that I had embarked on a journey to discover myself as a person of color, to discover the rage and pain that had formed my Japanese-American identity, and that he would deny me this journey. He saw me as someone who would make him a victim, whose feelings on race were charged with arrogance and self-righteousness. And yet, on some level, I know he saw that my journey was good for me. I felt I was asking him to come on that journey with me.

Inevitably I wonder if my daughter will understand my perspective as a person of color. Will she identify with white friends, and be fearful and suspicious of my anger and frustration? Or will she be working from some viewpoint I can't quite conceive, some line that marks her as a person of color and white and neither, all at the same time, as some new being whose experiences I will have to listen to and learn from? How can I prepare her for that new identity?

Will it be fair or accurate or helpful for me to tell her, "Unless the world is radically different, on some level, you will still have to choose: Are you a person of color or not?"

It took me months to figure out what had gone down with Paula and Mark. Part of me wanted to let things go, but part of me knew that someday I'd have to talk to Samantha about race. If I avoided what was difficult in my own life, what would I be able to say to her? My black friend Alexs and I talked about how whites desperately want to do "the victim limbo," as he called it. Offered by many as a token of solidarity—"I'm just the same as you"—it's really a way of depoliticizing the racial question; it ignores the differences in power in this country that result from race.

When white people engage in conversation about racism, the first thing they often do, as Paula did with me, is the victim limbo: "I'm a woman, I know what prejudice is, I've experienced it." "I'm Jewish/working class/Italian in a WASP neighborhood, I know what prejudice is." The purpose of this is to show the person of color that he or she doesn't really experience anything the white person hasn't experienced, that the white person is a victim too. But Alexs and I both knew that the positions of a person of color and a white person in American society are not the same. "Whites don't want to give up their privilege and psychic comforts," said Alexs. "That's really why they're so angry. They have to choose whether they're going to give up power or fight for it."

Thinking this through, though, does not assuage the pain and bitterness I 35
feel about losing white friendships over race, or the distance I have seen open up between me and my white friends. Nor does it help me explain to my daughter

why we no longer see Paula or Mark. The compensation has been the numerous friendships that I've begun to have with people of color. My daughter will grow up in a household where the people who visit will be from a wider spectrum than were those Japanese Americans and whites who visited my parents' house in the suburbs of Chicago.

Not that teaching her about her Asian-American self has become any easier. My wife has been more conscious than I've been about telling Sam that she's Japanese. After playing with blond Shannon, the girl from next door, Sam said: "She's not Japanese, Mom. We're Japanese." "No," said Susie. "Daddy's Japanese, and you're part Japanese, but I'm not Japanese." Sam refused to believe this: "No, you're Japanese." After a few minutes, Susie finally sorted out the confusion. Sam thought being Japanese meant you had black hair.

For many liberal whites, what seems most important in any discussion of race is the need for hope, the need to find some link with people of color. They do not see how much that need serves as a tool of denial, how their claims of solidarity not only ignore real differences but also blot out the reality of people of color. How can we move forward, they ask, with all this rage you seem to feel? How can you stereotype me or group me in this category of whiteness?

I tell them they are still unwilling to examine what being white has meant to their existence. They think their rage at being classified as a white person is the same rage that people of color feel when they are being stereotyped. It is not. When whites feel anger about race, almost always they are feeling a threat to their comfort or power.

In the end, whites must exchange a hope based on naiveté and ignorance for one based on knowledge. For this naive hope denies connections, complexities. It is the drug of amnesia. It says there is no thread from one moment to the next, no cause and effect. It denies consequence and responsibility.

40 For my wife, this journey has been a difficult one. The arguments we have over race mirror our other arguments; at the same time, they exist in another realm, where I am a person of color and Susie is white. "I realize that in a way I've been passing too," she said a few months ago. "There's this comfort I've got to give up, this ease." At her clinic, she challenges the mainly white children's books in the waiting room, or a colleague's unconscious assumptions about Hmong families. More and more, she finds herself at gatherings where she as a white person is in the minority.

Breaking through denial, seeing how much needs to be changed, does not have to blunt the capacity for hope. For both of us, our daughter is proof of that capacity. And if I know that someday someone will call Samantha a gook, I know today she's a happy child. The love her mother and I share, the love we bear for her, cannot spare her from pain over race, and yet it can make her stronger. Sam will go further than we will, she will know more. She will be like nothing I can imagine, as I am like nothing my parents imagined.

Today my daughter told me she will grow up and work with her mother at the hospital. I'll be a grandpa and stay home and write poems and be with her children. Neither race nor ethnicity enters into her vision of the future. And yet they are already there, with our hopes, gathering shape.

QUESTIONS FOR DISCUSSION

1. Explain why Susie feels uneasy knowing that her husband may "cross [the] bridge" with Samantha by spending more time with an Asian-American community. Does the essay give reason to suggest her uneasiness is well founded?

2. Explain the logic behind Mura's inability to identify himself as Japanese and his concession that he is Japanese-American. Discuss the differences.

3. How does the controversy over a production of *Miss Saigon* lead to a protracted discussion of race between Mura and his two best white friends?

WRITING ASSIGNMENTS

1. Reaction Journal: At one point in this essay, Mura says he wants his daughter to inherit a different world from the one he lives in. Assume the role of Mura and write a letter to Samantha—a letter she isn't to open until her eighteenth birthday.

2. In paragraph 8 Mura catalogues six ways of viewing identity. Write an essay in which you discuss how Americans determine their individual and collective identities. Try to focus on Mura's concerns for himself and for his daughter. Feel free to incorporate the methods of determining identity he lists in paragraph 8.

Language

THE ROLE OF LANGUAGES other than English in American society has been debated since the country's beginnings. Benjamin Franklin was concerned about the large number of German-speaking immigrants in Pennsylvania, whose lack of English fluency prevented them from understanding and participating as informed citizens in issues of local and national significance. In the early twentieth century, Teddy Roosevelt linked language with national loyalty and unity, warning against the danger of the country's becoming a "polyglot boarding-house." Today the fear of political disunity resulting from linguistic diversity informs some of the arguments of the contemporary English Only movement. James Fallows in "Language" points out that the current high concentrations of Spanish-speaking immigrants, particularly in the American Southwest, raise in some people's minds the specter of separatist movements similar to that in the province of Quebec. Respondents to such arguments point to results of surveys such as the one conducted by the Rand Corporation in 1985 which indicated that 95 percent of American-born Mexican-Americans use English proficiently and that among the second generation more than 50 percent speak no Spanish at all. In light of such evidence, linguist Geoffrey Nunberg has wryly observed that "English needs protecting about as much as crabgrass." Nevertheless, the question of whether or not English needs *de jure* protection as the nation's official language to bolster its obvious *de facto* existence continues to be a major cultural debate. Involved are questions of education, social programs, and the relationship between national and group identity.

U.S. English, an organization founded by the late semanticist and U.S. Senator S. I. Hayakawa, is dedicated to passing a constitutional amendment stating that "the English language shall be the official language of the United States." Its tenets and rationale are set forth in the "U.S. English 1991—National Opinion Survey." U.S. English proponents believe that policies which make it possible for non-English speakers to function in their native languages in this country actually prevent them from becoming fluent in English. As a result they may be consigned to low-paying jobs and prevented from being fully functioning citizens. Although the movement has not been successful on the national level, it has, as Harvey A. Daniels points out in "The Roots of Language Protectionism," been instrumental in the passing of official-English legislation in sixteen states. Daniels sees the movement as "another incident in the long history of American intolerance of immigrants and minorities, another outburst of our fear and hatred of the stranger." Failure to learn English is sometimes regarded as a sign of "intransigence and ingratitude" toward the United States as host country, and in fact Jerre Mangione in "Talking American" describes his Uncle Nino's refusal to learn English as his way of making a statement about his tenuous commitment to the United States. Although there have not yet been significant changes in public policy as a result of English-only legislation, some argue that the existence of such laws provides sanction for preventing access to medical, legal, and other social services to non-English speakers. Perhaps the most visible arena for the language debate is public education.

There are three basic options for schooling second-language children: "sink or swim," English as a Second Language (ESL) instruction, and bilingual education. The "sink or swim" method involves mainstreaming second-language students into classes with native English speakers and hoping they will not fall too far behind in content learning while they pick up the new language. ESL instruction provides students with specially trained teachers who present to them a modified curriculum in English while focusing primarily on developing their language skills. In bilingual programs, instruction is provided in the students' native languages in content areas where their lack of English proficiency would retard if not actually prevent mastery of those subjects. Generally, ESL instruction is offered at the same time so that students are working toward English proficiency while keeping up with grade-appropriate content in their native languages. A range of responses to these programs from teachers, parents, and students reflects a number of factors, including political and economic considerations, ethnocentrism, funding, and the contradictory concerns about loss of ethnic identity and prospects for the future without a strong base in English. Fallows examines some of the commonly voiced arguments for and against bilingual education, concluding that "bilingual education is inflammatory in large part because of what it symbolizes, not because of the nuts and bolts of its daily operation." While most Mexican-American parents, according to Fallows, view bilingual education simply as a means of learning English, Spanish-speaking activists may view it as a symbol of long overdue acknowledgment of their cultural presence. Many non-Hispanic Americans, responding to this self-assertion, see it as a threat of nonassimilation leading to the eventual breakdown of national unity. Rosalie Pedalino Porter, disillusioned by her training and experience as a Transitional Bilingual teacher, raises as an additional concern the possibility that biculturalism in schools can serve in effect to resegregate "children along language and ethnic lines."

The relaxing of racial and ethnic quotas by the Immigration and Nationality amendments of 1965 and the resulting flood of new immigrants chiefly from the Third World exacerbated the problem of how best to educate large numbers of students with no English or limited English proficiency. The language debate as it relates to the schools involves not only questions of how to communicate curricular content (including English language) but also questions of the extent to which the curriculum should be altered to reflect the ethnic-cultural backgrounds of various student populations. The latter issue is frequently framed as the question that asks if culture maintenance is the job of the public schools. Thus, efficiency of learning and of acculturation is not always the primary focus of the debate, as language comes to be seen as representing a cluster of cultural issues revolving around ethnic identity. The extent to which other languages and cultures are welcomed in the schools can come to symbolize the affirmation or denigration of identities, the extending or denying of opportunities. Just as Paule Marshall in "From the Poets in the Kitchen" tells of the absence of any mention of African-American writers or historical figures during her grade school education, so Latinos, Chicanos, Asian-Americans, and other ethnic groups find the absence of representatives of their language tradition in their own education a loss. Marshall relates that it was only after she accidentally came across a volume of poetry by Paul Laurence Dunbar and recognized the experiences he was describing as her own that she began to dream of one day becoming a writer.

That one's experiences are not only expressed in but to some extent shaped by the language one speaks—language that is intimately associated with one's identity—emerges as a theme in this chapter. Marshall, reminiscing about the "rich legacy of language and culture" gleaned from the conversation of her mother and her mother's friends, observes that these women transformed the English learned in their Barbados schools into their own compelling and uniquely expressive idiom, with its distinctive rhythm, cadence, syntax, metaphors. This creative use of language was, she claims, empowering for those who in other areas of their lives were "the female counterpart of Ralph Ellison's invisible man," and it became for her an important means of connecting with her own culture. Similarly Jerre Mangione, explaining his immigrant mother's insistence that the family speak only Italian at home, says that for her, giving up her native tongue would have been equivalent to "renouncing her own flesh and blood." This connection between language and identity and the ways in which language defines a world of culture and relationships emerges as well when Richard Rodriguez recalls the feeling of intimacy associated with the sounds of the Spanish language in his home. When his parents spoke to him, he felt "embraced by the sounds of their words," sounds that said, "You belong here. We are family members. Related. Special to one another."

The psychological, political, and cultural issues that inform the language debate preclude the possibility of easy workable solutions. There seems to be no question that English is, in fact, the language of the United States, though it is not so mandated by the Constitution. The tough questions facing educators and policymakers now include how best to improve literacy in English among both immigrants and other minority groups while at the same time encouraging an enlightened recognition that knowledge of more than one language is a personal and national resource rather than a handicap.

LANGUAGE

JAMES FALLOWS

James Fallows (b. 1949), currently the Washington editor of The Atlantic, *graduated from Harvard in 1970 and studied economic development at Oxford as a Rhodes scholar. From 1977 to 1979 he was President Jimmy Carter's chief speechwriter. Fallows is the author of many articles and of* National Defense *(1981), which deals with the technology of modern warfare, and* More Like Us: Making America Great Again *(1989), which considers the connections between culture and economic performance. The following is a selection from his lengthy article "Immigration: How It's Affecting Us," which appeared in* The Atlantic *in 1983. In it, Fallows traces the evolution of his own thinking on the related issues of multilingualism and bilingual education as threats to national unity in the United States. Examining the facts of previous generations' linguistic assimilation and the goals of current bilingual and intensive-English programs in the schools, Fallows comes to understand the extent to which symbolism informs and clouds the issues in debates over the linguistic future of this country.*

◆ FREEWRITING

One of the many reasons non-English speaking residents of the United States are reluctant to give up their primary language has to do with the close connection they feel exists between their language and their culture. On the other hand, many English-speaking residents see such reluctance as a threat of nonassimilation leading to the eventual breakdown of national unity. Freewrite for ten or fifteen minutes on the issue of language and national identity.

Assume for the moment that legal immigrants make an economy more efficient. Does that tell us all we need to know in order to understand the impact on our society? A national culture is held together by official rules and informal signals. Through their language, dress, taste, and habits of life, immigrants initially violate the rules and confuse the signals. The United States has prided itself on building a nation out of diverse parts. *E Pluribus Unum* originally referred to the act of political union in which separate colonies became one sovereign state. It now seems more fitting as a token of the cultural adjustments through which immigrant strangers have become Americans. Can the assimilative forces still prevail?

The question arises because most of today's immigrants share one trait: their native language is Spanish.

From 1970 to 1978, the three leading sources of legal immigrants to the U.S. were Mexico, the Philippines, and Cuba. About 42 percent of legal immigration during the seventies was from Latin America. It is thought that about half of all illegal immigrants come from Mexico, and 10 to 15 percent more from elsewhere in Latin America. Including illegal immigrants makes all figures imprecise, but it seems reasonable to conclude that more than half the people who now come to the United States speak Spanish. This is a greater concentration of immigrants in one non-English language group than ever before.

Is it a threat? The conventional wisdom about immigrants and their languages is that the Spanish-speakers are asking for treatment different from that which has been accorded to everybody else. In the old days, it is said, immigrants were eager to assimilate as quickly as possible. They were placed, sink or swim, in English-language classrooms, and they swam. But now the Latin Americans seem to be insisting on bilingual classrooms and ballots. "The Hispanics demand that the United States become a bilingual country, with all children entitled to be taught in the language of their heritage, at public expense," Theodore White has written. Down this road lie the linguistic cleavages that have brought grief to other nations.

This is the way many people think, and this is the way I myself thought as I 5
began this project.

The historical parallel closest to today's concentration of Spanish-speaking immigrants is the German immigration of the nineteenth century. From 1830 to 1890, 4.5 million Germans emigrated to the United States, making up one third of the immigrant total. The Germans recognized that command of English would finally ensure for them, and especially for their children, a place in the mainstream of American society. But like the Swedes, Dutch, and French before them, they tried hard to retain the language in which they had been raised.

The midwestern states, where Germans were concentrated, established bilingual schools, in which children could receive instruction in German. In Ohio, German-English public schools were in operation by 1840; in 1837, the Pennsylvania legislature ordered that German-language public schools be established on an equal basis with English-language schools. Minnesota, Maryland, and Indiana also operated public schools in which German was used, either by itself or in addition to English. In *Life with Two Languages*, his study of bilingualism, François Grosjean says, "What is particularly striking about German Americans in the nineteenth century is their constant efforts to maintain their language, culture, and heritage."

Yet despite everything the Germans could do, their language began to die out. The progression was slow and fraught with pain. For the immigrant, language was the main source of certainty and connection to the past. As the children broke from the Old World culture and tried out their snappy English slang on their parents, the pride the parents felt at such achievements was no doubt mixed with the bittersweet awareness that they were losing control.

At first the children would act as interpreters for their parents; then they would demand the independence appropriate to that role; then they would yearn to escape the coarse ways of immigrant life. And in the end, they would be

Americans. It was hard on families, but it built an assimilated English-language culture.

The pattern of assimilation is familiar from countless novels, as well as from 10
the experience of many people now living. Why, then, is the currently fashionable history of assimilation so different? Why is it assumed, in so many discussions of bilingual education, that in the old days immigrants switched quickly and enthusiastically to English?

One reason is that the experience of Jewish immigrants in the early twentieth century was different from this pattern. German Jews, successful and thoroughly assimilated here in the nineteenth century, oversaw an effort to bring Eastern European Jews into the American mainstream as quickly as possible. In New York City, the Lower East Side's Hebrew Institute, later known as the Educational Alliance, defined its goal as teaching the newcomers "the privileges and duties of American citizenship." Although many Jewish immigrants preserved their Yiddish, Jews generally learned English faster than any other group.

Another reason that nineteenth-century linguistic history is so little remembered lies in the political experience of the early twentieth century. As an endless stream of New Immigrants arrived from Eastern Europe, the United States was awash in theories about the threats the newcomers posed to American economic, sanitary, and racial standards, and the "100 percent Americanism" movement arose. By the late 1880s, school districts in the Midwest had already begun reversing their early encouragement of bilingual education. Competence in English was made a requirement for naturalized citizens in 1906. Pro–English-language leagues sprang up to help initiate the New Immigrants. California's Commission on Immigration and Housing, for example, endorsed a campaign of "Americanization propaganda," in light of "the necessity for all to learn English—the language of America." With the coming of World War I, all German-language activities were suddenly cast in a different light. Eventually, as a result, Americans came to believe that previous immigrants had speedily switched to English, and to view the Hispanics' attachment to Spanish as a troubling aberration. . . .

The bilingual system is accused of supporting a cadre of educational consultants while actually retarding the students' progress into the English-speaking mainstream. In this view, bilingual education could even be laying the foundation for a separate Hispanic culture, by extending the students' Spanish-language world from their homes to their schools.

Before I traveled to some of the schools in which bilingual education was applied, I shared the skeptics' view. What good could come of a system that encouraged, to whatever degree, a language other than the national tongue? But after visiting elementary, junior high, and high schools in Miami, Houston, San Antonio, Austin, several parts of Los Angeles, and San Diego, I found little connection between the political debate over bilingual education and what was going on in these schools.

15 To begin with, one central fact about bilingual education goes largely unreported. It is a *temporary* program. The time a typical student stays in the program varies from place to place—often two years in Miami, three years in Los Angeles—but when that time has passed, the student will normally leave. Why, then, do bilingual programs run through high school? Those classes are usually for students who are new to the district—usually because their parents are new to the country.

There is another fact about bilingual education, more difficult to prove but impressive to me, a hostile observer. Most of the children I saw were unmistakably learning to speak English.

In the elementary schools, where the children have come straight out of all-Spanish environments, the background babble seems to be entirely in Spanish. The kindergarten and first- to third-grade classrooms I saw were festooned with the usual squares and circles cut from colored construction paper, plus posters featuring Big Bird and charts about the weather and the seasons. Most of the schools seemed to keep a rough balance between English and Spanish in the lettering around the room; the most Spanish environment I saw was in one school in East Los Angeles, where about a third of the signs were in English.

The elementary school teachers were mostly Mexican-American women. They prompted the children with a mixture of English and Spanish during the day. While books in both languages were available in the classrooms, most of the first-grade reading drills I saw were in Spanish. In theory, children will learn the phonetic principle of reading more quickly if they are not trying to learn a new language at the same time. Once comfortable as readers, they will theoretically be able to transfer their ability to English.

In a junior high school in Houston, I saw a number of Mexican and Salvadoran students in their "bilingual" biology and math classes. They were drilled entirely in Spanish on the parts of an amoeba and on the difference between a parallelogram and a rhombus. When students enter bilingual programs at this level, the goal is to keep them current with the standard curriculum while introducing them to English. I found my fears of linguistic separatism rekindled by the sight of fourteen-year-olds lectured to in Spanish. I reminded myself that many of the students I was seeing had six months earlier lived in another country.

20 The usual next stop for students whose time in bilingual education is up is a class in intensive English, lasting one to three hours a day. These students are divided into two or three proficiency levels, from those who speak no English to those nearly ready to forgo special help. In Houston, a teacher drilled two-dozen high-school-age Cambodians, Indians, Cubans, and Mexicans on the crucial difference between the voiced *th* sound of "this" and the voiceless *th* of "thing." In Miami, a class of high school sophomores included youths from Cuba, El Salvador, and Honduras. They listened as their teacher read a Rockwellesque essay about a student with a crush on his teacher, and then set to work writing an essay of their own, working in words like "garrulous" and "sentimentalize."

One of the students in Miami, a sixteen-year-old from Honduras, said that his twelve-year-old brother had already moved into mainstream classes. Linguists say this is a standard pattern for immigrant children. The oldest children hold on to their first language longest, while their younger sisters and brothers swim quickly into the new language culture.

The more I saw of the classes, the more convinced I became that most of the students were learning English. Therefore, I started to wonder what it is about bilingual education that has made it the focus of such bitter disagreement.

For one thing, most immigrant groups other than Hispanics take a comparatively dim view of bilingual education. Haitians, Vietnamese, and Cambodians are eligible for bilingual education, but in general they are unenthusiastic. In Miami, Haitian boys and girls may learn to read in Creole rather than English. Still, their parents push to keep them moving into English. "A large number of [Haitian] parents come to the PTA meetings, and they don't want interpreters," said the principal of Miami's Edison Park Elementary School last spring. "They want to learn English. They don't want notices coming home in three languages. When they come here, unless there is total noncommunication, they will try to get through to us in their broken English. The students learn the language *very* quickly."

Bilingual education is inflammatory in large part because of what it symbolizes, not because of the nuts and bolts of its daily operation. In reality, bilingual programs move students into English with greater or lesser success; in reality, most Spanish-speaking parents understand that mastery of English will be their children's key to mobility. But in the political arena, bilingual education presents a different face. To the Hispanic ideologue, it is a symbol of cultural pride and political power. And once it has been presented that way, with full rhetorical flourish, it naturally strikes other Americans as a threat to the operating rules that have bound the country together.

Once during the months I spoke with and about immigrants I felt utterly 25
exasperated. It was while listening to two Chicano activist lawyers in Houston who demanded to know why their people should be required to learn English at all. "It is unrealistic to think people can learn it that quickly," one lawyer said about the law that requires naturalized citizens to pass a test in English. "*Especially when they used to own this part of the country*, and when Spanish was the *historic language* of this region."

There is a historic claim for Spanish—but by the same logic there is a stronger claim for, say, Navajo as the historic language of the Southwest. The truth is that for more than a century the territory has been American and its national language has been English.

I felt the same irritation welling up when I talked with many bilingual instructors and policy-makers. Their argument boiled down to: What's so special about English? They talked about the richness of the bilingual experience, the importance of maintaining the children's abilities in Spanish—even though when I watched the instructors in the classroom I could see that they were teaching principally English.

In my exasperation, I started to think that if such symbols of the dignity of language were so provocative to me, a comfortable member of the least-aggrieved ethnic group, it might be worth reflecting on the comparable sensitivities that lie behind the sentiments of the Spanish-speaking.

Consider the cases of Gloria Ramirez and Armandina Flores, who taught last year in the bilingual program at the Guerra Elementary School, in the Edgewood Independent School District, west of San Antonio.

San Antonio has evaded questions about the balance between rich and poor 30
in its school system by carving the city up into independent school districts. Alamo Heights is the winner under this approach, and Edgewood is the loser. The Edgewood School District is perennially ranked as one of the poorest in the state. The residents are almost all Mexican-Americans or Mexicans. It is a settled community, without much to attract immigrants, but many stop there briefly on their way somewhere else, enough to give Edgewood a sizable illegal-immigrant enrollment.

In the middle of a bleak, sunbaked stretch of fields abutting a commercial vegetable farm, and within earshot of Kelly Air Force Base, sits Edgewood's Guerra School. It is an ordinary-looking but well-kept one-story structure that was built during the Johnson Administration. Nearly all the students are Mexican or Mexican-American.

Gloria Ramirez, who teaches first grade, is a compact, attractive woman of thirty-three, a no-nonsense veteran of the activist movements of the 1960s. Armandina Flores, a twenty-seven-year-old kindergarten teacher, is a beauty with dark eyes and long hair. During classroom hours, they deliver "Now, children" explanations of what is about to happen in both Spanish and English, although when the message really must get across, it comes in Spanish.

Both are remarkable teachers. They have that spark often thought to be missing in the public schools. There is no hint that for them this is just a job, perhaps because it symbolizes something very different from the worlds in which they were raised.

Gloria Ramirez was born in Austin, in 1950. Both of her parents are native Texans, as were two of her grandparents, but her family, like many other Mexican-American families, "spoke only Spanish when I was growing up," she says. None of her grandparents went to school at all. Her parents did not go past the third grade. Her father works as an auto-body mechanic; her mother raised the six children, and recently went to work at Austin State Hospital as a cleaner.

Ramirez began learning English when she started school; but the school, on 35
Austin's east side, was overwhelmingly Mexican-American, part of the same culture she'd always known. The big change came when she was eleven. Her family moved to a working-class Anglo area in South Austin. She and her brother were virtually the only Mexican-Americans at the school. There was no more Spanish

on the playground, or even at home. "My parents requested that we speak more English to them from then on," she says. "Both of them could speak it, but neither was comfortable."

"Before then, I didn't realize I had an accent. I didn't know until a teacher at a new school pointed it out in a ridiculing manner. I began learning English out of revenge." For six years, she took speech classes. "I worked hard so I could sound—like this," she says in standard American. She went to the University of Texas, where she studied history and philosophy and became involved in the Mexican-American political movements of the 1970s. She taught bilingual-education classes in Boston briefly before coming home to Texas.

Armandina Flores was born in Ciudad Acuña, Mexico, across the river from Del Rio, Texas. Her mother, who was born in Houston, was an American citizen, but *her* parents had returned to Mexico a few months after her birth, and she had never learned English. Flores's father was a Mexican citizen. When she reached school age, she began commuting across the river to a small Catholic school in Del Rio, where all the other students were Chicano. When she was twelve and about to begin the sixth grade, her family moved to Del Rio and she entered an American public school.

At that time, the sixth grade was divided into tracks, which ran from 6–1 at the bottom to 6–12. Most of the Anglos were at the top; Armandina Flores was initially placed in 6–4. She showed an aptitude for English and was moved up to 6–8. Meanwhile, her older sister, already held back once, was in 6–2. Her parents were proud of Armandina's progress; they began to depend on her English in the family's dealings in the Anglo world. She finished high school in Del Rio, went to Our Lady of the Lake College in San Antonio, and came to Edgewood as an aide in 1978, when she was twenty-two.

Considered one way, these two stories might seem to confirm every charge made by the opponents of bilingual education. Through the trauma of being plucked from her parents' comfortable Spanish-language culture and plunged into the realm of public language, Gloria Ramirez was strengthened, made a cosmopolitan and accomplished person. Her passage recalls the one Richard Rodriguez describes in *Hunger of Memory*, an autobiography that has become the most eloquent text for opponents of bilingual programs.

"Without question, it would have pleased me to hear my teachers address 40
me in Spanish when I entered the classroom," Rodriguez wrote. "I would have felt much less afraid. . . . But I would have delayed—for how long postponed?—having to learn the language of public society."

Gloria Ramirez concedes that the pain of confused ethnicity and lost loyalties among Mexican-Americans is probably very similar to what every other immigrant group has endured. She even admits that she was drawn to bilingual education for political as well as educational reasons. As for Armandina Flores, hers is a calmer story of successful assimilation, accomplished without the crutch of bilingual education.

Yet both of these women insist, with an edge to their voices, that their students are fortunate not to have the same passage awaiting them.

It was a very wasteful process, they say. They swam; many others sank. "You hear about the people who make it, but not about all the others who dropped out, who never really learned," Ramirez says. According to the Mexican-American Legal Defense and Education Fund, 40 percent of Hispanic students drop out before they finish high school, three times as many as among Anglo students.

"Many people around here don't feel comfortable with themselves in either language," Ramirez says. Flores's older sister never became confident in English; "she feels like a lower person for it." She has just had a baby and is anxious that he succeed in English. Ramirez's older brother learned most of his English in the Marines. He is married to a Mexican immigrant and thinks that it is very important that their children learn English. And that is more likely to happen, the teachers say, if they have a transitional moment in Spanish.

Otherwise, "a child must make choices that concern his survival," Ramirez 45
says. "He can choose to learn certain words, only to survive; but it can kill his desire to learn, period. Eventually he may be able to deal in the language, but he won't be educated." If the natural-immersion approach worked, why, they ask, would generation after generation of Chicanos, American citizens living throughout the Southwest, have lived and died without ever fully moving into the English-language mainstream?

These two teachers, and a dozen others with parallel experience, might be wrong in their interpretation of how bilingual education works. If so, they are making the same error as German, Polish, and Italian immigrants. According to the historians hired by the Select Commission, "Immigrants argued, when given the opportunity, that the security provided them by their cultures eased rather than hindered the transition." Still, there is room for reasonable disagreement about the most effective techniques for bringing children into English. A former teacher named Robert Rossier, for example, argues from his experience teaching immigrants that intensive courses in English are more effective than a bilingual transition. Others line up on the other side.

But is this not a question for factual resolution rather than for battles about linguistic and ethnic pride? Perhaps one approach will succeed for certain students in certain situations and the other will be best for others. The choice between bilingual programs and intensive-English courses, then, should be a choice between methods, not ideologies. The wars over bilingual education have had a bitter, symbolic quality. Each side has invested the issue with a meaning the other can barely comprehend. To most Mexican-American parents and children, bilingual education is merely a way of learning English; to Hispanic activists, it is a symbol that they are at last taking their place in the sun. But to many other Americans, it sounds like a threat not to assimilate.

QUESTIONS FOR DISCUSSION

1. What is the historical parallel between today's Spanish-speaking immigrants and the German immigrants of the nineteenth century? What effect did World War I have on German bilingualism?

2. Does Fallows believe that Hispanic students can learn English in bilingual programs? Explain his position.
3. Discuss the major differences and similarities between the experiences of Gloria Ramirez and Armandina Flores. How did their experiences contribute to their positions on bilingual education?
4. This selection is full of rhetorical questions as well as personal experience. Discuss the effectiveness of these strategies. What assumptions can you make about the audience for whom Fallows intended this essay?

WRITING ASSIGNMENTS

1. Reaction Journal: Assume the role of either Gloria Ramirez or Armandina Flores (the two teachers Fallows describes in his essay) and respond to the arguments of a parent who wants his or her Spanish-speaking child to be mainstreamed in English-only classes.
2. Write a brief essay in which you respond to one of the following assertions from "Language":
   a. "Bilingual education is inflammatory in large part because of what it symbolizes, not because of the nuts and bolts of its daily operation."
   b. "I began learning English out of revenge."
   c. "The choice between bilingual programs and intensive-English courses, then, should be a choice between methods, not ideologies."

THE FRACTURED LOGIC OF BILINGUAL EDUCATION

ROSALIE PEDALINO PORTER

As a non-English-speaking immigrant child in Newark, New Jersey, Rosalie Pedalino Porter experienced the pain and frustration of being unable to understand her teacher and classmates. In spite of this difficult early experience at school, Porter learned English and went on to college, an achievement that was beyond the expectations for a daughter in the Italian working-class culture in which she was raised. When she began a teaching career after raising her own children, it was as a Spanish teacher in an early bilingual program in Springfield, Massachusetts. Later Porter became Director of Bilingual Education and English as a Second Language for the public schools in Newton, Massachusetts.

Porter's early experiences teaching in a transitional bilingual program led her to believe that teaching students academic subjects in their native languages while providing them with instruction in English as a second language for only a small part of the day post-

pones unnecessarily both their social integration and their acquisition of the second language. In the following excerpt from her book Forked Tongue: The Politics of Bilingual Education *(1990), Porter raises the question of whether maintenance of students' cultures is the job of the public schools and warns against the kind of emphasis on biculturalism in the schools that can resegregate "children along language and ethnic lines."*

◆ FREEWRITING

In her essay Porter asks, "Is the maintenance of family cultures to be a mandated responsibility of the public schools?" Before reading this selection, freewrite for ten or fifteen minutes in response to the question.

My introduction to the American school system began when I entered a first-grade classroom not long after arriving in the United States at the age of six. Feelings of fearfulness at being separated from my family were heightened when I lost my way home on the first day of school. I wandered for what seemed miles in central Newark, New Jersey, crying, until I was brought home by a policeman who lived in our neighborhood.

During those first few months, the hours I spent in the classroom were a haze of incomprehensible sounds. I copied what the other children seemed to be doing, scribbling on paper as though I were writing; otherwise, I silently watched the behavior of teachers and students. Although I cannot recall the process of learning English and beginning to participate in the verbal life of the classroom, I know it was painful. I can remember, however, that within two years I felt completely comfortable with English and with the school community —how it happened I do not know. I suspect that a combination of factors worked in my favor: a close-knit family, personal motivation, good health, sympathetic teachers, peer acceptance, and who knows what other intangibles of time and place. When it finally began to happen, I remember the intense joy of understanding and being understood, even at a simple level, by those around me. . . .

In my generation, many immigrant children did not succeed either in learning English or in mastering academic subjects. It was this common immigrant experience of failure, the widespread dropping out of school, that gave rise in the 1960s to the demand for effective, humane language programs. The expectation among educators of those earlier times was that immigrant children would either "sink or swim." This cruel experience forced many to leave school early, prepared only for unskilled labor. This aborted schooling was not as serious a drawback then, however, because of the easy access to jobs in industry and agriculture. The current growth of a service/technological economy requires a much higher level of education for even entry-level jobs. . . .

The start of the civil rights push on behalf of language minority children coincided, happily, with the years when I, like other women with career interests, was able to return to my university studies to complete an undergraduate degree. My children were all in school, and it was an ideal time to resume my study of Spanish literature. The college of education began transmitting such a sense of excitement about their new program to train Spanish bilingual teachers that I eagerly changed my direction. The new method, designated Transitional Bilingual Education (TBE) but usually referred to simply as "bilingual education" or TBE, requires the teaching of all school subjects in the native language for several years, so that the students learn subject matter while making, with gradually increased language lessons, the transition from native language to English.

The call was out for anyone with strong skills in Spanish to join the new 5
wave. Chicano activists from California and the Southwest, as well as Puerto Rican professors from New York and Chicago, taught us about the history and literature of the Caribbean, the phonetics of Spanish and English, psycholinguistics, multicultural sensitivity, and many other skills to prepare us to be bilingual teachers in urban schools. I entered the field of bilingual education at its very beginning and have, therefore, a direct understanding of the way it has developed. My firsthand experience provides a vivid representation of the issues in educating language minority children, a topic too often discussed abstractly by the theoreticians and ideologues. . . .

In 1974, with a bachelor's degree and a view of myself, at age forty-three, as the oldest "new" teacher in the world, I began teaching in Springfield, Massachusetts. Here began, first, my excitement in being part of a new experiment in education and, later, the evolution of my thinking on the impractical aspects of bilingual education in the classroom. The Armory Street School had just been desegregated in a citywide master plan that reassigned fifth- and sixth-grade students to different schools to achieve racial balance. Among the 500 students at Armory 49 percent were blacks, 10 percent were Spanish-speakers, and the rest were white students from predominantly low-income families of Irish background in the "Hungry Hill" neighborhood. Kindergarten children living in the vicinity, more than half of whom were from Puerto Rican families, also attended the school.

My prescribed teaching duties were dauntingly varied. First, I was to teach the kindergarten children *in Spanish* for about an hour daily, developing the basic concepts of size, shape, colors, numbers, and letters—in short, those things typically taught to American kindergarteners. I also was to provide twenty to thirty minutes of English for these children, usually through stories, songs, and games. The rest of the day I was to teach fifth- and sixth-grade students their subject matter—mathematics, science, and social studies—in Spanish and give them intensive lessons in English as a Second Language (ESL), the generic label for the teaching of English speaking, reading, and writing skills to speakers of other languages. . . .

At the Armory Street School I also was teaching fifth- and sixth-grade students, who spent three hours or more with me daily. These students came to my room from their various homerooms for special instruction because the school did not have a large enough group of limited-English students to organize an entire bilingual classroom of fifth graders or sixth graders. Those whose English was sufficient to the tasks studied their subjects in their homeroom and came to me for English-language reading and writing; those whose English was very limited spent more time in my class, receiving instruction in the fifth- and sixth-grade math, science, and social studies curriculum in Spanish, in addition to an intensive English program.

We bilingual teachers were told by the citywide director of the program to teach spoken English but not to teach reading in English until the students could read *at grade level* in Spanish. Supposedly, the reading skills in Spanish would easily be transferred to English. This is, indeed, the common practice in bilingual programs across the country. Working with students who were ten to fourteen years old and who were not reading above the first- or second-grade level in Spanish, I doubted that this magic transfer of reading skills from Spanish to English would happen before they finished high school—if they stayed in school that long. . . .

Underlying these fanciful ideas is the decent notion of showing respect for 10
other languages and cultures, which is certainly laudable; however, too many practitioners of this idea operate on fractured logic. In my five years of bilingual teaching in Springfield, I interviewed at least 150 families when they first registered their children for school and then later at parent-teacher conferences. Almost always the discussion was in Spanish, and always I carefully explained the bilingual program we were providing for their children. Most parents showed little interest in the details of the program, but all were earnestly concerned that their children's schooling should give them opportunities not available to their parents. They were interested in how rapidly the children would learn English. The fact that there was a teacher who could speak their language made them all feel welcome in the school and gave them the confidence to discuss their hopes for the children's futures. This was the crucial factor in establishing a basis for contact and trust between home and school. They felt respected. As with many families from other cultures, they were ready to trust the judgment of the teacher on the kind of program that would help their children the most. They did not, as advocates led us to believe, demand native-language instruction and, in some cases, were strongly opposed to it. . . .

When strict bilingual education advocates speak of the great benefits of separating limited-English students from their classmates temporarily so that they can develop pride in their own language and culture and a sense of identity, they downplay the negative side of such an approach, namely, that this segregation reinforces the feeling of being different, of being a perpetual outsider. An integrative approach to bilingual education is difficult to achieve because the program itself is essentially segregative. All my experience bore this out.

One consummate irony came to light late in my Springfield career. I learned, through conversations with a few of the bilingual teachers, that they did not enroll their own children in the public schools but were struggling to pay the tuition required for parochial school. When I asked if they preferred to have their children receive a religious education, they said no, that they wanted their children in the parochial school *because it did not have a bilingual program and therefore the children were learning English rapidly.* It shocked me to hear from bilingual teachers that they would not have their own children in our program! . . .

Bilingual education, for its part, soon appended the word *bicultural* to its program title. The goals of a bilingual/bicultural education program became to help students learn English while being taught in their native language *and* to help students develop pride in their language and culture. The bicultural part of this education program was not only to distinguish between the stereotypical majority culture of white, middle-class America (itself a myth) and the language, customs, and values that the language minority child brings to school but also to promote respect for the culture of the minority child. From the laudable impulse to teach respect for all cultures, languages, and ethnic backgrounds came the new rhetoric of rights. The poster circulated by the National Association of Bilingual Education a few years ago succinctly phrased the demand: "I have a right to my language and my culture." Every child and family, in fact, has this right under the U.S. Constitution; I know of no law that abridges it. Nevertheless, the strong surge of ethnicity brought with it a central question that must be addressed: Is the maintenance of family cultures to be a mandated responsibility of the public schools?

Stephen Arons, a legal studies professor at the University of Massachusetts whose special area of interest is the right of families to teach their children at home, has joined the bicultural rights debate by characterizing home teaching as a First Amendment right. Arons asks whether limited-English students should have to sacrifice their cultural heritage as the price of a public education. He contends that "every family has the constitutional right—without government interference—to inculcate its values in its children so long as those values do not themselves contravene the Constitution."[1] Arons presents an extremely dire picture of the consequences of not supporting the home language and the transmission of the family's cultural values in the schools: the child's self-worth will suffer; the child will be subjected to a humiliation "as deep as any religious persecution, any racism, or any censorship of family beliefs."[2] He calls not only for First Amendment protection for the preservation of language minority family values but an additional First Amendment obligation *that these values must indeed be taught in the schools.* He even contends that we do not have the right to use public schooling to impose an official language, as we do not have the right to try to impose an official religion. His is the most extreme position I have encountered so far in the arena of cultural maintenance, and as such it may serve as a boundary point in the discussion of educational goals and language policies in our pluralist polity. There are, to be sure, some very basic problems with Arons's reasoning and with his absolutist approach. First, English is not an official language, and educators have not been promoting it as such. However, denying children the opportunity to learn the language of the majority society through the public schools would be a gross denial of their civil rights.

In South Africa, we should note, the imposition of mother-tongue instruction, which Arons demands for American children, is used as a way of maintaining the isolation of black South Africans and denying them economic opportunity. The two official languages of the country are English and Afrikaans. The Bantu languages are not used in business, government, or commerce, but the use of Bantu is mandated as the medium of instruction in the primary schools for African children. Many children do not go beyond that point in their schooling. A South African critic of apartheid writes incisively that

> Africans feel that mother-tongue instruction has the effect of cramping them intellectually within the narrow bounds of tribal society and diminishing the opportunity of intercommunication between the African groups themselves and the larger world. . . . They need to have access to technological skills, to world literature and, particularly those living in the towns, must have mastery of one of the official languages, preferably English.[3]

Parents in our country who would choose, for whatever reasons, to keep their children away from the majority language may seek some form of alternative private schooling or provide home schooling. That is a matter of family choice that in most places is not denied by public policy.

One must question any proposal that the mission, indeed, the responsibility, of the public schools is to teach the values of any one group of families. Such an objective would be counter to the fundamental nature of American education, which Horace Mann called "the great equalizer," as it provides the less privileged members of society with opportunities for social and economic advancement. John Dewey described "the office of the school environment" as the obligation "to see to it that each individual gets an opportunity to escape from the limitations of the social group in which he was born, and to come into living contact with a broader environment."[4]

Surely, one of the noblest goals of education in our pluralistic society is to open the minds of children to the variety of thoughts and values of the many groups that make up our country, not to teach each group, even if that were possible, only about its own family culture. Furthermore, we know better than to believe, in this rapidly changing, interdependent world, that any community's culture remains static. Indeed, in the best of circumstances, what is taught in the classroom may no longer be a reflection of the reality that families are actually living. This natural evolution is especially true of groups that have moved from agrarian life to the industrial centers, from hot to cold climates, or from extended, stable family structures to small, dispersed units struggling to adapt.

Finally, one must ask, How is such linguistic and cultural exclusivity compatible with our goal of bringing together minority and majority students in our schools to fulfill the dream some day of an integrated society? How does segregation by language and ethnic culture empower the powerless and give voice to the voiceless? Antonio Gramsci, the twentieth-century Italian philosopher and cultural critic, analyzed the linguistic diversity of the Italian nation within the framework of class division and political control. He outlined the logical consequences of linguistic provincialism:

> If it is true that every language contains the elements of a conception of the world and of a culture, it could also be true that from anyone's language one can assess the greater and lesser complexity of his conception of the world. Someone who only speaks dialect, *or understands the standard language incompletely*, [author's emphasis] necessarily has an intuition of the world which is more or less limited and provincial, which is fossilized and anachronistic in relation to the major currents of thought which dominate world history.[5]

Gramsci elsewhere defended the maintenance of the Italian dialects within the family, but he believed that "without the mastery of the common standard version of the national language, one is inevitably destined to function only at the periphery of national life, and, especially, outside the national and political mainstream."[6] Let me add a pertinent note. This morning, as I write, a summons arrived in the mail for my twenty-two-year-old son to serve on jury duty. Among the conditions that exempt people from jury service are mental or physical incapacity, age (over seventy or under eighteen), felony conviction, or the inability to speak or understand the English language—a telling cluster of handicaps! To be excluded from this important public responsibility, this basic democratic right to sit in judgment of one's peers, seems a fundamental loss to me. Unable to communicate adequately in the language of the society, one is then unable to participate equally and at first hand, without intermediaries, in the communal life of a free society.

Arons's ideas are only the most extreme example of one side of the public 20
dialogue on the role of bilingual/bicultural education in our multilingual, multicultural society. The unresolved issues in public education include integration versus segregation of bilingual students and a redefinition of the responsibilities of families versus the responsibilities of public institutions in the maintenance of native languages and cultures. The unresolved societal issues include the rights of children to cultural freedom versus the rights of families and communities to ethnic solidarity; open access by all citizens to all institutions versus ethnic cohesiveness of neighborhoods, communities, and schools; the role of language in preserving cultural or ethnic group identity; and the tension between desire of some groups to maintain their culture and the desire for inclusion in the mainstream for economic advancement. . . .

Different groups may have different attitudes toward education and the role it plays in fulfilling their needs, but the desire for betterment is basic to all. Surely there is no community that does not prize its children and their abilities to achieve a better life than their parents. This desire must be common to all groups, but especially to the disadvantaged, who have to be the most concerned that their children be saved from disastrous circumstances. It is the one sentiment expressed to me consistently by parents, literate or not—whether Puerto Rican, Chinese, Italian, or Greek. They hope that the schools will enable their children to have more fulfilling lives, and they strongly desire respect for their identity, the ethnic and linguistic culture that the family represents. I do not see evidence that the current ethnic groups want the maintenance or revival of their cultures in substantial or complete ways, but they do want to see their cultures recognized, as a necessary measure of respect. . . .

Those of us who have experienced culture and language shift—and we are many—have felt at different times both the sentimental longing for a seemingly simpler past of shared traditions, closer communities, and stable families and the sharp sense that our cultural symbols from the past cannot really shield us from the discontents of the modern world. Overcoming the discontents of minorities will not be achieved by having our schools emphasize biculturalism and resegregating children along language and ethnic lines, which are the realities in bilingual education classrooms. Biculturalism will not make up for the years of neglect of language minority children when they were invisible in the mainstream classroom or out of school at an early age.

Notes

1. Stephen Arons, "First Amendment Rights Are 'Crucial' in Educating Language-Minority Pupils," *Education Week*, 1 October 1986, p. 19.

2. Ibid.

3. Hilda Bernstein, "Schools for Servitude," in *Apartheid: A Collection of Writings on South African Racism by South Africans*, ed. Alex La Guma (New York: International Publishers, 1971), 34–35.

4. Quoted in Stephen Steinberg, *The Ethnic Myth: Race, Ethnicity, and Class in America* (New York: Atheneum, 1981), 128.

5. Quoted in Arturo Tosi, *Immigration and Bilingual Education* (Oxford: Pergamon Press, 1984), 167.

6. Ibid., 176.

QUESTIONS FOR DISCUSSION

1. Provide a historical explanation for the rise of "humane language programs" during the 1960s.

2. Explain what you perceive to be some of the fundamental characteristics of Transitional Bilingual Education (TBE). Discuss strengths and weaknesses.

3. What point does Porter wish to make by shifting her focus to South African bilingual education problems? How does she use the requirements for jury duty to argue against bilingual education.

4. Porter's essay, which is intended to be an argument, is written from the first-person point of view. How is the first person an effective rhetorical aid in persuasive writing? Can you think of ways in which it could be a detriment?

WRITING ASSIGNMENTS

1. Reaction Journal: Assume the school board in your community is considering a new bilingual/bicultural program. Based on your readings and your observations, write a letter in which you make recommendations.
2. Write a paragraph or two on the following assertions from this selection:
   a. "If it is true that every language contains the elements of a conception of the world and of a culture, it could also be true that from anyone's language one can assess the greater and lesser complexity of his conception of the world."
   b. "Such an objective [bilingual/bicultural education] would be counter to the fundamental nature of American education, which Horace Mann called 'the great equalizer.'"

U.S. ENGLISH—1991 NATIONAL OPINION SURVEY

RONALD SAUNDERS

Ronald Saunders is executive director of U.S. English, a public interest group that was founded by the late senator S. I. Hayakawa. Its members and supporters contend that having a common language is vital to maintaining "national unity and strength," and they support both state legislation and an amendment to the U.S. Constitution to provide legal protection to English as the official language of the United States. The following is an excerpt from an informational letter that accompanied a survey form and a petition requesting President Bush to support an "official language" amendment.

◆ FREEWRITING

Read the "U.S. English—1991 National Opinion Survey." Assume your state has a ballot question coming up to make English the official language. Does the "Survey" persuade you to vote in favor of the question? Before reading Harvey A. Daniels's rebuttal, consider what might be valid arguments against the U.S. English position.

Do you agree—English should be the official language of our government?"

Most people are shocked to learn that English is not already our official language. However, here are the facts:

FACT: The United States doesn't have an official language, even though over 148 language groups are represented within our nation.

FACT: In many U.S. schools, limited-English children are taught primarily in their own languages largely funded by our federal government. Many children have limited opportunities to learn English and maybe some never will.

FACT: In Arizona, a federal district court judge ruled that public employees are not required to speak English on the job.

FACT: 375 voting districts are required by our Federal government to provide voting ballots and election materials in foreign languages even though people can take translators into the booth or vote by absentee ballot. The question remains: Does this encourage true participatory democracy by an informed electorate?

As you can see, it's clear that English is not the official language of the U.S. In fact, a common language is no longer viewed as necessary by many elected officials and opinion leaders.

What's happened is that many of our leaders have followed a well-intended but mistaken policy of accommodating non-English-speaking immigrants in their native languages—rather than help them learn English.

Pursuing this misguided policy has created a terrible tragedy. . . .

- Growing numbers of Americans, especially recent immigrants, don't know English and have been led to believe that it isn't necessary.
- Non-English-speaking children in our schools are taught in their native languages while English instruction is neglected.
- Poor-paying jobs, discrimination and segregation await those who cannot speak English.

That's why our founder, former United States Senator S. I. Hayakawa, introduced *the first English Language Amendment in Congress.*

The amendment says powerfully, simply and directly: *The English language shall be the official language of the United States.*

He was deluged immediately with thousands of letters of support from Americans of all races and ethnic backgrounds.

But unfortunately, no organization existed back then to channel the concerns of these Americans or to work to pass the English Language Amendment.

Worse, many special interest groups that did exist—like the powerful National Education Association teachers union—had developed a vested interest in continuing unproven bilingual education programs. They lobbied hard to keep Senator Hayakawa's Amendment bottled up in Congress.

Having immigrated to the U.S. from Canada, he had thought that his colleagues in Congress, most native-born Americans, would join in recognizing the role of English as the common bond that unites all Americans regardless of race, creed, or national origin.

As a professor, researcher and author studying the field of language, it became clear to Senator Hayakawa that the English language is the social glue that binds the people of our nation—and that learning English opens the golden door to opportunity in America.

He was sure that Congress would welcome the opportunity to make English our official language. He was astounded to find out how terribly wrong he was.

President Theodore Roosevelt once said:

> "The one absolutely certain way of bringing this nation to ruin . . . would be to permit it to become a tangle of squabbling nationalities."

Just think of it. It's happening all around us, and right now:

- Youngsters can go through our public schools and graduate not knowing English. All their classes and tests are given in their native language. California schools alone provide instruction in at least 42 different languages!
- And the real victims? They're our non-English-speaking immigrants and their children. Isolated from the rest of our nation, they are doomed to illiteracy and poverty. Worse, they are easy prey for economic and political exploitation.
- Inefficient language divisions harm our ability to compete in world markets. *Or to command our Armed Forces.*
- And further, imagine our own children or grandchildren living in an America divided by language. Can we remain "one nation, indivisible" while divided along language and ethnic lines?

This is exactly the course set for us by special interests, who often overlook 20
the good of the nation.

In order to forestall this grim outlook, Senator Hayawaka, after retiring from the Senate launched a national nonprofit, nonpartisan public interest group to establish English as our official language.

That group is <u>U.S. ENGLISH.</u>

Our principal objectives are . . .

1. To make English the official language of the United States government through federal legislation.
2. To encourage each state to declare English its official language.
3. To make sure that all persons in the United States are guaranteed the opportunity to learn English.
4. To improve bilingual education in our schools so that children learn English in the most effective way possible.
5. To uphold the existing law making knowledge of English a requirement for immigrants obtaining U.S. citizenship.
6. To repeal laws mandating bilingual voting ballots, government licensing and similar uses.

Only eight years old, U.S. ENGLISH has already built a membership of over 400,000 concerned Americans. And we've already accomplished a great deal.

For example, before U.S. ENGLISH was founded, only four states had made English their official language. Today, through our efforts, the number of states with official English legislation is 18.

And since our start, Congress has finally adopted proposals to limit bilingual education to no more than three years for any child, and raised the funding level for innovative programs to teach English to immigrant children.

Our long and difficult efforts in Washington to pass legislation protecting English took a giant leap forward when the Language in Government Act (H. R. 123) was recently introduced. This bill designates English the official language of the Federal Government, and says that government has an "affirmative obligation to protect, preserve, and enhance the role of English as the official language of the U.S."

However, our battle in Congress remains an uphill fight with many special interest groups arrayed against us.

But we do have one powerful weapon our opponents lack—and that is *the force of public opinion on our side.*

A January 1991 Gallup/U.S. ENGLISH survey shows that 78% of Americans favor English as our official language. Now, it's critical that we channel this overwhelming public support and bring it to bear on the media, members of Congress and President Bush, to win their backing for our common language legislation. . . .

U.S. ENGLISH is committed to a nation united by a common language, not weakened or fragmented by competing language groups as in Canada. We're committed to ensuring that every person is given the opportunity to learn our common language so that everyone can participate in all our country has to offer.

Note: For study questions, see page 405.

THE ROOTS OF LANGUAGE PROTECTIONISM

HARVEY A. DANIELS

Harvey A. Daniels (b. 1947) is professor of education and chair of the Department of Interdisciplinary Studies at National-Louis University in Evanston, Illinois. He has authored or coauthored five books on language and education, among them Famous Last Words:

The American Language Crisis Reconsidered (1983) and Not Only English: Affirming America's Multilingual Heritage (1990), from which the following selection is taken. From 1986 to 1989 Daniels served as a member of the Commission on Language for the National Council of Teachers of English. During his tenure on this commission, the NCTE officially condemned the English-only movement. In "The Roots of Language Protectionism," Daniels reviews the arguments of English-only proponents who, he says, regard what they see as immigrants' refusal to learn English as evidence of their "intransigence and ingratitude." Daniels characterizes such opinions as part of "the long history of American intolerance of immigrants and minorities." In his response to this position, Daniels points to the possible rights denied and lives endangered if English-only legislation is enforced.

The United States has always been a multilingual country. The history of the American people, the story of the peoples native to this continent and of those who immigrated here from every corner of the world, is told in the rich accents of Cherokee, Spanish, German, Dutch, Yiddish, French, Menomonie, Japanese, Norwegian, Arabic, Aleut, Polish, Navajo, Thai, Portuguese, Caribbean creoles, and scores of other tongues. Of all the richnesses that define the complex culture of this nation, none is more sparkling, more fascinating, or more evocative of our diverse origins than our plural heritage of languages.

Through much of our history, Americans have viewed this linguistic diversity as either a blessing or a simple fact of life. The founding fathers carefully omitted any constitutional provision establishing an official language—indeed, many of the founders were German-English bilinguals themselves. From the earliest days of nationhood, through both law and custom, the use of various languages other than English has been officially sanctioned in education, government, and commerce. The public and private use of a variety of languages has usually been treated as business-as-usual in a nation of immigrants.

But as Americans, we have also shared and treasured English, by custom and practice, and without challenge, as our common national language. While we trace our origins among peoples of many languages, we have always had our strong lingua franca. Indeed, America has developed one of the most efficient patterns of linguistic assimilation in the world. For more than two centuries, non-English speakers arriving in America typically have moved from their native language, through a bilingual stage, to monolingual English-speaking within three generations—and among some of today's immigrants, the process is occurring in only two generations (Veltman 1988).

The predominance and civic necessity of English is unquestioned in America; indeed, few countries in the world enjoy such a well-established, stable national language standard. For just one contemporary example of this acceptance: among a sample of contemporary Hispanic immigrants, 98 percent believe their children must learn to speak English "perfectly" in order to succeed

—compared with 94 percent of Anglos holding the same opinion (Crawford 1989, 60). Of course, we Americans have also had our share of sociolinguistic conflicts, and . . . the most painful of these have occurred in the past seventy-five years. But still, the overwhelming fact of our national linguistic life has been the predominance of English and its remarkably quick mastery by new Americans.

5 Given this broad historic picture of linguistic stability and cultural consensus, then, it is somewhat surprising to find that language differences have become a searing political issue in the 1990s. Today, several powerful national lobbying groups are calling for the passage of both state and federal laws to officialize English, for cutbacks in bilingual education programs, and for a host of other legal measures designed to "legally protect" the common language. These groups argue that America is in a profound cultural crisis, that the very dominance of English is suddenly in peril, and that only concerted national legal action can save its central role in our culture. To these people, the image of Babel, a country confounded by a multiplicity of languages is not just a Biblical parable but an unfolding American reality.

According to U.S. English and other groups, the old pattern of language shift is no longer working; today's immigrants are different, and they are not assimilating like the Germans, Swedes, Poles, and Italians once did, Hispanics in particular are accused of actually *refusing* to learn English, instead demanding separate government-funded services delivered in their native language right to their ethnic neighborhoods. This new crop of immigrants, as one leader of the official English movement explains, prefers to hide in ethnic ghettos, "living off welfare and costing working Americans millions of tax dollars every year" (Horn, 1).

The American public has been stirred by such accusations. How dare immigrants withhold this minimal act of allegiance—of plain simple respect—refusing to learn the common language of their adopted homeland? One need not be an ultrapatriot to be offended by such apparent intransigence and ingratitude. Nor has it been difficult for protectionist groups to spin frightening propaganda out of contemporary headlines. "I'm furious, and I'm scared," begins a solicitation letter from the director of El-Pac, the political lobbying arm of U.S. English. "I'm furious that the presidential nominee of a major American political party delivered a large portion of his acceptance speech *in a foreign language*. . . . Dukakis crossed a line that has never been crossed before. He signaled to all Americans that, in his search for Hispanic votes, he is willing to *embrace a new way of life* for us all—official bilingualism" (Zall, 1).

Their fears stoked by such appeals, thousands of good-hearted, patriotic, loyal Americans—often consciously honoring their own immigrant ancestry—have voted in large majorities to support official-English referenda recently appearing on the ballot in many states. By now, sixteen states have passed some version of an official-English law, and many more are considering such legislation. These states and the dates of their legislation are listed below:

Arizona	1988
Arkansas	1987
California	1986
Colorado	1988
Georgia	1986
Florida	1988
Illinois	1969
Indiana	1984
Kentucky	1984
Mississippi	1987
Nebraska	1923
North Carolina	1987
North Dakota	1987
South Carolina	1987
Tennessee	1984
Virginia	1981

*Hawaii and Louisiana have laws which give legal status to multiple languages.

What have been the outcomes of these state official-English statutes? The laws passed in the last few years have had a largely symbolic impact thus far. But from each of the new official-English states come reports of uncivil confrontations: in Colorado, a bus driver orders Hispanic children to stop speaking Spanish on the way to school ("English Only," 1989, 6); in Denver a restaurant worker is fired for translating the menu for a Hispanic customer (EPIC, March/April, 1988); in Texas, Spanish-language radio stations are the subject of FCC petitions (Bikales 1985); in Coral Gables, Florida, a supermarket checker is suspended without pay for speaking Spanish on the job (Gavin 1988); in Huntington Beach, California, court translators are forbidden to use Spanish in personal conversations (EPIC, March/April, 1988).

10 Still, large-scale official changes have not yet occurred in most areas. Few public officials—especially elected ones—have been eager to enforce English-only laws, especially when doing so would effectively terminate a previously available public service, and some, like the mayors of Denver and San Antonio have been outwardly defiant. And courts have struck down some English-only rulings, such as the Huntington Beach translators' case noted above. But, always keeping up the pressure, U.S. English and other groups continue to file specific challenges to particular practices, and these will gradually work their way through the legal system. It is not yet clear how the courts will rule, especially when language issues conflict with civil rights, a collision which is bound to occur frequently in these disputes.

What are some of the uses of non-English languages that U.S. English and others will try to terminate under the new statutes? Below are listed some practices and situations already targeted for abolition by U.S. English in one or more states:

- translators in public hospitals
- 911 emergency service
- voting materials, instructions, and ballots
- court reporters and other legal services
- bilingual education in public schools
- school materials, parent conferences, report cards
- driver's license regulations and examinations
- non-English radio and television broadcasting
- non-English holdings in public libraries
- street signs, park names, commemorative naming of public sites
- directory assistance
- telephone books and yellow pages
- tourist information
- public housing listings and information
- bus and train schedules and signs
- general advertising, business signs, billboards, menus (Zall, Crawford 1989; *EPIC Events*, 1988, both issues)

This list is a reminder, perhaps, of the degree to which public and private services already are routinely provided in non-English languages throughout America, in many cases to ensure public safety or simple justice.

As the list also suggests, U.S. English will probably not be satisfied when all immigrants learn English—they seem also to want all public reminders of the existence of other languages removed from America. They do not want to have to hear any Spanish in public, see any billboards, flip past any TV channels in languages other than English. Indeed, many U.S. English documents describe it as a violation of English speakers' civil rights to hear "foreign" languages in the street, to be made to feel a stranger in one's own country.

And as the above list further demonstrates, some English-only adherents feel that death is not too severe a penalty for an immigrant's failure to speak English. The denial of translator services in hospitals is one of the most telling planks in the official-English platform. The Florida director of U.S. English has specifically called not just for the termination of the 17 employees who translate between doctors and Spanish-speaking patients at Dade County's Jackson Memorial County Hospital, but also for elimination of prenatal, postnatal, and postsurgical materials and conferences in non-English languages (Robbins

1985). U.S. English is willing, in other words, to risk the lives of fellow Americans in the name of its language standards. As one U.S. English leader declared, just before going off to run for Congress from a Florida district, people who cannot explain a fire location or an ongoing crime in English have no right to police and fire protection through the 911 emergency number ("Florida English," 1986).

U.S. English holds an analogous view of education. Adherents essentially insist that being schooled immediately and exclusively in English is more important than achieving literacy or learning subject matter. Never mind that such an approach violates the best-proven educational practices and guarantees unnecessary academic failure for many youngsters. As one widely distributed U.S. English promotional piece puts it, "If our society can't afford some scholastic failure, then we can't afford immigration" ("Frequently Used Arguments," U.S. English). U.S. English proponents describe it as unrealistic and unattainable for immigrant children to succeed in school at the same rate as American-born children. Accordingly, U.S. English and the other language restrictionist groups oppose bilingual education, which has been amply shown to be the most educationally effective and socially benevolent approach to the education of non-English-speaking students.

For the time being, the national English-only lobby seems only modestly 15
interested in enforcing its newly passed state laws. Instead, the movement's main energies are devoted to passing similar laws in additional states and attacking federal bilingual education policy. The overall strategy seems to be to get some official-English law on the books of a majority of states and to continually fan public resentment over schooling policies that "degrade English" and "cater" to immigrants. These activities seem aimed to develop momentum behind the English Language Amendment, the proposed federal constitutional amendment which has been stalled in committee for years, lacking the broad sponsorship that might coalesce if a snowballing public sentiment can be created.

Language Debates in the Twentieth Century

There has probably been more discord about language differences in America during the last seventy-five years than there was between Plymouth Rock and the turn of this century. A very distinct watershed occurred between 1915–20, when differences in language became a very contentious public issue. Emblematic of the period, Theodore Roosevelt asserted in 1919: "We have room for but one language here and that is the English language, for we intend to see that the crucible turns out people as Americans and not as dwellers in a polyglot boarding-house" (Crawford 1989, 23).

The increased concern with language differences was obviously related to the imminent World War, but it was also concurrent with a major shift in the quantity and type of immigration to the United States. After a steady flow of northern Europeans in the nineteenth century, there now appeared a growing number of southern and eastern European immigrants (members of the "Mediterranean" and "Alpine" races, according to the eugenicists of the day)—Italians, Poles, and Jews of various nationalities. This new type of immigrant was viewed darkly by many American politicians and educators, and thought to suffer from high levels of feeble-mindedness, disloyalty, Popery, and other shortcomings. In one of the more popular books of the day, Charles Benedict Davenport warned that

> the population of the United States will, on account of the great influx of blood from South-eastern Europe, rapidly become darker in pigmentation, smaller in stature, more mercurial, more attached to music and art, more given to crimes of larceny, kidnapping, assault, murder, rape, and sex-immorality . . . [and] the ratio of insanity in the population will rapidly increase (Davenport 1911, 219)

During this period there were vociferous debates over how—and whether—persons so alien to the American "Nordic" race could assimilate. There was a vocal national concern that these immigrants were simply not of the quality and character of English or Scandinavian stock. While Germans were still viewed as genetically superior to Mediterranean types, the outbreak of war made the Germans the most despised people of all. The German accent was virtually eradicated from public use in America within a few years. In 1915, 24 percent of American high school students were studying German; by 1922 only 1 percent were doing so. Indeed, this period of linguistic intolerance caused a catastrophic drop in enrollments in *all* foreign languages from which our educational system has never recovered (Crawford 1989, 24).

Around this time, the fledgling National Council of Teachers of English, in its first decade of existence, hopped on the protectionist bandwagon by cosponsoring a national event called "Better Speech Week." In schools throughout America, students were enlisted in "Ain't-less," "Final-G," and other assorted grammatical tag-days designed to heighten linguistic vigilance. The centerpiece of this annual festival, which ran for more than a decade, was the following pledge, recited by schoolchildren all around the country:

> I love the United States of America. I love my country's flag. I love my country's language. I promise:
> 1. That I will not dishonor my country's speech by leaving off the last syllable of words.
> 2. That I will say a good American "yes" and "no" in place of an Indian grunt "um-hum" and "nup-um" or a foreign "ya" or "yeh" and "nope."
> 3. That I will do my best to improve American speech by avoiding loud rough tones, by enunciating distinctly, and by speaking pleasantly, clearly, and sincerely.
> 4. That I will learn to articulate correctly as many words as possible during the year. (McDavid 1965, 9–10)

People familiar with the subsequent role of the NCTE in public language 20
debates may be surprised to hear of the organization's entry on the side of prescriptivism, even overt nativism. But after this inauspicious launching, the NCTE promptly abjured popular, seat-of-the-pants notions about American speech and committed itself to the scholarly study of language. . . .

Today, in the controversy over the officialization of English, we are refighting the same old sociolinguistic issues—the struggles of the 1970s, the 1920s, and other times and places. If anything is certain about the current episode, it is this: in fifty years, when we look back upon all this turmoil, we will recognize the English-only furor of the 1980s and 1990s as another incident in the long history of American intolerance of immigrants and minorities, another outburst of our fear and hatred of the stranger. Our era will seem and sound much like the early 1920s, and we will immediately notice the remarkable structural similarities between the immigration patterns—the sudden and large influx of ethnically diverse people from unfamiliar areas of the world.

In 1919, it seemed inconceivable that the American nation could possibly assimilate millions of dark-skinned, poor, largely Catholic southern European immigrants without being "polluted" and destroyed. And yet, of course, we did gradually absorb all those peoples, and we have been immeasurably enriched in every aspect of our culture by doing so. Now those once-sinister Italians, Poles, and Jews have joined the old-timers in wondering: Can America absorb millions of Hispanics and Asians without being distorted, watered-down, and ruined?

Also when we look back fifty or seventy-five years from now, we will see that the English-only movement was built on misinformation, ignorance, and fear, but not on hatred. Whatever the politics of its leaders, the rank and file supporters, the ordinary citizens who marked official-English ballots and wrote small donation checks to U.S. English were not bigots. These were well-meaning, patriotic American citizens who supported language restrictionism out of genuine fear for the future of their country, or because they did not understand how language is actually learned and used, or because they had simply forgotten about the linguistic discrimination faced by their own immigrant ancestors. We will look back on the English-only movement, in other words, as a socially acceptable form of ethnic discrimination that passed from the scene just as soon as people understood its hidden meanings, its consequences, and the inhospitable messages it has sent to millions of our fellow citizens.

References

Bikales, Gerda. [Executive Director of U.S. English.], "Petition for FCC Rule Making." Letter, 26 September 1985.

Crawford, James. *Bilingual Education: History, Politics, Theory, and Practice*, Trenton, N.J.: Crane Publishing Company, 1989.

Davenport, Charles Benedict. *Heredity in Relation to Eugenics*, New York: Henry Holt and Company, 1911.

"English Only Law Becomes a Matter of Interpretation." *Chicago Tribune*, *6*, 15 January 1989.

EPIC Events (newsletter of the English Plus Information Clearinghouse). Washington, D.C.: January/February, March/April 1988.

"Florida English." *Education Week*, 19 March 1986.

"Frequently Used Arguments Against the Legal Protection of English," Flyer. Washington, D.C.: U.S. English, n.d.

Gavin, Jennifer. "Pena Outlaws Bias Based on Language," *Rocky Mountain News*, 29 December 1988.

Horn, Jim. "English First" solicitation letter. Falls Church, Va.: Committee to Protect the Family, n.d.

McDavid, Raven, ed. *An Examination of the Attitudes of the NCTE Toward Language*. Champaign, Ill.: National Council of Teachers of English, 1965.

Robbins, Terry. "An Open Letter to All the Governors in the United States." Florida English Campaign, Dade County, 30 March 1985.

Veltman, Clavin J. *The Future of the Spanish Language in the United States*. Washington, D.C.: Hispanic Policy Development Project, 1988.

Zall, Barnaby. "EL-PAC" solicitation letter, n.d.

QUESTIONS FOR DISCUSSION

1. Comment on the format of the "Survey." Why do you think it is called a "1991 National Opinion Survey"?
2. Comment on two or three passages in the "Survey" that seem to you persuasive. Do the same for two or three passages that you question or find annoying.
3. How do the results of the Crawford poll mentioned in paragraph 4 of "The Roots of Language Protectionism" support Daniels's position?
4. Explain the biblical allusion in paragraph 5. How does Daniels ironically turn the Babel parable to his favor?
5. Why was the period from 1915 to 1920 a time that reflected a major shift in attitudes about language differences, a time when language differences became a very contentious public issue? Why does Daniels find it "somewhat surprising to find that language differences have become a searing political issue in the 1990s"?

WRITING ASSIGNMENTS

1. Reaction Journal: Now that you have read Daniels's argument, reconsider your original freewriting. Discuss how Daniels's argument affected your thinking.
2. Reread both selections and find examples of diction that is charged or slanted. Daniels observes, "Nor has it been difficult for protectionist groups to spin frightening propaganda out of contemporary headlines." Comment on such "propaganda" and then examine Daniels's diction, for example, his statement that "some English-only adherents feel that death is not too severe a penalty for an immigrant's failure to speak English." Write a paper based on your findings.

TALKING AMERICAN

JERRE MANGIONE

Jerre Mangione (b. 1909) was born in Rochester, New York, and raised by Sicilian relatives in the area he describes in his novel Mount Allegro *(1943). Educated at Syracuse, he worked for the government and in advertising and public relations before joining the faculty at the University of Pennsylvania.* Mount Allegro, *in which "Talking American" appears, has been acclaimed for its rendering of the immigrant experience. Although it is a novel, it forms a trilogy with two works of nonfiction that continue the author's ethnic observations abroad:* Reunion in Sicily *(1950) and* A Passion for Sicilians *(1968). His other books include two more novels, a brief record of immigration titled* America Is Also Italian *(1969), and a history of the Federal Writers Project,* The Dream and the Deal *(1971). In the following selection, the narrator, whose mother thought of giving up speaking Italian as "renouncing her own flesh and blood," explores the social and psychological meanings of languages.*

◆ FREEWRITING

Typically, young children and adolescents are occasionally embarrassed by the behavior and rules of their parents and/or other adult family members. Freewrite for ten or fifteen minutes on your remembrances of such embarrassments.

My father could be more severe than my mother, but usually he was gentle with us and even conspired with us occasionally when we tried to avoid some of the household rules my mother laid down. Probably the most repugnant rule of all was that we eat everything she cooked for us, regardless of whether or not we liked the food or were hungry.

Unless my father protested, she persistently fed us *verdura*, in the interests of health, usually dandelion or escarole or some other bitter member of the vegetable family. The more we complained about such dishes the more convinced she became that they were good for us. She was without mercy about such things. If one of us dared protest while we were at the table, she would inflict a second helping on him. In time, we learned the wisdom of pretending to look fairly enthusiastic about everything she cooked for us, regardless of how distasteful it seemed.

Another unpopular rule she vigorously enforced was that we speak no other language at home but that of our parents. Outside the house she expected us to speak English, and often took pride in the fact that we spoke English so well that almost none of our relatives could understand it. Any English we spoke at home, however, was either by accident or on the sly. My sister Maria, who often talked in her sleep, conducted her monologues in English, but my mother forgave her on the ground that she could not be responsible for her subconscious thoughts.

My mother's insistence that we speak only Italian at home drew a sharp line between our existence there and our life in the world outside. We gradually acquired the notion that we were Italian at home and American (whatever that was) elsewhere. Instinctively, we all sensed the necessity of adapting ourselves to two different worlds. We began to notice that there were several marked differences between those worlds, differences that made Americans and my relatives each think of the other as foreigners.

5 The difference that pained me most was that of language, probably because I was aware of it most often. Child that I was, I would feel terribly embarrassed whenever my mother called to me in Italian while I was playing on the street, with all my playmates there to listen; or when she was buying clothes for me and would wrangle in broken English with the salesmen about the price.

My mother took no notice of such childish snobbery. As long as I remained under her jurisdiction, she continued to cling to her policy of restricting the family language to Italian. 'I might as well not have my children if I can't talk with them,' she argued. She considered it sinful for relatives to permit their children to speak a language which the entire family could not speak fluently, and claimed that if she were to cast aside Italian, the language of her forefathers, it would be like renouncing her own flesh and blood.

There was only one possible retort to these arguments but no one dared use it: the language we called Italian and spoke at home was not Italian. It was a Sicilian dialect which only Sicilians could understand. I seldom heard proper Italian spoken, except when my Uncle Nino made speeches or when one of my relatives would meet an Italian or another Sicilian for the first time. Proper Italian sounded like the melody of church bells and it was fresh and delicate compared to the earthy sounds of the dialect we spoke. Yet it was hard to understand how two persons could carry on an honest conversation in a language so fancy.

My Uncle Nino claimed that Italian was "feminine" and Sicilian "masculine." He also said that the only reason Sicilians ever addressed each other in proper Italian was to show off their schooling and prove to each other that they were not peasants. He probably was right, for I noticed that the ostentation of speaking proper Italian was dropped as soon as two Sicilians had known each other for an evening and showed any desire to be friends. Anyone who persisted in speaking Italian after that was considered a prig or, at least, a socialist.

But if my relatives were under the impression that they were speaking the same dialect they brought with them from Sicily, they were mistaken. After a few years of hearing American, Yiddish, Polish, and Italian dialects other than their own, their language gathered words which no one in Sicily could possibly understand. The most amazing of these were garbled American words dressed up with Sicilian suffixes—strange concoctions which, in later years, that non-

Sicilian pundit, H. L. Mencken, was to include in his book, *The American Language*.

Mr. Mencken's collection of Italian-American words is a good indication of 10
what happened to the vocabulary of my relatives. Such words as *minuto* for minute, *ponte* for pound, *storo* for store, *barra* for bar, *giobba* for job were constantly used as Sicilian words.

One word that Mr. Mencken should include in the next edition of his book is *baccauso*, which has been in my relatives' vocabulary as far back as I can remember. My parents probably picked it up from other American Sicilians when they first arrived in Rochester. Certainly, the word had no relation to their current mode of city life. It was used when referring to "toilet" and was obviously derived from the American "backhouse" that flourished in earlier and more rural America. Not until a few years ago when I first visited Italy, a nation without backhouses, and mystified Sicilians there by using the word, did I become aware of its Chic Sale derivation. Yet I had been using *baccauso* for a lifetime, always under the impression it was an authentic Sicilian word.

Even my father felt inhibited by my mother's determination to keep English out of the house, and would only speak the language when it was absolutely necessary or when my mother was not present. My father's English was like no one else's in the world. Yet it could be understood more easily than the English spoken by most of my Sicilian relatives. All that he knew of the language he managed to pick up during his first six months in America. His first factory *bosso*, a noisy Irishman, provided the incentive. My father wanted to learn enough English so that he could talk back to him. He was most successful; the boss fired him the first time he understood what he was saying.

So elated was my father with the amount of English he absorbed in a half-year that he stopped learning the language then and there and never made any further conscious effort to add to his vocabulary or improve his grammar. But he made the most of what he knew, and in a few years had developed a system of speaking English which defied all philological laws but could be understood by most Americans after about five minutes of orientation. Probably the most astonishing aspect of his system was that he used only one pronoun—"she"—and only one tense—the present.

The little English my mother knew she acquired from my father. But she spoke the language without any system, groping for nearly all the words she used, without any of my father's wonderful sureness. Although she had been in America as long as he, she had never had daily contact with persons who spoke only English. The tailor factories, where she worked when she arrived, were nearly all filled with men and women who had recently come from Italy and spoke only their native tongue.

The stores where she did her shopping every day were operated by Italians 15
whose customers were all Italians. The Poles and the Jews who made up a large part of Mount Allegro stuck to their native languages most of the time. My mother had little to do with them. She exchanged greetings with all of them, but you did not need to know much English to keep on friendly terms with a neigh-

bor. A smile or an occasional gift of cooked spaghetti served the purpose just as effectively.

My Uncle Luigi, more than any other of my relatives, had to depend on his smiles and charms to maintain good relations with Americans. His English was so rudimentary that it could be understood only by Sicilians. In view of his burning ambition to marry a slim widow with a fat bank account, his scant knowledge of the language proved something of a handicap. Most of the Italian widows he knew were fat and had very slim bank accounts. The few widows he met who qualified did not know a word of Italian.

It is possible that had he been able to speak English with any fluency, he might have married one of them, for he was six feet tall, and handsome in a gaunt and silvery way. He had been a widower for such a long time that his eyes had begun to dance again like those of a young bachelor. Yet despite all this and his most earnest efforts, he found that his sign language and his eye-rolling were not sufficient to establish communication with a rich widow's heart.

In spite of his superior intellect, Uncle Nino never learned much English—chiefly because of an old grudge he bore against his wife. Whenever he quarreled with her he would shout that he had never intended to come to America in the first place and only did so because she so "blinded" him that he could not distinguish between love and common sense. Even when he was not quarreling with her, you would have surmised from hearing him talk that he was through with America and was returning to Sicily the very next day.

Since he had ranted in much the same way for nearly twenty years, none of his relatives, least of all his wife, took him seriously. Yet the fact remained that during all that time Uncle Nino considered himself little more than a transient who would some day persuade his wife that it would be far more comfortable to return to Sicily and live on the fat of the land he owned there than to exist in a callow city like Rochester and slave all week for a few strands of spaghetti.

His arguments did not impress his wife, possibly because it was she and not 20
he who slaved all week. My Aunt Giovanna sewed buttonholes in a tailor factory, while he ran a small jewelry trade from his living-room, an occupation that left him with considerable time and energy to play briscola and threaten to leave America.

It was quite true that if he had not met my Aunt Giovanna, he probably would never have set foot outside of Sicily. As a young man he was managing a prosperous importing business in Palermo—so prosperous, my mother said, that he could bribe judges to change their decisions. And then my Aunt Giovanna came along. She was in the throes of conspiring to secure admission into the United States after having failed twice before. Both times her application had been rejected in the belief that she had trachoma, the eye disease that was often contracted by Sicilians living in towns where the water was bad.

On her first attempt to get to America she actually got as far as Ellis Island. But American officials seemed less susceptible to her beauty than the Italian officials who had gallantly helped to smuggle her through the red tape in Palermo. Ellis Island was little more than a prison in those days. For eight days she spent her time looking through iron bars at the Statue of Liberty and the New York skyline, and weeping.

Every morning an Irish policewoman who spoke Italian tried to make her tell how she had got on the boat without a passport. But my aunt never told. Finally the immigration officials realized they were wasting their time and shipped Aunt Giovanna back to Palermo.

When my Uncle Nino proposed three days after he met her, she consented, but only on condition that he take her to America. He gave up his thriving business, married her, and took her on a honeymoon to France, where they thought she would stand a better chance of getting a passport. At Havre she was again turned down. Uncle Nino got his passport without any trouble, but he saw little point in leaving his bride behind to go to a country that did not particularly attract him.

My Aunt Giovanna was never lacking in stubbornness. Against his better 25
judgment, she persuaded him to sail alone, arguing that once he was in the United States it would be a simple matter for him to make arrangements to send for her. Was she not his wife? Surely, American officials could not be so heartless as to permit red tape to separate newlyweds. Uncle Nino loved his wife too much to argue with her.

Her reasoning proved to be faulty. Uncle Nino's presence in the United States did not stir up any sentiments American officials might have for young newlyweds. He spent a miserable year in New York filling out endless forms, pining for his bride, and cursing the moment he had given in to her arguments. He was about to return to Europe and take her back to Sicily, when word came that Aunt Giovanna had been able to persuade the French immigration officials that there was nothing wrong with her eyes that a less tearful existence could not remedy.

He had never forgiven her for those lonely months he spent in New York waiting for her. And after twenty years of America he was still angry with her for having wrenched him away from a successful career to a makeshift existence in a strange land where he had to depend largely on his wife's earnings.

If it had not been for this old grudge, Uncle Nino might have mastered English.

"He who knows the English language will go forward," he was fond of saying. But he himself made not the slightest effort to learn it. "Why should I try to master a language as difficult as English? By the time I learned to speak it properly, it would be time for me to die. If your demands are as simple as mine, it is not hard to get whatever you want without knowing the language."

He liked to illustrate this point with a story he heard about the first Italians 30
who came to Rochester.

"In the early days Italians were disliked far more than they are now," he said. "They could not speak a word of English; at least I can fool an American into believing that I know what he is talking about, but they didn't even know enough English to do that. Nor did they get much chance to associate with Americans.

"The men were good strong workers but the Americans regarded them as bandits and intruders, and their employers treated them as though they were nothing but workhorses. They all forgot that they had been foreigners once too, and they made life as miserable as possible for them.

"Although the Italians had money, the storekeepers would not sell them food and the landlords would not rent them homes. For many weeks they were forced to live in boxes and tents and depend on *cicoria* for their main food. Now, *cicoria* is one of the most nutritious foods God planted in this earth, but even *cicoria* can become boring as a steady diet.

"The men had tried praying to God, begging Him to remind the Americans that they were *Cristiani* like themselves. But that didn't help. They became desperate. What was the use of earning money if you could not buy the things you needed most? One afternoon they armed themselves with pickaxes and marched into one of the largest grocery stores in town. While they stood by with their pickaxes poised over their heads, their leader addressed himself to the chief clerk.

"The leader did not know a word of English. He made motions with his 35
hands and his mouth to show that they were all very hungry. He also made it clear that unless the men were allowed to purchase food, they would tear up the store with their pickaxes. The clerk was a very understanding fellow and sold them all the food they wanted.

"Their success went to their heads. Now that they could buy food, they began to wish for real houses to eat it in. Even then Rochester was a miserably damp and rainy town, and a tent or a box was no way to keep snug. Once more the men got out their pickaxes and called on the grocery clerk. Again the clerk had no difficulty making out what they wanted. He begged them to calm down and indicated that he would try to help them.

"A few minutes later the police arrived. The clerk told them what the Italians wanted. The police told the Town Council, and the authorities told the landlords. In a few days the men were moved from their tents and shanties into real homes. These same Italians now have children who are some of the leading doctors, lawyers, and druggists in town. There's no doubt about it: you have to ask for whatever you want in this world, and prayer isn't always the way to ask."

QUESTIONS FOR DISCUSSION

1. What was Mangione's mother's "most repugnant" household rule? How did his mother's rule about speaking Italian at home and English away from home affect Mangione's childhood experiences?

2. In paragraphs 9–11 Mangione makes some interesting observations about the ethnic transformations of American words that H. L. Mencken found so fascinating. Discuss some of these observations.

3. The selection is written from the first-person point of view of an adult remembering childhood experiences. Explain why this point of view is particularly effective.

WRITING ASSIGNMENTS

1. Reaction Journal: Based on this and other selections in the text and on your own experiences and observations, write an essay in which you discuss the advantages and disadvantages of Mangione's mother's rule that only Italian be spoken at home.

2. All individuals have language and speaking habits that are uniquely their own. Such individual traits may be more pronounced for nonnative speakers; nevertheless, they do exist for native speakers as well. Review Mangione's essay, paying particular attention to paragraphs 10–17. Write an essay in which you describe individual language traits of selected members of your greater family. Be certain to use concrete examples, and remember that native speakers also develop their own language idiosyncrasies.

THE EDUCATION OF RICHARD RODRIGUEZ

RICHARD RODRIGUEZ

Richard Rodriguez (b. 1944), the son of working-class Mexican-American parents, learned to speak English when he entered elementary school in Sacramento. He earned an undergraduate degree at Stanford University, a master's degree at Columbia University, and a Ph.D. in English literature at the University of California at Berkeley, where he also taught, before devoting himself to writing, lecturing, and consulting on educational issues. His essays on the cultural and educational aspects of the language debate have appeared in many magazines and professional journals. He is the author of Hunger of Memory *(1981), a collection of autobiographical essays, and* Mexico's Children *(1991). In the following essay, which first appeared in* The American Scholar *in 1981 and was later included in* Hunger of Memory, *Rodriguez describes the pulls of family and mainstream society in the lives of bilingual children, the losses and gains that accompany assimilation into public society.*

◆ FREEWRITING

All families, not only bilingual families, have their own language. Write about the intimate language of your own family. As you freewrite for ten or fifteen minutes, try to give specific examples of this "private" language.

I remember to start with that day in Sacramento—A California now nearly thirty years past—when I first entered a classroom, able to understand some fifty stray English words.

The third of four children, I had been preceded to a neighborhood Roman Catholic school by an older brother and sister. But neither of them had revealed very much about their classroom experiences. Each afternoon they returned, as they left in the morning, always together, speaking in Spanish as they climbed the five steps of the porch. And their mysterious books, wrapped in shopping-bag paper, remained on the table next to the door, closed firmly behind them.

An accident of geography sent me to a school where all my classmates were white, many the children of doctors and lawyers and business executives. All my classmates certainly must have been uneasy on that first day of school—as most children are uneasy—to find themselves apart from their families in the first institution of their lives. But I was astonished.

The nun said, in a friendly but oddly impersonal voice, "Boys and girls, this is Richard Rodriguez." (I heard her sound out: *Rich-heard Road-ree-guess.*) It was the first time I had heard anyone name me in English. "Richard," the nun repeated more slowly, writing my name down in her black leather book. Quickly I turned to see my mother's face dissolve in a watery blur behind the pebbled glass door.

Many years later there is something called bilingual education—a scheme pro- 5
posed in the late 1960s by Hispanic-American social activists, later endorsed by a congressional vote. It is a program that seeks to permit non-English-speaking children, many from lower-class homes, to use their family language as the language of school. (Such is the goal its supporters announce.) I hear them and am forced to say no: It is not possible for a child—any child—ever to use his family's language in school. Not to understand this is to misunderstand the public uses of schooling and to trivialize the nature of intimate life—a family's "language."

Memory teaches me what I know of these matters; the boy reminds the adult. I was a bilingual child, a certain kind—socially disadvantaged—the son of working-class parents, both Mexican immigrants.

In the early years of my boyhood, my parents coped very well in America. My father had steady work. My mother managed at home. They were nobody's victims. Optimism and ambition led them to a house (our home) many blocks from the Mexican south side of town. We lived among *gringos* and only a block from the biggest, whitest houses. It never occurred to my parents that they couldn't live wherever they chose. Nor was the Sacramento of the fifties bent on teaching them a contrary lesson. My mother and father were more annoyed than intimidated by those two or three neighbors who tried initially to make us unwelcome. ("Keep your brats away from my sidewalk!") But despite all they achieved, perhaps because they had so much to achieve, any deep feeling of ease, the confidence of 'belonging' in public was withheld from them both. They regarded the people at work, the faces in crowds, as very distant from us. They were the others, *los gringos*. That term was interchangeable in their speech with another, even more telling, *los americanos*.

I grew up in a house where the only regular guests were my relations. For one day, enormous families of relatives would visit and there would be so many people that the noise and the bodies would spill out to the backyard and front porch. Then, for weeks, no one came by. (It was usually a salesman who rang the doorbell.) Our house stood apart. A gaudy yellow in a row of white bungalows. We were the people with the noisy dog. The people who raised pigeons and chickens. We were the foreigners on the block. A few neighbors smiled and waved. We waved back. But no one in the family knew the names of the old couple who lived next door; until I was seven years old, I did not know the names of the kids who lived across the street.

In public, my father and mother spoke a hesitant, accented, not always grammatical English. And they would have to strain—their bodies tense—to catch the sense of what was rapidly said by *los gringos*. At home they spoke Spanish. The language of their Mexican past sounded in counterpoint to the English of public society. The words would come quickly, with ease. Conveyed through those sounds was the pleasing, soothing, consoling reminder of being at home.

During those years when I was first conscious of hearing, my mother and 10
father addressed me only in Spanish; in Spanish I learned to reply. By contrast, English (*inglés*), rarely heard in the house, was the language I came to associate with *gringos*. I learned my first words of English overhearing my parents speak to strangers. At five years of age, I knew just enough English for my mother to trust me on errands to stores one block away. No more.

I was a listening child, careful to hear the very different sounds of Spanish and English. Wide-eyed with hearing, I'd listen to sounds more than words. First, there were English (*gringo*) sounds. So many words were still unknown that when the butcher or the lady at the drugstore said something to me, exotic polysyllabic sounds would bloom in the midst of their sentences. Often, the speech of people in public seemed to me very loud, booming with confidence. The man behind the counter would literally ask, "What can I do for you?" But by being so firm and so clear, the sound of his voice said that he was a *gringo*; he belonged in public society.

I would also hear then the high nasal notes of middle-class American speech. The air stirred with sound. Sometimes, even now, when I have been traveling abroad for several weeks, I will hear what I heard as a boy. In hotel lobbies or airports, in Turkey or Brazil, some Americans will pass, and suddenly I will hear it again—the high sound of American voices. For a few seconds I will hear it with pleasure, for it is now the sound of *my* society—a reminder of home. But inevitably—already on the flight headed for home—the sound fades with repetition. I will be unable to hear it anymore.

When I was a boy, things were different. The accent of *los gringos* was never pleasing nor was it hard to hear. Crowds at Safeway or at bus stops would be noisy with sound. And I would be forced to edge away from the chirping chatter above me.

I was unable to hear my own sounds, but I knew very well that I spoke English poorly. My words could not stretch far enough to form complete thoughts. And the words I did speak I didn't know well enough to make into distinct sounds. (Listeners would usually lower their heads, better to hear what I was trying to say.) But it was one thing for *me* to speak English with difficulty. It was more troubling for me to hear my parents speak in public: their high-whining vowels and guttural consonants; their sentences that got stuck with 'eh' and 'ah' sounds; the confused syntax; the hesitant rhythm of sounds so different from the way *gringos* spoke. I'd notice, moreover, that my parents' voices were softer than those of *gringos* we'd meet.

I am tempted now to say that none of this mattered. In adulthood I am embarrassed by childhood fears. And, in a way, it didn't matter very much that my parents could not speak English with ease. Their linguistic difficulties had no serious consequences. My mother and father made themselves understood at the county hospital clinic and at government offices. And yet, in another way, it mattered very much—it was unsettling to hear my parents struggle with English. Hearing them, I'd grow nervous, my clutching trust in their protection and power weakened.

There were many times like the night at a brightly lit gasoline station (a blaring white memory) when I stood uneasily, hearing my father. He was talking to a teenaged attendant. I do not recall what they were saying, but I cannot forget the sounds my father made as he spoke. At one point his words slid together to form one word—sounds as confused as the threads of blue and green oil in the puddle next to my shoes. His voice rushed through what he had left to say. And, toward the end, reached falsetto notes, appealing to his listener's understanding. I looked away to the lights of passing automobiles. I tried not to hear anymore. But I heard only too well the calm, easy tones in the attendant's reply. Shortly afterward, walking toward home with my father, I shivered when he put his hand on my shoulder. The very first chance that I got, I evaded his grasp and ran on ahead into the dark, skipping with feigned boyish exuberance.

But then there was Spanish. *Español*: my family's language. *Español*: the language that seemed to me a private language. I'd hear strangers on the radio and in the Mexican Catholic church across town speaking in Spanish, but I couldn't really believe that Spanish was a public language, like English. Spanish speakers, rather, seemed related to me, for I sensed that we shared—through our language—the experience of feeling apart from *los gringos*. It was thus a ghetto Spanish that I heard and I spoke. Like those whose lives are bound by a barrio, I was reminded by Spanish of my separateness from *los otros*,* *los gringos* in power. But more intensely than for most barrio children—because I did not live in a barrio—Spanish seemed to me the language of home. (Most days it was only at home that I'd hear it.) It became the language of joyful return.

* The others.

A family member would say something to me and I would feel myself specially recognized. My parents would say something to me and I would feel embraced by the sounds of their words. Those sounds said: *I am speaking with ease in Spanish. I am addressing you in words I never use with* los gringos. *I recognize you as someone special, close, like no one outside. You belong with us. In the family.*

(Ricardo.)

20 At the age of five, six, well past the time when most other children no longer easily notice the difference between sounds uttered at home and words spoken in public, I had a different experience. I lived in a world magically compounded of sounds. I remained a child longer than most; I lingered too long, poised at the edge of language—often frightened by the sounds of *los gringos*, delighted by the sounds of Spanish at home. I shared with my family a language that was startlingly different from that used in the great city around us.

For me there were none of the gradations between public and private society so normal to a maturing child. Outside the house was public society; inside the house was private. Just opening or closing the screen door behind me was an important experience: I'd rarely leave home all alone or without reluctance. Walking down the sidewalk, under the canopy of tall trees, I'd warily notice the —suddenly—silent neighborhood kids who stood warily watching me. Nervously, I'd arrive at the grocery store to hear there the sounds of the *gringo*—foreign to me—reminding me that in this world so big, I was a foreigner. But then I'd return. Walking back toward our house, climbing the steps from the sidewalk, when the front door was open in summer, I'd hear voices beyond the screen door talking in Spanish. For a second or two, I'd stay, linger there, listening. Smiling, I'd hear my mother call out, saying in Spanish (words): "Is that you, Richard?" All the while her sounds would assure me: *You are home now; come closer; inside. With us.*

"*Sí,*" I'd reply.

Once more inside the house I would resume (assume) my place in the family. The sounds would dim, grow harder to hear. Once more at home, I would grow less aware of that fact. It required, however, no more than the blurt of the doorbell to alert me to listen to sounds all over again. The house would turn instantly still while my mother went to the door. I'd hear her hard English sounds. I'd wait to hear her voice return to soft-sounding Spanish, which assured me, as surely as did the clicking tongue of the lock on the door, that the stranger was gone.

Plainly, it is not healthy to hear such sounds so often. It is not healthy to distinguish public words from private sounds so easily. I remained cloistered by sounds, timid and shy in public, too dependent on voices at home. And yet it needs to be emphasized: I was an extremely happy child at home. I remember many nights when my father would come back from work, and I'd hear him call out to my mother in Spanish, sounding relieved. In Spanish, he'd sound light and free notes he never could manage in English. Some nights I'd jump up just at hearing his voice. With *mis hermanos** I would come running into the room where he was with my mother. Our laughing (so deep was the pleasure!) became screaming. Like others who know the pain of public alienation, we transformed the knowledge of our public separateness and made it consoling—the reminder of intimacy. Excited, we joined our voices in a celebration of sounds. *We are speaking now the way we never speak out in public. We are alone—together*, voices sounded, surrounded to tell me. Some nights, no one seemed willing to loosen the hold sounds had on us. At dinner, we invented new words. (Ours sounded Spanish, but made sense only to us.) We pieced together new words by taking, say, an English verb and giving it Spanish endings. My mother's instructions at bedtime would be lacquered with mock-urgent tones. Or a word like *sí* would become, in several notes, able to convey added measures of feeling. Tongues explored the edges of words, especially the fat vowels. And we happily sounded that military drum roll, the twirling roar of the Spanish *r*. Family language: my family's sounds. The voices of my parents and sisters and brother. Their voices insisting: *You belong here. We are family members. Related. Special to one another. Listen!* Voices singing and sighing, rising, straining, then surging, teeming with pleasure that burst syllables into fragments of laughter. At times it seemed there was steady quiet only when, from another room, the rustling whispers of my parents faded and I moved closer to sleep.

QUESTIONS FOR DISCUSSION

1. How wise was the decision of Rodriguez's parents to send him to a school where all his classmates were English-speaking?
2. Discuss the following:
   a. "Not to understand this [a child's using his family's language in school] is to misunderstand the public uses of schooling and to trivialize the nature of intimate life."
   b. "The confidence of 'belonging' in public was withheld from them [my parents] both."
   c. "The language of their [my parents'] Mexican past sounded in counterpoint to the English of public society."
   d. "In adulthood I am embarrassed by childhood fears."
   e. "It is not healthy to distinguish public words from private sounds so easily."
3. The image in paragraph 4 of the "watery blur behind the pebbled glass door" is just one of several examples of figurative language. Find other examples and discuss what such figures contribute to Rodriguez's style.

* My brothers.

WRITING ASSIGNMENTS

1. Rodriguez focuses on public language and its effect on private language, family language. Review your freewriting activity and discuss how the language you use with your family differs from your more public language. For example, do you have any special words, expressions, jokes, that only members of your family can fully understand or appreciate? Write an essay about the differences between these two language worlds. Be certain to discuss why the two worlds exist for most of us.

2. If you were brought up in a bilingual family, write an essay about your experiences in both languages. If you were brought up in an English-only family, write about your experiences as a student in a foreign language program or as a visitor to a different language culture. If you can do neither of these, consider writing about whether or not you're missing something important.

FROM THE POETS IN THE KITCHEN

PAULE MARSHALL

Born of West Indian parents in Brooklyn, New York, Paule Marshall (b. 1929) received her bachelor's degree from Brooklyn College. She published her first novel, Brown Girl, Brownstones, *in 1959. Her other novels include* Soul Clap Hands and Sing *(1961) and* The Chosen Place, the Timeless People *(1969). "From the Poets in the Kitchen" (1983) appears in her collection* Reena and Other Stories. *In this essay Marshall describes the "rich legacy of language and culture" she gleaned as a child from the exuberant conversation of her mother and her mother's Barbadian friends—conversation that transformed school English into an idiom of their own. In their creative and empowering use of language, "these unknown bards" transformed their lives as well.*

◆ FREEWRITING

In this essay Marshall quotes the Polish writer Czeslaw Milosz: "Language is the only homeland." Before you read the following selection, freewrite for ten or fifteen minutes on what this statement suggests to you.

Some years ago, when I was teaching a graduate seminar in fiction at Columbia University, a well known male novelist visited my class to speak on his development as a writer. In discussing his formative years, he didn't realize it but he seriously endangered his life by remarking that women writers are luckier than those of his sex because they usually spend so much time as children around their mothers and their mothers' friends in the kitchen.

What did he say that for? The women students immediately forgot about being in awe of him and began readying their attack for the question and answer period later on. Even I bristled. There again was that awful image of women locked away from the world in the kitchen with only each other to talk to, and their daughters locked in with them.

But my guest wasn't really being sexist or trying to be provocative or even spoiling for a fight. What he meant—when he got around to explaining himself more fully—was that, given the way children are (or were) raised in our society, with little girls kept closer to home and their mothers, the woman writer stands a better chance of being exposed, while growing up, to the kind of talk that goes on among women, more often than not in the kitchen; and that this experience gives her an edge over her male counterpart by instilling in her an appreciation for ordinary speech.

It was clear that my guest lecturer attached great importance to this, which is understandable. Common speech and the plain, workaday words that make it up are, after all, the stock in trade of some of the best fiction writers. They are the principal means by which characters in a novel or story reveal themselves and give voice sometimes to profound feelings and complex ideas about themselves and the world. Perhaps the proper measure of a writer's talent is skill in rendering everyday speech—when it is appropriate to the story—as well as the ability to tap, to exploit, the beauty, poetry and wisdom it often contains.

"If you say what's on your mind in the language that comes to you from 5
your parents and your street and friends you'll probably say something beautiful. Grace Paley tells this, she says, to her students at the beginning of every writing course.

It's all a matter of exposure and a training of the ear for the would-be writer in those early years of apprenticeship. And, according to my guest lecturer, this training, the best of it, often takes place in as unglamorous a setting as the kitchen.

He didn't know it, but he was essentially describing my experience as a little girl. I grew up among poets. Now they didn't look like poets—whatever that breed is supposed to look like. Nothing about them suggested that poetry was their calling. They were just a group of ordinary housewives and mothers, my mother included, who dressed in a way (shapeless housedresses, dowdy felt hats and long, dark, solemn coats) that made it impossible for me to imagine they had ever been young.

Nor did they do what poets were supposed to do—spend their days in an attic room writing verses. They never put pen to paper except to write occasionally to their relatives in Barbados. "I take my pen in hand hoping these few lines will find you in health as they leave me fair for the time being," was the way their letters invariably began. Rather, their day was spent "scrubbing floor," as they described the work they did.

Several mornings a week these unknown bards would put an apron and a pair of old house shoes in a shopping bag and take the train or streetcar from our section of Brooklyn out to Flatbush. There, those who didn't have steady jobs would wait on certain designated corners for the white housewives in the neighborhood to come along and bargain with them over pay for a day's work cleaning their houses. This was the ritual even in the winter.

Later, armed with the few dollars they had earned, which in their vocabulary became "a few raw-mouth pennies," they made their way back to our neighborhood, where they would sometimes stop off to have a cup of tea or cocoa together before going home to cook dinner for their husbands and children.

The basement kitchen of the brownstone house where my family lived was the usual gathering place. Once inside the warm safety of its walls the women threw off the drab coats and hats, seated themselves at the large center table, drank their cups of tea or cocoa, and talked. While my sister and I sat at a smaller table over in a corner doing our homework, they talked—endlessly, passionately, poetically, and with impressive range. No subject was beyond them. True, they would indulge in the usual gossip: whose husband was running with whom, whose daughter looked slightly "in the way" (pregnant) under her bridal gown as she walked down the aisle. That sort of thing. But they also tackled the great issues of the time. They were always, for example, discussing the state of the economy. It was the mid and late '30's then, and the aftershock of the Depression, with its soup lines and suicides on Wall Street, was still being felt. . . .

There was no way for me to understand it at the time, but the talk that filled the kitchen those afternoons was highly functional. It served as therapy, the cheapest kind available to my mother and her friends. Not only did it help them recover from the long wait on the corner that morning and the bargaining over their labor, it restored them to a sense of themselves and reaffirmed their self-worth. Through language they were able to overcome the humiliations of the work-day.

But more than therapy, that freewheeling, wide-ranging, exuberant talk functioned as an outlet for the tremendous creative energy they possessed. They were women in whom the need for self-expression was strong, and since language was the only vehicle readily available to them they made of it an art form that—in keeping with the African tradition in which art and life are one—was an integral part of their lives.

And their talk was a refuge. They never really ceased being baffled and overwhelmed by America—its vastness, complexity and power. Its strange customs and laws. At a level beyond words they remained fearful and in awe. Their uneasiness and fear were even reflected in their attitude toward the children they had given birth to in this country. They referred to those like myself, the little Brooklyn-born Bajans (Barbadians), as "these New York children" and complained that they couldn't discipline us properly because of the laws here. "You can't beat these children as you would like, you know, because the authorities in this place will dash you in jail for them. After all, these is New York children."

Not only were we different, American, we had, as they saw it, escaped their ultimate authority.

Confronted therefore by a world they could not encompass, which even limited their rights as parents, and at the same time finding themselves permanently separated from the world they had known, they took refuge in language. "Language is the only homeland," Czeslaw Milosz, the emigré Polish writer and Nobel Laureate, has said. This is what it became for the women at the kitchen table. 15

It served another purpose also, I suspect. My mother and her friends were after all the female counterpart of Ralph Ellison's invisible man. Indeed, you might say they suffered a triple invisibility, being black, female and foreigners. They really didn't count in American society except as a source of cheap labor. But given the kind of women they were, they couldn't tolerate the fact of their invisibility, their powerlessness. And they fought back, using the only weapon at their command: the spoken word.

Those late afternoon conversations on a wide range of topics were a way for them to feel they exercised some measure of control over their lives and the events that shaped them. "Soully-gal, talk yuh talk!" they were always exhorting each other. "In this man world you got to take yuh mouth and make a gun!" They were in control, if only verbally and if only for the two hours or so that they remained in our house.

For me, sitting over in the corner, being seen but not heard, which was the rule for children in those days, it wasn't only what the women talked about—the content—but the way they put things—their style. The insight, irony, wit and humor they brought to their stories and discussions and their poet's inventiveness and daring with language—which of course I could only sense but not define back then.

They had taken the standard English taught them in the primary schools of Barbados and transformed it into an idiom, an instrument that more adequately described them—changing around the syntax and imposing their own rhythm and accent so that the sentences were more pleasing to their ears. They added the few African sounds and words that had survived, such as the derisive suck-teeth sound and the word "yam," meaning to eat. And to make it more vivid, more in keeping with their expressive quality, they brought to bear a raft of metaphors, parables, Biblical quotations, sayings and the like:

"The sea ain' got no back door," they would say, meaning that it wasn't like a house where if there was a fire you could run out the back. Meaning that it was not to be trifled with. And meaning perhaps in a larger sense that man should treat all of nature with caution and respect. 20

"I has read hell by heart and called every generation blessed!" They sometimes went in for hyperbole.

A woman expecting a baby was never said to be pregnant. They never used that word. Rather, she was "in the way" or, better yet, "tumbling big." "Guess who I butt up on in the market the other day tumbling big again!"

And a woman with a reputation of being too free with her sexual favors was known in their book as a "thoroughfare"—the sense of men like a steady stream of cars moving up and down the road of her life. Or she might be dubbed "a free-bee," which was my favorite of the two. I liked the image it conjured up of a woman scandalous perhaps but independent, who flitted from one flower to another in a garden of male beauties, sampling their nectar, taking her pleasure at will, the roles reversed.

And nothing, no matter how beautiful, was ever described as simply beautiful. It was always "beautiful-ugly": the beautiful-ugly dress, the beautiful-ugly house, the beautiful-ugly car. Why the word "ugly," I used to wonder, when the thing they were referring to was beautiful, and they knew it. Why the antonym, the contradiction, the linking of opposites? It used to puzzle me greatly as a child.

There is the theory in linguistics which states that the idiom of a people, the 25
way they use language, reflects not only the most fundamental views they hold of themselves and the world but their very conception of reality. Perhaps in using the term "beautiful-ugly" to describe nearly everything, my mother and her friends were expressing what they believed to be a fundamental dualism in life: the idea that a thing is at the same time its opposite, and that these opposites, these contradictions make up the whole. But theirs was not a Manichaean brand of dualism that sees matter, flesh, the body, as inherently evil, because they constantly addressed each other as "soully-gal"—soul: spirit; gal: the body, flesh, the visible self. And it was clear from their tone that they gave one as much weight and importance as the other. They had never heard of the mind/body split.

As for God, they summed up His essential attitude in a phrase. "God," they would say, "don' love ugly and He ain' stuck on pretty."

Using everyday speech, the simple commonplace words—but always with imagination and skill—they gave voice to the most complex ideas. Flannery O'Connor would have approved of how they made ordinary language work, as she put it, "double-time," stretching, shading, deepening its meaning. Like Joseph Conrad they were always trying to infuse new life in the "old old words worn thin . . . by . . . careless usage." And the goals of their oral art were the same as his: "to make you hear, to make you feel . . . to make you *see*." This was their guiding esthetic. . . .

I was sheltered from the storm of adolescence in the Macon Street library, reading voraciously, indiscriminately, everything from Jane Austen to Zane Grey, but with a special passion for the long, full-blown, richly detailed 18th- and 19th-century picaresque tales: "Tom Jones," "Great Expectations," "Vanity Fair."

But although I loved nearly everything I read and would enter fully into the lives of the characters—indeed, would cease being myself and become them—I sensed a lack after a time. Something I couldn't quite define was missing. And then one day, browsing in the poetry section, I came across a book by someone called Paul Laurence Dunbar, and opening it I found the photograph of a wistful, sad-eyed poet who to my surprise was black. I turned to a poem at random. "Little brown-baby wif spak'klin'/eyes/Come to yo' pappy an' set on his knee." Although I had a little difficulty at first with the words in dialect, the poem spoke to me as nothing I had read before of the closeness, the special relationship I had had with my father, who by then had become an ardent believer in Father Divine and gone to live in Father's "kingdom" in Harlem. Reading it helped to ease somewhat the tight knot of sorrow and longing I carried around in my chest that refused to go away. I read another poem. "'Lias! 'Lias! Bless de Lawd!/Don' you know de day's/erbroad?/Ef you don' get up, you scamp/Dey'll be trouble in dis camp." I laughed. It reminded me of the way my mother sometimes yelled at my sister and me to get out of bed in the mornings.

And another: "Seen my lady home las' night/Jump back, honey, jump back. /Hel' huh han' an' sque'z it tight . . ." About love between a black man and a black woman. I had never seen that written about before and it roused in me all kinds of delicious feelings and hopes.

And I began to search then for books and stories and poems about "The Race" (as it was put back then), about my people. While not abandoning Thackeray, Fielding, Dickens and the others, I started asking the reference librarian, who was white, for books by Negro writers, although I must admit I did so at first with a feeling of shame—the shame I and many others used to experience in those days whenever the word "Negro" or "colored" came up.

No grade school literature teacher of mine had ever mentioned Dunbar or James Weldon Johnson or Langston Hughes. I didn't know that Zora Neale Hurston existed and was busy writing and being published during those years. Nor was I made aware of people like Frederick Douglass and Harriet Tubman—their spirit and example—or the great 19th-century abolitionist and feminist Sojourner Truth. There wasn't even Negro History Week when I attended P.S. 35 on Decatur Street!

What I needed, what all the kids—West Indian and native black American alike—with whom I grew up needed, was an equivalent of the Jewish shul, someplace where we could go after school—the schools that were shortchanging us—and read works by those like ourselves and learn about our history.

It was around that time also that I began harboring the dangerous thought of someday trying to write myself. Perhaps a poem about an apple tree, although I had never seen one. Or the story of a girl who would magically transplant herself to wherever she wanted to be in the world—such as Father Divine's kingdom in Harlem. Dunbar—his dark, eloquent face, his large volume of poems—permitted me to dream that I might someday write, and with something of the power with words my mother and her friends possessed.

When people at readings and writers' conferences ask me who my major influences were, they are sometimes a little disappointed when I don't immediately name the usual literary giants. True, I am indebted to those writers, white and black, whom I read during my formative years and still read for instruction and pleasure. But they were preceded in my life by another set of giants whom I always acknowledge before all others: the group of women around the table long ago. They taught me my first lessons in the narrative art. They trained my ear. They set a standard of excellence. This is why the best of my work must be attributed to them; it stands as testimony to the rich legacy of language and culture they so freely passed on to me in the wordshop of the kitchen.

QUESTIONS FOR DISCUSSION

1. Marshall maintains that she "grew up among poets." Explain what she means when she refers to her mother and her mother's group of friends as poets.
2. Marshall's mother and her mother's friends felt their children, these "New York children," were difficult to raise because they "escaped their ultimate authority." Explain.
3. Explain why Marshall begins this selection by describing a "well-known male novelist" who was once a guest in a graduate seminar she was teaching.

WRITING ASSIGNMENTS

1. Reaction Journal: Review your freewriting for this selection. Freewrite again for ten or fifteen minutes. This time compare your response to what Milosz's statement appears to mean to Marshall.
2. Write a paragraph in response to two of the following:
    a. Describe the "idiom" of the "kitchen poets."
    b. Discuss the notion of language as therapy.
    c. Explain the use of "ugly" in the antonym "beautiful-ugly."
    d. Explain how Marshall's mother was able to make ordinary language work "overtime."
3. Identify someone from your own family or group of friends who speaks in a colorful if not poetic idiom. Write an essay in which you discuss this idiom. Be certain to show in a concrete manner how this person makes ordinary language work "overtime."

Education

IN A NATION OF IMMIGRANTS, public schooling faces special challenges. As Jane Addams, an early advocate for educational and social welfare issues, pointed out in 1908, the public school is the primary agency that introduces children to American life. A powerful tool of assimilation and a reflector of the general culture, public education transmits values as well as subject matter. In countries with more or less homogeneous populations, conflicts between public values and family values may appear primarily along class lines, but in a country of great ethnic diversity, such conflicts are compounded by ethnic differences in behavior and communication styles. Questions of how most effectively and humanely to accommodate these differences where they meet in the public schools have long been a focus of educational debate in the United States. While the particular racial and ethnic features of new Americans have changed and will continue to change, the basic issues persist. Jane Addams's pleas that teachers be knowledgeable about the traditions and values of their students and that schools take care not to cut students off from these traditions and values echo in contemporary efforts to provide a more balanced, truly multicultural curriculum.

When first established in the United States, public schooling had two principal aims—shaping a national character by encouraging personal identification with and loyalty to common principles of government and improving individual and national material well-being. The first of these aims—forging a unified identity out of ethnic diversity—seemed to require giving up those parts of one's identity that appeared "foreign" and taking on the values and behavioral norms reflected in the public schools. That these values and behaviors happened to be associated with nondenominational Protestantism is a result of the common background of the majority of public school teachers. When the current system of universal, free, tax-supported education was instituted in 1840, many of its strong advocates were Protestant ministers and the majority of its teachers were products of Protestant colleges that specialized in teacher training. The relative homogeneity of the teaching force ensured a considerable amount of standardization from school to school and state to state despite the local control characteristic of a decentralized system. Well into the twentieth century, adult evening schools as well as public day schools focused not only on the achievement of English literacy and allegiance to democratic political principles, but on the acquisition of the Protestant work ethic as well as certain norms of personal and domestic hygiene. In "College," Anzia Yezierska remarks on the "spick-and-span cleanliness" of her classmates who smelled of "soap and bathing" and even whose "black shoes had a clean look." Marilyn French's character Bella, in "First Day at School," remembers that when her mother first took her to school, the principal "looked at Momma as if she were dirty." The American preoccupation with cleanliness was a cultural feature unfamiliar to many immigrants forced to live in airless, overcrowded tenements, and the teaching of hygiene became one of the missions of the public schools. In "The Lower East Side," Samuel G. Freedman reports that during the late nineteenth and early twentieth centuries the schools on New York's Lower East Side taught hygiene, etiquette, and patriotism. No doubt this emphasis on hygiene and etiquette is one of the features Jane Addams had in mind when she warned against insisting on the kind of "superficial Americanism" that can cause intergenerational rifts within immigrant families.

Today there is renewed awareness of the kinds of behaviors leading to and resulting from conflicting value systems within the educational experience. Sarah Nieves-Squires, reporting on the experiences of Hispanic women in higher education in "Hispanic Women on Campus," points to some of the cultural differences and stereotyping that make the campus a more problematic environment for Hispanic students and faculty than for their Anglo counterparts. When the reasons for misunderstandings are not examined and appropriate intervention provided, minority students sometimes adopt behavior patterns that make their success within the existing educational system impossible. In "The Hidden Hurdle," Sophronia Scott Gregory describes the "sad irony" that academic achievement has made some black students targets for the ridicule of their peers who regard success in school as a rejection of black identity.

Such self-defeating defenses can also appear among students of any racial or ethnic background who have been identified as less able students. Mike Rose describes how he became a "mediocre student and a somnabulant problem solver" as he conformed to the norms of the vocational track to which he had been assigned through an administrative error ("I Just Wanna Be Average"). The defenses against denigration and low expectation that one cultivates by rejecting intellectual stimuli and feigning boredom ("flaunt ignorance, materialize your dreams") exact, as Rose points out, a terrible price.

The price Rose speaks of is a personal, not an economic one. Even if his fellow vocational students went on to become economically successful skilled workers, Rose suggests that their education would have taken away from them more than it gave them. Similarly, W. E. B. Du Bois, distinguished scholar, teacher, historian, and advocate for complete racial equality, argued in 1903 against the sorts of stereotyping that by limiting the scope of education available to particular groups dares to "regard human beings as among the material resources of a land to be trained with an eye single to future dividends." Relegating certain people to certain prospects by providing them with a limiting rather than a liberating education may lead to improved national and perhaps even individual prosperity. But such a course disregards the roles of aspiration and ideals in the formation of personal and national character.

The public schools must be concerned with the philosophical issues that inform decisions about what kind of education will best prepare students for their roles as wage earners, involved citizens, and fulfilled individuals. In addition, there are practical considerations and financial challenges for school systems struggling to accommodate large numbers of non-English-speaking students. Freedman reports that in 1900, burdened by a rapidly expanding immigrant population, overcrowded public schools in New York City turned away 1,100 eligible children and assigned 70,000 more to part-time classes. While students are no longer turned away, problems of inadequate facilities, personnel, and funding continue to plague many urban school systems. The arrival of more than 25,000 Southeast Asians in Lowell, Massachusetts, during a short period in the 1980s had a powerful impact on that city's school system. Within two years the school population grew by 2,000 students. The subsequent rise in the school budget left the city, in the words of its mayor, "financially devastated," while students themselves were too often left to flounder in overcrowded schools with teachers not trained to meet their cultural and linguistic needs.

Although public schooling in the United States has not always been responsive to the needs of its students, the tradition of local control has allowed concentrated ethnic communities a degree of influence on their schools. Language is the most prominent example of such influence. As early as the midnineteenth century, some non-English-speaking groups were able to get their own languages into the public schools, either as the media of instruction or as second-language studies. Nevertheless, the commitment of both schools and immigrant parents to assimilation was strong, and use of native languages in the schools was regarded as easing the inevitable and desired transition from one culture to another. Today the debate over whether or to what extent instruction should be in languages other than English continues (see "Language," pages 378–394, 412–418), informed by cultural as well as cognitive considerations.

Within the past decade there have been major changes in curriculum and methodology in response to hypotheses about the psychological and sociological factors that bear on school success. Specifically devised multicultural approaches have done away with the earlier fiction of common European ancestry and strive to acknowledge and respect cultural differences (see "Controversy: A Casebook on Multicultural Education"). There is a renewed effort to teach toleration and respect for others, to utilize the many resources minority and immigrant children bring to the classroom. It remains to be seen whether the schools are capable of legitimizing and destigmatizing a wide variety of cultures in a nondivisive way, while also encouraging a sense of national unity. If so, perhaps they can become, as Jane Addams hoped, the vehicles for giving "each child the beginnings of a culture so wide and deep and universal that he can interpret his own parents and countrymen by a standard which is world-wide and not provincial."

THE LOWER EAST SIDE

SAMUEL G. FREEDMAN

Samuel G. Freedman, a former reporter for the New York Times *and a frequent writer for* Rolling Stone, *has won a number of awards for investigative reporting and feature writing. He has also taught in the Graduate Departments of Theater and Journalism at Columbia University. In writing* Small Victories *(1990), Freedman followed a teacher through an academic year at Seward Park High School in New York's Lower East Side to learn how a school that serves America's newest immigrants is functioning amidst overcrowded conditions and a population burdened by tremendous social problems. In this selection from the book, Freedman sketches the social and educational conditions prevailing in immigrant neighborhoods in New York City up through the mandating of comprehensive neighborhood high schools in 1920.*

◆ FREEWRITING

In paragraph 9 Elwood P. Cubberly describes the "task" of public education in immigrant neighborhoods in the early years of the twentieth century. Read his description and freewrite for ten or fifteen minutes on the relevance of his words as we approach the twenty-first century.

The Lower East Side began its march to notoriety with an accident of topography. In southern Manhattan, near the present-day site of the Criminal Courts building on Centre Street, the land sagged into a marsh and a pond known as the Collect. Tanneries had sprung up around the Collect in the late 1700s, the better to dispose of carcasses, and the resulting stench and disease drove the wealthier residents uptown. So, too, did the tendency of structures to sink into the swampy soil, even after the Collect was drained and filled in 1808. A sanitary inspector for the city put it plainly: This land was "undesirable for a good class of population."

Its inheritors were, by one concise description, "freed slaves and hapless immigrants," predominantly Irish peasants fleeing the potato famine and the land-enclosure movement. They named their neighborhood Five Points for the corners created by its main intersection, since little about the area justified its prior title, Paradise Square. Forty-five thousand people lived in a square quarter-mile, piling two dozen to a room in cellars, backyard tenements, and abandoned mansions. One converted brewery was the original "Den of Thieves," and an adjacent passageway earned the monicker "Murderers' Alley."

By 1850, 26 percent of the population of New York (133,000 of 513,000) had been born in Ireland, and in Five Points, where Gaelic sometimes seemed the mother tongue, the proportion hovered closer to 70 percent. Congested and miserable, many of the immigrants sought identity in gangs, thieving and brawling and more rarely killing as troops of the Shirt Tails and the Plug Uglies, the Forty Thieves and the Dead Rabbits. But many more Irish immigrants submitted to the harsh doctrine of legal employ, the men toiling as manual laborers for fifty cents a day, the women hiring themselves out as maids for one dollar a week. As one newspaper of the time noted, "There are several sorts of power working at the fabric of this Republic—water power, steam power and Irish power. The last works hardest of all."

Still, the surrounding city saw what it always would see on the Lower East Side—an alien menace, teeming. Matthew Hale Smith wrote of the Irish poor: "Their homes are in the dens and stews of the city, where thieves, vagabonds and gamblers dwell. With the early light of morning they are driven from their vile homes to pick rags and cinders, collect bones and steal. They fill the galleries of the low theater, they are familiar with every form of wickedness and crime." As for education, Smith remarked that the children of Five Points were "too dirty, too ragged and carry too much vermin about them to be admitted to the public schools."

Wretched and oppressed as the early immigrants on the Lower East Side 5
were, their lot appeared enviable to millions of Eastern European Jews, afflicted by poverty, conscription, and pogroms. From 1880 to 1924, when the adoption of immigration quotas stanched the flow, two million Jews reached America. Talmudic scholars and illiterate peasants, lumber dealers and innkeepers, minstrels and factory owners, they poured into the Lower East Side, forming a Yiddish-speaking city within a city, with its own newspapers and magazines, banks and synagogues, nursing homes and mutual aid societies. Adjacent quarters swarmed with Italians, Greeks, Chinese, Germans, Irish, and blacks, transforming southeastern Manhattan into what Abraham Cahan dubbed "the metropolis of the ghettoes of the world."

Barely recovered from steerage, Jews shoved themselves into sunless tenements, three or four families to a floor, six or seven floors to a building, by their desperation raising the population density on some blocks to 968 people per acre, the highest in the world save for Bombay. "The architecture," Arnold Bennett wrote, "seems to sweat humanity at every window and door." The nascent middle-class aside, most turn-of-the-century Jewish immigrants held menial jobs. Some 25,000 peddlers sold pots, socks, pans, shoes, pickles, shirts, tools, seltzer, sweet potatoes, and Indian nuts. Another 200,000 Jews worked in garment factories, many of them owned by the more prosperous and assimilated German "uptown Jews," none of them protected by child-labor and occupational-safety laws until after 146 girls and women perished in the 1911 Triangle Shirtwaist Company fire.

Articles about "the Jewish problem," a staple of New York journalism, identified Eastern European immigrants as "ignorant," "primitive," and "the dregs of society." The novelist Henry James wrote of the Lower East Side in *The American Scene:* "It was like being at the bottom of some vast aquarium surrounded by innumerable fish with overdeveloped proboscis bumping together

. . . Here was multiplication with a vengeance." German Jews contributed to the lexicon of bigotry with *kike*, their slur against Eastern European Jews whose name often ended in "ky."

There was real and bitter debate on whether these inferiors could be saved, or whether America needed to be saved from them. The nativists triumphed when Congress passed the Johnson-Reed Act of 1924, restricting immigration by 75 percent, establishing quotas based on national origins, and vowing to preserve "the racial preponderance of the basic strain of our people." But more progressive minds prevailed on the issue of education. Major cities needed compulsory schooling, at least on the elementary level, for the same reason they needed professional police forces—to regulate the rabble and so protect themselves. Teaching the poor, by this thinking, had no intrinsic merit; it justified itself only as a balance wheel, a vast threshing machine.

"Our task," wrote Elwood P. Cubberly, the leading education historian of the early twentieth century, "is to break up these . . . [ethnic] settlements, to assimilate and amalgamate these people as part of our American race, and to implant in their children, so far as can be done, the Anglo-Saxon conception of righteousness, law and order, and popular government, and to awaken in them a reverence for our democratic institutions and for those things in our national life which we as a people hold to be of abiding worth." A New York state senator conveyed the theory more succinctly: "They will be elevated and lifted out of the swamp into which they were born and brought up."

The children of the Lower East Side were taught hygiene, etiquette, and 10
patriotism; they were expected to master serving manners and carry clean handkerchiefs. As if deliberately to defame the Jewish heritage of most pupils, each school day opened with a recitation of the Lord's Prayer, a New Testament invocation, and often proceeded in home economics to handling meat and milk together, a violation of kosher dietary laws. Textbooks of the period presented all ethnic and racial minorities—except the English, Scots, Germans, and Scandinavians—in various shades of debauchery, larceny, and sloth. Reality was not the battlefield; perception was, particularly the perception of foreignness.

However the elementary schools performed in assimilating immigrants, they showed severe problems in educating them. Overcrowded schools turned away 1,100 eligible children in 1900, while relegating 70,000 others to part-time classes. . . . Forty percent of the city's pupils lagged behind their grade level, and, according to a 1913 survey, only one-third of those entering the first grade graduated from the eighth. Not that the attrition troubled most educators. Industrial jobs and apprenticeships awaited the Lower East Side's dropouts, especially in the booming Brownsville district in Brooklyn. Teachers saw students' failures, David B. Tyack wrote, "not as a reflection of their own inabilities as instructors, but as evidence of the students' personal and moral recalcitrance."

Even for those who did manage it, elementary school graduation held a certain finality. In her unsentimental memoir, *A Wider World*, Kate Simon recalled receiving a rose and an ice-cream cone for the occasion, because "in the houses of immigrants . . . eight years in elementary school meant a long and broad education." In a 1910 tally, only 6,000 of the 191,000 Jewish pupils in New York were attending high school.

Larger aspirations, in any case, were irrelevant before the turn of the century. New York, a city of nearly 3.4 million, did not have a single public high school. The wellborn went to private academies, the future priests to parochial institutions, and all the rest to work. The concept of free secondary education had to be imported from Brooklyn, then a separate city, and it was not until 1897 that New York inaugurated its first public high school, Boys High School, soon to be followed by Girls High School and Mixed High School. Public in name only, these schools served a small, select population and attracted a faculty from the Ivy League, the Little Three, and other private colleges.

William H. Maxwell, the superintendent of schools and a Scottish immigrant himself, did promise a free education to every elementary school graduate, even as he opined that the handful of existing high schools could meet the demand for the next fifty years. His prediction seemed sound enough, considering that less than 5 percent of the city's students were enrolled in high schools and that those institutions were deliberately situated far from the crowded immigrant ghettoes. Maxwell, unfortunately, had not reckoned on the subway.

Once the Interborough Rapid Transit lines opened in 1904, the most im- 15
poverished immigrant could reach any of the three new high schools for a few cents. Enrollment in high schools citywide soared from 6,556 in 1898 to 63,000 in 1914, with well over half the elementary school alumni taking up Maxwell's offer. Some people, it seemed, just didn't know their place. So Maxwell tried to bring the appropriate place to them. He erected two vocational high schools, Manual Training for boys and Washington Irving for girls, on the northern border of the Lower East Side. No less an authority than Elwood P. Cubberly, after all, had urged educators to divest themselves of "the exceedingly democratic idea that all are equal, and that our society is devoid of classes."

But even the system of trade and academic schools soon proved inadequate. As New York's population ballooned toward 5.6 million in 1920, virtually every high school in the city burst its bounds, stacking 40 or 60 pupils in a class and cleaving its schedule into dual sessions. The battle had been lost. Neighborhoods would get their own high schools, even a neighborhood as disparaged as the Lower East Side.

QUESTIONS FOR DISCUSSION

1. Freedman suggests why the Irish immigrants formed street gangs. What is his reasoning? Do you see similar reasons that contribute to the formation of gangs in the inner city today?

2. Explain the origin of the ethnic slur "Kike." What group first used the term? Explain the origins of similar racial slurs.

3. What does Freedman gain by opening this selection with a description of the Collect?

4. Does Freedman manage to sustain a tone of "historical objectivity" in this selection? Point to specific sentences that demonstrate that he does or does not.

WRITING ASSIGNMENTS

1. Reaction Journal: Freewrite for ten or fifteen minutes on how well you feel public schools are meeting the special needs of minority students. Meet with three or four of your classmates and discuss your opinions. Make a list of your suggestions and share them with the whole class.

2. Freedman points to many problems that plagued urban schools nearly a century ago. How successfully have these problems been solved? Based on your reading, research, and personal experiences, write an essay in which you compare today's problems with those that Freedman describes.

THE HIDDEN HURDLE

SOPHRONIA SCOTT GREGORY

In "The Hidden Hurdle," Sophronia Scott Gregory (b. 1966) describes the dilemma faced by some black students whose school success causes their peers to accuse them of "acting white." Faced with this situation, talented students will sometimes yield to the pressure and adopt what sociologists have called the "oppositional behavior" of their peers—in this case, as Gregory points out, "sabotaging their own learning in order to fit in with peers." "The Hidden Hurdle" originally appeared in Time *in 1992.*

◆ FREEWRITING

Bright students who achieve high marks and set high standards for themselves are often ridiculed by less motivated students. This type of peer ridicule is sometimes called "nerd bashing." But whatever it is called, it is clearly an anti-achievement ethic that most adolescents and even young children experience or at least observe. Freewrite for ten or fifteen minutes on occasions when you observed incidents of this kind of peer pressure.

When it comes to achieving in school, Za'kettha Blaylock knows that even dreaming of success can mean living a nightmare. She would, above all things, like to work hard, go to college and become a doctor. But to many other black 14-year-old girls in her corner of Oakland, these ideas are anathema. The telephone rings in her family's modest apartment, and the anonymous voice mur-

murs daggers. "We're gonna kill you," the caller says. Za'kettha knows the threat comes from a gang of black girls, one that specializes not in drugs or street fights but in terrorizing bright black students. "They think that just because you're smart," says the eighth-grader, "they can go around beating you up."

Of all the obstacles to success that inner-city black students face, the most surprising—and discouraging—may be those erected by their own peers. Many children must also cope with broken families, inadequate schools and crumbling communities that do not value academic achievement as essential to survival and prosperity. But the ridicule of peers cuts most deeply of all. Students like Za'kettha find themselves reviled as "uppity," as trying to "act white," because many teenagers have come to equate black identity with alienation and indifference. "I used to go home and cry," says Tachelle Ross, 18, a senior at Oberlin High in Ohio. "They called me white. I don't know why. I'd say, 'I'm just as black as you are.'. . ."

The phrase "acting white" has often been the insult of choice used by blacks who stayed behind against those who moved forward. Once it was supposed to invoke the image of an African American who had turned his back on his people and community. But the phrase has taken an ominous turn. Today it rejects all the iconography of white middle-class life: a good job, a nice home, conservative clothes and a college degree.

In the smaller world of high school, the undesirable traits are different, but the attitude is the same. Promising black students are ridiculed for speaking standard English, showing an interest in ballet or theater, having white friends or joining activities other than sports. "They'll run up to you and grab your books and say, 'I'll tear this book up,'" say Shaquila Williams, 12, a sixth-grader at Webster Academy in East Oakland. "They'll try and stop you from doing your work." Honor students may be rebuked for even showing up for class on time.

5 The pattern of abuse is a distinctive variation on the nerd bashing that almost all bright, ambitious students—no matter what their color—face at some point in their young lives. The anti-achievement ethic championed by some black youngsters declares formal education useless; those who disagree and study hard face isolation, scorn and violence. While educators have recognized the existence of an anti-achievement culture for at least a decade, it has only recently emerged as a dominant theme among the troubles facing urban schools.

The label "acting white" and the dismissal of white values are bound up in questions of black identity. "If you see a black girl," explains Kareema Matthews, a street-smart 14-year-old from Harlem, "and she's black, not mixed or anything, and she wants to act like something she's not, in these days nobody considers that good. She's trying to be white. That's why nobody likes her. That's how it is now." But when asked what it is to be black, Kareema pauses, "I don't have the slightest idea."

The right attitude, according to the targets of ridicule, would be shown by skipping class, talking slang and, as Tachelle says, 'being cool, not combing your hair. Carrying yourself like you don't care." Social success depends partly on academic failure; safety and acceptance lie in rejecting the traditional paths to self-improvement. "Instead of trying to come up with the smart kids, they try to bring you down to their level," says eighth-grader Rachel Blates of Oakland. "They don't realize that if you don't have an education, you won't have anything —no job, no husband, no home."

It is a sad irony that achievement should have acquired such a stigma within the black community. Hard work, scholarship and respect for family values have long been a cornerstone of black identity. In the years before the Civil War, many black slaves risked their lives learning how to read. In 1867, just four years after the Emancipation Proclamation, African Americans founded Morehouse and Howard universities. According to the Bureau of the Census, between Reconstruction and 1910, the literacy rate among Southern blacks climbed from 20% to 70%. "There has always been a strong pressure toward educational achievement," says Mac Kendall, director of elementary education for the Atlanta public schools. Kendall, who grew up in semirural Thomasville, Ga., recalls, "My mother was not a lettered woman by any means, but she said, with a good education, you could turn the world upside down. That was a strong common linkage among all black people, and it was instilled early on."

Some education experts associate the rise of the culture of anti-achievement with the advent of public school desegregation and the flight of the black middle class to the suburbs. That left fewer role models whose success reinforced the importance of education and more children from families who found little grounds for hope in schools that were decaying.

The civil-rights movement did produce pockets of progress: the number of 10
black managers, professionals and government officials rose 52% in the past decade. Black enrollment in colleges has climbed steeply. In 1990, 33% of all black high school graduates went on to college, in contrast to 23% in 1967. Since 1976, black Scholastic Aptitude Test scores have increased by a greater percentage than those of either whites or Asians. Still blacks have higher truancy rates, and in spite of the gains, the test scores of African Americans remain the lowest among large ethnic groups. The high school dropout rate among young blacks averages 7.7%, nearly twice that of their white peers, at 3.9%.

As more black teachers and administrators reach positions of power in the public school system, the anti-achievement ethic presents a special challenge to them as educators. For years, the failure of black students to succeed in white-run schools was attributed in large part to institutional racism. But some black educators are reassessing the blame. "It's absolutely ridiculous for us to be talking about what's happening to black youngsters when you've got a 90% African-American staff teaching a 95% black student body," says Franklin Smith, who is superintendent of schools in Washington and black himself. "If you can't prove what you believe here in Washington, then you might as well forget it anywhere in this country."

The effort to reverse the pattern of black failure has prompted educators like Smith to try many experiments—Afrocentric curriculums, academic-achievement fairs and efforts to establish black all-male public schools that focus on building self-esteem. The reform movements seek to revive in black students the value system that prizes education as, among other things, a way out of poverty. "We dropped the ball," laments Trinette Chase, a Montgomery County, Md., mother. "Our generation failed to pass on the value of an education."

It is a truism to say the problem most often begins at home. When parents are not able to transmit the values of achievement, the ever present peer group fills the vacuum. Moniqua Woods, 12, a student in the Webster Academy in Oakland, says it is easy to spot neglected children because they "come to school every day yawning and tired. You know they stayed out late that night." Concurs classmate Mark Martin, also 12: "Some of the kids' parents are on drugs. You go in their house, and you can smell it." Such a homelife can further strengthen the attitude that school does not matter, especially if the parents themselves are without a diploma.

Kiante Brown, 15, of Oakland, knows this all too well. His mother is a recovering crack addict who, he says, pays little attention to his comings and goings, and he hasn't seen his father in two years. Kiante used to spend his afternoons selling drugs on street corners. What little education he has came in bits and pieces; he has missed so much school he'll have to repeat the eighth grade. "I didn't really drop out, but I haven't been going to school much," he says. "For a while my mom told me to get up and go to school, but she really doesn't say nothing about it anymore."

15 Teachers may try to move in where parents have retreated. But with class sizes increasing and school violence growing, it is often all educators can do to maintain minimal order, much less give individual attention to any child. Some teachers admit that the insidious attitudes creep into the classroom. It becomes a self-fulfilling prophecy: when teachers have lower expectations for their black students, they give them less attention and do not push them as hard to do well. Such stereotypes have crossed racial barriers to the point where even black teachers may hold these same attitudes. "If teachers feel they cannot make any headway with a youngster," says Richard Mesa, superintendent of Oakland public schools, "they may write him off."

It is especially painful for teachers to watch their most talented students sabotage their own learning in order to fit in with peers. "Some of them feign ignorance to be accepted," says Willie Hamilton, the principal of Oakland's Webster Academy. Seneca Valley's Martine Martin observed this self-destructive pattern when she formed a program for "at risk" black females at one of her previous schools. The group originally comprised girls who were pregnant or uninterested in learning. But then, little by little, Martin noticed honor students showing up in her program because they thought it was cool.

The environment outside the classroom also leaves its mark inside. The persistence of recession has made it even more difficult to inspire black students to do well in school with the carrot of a job. "The lack of association between education and post-school employment has discouraged a lot of young people," says William Julius Wilson, professor of sociology and public policy at the University of Chicago. "They see that whether you graduate from high school or you drop out, you're still going to be hanging around on a corner or the best job you're going to find is working at a McDonald's. After a time they develop a view that you're a chump if you study hard."

Many successful black role models feel the need to "give something back," by reaching out to inner-city youths. But some are finding it hard to make the connection. Meeting with a group of young inmates from a correctional facility, Robert Johnson, founder and CEO of Black Entertainment Television, faced some hostile young men and responded in kind. "I told them they were playing themselves into the hands of people who don't care about them. That if they think the way to pull themselves up is to get into the drug trade, rob, shoot and steal they were going to lose."

But teenagers who have trouble identifying with Johnson choose their role models accordingly. "There's a lot of violence and a lot of drugs where I grow up," says Harlem teenager Marcos Medrano, 15, whose role model is macho actor Steven Seagal. "I went to a party, and there was a shoot-out. You're constantly living in danger. Who you gonna look up to? Bill Cosby or somebody that comes out shooting a lot?"

Successful blacks can be intimidating for the young, especially if they dress 20
in suits and "sound white." Some suspect that the ease with which successful blacks move in a white world means that they have denied their heritage. "It's devastating for them because you begin to get this stereotype thinking that all blacks when they get to a certain level try to become white by assimilating themselves with whites," says Dorothy Young, principal of the Delano Elementary School on the west side of Chicago. "And that's not true. But once that seed is planted in any form, that seed is going to grow."

The need to define their identity may lead young blacks to reject the values of achievement; but, according to Rutgers anthropologist Signithia Fordham, this does not mean they think being black is *only* about failure. "They may not be able to articulate fully what it means to be black, but they're more attuned to why it is they don't want to be white," she says of black students she researched. "They know they want very much to remain connected to the black community. They want to be successful on their own terms."

There are, of course, many schools that can point to their success stories, to students who overcame all the private obstacles to graduation, often with the help of innovative programs. In Cleveland, the Scholarship-in-Escrow program was set up by local businessmen in 1987. To encourage students to work toward college, the program offers cash incentives—$40 for each A they earn, $20 for each B—which go into an escrow account for their tuition. Since its inception, SIE has paid $469,300 in earned funds for 2,199 graduates. "It's good to know that money is being put away for you," says Faith Bryant, an 11th-grader at John Adams High School. "I had always dreamed of being successful, but now I know I have a way to do it."

The hope for these students lies in their understanding that no one group in society has a monopoly on success. "As long as you're able to term success as being black or white or red," says Oberlin's Sherman Jones, a placement specialist for the Jobs for Ohio's Graduates program, "as long as we put conditions and colors on success then it'll be difficult for our kids." Destroying such misconceptions is not easy, especially when they are old and deeply rooted. But given time, perhaps "acting white" can be a phrase retired to the history books as the emblem of a misguided attitude that vanished in the light of black achievement.

QUESTIONS FOR DISCUSSION

1. Respond to the technique Gregory employs to introduce her thesis. How does her closing relate to her opening paragraph? Is her use of concrete examples appropriate and convincing?
2. Those African-American students who reject the anti-achievement culture Gregory describes are often accused by their peers of "acting white." Discuss the relationship between black identity and this "hidden hurdle."
3. What are some possible solutions that you can suggest to such anti-achievement bias?

WRITING ASSIGNMENTS

1. Reaction Journal: Write a letter to Za'Kettha Blaylock. Demonstrate how you have observed "nerd bashing" and how you have felt such anti-achievement bias. In your letter suggest what she can do. Can you show her that such peer pressure, although stronger in the African-American community, is not unique to it?
2. Write an essay in which you discuss ways in which our schools, our families, and even our media have unwittingly encouraged anti-achievement bias. After you have described the problem, suggest some solutions.

HISPANIC WOMEN ON CAMPUS

SARAH NIEVES-SQUIRES

Sarah Nieves-Squires (b. 1938), a native of Puerto Rico, is an associate professor of education and sociology at Lesley College. She served previously as the director of Harvard University's health professions program. In the following excerpt from her paper published in 1991 by the Association of American Colleges as part of its Project on the Status and Education of Women, Nieves-Squires suggests some of the factors that complicate academic life for Hispanic women.

◆ FREEWRITING

In this selection, Nieves-Squires points out that a major cause of stress for members of minority cultures is the conflict of their values with the values of the dominant culture. Before reading this selection, freewrite for ten or fifteen minutes. Try to find concrete examples that demonstrate such conflicts. Draw from your reading and from your experiences.

Cultural Differences

For many Hispanic women, the major cause of stress is cultural conflict. In addition to facing difficulties that women or any minority member might experience, they also must deal with different cultural expectations. Meléndez and Petrovich point out that "many attitudes and values of the university culture are at odds with the character of Hispanic interpersonal relationships, forms of communication, and sex-role expectations."[1]

Meléndez and Petrovich also note, for example, that Hispanic culture encourages tolerance of different opinions. Challenging someone's statements, trying to change another person's opinion, or debating issues can be viewed as a sign of disrespect. Not only does such a tradition of academe make some Hispanics uncomfortable, but the reluctance of Hispanics to participate in such behavior may be misinterpreted by faculty members as a lack of interest or ability; the classroom silence of a Hispanic may be due to politeness rather than a lack of independent thinking.[2]

Cooperation and group cohesiveness are very important values in Hispanic culture. The competitiveness of academe, with its strong emphasis on individual achievement, can be a source of conflict for Hispanics. "While Hispanics need to learn to survive and thrive in a competitive environment, they may well need a period of transition before they can tackle individual and competitive projects. Professors can help by permitting students to do some group projects. Non-Hispanic students could also benefit from opportunities to develop cooperation skills."[3]

The way in which professors relate to students in conversation about their work reflects these cultural difference. "Anglo professors . . . are often task oriented and get right to the point in conferences with students. Hispanic students are used to professors asking about their families, vacations, hobbies, and so forth, before discussing business. The immediate discussion of the business at hand is considered indifferent and cold."[4] Thus professors may be viewed as rejecting students even when they are not. More importantly, a professor who shows personal interest in a student and provides encouragement can enhance markedly the student's motivation and performance. This is true for all students, not just Hispanic women.

Similarly, expectations of friendship and peer relationships may be different 5
for Hispanics. Hispanics often spend a good deal of time building relationships.

Friendships are deep and require loyalty. “The informal casualness of acquaintances in the dominant culture, along with the different expectations of friendships, may complicate the task of making friends and exacerbate feelings of isolation.”[5]

Other differences also may lead to misunderstandings between Hispanics and others. The closer personal space that is comfortable for some Hispanics may make Anglos uncomfortable or may be perceived as inviting intimacy. A warm smile may be mistaken for a flirtatious one. Overt hand and arm gestures, coupled with a Spanish accent, may be perceived as a lack of verbal ability. Moreover, “Hispanics of the same sex stand very close together, while members of the opposite sex stand further apart than Anglos do. Hispanic friends of the same sex touch each other quite frequently, whereas those of the opposite sex do not touch each other at all.”[6] Thus closeness, hugging, and kissing among Hispanic women may be misinterpreted as homosexual behavior.

In Hispanic cultures, looking someone directly in the eye is often considered a challenge or a sign of disrespect. In contrast, in the dominant culture—and particularly in the classroom—eye contact means attentiveness. Thus the stage is set for misperception and misunderstanding. The Hispanic female student may feel embarrassed when her male professor looks directly at her. The professor, noting that the student did not maintain eye contact, may conclude that she is not paying attention, is not interested in the materials, or is too passive to interact with the professor.[7]

Ignorance of Hispanic customs and beliefs can prompt non-Hispanics to misunderstand the motivation and behavior of Hispanics. Social contacts are problematic when compounded by stereotypes. Many non-Hispanics' knowledge of Hispanic culture derives from stereotypes perpetuated in the media. Their knowledge of Puerto Ricans comes from *West Side Story*; *La Bamba* and *El Norte* complete the picture for Central and Mexican Americans. Some people do not differentiate among the various Hispanic groups but have one stereotype for all.

The stereotypes of Hispanic women are compounded by stereotyped attitudes and views of women in general. One of the major assumptions about Hispanic women is that they focus only on home and family. “The image of dutiful daughters, wives, and mothers . . . is a negative one in this society because the sense of duty is linked to subservience and dependency. Hispanic women are seen as content with being sex objects and decorative figures who are required to obtain less education than their male counterparts because they are less capable of using it. . . . These negative images . . . lead to the stereotyping of Hispanic-American women as powerless, pathological, and prayerful, and dutiful family members.”[8]

A woman dean at a private university comments: “I suspect that being a 10
woman became more important in this [institution] than being Puerto Rican. It has always been difficult for me to tell what it is that is really disturbing people who I don't feel should otherwise be disturbed—my gender? my being Puerto

Rican? or my political views? At any rate, I say I suspect being a woman was more important because when our printer came . . . to deliver an order, he yelled to the white male assistant dean, 'Hey, I hear you got a woman!' meaning a woman boss."[9]

Notes

1. Sara E. Meléndez and Janice Petrovich, "Hispanic Women Students in Higher Education: Meeting the Challenge of Diversity," in *Educating the Majority: Women Challenge Tradition in Higher Education*, ed. Carol S. Pearson, Donna Shavlik, and Judith Touchton (Washington, DC: American Council of Education/Macmillan Series on Higher Education, 1989), 60.
2. *Ibid.*, 61.
3. *Ibid.*, 62.
4. *Ibid.*
5. *Ibid.*, 61.
6. *Ibid.*, 64.
7. *Ibid.*, 63.
8. Shelby Lewis with Owanah Anderson, Lucie Cheng, Arlene Fong Craig, Njeri Jackson, Isabella Jenkins, Barbara Jones, Saundra Rice Murray, Marge Rosensweig, Patricia Bell-Scott, and Bonnie Wallace, "Achieving Sex Equity for Minority Women," in *Handbook for Achieving Sex Equity*, ed. Susan S. Klein (Baltimore: Johns Hopkins University Press, 1989), 376.
9. Quoted in Clara E. Rodriguez, "On the Declining Interest in Race," 20.

QUESTIONS FOR DISCUSSION

1. Explain why the classroom silence of Hispanic women may be due to politeness rather than to lack of independent thinking. Also, according to Nieves-Squires, how might cultural conflict become an issue in a professor/student conference?
2. Discuss how the Hispanic response to the following circumstances might lead to cultural conflict on a university campus:
   a. peer relationships
   b. personal space
   c. hand and arm gestures
   d. eye contact
3. Nieves-Squires asserts that "stereotypes of Hispanic women are compounded by stereotyped attitudes and views of women in general." Explain her position.

WRITING ASSIGNMENTS

1. Reaction Journal: Write a paragraph on Nieves-Squires' focus in this selection. Is her focus more on gender differences or on Hispanic cultural differences? Is she able to make the two distinct, or does she intend for the two to become a single focus?

2. Interview a member of a minority culture and/or draw upon your own experiences with potential conflicts created by differences between minority cultures and the dominant culture. Use your freewriting to help develop an essay in which you demonstrate such conflicts as concretely as possible.

FROM NARRATIVE OF THE LIFE OF FREDERICK DOUGLASS, AN AMERICAN SLAVE

FREDERICK DOUGLASS

Born and raised as a slave, Frederick Douglass (1817–1895) became an internationally famous abolitionist. Escaping to Massachusetts at the age of twenty-one, Douglass initially supported himself as a laborer and later became a featured speaker at antislavery meetings in the United States and Europe. North Star, *a newspaper he began for blacks, was an influential voice in the abolitionist movement. In this selection from his autobiography, published in 1845, Douglass describes how he learned to read and write and how he came to realize that literacy was the key to freedom.*

◆ FREEWRITING

In this selection from his autobiography describing his experiences as an American slave, Frederick Douglass tells how a master felt that knowing how to read and write would forever make Douglass unfit to be a slave. Freewrite for ten or fifteen minutes and anticipate what Douglass will say about this apparent incompatibility of slavery and literacy.

Very soon after I went to live with Mr. and Mrs. Auld, she very kindly commenced to teach me the A, B, C. After I had learned this, she assisted me in learning to spell words of three or four letters. Just at this point of my progress, Mr. Auld found out what was going on, and at once forbade Mrs. Auld to instruct me further, telling her, among other things, that it was unlawful, as well as unsafe, to teach a slave to read. To use his own words, further, he said, "If you give a nigger an inch, he will take an ell. A nigger should know nothing but to obey his master—to do as he is told to do. Learning would *spoil* the best nigger in the world. Now," said he, "if you teach that nigger (speaking of myself) how to read, there would be no keeping him. It would forever unfit him to be a slave. He would at once become unmanageable, and of no value to his master. As to himself, it could do him no good, but a great deal of harm. It would make him discontented and unhappy." These words sank deep into my heart, stirred up sentiments within that lay slumbering, and called into existence an entirely new train of thought. It was a new and special revelation, explaining dark and mysterious things, with which my youthful understanding had struggled, but struggled in vain. I now understood what had been to me a most perplexing difficulty—to wit, the white man's power to enslave the black man. It was a grand achievement, and I prized it highly. From that moment, I understood the pathway from slavery to freedom. It was just what I wanted, and I got it at a time when I the least expected it. Whilst I was saddened by the thought of losing the aid of my kind mistress, I was gladdened by the invaluable instruction which, by the merest accident, I had gained from my master. Though conscious of the difficulty of learning without a teacher, I set out with high hope, and a fixed purpose, at whatever cost of trouble, to learn how to read. The very decided manner with which he spoke, and strove to impress his wife with the evil consequences of giving me instruction, served to convince me that he was deeply sensible of the truths he was uttering. It gave me the best assurance that I might rely with the utmost confidence on the results which, he said, would flow from teaching me to read. What he most dreaded, that I most desired. What he most loved, that I most hated. That which to him was a great evil, to be carefully shunned, was to me a great good, to be diligently sought; and the argument which he so warmly urged, against my learning to read, only served to inspire me with a desire and determination to learn. In learning to read, I owe almost as much to the bitter opposition of my master, as to the kindly aid of my mistress. I acknowledge the benefit of both. . . .

I lived in Master Hugh's family about seven years. During this time, I succeeded in learning to read and write. In accomplishing this, I was compelled to resort to various stratagems. I had no regular teacher. My mistress, who had kindly commenced to instruct me, had, in compliance with the advice and direction of her husband, not only ceased to instruct, but had set her face against my being instructed by any one else. It is due, however, to my mistress to say of her, that she did not adopt this course of treatment immediately. She at first lacked the depravity indispensable to shutting me up in mental darkness. It was at least necessary for her to have some training in the exercise of irresponsible power, to make her equal to the task of treating me as though I were a brute.

My mistress was, as I have said, a kind and tender-hearted woman; and in the simplicity of her soul she commenced, when I first went to live with her, to treat me as she supposed one human being ought to treat another. In entering upon the duties of slaveholder, she did not seem to perceive that I sustained to her the relation of a mere chattel, and that for her to treat me as a human being was not only wrong, but dangerously so. Slavery proved as injurious to her as it did to me. When I went there, she was a pious, warm, and tender-hearted woman. There was no sorrow or suffering for which she had not a tear. She had bread for the hungry, clothes for the naked, and comfort for every mourner that came within her reach. Slavery soon proved its ability to divest her of these heavenly qualities. Under its influence, the tender heart became stone, and the lamblike disposition gave way to one of tiger-like fierceness. The first step in her downward course was in her ceasing to instruct me. She now commenced to practise her husband's precepts. She finally became even more violent in her opposition than her husband himself. She was not satisfied with simply doing as well as he had commanded; she seemed anxious to do better. Nothing seemed to make her more angry than to see me with a newspaper. She seemed to think that here lay the danger. I have had her rush at me with a face made all up of fury, and snatch from me a newspaper, in a manner that fully revealed her apprehension. She was an apt woman; and a little experience soon demonstrated, to her satisfaction, that education and slavery were incompatible with each other.

From this time I was most narrowly watched. If I was in a separate room any considerable length of time, I was sure to be suspected of having a book, and was at once called to give an account of myself. All this, however, was too late. The first step had been taken. Mistress, in teaching me the alphabet, had given me the *inch*, and no precaution could prevent me from taking the *ell*.

5 The plan which I adopted, and the one by which I was most successful, was that of making friends of all the little white boys whom I met in the street. As many of these as I could, I converted into teachers. With their kindly aid, obtained at different times and in different places, I finally succeeded in learning to read. When I was sent of errands, I always took my book with me, and by going one part of my errand quickly, I found time to get a lesson before my return. I used also to carry bread with me, enough of which was always in the house, and to which I was always welcome; for I was much better off in this regard than many of the poor white children in our neighborhood. This bread I used to bestow upon the hungry little urchins, who, in return, would give me that more valuable bread of knowledge. I am strongly tempted to give the names of two or three of those little boys, as a testimonial of the gratitude and affection I bear them; but prudence forbids;—not that it would injure me, but it might embarrass them; for it is almost an unpardonable offence to teach slaves to read in this Christian country. It is enough to say of the dear little fellows, that they lived on Philpot Street, very near Durgin and Bailey's ship-yard. I used to talk this matter of slavery over with them. I would sometimes say to them, I wished I could be as free as they would be when they got to be men. "You will be free as soon as you are twenty-one, *but I am a slave for life!* Have not I as good a right to be free as you have?" These words used to trouble them; they would express for me the liveliest sympathy, and console me with the hope that something would occur by which I might be free.

I was now about twelve years old, and the thought of being *a slave for life* began to bear heavily upon my heart. Just about this time, I got hold of a book entitled "The Columbian Orator." Every opportunity I got, I used to read this book. Among much of other interesting matter, I found in it a dialogue between a master and his slave. The slave was represented as having run away from his master three times. The dialogue represented the conversation which took place between them, when the slave was retaken the third time. In this dialogue, the whole argument in behalf of slavery was brought forward by the master, all of which was disposed of by the slave. The slave was made to say some very smart as well as impressive things in reply to his master—things which had the desired though unexpected effect; for the conversation resulted in the voluntary emancipation of the slave on the part of the master.

In the same book, I met with one of Sheridan's mighty speeches on and in behalf of Catholic emancipation. These were choice documents to me. I read them over and over again with unabated interest. They gave tongue to interesting thoughts of my own soul, which had frequently flashed through my mind, and died away for want of utterance. The moral which I gained from the dialogue was the power of truth over the conscience of even a slaveholder. What I got from Sheridan was a bold denunciation of slavery, and a powerful vindication of human rights. The reading of these documents enabled me to utter my thoughts, and to meet the arguments brought forward to sustain slavery; but while they relieved me of one difficulty, they brought on another even more painful than the one of which I was relieved. The more I read, the more I was led to abhor and detest my enslavers. I could regard them in no other light than a band of successful robbers, who had left their homes, and gone to Africa, and stolen us from our homes, and in a strange land reduced us to slavery. I loathed them as being the meanest as well as the most wicked of men. As I read and contemplated the subject, behold! that very discontentment which Master Hugh had predicted would follow my learning to read had already come, to torment and sting my soul to unutterable anguish. As I writhed under it, I would at times feel that learning to read had been a curse rather than a blessing. It had given me a view of my wretched condition, without the remedy. It opened my eyes to the horrible pit, but to no ladder upon which to get out. In moments of agony, I envied my fellow-slaves for their stupidity. I have often wished myself a beast. I preferred the condition of the meanest reptile to my own. Any thing, no matter what, to get rid of thinking! It was this everlasting thinking of my condition that tormented me. There was no getting rid of it. It was pressed upon me by every object within sight or hearing, animate or inanimate. The silver trump of freedom had roused my soul to eternal wakefulness. Freedom now appeared, to disappear no more forever. It was heard in every sound, and seen in every thing. It was ever present to torment me with a sense of my wretched condition. I saw nothing without seeing it, I heard nothing without hearing it, and felt nothing without feeling it. It looked from every star, it smiled in every calm, breathed in every wind, and moved in every storm.

QUESTIONS FOR DISCUSSION

1. Even though Douglass learned basic reading skills from his master's wife, he felt he owed "almost as much" for the "instruction . . . [he] had gained from [his] master." Explain this apparent contradiction.

2. Why did Douglass believe that slavery was at least as injurious to his mistress as it was to him?

3. At one point in this selection Douglass asserts that he "envied [his] fellow-slaves for their stupidity." Comment on this attitude.

4. Mention some of the features that give Douglass's prose such a distinct voice. What does the author do to make his voice seem so alive and convincing?

WRITING ASSIGNMENTS

1. Reaction Journal: Write a one-paragraph summary in which you explain just how Douglass learned to read.

2. Write a brief essay in which you describe the process you went through to learn some skill or discipline. Learning to swim, to ride a bicycle, to dance, or to play a musical instrument, are among many possible topics. Pay close attention to Douglass's style, and write your essay in the first person. Try to find aspects of Douglass's style that you can imitate in your essay.

COLLEGE

ANZIA YEZIERSKA

Anzia Yezierska (1883?–1970) was born in the Russian part of Poland and emigrated with her family to the United States as a young girl. Determined to escape the conditions of ghetto life through education, she attended night school and graduated from the Teachers College of Columbia University in 1904. By the 1920s she had become a successful writer. Her stories, one of which won the O. Henry Prize for the best story of 1919, focus on the lives of immigrant Jews living in New York's Lower East Side. Yezierska published five novels and several volumes of short stories now collected in the volume How I Found America. *The following selection from her autobiographical novel* Bread Givers *(1925) describes the disillusioning experiences of a poor immigrant girl during her freshman year at an American college.*

◆ FREEWRITING

Write two paragraphs describing your first few days at your college. In the first describe your response to the physical environment, and in the second develop one concrete incident that demonstrates how you felt—afraid, anxious, welcome?

That burning day when I got ready to leave New York and start out on my journey to college! I felt like Columbus starting out for the other end of the earth. I felt like the pilgrim fathers who had left their homeland and all their kin behind them and trailed out in search of the New World.

I had stayed up night after night, washing and ironing, patching and darning my things. At last, I put them all together in a bundle, wrapped them up with newspapers, and tied them securely with the thick clothes line that I had in my room on which to hang out my wash. I made another bundle of my books. In another newspaper I wrapped up my food for the journey: a loaf of bread, a herring, and a pickle. In my purse was the money I had been saving from my food, from my clothes, a penny to penny, a dollar to a dollar, for so many years. It was not much but I counted out that it would be enough for my train ticket and a few weeks start till I got work out there.

It was only when I got to the train that I realized I had hardly eaten all day. Starving hungry, I tore the paper open. *Ach!* Crazy-head! In my haste I had forgotten even to cut up the bread. I bent over on the side of my seat, and half covering myself with a newspaper, I pinched pieces out of the loaf and ripped ravenously at the herring. With each bite, I cast side glances like a guilty thing; nobody should see the way I ate.

After a while, as the lights were turned low, the other passengers began to nod their heads, each outsnoring the other in their thick sleep. I was the only one on the train too excited to close my eyes.

Like a dream was the whole night's journey. And like a dream mounting on 5
a dream was this college town, this New America of culture and education.

Before this, New York was all of America to me. But now I came to a town of quiet streets, shaded with green trees. No crowds, no tenements. No hurrying noise to beat the race of the hours. Only a leisured quietness whispered in the air: Peace. Be still. Eternal time is all before you.

Each house had its own green grass in front, its own free space all around, and it faced the street with the calm security of being owned for generations, and not rented by the month from a landlord. In the early twilight, it was like a picture out of fairyland to see people sitting on their porches, lazily swinging in their hammocks, or watering their own growing flowers.

So these are the real Americans, I thought, thrilled by the lean, straight bearing of the passers-by. They had none of that terrible fight for bread and rent that I always saw in New York people's eyes. Their faces were not worn with the hunger for things they never could have in their lives. There was in them that sure, settled look of those who belong to the world in which they were born.

The college buildings were like beautiful palaces. The campus stretched out like fields of a big park. Air—air. Free space and sunshine. The river at dusk. Glimmering lights on passing boats, the floating voices of young people. And when night came, there were the sky and the stars.

This was the beauty for which I had always longed. For the first few days I could only walk about and drink it in thirstily, more and more. Beauty of houses, beauty of streets, beauty shining out of the calm faces and cool eyes of the people! Oh—too cool. . . .

How could I most quickly become friends with them? How could I come into their homes, exchange with them my thoughts, break with them bread at their tables? If I could only lose myself body and soul in the serenity of this new world, the hunger and the turmoil of my ghetto years would drop away from me, and I, too, would know the beauty of stillness and peace.

What light-hearted laughing youth met my eyes! All the young people I had ever seen were shut up in factories. But here were young girls and young men enjoying life, free from the worry for a living. College to them was being out for a good time, like to us in the shop a Sunday picnic. But in our gayest Sunday picnics there was always the under-feeling that Monday meant back to the shop again. To these born lucky ones joy seemed to stretch out forever.

What a sight I was in my gray pushcart clothes against the beautiful gay colours and the fine things those young girls wore. I had seen cheap, fancy style, Five- and Ten-Cent Store finery. But never had I seen such plain beautifulness. The simple skirts and sweaters, the stockings and shoes to match. The neat finished quietness of their tailored suits. There was no show-off in their clothes, and yet how much more pulling to the eyes and all the senses than the Grand Street richness I knew.

And the spick-and-span cleanliness of these people! It smelled from them, the soap and the bathing. Their fingernails so white and pink. Their hands and necks white like milk. I wondered how did those girls get their hair so soft, so shiny, and so smooth about their heads. Even their black shoes had a clean look.

Never had I seen men so all shaved up with pink, clean skins. The richest store-keepers in Grand Street shined themselves up with diamonds like walking jewellery stores, but they weren't so hollering clean as these men. And they all had their hair clipped so short; they all had a shape to their heads. So ironed out smooth and even they looked in their spotless, creaseless clothes, as if the dirty battle of life had never yet been on them.

I looked at these children of joy with a million eyes. I looked at them with my hands, my feet, with the thinnest nerves of my hair. By all their differences from me, their youth, their shiny freshness, their carefreeness, they pulled me out of my senses to them. And they didn't even know I was there.

I thought once I got into the classes with them, they'd see me and we'd get to know one another. What a sharp awakening came with my first hour!

As I entered the classroom, I saw young men and girls laughing and talking to one another without introductions. I looked for my seat. Then I noticed, up in front, a very earnest-faced young man with thick glasses over his sad eyes. He made me think of Morris Lipkin, so I chose my seat next to him.

"What's the name of the professor?" I asked.

"Smith," came from his tight lips. He did not even look at me. He pulled himself together and began busily writing, to show me he didn't want to be interrupted.

I turned to the girl on my other side. What a fresh, clean beauty! A creature of sunshine. And clothes that matched her radiant youth.

"Is this the freshman class in geometry?" I asked her.

She nodded politely and smiled. But how quickly her eyes sized me up! It was not an unkind glance. And yet, it said more plainly than words, "From where do you come? How did you get in here?"

Sitting side by side with them through the whole hour, I felt stranger to them than if I had passed them in Hester Street. Wasn't there some secret something that would open us toward one another?

In one class after another, I kept asking myself, "What's the matter with me? Why do they look at me so when I talk with them?"

Maybe I'd have to change myself inside and out to be one of them. But how?

The lectures were over at four o'clock. With a sigh, I turned from the college building, away from the pleasant streets, down to the shabby back alley near the post office, and entered the George Martin Hand Laundry.

Mr. Martin was a fat, easy-going, good-natured man. I no sooner told him of my experience in New York than he took me on at once as an ironer at fifty cents an hour, and he told me he had work for as many hours a day as I could put in.

I felt if I could only look a little bit like other girls on the outside, maybe I could get in with them. And that meant money! And money meant work, work, work!

Till eleven o'clock that night, I ironed fancy white shirtwaists.

"You're some busy little worker, even if I do say so," said Mr. Martin, good-naturedly. "But I must lock up. You can't live here."

I went home, aching in every bone. And in the quiet and good air, I so overslept that I was late for my first class. To make matters worse, I found a note in my mailbox that puzzled and frightened me. It said, "Please report at once to the dean's office to explain your absence from Physical Education I, at four o'clock."

A line of other students was waiting there. When my turn came I asked the secretary, "What's this physical education business?"

"This is a compulsory course," he said. "You cannot get credit in any other course unless you satisfy this requirement."

At the hour when I had intended to go back to Martin's Laundry, I entered the big gymnasium. There were a crowd of girls dressed in funny short black bloomers and rubber-soled shoes.

The teacher blew the whistle and called harshly, "Students are expected to report in their uniforms."

"I have none."

"They're to be obtained at the bookstore," she said, with a stern look at me. "Please do not report again without it."

I stood there dumb.

40 "Well, stay for today and exercise as you are," said the teacher, taking pity on me.

She pointed out my place in the line, where I had to stand with the rest like a lot of wooden soldiers. She made us twist ourselves around here and there, "Right face!" "Left face!" "Right about face!" I tried to do as the others did, but I felt like a jumping-jack being pulled this way and that way. I picked up dumbbells and pushed them up and down and sideways until my arms were lame. Then she made us hop around like a lot of monkeys.

At the end of the hour, I was so out of breath that I sank down, my heart pounding against my ribs. I was dripping with sweat worse than Saturday night in the steam laundry. What's all this physical education nonsense? I came to college to learn something, to get an education with my head, and not monkeyshines with my arms and legs.

I went over to the instructor. "How much an hour do we get for this work?" I asked her, bitterly.

She looked at me with a stupid stare. "This is a two-point course."

45 Now I got real mad. "I've got to sweat my life away enough only to earn a living," I cried. "God knows I exercised enough, since I was a kid—"

"You properly exercised?" She looked at me from head to foot. "Your posture is bad. Your shoulders sag. You need additional corrective exercises outside the class."

More tired than ever, I came to the class next day. After the dumbbells, she made me jump over the hurdles. For the life of me, I couldn't do it. I bumped myself and scratched my knees on the top bar of the hurdle, knocking it over with a great clatter. They all laughed except the teacher.

"Repeat the exercise, please," she said, with a frozen face.

I was all bruises, trying to do it. And they were holding their sides with laughter. I was their clown, and this was their circus. And suddenly, I got so wild with rage that I seized the hurdle and right before their eyes I smashed it to pieces.

50 The whole gymnasium went still as death.

The teacher's face was white. "Report at once to the dean."

The scared look on the faces of the girls made me feel that I was to be locked up or fired.

For a minute when I entered the dean's grand office, I was so confused I couldn't even see.

He rose and pointed to a chair beside his desk. "What can I do for you?" he asked, in a voice that quieted me as he spoke.

55 I told him how mad I was, to have piled on me jumping hurdles when I was so tired anyway. He regarded me with that cooling steadiness of his. When I was through, he walked to the window and I waited, miserable. Finally he turned to me again, and with a smile! "I'm quite certain that physical education is not essential in your case. I will excuse you from attending the course."

After this things went better with me. In spite of the hard work in the laundry, I managed to get along in my classes. More and more interesting became the life of the college as I watched it from the outside.

What a feast of happenings each day of college was to those other students. Societies, dances, letters from home, packages of food, midnight spreads and even birthday parties. I never knew that there were people glad enough of life to celebrate the day they were born. I watched the gay goings-on around me like one coming to a feast, but always standing back and only looking on.

One day, the ache for people broke down my feelings of difference from them. I felt I must tear myself out of my aloneness. Nothing had ever come to me without my going out after it. I had to fight for my living, fight for every bit of my education. Why should I expect friendship and love to come to me out of the air while I sat there, dreaming about it?

The freshman class gave a dance that very evening. Something in the back of my head told me that an evening dress and slippers were part of going to a dance. I had no such things. But should that stop me? If I had waited till I could afford the right clothes for college, I should never have been able to go at all.

I put a fresh collar over my old serge dress. And with a dollar stolen from 60
my eating money, I bought a ticket to the dance. As I peeped into the glittering gymnasium, blaring with jazz, my timid fears stopped the breath in me. How the whole big place sang with their light-hearted happiness! Young eyes drinking joy from young eyes. Girls, like gay-coloured butterflies, whirling in the arms of young men.

Floating ribbons and sashes shimmered against men's black coats. I took the nearest chair, blinded by the dazzle of the happy couples. Why did I come here? A terrible sense of age weighed upon me; yet I watched and waited for someone to come and ask me to dance. But not one man came near me. Some of my classmates nodded distantly in passing, but most of them were too filled with their own happiness even to see me.

The whirling of joy went on and on, and still I sat there watching, cold, lifeless, like a lost ghost. I was nothing and nobody. It was worse than being ignored. Worse than being an outcast. I simply didn't belong. I had no existence in their young eyes. I wanted to run and hide myself, but fear and pride nailed me against the wall.

A chaperon must have noticed my face, and she brought over one of those clumsy, backward youths who was lost in a corner by himself. How unwilling his feet as she dragged him over! In a dull voice, he asked, "May I have the next dance?" his eyes fixed in the distance as he spoke.

"Thank you. I don't want to dance." And I fled from the place.

I found myself walking in the darkness of the campus. In the thick shadows 65
of the trees I hid myself and poured out my shamed and injured soul to the night. So, it wasn't character or brains that counted. Only youth and beauty and

clothes—things I never had and never could have. Joy and love were not for such as me. Why not? Why not? . . .

I flung myself on the ground, beating with my fists against the endless sorrows of my life. Even in college I had not escaped from the ghetto. Here loneliness hounded me even worse than in Hester Street. Was there no escape? Will I never lift myself to be a person among people?

I pressed my face against the earth. All that was left of me reached out in prayer. God! I've gone so far, help me to go on. God! I don't know how, but I must go on. Help me not to want their little happiness. I have wanted their love more than my life. Help me be bigger than this hunger in me. Give me the love that can live without love. . . .

Darkness and stillness washed over me. Slowly I stumbled to my feet and looked up at the sky. The stars in their infinite peace seemed to pour their healing light into me. I thought of the captives in prison, the sick and the suffering from the beginning of time who had looked to these stars for strength. What was my little sorrow to the centuries of pain which those stars had watched? So near they seemed, so compassionate. My bitter hurt seemed to grow small and drop away. If I must go on alone, I should still have silence and the high stars to walk with me.

QUESTIONS FOR DISCUSSION

1. What can a careful reader infer about the author's home in New York by examining her response to the students who attend the university and to the physical aspects of the college environment?
2. Yezierska compares college life for the students she observes to Sunday picnics she remembers. What are the similarities, and what is the one big difference?
3. Explain the source of the newfound resolve she demonstrates in the concluding paragraph.

WRITING ASSIGNMENTS

1. Reaction Journal: Assume that you are adjusting to life at your own college, and write a letter to Ms. Yezierska in which you advise her on what she can do to adjust to such a different life-style and culture. Assume that she is attending a college with which you are familiar, and make your own experiences part of your advice.
2. Assume the role of Anzia Yezierska. On the day after the class dance, write a letter home. Assume that this letter is your first since you left for college, and use the concrete information in the selection to develop your letter. If you prefer, you may write to your (Yezierska's) best friend on Hester Street.

FIRST DAY AT SCHOOL

MARILYN FRENCH

Marilyn French (b. 1929), author of the best-selling novels The Women's Room *(1977),* The Bleeding Heart *(1981), and* Her Mother's Daughter *(1987), holds undergraduate and graduate degrees from Hofstra College and a Ph.D. from Harvard University. In addition to fiction she has published two works of literary criticism,* The Book as World: James Joyce's "Ulysses" *(1976) and* Shakespeare's Division of Experience (1981), *and a work of social criticism,* Beyond Power: On Women, Men, and Morals. Her Mother's Daughter *tells the story of four generations of women. The following selection from this novel describes both the humiliation and determination of Bella, the non-English-speaking child of Polish immigrants, as she begins school in the Williamsburg section of Brooklyn.*

◆ FREEWRITING

This selection is a fictional account of a young Polish girl's first days at school in America. Freewrite for ten or fifteen minutes as you try to remember as much as you can about your own first days at school.

When Bella was five and a half, Momma sent her to school. She had a new dress, and stiff new boots, and a pair of eyeglasses. Momma kept reminding her she was not to lose them or break them. Momma gave her directions, and kissed her, but only perfunctorily, for she worried about Euga, who had a cold. Momma was carrying her around, bouncing her, talking to her to keep her from crying, but she still cried.

Bella walked the streets very carefully, reaching up every few seconds to touch her eyeglasses, to make sure they were still on her head. She found the building, and went where Momma said, into the office. There a grey-haired woman looked up and spoke to her. Bella simply stood there. She could not understand what the woman was saying. It was some sound like "o," but it meant nothing to Bella. Finally, the woman waved her hand at Bella, as if she wanted her to leave, and returned to her work. When Bella did not move, the woman came out from behind the high desk, and took Bella by the arm and thrust her out the door.

Bella sat on the curb and cried. She was afraid to go home, where the servant girl would mock her, or worse. She was afraid to go to Poppa's shop, because she was not allowed to go there unless Momma took her. She stayed on the curb, lifting one foot, then the other, for her feet hurt in the stiff new boots. She watched the trolleys, the great drays that sometimes passed, the iceman's wagon. She was hungry. She stayed until the school doors burst open and the children sprang out like peas ejected from a BB gun, and ran in all directions shouting, teasing, laughing. She stood up and turned around and looked at them. Why were they better than she was? Why were they allowed in the school and she not? She felt near tears again, but did not want to cry in front of them. She waited until most of the children were gone, and then set off toward home.

Her body was stiff with terror. What would Momma and Poppa say about her when they found out the school didn't want her? A school that took all the other children, even those from their block, for she'd seen Jan Szcepanski and Myron Goldstein running past her on their way home. But if they didn't find out, what would she do then? Would she have to come here every day and sit on the curb? Suppose it rained? Or snowed?

She remained tense and stiff as she entered the house, but only the servant 5
girl was there, and she said nothing. And when Momma came home early to nurse the baby, she was busy, and then she had to get dinner. Bella stayed out of the way, on the floor behind the bed, staring at the grain of the wood floor. And then, when Poppa came, Bella shuddered, but he said nothing either, not even when they all sat down to dinner. Maybe they would never find out.

But then, after dinner, it was Eddie who brought it up—oh, Eddie! her face pleaded with him, but he did not stop. He asked her who her teacher was and if she was in that ugly corner room that got so hot and had paint peeling from the ceiling in big flakes that drifted down and settled on your head making everybody laugh and point to you.

Bella couldn't speak, but Eddie kept it up. Finally, he pointed to her laughing, "Cat got your tongue? I bet you didn't even *go* to school, scaredy-cat! I bet you were too scared!"

"I did! I did!" she protested, her face hot in splotches.

"Then what's your teacher's name?"

Bella burst into tears. 10

By this time, Momma and Poppa were paying attention, and they listened when Bella, sobbing and sniffling, told how she'd been expelled from school before she even entered. Poppa was angry, but not with her. She would go again tomorrow, they decided, but Momma would go with her.

The next day, she put on her new dress, which was wrinkled and dirty from sitting on the curb, and the stiff new boots and the new eyeglasses, and went with Momma back to the office of the terrible woman. And Momma talked to the woman in the same kind of words the woman used, and the woman made a face at Bella and looked at Momma as if she were dirty—although Momma had worn her hat, her black hat with the veil, that Bella loved. The woman pushed a piece of paper at Momma and Momma wrote things on it. Then the woman took Bella into the hall and down a long corridor with doors in it, and opened one of the doors and said something incomprehensible to Bella and took her in and whispered to a lady who was standing in front of lots of other children Bella's size who were sitting at little desks.

Bella's heart leaped. Would *she* be allowed to sit at a little desk like that and write on paper with a pen, the way they were doing? Bella had never held a pen. The terrible woman went out and the lady—she must be the teacher, Bella wanted to know her name, suppose Eddie asked her!—said something to Bella. But Bella just stood there. So the lady came to Bella and took her hand and led her to a little desk. Bella slid into the seat and smiled a dazzled, grateful, happy smile at the lady. And the lady spoke to her, kindly, to her, Bella, right in front of all the children! Bella stopped smiling, and lines of anxiety formed on her forehead. Would it be like this all the time? The teacher had stopped speaking; she sighed and her shoulders drooped, and she went to the big desk in front of the room and came back to Bella and put a piece of paper and a pen on Bella's desk. Bella understood that she was supposed to have her own pen and paper, and was humiliated. She knew the other children thought she was so poor she could not afford pen and paper. The teacher poked open the lid of the inkwell and showed Bella how to dip a pen in it, and how to hold the pen to write. But when Bella tried it, she made a big blot. The teacher sighed again, marched to the desk, and slammed a blotter down. Then she returned to the front of the class and said something. Bella heard her own name—Isabella Brez. That was all she understood.

Her heart was squeezed tight. She could hear the word "stupid, stupid" running through her brain, and knew that was what they all thought—the teacher and the terrible woman and all the children. And she *was* stupid. That was why she could not understand their words. They all understood each other, even Alicia from the next block, who was sitting in the first row giggling behind her hand and glancing at Bella. But she would not cry. She would try to conceal her stupidity, so that people would not laugh at her. She practiced with her pen.

She watched the other children following the teacher's directions, and she 15
did whatever they did. Even in kindergarten, they taught words to this potpourri of children from different backgrounds, and Bella copied meaningless words from the blackboard: BOY GIRL DOG CAT. In time, she came to understand what these words meant, but she could not put them in a sentence.

She went home that day and sat quietly waiting until Momma arrived. Then Bella told her she had to have a pen, a tablet, and a blotter. Momma said she had no money. Bella threw a tantrum. So astonishing was this to Momma that she left the house and walked back to the shop and got a nickel from Poppa and returned and gave it to Bella. With a shaky pride—only partly believing she had accomplished this—Bella walked to the stationery store on the corner clutching her nickel, directed the purchase of the tools of her education, and with great dignity, returned home.

QUESTIONS FOR DISCUSSION

1. At what point in this selection did you realize that much of Bella's terror resulted from her not knowing English?
2. Although most of this selection focuses on Bella's first days at school, some attention is directed to her family. What can you infer about Bella's family and home environment?
3. French describes a young girl's terror in this story. What details does she choose to show this fear?

WRITING ASSIGNMENTS

1. Reaction Journal: Assume the role of a high school graduate of Polish descent living near Bella who has been through the same school system. Write a letter to Bella's mother advising her how to prepare her daughter for the first few days in your American school system.
2. Reread your freewriting for this selection and write a narrative account of your first day at school. Establish how you felt and make that mood the dominant impression of your narrative. Don't be afraid to make up a few details as long as you are honest to the overall impression.

"I JUST WANNA BE AVERAGE"

MIKE ROSE

Mike Rose (b. 1944) is associate director of UCLA Writing Programs. The child of immigrants, Rose grew up in a poor neighborhood on the south side of Los Angeles a mile and a half northwest of Watts. He has written widely on language and literacy, drawing on his experiences in the Teacher Corps, a federal program which places teacher interns in depressed areas of the country, in Veterans and CETA programs for adults from the underclass, and in college programs for students designated as "remedial." His writing is informed by a dissatisfaction with the kind of teaching that slots and categorizes rather than shapes and fosters, and by his belief in the way lives can be turned around through encouragement and culturally sensitive pedagogy. In this selection from Lives on the Boundary *(1989), Rose describes his own experience as a student in the high school vocational track, where he learned firsthand how students who are labeled unprepared can become alienated in school because of race, class, poverty, and cultural difference.*

◆ FREEWRITING

In paragraph 9 Rose talks about a secondary school curriculum that "isn't designed to liberate you but to occupy you." Think about your own high school curriculum and write for ten or fifteen minutes about whether it liberated you or occupied you.

My parents used to say that their son would have the best education they could afford. Maybe I would be a doctor. There was a public school in our neighborhood and several Catholic schools to the west. They had heard that quality schooling meant private, Catholic schooling, so they somehow got the money together to send me to Our Lady of Mercy, fifteen or so miles southwest of Ninety-first and Vermont.

It took two buses to get to Our Lady of Mercy. The first started deep in South Los Angeles and caught me at midpoint. The second drifted through neighborhoods with trees, parks, big lawns, and lots of flowers. The rides were long but were livened up by a group of South L.A. veterans whose parents also thought that Hope had set up shop in the west end of the county. There was Christy Biggars, who, at sixteen, was dealing and was, according to rumor, a pimp as well. There were Bill Cobb and Johnny Gonzales, grease-pencil artists extraordinaire, who left Nembutal-enhanced swirls of "Cobb" and "Johnny" on the corrugated walls of the bus. And then there was Tyrrell Wilson. Tyrrell was the coolest kid I knew. He ran the dozens like a metric halfback, laid down a rap that outrhymed and outpointed Cobb, whose rap was good but not great—the curse of a moderately soulful kid trapped in white skin. But it was Cobb who would sneak a radio onto the bus, and thus underwrote his patter with Little Richard, Fats Domino, Chuck Berry, the Coasters, and Ernie K. Doe's mother-in-law, an awful woman who was "sent from down below." And so it was that Christy and Cobb and Johnny G. and Tyrrell and I and assorted others picked up along the way passed our days in the back of the bus, a funny mix brought together by geography and parental desire.

Entrance to school brings with it forms and releases and assessments. Mercy relied on a series of tests, mostly the Stanford-Binet, for placement, and somehow the results of my tests got confused with those of another student named Rose. The other Rose apparently didn't do very well, for I was placed in the vocational track, a euphemism for the bottom level. Neither I nor my parents realized what this meant. We had no sense that Business Math, Typing, and English-Level D were dead ends. The current spate of reports on the schools criticizes parents for not involving themselves in the education of their children. But how would someone like Tommy Rose, with his two years of Italian schooling, know what to ask? And what sort of pressure could an exhausted waitress apply? The error went undetected, and I remained in the vocational track for two years. What a place.

Students will float to the mark you set. I and the others in the vocational classes were bobbing in pretty shallow water. Vocational education has aimed at increasing the economic opportunities of students who do not do well in our schools. Some serious programs succeed in doing that, and through exceptional teachers—like Mr. Gross in *Horace's Compromise*—students learn to develop hypotheses and troubleshoot, reason through a problem, and communicate effectively—the true job skills. The vocational track, however, is most often a place for those who are just not making it, a dumping ground for the disaffected. There were a few teachers who worked hard at education; young Brother Slattery, for example, combined a stern voice with weekly quizzes to try to pass along to us a skeletal outline of world history. But mostly the teachers had no idea of how to engage the imaginations of us kids who were scuttling along at the bottom of the pond.

And the teachers would have needed some inventiveness, for none of us was 5
groomed for the classroom. It wasn't just that I didn't know things—didn't know how to simplify algebraic fractions, couldn't identify different kinds of clauses, bungled Spanish translations—but that I had developed various faulty and inadequate ways of doing algebra and making sense of Spanish. Worse yet, the years of defensive tuning out in elementary school had given me a way to escape quickly while seeming at least half alert. During my time in Voc. Ed., I developed further into a mediocre student and a somnambulant problem solver, and that affected the subjects I did have the wherewithal to handle: I detested Shakespeare; I got bored with history. My attention flitted here and there. I fooled around in class and read my books indifferently—the intellectual equivalent of playing with your food. I did what I had to do to get by, and I did it with half a mind.

But I did learn things about people and eventually came into my own socially. I liked the guys in Voc. Ed. Growing up where I did, I understood and admired physical prowess, and there was an abundance of muscle here. There was Dave Snyder, a sprinter and halfback of true quality. Dave's ability and his quick wit gave him a natural appeal, and he was welcome in any clique, though he always kept a little independent. He enjoyed acting the fool and could care less about studies, but he possessed a certain maturity and never caused the faculty much trouble. It was a testament to his independence that he included me among his friends—I eventually went out for track, but I was no jock. Owing to the Latin alphabet and a dearth of *R*s and *S*s, Snyder sat behind Rose, and we started exchanging one-liners and became friends.

There was Ted Richard, a much-touted Little League pitcher. He was chunky and had a baby face and came to Our Lady of Mercy as a seasoned street fighter. Ted was quick to laugh and he had a loud, jolly laugh, but when he got angry he'd smile a little smile, the kind that simply raises the corner of the mouth a quarter of an inch. For those who knew, it was an eerie signal. Those who didn't found themselves in big trouble, for Ted was very quick. He loved to carry on what we would come to call philosophical discussions: What is courage? Does God exist? He also loved words, enjoyed picking up big ones like *salubrious* and *equivocal* and using them in our conversations—laughing at himself as the word hit a chuckhole rolling off his tongue. Ted didn't do all that well in school—baseball and parties and testing the courage he'd speculated about took up his time. His textbooks were *Argosy* and *Field and Stream*, whatever newspapers he'd find on the bus stop—from *the Daily Worker* to pornography—conversations with uncles or hobos or businessmen he'd meet in a coffee shop, *The Old Man and the Sea.* With hindsight, I can see that Ted was developing into one of those rough-hewn intellectuals whose sources are a mix of the learned and the apocryphal, whose discussions are both assured and sad.

And then there was Ken Harvey. Ken was good-looking in a puffy way and had a full and oily ducktail and was a car enthusiast . . . a hodad. One day in religion class, he said the sentence that turned out to be one of the most memorable of the hundreds of thousands I heard in those Voc. Ed. years. We were talking about the parable of the talents, about achievement, working hard, doing the best you can do, blah-blah-blah, when the teacher called on the restive Ken Harvey for an opinion. Ken thought about it, but just for a second, and said (with studied, minimal affect), "I just wanna be average." That woke me up. Average?! Who wants to be average? Then the athletes chimed in with the clichés that make you want to laryngectomize them, and the exchange became a platitudinous melee. At the time, I thought Ken's assertion was stupid, and I wrote him off. But his sentence has stayed with me all these years, and I think I am finally coming to understand it.

Ken Harvey was gasping for air. School can be a tremendously disorienting place. No matter how bad the school, you're going to encounter notions that don't fit with the assumptions and beliefs that you grew up with—maybe you'll hear these dissonant notions from teachers, maybe from the other students, and maybe you'll read them. You'll also be thrown in with all kinds of kids from all kinds of backgrounds, and that can be unsettling—this is especially true in places of rich ethnic and linguistic mix, like the L.A. basin. You'll see a handful of students far excel you in courses that sound exotic and that are only in the curriculum of the elite: French, physics, trigonometry. And all this is happening while you're trying to shape an identity, your body is changing, and your emotions are running wild. If you're a working-class kid in the vocational track, the options you'll have to deal with this will be constrained in certain ways: You're defined by your school as "slow"; you're placed in a curriculum that isn't designed to liberate you but to occupy you, or, if you're lucky, train you, though the training is for work the society does not esteem; other students are picking up the cues from your school and your curriculum and interacting with you in particular ways. If you're a kid like Ted Richard, you turn your back on all this and let your mind roam where it may. But youngsters like Ted are rare. What Ken and so many others do is protect themselves from such suffocating madness by taking on with a vengeance the identity implied in the vocational track. Reject the confusion and frustration by openly defining yourself as the Common Joe. Champion the average. Rely on your own good sense. Fuck this bullshit. Bullshit, of course, is everything you—and the others—fear is beyond you: books, essays, tests, academic scrambling, complexity, scientific reasoning, philosophical inquiry.

10 The tragedy is that you have to twist the knife in your own gray matter to make this defense work. You'll have to shut down, have to reject intellectual stimuli or diffuse them with sarcasm, have to cultivate stupidity, have to convert boredom from a malady into a way of confronting the world. Keep your vocabulary simple, act stoned when you're not or act more stoned than you are, flaunt ignorance, materialize your dreams. It is a powerful and effective defense—it neutralizes the insult and the frustration of being a vocational kid and, when perfected, it drives teachers up the wall, a delightful secondary effect. But like all strong magic, it exacts a price.

QUESTIONS FOR DISCUSSION

1. Specifically, where is the high school that Rose attended? Why does he go to that particular school? Why is the vocational track a "euphemism for the bottom level"? How did Rose happen to be placed in this curriculum?
2. What type of students are Dave Snyder, Ted Richard, and Ken Harvey? Be specific. Does the author treat these three as individuals or types?
3. Discuss the effectiveness of the water metaphor in paragraph 4. Find other examples of figurative language in this selection.

WRITING ASSIGNMENTS

1. Rose addresses the issue of students coping with a curriculum rather than engaging in it and the need to survive in a curriculum that does not meet students' needs. Write a letter to your high school principal in which you discuss whether or not his curriculum met your needs. Feel free to offer constructive suggestions as long as you are concrete and logical.
2. In paragraphs 6 through 9 Rose describes three specific students with objective distance. Assume such a role and look back on your high school classmates. In an essay describe three students and show how they "typify" the larger group.

Confrontations

THE EXTENT TO WHICH American multiculturalism will succeed depends largely on the ways in which cultural differences among groups are reconciled, tensions resolved. Cross-cultural encounters between newcomers and natives began when the first European explorers and settlers arrived, and the character of the country ever since has been shaped by the history of ethnic and racial interactions between new arrivals and established citizens and among various minorities. The tenor of these encounters has ranged from amicable to confrontational. Some have sought accommodation while others have exploited conflict. With the arrival of each new group come not only new and valuable resources but also temporary economic burdens, unfamiliar languages and customs, and long-term competition for jobs and goods. Too often fears of the unfamiliar and of the possibility of losing social, political, and economic status have caused group interaction to be marked by the kind of bigotry, racism, and xenophobia satirized in Tom Lehrer's song "National Brotherhood Week." The anti-Catholic riots and the rise of nativism in the mid-1800s, the anti-Chinese riots in the West during the 1870s and 1880s, segregation laws limiting the freedom of African-Americans, anti-Semitic conspiracy theories of the 1890s, the anti-immigration legislation of 1921 and 1924, Ku Klux Klan terrorism, limited access to jobs, prestigious colleges and professional societies, and street violence often racially motivated as in the 1992 riots in Los Angeles are some of the unfortunate realities of life in this multiethnic, multiracial society.

During the past three decades, the pace of interaction among minority and immigrant groups has increased. Urban neighborhoods previously marked off into rigid and often voluntary ethnic enclaves have shown greater levels of integration. Neighborhoods once exclusively Italian or Chinese have become ethnically mixed. On the streets of Manhattan's Lower East Side, a reporter observed in 1972 that one might see "an Italian religious procession on Mott Street, with nearly all onlookers Chinese, or glimpse Italian barbers shearing Asian locks. In one store Italians are playing cards; next door, Chinese are playing Mah-Jongg." Unfortunately, however, increased contact does not always lead to harmonious relations.

Ethnic separation of newcomers from each other and from the American-born, particularly in large cities, prevailed from the mid-nineteenth century until the 1970s. In industrial towns the establishment of discrete ethnic enclaves was promoted by the importing and housing of immigrant labor. There was ethnic separation by occupation as well, since immigrants were often imported to fill particular industrial needs. The pattern of ethnic segregation was supported not only by industry but also by specious application of new discoveries in the science of heredity to theories of racial typing during the early nineteenth century, and these theories extended to African-American as well as immigrant populations. One observer of American neighborhoods during the early twentieth century remarked that in the larger cities "we see a conglomeration of colonies and ghettos and immigrant sections . . . with settlement quite as un-American as anything to be found abroad."

Early encounters between settlers and Native American peoples—and subsequent policies regarding removal of these peoples from frontier areas—reflected virtually no concern about integration or assimilation. The settlers' obsession with acquiring Native American lands predictably led to many clashes. Events like the attack on Lancaster, Massachusetts, during King Philip's War (1675–1676) led to portrayals of Native Americans as "merciless heathens."

Not only did the desire for land play a large part in defining relationships between settlers and Native Americans, but the mid-nineteenth-century need for settlers and laborers affected relationships between groups during that century. Floods of immigrants responding to the absence of immigration restrictions and the call for cheap labor took advantage of the availability of farmland on the prairies and crowded into tenement districts in U.S. cities. The lack of regulations regarding the entry of immigrants is one reason why many of these unscreened arrivals ended up in almshouses, mental institutions, and prisons, thereby causing stereotyping of certain groups as shiftless, mentally inferior, or dangerous. Among the first to come in numbers large enough to cause concern were the Irish. Irish immigration increased from 200,000 in the 1830s to 781,000 in the 1840s and 914,000 in the 1850s. The competitive strain that this massive immigration placed on poor, unskilled native workers, combined with the perceived threat posed by a rapidly increasing Catholic minority, resulted in street fighting and the burning of churches in cities along the East Coast. In "Anti-Irish Nativism," William Shannon details one such episode, the burning of the Ursuline Convent in Charlestown, Massachusetts, in 1831.

There had been a history of anti-Catholic sentiment even among such leaders as John Jay, Patrick Henry, John Adams, and Alexander Hamilton, but until 1820 the small number of Catholics in the United States was not perceived as posing a threat to American political unity. Shannon points out that the nativist crusade, sparked at midcentury by Catholic immigration, was, in fact, a response to economic conditions. That the antagonism was expressed in religious terms merely supplied a "respectable pretext" for the movement. In the 1840s and 1850s the nativist movement, with an antiforeign and anti-Catholic agenda, gained momentum. Spokespeople like inventor Samuel F. B. Morse fanned fears of foreign (and specifically Catholic) influence by warning that "popery is opposed in its very nature to Democratic Republicanism; and it is, therefore, as a political system, as well as a religious, opposed to civil and religious liberty and consequently to our form of government." In the 1850s, the Know-Nothing Party, appearing on the ballot as the American Party, was organized. The only xenophobic, nativist party to wield appreciable strength in state and national elections, the Know-Nothing Party was dedicated to excluding all immigrants, especially Roman Catholics, from positions of power and profit. Its members proposed such measures as making immigrants wait twenty-one years before becoming eligible for naturalization and barring them from holding public office. It was only the continued need for workers that prevented a call for a complete stop to immigration. In the state legislative elections of 1854, the Know-Nothing Party carried Massachusetts, Delaware, and (in alliance with the Whigs) Pennsylvania. By 1856 nativists held seven governorships, eight U.S. Senate seats, and 104 seats in the U.S. House of Representatives. Nativist following, however, fell off with the 1856 nomination of Millard Fillmore, regarded in the north as a supporter of slavery, and with the increasing national debate over slavery. By the turn of the century, the Irish Catholics, because of their numbers and their experience negotiating difficult political waters in Ireland, became a potent political force. They came to dominate political life in Boston and New York. Today it is difficult to understand why, when John F. Kennedy, a fourth-generation American, became the second Catholic nominee for the presidency, he was repeatedly challenged, because of his religion, to prove himself "American" enough to hold that office.

Although group conflicts are frequently expressed as religious or racial intolerance, they are often driven by fears of economic and social upheaval. It is easy for a group that has been established in a country for a number of years or generations to harbor resentment against new arrivals who receive tax-supported social services and/or begin to prosper shortly after their arrival. Tough economic conditions compound these feelings. The populist revolt of the 1890s, with its anti-Semitic theories of an international Jewish monetary conspiracy, has been ascribed to the tightness of money during that era and the difficulties faced by largely Protestant farmers. The revival of Ku Klux Klan terrorism and religious hatred during the Great Depression is further evidence of the link between economic instability and intolerance. Just as the inundation by Irish-Catholic immigrants seemed to threaten the economic and social order of the 1830s, '40s, and '50s, so the waves of immigrants from Russia (largely Jews) and from Southern Europe beginning in 1890 brought renewed fears.

But economic competition is not the only factor affecting group relations. The degree to which established residents have to come into contact with immigrant groups also affects their tolerance of them. The rise of the cities and the ascendancy of industry and commerce over farming brought groups into more intimate contact with each other. Roy L. Garis, an economist writing during the 1920s and '30s, observed that even in colonial times the American people opposed the arrival of immigrants "when they had to associate with them and enter into competition with them; . . . so long as there was plenty of land—a frontier —and the immigrants were willing to go into it, the problem was not acute." The visibility of the so-called new immigration raised fears. Furthermore, the "old" immigration (prior to 1890) came mostly from Great Britain and Ireland and Northern Europe and was therefore predominantly from Anglo-Saxon-Germanic Protestant background, while the "new" immigrants came mostly from Southern and Eastern Europe. The shift in immigration patterns from countries with universal education to those with less-educated populations, from countries more progressive in agriculture, industry, and government to those less developed, and from Teutonic to Latin, Slavic, and Jewish racial stocks raised fears of fundamental changes to the American population. The anti-immigration laws of 1921 and 1924, which ended unrestricted immigration and established discriminatory national and racial quotas, were a direct response to fears of anarchy and racial "contamination."

The new science of heredity that began to come out of Europe around 1900 emphasized the primacy of nature over nurture. One's genetic code, apparently, dictated the type of person one would become, regardless of environmental influence. Sir Francis Galton, England's foremost Darwinian scientist, had for some years been doing statistical studies on the inheritance of human abilities and deficiencies. His belief in the perfectability of humanity through selective breeding, offering as it did a scientific solution to social problems, had great appeal in the decades around the turn of the century. The eugenics movement in the United States, which was dedicated to maintaining or improving the physical and mental quality of the American population through controlling heredity, had definite racial and nativist implications. The immigration question became a biological one, and talk of exclusion took on a certain scientific respectability. Among the many crude interpretations of Mendelian genetics was one by Madison Grant, founder and later chairman of the New York Zoological Society. His *The Passing of the Great Race* (1916) proposed that mixing races results in a race "reverting to the more ancient, generalized, and lower type." The Jews were the "ancient race" against which his venom was particularly directed. "The cross," he wrote, "between any of the three European races and a Jew is a Jew." Drawing implications about superior morality and character from theories of evolution and genetics, the eugenics movement arrived at conclusions that class is dependent on race and proceeded to ascribe all the higher qualities to the Nordic race. Grant and his sympathizers went so far as to attack democracy as being inconsistent with supposed scientific truths about heredity, and Christianity as favoring the weak and thus undermining racial pride. Through the work of Grant and others, pseudoscientific theories proclaiming racial determination of culture provided an ideology for racism.

During the first half of the twentieth century, the two groups that felt the sting of racism most strongly were the blacks and the Jews. Indeed, as James McPherson points out in "To Blacks and Jews: *Hab Rachmones*," blacks and Jews had a sympathetic relationship for the first four decades of this century, based, at least in part, on a sense of common trials. The Yiddish press presented black suffering as parallel to that of Jews, and Jews played an active role in furthering black causes, providing financial and legal support, and acting as go-betweens for blacks and whites. McPherson sees the falling-out between Jews and blacks as beginning in the late 1960s, when the Israeli victory in the Six-Day War (1967) underlined a basic difference in terms of identity and political position between these two groups. Reassertion of Jewish nationhood provided a political basis for Jewish identity outside the United States. Blacks, while feeling an intense identification with Africa, have no such established homeland to return to, and must work out their special racial and social problems here in the United States. Elaine H. Kim's remarks on racial dynamics in her discussion of the open conflicts between African-Americans and Korean-Americans in Los Angeles in May 1992 (in "They Armed in Self-Defense") provide one way of understanding the charges of racism and anti-Semitism exchanged between blacks and Jews. The American system, Kim feels, places minorities in competition with each other "in a zero-sum game over the crumbs of a broken society, a war in which the advancement of one group means deterioration for the other." One way of advancing economically and socially in such a competition is to find common ground with the majority. Arthur Hertzberg's observation that "anti-Semitism is the way blacks join the majority. Racism is the way Jews join the majority" (McPherson, "To Blacks and Jews: *Hab Rachmones*") is a grim comment on what happens to human values when one engages in such a game.

When gains made by one group are seen as losses suffered by another, competition for a good life and the goods associated with that life inevitably pits group against group. Dawn Kelly, one of the students interviewed by Studs Terkel in "Campus Life," sees a conspiracy not to let blacks rise socially and economically, while Jennifer Kasko, another student, is disheartened when she sees some classmates basing black pride on efforts "to surpass the white race." In "Us and Them," Arthur Hu reflects on the black-Korean conflicts brought to national attention in the rioting in Los Angeles during which eight out of ten Korean stores in South-Central L.A. were burned or looted. He believes that the only way out of this sort of violence is to teach within the family the values of resourcefulness and industry and to stress the negative effects of hatred, killing, lying, and stealing. The beginning of harmony is individual responsibility for oneself and one's neighbor, individual commitment to the fact that a person is not defined by his or her class, color, or gender. The alternative, in addition to violence, is the kind of negativism expressed by the narrator's friend in a passage that follows the chapter from Tomás Rivera's . . . *'Y No Se lo Tragó la Tierra* included in our text. He advises the young narrator not to worry about school and preparing for a career. "The downtrodden," he says, "will always be downtrodden. Things can't get any worse." It's the ones who have already achieved something who have to worry, for they "have something to lose." The possibility of achieving gains through personal effort does not enter into such a view. Trapped in an Us versus Them mentality, with no reference for an achievement-based sense of self-worth, these young people see the life that stretches out before them only as a game of losses, a game that a multicultural nation can ill afford to endorse.

ANTI-IRISH NATIVISM

WILLIAM V. SHANNON

William V. Shannon (1927–1988) served as ambassador to Ireland from 1977 to 1981. Before that he was a Washington correspondent and columnist for the New York Post *and other newspapers and a member of the* New York Times *editorial board. From 1981 until his death he was a professor at Boston University. Among his writings are* The Heir Apparent: Robert Kennedy and the Struggle for Power *(1967) and* They Could Not Trust the King: Nixon, Watergate and the American People *(1974). In the following selection from* The American Irish *(1963), Shannon describes nativist attacks on Irish immigrants during the pre–Civil War era.*

◆ FREEWRITING

The opening sentence of the introduction to this section reads, "The extent to which the ongoing U.S. experiment in multiculturalism will succeed depends largely on the ways in which cultural differences among groups are reconciled, tensions resolved." Think about how cross-cultural encounters have or have not been resolved in your region. Freewrite for ten or fifteen minutes on the ways confrontation and accommodation have been employed to reconcile such encounters.

The style of life among the Irish contrasted markedly with the Yankee spirit of native Protestant Americans. The Irish were as different as could be imagined in mood and tempo from those natives of Anglo-Saxon Puritan stock whom Whittier described:

> Church-goers, fearful of the unseen Powers
> But grumbling over pulpit tax and pew-rent,
> Saving, as shrewd economists, their souls
> And winter pork with the least possible outlay
> Of salt and sanctity.

The Yankee, too, was present in the growing cities. Indeed, in their original form the cities had been his creation, and he resented the coming of these Irish intruders. The Yankee peddler, famed in song and story, was the archetype of the early nineteenth century city man. His values were those of the prudent merchant and banker, the rising tradesman, the thrifty, hardworking craftsman. The city's original ethos was a flinty blend of the gospel according to Calvin and the gospel according to Franklin's "Poor Richard." "Early to bed and early to rise makes a man healthy, wealthy and wise" was the native community's guiding maxim if not always its invariable practice. Individual effort, thrift, caution, sobriety, and a canny, tight-lipped self-reliance were its prevailing values.

The newer Irish challenged the code of the community at almost every point. Impoverished on their arrival, ignorant of skilled trades, bereft of any apprenticeship training, they had nothing to offer but their hands and their willingness to work. As day laborers, they competed for the tough and menial jobs and were at the mercy of every shift in the job market. Their presence on the scene in large and growing numbers threatened the old occupational structure of master, journeyman, and apprentice. The native working classes feared and hated them.

The native middle classes worried about the Irish from another vantage point, seeing in them the nucleus of a permanently depressed laboring class. The natives did not foresee the extent to which industry would expand and how important a resource the Irish laborers would be in this industrial expansion. What they did see was that the Irish, crowding into the cities, posed problems in housing, police, and schools; they meant higher tax rates and heavier burdens in the support of poorhouses and private charitable institutions. Moreover, the Irish did not seem to practice thrift, self-denial, and other virtues desirable in the "worthy, laboring poor." They seemed drunken, dissolute, permanently sunk in poverty. Here appearances were partly deceiving. The Irish of the first generation, that is, those who were born in Ireland and made the great journey to America, did not usually conform to native Protestant values and practices. And this was true whether it was the first generation that came in 1845, in 1880, or in 1910. It was rare for an Irishman of the first generation to have a rags-to-riches success story; to rise economically in the customary American fashion demanded more in terms of relentless perseverance, financial acumen, familiarity with new ways, and plain good luck than the Irish were able to summon from themselves or their environment. This was a task for the second and third and succeeding generations. But within the bounds of what was humanly possible, the Irish laborers and housemaids of the first generation were not so thriftless as the native stereotype of them suggested. Remittances to Ireland from individuals in this country were at the rate of $1,000,000 annually in the 1840's and rose to ten times that figure over the next twenty years. Thousands of individuals earning only fifty cents a day or, in the case of domestic servants, a dollar a week were methodically saving pennies and quarters to send to dependents in the old country. The Emigrant Industrial Savings Bank of New York, chartered by the Irish Emigrant Society in 1851, opened with 2,300 depositors whose average savings were $238.56. In the next thirty years, this bank alone sent $30,000,000 in remittances to Ireland.[1]

The two-fisted aggressiveness of the Irish, however, seemed to confirm the 5
contrary image. The Irishman first entered the popular folklore and the comic stage in the guise of the "the bhoy"—the swaggering, rough-talking, free-swinging tough. Irish gangs battled fiercely on election days. In the famous Astor Place Riot in New York, they mobbed the performance of William Macready, an English actor, when he tried to present a production of *Macbeth* competing with

one by Edwin Forrest, the theatrical favorite of the Irish. When the police attempted to quell the riot, one Irishman tore open his shirt, bared his chest, and shouted, "Fire into this! Take the life of a free-born American for a bloody English actor! Do it! Ay, you darsen't!"

When Protestants marched on the anniversary of the Battle of Boyne, the Irish broke up their parades. When the Prince of Wales visited New York in 1860, an Irish regiment embarrassed the city fathers by refusing to parade in his honor.

"It is a fact," declared Samuel F. B. Morse, the inventor of the telegraph and a foremost nativist of the period, "that an unaccountable disposition to riotous conduct has manifested itself within a few years when exciting topics are publicly discussed, wholly at variance with the former peaceful, deliberative character of our people."

The Irish did not enter city politics. They erupted. Their politicians pressed to the fore; their priests raised new issues of religious discrimination in the public schools. The activities of both disturbed the smug, clublike atmosphere in which the large towns had formerly been governed. Their "grating brogue" was heard everywhere.

If Irish manners were objectionable to the Yankee community, their morals seemed deplorable. There were two thousand saloons in lower New York City alone by 1840. Not all of them were Irish-run or Irish-patronized, but there was no doubt that the status of the liquor seller was different in the Yankee and Irish communities. In the former, he tended increasingly to be a pariah; in the latter, he was a respected figure. The Irish had their own temperance leader in Father Theobald Mathew who came from Ireland in the 1840's to preach the cause of total abstinence, but he was an isolated figure compared to the solid phalanx of Protestant clergymen who inveighed Sunday in and Sunday out against the evils of "Demon Rum." How could the ministers dry up the land when every day some new Irishman was selling or buying "a drop of the creature"?

The Irish could also produce and esteem a figure like John "Old Smoke" 10
Morrissey. John, born in Tipperary and brought as a child to the river town of Troy, New York, was a great "broth of a bhoy." In 1853, at twenty-two, he won the American heavyweight championship from Yankee Sullivan in a bare-knuckles bout lasting thirty-seven rounds (Yankee Sullivan retired to California where Vigilantes put him in jail and an unknown assailant strangled him to death.) "Old Smoke" Morrissey earned his name when he tipped over a stove in a barroom in the course of a friendly difference of opinion, fell on his back on the burning coals, but rose, coattails smoking, and knocked out his adversary. Unlike Sullivan, he died quietly in his bed twenty-five years later. In the interim, he served in Congress, amassed a fortune of two million dollars, and founded the first fashionable gambling salon in America at Saratoga Springs.

Prizefighting was illegal and so was gambling. The Irish dominated both, and the natives were scandalized.

The mood of the era before the Civil War was dynamic and expansive; it spoke naturally in a raucous tone. As one observer remarked, "The cities of

America were not clean, spotless havens of virtue before the immigrants came and they would not be if all the immigrants suddenly disappeared." Nevertheless, the older elements of the community understandably associated the quickened tempo, the heightened tension, and the unexpected stresses of the growing cities with the most conspicuous newcomers—the Irish.

The natives responded in convulsive bursts of violence and prolonged withdrawals. A native mob burned a convent in Charlestown, Massachusetts, in 1831; another mob sacked a Catholic Church in Philadelphia in 1846; respectable ministers and civic leaders endorsed the comic opera "disclosures" of Maria Monk in the late 1830's; and reputable politicians flirted with organized bigotry on and off for thirty years, culminating in the brief Know-Nothing upheaval of 1854-1858. Meanwhile, Yankee employers everywhere in the seaboard cities published advertisements, "No Irish Need Apply." It is not easy to distinguish to what extent the Nativist crusade of these three decades was directed against Catholicism as such or against the Irish, but it appears that the prevailing motive was an antipathy to the Irish as an alien group. They threatened the patterns of job and trade competition, the old values, the homogeneity of the once-small cities. Religious sentiment was probably an available, respectable pretext rather than the motive for action. The old community, particularly its lower-middle class and working class, feeling threatened, found the religious differences an easy rationale, sanctioned by the anti-Catholic tradition of the colonial era. The Irish workingman in the next block and not the Pope in Rome was the real enemy.[2]

The raid on the Charlestown convent represented the first *démarche* of the Boston workingmen against the Irish. It was also a gesture of defiance against a darkening future. Boston in 1830 was economically a sick city; only half of the persons born there in 1790 still dwelt in the city by 1820. Only emigration from the farming hinterland prevented the city from suffering an absolute shrinkage in population. The old trade with the Far East, the glittering superstructure of the city's former maritime supremacy, had declined. New York, even before the opening of the Erie Canal in 1825, had pulled ahead in prosperity. The growth of factory towns along nearby rivers where electric current was cheap provided Boston entrepreneurs with new wealth, but afforded native craftsmen a glimpse of a dark future in which the factory system would be triumphant.[3] Hemmed in by these pressures, the workingmen searched for a scapegoat.

The imposing red-brick convent conducted by the Ursuline Nuns on the 15
crest of Mount Benedict Hill in Charlestown across the Charles River from Boston was a convenient symbol. Ironically, the pupils in this convent, established in 1818, were drawn largely not from Catholic but from wealthy liberal Protestant homes. The hold of orthodox Congregationalism was breaking down under the impact of liberal Unitarian and Transcendentalist ideas about religion. A number of parents who desired a more cosmopolitan kind of education for their daughters than could be obtained in the female seminaries run by the Congregational Church entered them in the Ursuline Convent. All the hatreds born of the struggle then going on between liberal and fundamentalist religion in Mas-

sachusetts thus became centered on the Charlestown convent. "To the lower classes, with whom Congregationalism was a sacred creed, Catholics and Unitarians seemed to be combining against their religion."

On Sunday evening, August, 11, 1831, after weeks of rising tension, a mob gathered before the convent. The Mother Superior pleaded with the crowd to go away. When her entreaties failed, she tried intimidation.

"The Bishop has twenty thousand Irishmen at his command in Boston," she cried.

Her threat was not only injudicious but also inaccurate (it is doubtful if there were that many Irish adults in Boston in that year). By prearranged signal, mob leaders ignited barrels of tar in a neighboring field. Fire bells began ringing. Hundreds of persons streamed up the hill to join the crowd and watch the fun. As midnight approached, a gang of forty or fifty men forced their way into the convent. The Mother Superior, the dozen nuns, and some sixty frightened pupils fled by the rear entrance. The gang set fire to the building and a neighboring farmhouse owned by the order. The crowd stood and cheered as the two buildings went down in flames.

Eight men were ultimately accused of arson in connection with the burning of the convent, but their trial was an orgy of anti-Catholic prejudice. All but one was swiftly acquitted, and the latter was pardoned soon after when leading Boston Catholics, in a gesture of conciliation, signed a petition asking clemency. The nuns resumed teaching a year later in another Boston suburb, but few pupils cared to risk studying with them. In 1838 the Ursulines abandoned their work in Boston and withdrew to Canada.[4]

The burning of the convent brought the smoldering fires of anti-Catholic, 20
anti-Irish feeling to the surface of national life. Equally incendiary in its own way was the publication in 1836 of Maria Monk's *Awful Disclosures*. In this inspired work of fiction, the author told of her education in a Catholic convent in Montreal, her conversion to Catholicism, her decision to become a nun, and her subsequent shocking discoveries. The Mother Superior of the Convent instructed her, she reported, to "obey the priests in all things," and this, she discovered, meant "to live in the practice of criminal intercourse with them." The children born of these liaisons were, she reported, baptized and immediately strangled. Nuns who refused to cooperate were murdered. Hers was a colorful picture of convent life complete with mass graves in the basement, a secret passageway to the priest's quarters, and midnight orgies. Maria explained that having become pregnant after relations with a priest, she had fled to New York to save the life of her unborn child.

Awful Disclosures, which apparently was ghosted by a professional writer, had a tremendous vogue. Maria was taken up by a sponsoring committee of Protestant clergymen and enjoyed a brief personal success. But then her mother in Montreal disclosed that Maria had never been a resident in the convent described in the book, that she had instead been in a Catholic asylum for delinquent girls, and had run away with the help of a former boyfriend, the probable father of her child. Maria's associates in the writing of the book cheated her out of most of the profits. When she gave birth to a second fatherless child, she did not bother to name him after a priest. One Protestant journal insisted her second pregnancy was arranged by crafty Jesuits to discredit her revelations, but the explanation did not catch on. Her respectable defenders deserted her, and she disappeared into obscurity. Years later she was arrested for picking the pockets of a man in a house of prostitution, and she died in prison. But the book outlived its nominal author. It went through twenty printings, sold 300,000 copies, and down to the Civil War served as the "Uncle Tom's Cabin" of the Know-Nothing movement.*

The most serious outburst of violence came in Philadelphia, the City of Brotherly Love. In 1843 Bishop Francis Kenrick persuaded the school board to permit Catholic children to read the Douai rather than the King James version of the Bible in the public schools. Catholic children were also excused from the religious instruction that was then a customary part of the curriculum. Nativists attacked this decision as interference by a "foreign prelate" in American education. Mass meetings were held in Independence Square to denounce the change. In May 1844, a Protestant group invaded the Philadelphia suburb of Kensingston, an industrial section where the Irish predominated, to hold a protest meeting. This gesture of defiance produced street fighting in which the Irish drove off their antagonists. The nativists then called a mass meeting for the following Monday, May 6th, in the same neighborhood and appealed to their supporters to turn out in force. The second meeting resulted in a far more serious melee in which one man was killed. This pitched battle touched off three days of general rioting. Protestant mobs roamed the streets of Kensington, setting blocks of houses in flames, and burning two Catholic churches.

An uneasy quiet reigned for several weeks. Then, on July 4th, the holiday was converted into a testimonial to those nativist dead who had fallen in the May rioting. Seventy thousand persons paraded behind the carriages of the widows and children of these men in downtown Philadelphia. The next day street fighting broke out again. This time the focus of attack was St. Philip de Neri Church in Southwark, another suburb, where the pastor had stored guns in the basement of the church as a precautionary measure. When the rumor of the existence of this cache spread, hostile crowds gathered. Separate searches by the sheriff and by a committee of twenty drawn from members of the crowd turned up eighty-seven guns and a quantity of ammunition. When the crowd still did not disperse, the governor sent militia to protect the church. By nightfall of the second day, "a company of troops had turned the square on which the church was located into an armed fortress with barricades erected and cannon commanding the principal avenues of approach." The rioters obtained a cannon of their own and fired into the soldiers massed before the church doors. The troops returned the attack, and the sound of cannon and musket fire rang across the square for several hours.

* The book was again in circulation on a small scale in the presidential campaign of 1960.

Meanwhile, gangs roamed the streets looking for Irishmen. Priests and nuns went into hiding. Thousands of Catholics fled the city. Before these days of open civil war had passed, thirteen persons had been killed and more than fifty were wounded, most of them nativists who had engaged the militia in combat.[5]

The burning of churches and the open war in the streets of Philadelphia 25
caused a strong backlash of public disapproval of the nativists. The middle and upper classes drew back in fear from a movement that seemed to be reenacting the horrors of the French Revolution. The diary entries of a wealthy New Yorker, George Templeton Strong, record the change in opinion in respectable circles during that tumultuous spring and early summer. On April 10th he rejoiced in the victory of the nativists in the New York municipal elections: "Hurrah for the Natives!" he wrote. "Such a blow hasn't fallen on the Hibernian race since the days of Earl Strongbow."

On May 8th, when news reached New York of the first outbreak of rioting, he wrote: "Great row in Philadelphia. . . . This'll be a great thing for the Natives, strengthen their hands amazingly if judiciously used."

Two months later when the fighting broke forth again, he took a darker view. "Civil war raging [in Philadelphia]," he wrote on July 8th. "Mob pelting the military, not with paving stones, but with grapeshot and scrap-iron out of ten-pounders; the state of things in that city is growing worse and worse every day.

"I shan't be caught voting for a 'Native' ticket again in a hurry," he concluded.[6]

The nativist movement rose and fell in successive waves of passion. In reaction to the episodes in Philadelphia, the movement ebbed for nearly a decade. It did not, however, go out of existence. By the 1840's a broad network of nativist societies, religious propaganda organizations, magazines and newspapers was in existence. Books attacking Catholics had become staples in the publishing industry. One writer observed as early as 1835 that the abuse of Catholics "is a regular trade and the compilation of anti-Catholic books . . . has become a part of the regular industry of the country, as much as the making of nutmegs or the construction of clocks."

The last great surge of nativism came in 1854 with the emergence of the 30
American, or Know-Nothing, Party. (The party drew its name from the fact that members of the Order of the Star-Spangled Banner, a secret nativist organization, when asked about their activities said, "I know nothing.") In the elections of 1854–1855, the Know-Nothings scored unexpectedly sweeping victories. The party and its allies carried Maryland, Delaware, Kentucky, and most of New England and showed strength in other parts of the country. About seventy-five congressmen were elected, pledged to do battle against the Pope and his American adherents. The size of the victory was deceptive. In retrospect, it is clear that the Know-Nothing Party was a halfway house for voters seeking a new political home. The ravaging struggle over slavery was tearing apart the dying Whig Party and transforming the Democratic Party. The new Republican Party, pledged to halt the extension of slavery, had just been born. In this period of

rapid political flux, the Know-Nothings represented an effort to divert attention away from the slavery issue to the "safer" issues of anti-Catholicism and anti-immigration about which the native community could more easily agree.

Massachusetts was the stronghold of the Know-Nothings. There they captured the governorship, all state offices, and huge majorities in both houses of the legislature. The election represented a real coming to power of the embittered lower classes of the native community. Of the 378 members of the lower house of the legislature, only thirty-four had ever served in office before. The great majority were "mechanics, laborers, clerks, school teachers, and ministers who understood nothing of the governmental processes and were ill-equipped to learn." The disorganized, disorderly legislative session passed little important legislation. A committee appointed to investigate convents became the butt of jokes in the newspapers. On a visit to Lowell, members of the committee charged to the state their liquor bills and also expenses incurred in their off-duty relations with a lady "answering to the name of Mrs. Patterson." The scandal became so great the legislature canceled the rest of the investigation and expelled the chairman of the committee from the legislature. Before adjourning, the members voted themselves a pay increase. At the next election, only one-sixth of the members were reelected.[7]

The fiasco in Massachusetts and the ineffectiveness of Know-Nothing legislators in other states contributed to the party's rapid decline. By 1860 it had dwindled to an inconsequential faction. Life in the cities, however, retained its violent tone. In the years just before the Civil War, a nativist mob of fifteen hundred persons rioted in the Irish districts of Lawrence, Massachusetts, burning homes and churches; in Baltimore eight men were killed in election-day battles between Know-Nothings and Democrats, and in New York, Philadelphia, and other cities violence flared sporadically.

Throughout these strife-torn decades of the 1840's and 1850's, however, each week during the spring and summer months vessels arrived in Atlantic Coast seaports carrying more Irish to America. While the battle raged intermittently in the streets between the Irish and the natives, the reinforcements poured forth from steerage. The Irish were slowly winning the battle for the city against the Protestant lower classes by sheer force of numbers.

Notes

1. Robert Ernst, *Immigrant Life in New York City, 1825–1863* (King's Crown Press, New York, 1949), p. 133.

2. John Higham, *Strangers in the Land: Patterns of American Nativism 1860–1925* (Rutgers University Press, New Brunswick, N.J., 1955), Chapter One.

3. Oscar Handlin, *Boston's Immigrants, 1790–1880* (Harvard University Press, Rev. Ed., Cambridge, Mass., 1959), pp. 14–15.

4. Ray A. Billington, *The Protestant Crusade, 1800–1860* (Macmillan, New York, 1938; reissued, Rinehart, New York 1952), pp. 72–76.

5. Billingham, *op. cit.*, pp. 220–231.

6. Strong, *Diary.* These entries are in the volume for 1835–1849, pp. 228, 232–233, 240.
7. Billington, *op. cit.*, pp. 412–416.

QUESTIONS FOR DISCUSSION

1. In paragraph 13, Shannon points out that it was difficult to determine whether anti-Catholic nativist crusades were against Catholicism or against the Irish. Explain.
2. One of the reasons for anti-Irish sentiment in Boston was the city's abrupt decline in prosperity in the early years of the nineteenth century. Mention some of the causes of the decline.
3. Shannon is skilled in his retelling of historical events. Locate some passages and comment on their effectiveness.

WRITING ASSIGNMENTS

1. Reaction Journal: After you have read this selection carefully, write an accurate summary of its major points in no more than two hundred words.
2. Write a paragraph or two in which you explain and discuss two of the following:
   a. "The Irish workingman in the next block and not the Pope in Rome was the real enemy."
   b. "The burning of churches and the open war in the streets of Philadelphia caused a strong backlash of public disapproval of the nativists."
   c. "In this period of rapid political flux, the Know-Nothings represented an effort to divert attention away from the slavery issue to the 'safer' issues of anti-Catholicism and anti-immigration about which the native community could more easily agree."
3. Notice the color and style with which Shannon writes historical narrative. Research a historical incident of some local importance and write a brief narrative in which you imitate Shannon's prose.

THE CHINESE MUST GO

BETTY LEE SUNG

Betty Lee Sung (b. 1948), an American-born Chinese, has lived in China and traveled widely throughout Asia. She speaks three Chinese dialects and for five years wrote a special program on the Chinese in the United States for the Voice of America. Her numerous works on the Chinese-American experience include Chinese Immigrant Children in New York City: The Experience of Adjustment *(1987), which she wrote, and* Chinese American Intermarriage *(1990), which she edited. In the following selection from* Mountain of Gold: The Story of the Chinese in America *(1967), Sung details some of the incidents of discrimination and violence against Chinese laborers in the western United States during the last half of the nineteenth century.*

◆ FREEWRITING

The introduction to this section states that "although group conflicts are frequently expressed as religious or racial intolerance, they are often driven by fears of economic and social upheaval." Freewrite for ten or fifteen minutes on how applicable this comment is to cultural conflict in your region.

In 1870, there were 63,000 Chinese in the United States, 99 percent of whom were on the west coast. Every tenth person in California in 1860 was Chinese. Their large numbers, their physical differences, the retention of their national dress, the custom of wearing their hair in pigtails, their habits and traditions, so incomprehensible to the Occidental mind, made them a target easy to spot.

When employment with the railroad ceased, the Chinese sought work in the mines, on the farms, in land reclamation, in domestic service, and in the cigar and woolen factories. These were jobs which the white man scorned, for the white man was looking for a quick bonanza. Nevertheless, they were jobs that gave the Chinese employment while the white man was out of work.

So whereas the Chinese had been praised for their industry, their honesty, their thrift, and their peaceful ways, they were now charged with being debased and servile coolies, clannish, dangerous, deceitful, and vicious. They were accused of being contract laborers, although there was no shred of evidence to show that the Chinese were anything but Argonauts of a different skin coloring. Degenerate traits were ascribed to them, in direct contradiction to the praises heaped upon them a few years earlier. The workingmen accused them of undermining the white man's standard of living. It was alleged they could work for less because they subsisted on next to nothing. The word was spread that the land and rail monopolies hired Chinese instead of white men because the Chinese accepted employment at any price. Yet the books kept by Charles Crocker of the Central Pacific showed that white men were paid at the rate of $35 per month plus keep, and the Chinese were paid $35 per month without keep, mainly because the Chinese preferred cooking their own food.

The charge of accepting slave wages was shortly disproved after the exclusion laws took effect. The drastic curtailment in immigration brought about a shortage in Chinese laborers. Quick to take advantage of the situation, Chinese laborers demanded and got higher wages for their services—this in spite of a surplus in white labor.

However, reason and fact could not prevail. Elmer Clarence Sandmeyer wrote: "... there would have been a depression in the 1870s if the entire population had been made up of lineal descendants of George Washington. . . . If the Chinese in California were white people, being in all other respects what they are, I do not believe that the complaints and warfare against them would have existed to any considerable extent."[1] But once the charges were made, they spread like a prairie fire, fanned red-hot by Dennis Kearney.*

Kearney invariably began his speeches with an attack upon the monopolies —the rich, huge corporate enterprises. He pointed out their owners' ornate mansions on Nob Hill and blamed these moguls for the plight of the workingmen. He accused the Chinese of working hand-in-hand with monopolies, of accepting slave wages, and of robbing the white man of his job. His wrath was directed against both the Chinese and the land and rail monopolies, but the latter were powerful, impregnable, organized, while the Chinese were docile, eager to avoid conflict, and ineffectual in court because their testimony could not be accepted as evidence. Kearney's speeches always ended with the slogan, "The Chinese must go!" So the blame fell upon the Chinese, and thus supplied with a hate object, the frenzied, incited mob would dash off to another orgy of attacks upon the defenseless Chinese.

During this period, the Chinese were stoned and robbed, assaulted and murdered. Hoodlums would organize attacks against the Chinese camps as sport, for they knew the Chinese could not obtain redress.

In the spring of 1876, the Chinese were driven from small towns and camps, their quarters burned. Some Chinese were killed or injured. In June of 1876, a violent attack was made upon them at Truckee.

In 1877, employers of Chinese labor in Chico received threatening letters. In March of that year, six tenant farmers were attacked and five killed. The murderer who was caught confessed to being under orders from the Workingmen's Party.

In July 1877, a great riot broke loose. Twenty-five wash houses were burned, and there followed an outbreak of riots. For months afterwards, no Chinese was safe on the streets. Arson and personal abuse spread to adjacent counties. Chinese laundries were burned and when occupants tried to escape, they were shot or left to die in flaming buildings.

In 1878, the entire Chinese population of Truckee was rounded up and driven from town.

In 1885, the infamous massacre of 28 Chinese in Rock Springs, Wyoming, occurred. Many others were wounded and hundreds were driven from their homes.

In 1886, Log Cabin, Oregon, was the scene of another brutal massacre.

Professor Mary Coolidge wrote: "During the years of Kearneyism, it is a wonder that any Chinese remained alive in the U.S."

* an influential labor union leader.

Murdering Chinese became such a commonplace occurrence that the news- 15
papers seldom bothered to print the stories. Police officials winked at the attacks, and politicians all but incited more of the same. There were thousands of cases of murder, robbery, and assault, but in only two or three instances were the guilty brought to justice.

If murders were commonplace, the indignities, abuse, brutalities, and injustices practiced against the Chinese were outrageous. An oldtimer told of the indignities he suffered at the hands of drunken white men:

> Every Saturday night, we never knew whether we would live to see the light of day. We operated a laundry near a mining camp. Saturday was the night for the miners to get drunk. They would force their way into our shop, wrest the clean white bundles from the shelves and trample the shirts which we so laboriously finished. If the shirts were torn, we were forced to pay for the damages. One night, one of the miners hit his face against the flat side of an iron. He went away, but we knew that our lives were now in danger so we fled, leaving all of our possessions and money behind. The miner came back with a mob who ransacked our shop, robbed us of the $360 that was our combined savings and set fire to the laundry. We were lucky to escape with our lives, so we came east.

Whereas most Chinese had gone straight to San Francisco upon their arrival in the United States, they now began to disperse. Some had already gone north to work on the Northern Pacific and Canadian Pacific Railroads. Others sought work in the silver and coal mines of Nevada, Oregon, Wyoming, and Colorado. But prejudice and hatred confronted them everywhere. The anti-Chinese sentiments had spread like a cancerous growth to other parts of the West.

On February 11, 1870, a joint resolution passed the legislature of the Territory of Colorado, affirming the desirability of Chinese immigration. "The preamble stated that the immigration of Chinese labor to Colorado was calculated to hasten the development and early prosperity of the Territory by supplying the demand for cheap labor. It was, therefore, resolved that such immigration should be encouraged by legislation that would guarantee the immigrants security of their persons and property."[2] Ten years later, the seeds of hatred sprouted in Colorado. Anti-Chinese feelings reached their pitch in Denver for the November elections, and these feelings soon gave way to open violence.

There were two versions to the story of how one riot started. The *Rocky Mountain News* version was that a Chinese laundryman charged ten cents more than a white customer was willing to pay. An argument ensued, whereupon the Chinese slapped the white man in the face with a knife. The injured man ran into the streets and a crowd gathered, so the Chinese fired a gun into the crowd.

The other version was revealed in a government publication as a result of an 20
investigation to determine if indemnity was due the Chinese. The riots, said the

government publication, began when a game of chance between two Chinese was broken up by a couple of drunken white men. Both versions then agreed about the crowd that gathered.

Because only fifteen policemen were on the Denver force, the Mayor called out the fire department, promising the crowd a drenching if they did not disperse. The crowd became so angry that they began a destructive rampage lasting throughout the night. Every Chinese laundry, business, and home was destroyed. The Mayor, with his pitiful law-enforcement staff, was helpless. An appeal was made to the Governor for help. A light artillery battery and the Governor's guards were dispatched to Denver. The Chinese were rounded up and locked in jail for their own safety. One Chinese was killed and several white men wounded, but the homes and property of the Chinese were completely destroyed.

The Chinese had no recourse. Neither the state, the federal, nor the Chinese government provided them any protection. China had not wanted her citizens to roam abroad.

Notes

1. Elmer Clarence Sandmeyer, *The Anti-Chinese Movement in California* (Urbana, Ill.: University of Illinois Press, 1939), p. 88.
2. "The Chinese in Colorado," *Colorado Magazine* (October, 1952), p. 273.

QUESTIONS FOR DISCUSSION

1. What was the nature of the anti-Chinese sentiment when it first began to develop? How was the sentiment related to the curtailment of immigration by the exclusion laws?
2. E. C. Sandmeyer, an authority on the anti-Chinese movement in California, wrote that "there would have been a depression in the 1870s if the entire population had been made up of lineal descendants of George Washington." Explain what he meant.

WRITING ASSIGNMENTS

1. Reaction Journal: Write a letter to an editor of a local paper about a minority group in your region that has been victimized by intolerance. Identify the source of the conflict and suggest what members of both majority and minority groups might do to improve relations.
2. Examine your freewriting and compose an essay in which you apply your ideas to Sung's anti-Chinese riots. If you prefer, show how your ideas relate to any other group conflicts with which you are familiar either through your reading or your personal experiences.

TO BLACKS AND JEWS: *HAB RACHMONES*

JAMES A. MCPHERSON

James A. McPherson (b. 1943) attended segregated schools in his native Georgia before going to Morris Brown College in Atlanta and to Harvard Law School. He has been a journalist and a lecturer at several universities and has published two volumes of short stories: Hue and Cry *(1969) and* Elbow Room *(1977), which won the Pulitzer Prize. The following essay was originally published in the journal* Tikkun *in 1989 and subsequently included in* The Best American Essays, 1990. *In this essay, McPherson traces the history of the relationship between American Jews and blacks and examines the sources of tension between the two groups.*

◆ FREEWRITING

In paragraph 17, McPherson quotes Hertzberg's comment that individual blacks and Jews "have the capacity to package themselves in order to make it in terms the white majority can understand." Do you think the same applies to other minority groups, including white ethnics? Freewrite for ten or fifteen minutes on such "packaging jobs" that you have observed or read about.

About 1971, Bernard Malamud sent me a manuscript of a novel called *The Tenants*. Malamud had some reservations about the book. Specifically, he was anxious over how the antagonism between Harry Lesser, a Jewish writer, and Willie Spear, a Black writer, would be read. We communicated about the issue. On the surface, Malamud was worried over whether he had done justice to Willie Spear's black idiom; but beneath the surface, during our exchange of letters, he was deeply concerned about the tensions that were then developing between Black intellectuals and Jewish intellectuals. I was living in Berkeley at the time, three thousand miles away from the fragmentation of the old civil rights coalition, the mounting battle over affirmative action, and most of the other incidents that would contribute to the present division between the Jewish and Black communities.

I was trying very hard to become a writer. As a favor to Malamud, I rewrote certain sections of the novel, distinguished Willie Spear's idiom from Harry Lesser's, and suggested several new scenes. I believed then that the individual human heart was of paramount importance, and I could not understand why Malamud had chosen to end his novel with Levenspiel, the Jewish slumlord who owned the condemned building in which the two antagonists lived, pleading with them "*Hab rachmones*" ("Have mercy"). Or why Levenspiel begs for mercy 115 times. Like Isaac Babel, I felt that a well-placed period was much more effective than an extravagance of emotion. Malamud sent me an autographed copy of the book as soon as it was printed. Rereading the book eighteen years later, I now see that, even after the 115th plea for mercy by Levenspiel, there is no period and there is no peace.

Well-publicized events over the past two decades have made it obvious that Blacks and Jews have never been the fast friends we were alleged to be. The best that can be said is that, at least since the earliest decades of this century, certain spiritual elites in the Jewish community and certain spiritual elites in the Black community have found it mutually advantageous to join forces to fight specific obstacles that block the advancement of both groups: lynchings, restrictive housing covenants, segregation in schools, and corporate expressions of European racism that target both groups. During the best of times, the masses of each group were influenced by the moral leadership of the elites. From my reading of the writers of the extreme right wing, in whose works one can always find the truest possible expression of white racist sentiment, I know that the Black and Jewish peoples have historically been treated as "special cases." The most sophisticated of these writers tend to examine the two groups as "problems" in Western culture. Both share incomplete status. Both are legally included in Western society, but for two quite different reasons each has not been fused into the "race."

Until fairly recently, Jews were considered a "sect-nation," a group of people living within Western territorial states and committed to a specific religious identity. This extraterritorial status allowed Jews to convert and become members of a confessional community, as was often the case in Europe, or to drop any specific religious identification and become "white," as has often been the case in the United States.

This second Jewish option is related, in very complex ways, to the special 5
status of Black Americans and thus to the core of the present Black-Jewish problem. The romantic illusions of Black nationalism aside, black Americans have not been Africans since the eighteenth century. Systematic efforts were made to strip Black slaves of all vestiges of the African cultures from which they came. The incorporation of European bloodlines, from the first generations onward, gave the slaves immunities to the same diseases, brought by Europeans to the Americas, that nearly decimated America's indigenous peoples. The slave ancestors of today's thirty or so million Black Americans took their ideals from the sacred documents of American life, their secular values from whatever was current, and their deepest mythologies from the Jews of the Old Testament. They were a self-created people, having very little to look back on. The one thing they could not acquire was the institutional protection, or status, that comes in this country from being classified as "white." And since from its very foundation the United States has employed color as a negative factor in matters of social mobility, we Black Americans have always experienced tremendous difficulties in our

attempts to achieve the full rewards of American life. The structure of white supremacy is very subtle and complex, but the most obvious thing that can be said about it is that it "enlists" psychologically those whites who view their status as dependent on it. It has the effect of encouraging otherwise decent people to adopt the psychological habits of policemen or prison guards.

Given this complex historical and cultural reality, most Black Americans, no matter how wealthy, refined, or "integrated," have never been able to achieve the mobility and security available to whites. Jewish Americans, by contrast, have this option, whether or not they choose to exercise it. Blacks recognize this fact, and this recognition is the basis of some of the extreme tension that now exists between the two groups. While Jews insist that they be addressed and treated as part of a religious community, most Black Americans tend to view them as white. When Jews insist that Jewish sensitivities and concerns be recognized, Black Americans have great difficulty separating these concerns from the concerns of the corporate white community.

And yet, despite the radically different positions of the two groups, there has been a history of alliances. Perhaps it is best to say that mutual self-interest has defined the interaction between Blacks and Jews for most of this century. In her little-known study *In the Almost Promised Land*, Hasia R. Diner has traced the meeting and mutual assessment of the two peoples as presented in the Yiddish press to the two million Jewish immigrants from Eastern Europe and Russia who came to the United States during the first four decades of this century. Community papers like the *Tageblatt* and the *Forward* forged a socialistic language that brought together Jewish immigrants from different backgrounds, that helped them acculturate, and that advised them about the obstacles and opportunities they would find in America. These papers gave more attention to Black American life than to any other non-Jewish concern. They focused on Black marriage and family, on Black crime, on Black "trickery and deception," and on Black education, entertainment, and achievement. They linked Black suffering to Jewish suffering. Diner writes:

> The Yiddish papers sensed that a special relationship existed between blacks and Jews and because of this the press believed that the two groups were captivated by each other. . . . Jews believed that a history of suffering had predisposed Jews toward understanding the problems of blacks. ("Because we have suffered we treat kindly and sympathetically and humanly all the oppressed of every nation.")

The central theme was that Black people were America's Jews. Historical parallels were emphasized: the Black Exodus from the South was compared to the Jewish Exodus from Egypt and to the Jewish migration from Russia and Germany.

But there were much more practical reasons why the two groups—one called "white," the other defined by caste; one geared to scholarship and study, the other barely literate; one upwardly mobile, the other in constant struggle merely to survive—managed to find common ground during the first four decades of this century. There was the desperate Black need for financial, legal, and moral support in the fight against racism, lynchings, and exclusion from the institutions of American life. There was the Jewish perception that many of the problems of exclusion faced by Black people were also faced by Jews. Diner writes:

> Black Americans needed champions in a hostile society. Jewish Americans, on the other hand, wanted a meaningful role so as to prove themselves to an inhospitable [society]. . . . Thus, American Jewish leaders involved in a quest for a meaningful identity and comfortable role in American society found that one way to fulfill that search was to serve as the intermediaries between blacks and whites. The Jewish magazines defined a mission for Jews to interpret the black world to white Americans and to speak for blacks and champion their cause.

Diner is describing the "interstitial" role, traditionally assumed by Jewish shopkeepers and landlords in Black communities, being extended into the moral sphere. Given the radical imbalance of potential power that existed between the two groups, however, such a coalition was fated to fail once American Jews had achieved their own goals.

10 For mutually self-interested reasons, I believe, the two groups began a parting of the ways just after the Six Day War of 1967. The rush of rationalizations on both sides—Jewish accusations of Black anti-Semitism, Black Nationalist accusations of Jewish paternalism and subversion of Black American goals—helped to obscure very painful realities that had much more to do with the broader political concerns of both groups, as they were beginning to be dramatized in the international arena, than with the domestic issues so widely publicized. Within the Black American community, even before the killing of Martin King, there arose a nationalistic identification with the emerging societies of newly liberated Africa. In the rush to identify with small pieces of evidence of Black freedom *anywhere* in the world, many Black Americans began to embrace ideologies and traditions that were alien to the traditions that had been developed, through painful struggle, by their earliest ancestors on American soil.

A large part of this romantic identification with Africa resulted from simple frustration: the realization that the moral appeal advocated by Martin King had authority only within those southern white communities where the remnants of Christian tradition were still respected. The limitations of the old civil rights appeal became apparent when King was stoned while attempting to march in Cicero, Illinois, in 1966. We Black Americans discovered that many ethnic Americans, not just southern whites, did not care for us. The retrenchment that resulted, promoted by the media as Black Nationalism, provided convenient excuses for many groups to begin severing ties with Black Americans. Expressions of nationalism not only alienated many well-meaning whites; they had the effect of discounting the Black American tradition of principled struggle that had produced the great leaders in the Black American community. To any perceptive listener, most of the nationalistic rhetoric had the shrillness of despair.

For the Jewish community, victory in the Six Day War of 1967 caused the beginning of a much more complex reassessment of the Jewish situation, one based on some of the same spiritual motivations as were the defeats suffered by Black Americans toward the end of the 1960s. The Israeli victory in 1967 was a *reassertion* of the nationhood of the Jewish people. But, like the founding of Israel in 1948, this reassertion raised unresolved contradictions. My reading teaches me that, until the twentieth century, Zion to most Jews was not a tangible, earthly hope, but a mystical symbol of the divine deliverance of the Jewish nation. Zion was a heavenly city that did not yet exist. It was to be planted on earth by the Messiah on the Day of Judgment, when historical time would come to an end. But the Jewish experience in Europe seems to have transformed the dream of a heavenly city into an institution in the practical world. This tension has turned the idea of the Jews as a nation existing as the community of the faithful into the idea of Israel as a Western territorial sovereign. Concerned for its survival, Israel has turned expansionist; but the price it has paid has been the erosion of its ethical identity. It is said that the world expects more from the Jews than from any other people. This deeply frustrating misconception, I believe, results from the dual premise (religious and political) of the State of Israel. I also believe that American Jews are extraordinarily frustrated when they are unable to make non-Jews understand how sensitive Jews are to uninformed criticism after six thousand years of relentless persecution.

The majority of Black Americans are unaware of the complexity of the meaning of Israel to American Jews. But, ironically, Afro-Zionists have as intense an emotional identification with Africa and with the Third World as American Jews have with Israel. Doubly ironic, this same intensity of identification with a "Motherland" seems rooted in the mythologies common to both groups. In this special sense—in the spiritual sense implied by "Zion" and "Diaspora" and "Promised Land"—Black Americans *are* America's Jews. But given the isolation of Black Americans from any meaningful association with Africa, extensions of the mythology would be futile. We have no distant homeland preparing an ingathering. For better or worse, Black Americans are *Americans*. Our special problems must be confronted and solved here, where they began. They cannot be solved in the international arena, in competition with Jews.

Related to the problem of competing mythologies is a recent international trend that, if not understood in terms of its domestic implications, will deepen the already complex crisis between Blacks and Jews. The period of European hegemony, mounted in the fifteenth century and consolidated in the nineteenth, imposed on millions of non-European people values and institutions not indigenous to their cultural traditions. One of these institutions was the nation-state. Since the end of World War II, the various wars of independence in India, Asia,

Africa, and elsewhere have exposed the fact that a European invention does not always meet the mythological, linguistic, and cultural needs of different ethnic groups competing within artificial "territorial states." We sometimes forget that it took many centuries for Europeans to evolve political forms suited to their own habits. Since the 1950s, colonized people have begun to assert their own cultural needs. The new word coined to define this process is "devolutionism." While devolutionism is currently a Third World phenomenon, two of the most prominent groups within the territorial United States, because of their unique origins, can be easily drawn into this struggle: Black Americans, because of our African origins and our sympathy for the liberation struggle currently taking place in South Africa; and Jews, because of their intense identification with Israel. Given the extent of Israeli involvement in South Africa, and given the sympathy many Black Americans feel for Black South Africans and Palestinians, it is only predictable that some Black Americans would link the two struggles. My deepest fear is that the dynamics of American racism will force Black Americans into a deeper identification with the Palestinians, thus incorporating into an already tense domestic situation an additional international dimension we just do not need. The resulting polarization may well cause chaos for a great many people, Blacks and Jews included.

I have no solutions to offer beyond my feeling that we should begin talking 15
with each other again.

I remember walking the streets of Chicago back in 1972 and 1973, gathering information for an article on Jewish slumlords who had "turned" white neighborhoods and then sold these homes at inflated prices to poor Black people, recent migrants from the South, on installment purchase contracts. I remember talking with Rabbi Robert Marx, who sided with the buyers against the Jewish sellers; with Gordon Sherman, a businessman who was deeply disturbed by the problem; with Marshall Patner, a lawyer in Hyde park; and with other Jewish lawyers who had volunteered to work with the buyers in an attempt to correct the injustice. I spent most of a Guggenheim Fellowship financing my trips to Chicago. I gave the money I earned from the article to the organization created by the buyers. And although the legal case that was brought against the sellers was eventually lost in federal district court, I think that all the people involved in the effort to achieve some kind of justice found the experience very rewarding. I remember interviewing poor Black people, the victims, who did not see the sellers as Jews but as whites. I remember interviewing Mrs. Lucille Johnson, an elderly Black woman who seemed to be the spiritual center of the entire effort. Her influence could get smart Jewish and Irish lawyers to do the right thing, as opposed to the legal thing. I asked her about the source of her strength. I still remember her reply:

> The bad part of the thing is that we just don't have what we need in our lives to go out and do something, white or black. We just don't have *love*. . . . But this ain't no situation to get hung up on color; getting

> hung up on some of God's love will bail us out. I think of "Love one another" and the Commandments. If we love the Lord our God with all our hearts and minds, and love our neighbors as ourselves, we done covered them Commandments. And "Let not your heart be troubled; he that believes in God believes also in me."

I think there was, a generation or two ago, a group of stronger and wiser Black and Jewish people. I think they were more firmly grounded in the lived mythology of the Hebrew Bible. I think that, because of this grounding, they were, in certain spiritual dimensions, almost one people. They were spiritual elites. Later generations have opted for more mundane values and the rewards these values offer. Arthur Hertzberg told me, "Anti-Semitism is the way Blacks join the majority. Racism is the way Jews join the majority. Individuals in both groups have the capacity to package themselves in order to make it in terms the white majority can understand."

Certain consequences of the Black-Jewish alliance cannot be overlooked. The spiritual elites within both groups recognized, out of common memories of oppression and suffering, that the only true refuge a person in pain has is within another person's heart. These spiritual elites had the moral courage to allow their hearts to become swinging doors. For at least six decades these elites contributed to the soul of American democracy. Their influence animated the country, gave it a sense of moral purpose it had not known since the Civil War. The coalition they called into being helped to redefine the direction of the American experience and kept it moving toward transcendent goals. With the fragmentation of that coalition, and with the current divisions among its principals, we have fallen into stasis, if not into decadence. Bernard Malamud's Levenspiel the landlord would like to be rid of his two troublesome tenants. I have no solutions to offer. But, eighteen years later, I want to say with Malamud: Mercy, Mercy, Mercy, Mercy, Mercy, Mercy, Mercy, Mercy, Mercy, Mercy

I want to keep saying it to all my friends, and to all my students, until we are strong enough to put a period to this thing.

QUESTIONS FOR DISCUSSION

1. In what respects do African-Americans and Jews both share "incomplete status" in Western culture? Discuss how this relationship at once draws them together and pulls them apart.
2. Explain why McPherson regards as a "misconception" the commonly held belief that "the world expects more from the Jews than from any other people."
3. Define "devolutionism" and show how it can lead to hostile relationships between African-Americans and Jews.
4. Discuss how effectively McPherson uses Bernard Malamud's *The Tenants* to open and close his essay. Be certain to show how he relates his experience with Malamud and the novel with the ideas in this selection.

WRITING ASSIGNMENTS

1. Reaction Journal: McPherson writes that "the central theme" of Hasia R. Diner's study "was that Black people were America's Jews." Assume the role of a Jewish student, and write a letter to an African-American friend in which you explain what Diner was saying. Refer to the ideas in McPherson's essay, and show how his comments are of mutual interest.

2. McPherson suggests that American blacks and Jews share the "same intensity of identification with a 'Motherland.'" Write a brief but developed explanation of what he means, and show how this problem of competing mythologies affects the relationship.

FROM . . . Y NO SE LO TRAGÓ LA TIERRA (. . . AND THE EARTH DID NOT PART)

TOMÁS RIVERA

Tomás Rivera (1935–1984) was born in Texas to parents who had emigrated from Mexico in the 1920s. Along with other migrant farm workers, Rivera and his family traveled north yearly, sometimes as far as Michigan and Minnesota. In spite of the difficulties of accommodating schooling to the family's frequent relocations and his own work in the fields, Rivera graduated from high school and went on to earn a Ph.D. in Spanish literature from the University of Oklahoma in 1969. After teaching English at the high school and college levels, Rivera served in various administrative posts at the University of Texas at San Antonio and at El Paso. From 1979 until his death he was chancellor of the University of California at Riverside. Widely honored for his work on the problems of Chicano students, Rivera also served on the board of the National Chicano Council on Higher Education.

In 1971 Rivera's novel . . . Y No Se lo Tragó la Tierra *(later translated into English as* . . . And the Earth Did Not Part*), which relates the events of one year in the 1940s through the eyes of a migrant farm-worker child, won the Quinto Sol Prize for Chicano literature. He is also the author of essays, the poetry collection* Always and Other Poems *(1973), and a collection of short stories published posthumously in 1988,* La Cosecha (The Harvest). *The following excerpt from the novel, in which the narrator suffers anxiety about what effect his expulsion from school will have on his family's ambitions for a better future, demonstrates a stream-of-consciousness style of narration.*

◆ FREEWRITING

Recall an incident that you experienced as a young child that you were ashamed of and that you wanted to keep hidden from your parents. Freewrite for ten or fifteen minutes and describe the incident. Try to remember your impressions—real and imagined.

It is very painful. That's why I hit him. And now what do I do? Maybe they didn't expel me from school. Maybe it isn't true after all. Maybe not. *Of course it is.* Sure, it's true, they did expel me. And now what can I do?

I think it all started when I felt shame and anger both at the same time. I don't even want to get home. What am I going to tell my mother? What about when my father comes home from the fields? They'll spank me for sure. But one feels shame and anger. It's always the same in these northern schools. Everyone just stares at you up and down. Then they laugh at you, and the teacher with that Popsicle or Eskimo Pie stick trying to find lice on your head. One feels shame. And when they turn up their noses, one feels anger. I think it's better to stay here in the ranch, here among the trees and chicken coops; or out in the field where one at least feels free, more at ease.

"Hurry up, son, we're almost at school."

"Are you going to take me to the principal?"

"Heck no, don't tell me you can't speak English yet. Look, there is the front door. If you don't know where to go, just ask. Ask, don't be timid. Don't be afraid."

"Why don't you come with me?"

"Don't tell me you're afraid. Look, that must be the entrance. Here comes a man. Alright, behave well, ok?"

"But why won't you help me?"

"Good Lord, you can handle it. Don't be afraid."

It's always the same thing. They take you to the nurse and the first thing she does is look for lice. It's really the fault of those old ladies. On Sundays they sit out in front of the chicken coops and clean one another of lice. The gringos drive back and forth in their cars staring and pointing at them. Father is right in saying they're like monkeys in a zoo. But it's not all that bad.

"Look, mother, What do you think? They pulled me out of the classroom as soon as I arrived and they took me to the nurse who was all dressed in white. They made me take off all my clothes and they examined me all over down to my butt. But where they took the longest was on my head. I had washed it, right? Well, the nurse brought out a jar that looked like vaseline but smelled like worm killer. Do I still smell like that? And she rubbed it all over my head. It itched. Then she started to part my hair with a pencil. After a while they let me go, but I was very embarrassed because I had to take off my pants and even my shorts in front of the nurse."

But now what can I tell them? That they threw me out of school? It wasn't all my fault. From the very beginning I didn't like that gringo.* He didn't laugh at me. He just kept staring at me, and when they put me in the corner away from the others every few minutes he turned around, then he would give me the finger. I was angered, but more than anything I felt shame because I was away from all the others and they could all see me better there. And when it was my turn to read, I couldn't. I listened to myself. I couldn't hear the words come out . . . this cemetery doesn't even frighten me. That's what I like best about going and coming from school. How green it is! Everything so level. All the lanes are paved. It even looks like a golf course. Now I won't have time to run up through the hills and slide and tumble down. Not even time to lie down on the grass and listen to all the different sounds. Last time I counted twenty-six . . . if I hurry maybe I can tag along with doña† Cuquita. She leaves for the dump about this time, when the sun isn't too hot.

> Be careful, children. Just be careful not to step where there's burning underneath. Wherever you see smoke rising, that means there are coals under there. I know very well why I'm telling you this; I was badly burned; I still have the scar . . . Look, each of you pick up a long stick and turn over the trash vigorously. If the keeper of the dump comes to see what we're doing, tell him we came to throw something away. He's a good man, but he likes to keep those dirty little books that people throw away sometimes . . . look out for the train when you cross that bridge. A man was killed there last year . . . he was caught in the middle of the bridge and he couldn't make it to the other side . . . Did they give you permission to come with me? . . . Don't eat anything until after you wash it.

But if I go with her and not tell my parents they'll give me another thrash- 5
ing. What am I going to tell them? Maybe they didn't expel me. *Sure, man, sure they did!* What if they didn't. *Sure they did.* What am I going to tell them? But it wasn't entirely my fault. I just had to urinate. When I was standing there at the latrine he was the one who started to pick on me.

> "Hey, Mex. . . . I don't like Mexicans because they steal. You hear me?"
> "Yes."
> "I don't like Mexicans. You hear, Mex?"
> "Yes."
> "I don't like Mexicans because they steal. You hear me?"
> "Yes."

I remember the first time I had a fight at school. I was very afraid because everything had been planned ahead of time. It wasn't over anything in particular.

* white, non-Hispanic.
† a title of respect.

It was just that some of the boys who were in the second grade and old enough to have mustaches started pushing us against each other. They kept it up until we started to fight, probably out of fear. They started pushing me toward Ramiro. We were about a block away from school. Then we started to wrestle and to hit back. A couple of ladies came out and pulled us apart. Ever since then I started feeling much bigger. But up until the fight started I was scared.

This time it was different. He didn't even warn me. I just felt a hard blow on my ear and I heard sounds like the ones you hear when listening to shells at the beach. I can't even remember how nor when I hit him, but I know I hit him because they told the principal that we were fighting in the restroom. Maybe they didn't throw me out? *Sure they did.* I wonder who called the principal. And the janitor was all scared and held his broom up in the air, ready to squash me if I tried to escape.

> "The Mexican kid got in a fight and beat up a couple of our boys . . . no, not bad . . . but what do I do?"
>
> " . . . . "
>
> "No, I guess not. They could care less if I expel him . . . they need him in the fields."
>
> " . . . . "
>
> "Well, I just hope our boys don't make too much about it to their parents. I guess I'll just throw him out."
>
> " . . . . "
>
> "Yeah, I guess you're right."
>
> " . . . . "
>
> "I know you warned me, I know, I know . . . but . . . yeah, ok."

But how could I leave school if everyone at home wanted me to go to school. Anyway, the janitor was ready. He had his broom up in the air ready for anything . . . and then they just told me to go away.

This is half the distance home. This cemetery is really pretty. It doesn't resemble the one in Texas in the least. That one is really frightening. I don't like it. What really frightens me most is when we're leaving a burial and I look up and read on the archway of the entrance the words that say, *do not forget me*. I seem to hear all the dead who are buried there say these words; and then the sound of these words runs through my head. Sometimes, even if I don't look up when I go through the doorway, I see them. But not this cemetery. This one is so pretty. Nothing but grass and trees; I think that is probably the reason why people here don't even cry when they bury someone. I like to play here. I wish they would let us fish in the little stream that passes through here; there are many fish. But that's impossible, you even need a fishing license; and to top it off they won't even sell us one because we're from out of state.

I won't be able to go to school anymore. What am I going to tell them? I've 10
been told so many times that one's teachers are like second parents . . . and now? When we return to Texas everyone will know about it too. Mother and Father will be angry; maybe they'll do more than just spank me. And then my uncle and

my grandfather will also find out. Perhaps they'll send me to a reform school like I've heard them talk about. In there they make you behave if you're bad. They're pretty strict with you. When you come out you're smooth as silk. But, maybe they didn't expel me, *sure they did*, maybe not, *of course they did*. I could pretend I was going to school and I could stay here at the cemetery. That would be best. But after that? I could tell them I lost my report card. But wouldn't I still be in the same grade? What I regret most is that now I will not be able to be a telephone operator as my father wants me to be. You need to finish school for that.

> "Vieja,* tell the boy to come out . . . look, compadre,† ask your godchild what he wants to be when he grows up and he has finished school."
> "What are you going to be, son?"
> "I don't know."
> "Tell him! Don't be embarrassed, he's your godfather."
> "What are you going to be, son?"
> "Telephone operator."
> "Really?"
> "Yes, compadre, you wouldn't believe it but my son is really set on that. Everytime we ask him he says he wants to be a telephone operator. I think they're well paid. I told my boss about it the other day and he laughed. He probably thinks that my son can't do it, but the fact is that he doesn't know him, he's smarter than anything. I just pray that God helps him finish school and that he becomes one."

That was a good movie. The telephone operator was the main character. I think that that is why my father wanted me to study that as soon as I finished school. But . . . maybe they didn't expel me. What if it isn't true? What if it isn't? *Sure, it is*. What will I tell them? What will I do? Now they won't be able to ask me what I want to be when I grow up. Maybe they didn't. *Sure they did*. What can I do? It hurts and it is embarrassing at the same time. I'd better stay here. No, better not. Mother gets so scared, just as she does when there's thunder and lightning. I have to tell them. Now when my godfather comes to visit I'll just hide. No use asking me anything. What's the use of reading to him as my father makes me do when he comes to visit us. What I'll do when he comes is to hide behind the large locker or under the bed. That way Father and Mother won't be ashamed of me. What if they didn't expel me? What if they didn't? *Sure they did*.

QUESTIONS FOR DISCUSSION

1. In the second paragraph, Rivera's youthful narrator says he "felt shame and anger both at the same time." Describe what embarrassed the young boy and what angered him.

* old woman; term of endearment for spouse
† godfather; buddy

2. Discuss the importance of the cemetery the young narrator mentions twice.

3. According to the narrator, what is it that hurts about the long-term effects of his trouble? Account for the negativism that permeates this selection.

4. Would this selection be more or less effective if Rivera's organization were more conventional? Explain your response.

WRITING ASSIGNMENTS

1. Writing Journal: Even the appearance of this selection on the page is fragmented, and a quick reading will reveal that the content is also fragmented as this young Mexican-American responds privately to real and imagined events that surround a childhood incident. Write a paragraph or two in which you comment on the way that Rivera has written this piece.

2. Write an essay based on the childhood recollection in your freewriting. Write from the point of view you had at a young age. Try to experiment with structure and technique, using Rivera's approach as a model.

US AND THEM

ARTHUR HU

Arthur Hu is a columnist for the San Francisco–based Asian Week. *The following essay appeared in June 1992 in* The New Republic, *shortly after the riots in South-Central Los Angeles following the verdict in the Rodney King case. Hu sees a double standard in the media's reporting of racial incidents, a reluctance to identify black violence directed toward Asians or whites as equally racist as Asian or white violence toward blacks. Only through individualism and self-reliance, Hu feels, will there be an end to the destructive behaviors that grow out of racial tensions.*

◆ FREEWRITING

Read the opening paragraph of each of the following essays. Anticipate the two responses to the Los Angeles riots that followed the first Rodney King verdict. Freewrite for ten or fifteen minutes on what you expect Hu and Kim to do in their respective writings.

Spike Lee's vision of violence has truly become the Real Thing. Throughout the time of the conflagration in Los Angeles, I saw virtually no Asian Americans called on to explain the situation from their point of view. Yet Asians were not just victims of collateral damage; they were often a strategic target. Although much of what went on was black violence directed at Asians, the only racism that was lamented in the mainstream media was white violence against blacks.

The unfortunate timing of the mild sentence given to Soon Ja Du for shooting Latasha Harlins about a year ago in Los Angeles was a key factor in the degree of black outrage that resulted in the rioting of April 29 and 30. Activists of ill will had already spread the word that a black girl had been shot in the back by a Korean merchant over a carton of juice. They didn't mention that the woman running the store had been assaulted by the girl before she fired, or that the context for this action was widespread violence against Korean shopkeepers. Korean entrepreneurs in South-Central Los Angeles ran a 1 in 250 chance of being killed while pursuing their business last year, about the same odds as a tour of duty in Vietnam. Stretch that to a career of thirty years, and the chances go up to 1 in 16, not a much better chance of survival than their young black male customers. Around eight out of ten Korean stores were burned or looted in the riots. 100 in Koreatown alone. Three of the fifty-one killed were Asian—a high proportion when you consider that Asians constitute less than 0.5 percent of the population in South-Central Los Angeles.

Racist remarks were parlayed without comment by the various local and national news media and talk shows, as if one kind of racism were morally appropriate and another weren't: "Those Koreans don't respect us. . . . Those whites are subhuman, they don't even belong here. . . . The Koreans were part of the system, and so are you! . . . Burn the Chinese stores! Fuck the Koreans, we're glad they're gone. . . . Well, burning an apartment is a tragedy, but the liquor stores had to go. . . . We're sick of 400 years of oppression by Koreans!"

It is not as if Korean-Americans are far more economically powerful than black Americans. Even though household incomes were close to the national average, extended and intact families meant that Koreans in 1980 (the latest Census figures available) had a per capita income of only $5,544, which was closer to the $4,545 for blacks than the $7,808 for whites. The average small store brings in no more money than a good union manufacturing job. The difference is that Koreans have the highest number of self-employed of any ethnic group, and their willingness to work very hard for very little money gives them a competitive advantage in inner-city neighborhoods where supermarkets fear to tread. Blacks have also generally ceded the worst entry-level jobs such as janitors and maids to immigrants. Thus Latinos and Asians toil at subminimum wages, living in tiny cubicles and shacks in order to send money to their families in the old country, while many black teens turn their noses at jobs at McDonald's or Safeway at double the minimum wage.

One-hundred-and-twelve-hour work weeks, plus unpaid family labor, is 5
common among Koreans. Many have college degrees that won't get them decent jobs because of discrimination or language problems. Asian students who

live in housing projects and go to inner-city schools rack up grades, test scores, and graduation rates that are the envy of white suburban students. Koreans don't get special loans; they just work three jobs, save, sacrifice, and borrow from loan pools built by family and friends. It seems that Koreans are despised solely because they are the smallest local representative of the "capitalist system," or are of a different race and culture.

Many Asian Americans feel frustrated by the double standards involved in the reporting of criminal cases. In the King case, the race of the policemen, Rodney King, and his jurors was considered relevant. But consider the case of Gregory Calvin Smith, a black man who raped twenty women in San Jose, California. Half his victims were Asian. He got a death sentence for raping and shooting a Japanese exchange student. Yet Smith's picture was never shown; mention of his race was omitted in every article and local TV story. If the King case had been covered without reference to race, the L.A. riot may never have erupted. It's good the Asians don't have an Al Sharpton who can exploit such situations, but Asian resentment and confusion is inevitable when even Asian American leaders minimize the existence of anti-Asian prejudice when it is perpetrated by black Americans.

Many residents of South-Central already realize how, as one told the Los Angeles *Times*, "those damn fools destroyed our neighborhood for nothing." It's not the Koreans who now have no place to cash their checks and no place to buy their groceries. When the supermarket chains leave for good, many will wish for the Koreans to return.

My son is eight months old today. I'm going to teach him not to hate, not to kill, not to lie, and not to steal. I will show him how to fend for himself and his family by using his own resources and industry. I pray that one day everybody else can do the same. I know it's harder when you are poor, but there is no other way. Because only when that day comes will riots like those we've just witnessed in L.A. be a distant memory.

Note: For Study Questions, see pages 495–496.

THEY ARMED IN SELF-DEFENSE

ELAINE H. KIM

Elaine H. Kim (b. 1942) is a professor of Asian American studies at the University of California, Berkeley. The following essay appeared in Newsweek *in May 1992, two weeks after the post–Rodney King-verdict rioting in Los Angeles during which the Korean section of the city suffered heavy damage. Kim sees the racial tensions between blacks and Koreans as an inevitable product of a social system "in which the advancement of one group means deterioration for the other."*

When images of armed Korean shopkeepers and headlines about conflicts between African-Americans and Korean-Americans were suddenly beamed from Los Angeles two weeks ago, seemingly out of nowhere and without history or context, I knew it was another case of visual media racism. The disembodied images implied that both groups come from cultures more violent and racist than the dominant culture. They also diverted attention away from a long tradition of racial violence that was not created by African-Americans or Korean-Americans.

The tensions among people of color are rooted in racial violence woven into U.S. history for the past 500 years and evidenced today in a judicial system that can allow the men who beat Rodney King to escape conviction. The so-called black-Korean problem is a decontextualized manifestation of a much larger problem. The roots lie not in the Korean-immigrant-owned corner store situated in a community ravaged by poverty and police violence, but stretch far back to the corridors of corporate and government offices in Los Angeles, Sacramento and Washington, D.C. Without an understanding of our histories, Korean-Americans and African-Americans, it seems, are ready to engage in a zero-sum game over the crumbs of a broken society, a war in which the advancement of one group means deterioration for the other.

I have lived all my life in the United States. Even though people still compliment me occasionally on my ability to speak English and ask me when I am returning to "my country," I don't consider myself Korean. I am Korean-American. My consciousness was shaped by the civil-rights movement led by African-Americans, who taught me to reject the false choice between being treated as a perpetual foreigner and relinquishing my own identity for someone else's Anglo-American one. For me, African-Americans permanently redefined the meaning of "American." I came to understand how others had also been swept aside by the dominant culture: my schooling offered nothing about Chicanos or Latinos, and most of what I was taught about African-Americans was distorted to justify their oppression and vindicate the forces of that oppression.

Likewise, Korean-Americans have been and continue to be used for someone else's agenda and benefit, whether we are hated as foreigners who refuse to become "good Americans," stereotyped as diligent work machines or simply treated as if we do not exist. Throughout my childhood, the people who continually asked, "What are you?" knew nothing of Korea or Koreans. "Are you Chinese or Japanese?" they would ask confidently, as if there were no other possibilities. The "world history" courses I took started with Greece and Rome; China and Japan were barely mentioned—and Korea never was.

Like many Korean exiles whose political consciousness ripened under Japa- 5
nese colonialism, my father was a fierce nationalist fond of talking about Ko-

reans as a people of great courage and talent. When we were small, he regaled us with tales of heroes like Sohn Kee-chung, the Korean marathon runner who proved the bankruptcy of Hitler's notion of the Aryan "master race" when he won a gold medal in the 1936 Olympics in Nazi Germany. My father also claimed that Koreans were responsible for astounding and important inventions, such as gunpowder and movable type, as well as one of the world's oldest astronomical observatories.

Gold medal: Although I searched and searched, I could find no trace, in the America outside our house, of the things my father told us about. Because of Korea's suzerain relationship with China, Korean inventions such as gunpowder are commonly thought to be Chinese. Likewise, Sohn Kee-chung ran the marathon in a Japanese uniform because Korea was a colony of Japan at the time. The gold medal went to Japan. Later, I began to wonder if my father had made up these things. It was almost as if Korea had never existed, or its existence made no difference.

Why did my parents talk so much about Korea? After all, they both lived most of their lives in the United States. Why didn't they take on an "American" identity? My mother grew up on the plantations and tenant farms of Hawaii and California. Although she did not visit Korea until she was in her 60s, she considered herself a Korean. My father came to Chicago as a foreign student in 1926. He lived in the United States for 63 years. My parents didn't embrace an American identity because racism did not give them that choice. My mother arrived in Hawaii as an infant in 1903, but she could not vote until she was in her 50s, when laws prohibiting persons born in Korea from becoming naturalized U.S. citizens were overturned. My father never became a U.S. citizen, at first because he was not allowed to and later because he did not want to. He kept himself going by believing that he would return to Korea in triumph someday. Instead, he died in Oakland at 88, and we buried him in Korea in accordance with his wishes.

When the Los Angeles Police Department and the state government failed to respond to the initial outbreak of violence in South-Central, I suspected that Korean-Americans were being used as human shields to protect the real source of rage. Surveying the charred ruins of Koreatown, Korean-American newcomers must feel utterly betrayed by what they had believed was a democratic system that would protect life, liberty and property. The shopkeepers who trusted the government to protect them lost everything. In a sense, they may have finally come to know what my parents knew more than half a century ago: that the American Dream is only an empty promise.

I only hope that we can turn our outrage into energy, because I still want to believe the promise is real.

QUESTIONS FOR DISCUSSION

1. Hu and Kim respond quite differently to the Rodney King case. Explain what the King case was and compare their two responses to it.

2. Why, according to Hu, were Korean-owned shops destroyed during the Los Angeles riots? What reasons does Kim offer?

3. How would Kim respond to Hu's assertion that "it seems that Koreans are despised solely because they are the smallest local representative of the 'capitalist system,' or are of a different race and culture"?

4. How would Hu respond to Kim's assertion that "the so-called black-Korean problem is a decontextualized manifestation of a much larger problem"?

5. Why is it so important for Kim to make such a sharp distinction between being Korean and being Korean-American?

WRITING ASSIGNMENTS

1. Reaction Journal: Assume the role of Arthur Hu and write a letter in response to Kim's article. Then assume the role of Elaine Kim and write a response to Hu.

2. Kim's and Hu's essays represent two very different viewpoints on the same subject. In each case, a Korean-American writer addresses the relationships between Korean-Americans and African-Americans and how the Los Angeles riots of 1992 affected the relationships. The contrasts are numerous in the two selections, and the similarities are few. Write an essay in which you compare the two viewpoints and techniques.

CAMPUS LIFE

STUDS TERKEL

Studs Terkel (b. 1912) grew up in Chicago and graduated from the University of Chicago and the Chicago Law School. He has had a career in radio, as an actor in soap operas, disc jockey, sports commentator, talk-show host, and in television as an interviewer and social commentator. Among his several books are Division Street: America *(1966),* Hard Times *(1970), an oral history of the Depression,* Working *(1974), and* American Dreams: Lost and Found *(1980). "Campus Life" is an excerpt from his most recent book,* Race: How Blacks and Whites Think and Feel about the American Obsession *(1992). Two young women Terkel interviewed comment on racial tensions they have observed in school and reveal as well the sources of some of their own attitudes toward other racial and ethnic groups.*

◆ FREEWRITING

Before reading Terkel's selection, think about examples of racism and/or prejudice that you have witnessed on your campus or in your community. Freewrite for ten or fifteen minutes on race relations. Give concrete examples, and feel free to consider causes and solutions as you write.

Dawn Kelly

She is twenty-one, in her third year at the University of Illinois, Chicago. Aside from being a student member of the unversity's board of trustees, she was elected president of the student government. "I had white, Asian, Palestinian, and Hispanic students campaigning for me, as well as black."

She had attended a parochial high school, "a good one. I didn't have any black teachers, but my mother compensated for that. She always kept us in tune with our history and ourselves. I cried when they didn't acknowledge Dr. King's birthday. My mother said, 'Why cry? Fight back.' We had chapel which all the students attended. I did one of Dr. King's speeches as a tribute to him. They were forced to recognize him one way or another, even if we didn't have school out. That was my mother's idea. The majority of the students complimented me."

Her sixteen-year-old sister attends the same parochial school and her thirteen-year-old brother won a scholarship in a prep school out West. She plans to earn her Ph.D. and teach African-American literature.

Right now I'm a bit perplexed about things going on in my life. I'm affected quite emotionally. A lot of young African-Americans sit around and don't realize that our parents fought for us to be in universities and restaurants. We've become quite comfortable. Some think I'm overreacting. They say, "Dawn, you're too emotional."

In the last two years, I've seen racism and hate, and it disturbs me. I would 5
say that the majority of the people in the world are good—white and black, of all colors. Even here at the university. I think it's always a few bad apples.

The problem started when a female black student was walking through the dormitory early in the evening. She was grabbed by a group of white males who said all kinds of derogatory things to her. When she screamed, they ran away. She can identify one of the men, but she won't testify because she's afraid the university will not back her and the guys may come back. So she's moved home, off the dormitories. I said I'd go to the police with her, but she always stands me up. She's afraid and she has every right to be.

There was a black female resident advisor in the dormitory. A black penis from a cadaver was hung on her door, with a note: "Next time it might be one of your body parts." It was signed by the KKK. She moved home, terrified. I would have felt terribly guilty if something had happened to her, without standing up and saying something. Anyone who would do something so morbid is not joking. Right now, the tensions are so thick you can cut it with a knife.

There's a second student paper on the campus. It's run by the more progressive ones, most of them white. They've printed articles exposing much of the racism and have received hate letters from the Klan.

I think it stems from the country itself. These crimes aren't prosecuted as harshly as they can be. Therefore it gives students as well as other people the impression that they can do whatever they want to do and they'll get away with it.

10 I eat with white kids at the cafeteria, but most black students don't. You can see Asian kids in one corner, Hispanics in another, whites, blacks, all pretty well segregated. You have individual intermingling, but not groups.

The feeling has always been there, and I blame myself as well as others for not taking a stand before. My mother has totally come down on me. She's a very strong woman. She raised my brother, my sister, and me by herself. She felt I was too passive.

It's one thing to go to school together, but to live right next to each other, sleep in the same room, that's another story. Most white students come from the suburbs and have been isolated, have not encountered various cultures. I think they've lost out on a lot. And that leads to racism, too. That's why we're pushing for multicultural courses on campus. If you would study accounts where blacks and Asians and Latinos have contributed to society, your respect level would be a lot higher. They just don't know.

We've had different accounts of the tensions. Some of my friends had problems with white roommates who don't want to listen to their music or have their friends over. There's a cultural gap. I had a friend who listens to Louis Farrakhan. She has tapes of his sermons. When she listens, not loud, it would disturb her roommate. I guess it's because of his black-nationalistic overtones. I pretty much agree with him, but I guess it would probably frighten the average white person. Our music is different, our culture is different. One person might want to listen to Prince, another to Led Zeppelin, and you'd have a clash.

I appreciate Farrakhan because he's not afraid to tell the truth. People think he's a racist, but he's not. He has an endearment toward his people and wants to see them with empowerment, with a decent standard of living. I think the average white person is afraid to hear the truth.

15 We may have alienated a lot of white kids, not intentionally. Any time you stand up for something, most people think it threatens them. I don't think most of them are racists, but they feel alienated. When you look at them as you might look at anybody, they think you're seeing them as white racists. It's not that way at all. You're just trying to stand up for what's right. In our coalition, we have some white students and Jewish students, as well.

Jewish people in this country even today are discriminated against. Many people don't consider them Anglo or white. They're considered different.

A lot of people think Farrakhan is anti-Semitic. I disagree. He's just calling what he sees. That happens so much in this society, where people have this thing. Many black people feel that Jewish people think they're better and that blacks are on a different level. This feeling exists; we have to be honest.

I think Jewish history and black history parallel one another. I had a black professor who said if you want to know success, read Jewish history. They've been through degrading things, starting all the way back from Egypt and up into the forties and Hitler's Germany. The one thing I can respect about people of Jewish descent is that another Holocaust will never happen because they won't let people forget it.

African-Americans have a problem with celebrating slavery. I think if you celebrate what has been, you can move to higher ground. If you can celebrate your ancestors for dying so that you can move ahead, society won't forget it. Nobody is going to try that with Jews anymore, because they're not going to let it. People won't mess with them because they stood their ground. If we take that stance, it won't happen to us again either. If we said, "We're not going to let you pull at our sisters in the dorm," it wouldn't happen.

I feel that by nature blacks are a forgiving people. They're not racist. I hate 20
it when people throw around the terms reverse racism. I can be prejudiced but not racist. To be a racist, you have to be able to oppress another race. To do that, you have to have economic and political power. Blacks don't have that; whites do. Being prejudiced is something else. You have to prejudge. Many blacks may prejudge whites, because of all their past experiences.

For my grandmother or my great-aunts to have any love for the white race, considering what they've done to us, means they have a true forgiving quality within them. We think about those terrible things and they're not too long ago. They're in my mother's history.

Her family left the South because her brother, who worked in a gas station, beat up the white boy who tried to take his money. He was a great mechanic and got all his money in tips. He helped take care of the family. How was he gonna let this guy come in and take his money and not have a penny to bring home?

That day he told my great-grandmother what happened. She didn't waste any time. They left antique furniture, they left most of their belongings. Whatever they could carry, they threw in a bag, got on a train, and came North. He couldn't tell a white jury or a white judge, "I hit him because he tried to steal from me." He wouldn't have been believed. So for my mother, my uncle, or my great-grandmother, who is now passed, to have any love or respect for the white race, it's a quality in us.

The white kids on campus can't quite comprehend this because it's never happened to them. I've had people ask, "Why do you make such a big deal?" They truly don't understand, not that they're racist.

For one thing, we don't have an African-American cultural center. We've 25
been waiting for one for twenty years. It's a pity for a school that claims to have an urban mission not to have a center that celebrates African history and African art. We wanted to bridge the gap between the black community and the university. What was happening to black and Latino women on the campus was simply a sign of total disregard for us. They disrespect us because they feel we're noth-

ing, we're not intellectual, we're barbaric. So we black women like these type of things, like to be grabbed.

I think this is what a lot of whites believe. I think a lot of blacks believe it, too. We've been degraded so much that we have imbedded in our minds that maybe we're not that good. Maybe that's why so many black students don't excel in school. They feel, "I can't do it. I'm not as intelligent as Susie, the blonde sitting next to me. I lack something." If you grow up in the Chicago public-school system and this is taught you, it's eventually going to affect you. It's conditioning.

I think society has set it up this way. We don't want to see the true quality of life for everybody. We will let a few people of color—I don't like the word minorities, we're over eighty percent of the world—get to the top. They'll let a couple of us get Ph.D.s, become doctors, lawyers. After that, you have people laying by the wayside, people starving, homeless, without education.

You sit in a class and people tell you if you have full lips, darker skin, look a certain way, you're not pretty. This must affect children. I've seen numerous cases where darker students have been shunned and I've been accepted because I'm fair-skinned. Do we have to look European to be beautiful? That's what TV shows us. It's all over.

I see a country and I see a world that's going to have to change. I truly believe it's too late. We have no spirituality anymore. We have no belief in anything anymore but what we can make, what we can synthesize. We're even trying to make babies different ways but the natural way. We're coming up with all these things that are destroying the earth.

The white man has destroyed the earth. He raped Africa, he raped America. Now we say our ozone layer is ruined. You look outside and it's sixty degrees in December. What are we gonna do, patch it up with Band-Aids? I think the world is going and it's just a matter of time before we all just self-destruct. I think it's over. Maybe that's why so many people are not afraid to stand up—because I truly don't think there's anything to fear in the end.

I believe there's a higher power that I'm going to have to face for my wrongs. Everyone else will, too. It's going to be a final judgment. A lot of my friends feel it, too.

Yet, African-Americans have a will to live and to fight.

Jennifer Kasko

Chester Kasko's daughter. She is twenty-three, a graduate of an Illinois university, where she majored in education.

"I have a very hard time finding a job. Right now my pocketbook is depleted."

She describes the neighborhood in which she lives as predominantly white, no black people. "It's secluded, a white island. Blue-collar. They've closed the steel mills down and men who have worked there for thirty, forty years have lost everything. They've lost their pride."

When the time came for desegregation of the schools, we had black children bused in. The neighborhood didn't fight it, but they didn't like it. There wasn't any problem with the little children. They didn't know any better. At first, the older children resented it. They felt they were being invaded and losing what their parents had worked so hard for. I was in ninth grade at the time. There weren't any out-and-out blows. What I remember was everyone would give the bus the finger.

I didn't do it myself, but my friends did. My dad had always taught at a school where there were black people, and I was always around. I was always taught not to be prejudiced, not to hate. We'd go to all the school functions. I'd ride the bus to his school through all the rough neighborhoods. Some of his students would say, "Are you crazy taking the bus? *We* don't even like to take the bus." They were scared, telling me about getting purses stolen, intimidation. My sister and I just sat there and were left alone. We were the only whites on the bus and weren't scared at all. It was almost an adventure.

They would say to us, "Are you Kasko's daughters?" They were thrilled to see us, always nice and receptive. We used to play with the black boys on the days teachers made out the grades. There was no problem until one day the school secretary, a black female, told my father it was wrong for us to play together. Until then, we had a great time and couldn't wait till records day. The next year, we weren't allowed to come anymore.

At my school, even though the black kids were there now, we were actually separate in the same classroom. They'd hang around with their group and we'd hang around with ours. It seemed like the white kids were scared of the others. I'm sure it had something to do with the way they were brought up. They never had exposure.

A lot of my friends' parents would refer to them as niggers. One of my 40
friend's dad worked in Republic Steel. He was laid off and a black man was hired in his place. So he had a real vendetta against him: "The niggers are going to take over everything." I always took it with a grain of salt. I thought he was just angry.

At high school, parochial, it was sixty, twenty, twenty—sixty percent white, twenty percent black, twenty percent Hispanic. Surprisingly, we got along with everyone. When it was our year for Homecoming Queen, the runner-up was black.

We began to notice the problem with the younger students. The freshmen. This was about 1983. It's when Mayor Byrne and Harold Washington were going at it. The girls would wear their Washington buttons on uniform skirts. In obscene places. They were vulgar and would scream down the hall. The girls in our year were quieter, more docile.

The younger girls would tend to carry these heavy bags and would be inconsiderate to others on the stairs. It almost made us not like them. Because of this, the white kids were getting more angry and less tolerant.

At college, our dorm had sixty girls on a floor. Probably two-thirds white and one-third black. Our racial problems started when somebody reported that a couple of black girls had men in their room past hours. They accused our group as the ones who called. It wasn't true, because we had guys after hours, too. So it would have hurt us to call. But they wouldn't listen. We did it, that's all there was to it.

Now they started to leave their doors open and play their music really loud. 45
They'd just keep the same beat for hours. They'd do it purposely, while we tried to study. They joined a black sorority, and things started missing from our rooms. A black girl who was ousted by the others told us that was one of the things they had to do: steal something from white girls.

Did you believe her?

She said it. I heard her. I had a white Swatch watch that I got for my graduation from my brother and sister. Everyone knew I left my room unlocked. I was brought up to be not so protective of everything. I really never had that much. I was a little too open. I know that theft happens in every college and all that.

After that, I locked my room all the time. I was angry because I don't have a lot of nice things. Now I'm a lot less trusting. College really hardened me.

The only reason I got financial aid was that my parents got divorced. It made me angry that several friends couldn't go away to school. Their parents—one a fireman, another a policeman—worked hard all their life to put food on the table. And they couldn't get financial aid. Our parents work hard and don't make that much, just enough to get by, and they get nothing.

Just because a person's a minority, they get financial aid. Some of the kids 50
on my floor laugh about it. "You white people are so stupid. You're supposed to lie to get financial aid." It just bothers me that there's all the people, welfare. It should be even. Everybody should get it, no matter what.

I've been taught not to be prejudiced all my life, but it's hard when you see people getting something for nothing and expecting it. I am tired of people telling me that I owe them for something I haven't even done. I haven't gotten anything free in my life. I've worked hard for everything that I have.

I did my first year of teaching with the Chicago Archdiocese at an all-black school in Harvey. We did have a few Mexican children. I had parents tell me I was picking on their children because I was prejudiced. One parent wanted me to spend extra time with her son. I would have loved to do so, but I had thirty other children in the class and this child was actually learning-disabled and needed special help. She said I owe her. I don't know what she meant. I guess I owe her from years past.

I got along with most parents, and if I had a problem, they were receptive. A lot of parents worked all day and the baby-sitter was a TV set. They worked very hard, the parents, mostly single. The older sister of one of my students was shot dead at a drug dealer's house. I didn't know it, so I was yelling at the kid to sit down and get to work. I had no idea what this poor child had gone through. One day he exploded and I found out. I should be empathetic to what my students have to go through. But I've never been exposed to anything like this before.

I don't have any real close black friends any more. Last year I worked with a girl and she was something else. She was very open and had the system down pat. She said, "You pay your utility bill? Why don't you just move? You pay your Visa bill? Why don't you just change your name?" She'd use her daughter's social-security number and this and that. We spent every day together. I was just fascinated by her. I was wondering if this was characteristic of young black people.

I believe they feel they should get something for nothing. Not most, no. 55
Most those I come in contact with are self-sufficient. What I tried to instill in my students was that God helps those who help themselves. I could use the world "God" because I was in a Catholic school. [*Laughs.*]

Do you think your friend might have been putting you on?

No, she had it down pat. And I used to be so idealistic, thinking everybody in the world could get along. I admired Martin Luther King very much. I loved him. I believe that no person should sit in back of the bus, should have to use a different washroom. A person's a person, no matter what.

But people like Louis Farrakhan and Jesse Jackson are hurting the black culture, because they're telling them it's the white people's fault. You should have pride in your heritage, but not pride in your race over another race.

I went to an Operation Push rally when I was in grammar school. We performed there as baton twirlers. I was about ten. I remember his actual words. To give yourself pride. That was good. But when he said you have to surpass the white race, it just turned sour in my stomach.

They say that most of the people in the projects are black female heads of 60
families. What happened to all the black males that are fathers of these children? This is probably a very racist statement on my part, but I feel the black males should take responsibility for their families.

I still have that bit of adventure in me, but I don't ride the El anymore, like I used to. I'm scared on that. Blacks as well as whites are scared. I used to take that as a way to the Cubs game, to the Sox game. Not anymore.

I don't like some of my thoughts and feelings. I used to feel so different. Welfare has created a subculture, and I don't like that I feel angry about it. It's not a Christian feeling. It's not a helpful, understanding feeling. It's more of a bitter feeling. Even though I was brought up not to be prejudiced, I've almost been conditioned over the years towards being prejudiced. I hate to admit that I am.

I long for the time that I was able to play with Kenneth and Fitzgerald in the school yard and not give a second thought to it. I don't like the hatred that's happening in our society. I just feel there's gotta be some other answer out there. But I don't know what. My eyes have been opened to a lot of things I don't like that much.

QUESTIONS FOR DISCUSSION

1. Obviously, there are many differences that separate Dawn Kelly and Jennifer Kasko. Think about the two interviewees, and mention some of the similarities, which are less conspicuous.

2. What are some concrete examples of racial confrontations that Kelly and Kasko mention?

3. Kelly feels that one cause of racist behavior is the fact that most white students come from the suburbs. Explain what she means.

4. Kelly and Kasko mention Louis Farrakhan in very different contexts and with very different attitudes. Who is Farrakhan? Contrast Kelly's and Kasko's attitudes toward him.

5. Kelly suggests African-Americans have much to learn from Jewish history. Explain.

WRITING ASSIGNMENTS

1. Reaction Journal: Write a letter to the editor of your school or local newspaper in which you present examples of racism on your campus or in your community. Point to causes, and by all means discuss solutions.

2. Form a group with several of your fellow students and discuss the letters that you wrote to the newspapers. How much do the members of the group agree on what racism is? What do they see as possible causes of the conflicts, and what do they suggest might be done to accommodate all groups?

3. Write an essay in which you compare and contrast Kelly's and Kasko's observations and conclusions.

4. Interview a student from another race. Pay close attention to Terkel's techniques of writing interviews as you write your own.

Suggestions for Discussion and Writing

1. Reread the first paragraph of the introduction to "Neighborhoods." Write an extended definition of "neighborhood" in which you synthesize the ideas of the writers in this chapter with your own sense of neighborhood. Develop your definition with specific references to the readings and concrete illustrations from your experience.
2. Some social scientists argue that there are many people who have never lived in a neighborhood and that the power of the neighborhood has diminished in modern times. Write an essay in which you examine this idea and argue for or against it on the basis of personal experience, discussion with your family and others, and readings in this chapter.
3. The introduction to "Family" asserts that "one of the chief roles of any family structure is to transmit culture, and to this end respect for tradition on the part of both parent and child is essential." Lawrence H. Fuchs writes that American families are characterized by independence of individual members rather than mutual dependence. Monica McGoldrick shows how class and cultural differences are major determiners of the family experience. Write an essay in which you explore one or more of these ideas. Make direct reference to at least two of the following writers: James T. Farrell, G. S. Sharat Chandra, James M. Freeman, Shirley Ann Grau, and David Mura.
4. Write an essay in which you compare your family life and values to those of a friend, if possible one from a different ethnic background. Make specific reference to the writings in this unit and to your and your friend's personal experiences.
5. You have been invited to give a talk to a group of international students in this country on some of our language controversies. Make use of the material in "Language." Wherever applicable, refer to the experiences of Jerre Mangione, Richard Rodriguez, and Paule Marshall.
6. Public schools in the United States have often functioned as a means of acculturation and reflection of the dominant culture. The goal of public education has been to transmit values as well as subject matter. The degree of success clearly varies from time to time and place to place. In the past two decades there have been major curricular and other changes in recognition of our diversity. (The question of multicultural education is explored in the last unit of this text.) Write an essay in which you describe how well the schools met the needs of Anzia Yezierska, Bella (in Marilyn French's "First Day at School"), and Mike Rose. Then talk about how your own school experiences met your needs and reflected your particular values and culture.

7. "Confrontations" provides several examples of hostile and violent intergroup encounters. In the course of your own continuing response to assignment four at the end of the **National Identity and Cultural Pluralism** unit, you have recorded a number of instances of cultural confrontations and accommodations. Referring to this material and to the selections in "Confrontations," write an essay in which you analyze the nature of intergroup confrontations. Your essay should make specific reference to one or two of the essays in "Confrontations" as well as to some of the materials and personal experiences you collected in your journal.

Return to assignment one at the end of "National Identity and Cultural Pluralism." Reevaluate and refine your initial thoughts on group identity.

Return to assignment three at the end of "National Identity and Cultural Pluralism" and continue to update your collection of news and opinion items on the pluralism-tribalism controversy.

Return to assignment four at the end of "National Identity and Cultural Pluralism." Make additional entries in your journal on the theme of Confrontation and Accommodation.

PART

IV

CONTROVERSY: A CASEBOOK ON MULTICULTURAL EDUCATION

I'm sitting in my history class,
The instructor commences rapping,
I'm in my U.S. History class,
And I'm on the verge of napping.

The Mayflower landed on Plymouth Rock.
Tell me more! Tell me more!
Thirteen colonies were settled.
I've heard it all before.

What did he say?
Dare I ask him to reiterate?
Oh, why bother,
It sounded like he said,
George Washington's my father.

I'm reluctant to believe it,
I suddenly raise my mano.
If George Washington's my father,
Why wasn't he Chicano?

—THE IMMIGRANT EXPERIENCE, *RICHARD OLIVAS*[1]

[1] Olivas, Richard. "The Immigrant Experience." *Mexican-American Authors.* Ed. Américo Paredes and Raymond Paredes. Boston: Houghton Mifflin, 1972. 150.

Controversy: A Casebook on Multicultural Education

The selections in this unit may serve as the basis for a controlled research project on the subject of multicultural education. The purpose of such a casebook is to present various viewpoints on an issue, thus providing in one volume sources a student may draw upon in devising and supporting a thesis. You may find it useful to refer also to relevant essays in other sections of this book as you choose your topic and develop your paper.

One of the primary questions being debated by American educators today is to what extent school and college curricula should draw attention to the diversity of this country and the history and concerns of its various racial and ethnic groups. Arguments in favor of greater emphasis on ethnicity—especially of minority groups—sometimes approach the debate from a psychological standpoint, maintaining that seeing one's values and concerns reflected in educational materials is empowering, leading to improved self-image and more effective learning. Thus, it is argued, a "Eurocentric" curriculum in effect disadvantages students who are not of white European descent. Opponents frequently argue that the interests of the nation as a whole, and thus of the individuals who compose it, are best served by a curriculum emphasizing the elements that unite rather than divide us. But of course the issues are much broader and often very complex. As you read through the selections in this unit you will find that the authors present differing viewpoints on this far-reaching debate. In fact, even the definition of "multicultural education" is far from settled. You will probably find it useful to take some preliminary notes as you read each piece in order to record the author's major points for your future reference. This will allow you to identify which pieces are most relevant to the focus of your own essay.

Suggestions for a Research Paper

1. *Summary and Evaluation.* Whatever your topic, you will probably want to summarize several of the essays in the casebook. Whether your purpose is primarily to present information or to argue in favor of a particular position,

you should make certain that, one way or another, you have provided your reader with a spectrum of opinion. Done thoroughly and with judicious use of quotation and paraphrase, such a summary, together with an evaluation on your part, could be enough for a research report.

2. *Evaluation of Specific Proposals and Programs.* Discuss several relevant readings from the Casebook and provide information on curricula in schools you have attended and the college you are now attending. Show how these curricula relate to the proposals and programs presented in the readings. Consider, among other things, the ethnic composition of the student body. (You may also wish to refer to college catalogues in your library.)

3. *Evaluation of This Textbook.* Select a number of readings from earlier sections of this book that you would recommend for inclusion in a multicultural course. Defend your choice by referring specifically to some of the points about the function of a multicultural curriculum the authors make in the Casebook. Which authors in the Casebook would approve of your selections? Which would disapprove? Why?

4. *Multicultural Education and Language.* Select two or three readings in the "Language" chapter and show how they are relevant to the multicultural education controversy.

5. *Multicultural Education and Other Education Issues.* Select two or three readings in the "Education" chapter, and show how they are relevant to the multicultural education controversy.

6. *Multicultural Education and Cultural Enrichment.* Consider Ishmael Reed's statement that the alternative to multiculturalism is a "humdrum homogeneous world of all brains but no heart . . . a world of robots with human attendants bereft of imagination, of culture." Discuss the contribution of ethnic groups to cultural enrichment through music, art, and literature. Show how some of the writers in the Casebook would respond to incorporating such ethnic culture into the curriculum.

7. *Multicultural Education and a Specific Ethnic Group.* Select a chapter from "Ethnic Journeys," and relate the history and concerns of a specific ethnic group to the essays in the Casebook.

8. *Multicultural Education, Empowerment, and Self-Esteem.* The extent to which an individual is empowered by his or her group identity and the importance of self-esteem arise in several of the readings in the Casebook. They are explored as well in essays such as those by Shelby Steele, Stokely Carmichael/Charles V. Hamilton, and Michael Novak. Discuss these or other readings, and show how they are relevant to multicultural education.

9. *Multicultural Education and National Identity and Cultural Pluralism.* Explore the impact of a multicultural curriculum on the formation of a national identity.

10. *Multicultural Education and Confrontation and Accommodation.* Alice Chandler states that the United States must choose between a path of cultural reconciliation and one of "cultural and social apartheid." Explore the impact of multicultural education on the development of ethnic harmony or conflict.

Note on Documentation

Writing that uses information from sources—through quotation, summary, paraphrase, facts not common knowledge—must acknowledge these sources. In place of the traditional footnotes or endnotes, many academic disciplines now present the reference in parentheses within the text of the paper. Complete bibliographical information for the sources referred to in such in-text citations is included at the end of the paper in a list of works cited. Different disciplines follow different formats for both citations and bibliography. The Modern Language Association (MLA) system, described below, is used in English and the humanities. The American Psychological Association (APA) system is used in the social sciences.

According to the MLA system, in-text citations must include the author's last name and the page number where the original material may be found. The bracketed numbers in the selections indicate the page numbers in the original published versions. Including the author's name in your own sentence will allow you to keep the parenthetical citation brief and thus minimize interruption to your own text. The first time you mention an author's name in your text, use his or her full name. Thereafter, refer to the author by last name only. A standard handbook will provide a full description of both the MLA and APA systems of documentation. Included here are only those portions of the MLA system that you will need to use in referring to materials in the casebook and earlier sections of this text.

MLA In-Text Citations

Author(s) Mentioned in Text, Page Number in Parentheses:

In attempting to define what makes an American, Lewis Lapham observes that Americans share "a common temperament and habit of mind" rather than particular political or ideological positions (36).

Responding to the charge that Black Power preaches reverse racism, Stokely Carmichael and Charles V. Hamilton distinguish between racism, which has as its purpose subjugation, and Black Power, which aims at achieving black self-identity (191).

Author(s) and Page Number in Parentheses:

Adopting an anti-intellectual stance as a defense against educational experiences that denigrate their own abilities and cultural backgrounds, students may "flaunt ignorance, materialize [their] dreams. It is a powerful and effective defense. . . . But like all strong magic, it exacts a price" (Rose 459).

Racism excludes others for the purpose of subjugating them; Black Power excludes others for the purpose of achieving self-determination (Carmichael and Hamilton 191).

Format for Works Cited

The list of works cited, which appears at the end of a paper, gives the complete publishing information for each item cited in the paper. The list should be printed on a separate page titled "Works Cited," and items should be listed alphabetically by authors' last names. When a work has two or three authors, it is listed in alphabetical sequence according to the first author's last name. Complete publication information for the selections in the Casebook is given at the bottom of the first page of each piece in correct MLA style. For the purpose of your research paper on multicultural education, you will also need to know the format for citing a selection that appears in a collection. The entry below demonstrates this format as well as the format for a work with two authors:

> Carmichael, Stokely, and Charles V. Hamilton. "Black Power." *Face to Face: Readings on Confrontation and Accommodation in America.* Ed. Joseph A. Zaitchik, William H. Roberts, Holly C. H. Zaitchik. Boston: Houghton Mifflin, 1994. 186–92.

If in your paper you refer to any of the materials in this text that were written by the editors (introductions, preface, and so forth), you will list the text on your "Works Cited" page as follows:

> Zaitchik, Joseph A., William H. Roberts, Holly C. H. Zaitchik, eds. *Face to Face: Readings on Confrontation and Accommodation in America.* Boston: Houghton Mifflin, 1994.

AMERICA: THE MULTINATIONAL SOCIETY*

ISHMAEL REED

Writer and educator Ishmael Reed (b. 1938) has been the recipient of NEA and Guggenheim fellowships and has lectured at numerous colleges and universities. He is the editorial director of Yardbird Press and a contributing editor to the New York Times, *the* Los Angeles Times, *and* Ramparts. *His writings include the novels* Mumbo Jumbo *(1972),* The Last Days of Louisiana Red *(1974), and* Flight to Canada *(1976), and several volumes of poetry, including* Conjure *(1972) and* Chattanooga *(1973). The multimedia Bicentennial mystery* The Lost State of Franklin, *on which he collaborated with Carla Blank and Suzushi Hanayagi, won the Poetry in Public Places contest in 1975. In the following chapter from* Writin' Is Fightin': Thirty-seven Years of Boxing on Paper *(1988), Reed comments on the potential of the United States to become a place that acknowledges and celebrates its unique diversity.*

[51] At the annual Lower East Side Jewish Festival yesterday, a Chinese woman ate a pizza slice in front of Ty Thuan Duc's Vietnamese grocery store. Beside her a Spanish-speaking family patronized a cart with two signs: "Italian Ices" and "Kosher by Rabbi Alper." And after the pastrami ran out, everybody ate knishes.

—New York Times, *23 June 1983*

On the day before Memorial Day, 1983, a poet called me to describe a city he had just visited. He said that one section included mosques, built by the Islamic people who dwelled there. Attending his reading, he said, were large numbers of Hispanic people, forty thousand of whom lived in the same city. He was not talking about a fabled city located in some mysterious region of the world. The city he'd visited was Detroit.

A few months before, as I was leaving Houston, Texas, I heard it announced on the radio that Texas's largest minority was Mexican American, and though a foundation recently issued a report critical of bilingual education, the taped voice **[52]** used to guide the passengers on the air trams connecting terminals in Dallas Airport is in both Spanish and English. If the trend continues, a day will come when it will be difficult to travel through some sections of the country without hearing commands in both English and Spanish; after all, for some

* Reed, Ishmael. *Writin' Is Fightin'*. New York: Atheneum, 1988. (Note: The title of the above selection is actually the title of the chapter of Reed's book in which it appears. Therefore, since your citation will be to the original source, you will cite the book title rather than "America: The Multinational Society.")

western states, Spanish was the first written language and the Spanish style lives on in the Western way of life.

Shortly after my Texas trip, I sat in an auditorium located on the campus of the University of Wisconsin at Milwaukee as a Yale professor—whose original work on the influence of African cultures upon those of the Americas has led to his ostracism from some monocultural intellectual circles—walked up and down the aisle, like an old-time southern evangelist, dancing and drumming the top of the lectern, illustrating his points before some serious Afro-American intellectuals who cheered and applauded his performance and his mastery of information. The professor was "white." After his lecture, he joined a group of Milwaukeeans in a conversation. All of the participants spoke Yoruban, though only the professor had ever traveled to Africa.

One of the artists told me that his paintings, which included African and Afro-American mythological symbols and imagery, were hanging in the local McDonald's restaurant. The next day I went to McDonald's and snapped pictures of smiling youngsters eating hamburgers below paintings that could grace the walls of any of the country's leading museums. The manager of the local McDonald's said, "I don't know what you boys are doing, but I like it," as he commissioned the local painters to exhibit in his restaurant.

Such blurring of cultural styles occurs in everyday life in the United States 5
to a greater extent than anyone can imagine **[53]** and is probably more prevalent than the sensational conflict between people of different backgrounds that is played up and often encouraged by the media. The result is what the Yale professor, Robert Thompson, referred to as a cultural bouillabaisse, yet members of the nation's present educational and cultural Elect still cling to the notion that the United States belongs to some vaguely defined entity they refer to as "Western civilization," by which they mean, presumably, a civilization created by the people of Europe, as if Europe can be viewed in monolithic terms. Is Beethoven's Ninth Symphony, which includes Turkish marches, a part of Western civilization, or the late nineteenth- and twentieth-century French paintings, whose creators were influenced by Japanese art? And what of the cubists, through whom the influence of African art changed modern painting, or the surrealists, who were so impressed with the art of the Pacific Northwest Indians that, in their map of North America, Alaska dwarfs the lower forty-eight in size?

Are the Russians, who are often criticized for their adoption of "Western" ways by Tsarist dissidents in exile, members of Western civilization? And what of the millions of Europeans who have black African and Asian ancestry, black Africans having occupied several countries for hundreds of years? Are these "Europeans" members of Western civilization, or the Hungarians, who originated across the Urals in a place called Greater Hungary, or the Irish, who came from the Iberian Peninsula?

Even the notion that North America is part of Western civilization because our "system of government" is derived from Europe is being challenged by Native American historians who say that the founding fathers, Benjamin Franklin especially, were actually influenced by the system of **[54]** government that had been adopted by the Iroquois hundreds of years prior to the arrival of large numbers of Europeans.

Western civilization, then, becomes another confusing category like Third World, or Judeo-Christian culture, as man attempts to impose his small-screen view of political and cultural reality upon a complex world. Our most publicized novelist recently said that Western civilization was the greatest achievement of mankind, an attitude that flourishes on the street level as scribbles in public restrooms: "White Power," "Niggers and Spics Suck," or "Hitler was a prophet," the latter being the most telling, for wasn't Adolph Hitler the archetypal monoculturalist who, in his pigheaded arrogance, believed that one way and one blood was so pure that it had to be protected from alien strains at all costs? Where did such an attitude, which has caused so much misery and depression in our national life, which has tainted even our noblest achievements, begin? An attitude that caused the incarceration of Japanese-American citizens during World War II, the persecution of Chicanos and Chinese Americans, the near-extermination of the Indians, and the murder and lynchings of thousands of Afro-Americans.

Virtuous, hardworking, pious, even though they occasionally would wander off after some fancy clothes, or rendezvous in the woods with the town prostitute, the Puritans are idealized in our schoolbooks as "a hardy band" of no-nonsense patriarchs whose discipline razed the forest and brought order to the New World (a term that annoys Native American historians). Industrious, responsible, it was their "Yankee ingenuity" and practicality that created the work ethic. They were simple folk who produced a number of good poets, and they set the tone for the American writing style, of lean and spare lines, long **[55]** before Hemingway. They worshiped in churches whose colors blended in with the New England snow, churches with simple structures and ornate lecterns.

The Puritans were a daring lot, but they had a mean streak. They hated the 10
theater and banned Christmas. They punished people in a cruel and inhuman manner. They killed children who disobeyed their parents. When they came in contact with those whom they considered heathens or aliens, they behaved in such a bizarre and irrational manner that this chapter in the American history comes down to us as a late-movie horror film. They exterminated the Indians, who taught them how to survive in a world unknown to them, and their encounter with the calypso culture of Barbados resulted in what the tourist guide in Salem's Witches' House refers to as the Witchcraft Hysteria.

The Puritan legacy of hard work and meticulous accounting led to the establishment of a great industrial society; it is no wonder that the American industrial revolution began in Lowell, Massachusetts, but there was the other side, the strange and paranoid attitudes toward those different from the Elect.

The cultural attitudes of that early Elect continue to be voiced in everyday life in the United States: the president of a distinguished university, writing a letter to the *Times*, belittling the study of African civilizations; the television network that promoted its show on the Vatican art with the boast that this art represented "the finest achievements of the human spirit." A modern up-tempo state of complex rhythms that depends upon contacts with an international community can no longer behave as if it dwelled in a "Zion Wilderness" surrounded by beasts and pagans.

When I heard a schoolteacher warn the other night about **[56]** the invasion of the American educational system by foreign curriculums, I wanted to yell at the television set, "Lady, they're already here." It has already begun because the world is here. The world has been arriving at these shores for at least ten thousand years from Europe, Africa, and Asia. In the late nineteenth and early twentieth centuries, large numbers of Europeans arrived, adding their cultures to those of the European, African, and Asian settlers who were already here, and recently millions have been entering the country from South America and the Caribbean, making Yale Professor Bob Thompson's bouillabaisse richer and thicker.

One of our most visionary politicians said that he envisioned a time when the United States could become the brain of the world, by which he meant the repository of all of the latest advanced information systems. I thought of that remark when an enterprising poet friend of mine called to say that he had just sold a poem to a computer magazine and that the editors were delighted to get it because they didn't carry fiction or poetry. Is that the kind of world we desire? A humdrum homogeneous world of all brains but no heart, no fiction, no poetry; a world of robots with human attendants bereft of imagination, of culture? Or does North America deserve a more exciting destiny? To become a place where the cultures of the world crisscross. This is possible because the United States is unique in the world: The world is here.

FROM ONE NATION, MANY PEOPLES*

NEW YORK STATE SOCIAL STUDIES REVIEW AND DEVELOPMENT COMMITTEE

The following is an excerpt from the report made by the New York State Social Studies Review and Development Committee to the Commissioner of Education for the State of New York in June 1991. The Committee, consisting of twenty-four educators and scholars, was chaired by Edmund Gordon of Yale University and Francis Roberts of the Cold Spring Harbor Schools in New York. Among the Committee members were Nathan Glazer of the

* New York State Social Studies Review and Development Committee. *One Nation, Many Peoples: A Declaration of Cultural Interdependence*. Albany, N.Y.: New York State Education Department, 1991.

Harvard School of Education, Arthur Schlesinger, Jr., of the City University of New York, Asa Hilliard III, of Georgia State University, and several teachers and administrators in local school districts. The Committee was initially charged with developing criteria for review of the existing social studies curriculum in the State of New York, examining curriculum models which seemed promising, assessing the effectiveness of existing syllabi and recommending changes. Among the concerns of the Committee listed at the beginning of their report is the need for a balanced and pedagogically effective social studies curriculum to reference a variety of cultures and to respond to increasing demands by people of many different cultural backgrounds that the curriculum include their own histories and viewpoints.

[vii] The Committee was asked to review existing New York State social studies syllabi and to make recommendations to the Commissioner of Education designed to increase students' understanding of American culture and its history; the cultures, identities, and histories of the diverse groups which comprise American society today; and the cultures, identities, and histories of other people throughout the world.

In responding to this charge, the Committee members were mindful of four interrelated concerns.

1. Despite growing attention to the need for preparing young people to participate in the world community, the United States continues to be deeply involved in nation-building. The common school is generally viewed as one of the principal vehicles for building in our young people the attitudes, knowledge, skills and understandings essential to continuing national cohesion and viability. The teaching of the nation's history, our national traditions and values, and a common loyalty are purposes commonly accepted as appropriate to the social studies.
2. The present is unlike earlier periods in the history of this country, for now the various peoples who make up our nation, while anxiously embracing many of the advantages, opportunities and mores of this society, seem determined also to maintain and publicly to celebrate much that is peculiar to the cultures with which they identify. Recognizing the interdependence of cultures in this multi-cultural nation, yet unwilling to give up or celebrate in private that with which they have previously been identified, they insist that their participation be recognized, and that their knowledge and perspectives be treated with parity.
3. It is especially in the teaching and learning of geography and history in the 5
social studies that the nation has expected its schools to prepare students for citizenship. Yet it is also in the teaching and learning of this subject matter that the schools are expected to address the facts of diverse cultures, histories and world views. In a period of heightened consciousness about cultural identity, the problems of teaching and learning this subject matter are made

more difficult by lack of attention to this diversity and of reference to a variety of cultures.

4. Not only the world, but also our nation and the peoples who inhabit it, are changing. The nature of our knowledge and the criteria for being judged an educated person are changing, as are our conceptions of effective teaching and learning. Especially in the humanities and the social sciences, we are beginning to realize that understanding and the ability to appreciate things from more than one perspective may be as important as is factual knowledge, among the goals of education. One result of this changing perception is the Committee's assertion that the social studies should be concerned, not so much with "whose culture" **[viii]** and "whose history" are to be taught and learned, as with the development of intellectual competence in learners, with intellectual competence viewed as having as one of its major components the capacity to view the world and understand it from multiple perspectives. Thus the report takes the position that a few fundamental concepts should be the focus of teaching and learning in the social studies, with applications, contexts and examples drawn from multiple cultural sources, differing perspectives and diverse groups. Multicultural knowledge in this conception of the social studies becomes a vehicle and not the goal. Multicultural content and experience become instruments by which we enable students to develop their intelligence and to function as human and humane persons.

The Committee reviewed the existing syllabi and found them inadequate with reference to these concerns. By most acceptable standards of fairness and equitable treatment of the many cultural currents in our nation, the existing syllabi were found wanting, even though in many ways they are among the most advanced in the nation. They were found to contain insensitive language, to draw upon too narrow a range of culturally diverse contexts, and to omit content specific to some groups and areas of the world that some members of the Committee feel to be essential. Although the existing syllabi permit a high degree of freedom in the choice of materials, they can be criticized on the one hand for being insufficiently directive to insure certain types of coverage, and on the other hand for prescribing too heavy a load of specific content.

Thus the Committee recommends:

1. That the present New York State social studies syllabi be subjected to detailed analysis and revision to provide more opportunities for students to learn from multiple perspectives and to remove language which is insensitive or which may be interpreted as racist or sexist.
2. That appropriate mechanisms be set in place to produce a more long-term 10
revision of the syllabi, in order to better reflect the variety of cultural and social divisions extant in the nation's peoples; to be sensitive to the changing

nature of our knowledge and of the criteria by which educated persons are judged; and to make the tasks of teaching and learning the social studies manageable, as well as responsive to varied (and sometimes competing) interests.

3. That seven concepts guide social studies curriculum reform:

   a. Democracy: Democratic ideals as the foundation of American society.
   b. Diversity: Understanding and respecting others and oneself.
   c. Economic and Social Justice: Understanding personal and social responsibility for economic and social systems, and for their effects.
   d. Globalism: Recognizing interdependence and world citizenship.
   e. Ecological Balance: Recognizing responsibility for the global neighborhood.
   f. Ethics and Values: The pursuit of fairness and the search for responsibility.
   g. The Individual and Society: Seeing oneself as a participant in society.

   In order for these concepts to be realized in the social studies as experienced by students, teachers and others in the learning community, several changes will be required in the content, conditions and practice of teaching and learning in the social studies.

4. That the following principles for teaching and learning, therefore, guide the implementation of these changes:

   a. The selection of subject matter content should be *culturally inclusive*, based on up-to-date scholarship in history, the social sciences, and related fields.
   b. The subject matter content selected for inclusion should represent *diversity and unity* within and across groups.
   [ix] c. The subject matter content selected for inclusion should be set within the *context of its time and place*.
   d. The subject matter selected for inclusion should give *priority to depth over breadth*.
   e. Multicultural perspectives should *infuse the entire curriculum, prekindergarten through grade 12*.
   f. The subject matter content should be *treated as socially constructed* and therefore tentative—as is all knowledge.
   g. The teaching of social studies should *draw and build on the experience and knowledge that students bring to the classroom*.
   h. Pedagogy should incorporate a *range of interactive modes of teaching and learning* in order to foster understanding (rather than rote learning), examination of controversy, and mutual learning. . . .

[18] Specific Findings and Illustrations with Regard to the Present New York State Syllabi and Social Studies Program

This subsection serves its purpose by being illustrative, not exhaustive; the correction of each instance of the general problems cited here will be the work of a later phase of this project (whether re-working the current documents, or devising a new framework along the lines recommended by this Committee).

Number One:

Finding: Need for Multiple Perspectives. The Committee noted how frequently social studies slips into a "we-they" framework. All too often when communities are perceived as monolithic, it is common to teach from one perspective, usually that of the so-called dominant culture. For example, in the primary grades children examine neighborhoods and communities. Educators need to be aware that many of the typical features cited for study (such as banks, government buildings, department stores, and other major economic institutions) may not necessarily be present in inner-city or rural communities. Students need to be exposed to the strengths and potential of what does exist in their community, despite obstacles such as drugs and high visibility of crime. What does exist in the students' immediate real world should be used to help them become more aware of and sensitive to their civic responsibilities and possibilities in building their community. To take another instance, the story of the early colonization in the eastern U.S. has too often been told from the perspective of the colonists, not the Native Americans already settled on the land. Or the story of the western United States is told as one of westward expansion, assuming the perspective of the migrating Easterners and disregarding the native men and women already there or the long-established Hispanic influence and settlements in the West.

[19] *Related Finding: Unequal regard for the importance of national/regional bound-* 15
aries and distinctions. For example:

- In the syllabus for grades 9–10, all nations south of the United States are lumped together in the unit entitled "Latin America," tending to omit the information that a number of islands in the Caribbean and nations in Central and South America trace their traditions to non-Latin European nations, to Africa, India, and Indonesia, as well as to native roots. Attention is rarely paid to the complex and controversial relationship between Puerto Rico and the United States.
- The syllabus for grades 9/10 suggests (page 124): "Using pictures of Greek, Roman, and Oriental art and architecture, students could identify similarities." Does the term "Oriental" refer to Asians? If so, which Asians? The reference should be to specific Asian people, corresponding with the Greeks and Romans.
- Northern Africa often is implicitly or explicitly incorporated in the "Middle East" in the teaching of social studies at grade 6.

Related Finding: A disregard for the understanding and study of indigenous social, political, economic, and technological structures, and the precolonial histories of indigenous peoples. For example, the treatment of the European colonization of Africa in the syllabi inadequately addresses the great loss of lives and the eradication of many varieties of traditional culture and knowledge. Similarly, the long and rich history of India before the British conquest is not properly treated. The K–6 syllabi, for example, focus on celebrations such as Thanksgiving and Columbus Day without examining other perspectives than those of Europeans, such as the perspectives of Native Americans.
Related Finding: Effects are often seen as unidirectional (with the European participants as the actors) rather than bi-directional. For example, the syllabus for grades 9/10 recommends that teachers explore the effects of European rule on Africa with their students, but the effects that contact with Africa had on Europe—or the dehumanizing effects on Europeans of their role as colonizers—are not mentioned. In the syllabus for grades 7/8, the connection between Toussaint L'Ouverture's defeat of Napoleon in Haiti and the Louisiana Purchase is not made. In the grade 9/10 syllabus, the influence of Islam upon the religious, cultural, economic and political systems of lands extending from Spain to Sumatra is highlighted, but not the impact upon Islam of the peoples of these lands.
Related Finding: Complex and large-scale issues are often simplified because they are seen from a single, implicit perspective. For example, superficial discussions of the origins and eventual abolition of slavery in the Americas frequently omit the economic basis for the persistence of slavery as an institution. The syllabi for grades 7/8 and 11 do not adequately address the incarceration of Japanese Americans; nor do they discuss the deportation from the U.S. of thousands of people of Mexican origin in the 1920s, regardless of citizenship.

Recommendation: Social studies should be taught from multiple perspectives, global in scope. Beyond the successes, the complexities and shortcomings of U.S. policy should be explored.

Number Two:

Finding: Language Sensitivity. Although specific terms fall into and out of cur- 20
rency and the language of the syllabi may not be deliberately or intentionally sexist, racist, or prejudicial from the point of view of diversity and inclusiveness, the language used is often dated, narrow, and in some cases insensitive. For example, the syllabi refer to "slaves" **[20]** or "the everyday life of a slave," as if being a slave were one's role or status, similar to that of gardener, cook, or carpenter. To refer, rather, to "enslaved persons" would call forth the essential humanity of those enslaved, helping students to understand from the beginning the true meaning of slavery (in contrast to the sentimental pictures of contented slaves, still found in some texts).

Many geographical terms are Western-derived, sometimes almost unconsciously. Terms like "the Far East" should be replaced by ones like "East Asia."

Ideally, even the term "Middle East" should become "Southwest Asia and North Africa." To Native Americans, the Western Hemisphere is not "the New World." It was the newly arriving Europeans following Christopher Columbus who were new in the Western Hemisphere. Should the term "America" to mean only the United States be used sparingly and should the *hemispheric* meaning of the term be the usual usage?

Differential use of adjectives, the passive as opposed to the active voice, and other syntactic and semantic usages can betray unintended, unrecognized, but nonetheless real bias. For example, in the syllabus for grades 9/10, the African climate is described as essentially hostile to human migration ("There are few jungle environments in Africa and nearly 45% of the continent consists of desert or dry steppe . . ."), while that of Western Europe is described in the following terms: "Western Europe's environment exhibits great diversity in terms of physical geography and climate. Europeans have used technology to reshape their physical environment. Most of Western Europe has easy access to warm water ports. . . ." Why is desert seen as a hostile environment, but not freezing cold and snow?

Perhaps the most persistent and fundamental language problem in the teaching of social studies is the use of the terms "minority," "minorities," "minority persons" or "minority groups." Although commonly used, such terms nonetheless establish in the minds of all students inaccurate perceptions of the world and, increasingly, of our own nation. If social studies are to be taught from a global perspective, many of the so-called minorities in America are more accurately described as part of the world's majorities, a profoundly important point for young Americans who will come to maturity in the next century.

Recommendation: The syllabi and all related support materials and locally developed curricula should be regularly reviewed to insure that the language used is accurate and reflects current scholarship. Classroom instruction must include sensitivity to and awareness of the changing legitimacy of terms, such as the shift in meaning of terms such as "third world," "Negro," and "Oriental."

Number Three:

Finding: A limited range of examples. There is a tendency to use white male exam- 25
ples of achievement and to leave out examples of the contributions of women and of the many men and women of other than the traditional white groups. When women and people of color are mentioned, they are often marginalized as "other" groups "also" to be studied, implying that all the remaining content must not be about them. For example: the syllabus for grade 11 notes that "Inventions . . . in the 19th century were often the product of individual genius . . . , including that of lesser known, minority inventors." It recommends, under "Model Activities" on labor unionization: "Also examine the roles of women and racial/ethnic minorities at this time in labor history." Standard definitions of "achievement," too, omit the seemingly ordinary lives of people of all

groups—lives which, in aggregate, help us understand the human experience of a time and place.

As the January 1991 statement of the Executive Board of the Organization of American Historians points out:

> The history curricula of public schools should be constructed around the principle that all people have been significant actors in **[21]** human events. Students should therefore understand that history is not limited to the study of dominant political, social, and economic elites. It also encompasses the individual and collective quests of ordinary people for a meaningful place for themselves in their families, in their communities, and in the larger world.

Similarly, the multicultural complexity of individual cultures must be noted. Again, as observed in the statement of the Organization of American Historians, "the cultures of all peoples have become intermingled over time, often in subtle and complex ways." And although some will agree with V. S. Naipaul in seeing a new, emerging "universal civilization" (*New York Times*, November 5, 1990) dualities (or multiplicities) are everywhere apparent, as in the case of modern Japan, which may be seen as an "Asian" culture with "Western" technology.

Early in its work the *committee agreed that to reflect a multicultural perspective, the syllabi need not attempt to provide an encyclopedic list of every contribution by every person and group. Rather, as the emphasis shifts from an information-based to a conceptual curriculum, the syllabi should offer many appropriate examples of the experiences of many people and groups.* Further, the Committee believes that it can be particularly intriguing to students to examine with care what the elements are that hold together a nation or culture in spite of what are often great differences. This surely is one of the central questions to be considered in any course in American history.

Recommendation: The syllabi and other materials should provide teachers with several examples, drawn from different peoples, as appropriate to each topic. In this way, what begins to take shape in the mind of the student is an appreciation of the broader range of contributions of many people and groups to the building of our nation and the world.

Number Four

Finding: The visual environment of the classroom and school is a major educational ele- 30
ment. Maps and pictures hang on classroom walls, silently sending messages all day, all year. Many of the maps used in social studies are out of date; they often portray areas only from one perspective, not unlike the famous *New Yorker* cover showing the rest of the nation as a minor place west of the Hudson. For example, a map representing North America in 1700 might give the impression that nobody lived in the areas which were home to native peoples. Similarly, photo-

graphs on walls that show only white male inventors and heroes teach their own powerful, distorted lessons.

Recommendation: The visual environments of schools should reflect multicultural perspectives.

FOSTERING A MULTI-CULTURAL CURRICULUM: PRINCIPLES FOR PRESIDENTS*

ALICE CHANDLER

Alice Chandler (b. 1931) is President of the State University of New York at New Paltz. She wrote the following essay as part of an issues forum entitled "Fostering a Multi-Cultural Curriculum: Principles for Presidents," published by the American Association of State Colleges and Universities. Addressing college presidents, Chandler makes a case for "creating a multi-cultural curriculum [which] transcend[s] political viewpoints" and urges her colleagues to include the social and extracurricular dimensions of college life in their thinking about multicultural programming.

[3] What is Multi-Culturalism?

The word *multi-culturalism* carries with it many layers of meaning. Thinking about "multi-culturalism" can lead us toward:

- an acknowledgment of the rapidly changing demographic profile of American society, with its rising African American, Latino American, Asian American, and new immigrant populations
- an understanding of the need to bring educational equality to the under-represented minorities in American life and to bring them into the economic and social mainstream
- a new concept of American culture as a commingling of many distinctive strands, each equitably accepted within the fabric of our national life and all part of the rich interweaving of cultures that will be part of our emerging twenty-first-century civilization.

* Chandler, Alice. *Fostering a Multi-Cultural Curriculum: Principles for Presidents.* Washington, D.C.: American Association of State Colleges and Universities, 1992.

Thinking about multi-culturalism should call forth our idealism—our belief in the intrinsic worth and humanity of all those who live in America. But multi-culturalism also involves our self-interest. America is increasingly a racially and economically divided nation. We see the differential impact of these divisions most visibly in the disintegration and *de facto* segregation of many of our major cities, in the rising polarization and tensions resulting from these inequalities, and in the social costs we pay to sustain a system in which substantial portions of the population remain outside the mainstream of productive citizenry.

These social and economic divisions disadvantage us globally as well as nationally. This nation is already losing ground in the world economic market. As a demographically aging country, with a high standard of living and with high labor costs, it will certainly not succeed in the late twentieth and early twenty-first centuries unless and until it learns to use *all* of its available talent pool. That means educating and employing those persons of color who are all too often marginalized in American society.

Thinking about multi-culturalism can also remind us of its specific application to university campuses. It can remind us as educators that more than 25 percent of the presidents interviewed last year cited "racial intimidation and harassment" as a major problem on their campuses. It can also remind us of our responsibility as educators to champion multi-culturalism in its profoundest sense.

It is our responsibility as academic leaders to foster an understanding of our 5
emerging global and [4] multi-cultural society, to assist our faculty in exploring its intellectual and historic underpinnings, and to infuse that knowledge into the curriculum. It is our role, in short, to help create a "culture of cultures"— a base of knowledge and an approach to study that recognizes and appreciates the differences in cultures at the same time that it also identifies and celebrates the common humanity that binds them. Promoting multi-culturalism is an urgent task for educators, but it is no different academically from what we have always done—to discover, to analyze, to criticize, to synthesize, to transmit learning, and to use our new understandings to better understand ourselves and our society. . . .

Unity or Polarization?

American society faces an important choice: whether to adopt and reconcile its differing peoples and cultural traditions or to splinter into cultural and social apartheid.

The demographic changes in American society are fast moving and dramatic. American society is marked today by the rising presence of persons of color and by increased numbers of new immigrants, many of them persons of color as well. These changes are coming at the very time that we need to push for new labor sources and for heightened educational attainments across the population:

- By the year 2000, one-third of all school-age children will be African, Latino, Asian, or Native American.
- By the year 2020, that proportion will be two-fifths.

Such changes in American society are not new. During the late nineteenth and early twentieth centuries, America changed from a nation whose inhabitants were primarily of Western European and Nordic stock, to a nation largely populated by Eastern Europeans and Southern European immigrant groups. A labor-hungry United States welcomed these newcomers for the work they could do—at the same time that it was often contemptuous of the inferior racial "stock" they represented. Consciously and unconsciously, it also assimilated their cultures and their value systems until pizza became as American as apple pie and Catholicism and Judaism mingled with the native Protestantism to create a mosaic of religious beliefs.

Today's distinctions in culture are different from what they were in the past century. Despite their different backgrounds, the nineteenth-century [5] immigrants were all Europeans and, blond or brunette, still visibly "white." Today's so-called minority and immigrant groups represent a more complex commingling of cultures. Many of them are not of European origin, but come from Asia, Africa, the Caribbean, and Latin countries. Their traditions are an amalgam in many cases of earlier inheritances, often suppressed by slavery, and of American traditions and behaviors acquired over centuries or decades of residence here. Ironically, many African Americans have been in this country for centuries longer than those who perceive them as the "different" ones, and their culture often bears the impress of the American South. All of the so-called minority Americans—African, Latino, Asian, and other immigrant groups—are strongly influenced by the same modern technology and by the same media that affect the "majority" population. Whatever their origins, they are also immersed from birth in a Western tradition of laws and government. Less able to assimilate because of prejudice and bias, they are also less eager to assimilate than previous immigrant groups, more determined to retain their cultural and ethnic identity.

The history of the United States is a mixed picture of welcome and intoler- 10
ance for immigrant groups. The Know-Nothing Party of the 1840s took as its political platform opposition to Irish and Catholic Americans a full 25 years before the Ku Klux Klan began spewing its anti-African, anti-Semitic, anti-Catholic virulencies.

Today the fragmentation and polarization of American society is more complex. The boundaries between urban and suburban life separate racial minorities, and the cities themselves are ghettoized. Poverty lines follow geographic lines. Infant mortality for African Americans ranks 33rd among the 35 top nations in the world, and the life expectancy of a black male in Harlem is lower than the average life expectancy in Bangladesh.

The tensions, resentments and polarizations bred by an underlying social structure find reflection on our campuses today. Racial minorities and white students all too often meet as strangers who have inherited fears of each other. One-quarter of all college presidents and two-thirds of all presidents of research and doctorate institutions say racial tensions and hostilities are a moderate-to-major problem on their campus, reports Ernest Boyer. Social cleavages along racial and ethnic lines are widely visible.

To live harmoniously in this changing society of which their campuses are often a microcosm, college students will have to expand their understandings radically. They will have to include Africa, Asia, Latin America, and the Middle East in their knowledge base in the same way that they have always included Europe. This expansion of knowledge is needed for several reasons:

- to do justice to all groups in American society
- to help students of color feel more comfortable in American colleges and universities and, hence, more likely to enroll and to stay enrolled
- to create an environment that will move away from the dangerous polarization, rejection, and separatism that increasingly mark our society
- to combat the rising racism and xenophobia seen in America's society and reflected on college campuses
- to help college graduates, as the leaders of tomorrow's society, develop a new sense of national identity that will bind us more closely in the future
- to create college graduates who are prepared to live in a globalized world.

An intellectual understanding of our multicultural, international society cannot of itself eradicate prejudice and separatism. But it can create an environment in which there is a will to change.

Four Steps Toward Creating a Multi-Cultural Curriculum

Step One: Presidential Leadership

As with all curricular reform, creating a multi-cultural curriculum begins with 15
goal analysis and consensus building. It is not the president's role to create curriculum; that is the province of the faculty. But it is the president's role, together with the faculty and the academic administrators of the campus, to create a climate for change and to develop a consensus about the reasons for a more multi-cultural curriculum. These reasons include:

- the humanistic and intellectual importance of understanding the contributions of all cultures to our growing world civilization
- the personal developmental importance for *all* students to understand deeper cultural patterns and to recognize both the strengths and limitations of their own world views

- the personal importance for students of color to have their cultural contributions acknowledged and understood
- [6] the importance to campus civility of multi-cultural understandings in combatting prejudice, separatism, and fear
- the importance to American society of recognizing that culture is based on successful adaptation to given societal conditions and that the strengths of many cultures will need to combine with the Western tradition if American culture is to adapt productively to changing national and world conditions.

An intellectually coherent multi-cultural curriculum can help in enhancing the self-esteem of students of color, in developing greater commonalities among divided student groupings, and in assisting faculty in working with students from different cultural backgrounds. It can go far in bridging the polarization and separatism that increasingly divide our society.

Step Two: Curricular Audit

The next task belongs to the faculty and to its academic vice president and deans. Either a special task force or an academic standing committee should audit the curriculum to identify its strengths and weaknesses from a multi-cultural perspective. Where in the curriculum, it needs to be asked, are there courses dealing with international themes; with the multiple ethnic and racial strands in American culture and society; with issues of gender, race and ethnicity? Where is the curriculum obviously or not so obviously too narrow in its perspective? How would a campus envisage its ideal twenty-first century curriculum? How far and how fast can it move now?

The omissions in the current curriculum may be obvious simply by looking at the catalog. Does it show:

- lack of a world history course, absence of courses on Africa, Asia, the Middle East, or Latin America
- absence or paucity of courses on the "minority" or immigrant experience in American society or on feminism or other gender-related issues
- scarcity of foreign language and literature courses or the non-Western cultural heritage in the arts.

Some omissions may also be less obvious, occurring within course syllabi:

- the omission of female authors in a literature course
- the failure to look at Native American perspectives in an American history course
- the exclusion of historic and contemporary African American leaders from a modern politics course
- the use of psychological studies based only on male subjects

- a contemporary economics course that fails to include Japanese economics.

A completed curricular inventory would include: (1) a statement of multi- 20
cultural curricular goals and objectives, (2) a checklist of existing courses that include global and multi-cultural subject matter, (3) a list of recommended courses to be developed over the next five years, and (4) a set of guidelines for faculty teaching existing courses, indicating the possibilities for curricular revision and enrichment along multi-cultural and global dimensions.

Step Three: Intervention

This third step begins where Step Two leaves off—with the actual development of new courses and expanded syllabi. It would include:

- the development of new courses addressing specific cultural or inter-cultural relationships—e.g., a new course on "Twentieth-Century American Immigrants"
- complete revisions of existing courses to broaden their base—e.g., a "Modern History" course that becomes global rather than purely European and American
- revisions within syllabi to include relevant global or multi-cultural backgrounds—e.g., expansion of "History of the Novel" course to include *The Tale of Genji* (tenth-century Japan, female author) at one end and Zora Neale Hurston or James Baldwin at the other
- the elimination of hidden cultural assumptions—e.g., the need for discussion within a psychology course of the relevance of Freud's theories to non-Western societies.

Step Four: Faculty Development

In this step, as in hastening along Steps Two and Three, presidential leadership is again particularly necessary. To create a multi-cultural and global curriculum must over time involve a reallocation of resources. New faculty, with multi-cultural and international backgrounds and expertise, should be hired. Their perspectives and experience will, in many cases, give them a special role to play with students of color. They will also serve both as exemplars [7] of accomplishment to all students and as sources of specialized information and understandings within their disciplines. This hiring will be difficult, given limited availability pools and ever-tightening budgets, but it must remain a constant goal—to be accomplished with full-time tenure-track appointments where possible, but also lending itself to part-time and adjunct appointments, visiting professorships, workshops, seminars and modular courses.

The key to immediate and pervasive change is not the faculty of "Someday" but of Today. Given existing budgetary limitations, those faculty now on campus will be the majority for many years to come. Without their involvement, multicultural international themes will at best be peripheral or isolated, relegated to specialized programs such as "Black Studies" or "Women's Studies" but not mainstreamed within the curriculum. It is important that faculty see how their particular specialization fits within the broader outlines of multi-cultural understandings.

The retraining of faculty to teach a multi-cultural curriculum begins with their willingness to expand their existing range of expertise—to search out neglected areas of their disciplines and to include them in their research and their curricula. A legitimate summer project might well be the study of slave narratives or women artists or South American fiction. Encouragement should be given to faculty to expand their horizons in this way and to demonstrate their new expertise with new course syllabi, lectures, and reading lists. It is also important to help faculty and staff root out what may be their residual prejudices. The same criteria of knowledgeability, comprehensiveness, thoroughness, and objectivity must be applied to these new curricular and research ventures as are applied to all other academic endeavors. The rewards must not simply be acknowledgment of a job well done but the traditional academic rewards of advancement and merit increments, research and travel support. This retraining of individual faculty can benefit wider groups as well through brown bag luncheon lectures, seminars, workshops, and discussion groups involving colleagues from their own and other departments.

Students

Students are the beneficiaries of multi-cultural education. They should not be 25
passive recipients. The very nature of multi-cultural education involves a pluralism of perspectives. Students learn to see a subject not simply through the lens of their own cultural assumptions but from varying or reciprocal viewpoints. The history of South America is not simply the history of European advance. It is the reciprocal and equally valid viewpoint of the indigenous population as well and the ways in which its complex civilization met with the threat of European technological force. Such multi-cultural course work can be seen as having two advantages: (1) as specifically addressing the interests of non-Western students in the histories of their own backgrounds and origins, and (2) as contributing to the broadening of all students' intellectual horizons and the expansion of their capacity for critical thinking and for self-criticism.

Multi-cultural programming for students should also have a social and extracurricular dimension. Experiential activities for students, whether in the form of study abroad semesters or urban and rural area internships in a multi-cultural setting, can greatly expand the students' horizons. Student governments should be encouraged to build bridges among students through "unification" days, through ethnic and international festivals, through the sponsoring of artists and speakers from a wide range of backgrounds, and through social events that take students beyond the self-selection of friends and associates from backgrounds identical to their own. The college food service can also be enlisted in the preparation of ethnic and international foods, assisted by the students themselves. The art gallery and the music department have an especially important role to play.

Conflict and Controversy

The movement toward multi-culturalism has not occurred without controversy, and the debate is worthy of lengthier consideration than can be given here. The current drive toward an expansion of the canon and toward the recognition of cultural differences has been assailed as "canon-busting" and seen as part of the politicization of the campus. Critics such as William Bennett, Lynne Cheney, and Allan Bloom decry what they see as the loss of coherence in the curriculum and the substitution of a subversive agenda, promoting disarray and cultural relativism. Their views are given some validation by some of the more aggressive advocates of a multi-cultural agenda who use "multi-culturalism" as a vehicle for attacks on "Eurocentricity" and racial "oppression" within the existing curriculum. Even within the broad terrain of multi-culturalism there are significant and well-reasoned differences of approach as thoughtful and responsible individuals seek to integrate the new curriculum and the old.

Neither the fear of subverting Western culture nor the desire to smash it is valid, however. The incontrovertible reasons for creating a multi-cultural curriculum transcend political viewpoints, "right" or "left." They are rooted in the fundamental role of **[8]** education in discovering, interpreting, and transmitting all knowledge. A sound multi-cultural curriculum is vindicated by the very nature of American and global society and by the need to adapt our knowledge base to encompass a more complex vision of our humanity.

Multi-culturalism in the curriculum should fulfill much the same role that the traditional humanities have always played in creating imaginative empathy and in expanding our ability to look at the world through different eyes. That multi-cultural education may teach the varieties of human experience, social organization, and value systems need not be feared as ideologically subversive or threatening to the great Western traditions if it is recognized that there is a common humanity within these viewpoints and that the highest and most vital cultures are those that evolve actively to meet changing conditions. Nor need a multi-cultural curriculum be intellectually second rate, as some of its critics seem to fear, if the new courses and programs are subject to the same critical scrutiny that all other academic disciplines undergo. Far from teaching simplistic relativism, a more profound teaching of culture should show students how to evolve their own value systems more knowledgeably and to begin to function more effectively in the new multi-cultural and international world that is their inheritance.

Forging Ahead

Even if it had no practical applications, the expansion of the current curriculum 30
on most campuses to include multi-cultural and international studies would be justified by the very nature of current knowledge. But, as we have seen, it can have other values as well:

- in fostering greater mutual appreciation among diversified student populations
- in helping to combat the *de facto* apartheid that mars and erodes American life today
- in developing a greater ability to live with change.

Creating a multi-cultural curriculum takes vision, and knowledge, and skill. It calls for your insight and leadership as a college president. It calls for that willingness to integrate new knowledge and new understanding with the traditional learning that has always been the hallmark of human inquiry.

A DISSENTING OPINION*

ARTHUR M. SCHLESINGER, JR.

Arthur M. Schlesinger, Jr. (b. 1917), teaches at the graduate school at University Center of the City University of New York. He was an associate professor of history at Harvard University (1946 to 1954) and a special adviser to President Kennedy from 1961 to 1963. The recipient of two Pulitzer prizes, Schlesinger is a contributor to the Wall Street Journal *and many other publications. Among his many books are* A Thousand Days: John F. Kennedy in the White House *(1965), and* The Disuniting of America: Reflections on a Multicultural Society *(1991). As a member of the New York State Social Studies Review and Development Committee (see page 517), Schlesinger wrote the following "Dissenting Opinion," in which he voices his concern over what he describes as the report's "emphasis on cultivating and reinforcing ethnic differences." Schlesinger's is one of several responses to the process and conclusions of the committee filed by individual members and appended to its report.*

* Schlesinger, Arthur M., Jr. "A Dissenting Opinion." *One Nation, Many Peoples: A Declaration of Cultural Interdependence.* Albany, N.Y.: New York State Education Department, 1991. 45–47.

[45] I agree with many of the practical recommendations in the report. It is unquestionably necessary to diversify the syllabus in order to meet the needs of a more diversified society. It is unquestionably necessary to provide for global education in an increasingly interdependent world. Our students should by all means be better acquainted with women's history, with the history of ethnic and racial minorities, with Latin American, Asian and African history. Debate, alternative interpretations, "multiple perspectives" are all essential to the educational enterprise. I welcome changes that would adapt the curriculum to these purposes. If that is what the report means by multicultural education, I am all for it.

But I fear that the report implies much more than this. The underlying philosophy of the report, as I read it, is that ethnicity is the defining experience for most Americans, that ethnic ties are permanent and indelible, that the division into ethnic groups establishes the basic structure of American society and that a main objective of public education should be the protection, strengthening, celebration and perpetuation of ethnic origins and identities. Implicit in the report is the classification of all Americans according to ethnic and racial criteria.

These propositions are assumed rather than argued in the report. They constitute an ethnic interpretation of American history that, like the economic interpretation, is valid up to a point but misleading and wrong when presented as the whole picture.

The ethnic interpretation, moreover, reverses the historic theory of America—which has been, not the preservation and sanctification of old cultures and identities, but the creation of a *new* national culture and a *new* national identity. As Secretary of State John Quincy Adams told a German contemplating migration to these shores, those who would settle in America must recognize one necessity: "They must cast off the European skin, never to resume it. They must look forward to their posterity rather than backward to their ancestors."

Of course students should learn more about the rich variety of peoples and 5
cultures that have forged this new American identity. They also should understand the curse of racism—the great failure of the American experiment, the glaring contradiction of American ideals and the still-crippling disease of American society. But we should also be alert to the danger of a society divided into distinct and immutable ethnic and racial groups, each taught to cherish its own apartness from the rest.

While I favor curricular changes that make for more inclusive interpretations of past and present, I do not believe that we should magnify ethnic and racial themes at the expense of the unifying ideals that precariously hold our highly differentiated society together. The republic has survived and grown because it has maintained a balance between *pluribus* and *unum*. The report, it seems to me, is saturated with *pluribus* and neglectful of *unum*.

The first paragraph of the preamble notes that "no other country in the world is peopled by a greater variety of races, nationalities, and ethnic groups." It continues: "But although the United States has been a great asylum for diverse peoples, it has not always been a great refuge for diverse cultures." Both points are correct—but the report is oblivious to the historical fact that the second sentence explains the first.

[46] Why has the United States been thus far exempt from the "trends toward separation and dissolution" that, as the report later notes, are having such destructive effects in the Soviet Union, South Africa, Canada, Yugoslavia, Spain and the United Kingdom? The report replies with general statements about diversity as a source of strength. But diversity has not been a source of strength in the Soviet Union, South Africa, Canada, etc. Why has it been a source of strength in the United States?

Obviously the reason why the United States, for all its manifest failure to live up to its own ideals, is still the most successful large multi-ethnic nation is precisely because, instead of emphasizing and perpetuating ethnic separatism, it has assimilated immigrant cultures into a new *American* culture.

10 Most immigrants indeed came to America precisely in order to escape their pasts. They *wanted* to become Americans and to participate in the making of an American culture and an American national identity. Even black Americans, who came as involuntary immigrants and have suffered—still suffer—awful persecution and discrimination, have made vital contributions to the American culture in which they have grown up and of which they are an indispensable part.

The preamble rejects "previous ideals of assimilation to an Anglo-American model." Of course America derives its language and its primary political purposes and institutions from Great Britain. To pretend otherwise is to falsify history. To teach otherwise is to mislead our students. But the British legacy has been modified, enriched and reconstituted by the absorption of non-Anglo cultures and traditions as well as by the distinctive experiences of American life. That is why America today is so very different a nation from Britain. Assimilation does not equal Angloconformity.

But the report goes on to reject the very ideal of assimilation. I recognize that assimilation is a word that many now find upsetting. Even 'integration' seems to be out of fashion. The report does on occasion refer in general terms to the need for *unum* as well as for *pluribus*. The preamble observes, "Special attention will need to be given to those values, characteristics, and traditions which we share in common." I do not, however, find this concern much reflected in the body of the report or in the proposals for syllabus revision. Part II begins by describing "the search for common cultural grounds" as "more important than ever." This comment, if true, should give that search a much higher priority than it receives in the report. Buried toward the end is a comment on the importance of examining with care "what the elements are that hold together a nation or culture in spite of what are often great differences. This surely is one of the central questions to be considered in any course in American history." It surely is, but it is a central question that receives practically no attention in the proposals for curricular revision.

A basic question is involved: should public education seek to make our young boys and girls contributors to a common American culture? or should it strengthen and perpetuate separate ethnic and racial subcultures? The report places its emphasis on cultivating and reinforcing ethnic differences. Students, the report says, should be "continually" encouraged to ask themselves what their cultural heritage is, why they should be proud of it, "why should I develop an understanding of and respect for my own culture(s), language(s), religion, and national origin(s)." Would it not be more appropriate for students to be "continually" encouraged to understand the American culture in which they are growing up and to prepare for an active role in shaping that culture?

Am I wrong in sensing a certain artificiality and inauthenticity in all this? If the ethnic subcultures had genuine vitality, they would be sufficiently instilled in children by family, church and community. It is surely not the office of the public school to promote ethnic separatism and heighten ethnic tensions.

Should public education move in this direction, it will only increase the fragmentation, resegregation and self-ghettoization of American life. The bonds of national cohesion in the republic are sufficiently fragile already. Public education should aim to strengthen those bonds, not to weaken them. Of course Americans should be free (as they have always been, and have often done) to cultivate ancestral customs and traditions. **[47]** But the function of the schools is surely to teach what holds Americans together as well as to teach what sets them apart. The alternative to integration is disintegration.

What has held Americans together in the absence of a common ethnic origin has been the creation of a new American identity—a distinctive American culture based on a common language and common adherence to ideals of democracy and human rights, a culture to which many nationalities and races have made emphatic contributions in the past and will (one hopes) make emphatic contributions in the future. Our democratic ideals have been imperfectly realized, but the long labor to achieve them and to move the American experiment from exclusion to participation has been a central theme of American history. It should be a central theme of the New York social studies curriculum.

And it is important for students to understand where these democratic ideals come from. They come of course from Europe. Indeed, Europe is the *unique* source of these ideals—ideals that today empower people in every continent and to which today most of the world aspires. That is why it is so essential (in my view) to acquaint students with the western history and tradition that created our democratic ideals—and why it is so wrong to tell students of non-European origin that western ideals are not for them.

I regret the note of Europhobia that sometimes emerges in vulgar attacks on "Eurocentric" curriculums. Certainly Europe, like every other culture, has committed its share of crimes. But, unlike most cultures, it has also generated ideals that have opposed and exposed those crimes.

The report, however, plays up the crimes and plays down the ideals. Thus, when it talks about the European colonization of Africa and India, it deplores "the eradication of many varieties of traditional culture and knowledge." Like infanticide? slavery? polygamy? subjection of women? suttee? veil-wearing?

foot-binding? clitorectomies? Nothing is said about the influence of European ideas of democracy, human rights, self-government, rule of law.

Even Karl Marx was fairer to European colonization than that. “England,” 20
Marx said, “has to fulfill a double mission in India: one destructive, the other regenerating—the annihilation of old Asiatic society, and the laying of the material foundations of Western society in Asia. . . . The question is, can mankind fulfill its destiny without a fundamental revolution in the social state of Asia? If not, whatever may have been the crimes of England she was the unconscious tool of history in bringing about the revolution.”

I also am doubtful about the note occasionally sounded in the report that “students must be taught social criticism” and “see themselves as active makers and changers of culture and society” and “promote economic fairness and social justice” and “bring about change in their communities, the nation, and the world.” I very much hope that, as citizens, students will do all these things, but I do not think it is the function of the schools to teach students to become reformers any more than I ever thought it the function of the schools to teach them the beauty of private enterprise and the sanctity of the status quo. I will be satisfied if we can teach children to read, write and calculate. If students understand the nature of our western democratic tradition, they will move into social criticism on their own. But let us not politicize the curriculum on behalf either of the left or of the right.

I recognize that I am very much in the minority in these comments. But given basic philosophical disagreements with the report, I cannot conscientiously go along with my colleagues. I respect their serious concern and their devoted labor, and I have enjoyed my association with them. I would only beg them to consider what kind of nation we will have if we press further down the road to cultural separatism and ethnic fragmentation, if we institutionalize the classification of our citizens by ethnic and racial criteria and if we abandon our historic commitment to an American identity. What will hold our people together then?

THE CULT OF MULTICULTURALISM*

FRED SIEGEL

Fred Siegel (b. 1945) teaches humanities at Cooper Union in New York City and has written for magazines such as Commonweal, The Atlantic, *and* Society. *In the following*

* Siegel, Fred. “The Cult of Multiculturalism.” *The New Republic* 18 February 1991: 34–39.

excerpt from an essay that appeared in The New Republic *in 1991, Siegel discusses some of the changes that "multiculturalism's hard-liners" are effecting on American campuses.*

[35] The premise with which the multiculturalists begin is unexceptionable: that it is important to recognize and to celebrate the wide range of cultures that co-habit the United States. In what sounds like an inflection of traditional American pluralism, the multiculturalists argue that we must recognize difference, that difference is legitimate; in its kindlier versions, multiculturalism represents the discovery on the part of minority groups that they can play a part in molding the larger culture even as they are molded by it. And on the campus multiculturalism, defined more locally as the need to recognize cultural variations among students, has tried with some success to talk about how a racially and ethnically diverse student body can enrich everyone's education. Phillip Green, a political scientist at Smith and a thoughtful proponent of multiculturalism, notes that for a significant portion of the students, particularly minority students, the politics of identity is all-consuming. "Students" he says, "are unhappy with the thin gruel of rationalism. They require a therapeutic curriculum to overcome not straightforward racism but ignorant stereotyping."

But multiculturalism's hard-liners, who seem to make up the majority of the movement, damn as racism any attempt to draw the myriad of American groups into a common American culture. For these multiculturalists, differences are absolute, irreducible, intractable—occasions not for understanding but for separation. The multiculturalist, it turns out, is not especially interested in the great American hyphen, in the syncretistic (and therefore naturally tolerant) identities that allow Americans to belong to more than a single culture, to be both particularists and universalists.

This time-honored American mixture of assimilation and traditional allegiance is denounced as a danger to racial and gender authenticity. This is an extraordinary reversal of the traditional liberal commitment to a "truth" that transcends parochialisms. In the new race/class/gender dispensation (class being the least important of the three), universality is replaced by, among other things, feminist science, Nubian numerals (as part of an Afrocentric science), and what Marilyn Frankenstein of the University of Massachusetts describes as "ethnomathematics," in which the cultural basis of counting comes to the fore.

The multiculturalists insist on seeing all perspectives as tainted by the perceiver's particular point of view. Impartial knowledge, they argue, is not possible, because ideas are simply the expression of individual identity, or of the unspoken but inescapable assumptions that are inscribed in a culture or a language. The problem with this warmed-over Nietzscheanism is that it threatens to leave no ground for anybody to stand on. And so the multiculturalists make a leap, necessary for their own intellectual survival, and proceed to argue that there are some categories, such as race and gender, that do in fact embody an unmistakable knowledge of oppression. Victims are at least epistemologically lucky. Objectivity is a mask for oppression. And so an appalled former 1960s radical complained to me that self-proclaimed witches were teaching classes on witchcraft. "They're not teaching students how to think," she said, "they're telling them what to believe."

5 Multiculturalists attack the standard conceptual distinctions between rational/irrational, white/black, healthy/sick, male/female, history/myth, literacy/illiteracy as hidden expressions of a hierarchy designed to "privilege" the first half of the paired categories. But there's an irony here: what begins as an attempt to **[36]** expand our mental horizons ends up by giving the second half of the pairing superior standing and a rightful claim to power. For example, Houston Baker, Jr., a specialist in Afro-American literature and the Albert M. Greenfield Professor of Human Relations at the University of Pennsylvania, asserts that there is no need to mourn the passing "of the old order of literacy." Baker believes that if students can be freed from Western civilization, in the form of "whitemale" core reading lists (he compares the core reading lists to the deadly cores of a nuclear reactor), then "the powerful, syncretic, corporally minimalistic urgings of African American rap music signal this *défense légitime* of a new humanity and a new humanities that will outlast the 'crisis' and create new room for the new people." For Baker, the incoming president of the Modern Language Association, it is as if literacy were literally the problem.

But none of the reversals is as sad, as ridiculous, or as dangerous as the white/black reversal, wherein Herodotus and other ancient writers are combed for all references to North African and Levantine persons and events, and the myth of the African origins of all civilization displaces the conventional history of the Greek origins of Western culture. Classicists long ago concluded that all the African elements in the history of archaic Greece do not amount to an African origin for Western culture—but the multiculturalists are interested in feeling, not in learning. A prominent black professor who calls himself a "real world leftist" (and who asked to remain anonymous) explained to me the appeal of presenting a mythical African past as history: "It's easier for the faculty to level down by arguing that everything in the curriculum is just ideology than it is to pile on the work that's required, because deep in their hearts many of the ideologues don't believe that these minority kids can cut it." By contrast, "If you try to level up you face charges of racism."

Perhaps the most enabling fiction of multiculturalism is that there has been a single core curriculum composed of the canonical texts of Western civilization that is widely forced, with great harm to minorities, upon students across the country. "The classic texts of the Western tradition," a Wesleyan professor told me, "have been imposed on students as a form of male domination." A student leader at Stanford, where the recent public debate over the curriculum began, has insisted, "The implicit message of Western culture is, 'Nigger Go Home.'" Both speak to the notion that a core curriculum composed of such DWEMs (Dead White European Males) as Plato, Aristotle, Augustine, and Shakespeare has been required for virtually all college students. The truth is, however, that such cores hardly exist anymore. According to the National Endowment for the Humanities, 80 percent of college students graduate without a Western civilization course. Thirty-seven percent graduate without any history course at all.

A corollary fiction is that until the multiculturalists stepped into the breach, books about minority experiences in America were largely absent from the curriculum. In fact, one of the great academic achievements of the past quarter century has been the vast opening to new perspectives in Afro-American, women's, labor, and Third World history and literature. I repeatedly asked prominent academics across the country to name standard courses or texts at their own or other schools that failed to reflect the new scholarship and the diversity of American life. Not a single course or a single text was cited. Instead, as I was told by Paula Rothenberg—a professor at New Jersey's Paterson State College whose multicultural reader *Racism and Sexism: An Integrated Study*, has caused a stir on several campuses—the problem is "not specifics" but "a racism and a sexism which are pervasive" because they are largely "unconscious."

Her formulation has been widely echoed. Redemption, according to James Scanlon, dean of arts and sciences at Clarion State University in Pennsylvania, lies in "infusing race, ethnicity, and gender across the curriculum." Similarly, at Miami-Dade Junior College recent changes stipulate that "diversity" must be incorporated in every course. And "cooperation" is to weigh heavily in tenure and promotion decisions. At both schools there are plans to re-educate recalcitrant faculty. Gary Kelsey of Penn State, speaking for an increasing number of advisers and admissions counselors, insists that themes of "tolerance" should be integrated throughout the curriculum. "Faculty who fail to demonstrate an active agenda . . . to embrace the richness of diversity" should, Kelsey suggested, be told they will not be tenured.

10 The new bureaucratic factor, observes Adolph Reed, Jr., professor of political science at Yale, is the role of administrators. In the 1960s administrators, often academics themselves, were fighting to hold back ideologically driven changes; today they're initiating them. Drawing on the Carnegie Foundation's call for a more "caring" campus, and led by college presidents with "helping professionals" in tow, administrators are now redefining the purpose of higher education. Some colleges have in effect reverted to their earlier roles as religious/confessional institutions. Their job is no longer one of conveying knowledge: Why would it be, if knowledge is merely an instrument of power?

At Duke, close ties among the administration, the **[38]** support staff, and the "academic left" have led to a redefinition of goals. Duke's zeal doesn't stop with its orientation program. After a black student organization on campus alleged faculty racism, President Brodie promised to ferret out instances of subtle bias, which he called "the New Racism." Brodie has initiated a group with the Committee on Public Safety-like title of the "Committee to Address Discrimination in the Classroom." This body, which was given the charge of uncovering faculty racism in the classroom, found very little in the way of overt bias. But in its monitoring of the classroom it did discover examples of "disrespectful facial expressions or body language aimed at black students." The committee has promised to continue its work.

At the University of Texas at Austin, the required sensitivity is more localized if no less extreme. "The army hasn't been called in to UT and the university hasn't been closed," warned Barbara Harlow, a professor of English, "but we need to recognize that there are academic death squads operating on our campus." Harlow was speaking last fall at a rally on behalf of the new, politicized version of E306, a course required for the 60 percent of the first-year students who need remedial English. The rally, attended by half a dozen members of the English department, had been organized by minority activists. They rallied in support of what one faculty member approvingly called "the politicization of entering freshmen and their curriculum."

With encouragement from the dean of the College of Arts and Sciences, Texas's huge English department of more than eighty members, in a shift of resources, closed down its language lab, which had served primarily Hispanic, Asian, and other minority students struggling to master English. To remedy student writing and rhetoric problems, the department redesigned E306 around the theme of white male racism. The proposed texts for the remedial writing course are limited to Rothenberg's reader on racism; a series of 1950s Texas civil rights court cases; and a tract listing forty-six varieties of white male privilege.

Senior writing professor Maxine Hairston, a self-described liberal, sees the call for the politicization of E306 as a self-serving excuse to avoid the hard job of teaching the basics. "Probably only four of the eighty members of the Texas English department," she says, "believe that a central mission of their department is to teach people how to write." At a meeting of the faculty committee planning the course, some members complained that in the name of diversity a single mandatory reading list was being imposed in place of the variety offered in earlier versions of the course. The response, they told me, was that a range of opinions was not a good idea for the course. . . .

15 Many students, confronted with the new orthodoxy in its several manifestations, find it funny. Parodies and jokes about "de-cons," "PCs," and "multicult" are becoming campus commonplaces. (Q: What do you get when you cross a deconstructionist with a mafioso? A: Someone who makes you an offer you can't understand.) Multiculturalism is in trouble, says the University of Pennsylvania's Alan Kors, because "you can't distinguish between the parody and the 'real' thing."

But the thing *is* real. A great deal of what's turning the humanities in America into an intellectual backwater has already been institutionalized, with junior faculty and academic administrators alike having a vested interest in a multiculturalist curriculum. Finally the situation is not funny at all. The future may well lie with the Stanford student who, when asked about studying important non-Western trends such as Islamic fundamentalism and Japanese capitalism, responded, "Who gives a damn about those things? I want to study myself."

FROM MULTICULTURALISM: E PLURIBUS PLURES*

DIANE RAVITCH

Diane Ravitch (b. 1938), an adjunct professor of history and education at Teachers College, Columbia University, has written widely on the history of education. Her books include The Troubled Crusade: American Education, 1945–1980 *(1983). The following excerpt is from an essay that appeared in* The American Scholar *in 1990. In it, Ravitch notes with chagrin curricular changes that reflect a new kind of ethnocentrism springing from what she sees as a "particularist" distortion of multiculturalism.*

[339] As a result of the political and social changes of recent decades, cultural pluralism is now generally recognized as an organizing principle of this society. In contrast to the idea of the melting pot, which promised to erase ethnic and group differences, children now learn that variety is the spice of life. They learn that America has provided a haven for many different groups and has allowed them to maintain their cultural heritage or to assimilate, or—as is often the case—to do both; the choice is theirs, not the state's. They learn that cultural pluralism is one of the norms of a free society; that differences among groups are a national resource rather than a problem to be solved. Indeed, the unique feature of the United States is that its common culture has been formed by the interaction of its subsidiary cultures. It is a culture that has been influenced over time by immigrants, American Indians, Africans (slave and free) and by their descendants. American music, art, literature, language, food, clothing, sports, holidays, and customs all show the effects of the commingling of diverse cultures in one nation. Paradoxical though it may seem, the United States has a common culture that is multicultural.

Our schools and our institutions of higher learning have in recent years begun to embrace what Catherine R. Stimpson of Rutgers University has called "cultural democracy," a recognition that we must listen to a "diversity of voices" in order to understand our culture, past and present. This understanding of the pluralistic nature of American culture has taken a long time to forge. It is based on sound scholarship and has led to major revisions in what children are taught and what they read in **[340]** school. The new history is—indeed, must be—a warts-and-all history; it demands an unflinching examination of racism and discrimination in our history. Making these changes is difficult, raises tempers, and ignites controversies, but gives a more interesting and accurate account of

* Ravitch, Diane. "Multiculturalism: E Pluribus Plures." *The American Scholar* 59 (1990), 337–354.

American history. Accomplishing these changes is valuable, because there is also a useful lesson for the rest of the world in America's relatively successful experience as a pluralistic society. Throughout human history, the clash of different cultures, races, ethnic groups, and religions has often been the cause of bitter hatred, civil conflict, and international war. The ethnic tensions that now are tearing apart Lebanon, Sri Lanka, Kashmir, and various republics of the Soviet Union remind us of the costs of unfettered group rivalry. Thus, it is a matter of more than domestic importance that we closely examine and try to understand that part of our national history in which different groups competed, fought, suffered, but ultimately learned to live together in relative peace and even achieved a sense of common nationhood.

Alas, these painstaking efforts to expand the understanding of American culture into a richer and more varied tapestry have taken a new turn, and not for the better. Almost any idea, carried to its extreme, can be made pernicious, and this is what is happening now to multiculturalism. Today, pluralistic multiculturalism must contend with a new, particularistic multiculturalism. The pluralists seek a richer common culture; the particularists insist that no common culture is possible or desirable. The new particularism is entering the curriculum in a number of school systems across the country. Advocates of particularism propose an ethnocentric curriculum to raise the self-esteem and academic achievement of children from racial and ethnic minority backgrounds. Without any evidence, they claim that children from minority backgrounds will do well in school *only* if they are immersed in a positive, prideful version of their ancestral culture. If children are of, for example, Fredonian ancestry, they must hear that Fredonians were important in mathematics, science, history, and literature. If they learn about great Fredonians and if their studies use Fredonian examples and Fredonian concepts, they will do well in school. If they do not, they will have low self-esteem and will do badly.

At first glance, this appears akin to the celebratory activities associated with Black History Month or Women's History Month, when schoolchildren learn about the achievements of blacks and women. But the point of those celebrations is to demonstrate that neither race nor gender is an obstacle to high achievement. They teach all children that everyone, regardless of their race, religion, gender, ethnicity, or family origin, can achieve self-fulfillment, honor, and dignity in society if they aim high and work hard.

[341] By contrast, the particularistic version of multiculturalism is unabashedly fi- 5
liopietistic and deterministic. It teaches children that their identity is determined by their "cultural genes." That something in their blood or their race memory or their cultural DNA defines who they are and what they may achieve. That the culture in which they live is not their own culture, even though they were born here. That American culture is "Eurocentric," and therefore hostile to anyone whose ancestors are not European. Perhaps the most invidious implication of particularism is that racial and ethnic minorities are not and should not try to be part of American culture; it implies that American culture belongs only to those who are white and European; it implies that those who are neither

white nor European are alienated from American culture by virtue of their race or ethnicity; it implies that the only culture they do belong to or can ever belong to is the culture of their ancestors, even if their families have lived in this country for generations.

The war on so-called Eurocentrism is intended to foster self-esteem among those who are not of European descent. But how, in fact, is self-esteem developed? How is the sense of one's own possibilities, one's potential choices, developed? Certainly, the school curriculum plays a relatively small role as compared to the influence of family, community, mass media, and society. But to the extent that curriculum influences what children think of themselves, it should encourage children of all racial and ethnic groups to believe that they are part of this society and that they should develop their talents and minds to the fullest. It is enormously inspiring, for example, to learn about men and women from diverse backgrounds who overcame poverty, discrimination, physical handicaps, and other obstacles to achieve success in a variety of fields. Behind every such biography of accomplishment is a story of heroism, perseverance, and self-discipline. Learning these stories will encourage a healthy spirit of pluralism, of mutual respect, and of self-respect among children of different backgrounds. The children of American society today will live their lives in a racially and culturally diverse nation, and their education should prepare them to do so.

The pluralist approach to multiculturalism promotes a broader interpretation of the common American culture and seeks due recognition for the ways that the nation's many racial, ethnic, and cultural groups have transformed the national culture. The pluralists say, in effect, "American culture belongs to us, all of us; the U.S. is us, and we remake it in every generation." But particularists have no interest in extending or revising American culture; indeed, they deny that a common culture exists. Particularists reject any accommodation among groups, any interactions that blur the distinct lines between them. The brand of history that they espouse is one in which everyone is either a descendant of victims or **[342]** oppressors. By doing so, ancient hatreds are fanned and recreated in each new generation. Particularism has its intellectual roots in the ideology of ethnic separatism and in the black nationalist movement. In the particularist analysis, the nation has five cultures: African American, Asian American, European American, Latino/Hispanic, and Native American. The huge cultural, historical, religious, and linguistic differences within these categories are ignored, as is the considerable intermarriage among these groups, as are the linkages (like gender, class, sexual orientation, and religion) that cut across these five groups. No serious scholar would claim that all Europeans and white Americans are part of the same culture, or that all Asians are part of the same culture, or that all people of Latin-American descent are of the same culture, or that all people of African descent are of the same culture. Any categorization this broad is essentially meaningless and useless.

Several districts—including Detroit, Atlanta, and Washington, D.C.—are developing an Afrocentric curriculum. *Afrocentricity* has been described in a book of the same name by Molefi Kete Asante of Temple University. The Afrocentric curriculum puts Africa at the center of the student's universe. African Americans must "move away from an [*sic*] Eurocentric framework" because "it is difficult to create freely when you use someone else's motifs, styles, images, and perspectives." Because they are not Africans, "white teachers cannot inspire in our children the visions necessary for them to overcome limitations." Asante recommends that African Americans choose an African name (as he did), reject European dress, embrace African religion (not Islam or Christianity) and love "their own" culture. He scorns the idea of universality as a form of Eurocentric arrogance. The Eurocentrist, he says, thinks of Beethoven or Bach as classical, but the Afrocentrist thinks of Ellington or Coltrane as classical; the Eurocentrist lauds Shakespeare or Twain, while the Afrocentrist prefers Baraka, Shange, or Abiola. Asante is critical of black artists like Arthur Mitchell and Alvin Ailey who ignore Afrocentricity. Likewise, he speaks contemptuously of a group of black university students who spurned the Afrocentrism of the local Black Student Union and formed an organization called Inter-race: "Such madness is the direct consequence of self-hatred, obligatory attitudes, false assumptions about society, and stupidity."

The conflict between pluralism and particularism turns on the issue of universalism. Professor Asante warns his readers against the lure of universalism: "Do not be captured by a sense of universality given to you by the Eurocentric viewpoint; such a viewpoint is contradictory to your own ultimate reality." He insists that there is no alternative to Eurocentrism, Afrocentrism, and other ethnocentrisms. In contrast, the pluralist says, with the Roman playwright Terence, "I am a man: nothing **[343]** human is alien to me." A contemporary Terence would say "I am a person" or might be a woman, but the point remains the same: You don't have to be black to love Zora Neale Hurston's fiction or Langston Hughes's poetry or Duke Ellington's music. In a pluralist curriculum, we expect children to learn a broad and humane culture, to learn about the ideas and art and animating spirit of many cultures. We expect that children, whatever their color, will be inspired by the courage of people like Helen Keller, Vaclav Havel, Harriet Tubman, and Feng Lizhe. We expect that their response to literature will be determined by the ideas and images it evokes, not by the skin color of the writer. But particularists insist that children can learn only from the experiences of people from the same race.

10 Particularism is a bad idea whose time has come. It is also a fashion spreading like wildfire through the education system, actively promoted by organizations and individuals with a political and professional interest in strengthening ethnic power bases in the university, in the education profession, and in society itself. One can scarcely pick up an educational journal without learning about a school district that is converting to an ethnocentric curriculum in an attempt to give "self-esteem" to children from racial minorities. A state-funded project in a Sacramento high school is teaching young black males to think like Africans and to develop the "African Mind Model Technique," in order to free themselves of the racism of American culture. A popular black rap singer, KRS-One, complained in an op-ed article in the *New York Times* that the schools should be

teaching blacks about their cultural heritage, instead of trying to make everyone Americans. "It's like trying to teach a dog to be a cat," he wrote. KRS-One railed about having to learn about Thomas Jefferson and the Civil War, which had nothing to do (he said) with black history.

Pluralism can easily be transformed into particularism, as may be seen in the potential uses in the classroom of the Mayan contribution to mathematics. The Mayan example was popularized in a movie called *Stand and Deliver*, about a charismatic Bolivian-born mathematics teacher in Los Angeles who inspired his students (who are Hispanic) to learn calculus. He told them that their ancestors invented the concept of zero; but that wasn't all he did. He used imagination to put across mathematical concepts. He required them to do homework and to go to school on Saturdays and during the Christmas holidays, so that they might pass the Advanced Placement mathematics examination for college entry. The teacher's reference to the Mayans' mathematical genius was a valid instructional device: It was an attention-getter and would have interested even students who were not Hispanic. But the Mayan example would have had little effect without the teacher's insistence that the class study hard for a difficult examination.

[344] Ethnic educators have seized upon the Mayan contribution to mathematics as the key to simultaneously boosting the ethnic pride of Hispanic children and attacking Eurocentrism. One proposal claims that Mexican-American children will be attracted to science and mathematics if they study Mayan mathematics, the Mayan calendar, and Mayan astronomy. Children in primary grades are to be taught that the Mayans were first to discover the zero and that Europeans learned it long afterwards from the Arabs, who had learned it in India. This will help them see that Europeans were latecomers in the discovery of great ideas. Botany is to be learned by study of the agricultural techniques of the Aztecs, a subject of somewhat limited relevance to children in urban areas. Furthermore, "ethnobotanical" classifications of plants are to be substituted for the Eurocentric Linnaean system. At first glance, it may seem curious that Hispanic children are deemed to have no cultural affinity with Spain; but to acknowledge the cultural tie would confuse the ideological assault on Eurocentrism.

This proposal suggests some questions: Is there any evidence that the teaching of "culturally relevant" science and mathematics will draw Mexican-American children to the study of these subjects? Will Mexican-American children lose interest or self-esteem if they discover that their ancestors were Aztecs or Spaniards, rather than Mayans? Are children who learn in this way prepared to study the science and mathematics that are taught in American colleges and universities and that are needed for advanced study in these fields? Are they even prepared to study the science and mathematics taught in *Mexican* universities? If the class is half Mexican-American and half something else, will only the Mexican-American children study in a Mayan and Aztec mode or will all the children? But shouldn't all children study what is culturally relevant for them? How will we train teachers who have command of so many different systems of mathematics and science?

The efficacy of particularist proposals seems to be less important to their sponsors than their value as ideological weapons with which to criticize existing disciplines for their alleged Eurocentric bias. In a recent article titled "The Ethnocentric Basis of Social Science Knowledge Production" in the *Review of Research in Education*, John Stanfield of Yale University argues that neither social science nor science are objective studies, that both instead are "Euro-American" knowledge systems which reproduce "hegemonic racial domination." The claim that science and reason are somehow superior to magic and witchcraft, he writes, is the product of Euro-American ethnocentrism. According to Stanfield, current fears about the misuse of science (for instance, "the nuclear arms race, global pollution") and "the power-plays of Third World nations (the Arab oil boycott and the American-Iranian hostage **[345]** crisis) have made Western people more aware of nonscientific cognitive styles. These last events are beginning to demonstrate politically that which has begun to be understood in intellectual circles: namely, that modes of social knowledge such as theology, science, and magic are different, not inferior or superior. They represent different ways of perceiving, defining, and organizing knowledge of life experiences." One wonders: If Professor Stanfield broke his leg, would he go to a theologian, a doctor, or a magician? . . .

[346] Particularism is akin to cultural Lysenkoism, for it takes as its premise the spurious notion that cultural traits are inherited. It implies a dubious, dangerous form of cultural predestination. Children are taught that if their ancestors could do it, so could they. But what happens if a child is from a cultural group that made no significant contribution to science or mathematics? Does this mean that children from that background must find a culturally appropriate field in which to strive? How does a teacher find the right cultural buttons for children of mixed heritage? And how in the world will teachers use this technique when the children in their classes are drawn from many different cultures, as is usually the case? By the time that every culture gets its due, there may be no time left to teach the subject itself. This explosion of filiopietism (which, we should remember, comes from adults, not from students) is reminiscent of the period some years ago when the Russians claimed that they had invented everything first; as we now know, this nationalistic braggadocio did little for their self-esteem and nothing for their economic development. We might reflect, too, on how little social prestige has been accorded in this country to immigrants from Greece and Italy, even though the achievements of their ancestors were at the heart of the classical curriculum.

Filiopietism and ethnic boosterism lead to all sorts of odd practices. In New York State, for example, the curriculum guide for eleventh grade American history lists three "foundations" for the United States Constitution, as follows:

1. 17th and 18th century Enlightenment thought
2. Haudenosaunee political system

   a. Influence upon colonial leadership and European intellectuals (Locke, Montesquieu, Voltaire, Rousseau)
   b. Impact on Albany Plan of Union, Articles of Confederation, and U.S. Constitution

3. Colonial experience

Those who are unfamiliar with the Haudenosaunee political system might wonder what it is, particularly since educational authorities in New York State rank it as equal in importance to the European Enlightenment and suggest that it strongly influenced not only colonial leaders but the leading intellectuals of Europe. The Haudenosaunee political system was the Iroquois confederation of five (later six) Indian tribes in upper New York State, which conducted war and civil affairs through a council of chiefs, each with one vote. In 1754, Benjamin Franklin **[347]** proposed a colonial union at a conference in Albany; his plan, said to be inspired by the Iroquois Confederation, was rejected by the other colonies. Today, Indian activists believe that the Iroquois Confederation was the model for the American Constitution, and the New York State Department of Education has decided that they are right. That no other state sees fit to give the American Indians equal billing with the European Enlightenment may be owing to the fact that the Indians in New York State (numbering less than forty thousand) have been more politically effective than elsewhere or that other states have not yet learned about this method of reducing "Eurocentrism" in their American history classes.

Particularism can easily be carried to extremes. Students of Fredonian descent must hear that their ancestors were seminal in the development of all human civilization and that without the Fredonian contribution, we would all be living in caves or trees, bereft of art, technology, and culture. To explain why Fredonians today are in modest circumstances, given their historic eminence, children are taught that somewhere, long ago, another culture stole the Fredonians' achievements, palmed them off as their own, and then oppressed the Fredonians.

I first encountered this argument almost twenty years ago, when I was a graduate student. I shared a small office with a young professor, and I listened as she patiently explained to a student why she had given him a D on a term paper. In his paper, he argued that the Arabs had stolen mathematics from the Nubians in the desert long ago (I forget in which century this theft allegedly occurred). She tried to explain to him about the necessity of historical evidence. He was unconvinced, since he believed that he had uncovered a great truth that was beyond proof. The part I couldn't understand was how anyone could lose knowledge by sharing it. After all, cultures are constantly influencing one another, exchanging ideas and art and technology, and the exchange usually is enriching, not depleting.

Today, there are a number of books and articles advancing controversial 20
theories about the origins of civilization. An important work, *The African Origin*

of Civilization: Myth or Reality, by Senegalese scholar Cheikh Anta Diop, argues that ancient Egypt was a black civilization, that all races are descended from the black race, and that the achievements of "western" civilization originated in Egypt. The views of Diop and other Africanists have been condensed into an everyman's paperback titled *What They Never Told You in History Class* by Indus Khamit Kush. This latter book claims that Moses, Jesus, Buddha, Mohammed, and Vishnu were Africans; that the first Indians, Chinese, Hebrews, Greeks, Romans, Britains, and Americans were Africans; and that the **[348]** first mathematicians, scientists, astronomers, and physicians were Africans. A debate currently raging among some classicists is whether the Greeks "stole" the philosophy, art, and religion of the ancient Egyptians and whether the ancient Egyptians were black Africans. George G. M. James's *Stolen Legacy* insists that the Greeks "stole the Legacy of the African Continent and called it their own." James argues that the civilization of Greece, the vaunted foundation of European culture, owed everything it knew and did to its African predecessors. Thus, the roots of western civilization lie not in Greece and Rome, but in Egypt and, ultimately, in black Africa. . . .

[350] As a result of the 1987 revisions in American and world history, New York State had one of the most advanced multicultural history-social studies curricula in the country. Dozens of social studies teachers and consultants had participated, and the final draft was reviewed by such historians as Eric Foner of Columbia University, the late Hazel Hertzberg of Teachers College, Columbia University, and Christopher Lasch of the University of Rochester. The curriculum was overloaded with facts, almost to the point of numbing students with details and trivia, but it was not insensitive to ethnicity in American history or unduly devoted to European history.

But the Sobol task force* decided that this curriculum was biased and Eurocentric. The first sentence of the task force report summarizes its major thesis: "African Americans, Asian Americans, Puerto Ricans/Latinos, and Native Americans have all been the victims of an intellectual and educational oppression that has characterized the culture and institutions of the United States and the European American world for centuries."

The task force report was remarkable in that it vigorously denounced bias without identifying a single instance of bias in the curricular guides under review. Instead, the consultants employed harsh, sometimes inflammatory, rhetoric to treat every difference of opinion or interpretation as an example of racial bias. The African American consultant, for example, excoriates the curriculum for its "White Anglo-Saxon (WASP) value system and norms," its "deep-seated pathologies of racial hatred" and its "white nationalism"; he decries as bias the fact that children study Egypt as part of the Middle East instead of as part of Africa. Perhaps Egypt should be studied as part of the African unit (geographically, it is located on the African continent); but placing it in one region rather

* Task Force on Minorities: Equity and Excellence (1987).

than the other is not what most people think of as racism or bias. The "Latino" consultant criticizes the use of the term "Spanish-American War" instead of "Spanish-Cuban-American War." The Native American consultant complains that tribal languages are classified as "foreign languages."

The report is consistently Europhobic. It repeatedly expresses negative judgments on "European Americans" and on everything Western and European. All people with a white skin are referred to as "Anglo-Saxons" and "WASPs." Europe, says the report, is uniquely responsible for producing aggressive individuals who "were ready to 'discover, invade and conquer' foreign land because of greed, racism and national egoism." All white people are held collectively guilty for the historical **[351]** crimes of slavery and racism. There is no mention of the "Anglo-Saxons" who opposed slavery and racism. Nor does the report acknowledge that some whites have been victims of discrimination and oppression. The African American consultant writes of the Constitution, "There is something vulgar and revolting in glorifying a process that heaped undeserved rewards on a segment of the population while oppressing the majority."

The New York task force proposal is not merely about the reconstruction of 25
what is taught. It goes a step further to suggest that the history curriculum may be used to ensure that "children from Native American, Puerto Rican/Latino, Asian American, and African American cultures will have higher self-esteem and self-respect, while children from European cultures will have a less arrogant perspective of being part of the group that has 'done it all.'"

In February 1990, Commissioner Sobol asked the New York Board of Regents to endorse a sweeping revision of the history curriculum to make it more multicultural. His recommendations were couched in measured tones, not in the angry rhetoric of his task force. The board supported his request unanimously. It remains to be seen whether New York pursues the particularist path marked out by the Commissioner's advisory group or finds its way to the concept of pluralism within a democratic tradition. [See *One Nation, Many Peoples*, pages 517–525.]

The rising tide of particularism encourages the politicization of all curricula in the schools. If education bureaucrats bend to the political and ideological winds, as is their wont, we can anticipate a generation of struggle over the content of the curriculum in mathematics, science, literature, and history. Demands for "culturally relevant" studies, for ethnostudies of all kinds, will open the classroom to unending battles over whose version is taught, who gets credit for what, and which ethno-interpretation is appropriate. Only recently have districts begun to resist the demands of fundamentalist groups to censor textbooks and library books (and some have not yet begun to do so).

The spread of particularism throws into question the very idea of American public education. Public schools exist to teach children the general skills and knowledge that they need to succeed in American society, and the specific skills and knowledge that they need in order to function as American citizens. They receive public support because they have a public function. Historically, the public schools were known as "common schools" because they were schools for all, even if the children of all the people did not attend them. Over the years, the courts have found that it was unconstitutional to teach religion in the common schools, or to separate children on the basis of their race in the common **[352]** schools. In their curriculum, their hiring practices, and their general philosophy, the public schools must not discriminate against or give preference to any racial or ethnic group. Yet they are permitted to accommodate cultural diversity by, for example, serving food that is culturally appropriate or providing library collections that emphasize the interests of the local community. However, they should not be expected to teach children to view the world through an ethnocentric perspective that rejects or ignores the common culture. For generations, those groups that wanted to inculcate their religion or their ethnic heritage have instituted private schools—after school, on weekends, or on a full-time basis. There, children learn with others of the same group—Greeks, Poles, Germans, Japanese, Chinese, Jews, Lutherans, Catholics, and so on—and are taught by people from the same group. Valuable as this exclusive experience has been for those who choose it, this has not been the role of public education. One of the primary purposes of public education has been to create a national community, a definition of citizenship and culture that is both expansive and *inclusive*.

The curriculum in public schools must be based on whatever knowledge and practices have been determined to be best by professionals—experienced teachers and scholars—who are competent to make these judgments. Professional societies must be prepared to defend the integrity of their disciplines. When called upon, they should establish review committees to examine disputes over curriculum and to render judgment, in order to help school officials fend off improper political pressure. Where genuine controversies exist, they should be taught and debated in the classroom. Was Egypt a black civilization? Why not raise the question, read the arguments of the different sides in the debate, show slides of Egyptian pharaohs and queens, read books about life in ancient Egypt, invite guest scholars from the local university, and visit museums with Egyptian collections? If scholars disagree, students should know it. One great advantage of this approach is that students will see that history is a lively study, that textbooks are fallible, that historians disagree, that the writing of history is influenced by the historian's politics and ideology, that history is written by people who make choices among alternative facts and interpretations, and that history changes as new facts are uncovered and new interpretations win adherents. They will also learn that cultures and civilizations constantly interact, exchange ideas, and influence one another, and that the idea of racial or ethnic purity is a myth. Another advantage is that students might once again study ancient history, which has all but disappeared from the curricula of American schools. (California recently introduced a required sixth grade course in ancient civilizations, but ancient history is otherwise *terra incognita* in American education.)

[353] The multicultural controversy may do wonders for the study of history, which has been neglected for years in American schools. At this time, only half of our high school graduates ever study any world history. Any serious attempt to broaden students' knowledge of Africa, Europe, Asia, and Latin America will require at least two, and possibly three years of world history (a requirement thus far only in California). American history, too, will need more time than the one-year high-school survey course. Those of us who have insisted for years on the importance of history in the curriculum may not be ready to assent to its redemptive power, but hope that our new allies will ultimately join a constructive dialogue that strengthens the place of history in the schools.

As cultural controversies arise, educators must adhere to the principle of "E Pluribus Unum." That is, they must maintain a balance between the demands of the one—the nation of which we are common citizens—and the many—the varied histories of the American people. It is not necessary to denigrate either the one or the many. Pluralism is a positive value, but it is also important that we preserve a sense of an American community—a society and a culture to which we all belong. If there is no overall community with an agreed-upon vision of liberty and justice, if all we have is a collection of racial and ethnic cultures, lacking any common bonds, then we have no means to mobilize public opinion on behalf of people who are not members of our particular group. We have, for example, no reason to support public education. If there is no larger community, then each group will want to teach its own children in its own way, and public education ceases to exist.

History should not be confused with filiopietism. History gives no grounds for race pride. No race has a monopoly on virtue. If anything, a study of history should inspire humility, rather than pride. People of every racial group have committed terrible crimes, often against others of the same group. Whether one looks at the history of Europe or Africa or Latin America or Asia, every continent offers examples of inhumanity. Slavery has existed in civilizations around the world for centuries. Examples of genocide can be found around the world, throughout history, from ancient times right through to our own day. Governments and cultures, sometimes by edict, sometimes simply following tradition, have practiced not only slavery, but human sacrifice, infanticide, cliterodectomy, and mass murder. If we teach children this, they might recognize how absurd both racial hatred and racial chauvinism are.

What must be preserved in the study of history is the spirit of inquiry, the readiness to open new questions and to pursue new understandings. History, at its best, is a search for truth. The best way to portray this search is through debate and controversy, rather than through imposition of fixed beliefs and immutable facts. Perhaps the most dangerous aspect **[354]** of school history is its tendency to become Official History, a sanctified version of the Truth taught by the state to captive audiences and embedded in beautiful mass-market textbooks as holy writ. When Official History is written by committees responding to political pressures, rather than by scholars synthesizing the best available research, then the errors of the past are replaced by the politically fashionable errors of the present. It may be difficult to teach children that history is both important and uncertain, and that even the best historians never have all the pieces of the jigsaw puzzle, but it is necessary to do so. If state education departments permit the revision of their history courses and textbooks to become an exercise in power politics, then the entire process of state-level curriculum-making becomes suspect, as does public education itself.

The question of self-esteem is extraordinarily complex, and it goes well beyond the content of the curriculum. Most of what we call self-esteem is formed in the home and in a variety of life experiences, not only in school. Nonetheless, it has been important for blacks—and for other racial groups—to learn about the history of slavery and of the civil rights movement; it has been important for blacks to know that their ancestors actively resisted enslavement and actively pursued equality; and it has been important for blacks and others to learn about black men and women who fought courageously against racism and who provide models of courage, persistence, and intellect. These are instances where the content of the curriculum reflects sound scholarship, and at the same time probably lessens racial prejudice and provides inspiration for those who are descendants of slaves. But knowing about the travails and triumphs of one's forebears does not necessarily translate into either self-esteem or personal accomplishment. For most children, self-esteem—the self-confidence that grows out of having reached a goal—comes not from hearing about the monuments of their ancestors but as a consequence of what they are able to do and accomplish through their own efforts.

As I reflected on these issues, I recalled reading an interview a few years ago 35
with a talented black runner. She said that her model is Mikhail Baryshnikov. She admires him because he is a magnificent athlete. He is not black; he is not female; he is not American-born; he is not even a runner. But he inspires her because of the way he trained and used his body. When I read this, I thought how narrow-minded it is to believe that people can be inspired *only* by those who are exactly like them in race and ethnicity.

THE DEBATE HAS BEEN MISCAST FROM THE START*

HENRY LOUIS GATES, JR.

Henry Louis Gates, Jr. (b. 1950), is chairman of the Afro-American Studies Department and professor of English at Harvard University, where he also directs the W. E. B. Du Bois Institute for Afro-American Research. He holds an undergraduate degree from Yale Uni-

* Gates, Henry Louis, Jr. "The Debate Has Been Miscast from the Start." *The Boston Globe Magazine* 13 October 1991: 26, 36–38.

versity and a Ph.D. from Cambridge University. Gates is the editor of several books, including Reading Black, Reading Feminist: A Critical Anthology *(1990) and* Bearing Witness *(1991). His own book* The Signifying Monkey: Towards a Theory of Afro-American Literary Criticism *(1988) won an American Book Award in 1989. In the following essay, which appeared in* The Boston Globe Magazine, *Gates presents his belief that the role of educational institutions is to promote a balance between what he calls "that bygone model of monochrome homogeneity" and a "mindless celebration of difference"—a balance that seeks to understand cultural diversity in a context of mutual dependence.*

[26] What is multiculturalism and why are they saying such terrible things about it?

We've been told that it threatens to fragment American culture into a warren of ethnic enclaves, each separate and inviolate. We've been told that it menaces the Western tradition of literature and the arts. We've been told that it aims to politicize the school curriculum, replacing honest historical scholarship with a "feel good" syllabus designed solely to bolster the self-esteem of minorities. The alarm has been sounded, and many scholars and educators—liberals as well as conservatives—have responded to it. After all, if multiculturalism is just a pretty name for ethnic chauvinism, who needs it?

But I don't think that's what multiculturalism is—at least, I don't think that's what it ought to be. And because the debate has been miscast from the beginning, it may be worth setting the main issues straight.

To both proponents and antagonists, multiculturalism represents—either refreshingly or frighteningly—a radical departure. Like most claims for cultural novelty, this one is more than a little exaggerated. For the challenges of cultural pluralism—and the varied forms of official resistance to it—go back to the very founding of our republic.

In the university today, it must be admitted, the challenge has taken on a 5
peculiar inflection. But the underlying questions are time-tested. What does it mean to be an American? Must academic inquiry be subordinated to the requirements of national identity? Should scholarship and education reflect our actual diversity, or should they, rather, forge a communal identity that may not yet have been achieved?

For answers, you can, of course, turn to the latest jeremiad on the subject from, say, George Will, Dinesh D'Souza, or Roger Kimball. But in fact these questions have always occasioned lively disagreement among American educators. In 1917, William Henry [36] Hulme decried "the insidious introduction into our scholarly relations of the political propaganda of a wholly narrow, selfish, and vicious nationalism and false patriotism." His opponents were equally emphatic in their beliefs. "More and more clearly," Fred Lewis Pattee ventured in 1919, "is it seen now that the American soul, the American conception of democracy, Americanism, should be made prominent in our school curriculums, as a guard against the rising spirit of experimental lawlessness." Sound familiar?

Given the political nature of the debate over education and the national interest, the conservative penchant for charging the multiculturalists with "politics" is a little perplexing. For conservative critics, to their credit, have never hesitated to provide a political defense of what they consider to be the "traditional" curriculum: The future of the republic, they argue, depends on the inculcation of proper civic virtues. What these virtues are is a matter of vehement dispute. But to imagine a curriculum untouched by political concerns is to imagine—as no one does—that education can take place in a vacuum.

So where's the beef? Granted, multiculturalism is no panacea for our social ills. We're worried when Johnny can't read. We're worried when Johnny can't add. But shouldn't we be worried, too, when Johnny tramples gravestones in a Jewish cemetery or scrawls racial epithets on a dormitory wall? And it's because we've entrusted our schools with the fashioning of a democratic polity that education has never been exempt from the kind of debate that marks every other aspect of American political life.

Perhaps this isn't altogether a bad thing. As the political theorist Amy Gutmann has argued: "In a democracy, political disagreement is not something that we should generally seek to avoid. Political controversies over our educational problems are a particularly important source of social progress because they have the potential for educating so many citizens."

10 And while I'm sympathetic to what Robert Nisbet once dubbed the "academic dogma"—the ideal of knowledge for its own sake—I also believe that truly humane learning, unblinkered by the constraints of narrow ethnocentrism, can't help but expand the limits of human understanding and social tolerance. Those who fear that "Balkanization" and social fragmentation lie this way have got it exactly backward. Ours is a world that already is fissured by nationality, ethnicity, race, and gender. And the only way to transcend those divisions—to forge, for once, a civic culture that respects both differences and commonalities—is through education that seeks to comprehend the diversity of human culture. Beyond the hype and the high-flown rhetoric is a pretty homely truth: There is no tolerance without respect—and no respect without knowledge.

The historical architects of the university always understood this. As Cardinal Newman wrote more than a century ago, the university should promote "the power of viewing many **[37]** things at once as one whole, of referring them severally to their true place in the universal system, of understanding their respective values, and determining their mutual dependence." In just this vein, the critic Edward Said has recently suggested that "our model for academic freedom should therefore be the migrant or traveler: for if, in the real world outside the academy, we must needs be ourselves and only ourselves, inside the academy we should be able to discover and travel among other selves, other identities, other varieties of the human adventure. But, most essentially, in this joint discovery of self and other, it is the role of the academy to transform what might be conflict, or context, or assertion into reconciliation, mutuality, recognition, creative interaction."

But if multiculturalism represents the culmination of an age-old ideal—the dream known, in the 17th century, as *mathesis universalis*—why has it been the target of such ferocious attacks? On this point, I'm often reminded of a wonderfully wicked piece of 19th-century student doggerel about Benjamin Jowett, the great Victorian classicist and master of Balliol College, Oxford:

Here stand I, my name is Jowett,
If there's knowledge, then I know it;
I am the master of this college,
What I know not, is not knowledge.

Of course, the question of how we determine what is worth knowing is now being raised with uncomfortable persistence. So that in the most spirited attacks on multiculturalism in the academy today, there's a nostalgic whiff of the old sentiment: We are the masters of this college; what we know not is not knowledge.

I think this explains the conservative desire to cast the debate in terms of the West vs. the Rest. And yet that's the very opposition that the pluralist wants to challenge. Pluralism sees cultures as porous, dynamic, and interactive, rather than the fixed property of particular ethnic groups. Thus the idea of monolithic, homogeneous "West" itself comes into question (nothing new here: Literary historians have pointed out that the very concept of "Western culture" may date back only to the 18th century). But rather than mourning the loss of some putative ancestral purity, we can recognize what's valuable, resilient, even cohesive, in the hybrid and variegated nature of our modernity.

[38] Genuine multiculturalism is not, of course, everyone's cup of tea. Vulgar 15
cultural nationalists—like Allan Bloom or Leonard Jeffries—correctly identify it as the enemy. These polemicists thrive on absolute partitions: between "civilization" and "barbarism," between "black" and "white," between a thousand versions of Us and Them. But they are whistling in the wind.

For whatever the outcome of the culture wars in the academy, the world we live in is multicultural already. Mixing and hybridity is the rule, not the exception. As a student of African-American culture, of course, I've come to take this kind of cultural palimpsest for granted. Duke Ellington, Miles Davis, John Coltrane have influenced popular musicians the world over. Wynton Marsalis is as comfortable with Mozart as he is with jazz; Anthony Davis writes operas in a musical idiom that combines Bartok with the blues.

In dance, Judith Jamison, Alvin Ailey, Katherine Dunham all excelled at "Western" cultural forms, melding these with African-American styles to produce performances that were neither, and both. In painting, Romare Bearden and Jacob Lawrence, Martin Puryear and Augusta Savage learned to paint and sculpt by studying Western masters, yet each has pioneered the construction of a distinctly African-American visual art.

And in literature, of course, the most formally complex and compelling black writers—such as Jean Toomer, Sterling Brown, Langston Hughes, Zora

Hurston, Richard Wright, Ralph Ellison, James Baldwin, and Gwendolyn Brooks—have always blended forms of Western literature with African-American vernacular and written traditions. Then, again, even a vernacular form such as the spiritual took for its texts the King James version of the Old and New Testaments. Toni Morrison's master's thesis was on Virginia Woolf and Faulkner; Rita Dove is as comfortable with German literature as she is with the blues.

Indeed, the greatest African-American art can be thought of as an exploration of that hyphenated space between the African and the American. As James Baldwin once reflected during his long European sojourn, "I would have to appropriate these white centuries, I would have to make them mine. I would have to accept my special attitude, my special place in this scheme, otherwise I would have no place in any scheme."

"Pluralism," the American philosopher John Dewey insisted early in this 20
century, "is the greatest philosophical idea of our times." But he recognized that it was also the greatest problem of our times: "How are we going to make the most of the new values we set on variety, difference, and individuality—how are we going to realize their possibilities in every field, and at the same time not sacrifice that plurality to the cooperation we need so much?" It has the feel of a scholastic conundrum: How can we negotiate between the one and the many?

Today the mindless celebration of difference has proven as untenable as that bygone model of monochrome homogeneity. If there is an equilibrium to be struck, there's no guarantee we will ever arrive at it. The worst mistake we can make, however, is not to try.

Acknowledgments

(Continued from Copyright page)

Paula Gunn Allen "Where I Come from Is like This," from THE SACRED HOOP by Paula Gunn Allen. Copyright © 1986, 1992 by Paula Gunn Allen. Reprinted by permission of Beacon Press.

Stokely Carmichael and Charles V. Hamilton "Black Power," from BLACK POWER by Stokely Carmichael & Charles V. Hamilton. Copyright © 1967 by Stokely Carmichael and Charles Hamilton. Reprinted by permission of Random House, Inc.

Alice Chandler "Fostering a Multi-Cultural Curriculum: Principles for Presidents," April 1991. Copyright © 1991. Reprinted with permission of the American Association of State Colleges and Universities.

George J. Church "Hispanics: A Melding of Cultures" copyright © 1985 Time Inc. Reprinted by permission.

Tom Coakley "Burden of Arrival Is Felt by All," by Tom Coakley, January 22, 1989. Reprinted courtesy of *The Boston Globe.*

Judith Ortiz Cofer *Reaching for the Mainland* appearing in TRIPLE CROWN, Copyright © 1987 by Bilingual Press/Editorial Bilingue, Arizona State University, Tempe, AZ. Reprinted with permission.

Harvey A. Daniels "The Roots of Language Protectionism." *College Composition and Communication,* May 1992. Copyright 1992 by the National Council of Teachers of English. Reprinted with permission.

Carl N. Degler "The Forces That Shaped Modern America," excerpts from OUT OF OUR PAST by Carl N. Degler. Copyright © 1959, 1970 by Carl N. Degler. Reprinted by permission of HarperCollins Publishers.

Vine Deloria, Jr. "Indian Humor." Reprinted with the permission of Macmillan Publishing Company from CUSTER DIED FOR YOUR SINS: An Indian Manifesto by Vine Deloria, Jr. Copyright © 1969 by Vine Deloria, Jr.

Mary Crow Dog "We AIM Not to Please," from the book LAKOTA WOMAN by Mary Crow Dog with Richard Erdoes. Copyright © 1990 by Mary Crow Dog and Richard Erdoes. Used with the permission of Grove/Atlantic Monthly Press. Paperback available from HarperCollins, 10 East 53rd Street, NY, NY 10019.

Michael Dorris "Crazy Horse Malt Liquor and Other Cultural Metaphors." Copyright © 1992 by the New York Times Company. Reprinted by permission.

Ronald L. Fair "We Who Came After," from WE CAN'T BREATHE by Ronald L. Fair. Copyright © 1969 by R. Lyman, Inc. Reprinted by permission of HarperCollins Publishers.

James Fallows "Language." Reprinted with permission of the author.

James T. Farrell "Old Man Lonigan," from STUDS LONIGAN by James T. Farrell. Reprinted by permission of Vanguard Press, a division of Random House, Inc.

Samuel G. Freedman "The Lower East Side," from SMALL VICTORIES by Samuel G. Freedman. Copyright © 1990 by Samuel G. Freedman. Reprinted by permission of HarperCollins Publishers.

James M. Freeman "Undisciplined Children." Reprinted from HEARTS OF SORROW: VIETNAMESE-AMERICAN LIVES by James M. Freeman with the permission of the publishers, Stanford University Press copyright © 1989 by the Board of Trustees of the Leland Stanford Junior University.

Marilyn French "First Day at School." Copyright © 1987 by Belle-lettres, Inc. Reprinted by permission of Simon and Schuster, Inc.

Lawrence H. Fuchs "The American Way of Families," from FAMILY MATTERS by Lawrence H. Fuchs. Copyright © 1972 by Lawrence H. Fuchs. Reprinted by permission of Random House, Inc.

Henry Louis Gates, Jr. "The Debate Has Been Miscast from the Start," by Henry Louis Gates, Jr. First appeared in the *Boston Globe Magazine*. Copyright © 1991. Reprinted with permission of Brandt & Brandt Literary Agents, Inc.

Shirley Ann Grau "The Beginning," from NINE WOMEN by Shirley Ann Grau. Copyright © 1985 by Shirley Ann Grau. Reprinted by permission of Alfred A. Knopf, Inc.

Andrew M. Greeley "Social Turf," from WHY CAN'T THEY BE LIKE US? by Andrew M. Greeley. Copyright © 1971, 1970 by Andrew M. Greeley. Used by permission of the publisher, Dutton, an imprint of New American Library, a division of Penguin Books USA Inc.

Sophronia Scott Gregory "The Hidden Hurdle." Copyright © 1992 Time Inc. Reprinted by permission.

Oscar Handlin From *The Uprooted* by Oscar Handlin. Copyright 1951 © 1973 by Oscar Handlin. By permission of Little, Brown and Company.

Oscar Hijuelos "Visitors, 1965," from *Our House in the Last World*, by Oscar Hijuelos. Copyright © 1983 by Oscar Hijuelos. Reprinted by permission of Peresea Books, Inc.

Arthur Hu "Us and Them." Reprinted by permission of THE NEW REPUBLIC, © 1992, The New Republic, Inc.

Jesse Jackson From his Speech Before the Democratic National Convention, July 14, 1992, pp. 1–7.

Harriet Jacobs *From Incidents in the Life of a Slave Girl* by Harriet Jacobs. Copyright © 1988 Oxford University Press, Inc. Reprinted by permission.

Sarah Kemble Knight From *The Private Journey from Boston to New York*. Winship, George Parker, Ed., THE JOURNAL OF MADAM KNIGHT, Peter Smith Publisher, Inc.: 1935 Gloucester, MA.

Elaine H. Kim "They Armed in Self-Defense," from *Newsweek*, (May 18, 1992). Reprinted by permission of the author.

Andrew T. Kopan "Melting Pot: Myth or Reality?" from Edgar Epps: CULTURAL PLURALISM. Copyright © 1974 by McCutchan Publishing Corporation, Berkeley, California 94702. Permission granted by the publisher.

Lewis H. Lapham "Who and What Is American?" Copyright © 1991 by *Harper's Magazine*. All rights reserved. Reprinted from the January 1992 issue by special permission.

Tom Lehrer "National Brotherhood Week." © 1964 Tom Lehrer. Used by permission.

Nicholas Lemann "Clarksdale," from THE PROMISED LAND by Nicholas Lemann. Copyright © 1990 by Nicholas Lemann. Reprinted by permission of Alfred A. Knopf, Inc.

Lars Ljungmark "Swedish Exodus." Reprinted by permission of the Swedish-American Historical Society.

Dang Hong Loan "A Tragic Voyage." Reprinted from THE FAR EAST COMES NEAR: AUTOBIOGRAPHICAL ACCOUNTS OF SOUTHEAST ASIAN STUDENTS IN AMERICA, Lucy Nguyen-Hong-Nhiem and Joel Martin Halpern, eds. (Amherst: University of Massachusetts Press, 1989), copyright © 1989 by the University of Massachusetts Press.

Martin Luther King, Jr. "Letter from Birmingham Jail." Reprinted by arrangement with the Heirs of the Estate of Martin Luther King, Jr., c/o Joan Daves Agency as agent for the Proprietor. Copyright © 1963 by Dr. Martin Luther King, Jr. Copyright renewed 1991 by Coretta Scott King.

Malcolm X From THE AUTOBIOGRAPHY OF MALCOLM X by Malcolm X with Alex Haley. Copyright © 1964 by Alex Haley and Malcolm X. Copyright © 1965 by Alex Haley and Betty Shabezz. Reprinted by permission of Random House, Inc.

Jerre Mangione "Talking American," from *Mount Allegro: A Memoir of Italian American Life.* Jerre Mangione, 1981, © Columbia University Press, New York. Reprinted with the permission of the publisher.

Paule Marshall "From the Poets in the Kitchen." Copyright © 1983 by Paule Marshall. From the book REENA AND OTHER STORIES. Published by The Feminist Press at The City University of New York. All rights reserved.

James A. McPherson "To Blacks and Jews: *Hab Rachmones*," from *Tikkun, The Best American Essays.* Reprinted by permission of the author.

Monica McGoldrick "Ethnicity and Families," from *Ethnicity and Family Therapy*, ed. by Monica McGoldrick, John K. Pearce and Joseph Giordano. Copyright © 1982 by The Guilford Press. Reprinted by permission.

Margaret Mead and James Baldwin *A Rap on Race*, 1971, pp. 119–125. Reprinted with permission of the authors.

David Mura "Secrets and Anger." Reprinted with permission from *Mother Jones* magazine, © 1992, Foundation for National Progress.

Alixa Naff "Arabs in America," from Alixa Naff, "Arabs in the New World: A Historical Overview," from *Arabs in the New World: Studies in Arab-American Communities.* Copyright © 1983. Reprinted with permission.

Sarah Nieves-Squires "Hispanic Women on Campus," from *Project on the Status and Education of Women.* Copyright © 1990.

Michael Novak "How American Are You?" from *The Rediscovery of Ethnicity.* Copyright © 1973, James S. Ozer Publisher, Inc.

Richard O'Connor "The German-Americans: The Great White Whale." Copyright © 1968 by Richard O'Connor. Reprinted by permission of McIntosh and Otis, Inc.

Richard Olivas "The Immigrant Experience." Copyright © 1972, Richard Olivas.

Elena Padilla "Profound Changes," from UP FROM PUERTO RICO, Elena Padilla, 1958, © Columbia University Press, New York. Reprinted with the permission of the publisher.

Harry Mark Petrakis "A City Within a City." Copyright by Harry Mark Petrakis. Excerpted from *Reflections—A Writer's Life—A Writer's Work*, Lake View Press, Chicago, Illinois.

Rosalie Pedalino Porter "The Fractured Logic of Bilingual Education," from FORKED TONGUE: THE POLITICS OF BILINGUAL EDUCATION by Rosalie Pedalino Porter. Copyright © 1990 by Basic Books, Inc. Reprinted by permission of Basic Books, Inc., a division of HarperCollins, Publishers, Inc.

Diane Ravitch "Multiculturalism: E Pluribus Plures," from *The American Scholar*, Summer 1990. Reprinted with permission.

Ishmael Reed "America: The Multinational Society." Reprinted with the permission of Atheneum Publishers, an imprint of Macmillan Publishing from WRITIN' IS FIGHTIN' by Ishmael Reed. Copyright © 1983 by Ishmael Reed.

Aleksandra Rembiénska "A Polish Peasant Girl in America," from *America's Immigrants: Adventures in Eyewitness History*, ed. Rhoda Hoff. Copyright © 1967 Rhoda de Terra.

Tomas Rivera From Y NO SE LO TRAGO LA TIERRA (And the Earth Did Not Part). "It's That It Hurts," by Tomas Rivera translated by Evangelina Vigil Pinon is reprinted with permission from the publisher of *... y no se lo trago la tierra/ ... And the Earth Did Not Devour Him* (Houston: Arte Publico Press-University of Houston, 1987).

Clara E. Rodriguez "Salsa in the Melting Pot," from *The Boston Globe*, May 12, 1991. Reprinted with permission of the author.

Richard Rodriguez "The Education of Richard Rodriguez." Rodriguez, Richard, HUNGER OF MEMORY. Copyright © 1992 by David R. Godine. Used by permission.

Mike Rose "I Just Wanna Be Average." Reprinted with permission of The Free Press, a Division of Macmillan, Inc., from *Lives on the Boundary: The Struggles and Achievements of America's Underprepared* by Mike Rose. Copyright © 1989 by Mike Rose.

Ronald Saunders "U.S. English—1991 National Opinion Survey." Copyright © 1991, U.S. English.

Richard T. Schaefer "Model Minority?" from RACIAL AND ETHNIC GROUPS, 3/e by Richard T. Schaefer. Copyright © 1988 by Richard T. Schaefer. Reprinted by permission of HarperCollins Publishers.

Arthur M. Schlesinger, Jr. "A Dissenting Opinion," from the *Report of the Social Studies Syllabus Review Committee*, New York State Social Studies Syllabus Review Committee, May 23, 1991. Reprinted by permission of the author.

William V. Shannon "Anti-Irish Nativism." Reprinted from THE AMERICAN IRISH: A POLITICAL AND SOCIAL PORTRAIT by William V. Shannon (Amherst: University of Massachusetts Press, 1963, 1966), copyright © 1966 by William V. Shannon.

Fred Siegel from "The Cult of Multiculturalism." Reprinted by permission of THE NEW REPUBLIC, © 1991, The New Republic, Inc.

Shelby Steele "Individualism and Black Identity." Copyright © 1990 by Shelby Steele, from the book THE CONTENT OF OUR CHARACTER and reprinted with permission from St. Martin's Press, Inc., New York, NY.

Mario Suarez "El Hoyo." Reprinted from *Arizona Quarterly* vol. III, no. 2 (Summer 1947), by permission of the Regents of the University of Arizona.

Betty Lee Sung "The Chinese Must Go." Betty Lee Sung, MOUNTAIN OF GOLD: THE STORY OF THE CHINESE IN AMERICA, © 1967.

Studs Terkel "Campus Life," from Studs Terkel, *Race: How Blacks and Whites Think and Feel About the American Obsession*, 1992, pp. 202–206, 209–213. Copyright 1992 by Studs Terkel. Reprinted with permission of The New Press.

Luis Valdez and Stan Steiner from *Aztlan*. Reprinted by permission of Luis Valdez.

Elise Amalie Waerenskjold "Four-Mile Prairie—Four Letters from Texas," from *Land of Their Choice* ed., by Theodore C. Blegen. © 1955 by the University of Minnesota Press. Used by permission.

Mitsuye Yamada "Asian Pacific Women." Kitchen Table Women of Color Press.

Anzia Yezierska "College," from the novel BREAD GIVERS by Anzia Yezierska, first published in 1925 by Doubleday, re-issued by Persea Books, New York, 1975. Copyright, Louise Levitas Henriksen.

The publishers have made every effort to locate the owners of all selections of copyrighted works and to obtain permission to reprint them. Any errors or omissions are unintentional and corrections will be made in future printings if necessary.

Index

Instructor's Resource Manual
for

FACE *To* FACE

As part of Houghton Mifflin's ongoing commitment to the environment, this text has been printed on recycled paper.

Instructor's Resource Manual
for

FACE *To* FACE

Readings on Confrontation and Accommodation in America

JOSEPH ZAITCHIK
University of Massachusetts, Lowell

WILLIAM ROBERTS
University of Massachusetts, Lowell

HOLLY ZAITCHIK
Boston University

HOUGHTON MIFFLIN COMPANY BOSTON TORONTO
Geneva, Illinois *Palo Alto* *Princeton, New Jersey*

Sponsoring Editor:	Kristin Watts Peri
Associate Project Editor:	Danielle Carbonneau
Production/Design Coordinator:	Lucille Belmonte
Electronic Production Supervisor:	Victoria Levin
Senior Manufacturing Coordinator:	Priscilla Bailey
Marketing Manager:	George Kane

Printed in the U.S.A.

ISBN: 0–395–63687–6

123456789–AM–98 97 96 95 94

Contents

Preface

Although we believe that the story of *Face to Face* can best be told in the order in which we present the selections, we are aware that instructors will assign readings in a variety of ways. Some, following a series of rhetorical modes, will assign relevant selections from different chapters. Others, following a progression of writing assignments, may prefer to assign the four parts of the book in a different order. We are also aware that instructors will be selective in the use of the apparatus—the freewriting assignments and suggestions for discussion and writing—although we do believe that instructors should urge their students to read the introductions to each chapter at some point during the course. We have, therefore, in this manual, limited ourselves to what we believe will be most helpful to eclectic adopters—a summary/commentary of the selections and brief responses to the questions for discussion, with only occasional linkages to other readings and writing assignments.

To avoid needless and possibly annoying repetition, we have not repeated ourselves in the answers-to-questions material that appears in the summary/commentary paragraphs and have instead simply noted, "See above." Nor have we provided answers for questions that invite subjective responses. In such cases our comment is, "Answers will vary." As we have pointed out in the Preface for Students, the role of a textbook is not to preach but to help teach. This manual, in brief, functions as the textbook proper does—as a partner in a textbook-student-instructor collaborative.

PART I

NATIONAL IDENTITY AND CULTURAL PLURALISM

Michel Guillaume St. Jean de Crèvecoeur

FROM *Letters from an American Farmer*

Crèvecoeur was born in France, educated in England, and emigrated to Canada at the age of nineteen. He worked as a surveyor and cartographer under General Montcalm during the French and Indian War and, after being wounded at the Battle of Quebec, moved to New York and changed his name to J. Hector St. John. He traveled extensively in the frontier areas of New York, Vermont, and the Ohio Valley before marrying an American and settling down to farming in Orange County, New York, and writing about America. Arrested by the British during the Revolutionary War, Crèvecoeur eventually was allowed to leave the country in 1781 and in London sold his manuscripts that would become *Letters* before returning to France. In 1783 Crèvecoeur returned to New York as French consul. In *Letters,* a fictional narrator named James describes the physical and ideological characteristics of life in America. The general optimism of the *Letters* is evident in this brief excerpt in which Crèvecoeur envisions America as the great hope for the future of humankind, a place where the sciences and arts will flourish and "a new race of men" will be forged.

Margaret Mead and James Baldwin

FROM *A Rap on Race*

In this conversation, Mead and Baldwin consider the extent to which people identify with their ancestors, deriving dignity and pride from their connection with admired forebears. The authors begin on different sides of the question, with Mead stating, "We have to get rid of people being proud of their ancestors, because after all they didn't do a thing about it. . . . nobody has any right to be proud of his ancestors," and Baldwin responding that although he understands Mead's viewpoint, nonetheless, "Your ancestors give you, if you trust them, something to get through the world." They find common ground in agreeing that individuals *choose* their ancestors in the sense that they pick the people they care about and emulate. Mead introduces the anthropological term "mythical ancestors" to describe this phenomenon of spiritual ancestry, which can be as important in an individual's identity as his or her biological ancestry. Mead points out that in our culturally diverse society, where union is based on ideals rather than on common bloodlines, an individual can adopt as his or her spiritual ancestors models from many different ethnic backgrounds. Finally, their discussion touches on the ways in which identifying oneself as being *from* somewhere (biologically or geographically) can be heard as a way of setting oneself apart from—and sometimes above—others. The example of the American black's interpretation of the Puerto Rican's statement, "I'm from Puerto Rico" opens up possibilities for interesting discussion about the ambiguous ways in which where one comes *from* can function in our society. Students will readily supply examples of inter- and intratown rivalries, intergroup rivalries within a particular school, and even regional identities within the country as a whole, in which the area (and the people) from which one comes can be taken (whether intended or not) as a statement of superiority.

Questions for Discussion

1. and 2. Responses will of course vary. Some students will regard their ancestry as little more than an "accident of birth." Others will feel a link to their heritage and agree with Baldwin that it helps them "get through the world." Many will find a middle ground. Reference to the Preface for Students (pp. xix–xxi) may be helpful.

3. Mead and Baldwin reject the melting pot image because it suggests that people who migrated to this country are "melted" into something else, that is, they lose their ethnic identities. Another image might be more

apt—one that suggests all parts become one whole while group identity is maintained. Students may wish to discuss the images suggested in the second paragraph of the introduction to this unit.

Andrew T. Kopan
"Melting Pot: Myth or Reality?"

Kopan reviews the history of American immigration and explores the reasons why melting pot theory, which anticipated the fusion of various strains in American culture, has not held true. At the end of his essay he points to four factors that have contributed to the continuation of ethnic identities in this country, ranging from such external influences as nativist reaction to new waves of immigration to the internal desire (fueled in part by antiethnic discrimination) of various groups to protect their culture by forming "ethnic colonies." Noting that all of the migrations after about 1885 (when the majority of immigrants began arriving from southern and eastern Europe) were "regarded as unwelcome and socially destructive" by those who had arrived earlier, Kopan identifies a disturbing "ambivalence in the American character." The national ideal of equality and opportunity coexists with discrimination and exclusionary practices. For further exploration of nativist sentiment in the United States see the excerpt from Henry Pratt Fairchild's *The Melting Pot Mistake,* William V. Shannon's "Anti-Irish Nativism," and Betty Lee Sung's "The Chinese Must Go."

Questions for Discussion

1. In his first six paragraphs Kopan presents anecdotal data that adds credibility to his thesis. He established how immigration and pluralism have affected almost every aspect of U.S. history. The transition *but* that opens paragraph seven announces the thesis that America has also altered its immigrants.

2. After 1885 the majority of immigrants came from southern and eastern Europe. As nativism grew in response to immigration by unwelcome groups, the "confidence that they could be fused together waned."

3. a. This statement points to Kopan's thesis and serves as a transition that moves to a discussion of how America altered its immigrants.
   b. Before 1800 immigrant groups were mostly from northwestern Europe and, similar in culture and appearance, were easily assimilated.
   c. The ambivalence lies in the conflict between the ideal of equality and the practice of discrimination. Kopan goes on to show how this ambivalence has affected the development of American society.

d. Kopan refers to the pattern of developing cultures and subcultures. In paragraphs 24–27 he lists four major factors that "have contributed to the survival of ethnicity."

4. The "recurring nativism" refers to the phenomenon of how each "new" immigration group is regarded by established groups as inferior. Examples are abundant, and they will vary from period to period and region to region.

Michael Novak
"How American Are You?"

Novak argues that "accurate ethnic perception," achieved through the study of the historical contexts that have shaped the thinking and behavior of various ethnic groups, is essential if people in a culturally diverse society such as ours are going to live together with mutual understanding. Focusing on the experiences of working-class white ethnics as Poles, Italians, and Slavs, Novak observes that the prevailing myths that the United States is fundamentally an Anglo-Saxon nation and that ethnicity is "a dirty secret about which we should not speak, except . . . in hopes it would go away" has served to inhibit serious ethnic self-examination. Novak believes that ethnic differences are not about to disappear and that they inform behavior and perceptions in numerous tacit ways. Rather than looking forward to the disappearance of ethnic consciousness, Novak feels that we should acknowledge that "the preservation of ethnicity" is not only a "barrier against alienation and anomie" but also a "resource of compassion and creativity and intergroup learning." The "new ethnicity," which, according to Novak, "stresses the general contours of *all* ethnicity and notes analogies between the cultural history of the many groups," is cross-cultural and lead to mutual respect, peaceful coexistence, and meaningful political coalitions. Issues of "white racism," on the other hand, which pit white ethnics against blacks in many U.S. cities, serve to distract attention from the problems of *class* that plague both groups. An expanded understanding of ethnicity recognizes that "lower-middle-class blacks and white ethnics share more self-interests in common than either group does with any other." Such an understanding could provide the basis for effective coalitions leading to social amelioration. Because of what Novak calls "our pretensions of being *like* everyone else." Americans too often do not realize that intergroup misunderstandings are frequently a result of different *styles of communication* rather than fundamentally different attitudes. He calls for a new consciousness of cultural differences that will ultimately serve to unite rather than divide.

Questions for Discussion

1. Those who assimilate into a cultural mainstream in terms of power, wealth, or ideas may reject or ignore their ethnicity. Often, white, upper-class people simply perceive themselves as "Anglo-Saxon" and seem totally unaware of their personal ethnic histories.

2. The dictionary entry—especially the pejorative usages 3 and 4—supports Novak's contention that too many of us are "afraid of ethnicity!"

3. Responses will vary.

4. Novak argues that "one can still give blacks highest priority, but in an inclusionary way that aims at coalitions of whites and blacks on the grievances they have in common"(33).

Lewis H. Lapham
"Who and What Is American?"

Seeking to move beyond the current tendency for Americans to use "multiple adjectives [to qualify] the American noun" (female American, gay American, etc.), Lewis Lapham attempts to define the "centripetal forces that bind us together" as one people, the "traits of character or temperament" that Americans from all backgrounds share. He believes it is important to identify these traits because "we can speak plainly about our differences only if we know and value what we hold in common." At the base of the American character he finds an orientation toward the future rather than the past, a love of the freedoms that allow us to invent and reinvent ourselves. Desire to protect our own freedom brings with it the practical desire to protect also the freedoms of our fellow citizens. Lapham remarks, "We protect the other person's liberty in the interest of protecting our own," and thus there arises a mutual respect without which "the premise as well as the machinery of the American enterprise" cannot be sustained. Lapham's essay is filled with images of movement—journey, embarkation, voyage, pilgrimage: "the American," he claims, "is always on the way to someplace else (i.e., toward some undetermined future in which all will be well)." Insuring the possibility of the individual journey requires a cooperative effort. Lapham feels that the "multiple adjectives qualifying the American noun" cause us to focus on differences rather than commonalities and thus to fall into the ultimately self-destructive trap of identifying "others" to carry the blame for problems within society. He calls for "a more courageous understanding of ourselves," which will emphasize our mutual responsibility for the successes or failures of the American enterprise. Interesting avenues for discussion can be found in comparing the Novak and Lapham pieces. How does Novak's "new ethnicity" compare with Lapham's "more courageous understanding of ourselves"? What would Novak say about Lapham's characterization of the American as "adrift at birth in an existential void, inheriting nothing but the obligation to construct a plausible self" (18)?

Questions for Discussion

1. Lapham uses the noun/adjective relationship as one of the "strategies of division" that the media and politicians often employ. He thus introduces the divisive forces that emphasize ethnic differences, a topic that he develops in the following paragraphs. Additional metaphors occur, among other places, in paragraph 2 (markets) and paragraph 3 (dolls).

2. Lapham introduces the strategy of division in paragraph 1. In the rest of the essay he develops what he sees as the major causes for "false constructions of the American purpose and identity" (7).

3. a. Lapham argues that we focused our negative energy on the Soviet Union, the "monolithic evil." He suggests that now we have transferred that need for a "negative pole" to our own neighborhoods.
   b. Answers will vary on this as does scholarly opinion. However, Henry Lewis Gates, among others, has argued that the test remains the same no matter what race of the *qualified* teacher.
   c. Because we have little regard for history and because we don't allow ourselves to be defined by class privilege, we find ourselves having inherited "an obligation to construct a plausible self" (18).
   d. If we disregard the "plausible self" others construct, we reject the American notion of holding regard for individuality.
   e. Lapham argues that we must understand, appreciate, and even make jokes about our differences. We can only do so if we understand and value what we hold in common.

4. The closing is a succinct summary of Lapham's central point. It also provides a dramatic and memorable rhetorical hook to the opening.

PART II

ETHNIC JOURNEYS

Emma Lazarus
"The New Colossus"

Lazarus (1849–1887) was born in New York. Her *Poems and Translations* (1867) was a volume admired by Emerson, to whom she dedicated her second book of poetry, *Admetus and Other Poems* (1871). The daughter of a wealthy sugar merchant, Lazarus became very conscious of her Jewish heritage during the great migration of eastern European Jews, many of whom had been persecuted by the Czarist government in Russia. Her collection *Songs of a Semite* (1882) grew out of her response to these immigrants, as did "The New Colossus," which is inscribed on the base of the Statue of Liberty. Written in 1883 in the form of a Petrarchan sonnet, the poem contrasts the Colossus of Rhodes, "the brazen giant of Greek fame" who straddled the entrance to the harbor at Rhodes, to Bartholdi's statue in New York Harbor, with its "mild eyes" and maternal welcome. The message the statue speaks through "silent lips," however, is one not always upheld by the changing immigration laws of the United States. The national response to the arrival of the "huddled mass" and "wretched refuse" arriving during the late nineteenth century was not wholeheartedly enthusiastic and resulted, in fact, in the passage of restrictive immigration laws (see Introduction to "From Europe—The Huddled Masses").

Carl N. Degler
"The Forces That Shaped Modern America"

In this selection from his *Out of Our Past: The Forces That Shaped America,* Degler traces the origins of the American virtues of work and wealth to the influences of the Puritan and Quaker religions and to the abundance of land. The European feudal hierarchy based on ownership of land could not take hold in this country because the land that was the source of wealth was readily available to all. This abundance of land provided employment and the means to advancement for ever-increasing numbers of laborers. Thus, a fluid class structure based on individually accumulated—rather than inherited—wealth developed. Degler points out that Puritanism, by valuing productivity and proscribing idleness and drawing a close connection between economic success and godliness, bestowed a religious sanction on accumulating wealth through business. For the Puritans, hard work was pleasing to God, and the social obligation to increase the general welfare of the community as one's own wealth increased kept the work ethic from devolving into economic exploitation. Quakerism, with its injunctions to accumulate wealth through diligence and frugality and to avoid ostentation, fostered a similar linking of religious and economic virtues. Over time, as the theology faded from the ethic and the Puritan became the Yankee, the dominant values of work and wealth remained. Students can be asked if they see other values and qualities in the American character that support Degler's statement in paragraph 2 that "in a number of ways what American would be for generations to come was settled in the course of those first hundred years."

Questions for Discussion

1. This period was marked by significant developments in science and the spread of democratic ideals, religious toleration, and constitutional government. It was also the time of the settlement of America by English colonists. America was "fluid," and it was able to serve as a testing ground for many new, modern ideas.

2. and 3. In America land was almost free for the taking, something beyond the comprehension of land-starved Europeans. Americans became more adept at working with their hands. Such versatility undercut the traditional European subordination of labor and thus contributed to the development of a more flexible class structure.

Samuel Sewall

FROM *The Diary of Samuel Sewall*

These entries from his diaries reveal Sewall as a responsible member of his community, a loving husband and father, a man who, "having been long and much dissatisfied with the Trade of fetching Negroes from Guinea," wrote the first antislavery tract in North America, and a man of deep religious faith who felt the workings of God in every aspect of his life. While Sewall is most often remembered as one of the judges in the witchcraft trials in Salem, Massachusetts, in 1692, he is also the only one of those judges to later question the justice of the trials and to make a public statement of regret over his own participation. This statement appears in the entry for January 15, 1696/7. Sewall's first mention of the witchcraft trials is in his diary entry of April 11, 1692. The trials had at this point been going on for several weeks, and on this occasion John Procter, Elizabeth Procter, and Sarah Cloyse were examined and testimony against them taken from young girls. As a man of his time, Sewall did believe in witchcraft; *Exodus* 22:18 states, "You shall not suffer a witch to live" (which the Puritans and others interpreted to mean that witches must be executed). Prior to the hysteria of 1692, which led to the death of twenty persons, there had been six executions for witchcraft in Massachusetts. During the 1600s in England, hundreds of persons accused of witchcraft were put to death; in Scotland there were 3,400 such executions between 1580 and 1680, and on the continent from the fourteenth to the seventeenth century half a million persons were executed for witchcraft. Most of those in Britain and on the continent were executed by burning; none were burned in English America. The extent to which religion and self-examination to determine one's spiritual health pervaded all aspects of the lives of the Puritans is evident in Sewall's own self-examination in these entries and in his description of the spiritual turmoil within his fifteen-year-old daughter, who had been deeply affected by hearing and reading sermons. Sewall's statement of repentance for his participation in the witchcraft trials makes it clear that he believed that God intervened in people's daily lives, punishing sinfulness and rewarding virtue. In his unsuccessful wooing of Madam Winthrop we see the pragmatic side of Sewall as he tries to convince her of the financial and practical advantages of marrying him.

Sarah Kemble Knight

FROM *The Private Journal of a Journey from Boston to New York*

This brief excerpt from Knight's *Journal* reveals the adventurous spirit and fortitude of this woman who, in 1704 at thirty-eight, set out on horseback over rugged terrain from Boston to New Haven and New York City. Knight was a third-generation American, born in Boston and married to a shipowner many years her senior, who died before 1706. She distinguished herself in Boston as a preparer of legal documents and proprietress of a writing school. The 126-mile journey from Boston to New Haven, through wilderness with few roads, took five days of hard travel, which Knight records in detail. She undertook the journey in order to assist a relative in New Haven with some legal matters; after spending two months there, she went with another relative on a two-week visit to New York City. Knight's journal is of particular interest to social historians because of the detailed record it provides of daily life during the Colonial period. Her entry for December 6, for instance, includes a wealth of information on architecture, the decorative arts, social relationships, and eating habits among the citizens of New York.

William Byrd

FROM *The Secret Diary of William Byrd of Westover, 1709-1712*

In contrast to the portrait in Sewall's diary of a society very much caught up in serious self-examination of the soul, Byrd's diary is full of country walks, meetings with important people, flirtations and stolen kisses, petty quarrels with his wife, "flourishes" on the billiard table, beatings of slaves—all related with a detachment not found in the journals of either Sewall or Woolman. Byrd's is not a world in which actions had grave meaning or portent. If anything in his routine is neglected it is his prayers, and such omissions do not trouble his mind. Neither does he feel spiritually imperiled by his "wicked thoughts," lewd speech and actions, or arbitrary mistreatment of slaves. There is throughout the sense of comfortable confidence of one who expects the "good health, good thoughts, and good humor" he enjoys. He is, nonetheless, a man of learning, who read several modern languages in addition to the Hebrew, Latin, and Greek mentioned in these entries and whose personal library was the second largest in the American colonies. Interesting comparisons can be made among the worldviews reflected in the diaries of Sewall, Byrd, and Woolman.

John Woolman

FROM *The Journal of John Woolman*

Unlike the journals of Sewall and Byrd, Woolman's journal is a narrative rather than a series of discrete entries. In its synthesis of experiences and reflections, it is closer to spiritual autobiography than to journal. As a Quaker minister, Woolman traveled from New England to the Carolinas, visiting Colonial Quaker meetings. His observations of slavery in the South confirmed his desire to abolish slaveholding among Quakers. At a time when there was no organized abolitionist movement, Woolman waged a personal campaign, contacting slaveholders and writing essays that linked economic, political, and spiritual issues. Shortly after his death, the Friends did abolish slavery among their members and became as well a prominent voice in the call for national abolition of slavery. His early response to the killing of the robins that appears in this excerpt reflects Woolman's compassion for all living things. Students will be able to compare the positions of Woolman, Sewall, and Byrd on the issue of slavery and on the interrelationship of spiritual and worldly concerns in their lives.

Questions for Discussion

1. The preceding commentaries on the Sewall, Byrd, and Woolman journals outline several differences in attitude toward class, religion, economics and success, education, sex, and family.

2. Knight's journal entries reveal an open-minded woman of her times who is characterized by her energy, fortitude, warmth, compassion, and sense of humor. That she is receptive to diversity is apparent in her description of New York, a city she nevertheless left with "no little regret."

Iroquois Creation Myth

This myth explaining the creation of the Earth and the beginning of human life reflects the kind of spiritual union of the Native American with nature that Luther Standing Bear speaks of in "What the Indian Means to America." According to this myth, several creatures took part in creating the floating island that would be home to Hah-gweh-di-yu, the creator and protector, and his evil twin, Hah-gweh-da-ĕt-găh, the destroyer. Without the cooperative efforts of the Duck, the Beaver, the Muskrat, and the Turtle, there would have been no land on which humankind could grow, and it is the water birds who bear the fertile earth mother Ata-en-sic down onto the new-formed land. Students may wish to research some other creation myths from Native American mythology to explore whether common elements can be found. Closeness to the land and to nature will be a recurring theme. In the Tewa creation myth, for instance, people actually emerged from within the Earth, much as plants do, and their sacred ceremonial chambers were built beneath the ground to honor the life-giving Earth.

Questions for Discussion

1. See above.

2. When Hah-nu-nah the Turtle stirs, "the seas rise in the great waves, and . . . violent earthquakes yawn and devour." Hah-gweh-da-ĕt-găh "sundered the mountains . . . herded hurricanes in the sky which frowned with mad tempests." Students can be asked to work quotations into their sentences in answering this question.

Luther Standing Bear
"What the Indian Means to America"

Standing Bear states eloquently some of the values of the Native American way of life—brotherhood, generosity, honesty, justice, love of nature, respect for all life, faith in a good and omnipotent God. These values, Standing Bear asserts, are a natural part of the North American continent, "for the hand that fashioned the continent also fashioned the man for his surroundings" (2). A sharp contrast is drawn between these "natural" ways of the Native Americans and the ways of the descendants of European settlers who still, because of their comparatively recent arrival on the continent, do not understand the land. Standing Bear's rhetorical style is worth comment, particularly his use of rhythm and parallelism. Paragraph 25, with its powerful repetition of "when" clauses, is similar in style and effect to sections of Martin Luther King's "Letter from Birmingham Jail" (see especially paragraph 14). Interesting comparisons can be made between Standing Bear's sense of what the Indian means to America and Michael Dorris's observations on American pop culture's oddly inappropriate appropriation of Native American symbols in "Crazy Horse Malt Liquor and Other Cultural Metaphors."

Questions for Discussion

1. The fundamental spiritual law is that the land of America is still vested in the spirit of the Indian. The Indian is part of America's formative processes; the roots of the white man's "tree of life have not yet grasped the rock and soil" (4).

2. The white man relied on his written law and insisted that he had been guided by the will of his God. The final abuse was the excuse that the Indians were savages.

3. Indian songs and dances, "as varied as the emotions which inspire them," connect the Native American in an immediate and spiritual way to "Mother Earth." Without songs and dances, the Indian's spirit will die.

4. Standing Bear uses the familiar image of the Indian to signify pride and to elicit sympathy. The personal "I" demonstrates the author's loyalty to his people. The parallel structure and the rhetorical questions (paragraphs 14–16, for example) serve to dramatize the author's central message.

Vine Deloria, Jr.
"Indian Humor"

In this essay, Deloria focuses on the sense of humor that, contrary to "the image of the granite-faced grunting redskin . . . perpetuated by American mythology," pervades Native American culture. The examples of Indian humor Deloria provides demonstrate some of the social functions that humor plays within an ethnic or other identity group. Groups that have been the victims of stereotyping and insult humor directed at them by more dominant groups often retaliate and defend themselves with their own humor based on sarcasm, parody, and reversal. The Custer, Columbus, and BIA jokes described by Deloria fall into this category. But Deloria points out that Indian humor also contains a strong element of humorous self-deprecation and teasing used to defuse tensions, demonstrate humility, and reinforce solidarity. This essay could lead to a discussion of the function of various kinds of ethnic humor, both the confrontational humor that is directed at one group by another as a means of belittling and the gentler intragroup humor that consists of jokes members of a particular group tell about themselves.

Questions for Discussion

1. The different types of humor Deloria mentions are teasing, self-deprecation, jokes, and satire. Humor is "the cement" that holds the Native American community together. When people can laugh both at those who have insulted them and at themselves, they can survive.

2. This essay is an analysis in which Deloria divides humor into several categories. He develops each section with enough examples (e.g., Columbus and Custer jokes) to make his generalizations credible.

Mary Crow Dog
"We AIM Not to Please"

Crow Dog describes the "lift" the American Indian Movement (AIM) gave to Native Americans during the late 1960s and 1970s. She explains that "it defined our goals and expressed our innermost yearnings. It set a style for Indians to imitate." That style was one of hope and pride, of confidence, defiance, and political activism. Crow Dog notes that after the occupation of Alcatraz island in 1970, young Indian men no longer had "that hangdog reservation look" and that the new sense of unity and purpose inspired many Native Americans to give up self-destructive use of substances such as alcohol, marijuana, and glue. The Trail of Broken Treaties, a unified march on Washington, D.C., in the fall of 1972, culminating in the occupation of the BIA building on Constitution Avenue was for the participants a "baptism of fire." Crow Dog points out that the message that emerged from this event was twofold. First came the realization that rowdiness and daring actions attracted media attention to their cause. Second came a feeling of empowerment from having "faced White America collectively, not as individual tribes." Crow Dog admits that not all the actions of AIM were admirable and that tribal pride still sometimes stands in the way of Indian unity, but she feels that the movement helped bring Native Americans together in pursuit of common goals. Although AIM took some of its spirit and rhetoric from the various black movements, Crow Dog points out that a fundamental difference between the two groups is that blacks "want what the whites *have* . . . They want *in*. We Indians want *out!*" The events that Crow Dog relates and the seventy-one-day armed siege at Wounded Knee, South Dakota, in 1973 brought the separatist goals of the militant leadership of AIM into the national consciousness.

Questions for Discussion

1. Although the selection is reflective, the tone serves to convey the attitude of a militant movement and to show that Crow Dog's feelings have not altered significantly. The diction in paragraphs 13, 14, and 16 are among numerous examples of strident prose.

2. Crow Dog sees many parallels between the two minority groups' desires for change and recognition. She argues convincingly, however, that the African-Americans want what the whites have, the Native Americans do not.

3. The middle generation has been torn between two cultures, two value systems. The elderly never let go, and the young were prepared to romanticize their heritage. Similar attitudinal differences often exist among first-, second- and third-generation immigrant families.

Michael Dorris
"Crazy Horse Malt Liquor and Other Cultural Metaphors"

Dorris offers a bitter commentary on the ways in which the dominant culture has decontextualized and applied to its own activities and products certain features and symbols of Native American culture. To name an alcoholic beverage after a Native American leader when Native Americans suffer high rates of alcohol-related disability and death seems to Dorris inappropriate and insensitive. The Crazy Horse Malt Liquor marketing strategies, with their false evocation of a history not nearly as noble and romantic as what the labels suggest, are just one of a number of ways in which American society has insulted Native Americans while ignoring their problems. Dorris's bitterness emerges clearly in his final paragraph. An interesting comparison can be made between Dorris's sense of what the Native American means to America and Standing Bear's vision of what he or she *should* mean.

Questions for Discussion

1. The rhetorical questions in paragraphs 6 and 8, for example, add irony to Dorris's tone, and they force readers to consider obvious and uncomfortable answers. The thesis is not stated directly; rather, it is implied through numerous examples. The sarcasm of the closing is a powerful technique to emphasize the Native American point of view.

2. See above.

Paula Gunn Allen
"Where I Come from Is Like This"

Allen describes the ways in which the Indian and Anglo-European views of women differ. Among Native Americans, she explains, women are seen as "powerful, socially, physically, and metaphysically"—never as "mindless, helpless, simple, or oppressed." The expectations raised by these two conflicting traditions put Indian women in a "bicultural bind." There are, of course, other bicultural binds afflicting Native Americans. Allen mentions, for instance, that respectable, loving, civilized white people" often have distorted and simplistic views of Native Americans as either "howling, bloodthirsty beings" or "exotic curios." During her "formal, white, Christian education," Allen was introduced to these views, which contrasted sharply with Indian life as she knew it. She describes the loving, family-centered way of life she knew as a child and states that proximity to Anglo-European society has in fact had dehumanizing rather than "civilizing" effects on Native American society.

Questions for Discussion

1. and 2. Perceptions of Native American women vary from tribe to tribe, but no tribes "question the power of femininity." The image of menstruation serves to exemplify the strength and power of nonwhite notions of women. The author contrasts this reality with how whites believe Native Americans regard women. The dichotomy suggests the bicultural bind Native American women find themselves in.

3. The catalogue documents the importance of stories to Native Americans as well as revealing a strong mother/daughter bond. It contrasts with the less reliable "non-Indian" interpretations of Native American customs in paragraph 4.

Oscar Handlin

FROM *The Uprooted*

In his excerpt from his 1952 Pulitzer Prize-winning book, Handlin describes social and economic changes that led 35 million people to leave Europe for the United States during the eighteenth and nineteenth centuries. A dramatic rise in the population of Europe beginning in the eighteenth century strained the family- and village-centered social and economic structures. The number of children living to maturity meant larger families who could no longer be fed or employed on available land. When insular self-sufficiency shifted to a market economy, those with little land on which to raise marketable crops were severely disadvantaged. Crop failures created disastrous situations and provided the impetus for a move to the cities and abroad. With economic changes came changes in the static nature of the social order. The narrator in Abraham Cahan's *The Rise of David Levinsky,* crossing to New York on a Bremen steamship, remembers one response to his embarkation: "Are you crazy? You forget your place, young man!" With the dramatic movement of populations, one's "place" was no longer a known and inherited quality but something to be created. Handlin ends his list of the numbers coming to the United States from various countries with the question, "What manner of refuge lay there?"—a question that is answered in part by the selections that follow. It is a question students might be asked to answer after reading the solutions in this and other chapters in the Ethnic Journeys section of the text.

Questions for Discussion

1. See above.

2. The three phases are described in paragraphs 15-21. First, the few peasants with resources emigrated to the new world. Later, hundreds of thousands began to migrate after aid came from the gentry or the local parish. Finally, the new immigrants in the New World created a magnetic pole for those left behind.

Mary Gordon
"More that Just a Shrine: Paying Homage to the Ghosts of Ellis Island"

In this tribute to her ancestors and all the others who came to this country through the great immigration receiving center at Ellis Island, Gordon reflects the feelings of many Americans whose personal connection with American history began on this island in New York Harbor. Gordon focuses on the trials and traumas that marked the immigrants' first experiences of America. For her, Ellis Island represents "insecurity, obedience, anxiety, dehumanization, the terrified and careful deference of the displaced." Of the more than 16 million immigrants who arrived at Ellis Island, approximately 250,000 were rejected. Leading reasons for rejection were physical diseases that could pose health hazards to the general population, disabilities that could result in the inability to support oneself and thus in dependency on public support, and restrictions resulting from the influence of the eugenics movement. Gordon believes that the indignities suffered by many of the arrivals at Ellis Island were a result of the "eternal wrongheadedness of American protectionism and the predictabilities of simple greed." These experiences impressed upon these immigrants and their descendants a sense of not fully belonging here, a sense that "the country really belonged to someone else." She applauds their stoicism and determination in the face of these difficulties and tributes them with having added a lively spirit to American society.

Questions for Discussion

1. Answers will vary, of course, but many students will be surprised to discover that because of the shorter historical perspective of most of its citizens, their sense of America's history is quite different from that of "older" countries. Many students will regard their "personal history" as a history of another culture, the home of their forebears. A contrast of Gordon's attitude with Emma Lazarus's in "The New Colossus" might create a meaningful discussion.

2. The reasons for Gordon's reference to the Lazarus poem will become apparent in the discussion above. It is clear, though that Gordon does not see the same "symbolic" welcome for immigrants that Lazarus does.

Henry Pratt Fairchild

FROM *The Melting Pot Mistake*

The introduction to the Confrontations chapter gives some background on the eugenics movement in the United States, which was dedicated to maintaining or improving the mental and physical characteristics of the American population through controlling heredity. Applying evolutionary and genetic theories to the social realm, the eugenics movement posited a kind of hierarchy of moral and intellectual development along racial and ethnic lines. This kind of thinking provided a pseudoscientific respectability for nativist sentiments and influenced the restrictive immigration laws passed during the 1920s and defended by Fairchild. Students may well find Fairchild's views repugnant. He uses dehumanizing terms like "racial nondescripts," "mongrel," and "throwback," and invokes the dangerous concept of "racial purity." In addition, he begs the question by basing his argument on a false analogy between the mixing of human races and the cross-breeding of plants and animals. Fairchild praises the "outstanding characteristics" of what he calls the "English type" (which he says is also the "American type"). A "combination of a large amount of Nordic with smaller proportions of Mediterranean and Alpine." He states his belief that the racial mixing that would have taken place as a result of the unrestricted immigration of Chinese, Japanese, Hindus, blacks, and Malays would have resulted in a population "resembling much more closely a more primitive stage of human evolution." Fairchild's tone as he estimates of the "degree of . . . mongrelization" that will result from the genetic addition of "definitely esoteric elements" provides a striking contrast to the vision of racial mixing Margaret Mead presents in her conversation with James Baldwin.

Questions for Discussion

1. Fairchild reduces his brand of nativism to a biological issue as early as paragraph 2. It is important to point out that this selection was written nearly seventy years ago and is typical of one attitude that prevailed then. It is also important to point out that such pseudoscientific ethnocentric attitudes are still with us today.

2. One example is in paragraph 6, where Fairchild compares the pouring together of inert liquids to "race mixtures." In paragraph 10 he compares racial intermarriage to the cross-breeding of plants and animals. These analogies are effective only if we do not look at them closely;

when we do, we see that they are false analogies and distort rather than clarify.

3. He approves of changes in the immigration laws because the new laws will guarantee that the bulk of immigration is from northern and western Europe.

Richard O'Connor
"The German-Americans: The Great White Whale"

O'Connor describes the "Anglo-Teutonic amalgamation," the merging of Anglo-Saxon and German cultural entities, a cultural phenomenon by which Germans as a group have vanished into mainstream America. Although German influence on American society is obvious, the "ethnic disappearance" of this large ethnic group—i.e., their lack of a continued existence as an interest group or a voting block—is remarkable. O'Connor cites two major reasons for this disappearance. First, the German immigrants of the nineteenth century, many of whom were Protestant, well educated, and skilled workers or professionals, were much closer to the Anglo-Saxon center of American culture than other groups, such as the Irish, who arrived during the same period. A second factor contributing to their assimilation is that they represented a cross section of society rather than one particular religious, economic, or social segment.

Questions for Discussion

1. See above.

2. O'Connor ranks Scandinavians as "a close second" in successful assimilation. Answers will vary as students cite other groups that have been or are being drawn to the cultural center. In paragraphs 2-6 we find many examples of faint traces of German culture.

Lars Ljungmark

FROM *Swedish Exodus*

Ljungmark's description of the Swedish immigrants' passage to New York and on to Chicago and the Midwest during the 1800s is enlivened by letters written by immigrants to family and friends back home, menus from a steamship company, and useful English phrases from a Swedish-English handbook called *The Emigrant's Interpreter.* Ljungmark details the difficult conditions for steerage passengers, the pitfalls awaiting unsuspecting new arrivals in Chicago, and the isolation of frontier living. Forming small farming collectives enabled families to acquire equipment and maintain their farms even when it was necessary to work elsewhere during certain seasons to meet basic needs.

Questions for Discussion

1. Their greatest complaint was having to deal with passengers from other countries, particularly the Irish. Responses will vary.

2. The letters are more focused on hope and promise for a new and better life. The diaries often express disillusionment and describe hardships. Both letters and diaries add authenticity to the immigrant experience Ljungmark recounts.

Abraham Cahan

FROM *The Rise of David Levinsky*

In this excerpt from the early portion of his famous novel, Cahan conveys the feelings of anxiety, uncertainty, wonder, awe, admiration, and helplessness that crowd against each other in the consciousness of an immigrant newly arrived in nineteenth-century New York City. He describes an experience nearly universal for those beginning life in a newly adopted country—an experience that those who have not emigrated can share in some measure when they visit a foreign country alone. The narrator reports that the "unfriendly voices" of the immigration officials at Castle Garden "flavored all America with a spirit of icy hospitality that sent a chill through [his] very soul." Cahan provides a muted note of hopefulness as a counterpoint to his narrator's sense of abandonment at the end of the piece by having him remark that the first half-hour he spent alone in New York was one of the worst experiences of his thirty years in this country. The reader is thus left with a sense that there will soon be some relief from the narrator's "sickening sense of having been tricked, cast off, and abandoned." Selections like this one, Mary Gordon's, and others that reveal the trepidation with which immigrants begin their new lives can provide native-born American students with an enlightening view from the other side.

Questions for Discussion

1. Cahan uses a first-person narrator to convey the feelings of the immigrants. His detailed descriptions, authentic dialogue, and figurative language create a powerful mood. Students may be asked to underline what they regard as four or five of the most effective passages.

2. Psalm 104 is appropriate thematically since some of the verses are about the sea. The psalm also reinforces his faith; it reminds Cahan of "the way God took care of man and beast" and inspires him with hope for future.

Aleksandra Rembiénska
"A Polish Peasant Girl in America

Through Rembiénska's letters we are introduced to the circumscribed life and demanding work schedule experienced by many of those unskilled immigrants from eastern and southern Europe who comprised the bulk of the so-called new immigration in the early twentieth century. Domestic service was the most common source of employment for the women in this group, and although the schedule described by Rembiénska offered little opportunity for contact with American society, at least the living and working conditions were healthier than those in the tenements and unregulated sweatshops. Although Rembiénska says nothing about the conditions she left in Poland, her enthusiasm to help her brothers and sisters come to America indicates that, unsatisfactory as her life in domestic service is, it is an improvement over her life and prospects as a peasant in Poland. Her ambition is reflected not only in her desire to bring her siblings to this country but also in her moving from one position to another in order to obtain a higher salary.

Questions for Discussion

1. and 2. Responses will vary.

Harriet Jacobs

FROM *Incidents in the Life of a Slave Girl*

In this excerpt from her autobiography, Harriet Jacobs focuses on the peculiar morality of slaveholders who used their women slaves sexually and felt no compunction about playing the role of master to the slaves they had fathered. She describes her own "condition of shame and misery" in a household where both the master and his jealous wife hounded her relentlessly. While Jacobs maintains in this passage a consistently contemptuous attitude toward men who own slaves, her contempt for their wives is tempered by occasional sympathy for what they have to put up with from their husbands. With regard to her mistress's jealous rages she remarks, "I could not blame her," and later she expresses sympathy for the young women who marry slaveholders only to have their romantic illusions destroyed by their husbands' cavalier disregard of their wedding vows. In the very next paragraph, however, she describes the shameful treatment rendered by these women to the slave children fathered by their husbands. Jacobs seems to experience a kind of double vision, as both woman and slave, as she describes the behavior of these wives of slaveholders.

Questions for Discussion

1. The worst thing about being a "favorite" slave was her powerlessness in the face of a master's unwanted sexual advances.

2. The tone is courageous and convincingly antislavery. It is apparent Jacobs wished to reach white readers, especially Northern women. She showed how slavery corrupts the values of slave owners, both men and women.

3. Mrs. Flint detested Jacobs because she was aware of her husband's sexual indiscretions. Jacobs, on the other hand, pitied Mrs. Flint even though she knew she hated her presence. Both she and Mrs. Flint were helpless victims.

Martin Luther King, Jr. "Letter from Birmingham Jail"

King's defense of using nonviolent protest to draw attention to the injustice of segregation laws is an outstanding example of effective argumentation. King's control of tone, establishment of common ground with a hostile audience, rebuttal of opposing views, use of analogy, references to the Bible and to many secular and theological authorities, use of parallelism, placement of emotive language, and his employment of deductive logic (as, for instance, in the proof that segregation laws are unjust) are just some of the many avenues to explore in this exceptionally rich selection. Students should pay careful attention to King's diction (noting for instance that the work most frequently used to describe his feelings about the events in Birmingham and in the struggle for civil rights is "disappointed"), to the placement of his attacks on "white moderates" and the "white church," and to the placement (first in the essay) of his responses to the charges of those who opposed his actions in Birmingham. A comparison of the diction, tone, and message of this selection with that of the Malcolm X selection following it provides a sense of the very different approaches of two important black leaders in the struggle for racial justice.

Questions for Discussion

1. See above.

2. Answers will vary.

3. King argues we are obliged to obey just laws and, conversely, to disobey unjust laws. A just law is one that "squares" with moral law or with the law of God. An unjust law is one that degrades human personality and/or is imposed by one group on another group who had no say in its formation. Unjust laws are not rooted in eternal and natural law. Examples will vary and will likely be controversial; immigration laws, capital punishment, abortion, and censorship have been debated on such considerations.

Malcolm X

FROM *The Autobiography of Malcolm X*

In this selection from his autobiography, Malcolm X describes the mass rallies held by the Nation of Islam and the way in which he would prepare the audience to hear the preaching of the leader of the Nation of Islam, Elijah Muhammad. In contrast to the approach of Martin Luther King, Jr., that of Malcolm X during the period of his association with Elijah Muhammad is characterized by a fundamental and irreconcilable distrust of the white man, who is depicted as the "Caucasian devil slavemaster," the enemy of black people. Malcolm X ridicules King's commitment to civil disobedience, which he refers to here as "sitting-in, sliding-in, wading-in, eating-in, diving-in, and all the rest." The key to black empowerment according the Malcolm X does not lie in an appeal to what King would see as fundamental human reasonableness and compassion, the pursuit of shared goals, but in an embracing of the adversarial relationship between blacks and whites. The notion of separatism is introduced when Malcolm X remarks, "when we stay here among him [the white man], he continues to keep us at the very *lowest level* of his society!" (See Headnote and Introduction to this chapter, p. 159, for Malcolm X's views after his break with the Nation of Islam.)

Questions for Discussion

1. Spike Lee's film and increasing sales of *The Autobiography of Malcolm X* suggest that many now view Malcolm X as a political martyr. Students will find parallels in the lives and deaths of Martin Luther King, Jr., John F. Kennedy, and Robert F. Kennedy.

2. Answers will vary.

Stokely Carmichael (Kwame Toure) and Charles V. Hamilton "Black Power"

Carmichael and Hamilton define Black Power as black self-determination and self-identity and full participation in making the decisions that affect black people. They point out that in order to establish a bargaining position in a pluralistic society a group must achieve solidarity, and that solidarity can be achieved by cultivating self-sufficiency and self-definition. In the case of African-Americans, this means rejecting the values of the middle class, which Carmichael and Hamilton see as supporting a racist system based on "material aggrandizement." African-Americans must become leaders in their own communities, reject the notions of blacks as lazy, shiftless, apathetic, and redefine themselves as an energetic, determined, intelligent, peace-loving people. The authors observe that "before a group can enter the open society, it must first close ranks." Such closing of the ranks is sometimes viewed as reverse racism, a charge the authors rebut by pointing out that racism excludes for the purposes of subjugating those excluded, while Black Power advocates independent black initiative for the purpose of achieving self-determination. The "open society" of which Carmichael and Hamilton speak is one that is truly free and competitive. Because they believe that the values of middle-class American society do not truly support such openness, supporting instead "cloistered little closed societies tucked away neatly in tree-lined suburbia," the authors reject the assumption that the basic institutions of this society must be preserved.

Questions for Discussion

1. Answers will vary.
2. See above.
3. Answers will vary.

Shelby Steele
"Individualism and Black Identity"

Steele explains why, in their continuing search for a viable identity within American society, it is time for blacks to shift "from a wartime to a peacetime identity," from the kind of collective racial identity advocated by the Black Power movement to individual identity based on achievement. Steele states that the Black Power movement had the positive effect of giving blacks the "power to be racially unapologetic," but he feels that the kind of "adversarial, victim-focused identity" it promoted limited rather than expanded opportunities for individual blacks. He maintains that its focus on the continued victimization of blacks by whites implied that the fate of blacks was in society's control rather than in their own control and thus contributed to "demoralization and inertia" and debilitating self-doubt. In contrast, Steele reports that his own experience revealed, beyond "America's residual racism," a "remarkable range of opportunity." He advocates a new measure of black identity that will not equate lack of achievement with being "solidly Black," not judge those who move up in society as "somehow less black" and not associate academic achievement with whiteness (see also Sophronia Scott Gregory's "The Hidden Hurdle" in the chapter on Education). In contrast to Carmichael and Hamilton's belief that black solidarity is the necessary first step to establishing a "bargaining position" within American society, Steele makes a case for "individual effort within the American mainstream—rather than collective action against the mainstream—as our means of advancement."

Questions for Discussion

1. Steele feels that the Black Power movement provided him with a strong sense of racial identity but a diminished sense of individual identity. Steele's stance may surprise students, especially his argument that such racial pride leads to a self-image based on victimization.

2. Steele suggests that minorities often focus on their oppressors rather than on themselves. The resulting self-doubt and fear lead to what he calls an "inferiority anxiety." He argues that African-American culture needs to become more experienced in its use of freedom.

3. Answers will vary. Students may wish to take another look at the Preface for Students (pp. xix–xxi) and make use of their responses to assignments 1, 3, and 4 on pp. 40–41.

4. Steele feels such leaders put too much emphasis on victimization and suffering. He contends they must "tell us what they tell their own children at night": to work hard as individuals to achieve success.

Jesse Jackson
From his "Speech Before the Democratic National Convention, 1992"

In this speech at the convention that nominated Bill Clinton and Al Gore, Jackson calls for a moral vision that transcends race and politics, that turns "pain into partnership, not . . . into polarization." Stating that "we are more interdependent than we realize." Jackson emphasizes the need for a united effort in the "continuing struggle for justice and decency." In his sentence "We are inextricably bound together in a single garment of destiny" (paragraph 8) students may recognize echoes of Martin Luther King, Jr.'s "We are caught in an inescapable network of mutuality, tied in a single garment of destiny" (paragraph 4). They may recognize as well familiar rhetorical devices such as repetition (e.g., "In jail . . . In jail . . . In jail . . .," 15; "It was anti-Semitic and wrong . . . It was racist and wrong . . . And it is racist and wrong . . .," 10), and parallelism (e.g., the final sentence in 3). Jackson's message also has much in common with King's, as he appeals to individuals to "reach across the lines that divide by race, region, or religion." Reviewing the last five readings in this chapter, students will be able to contrast the predominantly confrontational stances of Malcolm X and Stokely Carmichael/Charles Hamilton with the more accommodational stances of King, Steele, and Jackson.

Questions for Discussion

1. See above.

2. Jackson uses history to support his argument for partnership rather than polarization. He cites historical incidents that all right-thinking people will regard as wrong—the internment of Japanese-Americans during World War II and the refusal of the United States to admit German Jews in 1939—and hopes to transfer his listeners' outrage at these happenings to current situations in Haiti and South Africa.

Clara E. Rodriguez
"Salsa in the Melting Pot"

Rodriguez uses the term "Latinos" for Americans of Puerto Rican, Mexican, Spanish-speaking Caribbean and South and Central American ancestry. She observes that this group, which will be the largest single minority in the United States by the year 2000, will "invigorate" many aspects of U.S. cultural life, but she feels that the most significant influence Latinos will have will be on the ways in which race is thought of. Rodriguez points out that whereas in the United States race is though of as a biologically determined black/white dichotomy, Latinos tend to perceive race as more cultural than biological. "In Latin America," she says, "race refers to a group of people who are felt to be somehow similar in their essential nature. That essential nature depends on biology but also physical appearance, class, education, manners and other 'social' variables." As evidence of the fact that people are beginning to reject the notion of race as merely biological without regard to culture, Rodriguez cites the dramatic increase in the numbers of individuals choosing not to define themselves on census reports as any of the "traditional" racial categories (white, black, Asian, Native American) and choosing instead to identify themselves as "other." The rapid growth of the Hispanic population in the United States, among which one finds some people with predominantly Caucasian, black, or Asian physical traits and many with characteristics that would lie between any of these on a racial continuum, has had a large influence on the need to rethink traditional categories. Rodriguez believes that moving away from what she calls the "dichotomous view of race in the United States" is a necessary step toward eliminating social inequities and realizing a truly pluralistic society.

Questions for Discussion

1. See above.

2. The social view that Rodriguez describes does not rely on a simple black/white dichotomy. The "social race" orientation of the Latinos forces others to examine what one is culturally rather than only what one is biologically, thus seeking commonality rather than differences as a basis for identification. Confrontation is more likely to erupt in a dichotomous situation.

Luis Valdez and Stan Steiner

FROM *Aztlan*

Valdez and Steiner point out that the term "New World" to describe the Americas of the European explorers is at best inaccurate since the Mexican civilization was already an old one before the arrival of the Spanish: "This was not a new world at all. It was an ancient world civilization based on a distinct concept of the universe." To distinguish themselves from the "long line of hyphenated-immigrants to the New World," those of Mexican heritage frequently choose to call themselves Chicanos, thereby rejecting what Valdez and Steiner describe as "efforts to make us disappear into the white melting pot. "Chicano," then, is a term of ethnic and racial pride to describe La Raza (La Raza de Bronce, the bronze race)—Mestizos who are racially "a powerful blend of indigenous America with European-Arabian Spain." The term "Aztlan" describes the cultural and racial amalgamation of La Raza. Valdez and Steiner's description of the mixing of races that occurred in Nueva España bears out Clara Rodriguez's thesis about the different way Latinos have of looking at race. The authors' observation that in spite of the range of color and features found among Chicanos, "we are casually labeled Caucasian" will remind students of the change in consciousness evident in recent census data reported by Rodriguez. The tone in this selection is bold and defiant, and students should note the diction and specifically the charged language which produces this tone. One notable example is at the end of paragraph 5, where the authors describe the barrio's "having survived even the subversive onslaught of the twentieth-century neon gabacho commercialism that passes for American culture." Valdez and Steiner describe the Chicano as created and energized by the spirit of the Revolution of 1910, the revolution of Emiliano Zapata and Pancho Villa, which the authors characterize as "a glorious affront to the aristocracy." Students will have various reactions to the tone of this essay and its implied political agenda. The ways in which this essay and the one by Clara Rodriguez differ may remind them of contrasts between the pieces by Malcolm X and Stokely Carmichael and those by Martin Luther King, Jr., and Jesse Jackson.

Questions for Discussion

1. The tone of this selection is angry and confrontational. Paragraphs 1 and 2 suggest the firm position that Valdez and Steiner take. The final sentence in paragraph 5 is one of many denunciations of "American culture." Paragraph 9 contains examples of effective figurative language.

2. The Meslizos have no race of their own. La Raza (the race) describes a people who are the products of a true melting pot process: "Miscegenation went joyously wild, creating the many shapes, sizes, and hues of La Raza" (4).

3. The barrio is "full of *chingaderas* imitating the way of the *patrón*. . . . Frijoles and tortillas remain, but the totality of the Indio's vision is gone" (6). Students will differ in their responses to this question, but will generally recognize the presence of the dominant American culture in other ethnic population centers. See especially "A Melding of Cultures," pp. 242-250.

Henry Gonzalez
"Reverse Racism"

In this 1969 speech to Congress, Gonzalez expresses his opposition to the confrontational tactics of the Mexican-American Youth Organization whose leader advocated violence as a means of resisting "'assimilating into this gringo society in Texas'" and accused those who opposed him as having "gringo tendencies." Gonzalez sees these actions and attitudes as examples of a "new racism" in Texas that emerged as a response to the region's history of racial politics and oppression against Mexican-Americans. Gonzalez is opposed to any kind of racism and to what he calls "the politics of confrontation," believing that seeking confrontation and fanning the flames of hatred cannot lead to the achieving of justice, that one cannot pursue "a just cause without unjust tactics." He feels that the new racism, a "reverse racism" of Mexican-Americans against whites, risks a confusion of seeking justice with seeking revenge and thereby threatens the country's progress toward unity and universal justice. Students might be encouraged compare Gonzalez's view of reverse racism with that in Carmichael and Hamilton's "Black Power."

Questions for Discussion

1. Gonzalez is addressing an audience that is reasonable and moderate. He makes this clear in his opening sentence. In paragraph 4 Gonzalez presents an analogy with two laws of physics to explain and reverse racism, an analogy appropriate to an educated audience.

2. The second law of physics Gonzalez cites in paragraph 4 is an effective means to begin to develop such a definition—"for a given force there is an equal and opposite reaction." Gonzalez argues that we must avoid adding the politics of race to the politics of confrontation; we can't have both justice and revenge.

Oscar Hijuelos
"Visitors, 1965"

In this excerpt from his novel *Our House in the Last World,* Hijuelos presents two different versions of the Cuban-American experience. Hector, whose parents Alejo and Mercedes have been in the United States for twenty years but have not experienced the upward mobility of the American dream, looks forward to the arrival of his aunt, uncle, and cousins with mixed emotions. For him they represent the "real Cubans," coming from a land he thinks of as a "dream house," where his mother "had once lived a life of style, dignity, and happiness." He has idealized memories of a childhood trip to Cuba. Anticipating the arrival of his relatives. Hector regrets his "unpracticed, practically nonexistent" Spanish and feels "sick at heart for being so Americanized." At the same time that he cherishes his notion of the "real" Cuba, however, he also has a fear of what he calls "Cubanness"—those aspects of his own Cuban-American experiences that are the antithesis of dignity and style. His father's drunkenness, the "dingy furniture and the cracking walls and the cheap decorative art, plaster statues, and mass-produced paintings" have made him want to distance himself from the language and culture of his parents. These contradictory feelings about what it means to be Cuban and his fear that his father's behavior and their dreary surroundings will reveal "just who the Santinios really were" cause Hector to be withdrawn in his dealings with his extended family. His brother remarks, "He's just dumb when it comes to being Cuban." When the relatives eventually move out on their own, Hector is "astounded" at their success in adjusting to their new lives and in acquiring the material possessions that his own family still could not afford. Students might consider the ways in which Hector's family differs from his aunt's who "did not allow the old world, the past, to hinder them." The two families may well have come to the United States with different expectations—one arriving before the revolution that made returning to Cuba virtually impossible, the other escaping gratefully from an oppressive regime. An interesting comparison can be made between Hector's and Richard Rodriguez's feelings toward the Spanish language and what it represents (see "The Education of Richard Rodriguez" in the Language chapter).

Questions for Discussion

1. Pedro and Luisa readily left their "old world" customs behind. As Hijuelos writes, "They did not cry but walked straight ahead." In many respects Alejo and Mercedes were never able to leave Cuba. Alejo was

more willing to accept Pedro's successes. Perhaps he knows Pedro and Luisa had to suffer much more in Cuba since they lived there after the revolution; perhaps he is simply not ambitious. Mercedes was unable to temper her jealousy,

2. Hector was clearly torn between the old Cuba represented by his parents and the new Cuba of his aunt and uncle. He struggled to understand his own cultural identity as he reconciled his "beautiful" memories with the ugly realities of his own life. He romanticized what Pedro and Luisa represented. He was tired of being so "Americanized," yet he must have been puzzled by Pedro and Luisa's rapid assimilation.

Elena Padilla
"Profound Changes"

In this excerpt from *Up from Puerto Rico,* Padilla examines the ways in which individuals and relationships change when Puerto Ricans come to the United States. She finds the ways in which these migrants view the new ways and values depends in large part on whether they think of themselves as settlers or transients. While the settler arriving in New York "expects to fulfill his social needs in relation to living in New York," the transient maintains strong emotional ties with the homeland, has a strong sense of his national identity as a Puerto Rican, and does not plan to stay in the United States permanently. Padilla notes that "social and cultural changes among Hispanos are a conscious preoccupation" among migrants, with some of the changes being regarded as good and some as bad. While most migrants see advantages in the better pay and greater availability of material goods in the United States, the changes in the expected behavior patterns of men, women, and children and in the kinds of relationships among family members draw mixed reviews from the individuals Padilla interviews. Students may find some connections between this essay and the selection from the Hijuelos novel. Toward the end of the Hijuelos piece, Hector, contemplating the success of his aunt's family and their apparently easy adjustment to life in the United States thinks, "They did not allow the old world, the past, to hinder them." Are there ways in which the two families demonstrate consciousness about their relationship to the United States?

Questions for Discussion

1. The transients, Padilla suggests, regard their future as gravitating toward Puerto Rico. On the other hand, migrants view their future as being "tied up with whatever life in New York may offer." Padilla uses the two types of immigrants to set up a contrast of reactions to life in the United States. The fundamental difference between settlers and transients is that the settler's life is organized in New York, while the transient's is both in New York and in Puerto Rico. She used experiences of specific immigrants to illustrate the different attitudes.

2. Some Puerto Ricans feel that when women get to New York, they "act too free." In Puerto Rico women are subservient, and in New York they are eager to test newfound freedoms. Padilla uses specific voices of "transient" immigrants to render such judgments.

George G. Church
"A Melding of Cultures"

Church describes the recent immigration of Hispanics to the United States, noting some of the demographic data on the various groups. He defines "Hispanic" as a catchall term, embracing people of "white, black, Indian and, frequently, thoroughly mixed ancestry who hail from countries that sometimes seem to have little in common except historical traditions and the Spanish language." Never before, Church observes, has the United States absorbed so many newcomers with the same language. The very size of the Spanish-speaking population allows for a considerable degree of insularity that, in combination with the youth and fertility of the population, can spark racism and Anglo fears of cultural inundation. Students will find connections between this essay and the pieces by Padilla and Hijuelos since Church considers the experiences of Cubans and Puerto Ricans among others. The questioning by some Hispanics of the desirability of giving up the Spanish language and traditions has a direct connection with the debate on multicultural education that is the topic of the final unit of this text.

Questions for Discussion

1. The first three paragraphs prepare the audience for the thesis by giving three specific and geographically diverse examples of Hispanic influence in the United States. The rest of the article explains how the Hispanic influence became so widespread and what types of social and economic developments we might expect.

2. Church points out that the Hispanic influence is not from one unified force. Rather, it comes from many different cultures. Answers will vary, but it seems likely students will agree that understanding Hispanics requires an understanding of their diversity.

Richard T. Schaefer
" 'Model Minority?' "

Schaefer probes the reality behind the model-minority view of Asian-Americans that is drawn from their academic and socioeconomic success as a group in comparison to other minority groups. He finds that the positive stereotype attached to Asian-Americans disregards the diversity of the group as a whole and does little to lessen anti-Asian discrimination. It may, in fact, exacerbate it by seeming to prove the American ideal of upward mobility and thus reflect badly on blacks and Hispanics who are not as a group achieving at a comparable level. (The black-Korean conflict that came to national attention during the 1992 rioting in Los Angeles is the subject of the essays by Arthur Hu and Elaine H. Kim in the Confrontations chapter.) In addition, Schaefer points out that this positive stereotyping may work to the disadvantage of some Asian-Americans since they are generally not considered eligible for some of the special considerations given to members of other minority groups. In his analysis of income and employment figures, Schaefer points out ways statistics can be misleading. His discussion of "family income" data, for instance, draws attention to the different ways in which families can use their income-producing potential and may remind students of the family of Pedro and Luisa in Hijuelos' "Visitors, 1965." The notion of a positive stereotype redounding to one's disadvantage may be a new idea to many students, but once introduced to it they will be able to relate it to experiences in their own families, schools, and communities.

Questions for Discussion

1. Asian-Americans live almost exclusively in urban areas where incomes tend to be higher and in regions where prevailing wages are higher. Also, on average they are better educated than whites.

2. Schaefer discusses the question of Asian "panethnic identity" and diversity in paragraphs 16-20. Students can be advised here to make use of reference works—almanacs, government publications, *The Harvard Encyclopedia of American Ethnic Groups,* and so on—and to report on their findings.

Mitsuye Yamada
"Asian Pacific Women and Feminism"

Yamada here addresses an issue of group identification introduced in the Preface for Students (pp. xix). Because one is a member of many groups simultaneously, the pressure to identify unequivocably with one in particular —to, as Yamada says, "sign a 'loyalty oath' favoring one over the other"— asks an individual in effect to ignore important aspects of him/herself. In Yamada's case, the conflict of identities arises when the women's movement fails to address the combination of sexism and racism faced by women of color, who need to be politically and socially active in affirming their ethnic identities as well as dealing with issues particular to women. Asian Pacific women, Yamada says, are expected to be rather passive and apolitical, a stereotype that is not true to the facts of their lives and that allows others to overlook their needs. She hopes that the women's movement will expand its awareness and agenda to include issues of race as well as gender. Yamada speaks of the "selective racism" in the United States, citing specifically the internment of Japanese-Americans during World War II. Yamada's sense that anti-Asian feeling is never far from the surface in the United States has unfortunately been confirmed by an increase in anti-Japanese activity in California. Officials believe that strained trade relations between the United States and Japan may be the immediate cause of this new hostility. For more on the internment experience, see Ted Nakashima's "Why Won't America Let Us Be Americans?" For more on the problems and concerns of women who are struggling to overcome both gender and ethnic stereotypes, see Sarah Nieves-Squires, "Hispanic Women on Campus" in the Education chapter.

Questions for Discussion

1. Asian women are stereotyped even by other women as being uniformly "passive, sweet, etc." They are regarded as having "no history behind [them] . . . as the least political, or the least oppressed, or the most polite." Yamada believes that the stereotype is false and Asian Pacific American women must educate the public, both men and women.

2. International conflicts, particularly in the Third World, lead to abrupt changes in attitude toward immigrants and minorities in the United States who are members of a group involved in the conflict. The outcry against Iranian students in America during the Iran Hostage Crisis was an example of "selective racism." The treatment of Japanese-Americans during World War II was another.

Ted Nakashima "Why Won't America Let Us Be Americans?"

Nakashima writes from personal experience of the internment of Japanese-Americans that began two months after the attack on Pearl Harbor. There seemed to be no actual national security issues behind the mass expulsion of Japanese-Americans from the West Coast, since individuals who were considered a threat had already been under close surveillance. Americans of German and Italian ancestry were not treated in this manner. The fact that the Japanese-American population was concentrated on the West Coast, however, contributed to unfounded rumors and fears of sabotage. There was no doubt some quelling of hysteria in the taking of action, no matter how irrational, in response to the attack. There was also economic gain for those who were able to acquire at bargain prices property hastily liquidated by departing Japanese-Americans. The internment not only deprived citizens of their civil rights but also violated the principles that one is innocent until proven guilty and that racial equality exists before the law. Students will be struck by Nakashima's thoroughly American voice and patriotic concerns, which underlie the insult and apparent senselessness of his internment.

Questions for Discussion

1. The tone is impassioned; he speaks as a patriotic American who has been betrayed. The answers to the rhetorical questions in paragraphs 11 and 17 are obvious and are clearly meant to disquiet non-Japanese-Americans. The irony in paragraph 15 serves the same purpose.

2. Mitsuye Yamada discusses such examples of selective racism in the preceding selection. See Questions for Discussion #2.

Carlos Bulosan
"Filipino Fruit Pickers"

Bulosan describes the brutalizing existence of migrant farm workers in the unregulated fruit-producing industry of the West Coast. Suspicion and betrayal among the workers themselves and persecution by white society marked the lives of the workers and their employers with uncertainty and danger. Undaunted by the cruelty that surrounded him, the young Bulosan remained an innocent, looking forward eagerly to going to California and to finding a better life among trustworthy companions.

Questions for Discussion

1. The setting is oppressive from the outset, consistent with the dilemma of the migrant Filipinos. "Hard light," "ugliness," and "treeless mountains" create a bleak mood. During the escape the setting parallels the motif of distance and loneliness—"the night was silent and the stars . . . were as far away as home." After the escape the setting reflects the tone of hope and promise—"cool wind" and "bright stream."

2. The movement suggested in the conclusion—from fear and despair to hope and promise—is typical of the immigrant experience.

Alixa Naff
"Arabs in America"

Naff provides an overview of Arab immigration to the United States from the late nineteenth century to the present. She reports that the early immigrants were mostly Christians from what is now Syria and Lebanon. The vast majority earned a living by peddling, a vocation which, because it involved constant travel and contact with native-born Americans, resulted in rapid acculturation. In contrast, the more recent Arab immigrants have been mostly Muslims with a strong sense of Arab nationalism and a desire to maintain their ethnic and religious traditions. Naff suggests that without the Post-World War II immigration, which increased interest in Arab culture, and political events in the Middle East, which have solidified the Arab-American community in the face of perceived hostility toward Arabs, "Syrian-Americans might have Americanized themselves out of existence." Like the Yamada and Nakashima essays, Naff's piece points to the ways in which international events affect ethnic consciousness in the United States.

Questions for Discussion

1. See above.

2. Arab families were changed by the influence of American values. The long working hours of fathers weakened paternal authority in Arab-American household. Women came to desire more freedom, and children were attracted to the culture of the American middle class.

Dang Hong Loan
"A Tragic Voyage"

While a student at the University of Massachusetts, Loan interviewed Ly, the subject of this essay. Ly's experiences of fleeing Vietnam are not unusual, as many refugees were taken advantage of by those arranging their passage, frequently in boats that were hardly seaworthy, and by pirates who preyed on such boats in the waters off Vietnam. It is likely that Vietnamese students will have had similar experiences or know of friends or family members who did.

Questions for Discussion

1. Answers will vary.

PART III

LIVING IN MULTICULTURAL AMERICA

Tom Lehrer
"National Brotherhood Week"

Lehrer's satiric songs treat serious and sacrosanct subjects with wry humor —the Catholic Church in "The Vatican Rag," college traditions in "Fight Fiercely Harvard," nuclear war in "We Will All Go Together When We Go," and cross-cultural relations in "National Brotherhood Week." Here, his ridiculing of insincere cosmetic gestures toward the ideal of brotherhood highlights the need to take a closer look at the stereotypes and prejudices that sometimes lurk below outward shows of civility. Recordings of Lehrer performing his works are available, and students would probably enjoy hearing the music that accompanies the lyrics. Much of the wry effect is achieved through a contrast between harsh lyrics and humorously inappropriate lighthearted rhythms and melodies.

Andrew M. Greeley
"Social Turf"

Greeley sees territoriality and the drive to preserve a neighborhood as "strongly rooted in the human condition." He maintains that territoriality is not just "geographic" but "interactional" as well. It is a phenomenon that involves a commitment to "the interaction network and the institutions which fill up . . . [a] geographic space." Since Greeley feels that this need to maintain attachments to a place and its special rituals and relationships is part of human nature, he rejects the concept that technological advances have somehow altered human beings' needs for attachments to particular places and practices. He believes that people's passionate commitments to maintaining their neighborhoods are genuine. Even though efforts to maintain the character of a neighborhood frequently result in hostility and in the exclusion of people from different ethnic or religious backgrounds, Greeley believes that these efforts do not spring simply from racism and bigotry but rather from deep psychological human needs. Greeley's notion of the importance of the network of interrelationships within a neighborhood is illustrated by several of the other selections in this chapter, and students might return to his definition of what constitutes the special attraction of a neighborhood as they read the pieces by Lemann, Suárez, Petrakis, and Fair.

Questions for Discussion

1. In his opening paragraph Greeley points out a documented need for man "to stamp out a certain amount of physical space as 'his own.'" He goes on to suggest that comparisons with animals are largely metaphorical and that man's "biological instinct" for territory is "profoundly affected by his social structure and culture."

2. Greeley contends that humans may have a need for turf, but he goes on to say that this need is much more interactional (social) than it is geographical. It is the desire for "social turf" that makes Americans, particularly Americans of ethnic background, committed to neighborhoods.

3. See above.

Nicholas Lemann
"Clarksdale"

In this portion of his description of life in a Mississippi Delta town, Lemann (pronounced "lemon") focuses on the different versions of reality accepted by residents of the white and black neighborhoods of Clarksdale. Stories and legends about encounters between the races abound in both neighborhoods, but it is the black people whose lives are most defined and circumscribed by the attitudes and beliefs of their white counterparts. Fear and shame at how the social practices of lower-class blacks will affect the whites' stereotyped views of all blacks creates a rift in the black community between the poor blacks, who live in the Roundyard section, and the middle-class blacks, who live in the Brickyard. The speed with which the neighborhood block club moves to acculturate poor country blacks who happen to move into the Brickyard is a sign of racial pride. Teaching new arrivals the "middle-class standards of household maintenance" is important not only in terms of how well the newcomers will fit in but also in terms of maintaining the neighborhood's dignified demeanor vis-à-vis white Clarksdale.

Questions for Discussion

1. Stories were essential to the African-American residents in poor Delta towns like Clarksdale because they provided blacks with a means to record their experiences and feelings. The stories, "gradually burnished into legend," kept their memories alive and permitted them to be told more openly as forms of entertainment. The stories became a type of code through which truths about black and white experiences in Clarksdale—especially of white racism—could be transmitted, often "under a mask of slightly uncomprehending servility."

2. Although the African-American middle class had many secrets in towns like Clarksdale, the most important secret of all was the family life of poor blacks. The lifestyle and manners of the poor blacks "made social segregation a necessity" for whites who were looking for justification for their racial attitudes.

Mario Suárez
"El Hoyo"

Suárez's description of the Tucson barrio emphasizes the great individual variety among the Chicanos who live there as well as the common cultural elements they all share. The Chicanos of El Hoyo are like *capirotada,* a universal dish that tastes different in every household. The Suárez piece bears out Greeley's theory of the "interactional" elements that give character and unity to a neighborhood. As Suárez points out, people don't live in El Hoyo because of its scenic beauty or its safety—houses are made of unplastered adobe, license plates, and abandoned car parts, and the Santa Cruz River frequently floods the area—but because of its spirit of generosity and solidarity.

Questions for Discussion

1. "'Chicano' is the short way of saying 'Mexicano,'" and "the long way of referring to everybody." Suárez describes *"capirotada"* in his final paragraph. He points out that although the ingredients are similar, each family prepares it differently. He compares this dish to the diversity among Chicanos in El Hoyo.

2. Among the disadvantages of living in El Hoyo are ugliness, congestion, and filth. Other problems come from a rising crime rate as well as an often rising Santa Cruz River. Suárez lists ironically under its advantages the fact that "bill collectors are less likely to find you." He goes on to point out the importance of a sustained Chicano culture and community spirit.

Tom Coakley
"Burden of Arrival Is Felt by All"

In this article from the Boston *Globe,* Coakley examines some of the problems faced by Southeast Asian refugees and immigrants and by the communities in which they settle. He focuses on the experiences of several Massachusetts cities that have received large numbers of Southeast Asians, describing both the demands that meeting the needs of these new residents places on schools, housing, and social services and the difficulties of adjustment faced by individuals. His use of statistics helps underline the urgency of the situation. The writing style in this piece might deserve some comment. Since it was written for a newspaper, it exhibits some of the characteristics associated with newspaper journalism. Students may notice, for instance, the preponderance of very short one- and two-sentence paragraphs, a format demanded by the narrow columns in a newspaper, and the fact that sentences are direct, generally following a subject-verb pattern rather than beginning with introductory phrases or dependent clauses.

Questions for Discussion

1. The communities are faced with special needs in education, health care, housing, and social services. But Coakley points out that the strain on municipal services does not equal the burden placed on refugees who often fled horrible situations only to find themselves victims of suspicion and racial hatred in the United States. Innovative federal and state programs like Massachusetts' Gateway Cities program are attempts at meeting the many needs of municipalities and of refugees.

2. "Secondary migrants" move within the United States after their initial arrival. They are attracted to such cities as Lowell, Massachusetts, after learning of job opportunities and the large numbers of fellow immigrants. The secondary migration is difficult to control, and the need for new services often is overwhelming.

3. The two examples represent the extremes of the immigrant experience. Nam Koeun's world is one of poverty and despair. Meng Kouch, on the other hand, has become successful and financially independent.

Elise Amalie Waerenskjold "Four-Mile Prairie—Four Letters from Texas"

Waerenskjold's letters reveal an energetic woman, much involved in the physical and spiritual life of her community. She comments on the state of the livestock, the efforts of the community to recruit a new minister, the tragedies caused by the consumption of alcohol, her efforts to persuade publishers to donate books for their reading club, and her giving birth to a son at the age of forty-four. The community of Norwegians, Swedes, and Danes emerges through her letters as a close-knit, caring community, eager to retain its Scandinavian ties but already convinced that Texas is the place to be. She contrasts the mutual supportiveness of her "neighbors in the country" with the unspecified but presumably more impersonal and independent ways of the "city women" who "follow the American customs."

Questions for Discussion

1. The Norwegians in rural Texas formed a close-knit community. They looked after one another and worked together to maintain their culture. The city Norwegians, on the other hand, followed the American customs. The settlers at Brownsboro drank heavily and took their church less seriously than their rural counterparts did.

2. She was impressed with Eielsen's tireless energy and commitment despite his old age. She was equally impressed by his refusal to accept offerings.

3. She is probably writing the letters to Norwegians who might be considering immigrating to the United States or perhaps a "secondary migration" to rural Texas. Letter three is more personal as she makes references that could only pertain to a family member or close friend.

Harry Mark Petrakis
"A City within a City"

Describing his ethnic Greek neighborhood in Chicago during the 1920s and '30s, Petrakis remarks that "there was a tangible smell to our neighborhood, a warmth and reassurance in recognizable faces and sociable friends." This combination of physical characteristics and comfortingly familiar relationships echoes Greeley's theory that the sense of belonging to a neighborhood has important social and psychological components. Petrakis's description is filled with nostalgia for this "kingdom of [his] childhood." As in all the great American cities where discrete islands of language, food, religion, and custom existed contiguous to each other, the Chicago Petrakis describes is clearly marked by ethnic boundaries. The Roman Catholic church and school across the street from his Greek parish school was, for Petrakis and his friends, "a foreign country." He describes these ethnic enclaves as "reservations of the city" and "province[s] of the land[s] from which our parents journeyed."

Questions for Discussion

1. The urban dwellings of immigrant neighborhoods tended to be crowded, identical, and nondescript. There was no common bond among the immigrant resident groups except that they all came from elsewhere. The first generation did its best to retain customs and traditions of the homelands, and the children tended not to relate to anything "American." For Petrakis, his earliest memories were of things Greek, not candy, baseball, and ice cream.

2. Paragraph 12 is one of several places where sensory detail abounds.

3. Petrakis's humor comes from honest and specific accounts of his childhood memories. The "libidinal" attraction to *Spicy Western* stories in paragraph 13 is one example. The descriptions of the students and the Greek school in paragraphs 22–24 is another example.

Ronald Fair
"We Who Came After"

Fair's narrative, in which a fictional narrator describes a black Chicago neighborhood of the 1930s and '40s, is an interesting companion piece to the Petrakis memoir. While both are filled with the enthusiasm and innocence of childhood, the Fair piece is informed by an adult sensibility that has come to see the dark underside of ghetto life. The contrast between the way the children felt and the way the adult narrator interprets their experiences is evident even in the first paragraph, where "poor," "deprived," and "hungry" were realities the "young," "excited," "busy" children were not aware of. The children's enthusiasm for their games, their feeling that storybook children in the country "had nothing on us," and the excitement generated by the arrival of peddlers with ice, fruit, and vegetables convey a feeling of camaraderie and community solidarity similar to that in the Petrakis memoir. But Fair's lengthy description of the ongoing battle against the rats casts an ominous shadow over the rest of the piece. The element of fear is present even in moments of exultant victory. In this world, poverty is one of the strongest bonds.

Questions for Discussion

1. White people appeared in Fair's childhood neighborhood only to exploit its poor residents. They came as peddlers with overpriced merchandise, as burial insurance representatives selling overpriced "pine box" burials, and as telephone company representatives removing some unfortunate's phone. Sampson, the ice man, was a role model for the neighborhood children. He was black, and he was successful and hardworking. He paid attention to the children by letting them feel they were helping him and by generally increasing their self-esteem.

2. The adults are in the background to give space and authenticity to the voice of children. Readers recognize, however, that behind the children's voices are loving yet poverty-stricken parents who, like their children, are trapped in the circumstances of their environment.

3. Such dialogue shows the resentment even young children had for the wealth and racism they associated with white people. The dialogue also reveals their innocence and their loyalty to their parents.

Lawrence H. Fuchs
"The American Way of Families"

Fuchs sees the American family system as different from those in other countries because it reflects the dominant American values of "personal independence and equality." He points out that this emphasis on independence contrasts with the ideal of maintaining "satisfying, pleasurable and continuous binding relationships," which is central to many cultures throughout the world. Two early forces that Fuchs believes helped shape the American family system are the Protestant belief in the individual's direct access to God, without the need of a priest as intermediary, and the combination of abundant land and shortage of labor. Dissident Protestantism, he states, "encouraged individualism for all against patriarchal rule," while the shortage of labor (and often of women too) increased the regard for women and children. Fuchs sees both pluses and minuses in the American ideal of personal independence, with the potential for loneliness and anxiety balanced by opportunities for self-expression and contributions to society. At the end of the selection he points to an issue that informs the conflicts within many immigrant families when he observes, "It is a question of your version of the good life." There are many versions of what kinds of relationships best meet the physical, emotional, and spiritual needs of human beings, and these versions vary cross-culturally and cross-generationally. The selections in the rest of this chapter reflect this variety.

Questions for Discussion

1. See above.

2. Fuchs says that Emerson preached that the individual should trust no one but him/herself. This attitude affected family identity as we became "the first culture in human history where an increasing number of people drew little psychological strength from roles or relationships." It should be pointed out that many readers of Emerson would argue that Fuchs is misinterpreting him. Perhaps some students could be assigned the task of reporting on this controversy.

Monica McGoldrick
"Ethnicity and Families"

McGoldrick points out that for patients coping with interpersonal conflicts, psychotherapy is facilitated by understanding how ethnicity affects "belief systems." Problems between generations and between partners in mixed marriages often grow out of ethnically defined differences in expectations about relationships and in ways of dealing with problems. Even the issue of what is regarded as a problem can be traced to ethnicity, and "families from different ethnic groups may have very different kinds of intergenerational struggles." In McGoldrick's description of the hypothetical WASP/Italian couple, students will find a concrete example of what Fuchs described as differing opinions about people's "emotional and spiritual needs."

Questions for Discussion

1. a. McGoldrick points out that we must come "to terms . . . with our ethnicity . . . to gain a perspective on the relativity of our belief systems." Customs vary from culture to culture. For example, Mexican-Americans have longer courtships and see early and middle childhood extend longer than it does in American families.
   b. The WASPS focus on the small nuclear family. They depend less on a network of kin and community. They are more prepared to achieve individual success and less prepared to contend with loss and tragedy.
   c. We sometimes misunderstand differences in family values by ascribing them to class rather than to ethnicity. The discussion of Puerto Ricans, Italians, and Greeks with similar rural, peasant backgrounds (paragraph 8) illustrates this point.

2. Families migrating with young children are "perhaps strengthened by having each other." It is more difficult, however, to migrate with adolescents because families will have less time as a unit before children move on. Also, adolescents feel peer pressure readily, and they are eager to acculturate. Generational differences often become substantial in such instances.

James T. Farrell
"Old Man Lonigan"

Patrick J. Lonigan's musings on the evening of his children's graduation from high school reveal his feelings about the importance of family and what he considers a proper upbringing. Relaxing on his porch in "burgher comfort" while the dinner dishes are being washed in the kitchen, Lonigan indulges in a fair amount of self-congratulation on his successes in business and family matters. Various forms of the words "content" and "comfortable" appear a number of times during his reverie. He takes pride in having been strengthened by hardship during the "ragged days" of his youth when his father was a "pauperized greenhorn," in his having "worked hard to win out in the grim battle," and most of all in his having met what he considers to be the responsibilities of a good father. He has no questions about these responsibilities, spelled out in the final paragraph, and does not hesitate to consider them "oughts" that other parents should adopt. It is interesting to note that his list of parental responsibilities consists entirely of doing and providing. Lonigan sees the role of father as provider, not confidant; having met all of what he regards as his paternal responsibilities, he still wonders what his son Bill thinks about.

Questions for Discussion

1. While relaxing on his porch after supper, Lonigan observes neighborhood children at play. This prompts him to reflect on his own childhood: "Golly, it would be great to be a kid again!" He feels that the fathers of the two children whom he compares to his own Martin and Loretta didn't look after them as much as he did his own children. He also doubts that the parents made the sacrifice to send the girl to Catholic school.

2. He knows he has been a good Catholic, a good father, and a good husband, and the three identities go together. The emphasis on religion in the final paragraph demonstrates how Lonigan's world has been defined by his church.

3. Lonigan seems to be satisfied with his past and content with his present: "Life was a good thing if you were Patrick J. Lonigan and had worked hard to win out in the grim battle, and God had been good to you."

G. S. Sharat Chandra
"Saree of the Gods"

Chandra's story of an Asian Indian couple transplanted to New York City dramatizes the strains that changing cultures places on relationships. Prapulla, "a proper Hindu wife, shy courteous and traditional," finds that her husband has embraced the trappings of American culture. While she holds fast to familiar traditions, he is eager to prove himself thoroughly acculturated, delighting in amazing his colleagues by ordering "corned beef on rye" at the deli and by showing off his newly acquired knowledge of German wines. Chandra's depiction of Shirley Dorsen, who drinks four cocktails to her husband's one, is not flattering and does little to contradict Prapulla's preconceived notion that women in America tend to drink too much, dress in a provocative manner, and engage in "sexual escapades." Prapulla's wedding saree, ruined by the brandy with which her "Americanized husband" hoped to impress his American guests, represents the changes that come with the new culture. Traditions are abandoned, as when Shekar, in response to the "disfigured or mutilated" silver avatars on his wife's saree, declares, "It's nothing!" Students may wish to speculate on how the relationship between Shekar and Prapulla will weather the transition to life in America. It has not had a propitious beginning.

Questions for Discussion

1. Prapulla worried over changes in her life. She wanted a place in New York where other Indian immigrants lived. She also worried about flying over Mount Everest because of her Hindu beliefs, and she worried about abruptly severing old relationships as well as managing her household without a maid-servant. But mostly she worried about differences in dress and sexual customs. Her cousin, who had lived in New York, told her, "Women there are just like women here!" Shekar, on the other hand, wanted to avoid other Asian immigrants. He wanted a chance to succeed on his own by assimilating rapidly.

2. Sarees had always been important to Prapulla, but now they were even more so since they became a symbol of all she had left behind in India. The fact that the saree was damaged by an American dinner guest is symbolically appropriate. To Prapulla, the wedding saree became her second self.

3. The story is told from Prapulla's point of view, which allows her inner fears, superstitions, and dreams to emerge as a central issue in the narrative. Because the reader is privy to these concerns s/he is more sympathetic toward Prapulla than s/he would be if the story were told from the point of view of Shekar (impatient with his wife's clinging to Indian ways) or one of the Americans (for whom these traditions and concerns hold no emotional content).

James M. Freeman
"Undisciplined Children"

Freeman has recorded the thoughts and experiences of an elderly Vietnamese refugee whose grandchildren, raised in America, have adopted American styles of behavior, rebelling against the strict control of their parents. But the speaker does not blame the general deterioration in respect and obedience entirely on the influences of American culture. He tells of his problems with his own older sons in Vietnam and observes that it is not true that the "difficulties with the Vietnamese family are a result of living in America." Nonetheless, the difficulties of maintaining strict control over children are exacerbated by living in a society that does not support this endeavor. Students will hear echoes of Fuchs in the final paragraph of this piece.

Questions for Discussion

1 and 2. In Vietnamese culture daughters are subject to different standards of parental discipline. Parents control their daughters until marriage, and for daughters "disobedience is unforgivable." Nevertheless, the narrator seems to have been more strongly affected by the disobedience of his sons. He does not feel his difficulties are simply a result of living in America, although that is clearly a factor. He points out that even in Vietnam, children do not always follow parents' wishes. His problems seem to come primarily from parental involvement in their children's marriages. The eldest son learned from a teacher that it is against the law to beat children in America.

3. The humor comes from the narrator's frankness and from his naivety. It is clear that he doesn't understand the changing marriage customs, and to his audience his inability to understand is a source of amusement, as is what will appear to American readers as his excessive meddlesomeness. The specific description of his sons' behavior in paragraphs 17–22 is an example of the source of the humor.

Shirley Ann Grau
"The Beginning"

The single black mother in Grau's story creates for her daughter a secure and loving environment in which she is "the queen of the world, the jewel of the lotus, the pearl without price [her] secret treasure." A capable and ambitious entrepreneur, the narrator's mother negotiates their way through a world full of "threats and pursuits and enemies to be avoided" and somehow manages, in spite of their often seedy surroundings, to make her daughter feel like a princess. What an observant reader may see as the reality of their situation does not really matter, for this is not the familiar story of someone who, having attained a mature point of view, recognizes and perhaps resents the poverty and deprivation of his or her early life (see, for instance, Ronald L. Fair's "We Who Came After"). Rather, the narrator of this story tells us that she "grew strong and resilient," internalizing "the castle and the kingdom" created in her mother's fantasy. If she was not actually a princess, she learned to think of herself as one, and she claims that this strong positive self-image made it possible for her to overcome the difficulties of being "a young black female of illegitimate birth."

Questions for Discussion

1. The persona's father was a Hindu from Calcutta, a salesman, the only man her mother had loved. Apart from a childhood attendant, "Miss Beauty," the narrator's mother seems to be her only companion. The narrator remarks, "After Miss Beauty's death, there was no one. I stayed by myself." Even when she attends school she describes herself as "always alone." The only schoolmate she mentions is "a moonfaced child" with rheumatoid arthritis, who died during their second year of high school.

2. The mysterious visitor who prompts the narrator's mother to brandish a pistol and ultimately to move is one incident that suggests less than happy experiences. The illegitimacy of her birth and other problems were hidden behind the "princess" world her mother created for her. The voice of childhood innocence allows Grau to present a story with an optimistic vision.

3. As a child she didn't realize all the faces in her world were black. The mother successfully protected her "princess" from reality. She remarks that when she attended Saint Mary's boarding school, hers was "the only dark face in a sea of Irish skin." With adulthood came her realization that she was "a young black female of illegitimate birth."

David Mura
"Secrets and Anger"

Mura, a third-generation Japanese-American who is married to a Caucasian American, came to realize the centrality of racial issues when he had to make decisions about how to raise his daughter. Although he himself was raised with a kind of "cultural amnesia," encouraged to blend in with the American cultural majority, he believes that the world his daughter grows up into will be a truly multicultural one in which individuals will no longer have to deny parts of their identity in order to conform to an unrealistic melting-pot model. For Mura, race has come to be a central defining feature in his own identity. As a Japanese-American, as opposed to a Japanese, he has come to understand the importance of seeing himself as a person of color. Mura believes that rather than denying differences between the experiences of whites and nonwhites in America, both whites and people of color must acknowledge the differences and deal with the sources of their anger about racism. Mura realizes how easy it would be to pretend that he could fulfill his duty to provide his daughter with a multicultural education by "teaching her *kanji* and how to conjugate Japanese verbs," but this would be avoiding the racial issues, stereotypes, and the "constant pressure [she will face] to forget that she is part Japanese American, to assume a basically white middle-class identity." Increased consciousness about race means for Mura an end to the denial of the importance of race to the fabric of American society. It opens the possibility of "exchang[ing] a hope [for racial harmony] based on naiveté and ignorance for one based on knowledge." Students may wish to explore connections between Mura's description of the "binary opposition of black and white" in American society and Clara Rodriguez's observations about the ways in which race is thought of in American versus Latin cultures in "From the Americas—The Cultural Rainbow" in Part II.

Questions for Discussion

1. Susie is afraid her relationship with her daughter will weaken if they become more involved in an Asian-American community. The prospect makes her uneasy because already strangers observing Samantha and Susie assume that the child is adopted and that Susie couldn't be her biological mother. Also, Susie is accustomed to being in the majority, and the prospect of finding herself in a situation in which her husband and daughter are part of something she is separate from disturbs her.

2. Being third-generation Japanese, Mura is aware of Japanese culture, but he is removed from it. Ironically, he discovered he is not Japanese while visiting Japan to write about the "cultural amnesia" of Japanese-Americans. His concession meant accepting the fact that his "identity would always be partially occluded" and that in America he would always see himself as a person of color.

3. Mura was disturbed by the production's stereotyping of Asian women into the Madame Butterfly role. He was also disturbed that no Asian-American actor had been given the chance to play the Eurasian lead. His American friends argued that who played the role wasn't as important as how the role was played. Mura felt the issue involved discrimination. His American friends placed emphasis on the issue of freedom in the arts.

James Fallows
"Language"

Fallows examines the "conventional wisdom" that a danger to national unity has arisen because Spanish-speaking immigrants are insisting on maintaining their own language and are to that end making demands on the educational and governmental systems that earlier immigrants, "eager to assimilate as quickly as possible," did not make. People who hold this view fear that bilingual education programs may provide the roots for political separatism by helping to maintain Spanish language and culture. When Fallows explores the history of the nineteenth-century German immigrants he finds that, like today's Spanish-speaking population, the Germans fought to maintain their language and culture. In spite of their efforts, however, the forces of assimilation prevailed and their language died out in the second generation. This process, Fallows believes, will have a similar effect on today's immigrants. Nonetheless, he points out, the debate over bilingual and intensive English programs is a heated one, mainly because bilingual education symbolizes different things to different factions—"To the Hispanic ideologue, it is a symbol of cultural pride and political power," while others see it "as a threat to the operating rules that have bound the country together." Fallows argues that each approach should be judged on its effectiveness in moving students into full participation in mainstream society rather than on what each symbolizes. He takes an interesting approach to this very sensitive issue, telling the reader in paragraph 5 that he used to be one of those who regarded special programs for Spanish speakers as a potential threat to national unity. This confession serves both as a foreshadowing of what his position on the debate will be at the end of the article and as a means of establishing common ground with those who disagree with that position. By characterizing himself as "a hostile observer" of bilingual programs, Fallows establishes a bond with those whom he knows to be his opposition. He takes the reader through his own process of discovery, frequently admitting his "irritation" and "exasperation." His frankness about the evolution of his thinking on the subject of bilingual programs is an important element in his argumentative strategy.

Questions for Discussion

1. The 4.5 million Germans emigrating to the U.S. from 1830 to 1890 accounted for one third of the total immigration during that period. They tried to retain their language and even sent their children to German-language and bilingual public schools. Nonetheless, the process of

assimilation proceeded, and the Germans became part of the English-language culture. Fallows argues that Hispanic linguistic assimilation will be similar. World War I hastened the linguistic assimilation of German-Americans since German was the language of the enemy.

2. Fallows came to see that the political debate about bilingual education has little to do with what goes on in the schools. He realized that these are *temporary* programs and that students learn English rapidly even when some of their content courses are taught in Spanish.

3. Ramirez and Flores are both bilingual teachers in San Antonio. Both came from Spanish-speaking families and both oppose the "natural-immersion" approach to learning English that they experienced as children. Ramirez was born in Austin and struggled to learn an accentless English when her family moved to an "Anglo" area. Flores lived in Mexico as a child and, like Ramirez, came to English late. Both teachers support transitional bilingual education so their students won't have to struggle with the same language "passage" they did, a passage which, as they point out, many Chicanos never successfully negotiate.

Rosalie Pedalino Porter
"The Fractured Logic of Bilingual Education"

Porter takes a stand against bilingual education programs in the public schools. She draws on her own experience in admitting that being put into an English-only environment can be painful, as a non-English-speaking child watches silently, copying behavior amidst a "haze of incomprehensible sounds." Nonetheless, she believes that bilingual programs can delay students' entry into mainstream classrooms and that the segregation they enforce on the student body has negative effects on the socialization of second-language students. While she approves in principle of the concept of showing respect for other languages and cultures, Porter does not feel that maintenance of other languages and cultures is the job of the public schools. When she was a bilingual teacher in Springfield, Massachusetts, Porter was surprised to find that several of her colleagues sent their own children to parochial schools, where they felt the absence of bilingual programs contributed to the children's rapid learning of English. Students should examine carefully the analogy she makes between bilingual programs in the U.S. and the mandated use of "mother-tongue instruction" (in the Bantu languages) in South Africa, which she claims has had the effect of limiting the opportunities of African children in a society where the two official languages are English and Afrikaans. They should also consider what authority Porter's own experiences add to her argument.

Questions for Discussion

1. Because immigrant children did not learn the language, they often experienced failure in school. Increased numbers of Asian and Hispanic immigrants forced schools to confront the issues of second-language pedagogy and to question the "sink or swim" attitude that had previously prevailed.

2. Responses will vary, but most students will recognize and describe the importance of learning the mainstream language gradually before completely letting go of their native language.

3. Porter uses the South African system as an argument against total bilingual education. She points out that the South Africans use it to deny blacks economic and linguistic equality. In effect it is used as a means

of forced isolation. She uses the requirements of jury duty to argue how important a knowledge of English is for meaningful U.S. citizenship.

4. The personal point of view is convincing because Porter uses her own experiences to bolster her authority and credibility. There is a danger of emotional adherence to one side of the issue.

Ronald Saunders
"U.S. English—1991 National Opinion Survey"

Saunders presents a case for the objectives of U.S. English, a group committed to maintaining the linguistic unity of the U.S. The group advocates making English "the official language of the United States government" through federal legislation, encouraging states to adopt similar legislation, making knowledge of English a requirement for citizenship, "repeal[ing] laws mandating bilingual voting ballots, government licensing and similar uses," and improving language education to insure that all persons in the U.S. have the opportunity to learn English in "the most effective way possible." Students should note the persuasive tactics Saunders employs. He cites the opinions of such respected figures as Theodore Roosevelt, who warned against the country's becoming "a tangle of squabbling nationalities," and linguist and senator S. I. Hayakawa, who regarded a common language as an essential unifying element. Saunders appeals to a number of very different factions by speaking of the use of taxpayers' money to fund the education of children in languages other than English, the victimization of non-English-speaking immigrants "doomed to illiteracy and poverty," and the potential inability of this country to "compete in world markets" or even *"to command our Armed Forces."* Such claims should be examined closely for their legitimacy and for their intended rhetorical effect.

Harvey A. Daniels
"The Roots of Language Protectionism"

Daniels rebuts the position of English-only proponents. He claims that "the public and private use of a variety of languages has usually been treated as business-as-usual in a nation of immigrants" and that such use of other languages does not threaten the strength and cultural primacy of the English language. He feels that the support which official-English legislation, such as that proposed by U.S. English, has found among "thousands of good-hearted, patriotic, loyal Americans" has been garnered largely through "frightening propaganda." English-only organizations have instilled unfounded fears about the stability and unity of the country and stirred up resentment against the alleged "intransigence and ingratitude" of recent immigrants. Although Daniels sees the effect of such legislation thus far as mostly "symbolic," he believes that it opens the door for some dangerous and discriminatory practices. Nonetheless, while Daniels is not overly generous in interpreting the politics of the movement's leaders, he is careful not to castigate the motives of those "ordinary citizens" ("well-meaning, patriotic American citizens") who have been moved to offer modest support. He believes that the English-only movement has been "built on misinformation, ignorance, and fear, but not on hatred" and that people will turn away from it when they understand that it is "a socially acceptable form of ethnic discrimination." Students should be encouraged to consider Daniels's imagined audience and how it affects his argumentative strategies.

Questions for Discussion

1. The title suggests a national consensus on the positions espoused by the U.S. English group.

2. Responses will vary.

3. The Crawford poll supports the notion of English as a national standard by reporting that 98 percent of current Hispanic immigrants believe their children must speak "perfect" English in order to succeed.

4. In the story of the Tower of Babel, people wanted to build a tower to reach heaven. God, unhappy with their overreaching, foiled their project by making them speak different languages. They were thus unable to communicate with each other and to cooperate in building the tower. Daniels cites historical precedent to show that in the U.S. a multiplicity of languages has resolved itself into an assimilated English-language culture. He makes those who invoke a similarity to Babel sound like Chicken Littles disregarding historical evidence.

5. Language differences became a prominent issue between 1915 and 1920 for two major reasons. First, World War I prompted an increase in nationalism. Second, and more directly, the increase in immigrants from Southern and Eastern Europe resulted in large second-language populations that seemed to some at the time unassimilable. In paragraph 5 Daniels points to our "broad historic picture of linguistic and cultural consensus." He claims that the fact that we are refighting the same old battles today is a sign of our national tendency to be intolerant of new immigrants.

Jerre Mangione
"Talking American"

In this selection from his novel *Mount Allegro,* Mangione explores the symbolic social functions of language. From the narrator's mother, who insists that only Italian be spoken in the home, to Uncle Nino, who distinguishes between the femininity and ostentation of Italian and the masculinity and honesty of Sicilian, to the narrator, who is embarrassed whenever his mother called to him in Italian while he was playing with friends, the sounds of particular languages and dialects are emotionally laden. Language emerges here as a powerful element in one's identity. For the narrator's mother, giving up speaking Italian would be like "renouncing her own flesh and blood." Uncle Nino, by refusing to learn English, makes a statement about his tenuous commitment to America. Students may want to consider what use the two sides in the English-only debate would make of the experiences described in this selection. English-only proponents might be irritated by what Uncle Nino's refusal to learn English "means," while its opponents would probably point to the obvious mastery of English and assimilation of the narrator, in spite of his having been raised in a fairly insular Italian subculture. The narrator's sense of living in two worlds—being, in this instance, "Italian at home and American . . . elsewhere"—is taken up in further detail in the following article by Richard Rodriguez.

Questions for Discussion

1. Mangione's mother allowed the family to speak only Italian at home. The children gradually acquired the notion that they were Italian at home and American everywhere else. The linguistic differences exaggerated the cultural differences in Mangione's childhood world.

2. Words such as *"minuto," "ponte," "storo," "barry,"* and *"giobba"* evolved by adding Sicilian suffixes to American words. The young Mangione grew up thinking these words were authentic Sicilian. When he tried to use them in Italy as an adult, he was surprised to discover they were meaningless.

3. The tone is innocent and honest. The anecdotes he relates about his family are nonjudgmental in accordance with the way a child views his/her world. By telling his own experiences in the first person, Mangione adds credibility to the events.

Richard Rodriguez
"The Education of Richard Rodriguez"

Rodriguez describes his childhood experiences in "a world magically compounded of sounds," where the "loud" and "hard" sounds of the English heard in public society contrasted with the soft, reassuring sounds of the Spanish spoken at home. Rodriguez lovingly describes the intimacy of the times at home when his family "joined [their] voices in a celebration of sounds," united by the language that separated them from the gringo world. Considering the joy he takes in this cloistered private world, students may be surprised when Rodriguez declares, "Plainly, it is not healthy to hear such sounds so often" in the final paragraph. Understanding what is "unhealthy," in Rodriguez's view, about spending too much time in the comforting, protective Spanish-speaking environment is the key to explaining his earlier negative comments on bilingual education (paragraph 5). Rodriguez shares Porter's concerns in "The Fractured Logic of Bilingual Education" about delaying too long the entry of second-language students into the "public world" of English-speaking American society.

Questions for Discussion

1. The point of the selection is that ultimately it was a wise decision to attend an English-speaking school. It caused difficulty at first for Rodriguez and his family, but the essay demonstrates how it enabled him to become comfortable with his public as well as his private language.

2. a. This statement prepares the reader for Rodriguez's opposition to bilingual education and for a central purpose of this selection—to distinguish between public and private languages. Rodriguez contends that no one speaks private or "family" language at school. And although this is more of an issue with non-English-speaking people, it is nonetheless an issue for all of us.
   b. Because his parents never fully understood English, they were never truly comfortable using the "public" language. They were therefore awkward and less than completely effective when they had to take part in public discourse.
   c. The private language was familiar, smooth, and harmonious. The public language of *los gringos* was harsh and full of tension.
   d. As a child, Rodriguez was made anxious by his parents' hesitant, confused English. In paragraph 15 he explains that their inability to communicate fluently in English weakened his "clutching trust in

their protection." The adult Rodriguez is ashamed to admit both how dependent he was as a child on the protective powers of his parents and his doubts about their ability to protect him.

e. See above.

3. Such instances certainly give credibility to Rodriguez's ability to use his "public" language effectively. Such figures also strengthen the personal tone of the essay. Paragraph 16 is another example of figurative language.

Paule Marshall
"From the Poets in the Kitchen"

Marshall describes her experiences growing up surrounded by the "beauty, poetry and wisdom" of the "freewheeling, wide-ranging, exuberant talk" that filled the kitchen as her mother and her friends "took refuge in language." After a day filled with the small and large indignities of performing housework in a white neighborhood, these women created their own language, the only medium available to them to fulfill their need for self-expression. This creative use of language, their "insight, irony, wit and humor," were weapons against "their invisibility, their powerlessness." Talk became their therapy. Marshall describes the ways in which they played with sound and syntax, creating rich images with everyday speech. She credits this early exposure to imaginative use of language with training her ear as a developing writer. These "poets in the kitchen" provided for Marshall exposure to the cultural and linguistic expression of the American black experience that was missing at that time from the grade school curriculum.

Questions for Discussion

1. Language was the medium for self-expression and self-fulfillment for these women. They used it imaginatively as poets do, creating special rhythms and textures to capture the essence of their experiences.

2. The mothers were uneasy and overwhelmed by the complexity of American life and culture. They felt American laws and customs were preempting their authority by forbidding them to beat their children.

3. The novelist was the catalyst that prompted Marshall to think of the important contributions her mother and her mother's friends made to her development of an appreciation for language. She identifies him as "male" to explain the women students' initial resistance to what they took as his chauvinistic view of women.

Samuel G. Freedman
"The Lower East Side"

In this selection from *Small Victories,* Freedman gives a brief history of New York's Lower East Side and its educational programs from the middle of the nineteenth century to the 1920s. He cites educational authorities and textbooks of the early twentieth century that expressed the prevailing notion that immigrants from places other than northern Europe and Britain were notable for their "personal and moral recalcitrance" and needed to be "elevated and lifted out of the swamp into which they were born and brought up." With no regard for the cultural backgrounds of their students, the schools of the Lower East Side went about the task of assimilation by teaching etiquette, patriotism, and "the Anglo-Saxon conception of righteousness, law and order." Training, rather than education, was the mission of these schools, which served to perpetuate class differences and inequities rather than provide ways out of poverty. Only with the opening of the subway in 1904 were immigrants provided access to the city's three public high schools, so taxing their capacity that the city erected two secondary schools in the northern section of the Lower East Side—both of them vocational rather than academic institutions. It was not until the 1920s that neighborhood high schools became a reality in the city. Freedman shows the connection between educational practices and the social and political climate of the twenties, a period of nativism and restricted immigration.

Questions for Discussion

1. The Irish immigrants lived in congested, miserable conditions in the Five Points neighborhood. The youth often joined gangs as a means of establishing identity amidst the squalor of their ghetto lives. The thieving that went with gang life provided an alternative to "the harsh doctrine of legal employ." Most students will probably agree that identity is one important reason inner-city youths join gangs today.

2. German Jews used *"kike"* to refer to Eastern European Jews whose names often ended in "ky." A dictionary will provide information on the origins of other slurs. Fuller entries will be found in Wentworth and Flexner's *Dictionary of American Slang.*

3. The description of the deplorable conditions of the Collect immediately attracts readers' attention. Readers want to know how people could possibly live in such a place, and Freedman's essay responds to that in-

terest. The history of the area as the site of tanneries helps explain why it became home to the poorest and newest immigrants.

4. Freedman is objective in the sense that he reports on conditions immigrants endured in the Lower East Side. He used strong, emotional language, but we sense it is warranted. To add to a sense of objectivity, he quotes from educators. Overall, he conveys a sense that the city of New York neglected the education and well-being of those living in the Lower East Side as long as it possibly could. The facts seem to support this opinion. Freedman maintains a balanced viewpoint. In the first sentence of paragraph 5, for instance, he describes the immigrants in the Lower East Side as "wretched and oppressed" but allows that still their position seemed "enviable" to Jews suffering oppression in Eastern Europe. Paragraph 14 proves false the prediction of Superintendent of Schools William H. Maxwell that the existing high schools would meet the needs of the population for the following twenty years, but Freedman admits that he could not have foreseen the advent of the rapid transit system and the difference it would make in the school population.

Sophronia Scott Gregory
"The Hidden Hurdle"

Gregory presents the dilemma faced by inner-city black students who are ridiculed by their peers for their academic achievement. Seeking to achieve a college degree, a good job, and a nice home is perceived by some blacks as evidence of "acting white," of turning one's back on the African-American community. Maintaining a black identity has come to mean adopting what social anthropologists call "oppositional behaviors." Oppositional identities evolve when a group, believing that they will never be treated like the dominant group, adopts values and behaviors that are not part of the dominant group. In the school environment, these include skipping class, not doing homework, and adopting an "I don't care" attitude. Gregory observes that "social success depends partly on academic failure: safety and acceptance lie in rejecting the traditional paths to self-improvement." Those who reject this "anti-achievement ethic" often become the targets of ridicule by their peers, who regard success as somehow antiblack. Thus, internal group dynamics contribute to school failure. The challenge, as Gregory points out, is to help young blacks understand "that no one group in society has a monopoly on success."

Questions for Discussion

1. Gregory uses the concrete illustration of Za'kettha Blaylock as a means of introducing the thesis of this selection. She shows an example of anti-achievement culture before she identifies it as her focus. The essay is full of concrete examples of such "nerd bashing." The concluding paragraph offers hope based on specific programs and studies that suggest ways to confront the problems Gregory has illustrated.

2. See above.

3. Answers will vary, but, among other things, students will probably mention development of racial pride, education, incentive programs, and role models.

Sarah Nieves Squires "Hispanic Women on Campus"

Nieves-Squires explains the culture- and gender-related causes of some of the difficulties Hispanic women have at American colleges. Among the cultural differences, she notes different styles in exchanging opinions, attitudes toward competitiveness, expectations about peer and teacher relationships, and nonverbal communication. Stereotypes of women and of Hispanic women in particular—"as powerless, pathological, and prayerful, and dutiful family members"—can further complicate these issues. A Puerto Rican woman dean interviewed by Nieves-Squires states that in her experience in the academic world she has found her gender to be more of a cause of comment and potential friction than her nationality.

Questions for Discussion

1. The selection demonstrates how the attitudes and values of university culture are at odds with Hispanic customs. For example, Hispanic culture encourages tolerance of different opinions rather than challenging new ideas. Hispanics value cooperation over competitiveness. In conferences Anglo professors are task-oriented, whereas Hispanic students expect casual conversation prior to a formal conference.

2. a. Hispanics tend to spend much time building relationships. Informal acquaintances of American university life may complicate feelings of isolation among Hispanics.
   b. Hispanics are comfortable with closer personal space than Anglos. Anglos may either be uncomfortable or perceive closer space as inviting intimacy. Hispanics of the same sex tend to stand close together, while members of the opposite sex stand further apart. This behavior may also be misinterpreted by Anglos.
   c. Overt hand and arm gestures may be perceived as a lack of verbal ability.
   d. In Hispanic culture looking someone directly in the eye is either a sign of disrespect or of challenge.

3. One of major assumptions about Hispanic women is that they focus only on home and family. The image of dutiful daughter and mother is a negative one because it is linked to subservience and dependency. Anglos often perceive Hispanic women as being content as sex objects.

Frederick Douglass
From *Narrative of the Life of Frederick Douglass, An American Slave*

Douglass tells that as a result of his master's injunction that teaching a slave to read "would forever unfit him to be a slave," he came to understand that learning to read was "the pathway from slavery to freedom." He claims to owe as much to his master for this insight as to his mistress, who, before her husband discovered she was doing so, provided Douglass with his first lessons. His master was right, for Douglass credits his reading of Sheridan's speeches on behalf of Catholic emancipation with giving shape to his hunger for freedom and his understanding of human rights.

Questions for Discussion

1. Douglass' master warned against teaching a slave to read: "If you teach that nigger [Douglass] how to read, there would be no keeping him. It would forever unfit him to be a slave." Douglass felt these words explained the white man's power to enslave the black man. From that moment he understood the value of freedom.

2. Slavery forced his mistress not to treat Douglass as a human being. At first she was humane and compassionate in the treatment of her slave, but finally she learned that to treat slaves as humans was dangerously wrong.

3. He envied the "stupidity" (illiteracy) of his fellow slaves because they didn't share his intellectual knowledge about the wrongs of his condition, nor did they understand the meaning of freedom. Reading "had given [him] a view of [his] wretched condition, without the remedy."

4. Douglass's voice is personal and powerful. His prose is concrete as he uses personal experience and observation to describe what he learned as well as how he learned it. His voice is full of condemnation, and he uses figurative language freely.

Anzia Yezierska
"College"

In this excerpt from her autobiographical novel, Yezierska contrasts her expectations of attending college with the realities she met on the campus and in the college town. The space, security, and quiet of the new environment was a dreamlike contrast to the crowded streets and tenements of the Lower East Side. Her "gray pushcart clothes" marked her as an outsider in the world of these people, whose "spotless, creaseless clothes" made them look "as if the dirty battle of life had never yet been on them." Yearning for the world of the intellect, the narrator is profoundly disappointed in the students who seem to value youth, beauty, and clothes over character or brains. Her strength and determination are evident at the end of the selection when, after her mortifying experience at the school dance, she is able to gain a universal perspective on her "little sorrow," drawing strength from the stars and her awareness of the vast amount of sorrow in the world. (Because this final scene is so painful, students are often relieved to know that as the novel progresses, the narrator, having broadened the students' understandings, becomes a popular and much respected member of the college community, earning a special ovation from her classmates at graduation.) The beginning of this piece provides an opportunity for students to consider the clues the author provides of the direction the narrative will take. Students might be asked at what point they first suspected that the narrator was going to be disillusioned.

Questions for Discussion

1. The contrasts between the two worlds are evident in the words she uses to describe them in paragraphs 6–14. The narrator associates the college town with "free space and sunshine," "calm security," "serenity," "beauty," and ownership in contrast to the Lower East Side with its crowds, tenements, noise, and worry. The contrast awes and thrills her, for at last she has entered the world of the "real Americans." It is not long, however, before she is disillusioned by the students' coolness. The fact that their coolness surprises her suggests that she is accustomed to warmer and more open relationships.

2. "The campus stretched out like fields of a big park" (9). Such observations, and her feelings that students were truly enjoying life, are remote to her immigrant experience, in which young people were shut up in

factories. The only similar sensation she recalls are Sunday picnics, but at Sunday picnics there was always the thought of Monday.

3. Her epiphanylike experience after a moment of deep despair strengthens her. Drawing resolve from the stars, which have seen so much suffering in the world, she realizes that her "little sorrow" is bearable and that—if she must—she will be able to face the challenges of this new life on her own.

Marilyn French
"First Day at School"

Bella's first experience in an English-speaking kindergarten classroom is at once humiliating and exhilarating. In Bella's eagerness to take part in the school activities and her determination to acquire the necessary supplies, French depicts the immigrant's vision of education as a means to assimilation and upward mobility. In Bella's self-doubts and feelings of stupidity because she cannot understand the language spoken by the teacher and the students, in her abrupt dismissal by the school principal, and in the weary resignation of the teacher confronting the task of teaching a non-English-speaking child, French shows us the strain that the sink-or-swim technique of English-only instruction places on both the student and the system. Bella seems to be a strong person, up to meeting the challenges of this new environment, yet one wonders what she would have done if her brother had not revealed to her parents her failure to gain admittance to the school on the first day.

Questions for Discussion

1. That Bella's terror results from her not knowing English became clear as early as the second paragraph. That terror is sustained until near the end of the selection.

2. After her parents realize they misjudged Bella's readiness for the independence associated with the first day at school, her family is supportive and understanding. It is clear they are poor and hardworking, but the parents do what they can to support their young daughter. The mother accompanies her to school, and she finds the money for Bella to purchase the supplies needed to restore her dignity. From a middle-class American point of view, however, it may seem surprising that Bella's mother sends the non-English-speaking kindergarten student into the school alone on the first day. The fact that her parents do not inquire about how her day at school went is even more surprising. Students will be able to contrast this behavior with that of their own parents. One gets the feeling, especially from paragraph 16, that Bella is a child who demands and therefore receives little attention.

3. The story is told from Bella's point of view, so we recognize her terror immediately. French shows us her fear in paragraph 3, and the tone is sustained until the final paragraph.

Mike Rose
"I Just Wanna Be Average"

Through Rose's description of his two years in the vocational track of his parochial high school we learn that the error which placed him there could have had disastrous consequences for his future. His father's two years of Italian schooling did not prepare him to be an advocate for his son in negotiating the bureaucracy of the school, and it was only by a fluke that Rose was rescued from the mind–deadening regimen ordained by the placement error. Rose's view is that the vocational-track curriculum is meant to "occupy" rather than "liberate" students and to train them for work that is not highly regarded. It is, in his harsh indictment, most often "a dumping ground for the disaffected." Ending up there is often a result of social class. In order to survive in an atmosphere in which they are publicly defined as "slow," students in the vocational track sometimes "take on with a vengeance" this implied identity. As a defense mechanism against the knowledge that they have not been given the tools with which to compete, they "shut down . . . reject intellectual stimuli or diffuse them with sarcasm . . . cultivate stupidity . . . flaunt ignorance, materialize [their] dreams." The process Rose describes is almost identical to the oppositional strategies described in Gregory's essay about black failure to achieve academically. In both cases, as Rose observes, the defense "exacts a price."

Questions for Discussion

1. Rose's parents sent him to a Catholic high school in West Los Angeles, approximately fifteen miles from their home. They chose this school so that "their son would have the best education they could afford." (See above for the answer to the rest of this question.)

2. Rose does not present stereotypes. His whole point is that, viewed with intelligence and compassion, all students have potential for growth. His description of these three schoolmates includes many individualizing details. Dave Snyder, a football player, was popular with everyone. Because Rose points out his independence, maturity, and quick wit, he emerges as an individual rather than a "typical jock." Ted Richard, a baseball player and "seasoned street fighter" who loved words and philosophical discussions, is someone Rose visualizes as becoming one of those "rough-hewn intellectuals." Ken Harvey, who appears to be a typical greaser, was, according to Rose, merely accepting the role assigned to him by the school, and the protective identity he assumed both cush-

ioned and limited him. Rose helps the reader see how the school made his oppositional behavior seem like a reasonable response. Students will see some similarity between Ken's situation and the behavior Gregory describes in "The Hidden Hurdle."

3. The water metaphor presents a clear image of rising to a specific level to survive. The metaphor is reintroduced in the opening sentence of paragraph 9. Another strong figure is introduced in the final paragraph.

CONFRONTATIONS

This chapter of the text may well be the most difficult to teach since it is devoted to an examination of serious confrontations among groups. To pretend that societal conflicts are limited to individuals within a group or between discrete groups and the dominant American culture would be to misrepresent the truth of ethnic and racial relations. We agree with sociologist Robin M. Williams, Jr., who contends in his book *Mutual Accommodation: Ethnic Conflict and Cooperation* that "denial or distortion of reality is a common defense against disliked information. It is by all odds the least adaptive and most dangerous of defenses" (405). There is certainly a temptation to gloss over problems, to avoid unpleasantness, but evasion cannot lead to resolution. Our purpose in assembling the materials in this chapter has been neither to vilify groups involved in intergroup conflicts nor to present packaged solutions, but rather to provide sources that will help readers analyze and understand the sources of some of these conflicts.

Students are undoubtedly aware, from exposure in various news media and perhaps from their own personal experiences, that ethnic and racial conflicts do exist in our society. If they have been working on the ongoing assignments that appear at the ends of Parts I, II, and III, they will have an increased awareness of how the issues of group identity, pluralism versus tribalism, and confrontation and accommodation are manifesting themselves in contemporary society. Actually talking about these problems in an honest and analytic way, however, may be a new experience for them. Some may question or even resent the raising of the topic of intergroup conflicts; others may be tempted to find their own biases vindicated by the perspectives voiced in some of the selections. Our own experiences in English as a Second Language and multicultural classes convinces us that it is possible to help students negotiate the charged atmosphere surrounding these conflicts. This chapter appears late in the text for two reasons. First, having been previously introduced to some of the difficulties, concerns, and achievements of individual ethnic and racial groups in earlier chapters, students will be able to approach the conflicts presented in a more informed manner; second, by the time a class arrives at this chapter, both teacher and students will have come to know each other and ideally will have established an atmosphere of respect and collaboration within the classroom that will facilitate the sensitive and mature analysis of the conflicts presented.

Social scientists who have studied group interactions believe that accommodation is a realistic goal. They point among other phenomena to the near extinction of what Williams calls "old-fashioned racialistic anti-Semitism" (6), a general decrease of prejudice and an acceptance of racial integration, the very successful desegregation of the Armed Services, passage of liberalized immigration legislation, and an increase in the numbers of people of color who hold elected offices. Changes in stereotypes have been greatly facilitated by images in the mass media. Programming and advertising on television have undergone radical changes in the past thirty years, and the new cultural sensitivity and inclusiveness of children's books and textbooks have contributed significantly to a new atmosphere of cultural awareness and respect. In concluding his discussion on the prospects for dealing with social conflicts, Williams speaks of the goal of a community's achieving "social maturity" (406). A mature society would be responsive to physical and social realities, would be committed to a system of beliefs and values including social integration, would recognize the inevitability of disagreement and conflict, and would support institutionalized methods of expressing and resolving conflicts. Social conflicts are difficult problems, defying simple solutions, but even partial solutions are goals worth striving for. In order to reach accommodation, it is necessary to come face to face with the causes of and responses to confrontation.

(References are to Robin M. Williams, Jr., *Mutual Accommodation: Ethnic Conflict and Cooperation.* Minneapolis: University of Minnesota Press, 1977.)

William V. Shannon
"Anti-Irish Nativism"

Shannon examines some of the events and speculates on the causes of the nativist crusade of 1840–1860. He points out that in the period preceding the Civil War, the prevailing spirit in America was "dynamic and expansive" and its tone "raucous." Transition to a factory system meant bad economic times for craftsmen, and as the cities and the tensions in them grew, many citizens associated "the heightened tension and the unexpected stresses . . . with the most conspicuous newcomers—the Irish." During the 1840s and '50s shiploads of Irish arrived on the East Coast, and because of their large numbers, these Irish immigrants threatened to dominate the urban Protestant lower classes economically and politically. Shannon sees economic factors as the real precipitators of anti-Irish sentiment, but religious differences provided a convenient lightning rod and functioned as a "respectable pretext" for violence. Shannon describes the burning of the Ursuline convent in Charlestown, Massachusetts, in 1831, the rioting between nativists and Catholics in Philadelphia in 1844, and the rise of the Know-Nothing Party.

Questions for Discussion

1. See above.

2. In 1830 Boston was economically weakened. Only half of the persons born there in 1790 remained by 1820. A decline in trade with the Far East led to a decline in the city's maritime supremacy. The growth of nearby factory towns led to further decline. For all of these reasons and more the Irish became the workingman's scapegoat.

3. The story of John Morrissey, the details of the raid on the Charlestown convent, and the riots in Philadelphia illustrate how Shannon uses concrete events, statistics, and quotations to bring the history of the era to life.

Betty Lee Sung
"The Chinese Must Go"

The title of Sung's essay is a slogan used by Dennis Kearney, an influential labor leader whose anti-Chinese rhetoric helped focus on Chinese laborers the anger and resentment resulting from the depression of the 1870s. When work on the transcontinental railroad was finished, the Chinese began to seek factory, domestic, mine, and farm work. Previously praised "for their honesty, their thrift, and their peaceful ways," the Chinese were suddenly seen as "undermining the white man's standard of living" and were characterized as "clannish, dangerous, deceitful, and vicious." Sung details some of the violence against the Chinese in California, Oregon, and Colorado during this period and quotes one scholar's comment that "during the years of Kearneyism, it is a wonder that any Chinese remained alive in the U.S."

Questions for Discussion

1. After the completion of the railroad, when Chinese workers began to take other jobs, white American workers no longer praised the Chinese for their industry and honesty. Now they accused them of undermining their standard of living by accepting slave wages, an accusation Sung disproves. These claims, in any event, were short-lived since the exclusion laws brought about a shortage of Chinese laborers and the Chinese were able to demand and get higher wages in spite of a surplus of white labor.

2. Sandmeyer felt that if the Chinese in California had been white, there would have been no complaints and no warfare against them. The problem was racial rather than economic; the depression was not caused by Chinese undermining of the economy.

James A. McPherson
"To Blacks and Jews: *Hab Rachmones*"

McPherson examines the tension between African-Americans and Jews, a tension he feels stems from resentment over the perception that Jews have the option, which blacks do not, of fully integrating and thus getting the benefits of "mobility and security available to whites." He points out that a sympathetic relationship existed between blacks and Jews for the first half of the twentieth century. The Yiddish press presented black suffering as parallel to that of the Jews, and Jews became active in championing black causes, acting as go-betweens between the black and white communities. The two groups began to part ways just after the Six Day War of 1967, an event that served as a reaffirmation of nationhood for the Jewish people. The existence of a strong Israel underlines differences between the fundamentally similar mythologies of the two people—it makes concrete the deeply felt Jewish ties with a "motherland," while the equally intense feelings of blacks for ties with Africa have not been realized. Thus there is what McPherson refers to as a "problem of competing mythologies." The black response to their isolation from "any meaningful association with Africa" was Black Nationalism, which alienated many whites. Also, American Jewish support of Israel and Israeli relations with South Africa exacerbated black-Jewish tensions among some African-Americans. He regrets the passing of what he believes was "a group of stronger and wiser Black and Jewish people" one or two generations ago, "spiritual elites" who forged a powerful coalition "out of common memories of oppression and suffering," and appeals for a return of such mutual empathy and understanding. He ends by quoting from Bernard Malamud's novel *The Tenants,* a story about the developing hostility between a black and a Jewish writer that ends with the appeal: "Hab rachmones" ("Have mercy").

Questions for Discussion

1. Both blacks and Jews have historically been excluded from mainstream American society—one for religion, the other for color. One thing that separates the two groups is that blacks cannot get the institutional protection that comes in this country from being classified as white. This is one of several issues that create tensions between the two groups.

2. He calls this view a "deeply frustrating misconception" that comes from the "dual premise (religious and political)" of Israel. Israel was established in a spirit of humanitarianism and high ethical expectations, and

some people have difficulty reconciling the religious/ethical nature of the country with its nationalist/political agenda. They therefore expect Jews to forgo the sorts of political agendas followed by all other sovereign nations.

3. "Devolutionism" is the term coined to describe the phenomenon of a colonized people seeking to assert their own cultural identities through language, myth, and other means. See above.

4. *The Tenants* addresses tensions that exist between black intellectuals and Jewish intellectuals. McPherson was personally involved with Malamud's project, and this provides an anecdotal opening for the essay. When he first read the manuscript, McPherson couldn't understand what he saw as the excessive begging for mercy in the book and the "extravagance of emotion." By referring to the novel at the end of this essay, McPherson provides a sense of closure for this essay. After eighteen years, he says, he now understands the novel and joins Malamud in the plea for mercy.

Tomás Rivera
From . . . *Y No Se lo Tragó la Tierra* (*. . . And the Earth Did Not Part*)

The young narrator in this excerpt from Rivera's novel is caught between his parents' hopes for his education and his experience of the indignities and prejudice he faces as the son of migrant workers at the schools "in the north." Expelled from school for having been drawn into a fight when he responded to ethnic insults and a punch, the boy feels trapped between the embarrassment and anger he feels at school and the whipping he faces at home for not having fulfilled his parents' hopes. His father's dreams that the boy will grow up to be a telephone operator rely on his negotiating the psychological minefield of the school, where he is submitted to humiliating examinations for lice and vermin and assumed to be in the wrong whenever trouble erupts. In the imagined conversation between the principal and someone who might be the school superintendent, the boy is not referred to by name but simply as "the Mexican kid." Expelling him appears to be the easiest solution since the authorities make the assumption that his parents "could care less" and will be happy to be able to have his help in the fields. The possibility that they aspire to something else for their son never occurs to them. Although the principal had apparently gone out on a limb in registering the boy, he now concedes to the person on the other end of the phone conversation, "I guess you're right . . . I know you warned me." He somewhat reluctantly accepts the prevailing opinion that Chicano farm workers are dirty, disruptive, and uninterested in education. Confronted with such stereotypes, it is hard for the narrator to imagine the possibility of climbing the socioeconomic ladder. Students will notice that the parent at the beginning of the story behaves in the same way Bella's mother did in Marilyn French's "First Day at School"—accompanying the child as far as the school building but not venturing inside—and may speculate on the reasons for this.

Questions for Discussion

1. See above.

2. The cemetery was a comfort to him. He enjoyed it as a part of his walk to school; it reminded him of a golf course. This cemetery, which is "really pretty," does not frighten him as the one in Texas did. He has memories of leaving the cemetery in Texas after a burial and hearing the

voices of the dead cry out, *"Do not forget me."* He has no such personal associations with this other cemetery.

3. See above.

4. The rambling, personal voice is appropriate. Rivera wants to show the fear, anger, and confusion of his youthful narrator. The unconventional organization emphasizes the confusion and the youthful flights of imagination and fear.

Arthur Hu
"Us and Them"

The "Us" and "Them" referred to in this essay are the Koreans and the blacks in Los Angeles. Hu is writing in the aftermath of the violence that erupted in South-Central Los Angeles in April 1992 following the first Rodney King verdict. Hu contends that previous racial tensions between blacks and Asians in the area had been fueled by what he calls the "double standards involved in the reporting of criminal cases." The media, Hu feels, publicize racism when it is white or Asian on black but do not give the same emphasis to race when the violence is black on Asian or black on white. He claims that racial remarks by blacks against Koreans and Asians in general following the 1992 riots "were parlayed without comment by the various local and national news media and talk shows, as if one kind of racism were morally appropriate and another weren't." Such a one-sided view, he says, which "minimize[s] the existence of anti-Asian prejudice when it is perpetrated by black Americans," causes "resentment and confusion" among Asian-Americans.

Elaine H. Kim
"They Armed in Self-Defense"

Like Arthur Hu in the previous article, Kim deplores the ways in which the media portray racism. Of the media coverage of the Los Angeles rioting in April 1992 Kim remarks, "It was another case of visual media racism." Unlike Hu, however, she does not see much hope for a resolution to the problems of racism since she believes it is, in effect, part of the agenda of the "dominant culture." Both Koreans and African-Americans, she claims, were portrayed as coming from "cultures more violent and racist than the dominant culture." She contends that "the so-called black-Korean problem" is one more example of the corruption of a social system that pits minorities against one another "in a zero-sum game over the crumbs of a broken society, a war in which the advancement of one group means deterioration for the other." Kim attacks "the corridors of corporate and government offices" for using minorities and the tensions they encourage among them for their own "agenda and benefit." She is unhappy about the ways in which Koreans, blacks, and Chicanos were ignored or misrepresented in her schooling and about the racism she claims kept her parents from wanted to taken on an American identity. She sees the destruction in Los Angeles' Koreatown as evidence that "the American Dream is only an empty promise."

Questions for Discussion

1. Rodney King is an African-American who was stopped, removed from his car, and beaten by Los Angeles police. The subsequent trial drew international attention, and the verdict, which found the police not guilty of excessive use of force and other charges, sparked riots in Los Angeles. Hu feels that the real victims were the Koreans whose property was destroyed by African-American rioters, resentful of the competitive edge the Koreans have achieved through their willingness to work hard. Hu complains that the Asians are not asked to express their point of view on racial issues and that their plight is ignored by white America. Kim feels the black/Korean problem is a manifestation of a much greater social problem. See above.

2. Hu feels the Koreans were a strategic target of African-American rioters inflamed by the rhetoric of racism. Kim feels that both blacks and Koreans are victims of U.S. racism, forced to fight "over the crumbs of a broken society."

3. Kim would agree, for she sees the capitalist system as institutionalizing racism for its own purposes. She sees the American Dream as a broken promise for both Koreans and African-Americans.

4. Hu would agree that there is a larger problem, particularly the ways in which the media distort racial issues, but he would disagree with what Kim points to as the problem. Hu focuses almost exclusively on what Kim calls the "decontextualized manifestation," trying to find within it the sources of the antagonism. He feels that African-Americans resent the success and enterprise of the Korean-Americans, who have the edge because of their willingness to work hard.

5. She makes the distinction because her consciousness was not shaped by Korean history. Rather, it was shaped by the civil rights movement led by black Americans.

Studs Terkel
"Campus Life"

Terkel interviewed Dawn Kelly, a twenty-one-year-old black college student, and Jennifer Kasko, a twenty-three-year-old white college graduate, about racial tensions on campus. Dawn, who says she is "disturbed" by the racism and hate she has seen, relates a frightening racial incident on her campus and explains that the reason why her family came north was that they believe her brother, who had beaten up a white boy in self-defense, would not have received fair treatment from a white judge or jury in the South. Although she says that she believes "the majority of the people in the world are good," she goes on to describe what sounds like a white conspiracy to keep blacks from rising in society. She concludes on a dismal note, predicting that the world is on the verge of self-destruction and blaming "the white man" who "has destroyed the earth," "raped Africa," and "raped America." Jennifer Kasko grew up in an all-white neighborhood but had warm relationships with the students at the mostly black schools where her father taught. She reports that when black students began to be bused into the white neighborhoods, many of the white adults and older children resented "being invaded." There was little mingling of the races at school, but real problems did not begin to occur until around 1983, during the heated mayoral contest between Jane Byme and Harold Washington. At her parochial high school, black students, she says became "vulgar" and "inconsiderate" and white students "angry and less tolerant." There is a notable difference between the first and second half of Jennifer's narration. As she describes racial tensions on her college campus and incidents that have occurred after college, her tone becomes accusatory. She describes herself as "angry" twice and says that "college really hardened [her]." Twice she refers to black people either "getting something for nothing" or feeling that they deserve to. She claims toward the end that Louis Farrakhan and Jesse Jackson are encouraging blacks to blame whites for their problems and thus adding fuel to already existing tensions.

Questions for Discussion

1. Responses will vary. Kelly and Kasko, an African-American college student and a white college graduate, both recognize the effects of racism in their lives and on their campuses. Kelly appears to be much more pessimistic at the end. They disagree on the role of people like Louis Farrakhan, but both seem to have been brought by their experiences to positions where they themselves are part of the problem. Kasko articu-

lates this at the end of her interview when she says she's "almost been conditioned over the years towards being prejudiced."

2. Both point to specific incidents of racism. Kelly points to episodes in which groups of white males terrorized a black female. She also points to more general problems between the races. Kasko mentions that her watch was stolen as part of a black sorority prank. She regards busing and group allegiance as sources of problems. She also says that some whites feel that a disproportionate amount of financial aid is awarded to black students.

3. Kelly feels that such students come from "isolated" pasts and have not developed an understanding of other cultures.

4. Kelly sees Farrakhan, a black nationalist leader of the Nation of Islam, as a figure who may have alienated whites. But she admires the fact that "he's not afraid to tell the truth" and that he is dedicated to seeing his people empowered. Kasko feels that Farrakhan is "hurting the black culture" because he focuses blacks' energies on blaming their problems on whites.

5. Kelly recognizes that Jewish history reveals much about dealing with hatred and discrimination. She respects the fact that the Jews won't let people forget the Holocaust and feels that this will keep another Holocaust from happening. She believes African–Americans need to make slavery a psychological monument in a similar way.

PART IV

CONTROVERSY: A CASEBOOK ON MULTICULTURAL EDUCATION

Richard Olivas
"The Immigrant Experience"

One of thirteen children, Richard Olivas (b. 1946) is the son of migrant workers who settled in San Jose in 1945. His father became a construction worker and his mother a cannery worker. In describing his early years Olivas refers to poverty and inadequate education and counseling, and notes that half of his siblings have been in prison at one time or another. Of his poem "The Immigrant Experience," which he wrote when he was an undergraduate at San Jose College, Olivas remarks, "It is my experience. It is the Chicano experience." Students may be interested in the tone of the poem, the attitude of the speaker. What has his experience of history curricula been? To what extent has he experienced multicultural perspectives in the classroom? Had the teacher actually said that George Washington was the *student's* father? Presumably he had referred to Washington as the "father of our country." The contrast between what we can assume the teacher said and what the student tells us he heard is significant. Proponents of multicultural education (such as the authors of the Report of the New York State Social Studies Review and Development Committee) might say that the student's willful dismissal of this national myth is a result of his having been alienated by culturally insensitive curricula. On the other hand, writers such as Ravitch and Schlesinger, who feel that the role of public education is to reinforce the *"unum"* rather than the *"pluribus,"* might point out that the student's education has failed to instill in him a sense of his national identity as an American. The readings in Part IV present a spectrum of opinion on how our educational system should respond to and shape the identities of American youth.

Ishmael Reed

"America: The Multinational Society"

Reed makes the point that the United States is in reality a "cultural bouillabaisse" and that to deny the rich mixing of cultures that has been going on since before the first European settlements is to ignore what is all around us. He claims that the "blurring of cultural styles" in the U.S. makes it virtually impossible to label anything as "foreign." The fear of "foreign" influences in areas such as educational curriculum relies on an assumption that what we have in place is a monocultural "Western" civilization. Even the concept of "Western civilization," Reed points out, is hard to define precisely, since the art, music, literature, and architecture of Europe have incorporated many influences from non-Western cultures. An insistence on monoculturalism, Reed warns, leads to intolerance—ultimately to the barbarism of Hitler, "the archetypal monoculturalist." In addition to pointing out the "multinational" realities of American culture, Reed has another purpose, which is to remind readers of some of the less-than-honorable behavior of the early European settlers. He mentions the intolerance of dissent, the extermination of the Indians, the witchcraft hysteria in Salem, Massachusetts—all of which illustrate "strange and paranoid attitudes toward those different from the Elect." Although Reed does not make any specific recommendations about school programs, one understands from his reaction to the schoolteacher who warned about "the invasion of the American educational system by foreign curriculums," that he is in favor of inviting the cultures of the students to enter the classroom. We have, he says, the unique potential of becoming "a place where the cultures of the world crisscross." In fact, we are already physically that place, and in order to fulfill an "exciting destiny," we need simply to acknowledge our diversity and encourage its expression.

New York State Social Studies Review and Development Committee from "One Nation, Many Peoples: A Declaration of Cultural Interdependence"

The committee was charged with the task of recommending changes in the New York State social studies curriculum in order to increase students' understanding of American history and culture, the diversity within America, and the histories and cultures of peoples throughout the world. In its report the committee notes that "the criteria for being judged an educated person are changing" and that the need to be able to "appreciate things from more than one perspective" calls for an approach to education that emphasizes this ability. Instead of drawing attention to "whose" cultures and histories are being taught, the curriculum should teach "the capacity to view the world and understand it from multiple perspectives." The committee also notes that there is an implicit conflict that needs to be acknowledged and addressed between the goals of nation-building and transmission of national values and traditions, which as considerations in devising a social studies curriculum, and the desire of many new Americans to hold onto their cultures and celebrate them publicly. Any revision of the curriculum must seek to accommodate both of these considerations. The committee found that the existing social studies syllabi they reviewed did not adequately meet their standards on several counts, including not being sufficiently culturally diverse, containing insensitive language, and being too prescriptive about some content while not sufficiently directive about others. They recommend that seven concepts should inform revised curricula: Democracy, Diversity, Economic and Social Justice, Globalism, Ecological Balance, Ethics and Values, and The Individual and Society. The excerpt included here lists four of the committee's seven "specific findings and illustrations."

Alice Chandler
"Fostering a Multi-Cultural Curriculum: Principles for Presidents

Chandler maintains that there are pressing reasons for educators to create multicultural curricula—reasons that "transcend political viewpoints." She points out that adopting a multicultural persepctive can appeal to both our "idealism" and our "self-interest," for acknowledging the worth of all peoples is part of the American credo and not doing so results in the kinds of "social and economic divisions [that] disadvantage us globally as well as nationally." Too often on college campuses, Chandler points out, "racial minorities and white students . . . meet as strangers who have inherited fears of each other." As incidents of "racial intimidation and harassment" increase on American college campuses, academic leaders must actively pursue ways of encouraging exploration and appreciation of differences among cultures while simultaneously "identif[ying] and celebrat[ing] the common humanity that binds them." She warns that not making an effort to "adopt and reconcile its differing peoples and cultural traditions" will result in America's "splinter[ing] into cultural and social apartheid." While acknowledging that during the late nineteenth and early twentieth centuries this country underwent a two-way assimilation as it changed and was changed by eastern and southern European immigrants, Chandler points out that the minority and immigrant groups of today "represent a more complex commingling of cultures." Kept from assimilating because of racial and cultural bias, many of them are also more interested than earlier immigrants in maintaining their cultural distinctiveness. Chandler makes a number of suggestions about how college administrators might go about achieving an "intellectually coherent multi-cultural curriculum," including examining existing syllabi for breadth of perspective on race, ethnicity, and gender, developing new courses, retraining faculty, and instituting "social and extracurricular" programming that will reflect a multicultural community.

Arthur M. Schlesinger, Jr.
"A Dissenting Opinion"

While he agrees with the necessity of "diversify[ing] the syllabus in order to meet the needs of a more diversified society" and to provide an education relevant to our "increasingly interdependent world," Schlesinger fears that the guidelines contained in the report of the New York State Social Studies Review and Development Committee put a dangerous emphasis on the perpetuation of ethnic identities. He calls "precarious" the ideals that unify and "hold our highly differentiated society together," and he feels that involving the public schools in the maintenance of ethnic identities jeopardizes the understanding of and commitment to a national identity. "The report," he believes, "is saturated with *pluribus* and neglectful of *unum.*" The curriculum, Schlesinger maintains, should have as a central theme "the long labor . . . to move the American experiment from exclusion to participation." Furthermore, he deplores the sort of Europe–bashing that sometimes emerges in curriculum revisions. He feels that in "play[ing] up the crimes and play[ing] down the ideals" of the European influence on other cultures the New York report politicizes the curriculum, ignores the "influence of European ideas of democracy, human rights, self–government, rule of law," and fails to give students what he considers to be an essential understanding of the Western ideals that shaped the ideals of the United States. Schlesinger elaborates on these viewpoints in *The Disuniting of America: Reflections on a Multicultural Society.* Students will find a similar argument in the selection from Diane Ravitch's "Multiculturalism: E Pluribus Plures."

Fred Siegel
"The Cult of Multiculturalism"

As can be divined from the title of his essay, Siegel attacks what he sees as the excesses of "multiculturalism's hard–liners." He characterizes this faction as regarding differences as "absolute, irreducible, intractable—occasions not for understanding but for separation"—and as maintaining that "impartial knowledge is impossible." These positions result in the maintaining of boundaries rather than the building of bridges and in a general watering down and antiintellectualizing of the curriculum. He states that some colleges, having given in to the new ideology, "have in effect reverted to their earlier roles as religious/confessional institutions." This "new orthodoxy," he maintains, is "turning the humanities in America into an intellectual backwater." He provides several examples of campuses where the curricula and the prevailing sentiments reflect a newly legitimized antirationalism and where a "leveling down" is tacitly agreed to be a way of avoiding charges of racism. Siegel's argument is strengthened by his citing of specific courses, texts, and spokespeople on both sides of the issue. The possibility that, according to one of Siegel's sources, students in some courses are being taught what to believe rather than how to think is an idea that students will probably want to respond to both from their own classroom experiences and from their ideas about the purposes of education.

Diane Ravitch
"Multiculturalism: E Pluribus Plures"

The ironic subtitle of this essay, "From Many Many," suggests that problems that Ravitch sees in what she calls the "pernicious" turn that multiculutralism has taken. She explains that "pluralistic multiculturalism," which seeks inclusiveness and the discovery of common ground, is being challenged by "a new particularist multiculturalism," which in the schools is manifesting itself in ethnocentric curricula. She maintains not only that the claims that ethnocentric curricula will "raise the self-esteem and academic achievement of children from racial and ethnic minority backgrounds" are unfounded but also that such curricula encourage in those who are "neither white nor European" an alienation from American culture. "Particularists," she claims, "reject any accommodation among groups, any interactions that blur the distinct lines between them," and embrace a simplistic view of history in which "everyone is either a descendant of victims or oppressors." This view of history heightens resentments and encourages the revival of "ancient hatreds." It rejects the possibility of universal values and common ground and forces individuals to choose among a variety of ethnocentrisms. Furthermore, it leads, according to Ravitch, to the kind of antirational relativism that rejects the notion "that science and reason are somehow superior to magic and witchcraft." Ravitch provides several examples of the ways in which some of the new "ethnocentric" curricula have incorporated particular versions of history, and she questions whether an ethnic or racial group really does recognize any benefit from the alleged accomplishments of its ancestors. Whether they do or not, Ravitch feels that the claim that they do rests on "the spurious notion that cultural traits are inherited," and thus implies "a dubious, dangerous form of cultural predestination." She, like Schlesinger, deplores the "Europhobic" nature of the New York State social studies curriculum and avers that the public schools "should not be expected to teach children to view the world through an ethnocentric perspective that rejects or ignores the common culture."

Henry Louis Gates, Jr. "The Debate Has Been Miscast from the Start"

Gates explains what multiculturalism "ought to be." Correctly understood, multiculturalism can help us "recognize what's valuable, resilient, even cohesive, in the hybrid and variegated nature of our modernity." In his fifth paragraph Gates cites the basic underlying questions that multiculturalism raises—questions about national identity and the relationship between diversity and "communal identity." He believes that those who fear that fragmentation will result from a study of our differences "have got it exactly backwards," for one has to come to know the "other" in order to respect him or her, and respect is a necessary component of toleration. Gates urges what might be thought of as a "sane" attitude toward multiculturalism—one that avoids the positions of both a "vulgar cultural national[ism]" and a "mindless celebration of difference." He joins Ishmael Reed in observing that "the world we live in is multicultural already."